D0397947

Foreword to "AM and PM Devotions"

When I read through Spurgeon's *Morning and Evening Devotions* in the morning, I find myself eagerly wanting to go ahead and read the corresponding evening devotion. These writings are so classic that they are always fresh and new. No matter how many times I read them, the Lord brings some new truth to my attention each time I scan the pages.

Charles Haddon Spurgeon was considered to be one of the mightiest preachers of all times. Weekly he preached to over 7,000 people and it is estimated that he addressed 10 million people in his lifetime. Wilbur M. Smith claimed, "No man in modern history who remained a pastor of one church has preached to as many people as did C. H. Spurgeon."

Spurgeon had a knowledge of Scripture that few could rival. He said, "I like to get a text and find out its meanings and gearings . . . and then I can talk about it." He found it difficult to choose just one text for a sermon, for to him the Bible was "an embarrassment of riches!"

These devotions, drawn from his skilled sermons and personal experiences, are a collection of riches that I know you will enjoy as much as I have. Always relevant, always timely, they will comfort, encourage, and teach you—morning and evening.

Jerry Falwell

MORNING
and
EVENING

Daily Readings

CHARLES H. SPURGEON

Complete and Unabridged

THE OLD-TIME GOSPEL HOUR
Lynchburg, Virginia

ISBN 0-8407-4166-9

"He wakeneth morning by morning. He wakeneth mine ear to hear as the learned." *Isaiah l. 4.*

" My soul shall be satisfied as with marrow and fatness: and my mouth shall praise Thee with joyful lips: when I remember Thee upon my bed, and meditate on Thee in the night watches."

Psalm lxiii. 5, 6.

EDITORIAL PREFACE

This edition of *Morning and Evening* is further evidence that Christians the world over continue to value and use the writings of Charles Haddon Spurgeon from year to year. Repeated reprintings of his valuable commentaries and of over two thousand published sermons have found their way into the libraries of pastors and Bible students who treasure and preach the Gospel of the grace of God.

Spurgeon was born in England at Kelveden, Essex, England, in 1834. His father and grandfather were both preachers, and the young and energetic Spurgeon preached his first sermon the same year he was converted, 1851. So great was his promise and so evident his preaching gifts, that he was called in 1854 to the pastorate of the New Park Street Chapel. It was here that the great Calvinist expositor and Baptist preacher John Gill had labored so long. Spurgeon was soon preaching to crowds of 6,000 in the great Metropolitan Tabernacle which was especially built for him. He died on January 31, 1892, and was much mourned by the Christian world.

Spurgeon was also a Calvinist. He believed in and expounded from the Scripture the truth that no one deserves to be saved, but that God chooses some, not all, for eternal salvation; that the elect sheep do not continue all their lives to resist the saving work of God; that the atonement of Christ was intended and designed to achieve, rather than to make merely possible, the full salvation of the elect of God. He believed also that man's heart was totally unable to desire or achieve the good of the Gospel, but that God must regenerate Mind, Emotion, and Will before the sinner really believes, and that the true saints will always perserve to the end.

The Free offer of this gracious Gospel was Spurgeon's life-work. As he said at the beginning of a sermon about our response to the preaching of the Word, "Brethren, it is a good thing to be under the sound of the Word of God."

Morning and Evening was written to bring the serious Christian under the sound of that Word at least twice a day. In this way the interpretation of reality which God gives us in His Word becomes the context of all our thought, the self-conscious presupposition of all truth.

The Publisher

" They did eat of the fruit of the land of Canaan that year."
Joshua v. 12.

SRAEL'S weary wanderings were all over, and the promised rest was attained. No more moving tents, fiery serpents, fierce Amalekites, and howling wildernesses: they came to the land which flowed with milk and honey, and they ate the old corn of the land. Perhaps this year, beloved Christian reader, this may be thy case or mine. Joyful is the prospect, and if faith be in active exercise, it will yield unalloyed delight. To be with Jesus in the rest which remaineth for the people of God, is a cheering hope indeed, and to expect this glory so soon is a double bliss. Unbelief shudders at the Jordan which still rolls between us and the goodly land, but let us rest assured that we have already experienced more ills than death at its worst can cause us. Let us banish every fearful thought, and rejoice with exceeding great joy, in the prospect that this year we shall begin to be " for ever with the Lord."

A part of the host will this year tarry on earth, to do service for their Lord. If this should fall to our lot, there is no reason why the New-year's text should not still be true. "We who have believed do enter into rest." The Holy Spirit is the earnest of our inheritance ; He gives us "glory begun below." In heaven they are secure, and so are we preserved in Christ Jesus ; there they triumph over their enemies, and we have victories too. Celestial spirits enjoy communion with their Lord, and this is not denied to us ; they rest in His love, and we have perfect peace in Him : they hymn His praise, and it is our privilege to bless Him too. We will this year gather celestial fruits on earthly ground, where faith and hope have made the desert like the garden of the Lord. Man did eat angels' food of old, and why not now ? O for grace to feed on Jesus, and so to eat of the fruit of the land of Canaan this year !

"We will be glad and rejoice in Thee."—Canticles i. 4.

WE will be glad and rejoice in Thee. We will not open the gates of the year to the dolorous notes of the sackbut, but to the sweet strains of the harp of joy, and the high sounding cymbals of gladness. "O come, let us sing unto the Lord : let us make a joyful noise unto the rock of our salvation." WE, the called and faithful and chosen, *we* will drive away our griefs, and set up our banners of confidence in the name of God. Let others lament over their troubles, we who have the sweetening tree to cast into Marah's bitter pool, with joy will magnify the Lord. Eternal Spirit, our effectual Comforter, we who are the temples in which Thou dwellest, will never cease from adoring and blessing the name of Jesus. *We* WILL, we are resolved about it, Jesus must have the crown of our heart's delight; we will not dishonour our Bridegroom by mourning in His presence. We are ordained to be the minstrels of the skies, let us rehearse our everlasting anthem before we sing it in the halls of the New Jerusalem. *We will* BE GLAD AND REJOICE : two words with one sense, double joy, blessedness upon blessedness. Need there be any limit to our rejoicing in the Lord even now ? Do not men of grace find their Lord to be camphire and spikenard, calamus and cinnamon even now, and what better fragrance have they in heaven itself? *We will be glad and rejoice* IN THEE. That last word is the meat in the dish, the kernel of the nut, the soul of the text. What heavens are laid up in Jesus ! What rivers of infinite bliss have their source, ay, and every drop of their fulness in Him ! Since, O sweet Lord Jesus, Thou art the present portion of Thy people, favour us this year with such a sense of Thy preciousness, that from its first to its last day we may be glad and rejoice in Thee. Let January open with joy in the Lord, and December close with gladness in Jesus.

" Continue in prayer."—Colossians iv. 2.

IT is interesting to remark how large a portion of Sacred Writ is occupied with the subject of prayer, either in furnishing examples, enforcing precepts, or pronouncing promises. We scarcely open the Bible before we read, " Then began men to call upon the name of the Lord ;" and just as we are about to close the volume, the " Amen " of an earnest supplication meets our ear. Instances are plentiful. Here we find a wrestling Jacob—there a Daniel who prayed three times a day—and a David who with all his heart called upon his God. On the mountain we see Elias ; in the dungeon Paul and Silas. We have multitudes of commands, and myriads of promises. What does this teach us, but the sacred importance and necessity of prayer ? We may be certain that whatever God has made prominent in His Word, He intended to be conspicuous in our lives. If He has said much about prayer, it is because He knows we have much need of it. So deep are our necessities, that until we are in heaven we must not cease to pray. Dost thou want nothing ? Then, I fear thou dost not know thy poverty. Hast thou no mercy to ask of God ? Then, may the Lord's mercy show thee thy misery ! A prayerless soul is a Christless soul. Prayer is the lisping of the believing infant, the shout of the fighting believer, the requiem of the dying saint falling asleep in Jesus. It is the breath, the watchword, the comfort, the strength, the honour of a Christian. If thou be a child of God, thou wilt seek thy Father's face, and live in thy Father's love. Pray that this year thou mayst be holy, humble, zealous, and patient ; have closer communion with Christ, and enter oftener into the banqueting-house of His love. Pray that thou mayst be an example and a blessing unto others, and that thou mayst live more to the glory of thy Master. The motto for this year must be, " Continue in prayer."

" Let the people renew their strength."—Isaiah xli. 1.

ALL things on earth need to be renewed. No created thing continueth by itself. "Thou renewest the face of the year," was the Psalmist's utterance. Even the trees, which wear not themselves with care, nor shorten their lives with labour, must drink of the rain of heaven and suck from the hidden treasures of the soil. The cedars of Lebanon, which God has planted, only live because day by day they are full of sap fresh drawn from the earth. Neither can man's life be sustained without renewal from God. As it is necessary to repair the waste of the body by the frequent meal, so we must repair the waste of the soul by feeding upon the Book of God, or by listening to the preached Word, or by the soul-fattening table of the ordinances. How depressed are our graces when means are neglected! What poor starvelings some saints are who live without the diligent use of the Word of God and secret prayer! If our piety can live without God it is not of divine creating; it is but a dream; for if God had begotten it, it would wait upon Him as the flowers wait upon the dew. Without constant restoration we are not ready for the perpetual assaults of hell, or the stern afflictions of heaven, or even for the strifes within. When the whirlwind shall be loosed, woe to the tree that hath not sucked up fresh sap, and grasped the rock with many intertwisted roots. When tempests arise, woe to the mariners that have not strengthened their mast, nor cast their anchor, nor sought the haven. If we suffer the good to grow weaker, the evil will surely gather strength and struggle desperately for the mastery over us; and so, mayhap, a painful desolation, and a lamentable disgrace may follow. Let us draw near to the footstool of divine mercy in humble entreaty, and we shall realise the fulfilment of the promise, "They that wait on the Lord shall renew their strength."

" I will give thee for a covenant of the people."—Isaiah xlix. 8.

JESUS Christ is Himself the sum and substance of the covenant, and as one of its gifts He is the property of every believer. Believer, canst thou estimate what thou hast gotten in Christ ? " In Him dwelleth all the fulness of the Godhead bodily." Consider that word " God " and its infinity, and then meditate upon "perfect man" and all his beauty ; for all that Christ, as God and man, ever had, or can have, is thine—out of pure free favour, passed over to thee to be thine entailed property for ever. Our blessed Jesus, as God, is omniscient, omnipresent, omnipotent. Will it not console you to know that all these great and glorious attributes are altogether yours ? Has he power ? That power is yours to support and strengthen you, to overcome your enemies, and to preserve you even to the end. Has He love ? Well, there is not a drop of love in His heart which is not yours ; you may dive into the immense ocean of His love, and you may say of it all, " It is mine." Hath He justice ? It may seem a stern attribute, but even that is yours, for He will by His justice see to it that all which is promised to you in the covenant of grace shall be most certainly secured to you. And all that He has as *perfect man* is yours. As a perfect man the Father's delight was upon Him. He stood accepted by the Most High. O believer, God's acceptance of Christ is thine acceptance ; for knowest thou not that the love which the Father set on a perfect Christ, He sets on thee *now ?* For all that Christ did is thine. That perfect righteousness which Jesus wrought out, when through His stainless life He kept the law and made it honourable, is thine, and is imputed to thee. Christ is in the covenant.

" My God, I am thine—what a comfort divine !
  What a blessing to know that the Saviour is mine !
  In the heavenly Lamb thrice happy I am,
  And my heart it doth dance at the sound of His name."

" The voice of one crying in the wilderness, Prepare ye the way of the Lord, make his paths straight."—Luke iii. 4.

THE voice crying in the wilderness demanded *a way for the Lord, a way prepared, and a way prepared in the wilderness.* I would be attentive to the Master's proclamation, and give Him a road into my heart, cast up by gracious operations, through the desert of my nature. The four directions in the text must have my serious attention.

Every valley must be exalted. Low and grovelling thoughts of God must be given up; doubting and despairing must be removed; and self-seeking and carnal delights must be forsaken. Across these deep valleys a glorious causeway of grace must be raised.

Every mountain and hill shall be laid low. Proud creature-sufficiency, and boastful self-righteousness, must be levelled, to make a highway for the King of kings. Divine fellowship is never vouchsafed to haughty, highminded sinners. The Lord hath respect unto the lowly, and visits the contrite in heart, but the lofty are an abomination unto Him. My soul, beseech the Holy Spirit to set thee right in this respect.

The crooked shall be made straight. The wavering heart must have a straight path of decision for God and holiness marked out for it. Double-minded men are strangers to the God of truth. My soul, take heed that thou be in all things honest and true, as in the sight of the heart-searching God.

The rough places shall be made smooth. Stumbling-blocks of sin must be removed, and thorns and briers of rebellion must be uprooted. So great a visitor must not find miry ways and stony places when He comes to honour His favoured ones with His company. Oh that this evening the Lord may find in my heart a highway made ready by His grace, that He may make a triumphal progress through the utmost bounds of my soul, from the beginning of this year even to the end of it.

" Grow in grace, and in the knowledge of our Lord and Saviour Jesus Christ."—2 Peter iii. 18.

" GROW in grace "—not in one grace only, but in *all* grace. Grow in that root-grace, *faith.* Believe the promises more firmly than you have done. Let faith increase in fulness, constancy, simplicity. Grow also in *love.* Ask that your love may become extended, more intense, more practical, influencing every thought, word, and deed. Grow likewise in *humility.* Seek to lie very low, and know more of your own nothingness. As you grow *downward* in humility, seek also to grow *upward*—having nearer approaches to God in prayer and more intimate fellowship with Jesus. May God the Holy Spirit enable you to *" grow in the knowledge of our Lord and Saviour."* He who grows not in the knowledge of Jesus, refuses to be blessed. To know Him is " life eternal," and to advance in the knowledge of Him is to increase in happiness. He who does not long to know more of Christ, knows nothing of Him yet. Whoever hath sipped this wine will thirst for more, for although Christ doth satisfy, yet it is such a satisfaction, that the appetite is not cloyed, but whetted. If you know the love of Jesus—as the hart panteth for the water-brooks, so will you pant after deeper draughts of His love. If you do not desire to know Him better, then you love Him not, for love always cries, "Nearer, nearer." Absence from Christ is hell; but the presence of Jesus is heaven. Rest not then content without an increasing acquaintance with Jesus. Seek to know more of Him in His divine nature, in His human relationship, in His finished work, in His death, in His resurrection, in His present glorious intercession, and in His future royal advent. Abide hard by the Cross, and search the mystery of His wounds. An increase of love to Jesus, and a more perfect apprehension of His love to us, is one of the best tests of growth in grace.

" And Joseph knew his brethren, but they knew not him."—
Gen. xlii. 8.

THIS morning our desires went forth for growth in our acquaintance with the Lord Jesus; it may be well to-night to consider a kindred topic, namely, *our heavenly Joseph's knowledge of us.* This was most blessedly perfect long before we had the slightest knowledge of Him. " His eyes beheld our substance, yet being imperfect, and in His book all our members were written, when as yet there was none of them." Before we had a being in the world we had a being in His heart. When we were enemies to Him, He knew us, our misery, our madness, and our wickedness. When we wept bitterly in despairing repentance, and viewed Him only as a judge and a ruler, He viewed us as His brethren well beloved, and His bowels yearned towards us. He never mistook His chosen, but always beheld them as objects of His infinite affection. " The Lord knoweth them that are His," is as true of the prodigals who are feeding swine as of the children who sit at the table.

But, alas! *we knew not our royal Brother*, and out of this ignorance grew a host of sins. We withheld our hearts from Him, and allowed Him no entrance to our love. We mistrusted Him, and gave no credit to His words. We rebelled against Him, and paid Him no loving homage. The Sun of Righteousness shone forth, and we could not see Him. Heaven came down to earth, and earth perceived it not. Let God be praised, those days are over with us; yet even now it is but little that we know of Jesus compared with what He knows of us. We have but begun to study Him, but He knoweth us altogether. It is a blessed circumstance that the ignorance is not on His side, for then it would be a hopeless case for us. He will not say to us, " I never knew you," but He will confess our names in the day of His appearing, and meanwhile will manifest Himself to us as He doth not unto the world.

" And God saw the light, that it was good : and God divided the light from the darkness."—Genesis i. 4.

LIGHT might well be good since it sprang from that fiat of goodness, " Let there be light." We who enjoy it should be more grateful for it than we are, and see more of God in it and by it. Light *physical* is said by Solomon to be sweet, but *gospel* light is infinitely more precious, for it reveals eternal things, and ministers to our immortal natures. When the Holy Spirit gives us *spiritual* light, and opens our eyes to behold the glory of God in the face of Jesus Christ, we behold sin in its true colours, and ourselves in our real position; we see the Most Holy God as He reveals Himself, the plan of mercy as He propounds it, and the world to come as the Word describes it. Spiritual light has many beams and prismatic colours, but whether they be knowledge, joy, holiness, or life, all are divinely good. If the light received be thus good, what must the *essential* light be, and how glorious must be the place where He reveals Himself! O Lord, since light is so good, give us more of it, and more of Thyself, the true light.

No sooner is there a good thing in the world, than *a division is necessary.* Light and darkness have no communion; God has divided them, let us not confound them. Sons of light must not have fellowship with deeds, doctrines, or deceits of darkness. The children of the day must be sober, honest, and bold in their Lord's work, leaving the works of darkness to those who shall dwell in it for ever. Our Churches should by discipline divide the light from the darkness, and we should by our distinct separation from the world do the same. In judgment, in action, in hearing, in teaching, in association, we must discern between the precious and the vile, and maintain the great distinction which the Lord made upon the world's first day. O Lord Jesus, be Thou our light throughout the whole of this day, for Thy light is the light of men.

"And God saw the light."—Genesis i. 4.

THIS morning we noticed the goodness of the light, and the Lord's dividing it from the darkness, we now note the special eye which the Lord had for the light. "God saw the light"— He looked at it with complacency, gazed upon it with pleasure, saw that it "was good." If the Lord has given you light, dear reader, He looks on that light with peculiar interest ; for not only is it dear to Him as His own handiwork, but because it is *like* Himself, for "He is light." Pleasant it is to the believer to know that God's eye is thus tenderly observant of that work of grace which He has begun. He never loses sight of the treasure which He has placed in our earthen vessels. Sometimes *we* cannot see the light, but *God* always sees the light, and that is much better than our seeing it. Better for the judge to see my innocence than for me to think I see it. It is very comfortable for me to know that I am one of God's people—but whether *I* know it or not, if the Lord knows it, I am still safe. This is the foundation, "The Lord knoweth them that are His." You may be sighing and groaning because of inbred sin, and mourning over your darkness, yet the Lord sees "light" in your heart, for He has put it there, and all the cloudiness and gloom of your soul cannot conceal your light from His gracious eye. You may have sunk low in despondency, and even despair ; but if your soul has any longing towards Christ, and if you are seeking to rest in His finished work, God sees the "light." He not only *sees* it, but He also *preserves* it in you. "I, the Lord, do keep it." This is a precious thought to those who, after anxious watching and guarding of themselves, feel their own powerlessness to do so. The light thus preserved by His grace, He will one day develop into the splendour of noonday, and the fulness of glory. The light within is the dawn of the eternal day.

" Casting all your care upon Him; for He careth for you."
1 Peter v. 7.

IT is a happy way of soothing sorrow when we can feel—" HE careth for *me*." Christian ! do not dishonour your religion by always wearing a brow of care; come, cast your burden upon your Lord. You are staggering beneath a weight which your Father would not feel. What seems to you a crushing burden, would be to Him but as the small dust of the balance. Nothing is so sweet as to

> " Lie passive in God's hands,
> And know no will but His."

O child of suffering, be thou patient; God has not passed thee over in His providence. He who is the feeder of sparrows, will also furnish *you* with what you need. Sit not down in despair ; hope on, hope ever. Take up the arms of faith against a sea of trouble, and your opposition shall yet end your distresses. *There is* One who careth for you. His eye is fixed on you, His heart beats with pity for your woe, and his hand omnipotent shall yet bring you the needed help. The darkest cloud shall scatter itself in showers of mercy. The blackest gloom shall give place to the morning. He, if thou art one of His family, will bind up thy wounds, and heal thy broken heart. Doubt not His grace because of thy tribulation, but believe that He loveth thee as much in seasons of trouble as in times of happiness. What a serene and quiet life might you lead if you would leave providing to the God of providence ! With a little oil in the cruse, and a handful of meal in the barrel, Elijah outlived the famine, and you will do the same. If God cares for you, why need you care too? Can you trust Him for your soul, and not for your body? He has never refused to bear your burdens, He has never fainted under their weight. Come, then, soul ! have done with fretful care, and leave all thy concerns in the hand of a gracious God.

" Now the hand of the Lord was upon me in the evening."—
Ezek. xxxiii. 22.

IN the way of *judgment* this may be the case, and, if so, be it mine to consider the reason of such a visitation, and hear the rod and Him that hath appointed it. I am not the only one who is chastened in the night season; let me cheerfully submit to the affliction, and carefully endeavour to be profited thereby. But the hand of the Lord may also be felt in another manner, *strengthening* the soul and lifting the spirit upward towards eternal things. O that I may in this sense feel the Lord dealing with me! A sense of the divine presence and indwelling bears the soul towards heaven as upon the wings of eagles. At such times we are full to the brim with spiritual joy, and forget the cares and sorrows of earth; the invisible is near, and the visible loses its power over us; servant-body waits at the foot of the hill, and the master-spirit worships upon the summit in the presence of the Lord. O that a hallowed season of divine communion may be vouchsafed to me this evening! The Lord knows that I need it very greatly. My graces languish, my corruptions rage, my faith is weak, my devotion is cold; all these are reasons why His healing hand should be laid upon me. His hand can cool the heat of my burning brow, and stay the tumult of my palpitating heart. That glorious right hand which moulded the world can new-create my mind; the unwearied hand which bears the earth's huge pillars up can sustain my spirit; the loving hand which incloses all the saints can cherish me; and the mighty hand which breaketh in pieces the enemy can subdue my sins. Why should I not feel that hand touching me this evening? Come, my soul, address thy God with the potent plea, that Jesu's hands were pierced for thy redemption, and thou shalt surely feel that same hand upon thee which once touched Daniel and set him upon his knees that he might see visions of God.

" For me to live is Christ."—Philippians i. 21.

THE believer did not always live to Christ. He began to do so when God the Holy Spirit convinced him of sin, and when by grace he was brought to see the dying Saviour making a propitiation for his guilt. From the moment of the new and celestial birth the man begins to live to Christ. Jesus is to believers the one pearl of great price, for whom we are willing to part with all that we have. He has so completely won our love, that it beats alone for Him; to His glory we would live, and in defence of His gospel we would die ; He is the pattern of our life, and the model after which we would sculpture our character. Paul's words mean more than most men think ; they imply that the *aim and end of his life was Christ*—nay, his life itself was Jesus. In the words of an ancient saint, he did eat, and drink, and sleep eternal life. Jesus was his very breath, the soul of his soul, the heart of his heart, the life of his life. Can you say, as a professing Christian, that you live up to this idea ? Can you honestly say that for you to live is Christ ? Your business—are you doing it *for Christ?* Is it not done for self-aggrandisement and for family advantage ? Do you ask, " Is that a mean reason ? " For the *Christian* it is. He professes to live for Christ; how can he live for another object without committing a spiritual adultery ? Many there are who carry out this principle in some measure; but who is there that dare say that he hath lived wholly for Christ as the apostle did ? Yet, this alone is the true life of a Christian—its source, its sustenance, its fashion, its end, all gathered up in one word— *Christ Jesus.* Lord, accept me ; I here present myself, praying to live only in Thee and to Thee. Let me be as the bullock which stands between the plough and the altar, to work or to be sacrificed ; and let my motto be, " Ready for either."

"My sister, my spouse."—Canticles iv. 12.

BSERVE the sweet titles with which the
heavenly Solomon with intense affection ad-
dresses His bride the church. *"My sister,"*
one near to me by ties of nature, partaker of the same
sympathies. *My spouse*, nearest and dearest, united
to me by the tenderest bands of love; my sweet companion, part of my own self. *My sister*, by my
Incarnation, which makes me bone of thy bone and
flesh of thy flesh; *my spouse*, by heavenly betrothal, in
which I have espoused thee unto myself in righteousness. *My sister*, whom I knew of old, and over whom
I watched from her earliest infancy; *my spouse*, taken
from among the daughters, embraced by arms of love,
and affianced unto me for ever. See how true it is
that our royal Kinsman is not ashamed of us, for He
dwells with manifest delight upon this two-fold relationship. We have the word "my" twice in our
version; as if Christ dwelt with rapture on His possession of His Church. "His delights were with the
sons of men," because those sons of men were His
own chosen ones. He, the Shepherd, sought the
sheep, because they were *His* sheep; He has gone
about "to seek and to save that which was lost,"
because that which was lost was *His* long before it
was lost to itself or lost to Him. The church is
the exclusive portion of her Lord; none else may
claim a partnership, or pretend to share her love.
Jesus, thy church delights to have it so! Let every
believing soul drink solace out of these wells. Soul!
Christ is near to thee in ties of relationship; Christ
is dear to thee in bonds of marriage union, and
thou art dear to Him; behold He grasps both of thy
hands with both His own, saying, *"My* sister, *my*
spouse." Mark the two sacred holdfasts by which thy
Lord gets such a double hold of thee that He neither
can nor will ever let thee go. Be not, O beloved,
slow to return the hallowed flame of His love.

" The iniquity of the holy things."—Exodus xxviii. 38.

WHAT a veil is lifted up by these words, and what a disclosure is made! It will be humbling and profitable for us to pause awhile and see this sad sight. The iniquities of our public worship, its hypocrisy, formality, lukewarmness, irreverence, wandering of heart and forgetfulness of God, what a full measure have we there! Our work for the Lord, its emulation, selfishness, carelessness, slackness, unbelief, what a mass of defilement is there! Our private devotions, their laxity, coldness, neglect, sleepiness, and vanity, what a mountain of dead earth is there! If we looked more carefully we should find this iniquity to be far greater than appears at first sight. Dr. Payson, writing to his brother, says, " My parish, as well as my heart, very much resembles the garden of the sluggard; and what is worse, I find that very many of my desires for the melioration of both, proceed either from pride or vanity or indolence. I look at the weeds which overspread my garden, and breathe out an earnest wish that they were eradicated. But why? What prompts the wish? It may be that I may walk out and say to myself, 'In what fine order is my garden kept!' This is *pride*. Or, it may be that my neighbours may look over the wall and say, ' How finely your garden flourishes!' This is *vanity*. Or I may wish for the destruction of the weeds, because I am weary of pulling them up. This is indolence." So that even our desires after holiness may be polluted by ill motives. Under the greenest sods worms hide themselves; we need not look long to discover them. How cheering is the thought, that when the High Priest bore the iniquity of the holy things he wore upon his brow the words, " HOLINESS TO THE LORD:" and even so while Jesus bears our sin, He presents before His Father's face not our unholiness, but his own holiness. O for grace to view our great High Priest by the eye of faith!

" Thy love is better than wine."—Canticles i. 2.

NOTHING gives the believer so much joy as fellowship with Christ. He has enjoyment as others have in the common mercies of life, he can be glad both in God's gifts and God's works; but in all these separately, yea, and in all of them added together, he doth not find such substantial delight as in the matchless person of his Lord Jesus. He has wine which no vineyard on earth ever yielded; he has bread which all the corn-fields of Egypt could never bring forth. Where can such sweetness be found as we have tasted in communion with our Beloved? In our esteem, the joys of earth are little better than husks for swine compared with Jesus, the heavenly manna. We would rather have one mouthful of Christ's love, and a sip of his fellowship, than a whole world full of carnal delights. What is the chaff to the wheat? What is the sparkling paste to the true diamond? What is a dream to the glorious reality? What is time's mirth, in its best trim, compared to our Lord Jesus in His most despised estate? If you know anything of the inner life, you will confess that our highest, purest, and most enduring joys must be the fruit of the tree of life which is in the midst of the Paradise of God. No spring yields such sweet water as that well of God which was digged with the soldier's spear. All earthly bliss is of the earth earthy, but the comforts of Christ's presence are like Himself, heavenly. We can review our communion with Jesus, and find no regrets of emptiness therein; there are no dregs in this wine, no dead flies in this ointment. The joy of the Lord is solid and enduring. Vanity hath not looked upon it, but discretion and prudence testify that it abideth the test of years, and is in time and in eternity worthy to be called *"the only true delight."* For nourishment, consolation, exhilaration, and refreshment, no wine can rival the love of Jesus. Let us drink to the full this evening.

"I will be their God."—Jeremiah xxxi. 33.

CHRISTIAN! here is all thou canst require. To make thee happy thou wantest something that shall *satisfy* thee ; and is not this enough ? If thou canst pour this promise into thy cup, wilt thou not say, with David, " My cup runneth over ; I have more than heart can wish " ? When this is fulfilled, " *I am thy God,*" art thou not possessor of all things ? Desire is insatiable as death, but He who filleth all in all can fill it. The capacity of our wishes who can measure? but the immeasurable wealth of God can more than overflow it. I ask thee if thou art not complete when God is thine ? Dost thou want anything but God ? Is not His all-sufficiency enough to satisfy thee if all else should fail ? But thou wantest more than quiet satisfaction; thou desirest *rapturous delight.* Come, soul, here is music fit for heaven in this thy portion, for God is the Maker of Heaven. Not all the music blown from sweet instruments, or drawn from living strings, can yield such melody as this sweet promise, "I will be their God." Here is a deep sea of bliss, a shoreless ocean of delight ; come, bathe thy spirit in it ; swim an age, and thou shalt find no shore ; dive throughout eternity, and thou shalt find no bottom. " *I will be their God.*" If this do not make thine eyes sparkle, and thy heart beat high with bliss, then assuredly thy soul is not in a healthy state. But thou wantest more than present delights—thou cravest something concerning which thou mayest exercise *hope;* and what more canst thou hope for than the fulfilment of this great promise, " I will be their God " ? This is the masterpiece of all the promises ; its enjoyment makes a heaven below, and will make a heaven above. Dwell in the light of thy Lord, and let thy soul be always ravished with His love. Get out the marrow and fatness which this portion yields thee. Live up to thy privileges, and rejoice with unspeakable joy.

" *Serve the Lord with gladness.*"—Psalm c. 2.

ELIGHT in divine service is a token of acceptance. Those who serve God with a sad countenance, because they do what is unpleasant to them, are not serving Him at all ; they bring the form of homage, but the life is absent. Our God requires no slaves to grace His throne ; He is the Lord of the empire of love, and would have His servants dressed in the livery of joy. The angels of God serve Him with songs, not with groans ; a murmur or a sigh would be a mutiny in their ranks. That obedience which is not voluntary is disobedience, for the Lord looketh at the heart, and if He seeth that we serve Him from force, and not because we love Him, He will reject our offering. Service coupled with cheerfulness is heart-service, and therefore true. Take away joyful willingness from the Christian, and you have removed *the test of his sincerity.* If a man be driven to battle, he is no patriot ; but he who marches into the fray with flashing eye and beaming face, singing, " It is sweet for one's country to die," proves himself to be sincere in his patriotism. Cheerfulness is *the support of our strength ;* in the joy of the Lord are we strong. It acts as *the remover of difficulties.* It is to our service what oil is to the wheels of a railway carriage. Without oil the axle soon grows hot, and accidents occur ; and if there be not a holy cheerfulness to oil our wheels, our spirits will be clogged with weariness. The man who is cheerful in his service of God, proves that obedience is his element ; he can sing,
    " Make me to walk in Thy commands,
     'Tis a delightful road."

Reader, let us put this question—do *you* serve the Lord *with gladness?* Let us show to the people of the world, who think our religion to be slavery, that it is to us a delight and a joy ! Let our gladness proclaim that we serve a good Master.

" There is laid up for me a crown of righteousness."
2 Timothy iv. 8.

DOUBTING one ! thou hast often said, " I fear I shall never enter heaven." Fear not ! all the people of God shall enter there. I love the quaint saying of a dying man, who exclaimed, " I have no fear of going home ; I have sent all before me ; God's finger is on the latch of my door, and I am ready for Him to enter." " But," said one, " are you not afraid lest you should miss your inheritance ? " " Nay," said he, " nay ; there is one crown in heaven which the angel Gabriel could not wear ; it will fit no head but mine. There is one throne in heaven which Paul the apostle could not fill ; it was made for me, and I shall have it." O Christian, what a joyous thought ! thy portion is secure ; " there remaineth a rest." " But cannot I forfeit it ? " No ; it is entailed. If I be a child of God I shall not lose it. It is mine as securely as if I were there. Come with me, believer, and let us sit upon the top of Nebo, and view the goodly land, even Canaan. Seest thou that little river of death glistening in the sunlight, and across it dost thou see the pinnacles of the eternal city ? Dost thou mark the pleasant country and all its joyous inhabitants ? Know, then, that if thou couldst fly across thou wouldst see written upon one of its many mansions, " This remaineth for such a one ; preserved for him only. He shall be caught up to dwell for ever with God." Poor doubting one, see the fair inheritance ; it is *thine.* If thou believest in the Lord Jesus, if thou hast repented of sin, if thou hast been renewed in heart, thou art one of the Lord's people, and there is a place reserved for thee, a crown laid up for thee, a harp specially provided for thee. No one else shall have thy portion, it is reserved in heaven for thee, and thou shalt have it ere long, for there shall be no vacant thrones in glory when all the chosen are gathered in.

" In my flesh shall I see God."—Job xix. 26.

ARK the subject of Job's devout anticipation—
"I shall see God." He does not say, "I shall
see the saints"—though doubtless that will be
untold felicity—but, "I shall see *God.*" It is not—
"I shall see the pearly gates, I shall behold the walls
of jasper, I shall gaze upon the crowns of gold," but
"I shall see God." This is the sum and substance of
heaven, this is the joyful hope of all believers. It is
their delight to see Him now in the ordinances by faith.
They love to behold Him in communion and in prayer;
but there in heaven they shall have an open and unclouded vision, and thus seeing "Him as He is," shall
be made completely like Him. *Likeness to God*—what
can we wish for more? And *a sight of God*—what can
we desire better? Some read the passage, "Yet, I shall
see God in my flesh," and find here an allusion to
Christ, as the "Word made flesh," and that glorious
beholding of Him which shall be the splendour of the
latter days. Whether so or not it is certain that
Christ shall be the object of our eternal vision; nor
shall we ever want any joy beyond that of seeing
Him. Think not that this will be a narrow sphere
for the mind to dwell in. It is but one source of
delight, but that source is infinite. All His attributes shall be subjects for contemplation, and as He is
infinite under each aspect, there is no fear of ex-
haustion. His works, His gifts, His love to us, and
His glory in all His purposes, and in all His actions,
these shall make a theme which will be ever new. The
patriarch looked forward to this sight of God as a
personal enjoyment. "Whom mine eye shall behold,
and not another." Take realising views of heaven's
bliss; think what it will be *to you.* "*Thine* eyes shall
see the King in His beauty." All earthly brightness
fades and darkens as we gaze upon it, but here is a
brightness which can never dim, a glory which can
never fade—"*I shall see God.*"

" These have no root."—Luke viii. 13.

Y soul, examine thyself this morning by the light of this text. Thou hast received the word with joy; thy feelings have been stirred and a lively impression has been made; but, remember. that to receive the word in the ear is one thing, and to receive Jesus into thy very soul is quite another; superficial feeling is often joined to inward hardness of heart, and a lively impression of the word is not always a lasting one. In the parable, the seed in one case fell upon ground having a rocky bottom, covered over with a thin layer of earth; when the seed began to take root, its downward growth was hindered by the hard stone, and therefore it spent its strength in pushing its green shoot aloft as high as it could, but having no inward moisture derived from root nourishment, it withered away. Is this my case? Have I been making a fair show in the flesh without having a corresponding inner life? Good growth takes place upwards and downwards at the same time. Am I rooted in sincere fidelity and love to Jesus? If my heart remains unsoftened and unfertilized by grace, the good seed may germinate for a season, but it must ultimately wither, for it cannot flourish on a rocky, unbroken, unsanctified heart. Let me dread a godliness as rapid in growth and as wanting in endurance as Jonah's gourd; let me count the cost of being a follower of Jesus, above all let me feel the energy of His Holy Spirit, and then I shall possess an abiding and enduring seed in my soul. If my mind remains as obdurate as it was by nature, the sun of trial will scorch, and my hard heart will help to cast the heat the more terribly upon the ill-covered seed, and my religion will soon die, and my despair will be terrible; therefore, O heavenly Sower, plough me first, and then cast the truth into me, and let me yield Thee a bounteous harvest.

" I have prayed for thee."—Luke xxii. 32.

OW encouraging is the thought of the Redeemer's never-ceasing intercession for us.
When we pray, He pleads for us ; and then
we are *not* praying, He is advocating our cause, and
by His supplications shielding us from unseen dangers.
Notice the word of comfort addressed to Peter—
"Simon, Simon, Satan hath desired to have you that
he may sift you as wheat ; but"—what ?   " But go and
pray for yourself."   That would be good advice, but
it is not so written.   Neither does he say, "But I
will keep you watchful, and so you shall be preserved."
That were a great blessing.   No, it is, *" But I have
prayed for thee,* that thy faith fail not."   We little know
what we owe to our Saviour's prayers.   When we preach
the hill-tops of heaven, and look back upon all the
way whereby the Lord our God hath led us, how
we shall praise Him who, before the eternal throne,
undid the mischief which Satan was doing upon
earth.   How shall we thank Him because He never
held His peace, but day and night pointed to the
wounds upon His hands, and carried our names
upon His breastplate !   Even before Satan had begun
to tempt, Jesus had forestalled him and entered a
plea in heaven.   Mercy outruns malice.   Mark, He
does not say, "Satan has sifted you, and therefore
I will pray," but " Satan hath *desired* to have you."
He checks Satan even in his very desire, and nips
it in the bud.   He does not say, "But I have desired
to pray for you."   No, but "I *have* prayed for you :
I have done it already ; I have gone to court and
entered a counterplea even before an accusation is
made."   O Jesus, what a comfort it is that thou
hast pleaded our cause against our unseen enemies ;
countermined their mines, and unmasked their am-
bushes.   Here is a matter for joy, gratitude, hope, and
confidence.

" Ye are Christ's."—1 Corinthians iii. 23.

"WE *are* Christ's." You are His by donation, for the Father gave you to the Son ; His by His bloody purchase, for He counted down the price for your redemption ; His by dedication, for you have consecrated yourself to Him ; His by relation, for you are named by his name, and made one of His brethren and joint-heirs. Labour practically to show the world that you are the servant, the friend, the bride of Jesus. When tempted to sin, reply, " I cannot do this great wickedness, for I am Christ's." Immortal principles forbid the friend of Christ to sin. When wealth is before you to be won by sin, say that you are Christ's, and touch it not. Are you exposed to difficulties and dangers ? Stand fast in the evil day, remembering that you are Christ's. Are you placed where others are sitting down idly, doing nothing ? Rise to the work with all your powers ; and when the sweat stands upon your brow, and you are tempted to loiter, cry, "No, I cannot stop, for I am Christ's. If I were not purchased by blood, I might be like Issachar, crouching between two burdens ; but I am Christ's, and cannot loiter." When the siren song of pleasure would tempt you from the path of right, reply, " Thy music cannot charm me ; I am Christ's." When the cause of God invites thee, give thyself to it ; when the poor require thee, give thy goods and thyself away, for thou art Christ's. Never belie thy profession. Be thou ever one of those whose manners are Christian, whose speech is like the Nazarene, whose conduct and conversation are so redolent of heaven, that all who see you may know that you are the Saviour's, recognising in you His features of love and His countenance of holiness. " I am a Roman ! " was of old a reason for integrity ; far more, then, let it be your argument for holiness, " I am Christ's ! "

" I have yet to speak on God's behalf."—Job xxxvi. 2.

WE ought not to court publicity for our virtue, or notoriety for our zeal ; but, at the same time, it is a sin to be always seeking to hide that which God has bestowed upon us for the good of others. A Christian is not to be a village in a valley, but " a city set upon a hill ;" he is not to be a candle under a bushel, but a candle in a candlestick, giving light to all. Retirement may be lovely in its season, and to hide one's self is doubtless modest, but the hiding of *Christ* in us can never be justified, and the keeping back of truth which is precious to ourselves is a sin against others and an offence against God. If you are of a nervous temperament and of retiring disposition, take care that you do not too much indulge this trembling propensity, lest you should be useless to the church. Seek in the name of Him who was not ashamed of you to do some little violence to your feelings, and tell to others what Christ has told to you. If thou canst not speak with trumpet tongue, use the still small voice. If the pulpit must not be thy tribune, if the press may not carry on its wings thy words, yet say with Peter and John, " Silver and gold have I none ; but such as I have give I thee." By Sychar's well talk to the Samaritan woman, if thou canst not on the mountain preach a sermon ; utter the praises of Jesus in the house, if not in the temple ; in the field, if not upon the exchange ; in the midst of thine own household, if thou canst not in the midst of the great family of man. From the hidden springs within let sweetly flowing rivulets of testimony flow forth, giving drink to every passer-by. Hide not thy talent ; trade with it ; and thou shalt bring in good interest to thy Lord and Master. To speak for God will be refreshing to ourselves, cheering to saints, useful to sinners, and honouring to the Saviour. Dumb children are an affliction to their parents. Lord, unloose all Thy children's tongues.

" Jehoshaphat made ships of Tharshish to go to Ophir for gold : but they went not ; for the ships were broken at Ezion-geber."—1 Kings xxii. 48.

SOLOMON'S ships had returned in safety, but Jehoshaphat's vessels never reached the land of gold. Providence prospers one, and frustrates the desires of another, in the same business and at the same spot, yet the Great Ruler is as good and wise at one time as another. May we have grace to-day, in the remembrance of this text, to bless the Lord for ships broken at Ezion-geber, as well as for vessels freighted with temporal blessings; let us not envy the more successful, nor murmur at our losses as though we were singularly and specially tried. Like Jehoshaphat, we may be precious in the Lord's sight, although our schemes end in disappointment.

The secret cause of Jehoshaphat's loss is well worthy of notice, for it is the root of very much of the suffering of the Lord's people; it was his alliance with a sinful family, his fellowship with sinners. In 2 Chron. xx. 37, we are told that the Lord sent a prophet to declare, " Because thou hast joined thyself with Ahaziah, the Lord hath broken thy works." This was a fatherly chastisement, which appears to have been blest to him; for in the verse which succeeds our morning's text we find him refusing to allow his servants to sail in the same vessels with those of the wicked king. Would to God that Jehoshaphat's experience might be a warning to the rest of the Lord's people, to avoid being unequally yoked together with unbelievers ! A life of misery is usually the lot of those who are united in marriage, or in any other way of their own choosing, with the men of the world. O for such love to Jesus that, like Him, we may be holy, harmless, undefiled, and separate from sinners; for if it be not so with us, we may expect to hear it often said, " The Lord hath broken thy works."

"The iron did swim."—2 Kings vi. 9.

THE axe-head seemed hopelessly lost, and as it was borrowed, the honour of the prophetic band was likely to be imperilled, and so the name of their God to be compromised. Contrary to all expectation, the iron was made to mount from the depth of the stream and to swim ; for things impossible with man are possible with God. I knew a man in Christ but a few years ago who was called to undertake a work far exceeding his strength. It appeared so difficult as to involve absurdity in the bare idea of attempting it. Yet he was called thereto, and his faith rose with the occasion ; God honoured his faith, unlooked-for aid was sent, and the iron did swim. Another of the Lord's family was in grievous financial straits, he was able to meet all claims, and much more if he could have realised a certain portion of his estate, but he was overtaken with a sudden pressure ; he sought for friends in vain, but faith led him to the unfailing Helper, and lo, the trouble was averted, his footsteps were enlarged, and the iron did swim. A third had a sorrowful case of depravity to deal with. He had taught, reproved, warned, invited, and interceded, but all in vain. Old Adam was too strong for young Melancthon, the stubborn spirit would not relent. Then came an agony of prayer, and before long a blessed answer was sent from heaven. The hard heart was broken, the iron did swim.

Beloved reader, what is thy desperate case ? What heavy matter hast thou in hand this evening ? Bring it hither. The God of the prophets lives, and lives to help His saints. He will not suffer thee to lack any good thing. Believe thou in the Lord of hosts ! Approach Him pleading the name of Jesus, and the iron shall swim ; thou too shalt see the finger of God working marvels for His people. According to thy faith be it unto thee, and yet again the iron shall swim.

" Mighty to save."—Isaiah lxiii. 1.

BY the words "to save" we understand the whole of the great work of salvation, from the first holy desire onward to complete sanctification. The words are *multum in parro ;* indeed, here is all mercy in one word. Christ is not only "mighty to save" those who repent, but He is able to make men repent. He will carry those to heaven who believe; but He is, moreover, mighty to give men new hearts and to work faith in them. He is mighty to make the man who hates holiness love it, and to constrain the despiser of His name to bend the knee before Him. Nay, this is not all the meaning, for the divine power is equally seen in the after-work. The life of a believer is a series of miracles wrought by "the Mighty God." The bush burns, but is not consumed. He is mighty to keep His people holy after He has made them so, and to preserve them in his fear and love until he consummates their spiritual existence in heaven. Christ's might doth not lie in making a believer and then leaving him to shift for himself; but He who begins the good work carries it on; He who imparts the first germ of life in the dead soul, prolongs the divine existence, and strengthens it until it bursts asunder every bond of sin, and the soul leaps from earth, perfected in glory. Believer, here is encouragement. Art thou praying for some beloved one ? Oh, give not up thy prayers, for Christ is "mighty to save." You are powerless to reclaim the rebel, but your Lord is Almighty. Lay hold on that mighty arm, and rouse it to put forth its strength. Does your own case trouble you ? Fear not, for His strength is sufficient for you. Whether to begin with others, or to carry on the work in you, Jesus is "mighty to save;" the best proof of which lies in the fact that He has saved *you.* What a thousand mercies that you have not found Him mighty to destroy !

" Beginning to sink, he cried, saying, Lord, save me."
Matt. xiv. 30.

SINKING *times are praying times* with the Lord's servants. Peter neglected prayer at starting upon his venturous journey, but when he began to sink his danger made him a suppliant, and his cry though late was not too late. In our hours of bodily pain and mental anguish, we find ourselves as naturally driven to prayer as the wreck is driven upon the shore by the waves. The fox hies to its hole for protection ; the bird flies to the wood for shelter ; and even so the tried believer hastens to the mercy seat for safety. Heaven's great harbour of refuge is All-prayer ; thousands of weather-beaten vessels have found a haven there, and the moment a storm comes on, it is wise for us to make for it with all sail.

Short prayers are long enough. There were but three words in the petition which Peter gasped out, but they were sufficient for his purpose. Not length but strength is desirable. A sense of need is a mighty teacher of brevity. If our prayers had less of the tail feathers of pride and more wing they would be all the better. Verbiage is to devotion as chaff to the wheat. Precious things lie in small compass, and all that is real prayer in many a long address might have been uttered in a petition as short as that of Peter.

Our extremities are the Lord's opportunities. Immediately a keen sense of danger forces an anxious cry from us the ear of Jesus hears, and with Him ear and heart go together, and the hand does not long linger. At the last moment we appeal to our Master, but His swift hand makes up for our delays by instant and effectual action. Are we nearly engulphed by the boisterous waters of affliction ? Let us then lift up our souls unto our Saviour, and we may rest assured that He will not suffer us to perish. When we can do nothing Jesus can do all things ; let us enlist His powerful aid upon our side, and all will be well.

" Do as Thou hast said."—2 Samuel vii. 25.

GOD'S promises were never meant to be thrown aside as waste paper ; He intended that they should be used. God's gold is not miser's money, but is minted to be traded with. Nothing pleases our Lord better than to see His promises put in circulation ; He loves to see His children bring them up to Him, and say, " Lord, do as Thou hast said." We glorify God when we plead His promises. Do you think that God will be any the poorer for giving you the riches He has promised ? Do you dream that He will be any the less holy for giving holiness to you ? Do you imagine He will be any the less pure for washing you from your sins ? He has said " Come now, and let us reason together, saith the Lord : though your sins be as scarlet, they shall be as white as snow; though they be red like crimson, they shall be as wool." Faith lays hold upon the promise of pardon, and it does not delay, saying, " This is a precious promise, I wonder if it be true ? " but it goes straight to the throne with it, and pleads, " Lord, here is the promise, 'Do as Thou hast said.'" Our Lord replies, " Be it unto thee even as thou wilt." When a Christian grasps a promise, if he do not take it to God, he dishonours Him ; but when he hastens to the throne of grace, and cries, " Lord, I have nothing to recommend me but this, 'Thou hast said it;'" then his desire shall be granted. Our heavenly Banker delights to cash His own notes. Never let the promise rust. Draw the word of promise out of its scabbard, and use it with holy violence. Think not that God will be troubled by your importunately reminding Him of His promises. He loves to hear the loud outcries of needy souls. It is His delight to bestow favours. He is more ready to hear than you are to ask. The sun is not weary of shining, nor the fountain of flowing. It is God's nature to keep His promises ; therefore go at once to the throne with "Do as thou hast said."

" But I give myself unto prayer."—Psalm cix. 4.

LYING tongues were busy against the reputation of David, but he did not defend himself; he moved the case into a higher court, and pleaded before the great King Himself. Prayer is the safest method of replying to words of hatred. The Psalmist prayed in no cold-hearted manner, he *gave himself* to the exercise—threw his whole soul and heart into it—straining every sinew and muscle, as Jacob did when wrestling with the angel. Thus, and thus only, shall any of us speed at the throne of grace. As a shadow has no power because there is no substance in it, even so that supplication, in which a man's proper self is not thoroughly present in agonising earnestness and vehement desire, is utterly ineffectual, for it lacks that which would give it force. " Fervent prayer," says an old divine, " like a cannon planted at the gates of heaven, makes them fly open." The common fault with the most of us is our readiness to yield to distractions. Our thoughts go roving hither and thither. and we make little progress towards our desired end. Like quicksilver our mind will not hold together, but rolls off this way and that. How great an evil this is! It injures us, and what is worse, it insults our God. What should we think of a petitioner, if, while having an audience with a prince, he should be playing with a feather or catching a fly ?

Continuance and perseverance are intended in the expression of our text. David did not cry once, and then relapse into silence ; his holy clamour was continued till it brought down the blessing. Prayer must not be our chance work, but our daily business, our habit and vocation. As artists give themselves to their models, and poets to their classical pursuits, so must we addict ourselves to prayer. We must be immersed in prayer as in our element, and so pray without ceasing. Lord, teach us so to pray that we may be more and more prevalent in supplication.

" I will help thee, saith the Lord."—Isaiah xli. 14.

THIS morning let us hear the Lord Jesus speak to each one of us : " I will *help* thee." " It is but a small thing for Me, thy God, to *help* thee.   Consider what I have done already.   What ! not help thee ?   Why, I bought thee with My blood. What ! not help thee ?   I have died for thee ; and if I have done the greater, will I not do the less ?   *Help* thee !   It is the least thing I will ever do for thee ; I *have* done more, and *will* do more.   Before the world began I chose thee.   I made the covenant for thee. I laid aside My glory and became a man for thee ; I gave My life for thee ; and if I did all this, I will surely help thee now.   In helping thee, I am giving thee what I have bought for thee already.   If thou hadst need of a thousand times as much help, I would give it thee ; thou requirest little compared with what I am ready to give.   'Tis much for thee to need, but it is nothing for me to bestow.   '*Help* thee ?'   Fear not !   If there were an ant at the door of thy granary asking for help, it would not ruin thee to give him a handful of thy wheat ; and thou art nothing but a tiny insect at the door of My all-sufficiency.   ' I will help thee.' "

O my soul, is not this enough ?   Dost thou need more strength than the omnipotence of the United Trinity ?   Dost thou want more wisdom than exists in the Father, more love than displays itself in the Son, or more power than is manifest in the influences of the Spirit ?   Bring hither thine empty pitcher ! Surely this well will fill it.   Haste, gather up thy wants, and bring them here—thine emptiness, thy woes, thy needs.   Behold, this river of God is full for thy supply ; what canst thou desire beside ?   Go forth, my soul, in this thy might.   The Eternal God is thine helper !.

" Fear not, I am with thee, oh, be not dismay'd !
I, I am thy God, and will still give thee aid."

" *The Messiah shall be cut off, but not for himself.*"—Dan. ix. 26.

BLESSED be His name, there was no cause of death in Him. Neither original nor actual sin had defiled Him, and therefore death had no claim upon Him. No man could have taken His life from Him justly, for He had done no man wrong, and no man could even have slain Him by force unless He had been pleased to yield Himself to die. But lo, one sins and another suffers. Justice was offended by us, but found its satisfaction in Him. Rivers of tears, mountains of offerings, seas of the blood of bullocks, and hills of frankincense, could not have availed for the removal of sin; but Jesus was cut off for us, and the cause of wrath was cut off at once, for sin was put away for ever. Herein is wisdom, whereby substitution, the sure and speedy way of atonement, was devised! Herein is condescension, which brought Messiah, the Prince, to wear a crown of thorns, and die upon the cross! Herein is love, which led the Redeemer to lay down His life for His enemies!

It is not enough, however, to admire the spectacle of the innocent bleeding for the guilty, we must make sure of our interest therein. The special object of the Messiah's death was the salvation of His church; have we a part and a lot among those for whom He gave His life a ransom? Did the Lord Jesus stand as our representative? Are we healed by His stripes? It will be a terrible thing indeed if we should come short of a portion in His sacrifice; it were better for us that we had never been born. Solemn as the question is, it is a joyful circumstance that it is one which may be answered clearly and without mistake. To all who believe on Him the Lord Jesus is a present Saviour, and upon them all the blood of reconciliation has been sprinkled. Let all who trust in the merit of Messiah's death be joyful at every remembrance of Him, and let their holy gratitude lead them to the fullest consecration to His cause.

B

" And I looked, and, lo, a Lamb stood on the mount Sion."
Revelation xiv. 1.

THE apostle John was privileged to look within
the gates of heaven, and in describing what
he saw, he begins by saying, "I looked, and,
lo, a Lamb!" This teaches us that the chief object
of contemplation in the heavenly state is "the Lamb
of God, which taketh away the sins of the world."
Nothing else attracted the apostle's attention so much
as the person of that Divine Being, who hath redeemed
us by his blood. He is the theme of the songs of all
glorified spirits and holy angels. Christian, here is
joy for thee ; thou hast looked, and thou hast seen the
Lamb. Through thy tears thine eyes have seen the
Lamb of God taking away thy sins. Rejoice, then.
In a little while, when thine eyes shall have been
wiped from tears, thou wilt see the same Lamb *exalted
on His throne.* It is the joy of thy heart to hold daily
fellowship with Jesus ; thou shalt have the same joy
to a higher degree in heaven ; thou shalt enjoy the
constant vision of His presence ; thou shalt dwell with
Him for ever. "I looked, and, lo, a Lamb!" Why,
that Lamb is heaven itself ; for as good Rutherford
says, "Heaven and Christ are the same thing ;" to be
with Christ is to be in heaven, and to be in heaven is
to be with Christ. That prisoner of the Lord very
sweetly writes in one of his glowing letters—"O
my Lord Christ, if I could be in heaven without thee,
it would be a hell ; and if I could be in hell, and
have thee still, it would be a heaven to me, for thou art
all the heaven I want." It is true, is it not, Christian?
Does not thy soul say so ?

> " Not all the harps above
> Can make a heavenly place,
> If God His residence remove,
> Or but conceal His face."

All thou needest to make thee blessed, supremely
blessed, is "to be with Christ."

"And it came to pass in an evening-tide, that David arose from off his bed, and walked upon the roof of the king's house."—2 Samuel xi. 2.

AT that hour David saw Bathsheba. We are never out of the reach of temptation. Both at home and abroad we are liable to meet with allurements to evil ; the morning opens with peril, and the shades of evening find us still in jeopardy. They are well kept whom God keeps, but woe unto those who go forth into the world, or even dare to walk their own house unarmed. Those who think themselves secure are more exposed to danger than any others. The armour-bearer of Sin is Self-confidence.

David should have been engaged in fighting the Lord's battles, instead of which he tarried at Jerusalem, and gave himself up to luxurious repose, for he arose from his bed at eventide. Idleness and luxury are the devil's jackals, and find him abundant prey. In stagnant waters noxious creatures swarm, and neglected soil soon yields a dense tangle of weeds and briars. Oh for the constraining love of Jesus to keep us active and useful ! When I see the King of Israel sluggishly leaving his couch at the close of the day, and falling at once into temptation, let me take warning, and set holy watchfulness to guard the door.

Is it possible that the king had mounted his housetop for retirement and devotion ? If so, what a caution is given us to count no place, however secret, a sanctuary from sin ! While our hearts are so like a tinder-box, and sparks so plentiful, we had need use all diligence in all places to prevent a blaze. Satan can climb housetops, and enter closets, and even if we could shut out that foul fiend, our own corruptions are enough to work our ruin unless grace prevent. Reader, beware of evening temptations. Be not secure. The sun is down but sin is up. We need a watchman for the night as well as a guardian for the day. O blessed Spirit, keep us from all evil this night. Amen.

" There remaineth therefore a rest to the people of God."
Hebrews iv. 9.

HOW different will be the state of the believer in heaven from what it is here! Here he is born to toil and suffer weariness, but in the land of the immortal, fatigue is never known. Anxious to serve his Master, he finds his strength unequal to his zeal: his constant cry is, " Help me to serve Thee, O my God." If he be thoroughly active, he will have much labour; not too much for his will, but more than enough for his power, so that he will cry out, " I am not wearied *of* the labour, but I am wearied *in it.*" Ah! Christian, the hot day of weariness lasts not for ever; the sun is nearing the horizon; it shall rise again with a brighter day than thou hast ever seen, upon a land where they serve God day and night, and yet rest from their labours. *Here,* rest is but partial, *there,* it is *perfect. Here,* the Christian is always unsettled; he feels that he has not yet attained. *There,* all are at rest; they have attained the summit of the mountain; they have ascended to the bosom of their God. Higher they cannot go. Ah, toil-worn labourer, only think when thou shalt rest for ever! Canst thou conceive it? It is a rest *eternal;* a rest that "remaineth." Here, my best joys bear "mortal" on their brow; my fair flowers fade; my dainty cups are drained to dregs; my sweetest birds fall before Death's arrows; my most pleasant days are shadowed into nights; and the flood-tides of my bliss subside into ebbs of sorrow; but *there,* everything is immortal; the harp abides unrusted, the crown unwithered, the eye undimmed, the voice unfaltering, the heart unwavering, and the immortal being is wholly absorbed in infinite delight. Happy day! happy day! when mortality shall be swallowed up of life, and the Eternal Sabbath shall begin.

" He expounded unto them in all the Scriptures the things concerning himself."—Luke xxiv. 27.

THE two disciples on the road to Emmaus had a most profitable journey. Their companion and teacher was *the best of tutors;* the interpreter one of a thousand, in whom are hid all the treasures of wisdom and knowledge. The Lord Jesus condescended to become a preacher of the gospel, and He was not ashamed to exercise His calling before an audience of two persons, neither does He now refuse to become the teacher of even one. Let us court the company of so excellent an Instructor, for till He is made unto us wisdom we shall never be wise unto salvation.

This unrivalled tutor used as His class-book *the best of books.* Although able to reveal fresh truth, He preferred to expound the old. He knew by His omniscience what was the most instructive way of teaching, and by turning at once to Moses and the prophets, He showed us that the surest road to wisdom is not speculation, reasoning, or reading human books, but meditation upon the Word of God. The readiest way to be spiritually rich in heavenly knowledge is to dig in this mine of diamonds, to gather pearls from this heavenly sea. When Jesus Himself sought to enrich others, He wrought in the quarry of Holy Scripture.

The favoured pair were led to consider *the best of subjects,* for Jesus spake of Jesus, and expounded the things concerning Himself. Here the diamond cut the diamond, and what could be more admirable? The Master of the House unlocked His own doors, conducted the guests to His table, and placed His own dainties upon it. He who hid the treasure in the field Himself guided the searchers to it. Our Lord would naturally discourse upon the sweetest of topics, and he could find none sweeter than his own person and work: with an eye to these we should always search the Word. O for grace to study the Bible with Jesus as both our teacher and our lesson!

" I sought him, but I found him not."—Canticles iii. 1.

TELL me where you lost the company of Christ, and I will tell you the most likely place to find Him. Have you lost Christ in the closet by restraining prayer? Then it is there you must seek and find Him. Did you lose Christ by sin? You will find Christ in no other way but by the giving up of the sin, and seeking by the Holy Spirit to mortify the member in which the lust doth dwell. Did you lose Christ by neglecting the Scriptures? You must find Christ in the Scriptures. It is a true proverb, " Look for a thing where you dropped it, it is there." So look for Christ where you lost Him, for He has not gone away. But it is hard work to go back for Christ. Bunyan tells us, the pilgrim found the piece of the road back to the Arbour of Ease, where he lost his roll, the hardest he had ever travelled. Twenty miles onward is easier than to go one mile back for the lost evidence.

Take care, then, when you find your Master, to cling close to Him. But how is it you have lost Him? One would have thought you would never have parted with such a precious friend, whose presence is so sweet, whose words are so comforting, and whose company is so dear to you! How is it that you did not watch him every moment for fear of losing sight of Him? Yet, since you have let Him go, what a mercy that you are seeking Him, even though you mournfully groan, "O that I knew where I might find Him!" Go on seeking, for it is dangerous to be without thy Lord. Without Christ you are like a sheep without its shepherd; like a tree without water at its roots; like a sere leaf in the tempest—not bound to the tree of life. With thine whole heart seek Him, and He will be found of thee: only give thyself thoroughly up to the search, and verily, thou shalt yet discover Him to thy joy and gladness.

" Then opened He their understanding, that they might understand the Scriptures."—Luke xxiv. 45.

HE whom we viewed last evening as opening Scripture, we here perceive opening the understanding. In the first work He has many fellow-labourers, but in the second He stands alone; many can bring the Scriptures to the mind, but the Lord alone can prepare the mind to receive the Scriptures. Our Lord Jesus differs from all other teachers; they reach the ear, but He instructs the heart; they deal with the outward letter, but He imparts an inward taste for the truth, by which we perceive its savour and spirit. The most unlearned of men become ripe scholars in the school of grace when the Lord Jesus by His Holy Spirit unfolds the mysteries of the kingdom to them, and grants the divine anointing by which they are enabled to behold the invisible. Happy are we if we have had our understandings cleared and strengthened by the Master! How many men of profound learning are ignorant of eternal things! They know the killing letter of revelation, but its living spirit they cannot discern; they have a veil upon their hearts which the eyes of carnal reason cannot penetrate. Such was our case a little time ago; we who now see were once utterly blind; truth was to us as beauty in the dark, a thing unnoticed and neglected. Had it not been for the love of Jesus we should have remained to this moment in utter ignorance, for without His gracious opening of our understanding, we could no more have attained to spiritual knowledge than an infant can climb the Pyramids, or an ostrich fly up to the stars. Jesus' College is the only one in which God's truth can be really learned; other schools may teach us what is to be believed, but Christ's alone can show us how to believe it. Let us sit at the feet of Jesus, and by earnest prayer call in His blessed aid that our dull wits may grow brighter, and our feeble understandings may receive heavenly things.

" Abel was a keeper of sheep."—Genesis iv. 2.

AS a shepherd Abel *sanctified his work to the glory of God, and offered a sacrifice of blood upon his altar, and the Lord had respect unto Abel and his offering.* This early type of our Lord is exceedingly clear and distinct. Like the first streak of light which tinges the east at sunrise, it does not reveal everything, but it clearly manifests the great fact that the sun is coming. As we see Abel, a shepherd and yet a priest, offering a sacrifice of sweet smell unto God, we discern our Lord, who brings before His Father a sacrifice to which Jehovah ever hath respect. Abel was hated by his brother—hated without a cause; and even so was the Saviour : the natural and carnal man hated the accepted man in whom the Spirit of grace was found, and rested not until his blood had been shed. Abel fell, and sprinkled his altar and sacrifice with his own blood, and therein sets forth the Lord Jesus slain by the enmity of man while serving as a priest before the Lord. " The good Shepherd layeth down His life for the sheep." Let us weep over Him as we view Him slain by the hatred of mankind, staining the horns of His altar with His own blood. *Abel's blood speaketh.* "The Lord said unto Cain, The voice of thy brother's blood crieth unto Me from the ground." The blood of Jesus hath a mighty tongue, and the import of its prevailing cry is not vengeance but mercy. It is precious beyond all preciousness to stand at the altar of our good Shepherd! to see him bleeding there as the slaughtered priest, and then to hear His blood speaking peace to all his flock, peace in our conscience, peace between Jew and Gentile, peace between man and his offended Maker, peace all down the ages of eternity for blood-washed men. Abel is the first shepherd in order of time, but our hearts shall ever place Jesus first in order of excellence. Thou great Keeper of the sheep, we the people of Thy pasture bless Thee with our whole hearts when we see Thee slain for us.

" Turn away mine eyes from beholding vanity; and quicken Thou me in Thy way."—Psalm cxix. 37.

THERE are divers kinds of vanity. The cap and bells of the fool, the mirth of the world, the dance, the lyre, and the cup of the dissolute, all these men know to be vanities; they wear upon their forefront their proper name and title. Far more treacherous are those equally vain things, the cares of this world and the deceitfulness of riches. A man may follow vanity as truly in the counting-house as in the theatre. If he be spending his life in amassing wealth, he passes his days in a vain show. Unless we follow Christ, and make our God the great object of life, we only differ in appearance from the most frivolous. It is clear that there is much need of the first prayer of our text.

"Quicken Thou me in Thy way." The Psalmist confesses that he is dull, heavy, lumpy, all but dead. Perhaps, dear reader, you feel the same. We are so sluggish that the best motives cannot quicken us, apart from the Lord Himself. What! will not hell quicken me? Shall I think of sinners perishing, and yet not be awakened? Will not heaven quicken me? Can I think of the reward that awaiteth the righteous, and yet be cold? Will not death quicken me? Can I think of dying, and standing before my God, and yet be slothful in my Master's service? Will not Christ's love constrain me? Can I think of His dear wounds, can I sit at the foot of His cross, and not be stirred with fervency and zeal? It seems so! No mere consideration can quicken us to zeal, but God Himself must do it, hence the cry, "Quicken Thou me." The Psalmist breathes out his whole soul in vehement pleadings: his body and his soul unite in prayer. "Turn away mine eyes," says the body: "Quicken Thou me," cries the soul. This is a fit prayer for every day. O Lord, hear it in my case this night.

" And so all Israel shall be saved."—Romans xi. 26.

WHEN Moses sang at the Red Sea, it was his joy to know that *all* Israel were safe. Not a drop of spray fell from that solid wall until the last of God's Israel had safely planted his foot on the other side the flood.   That done, immediately the floods dissolved into their proper place again, but not till then. Part of that song was, " Thou in thy mercy hast led forth the people which thou hast redeemed."   In the last time, when the elect shall sing the song of Moses, the servant of God, and of the Lamb, it shall be the boast of Jesus, " Of all whom thou hast given me, I have lost none."   In heaven there shall not be a vacant throne.

> " For all the chosen race
>   Shall meet around the throne,
> Shall bless the conduct of His grace,
>   And make His glories known."

As many as God hath chosen, as many as Christ hath redeemed, as many as the Spirit hath called, as many as believe in Jesus, shall safely cross the dividing sea. We are not all safely landed yet :

> " Part of the host have crossed the flood,
>   And part are crossing now."

The vanguard of the army has already reached the shore.   We are marching through the depths; we are at this day following hard after our Leader into the heart of the sea.   Let us be of good cheer : the rearguard shall soon be where the vanguard already is; the last of the chosen ones shall soon have crossed the sea, and then shall be heard the song of triumph, when all are secure.   But oh! if one were absent—oh! if one of his chosen family should be cast away—it would make an everlasting discord in the song of the redeemed, and cut the strings of the harps of paradise, so that music could never be extorted from them.

" He was sore athirst, and called on the Lord, and said, Thou hast given this great deliverance into the hand of Thy servant. and now shall I die for thirst?"—Judges xv. 18.

SAMSON was thirsty and ready to die. The difficulty was totally different from any which the hero had met before. Merely to get thirst assuaged is nothing like so great a matter as to be delivered from a thousand Philistines! but when the thirst was upon him, Samson felt that little present difficulty more weighty than the great past difficulty out of which he had so specially been delivered. It is very usual for God's people, when they have enjoyed a great deliverance, to find a little trouble too much for them. Samson slays a thousand Philistines, and piles them up in heaps, and then faints for a little water! Jacob wrestles with God at Peniel, and overcomes Omnipotence itself, and then goes "halting on his thigh!" Strange that there *must* be a shrinking of the sinew whenever we win the day. As if the Lord *must* teach us our littleness, our nothingness, in order to keep us within bounds. Samson boasted right loudly when he said, "I have slain a thousand men." His boastful throat soon grew hoarse with thirst, and he betook himself to prayer. God has many ways of humbling His people. Dear child of God, if after great mercy you are laid very low, your case is not an unusual one. When David had mounted the throne of Israel, he said, "I am this day weak, though anointed king." You must expect to feel weakest when you are enjoying your greatest triumph.

If God has wrought for you great deliverances in the past, your present difficulty is only like Samson's thirst, and the Lord will not let you faint, nor suffer the daughter of the uncircumcised to triumph over you. The road of sorrow is the road to heaven, but there are wells of refreshing water all along the route. So, tried brother, cheer your heart with Samson's words, and rest assured that God will deliver you ere long.

*" Son of man, What is the vine tree more than any tree,
or than a branch which is among the trees of the forest? "*
Ezekiel xv. 2.

THESE words are for the humbling of God's
people; they are called God's vine, but what
are they by nature more than others?   They,
by God's goodness, have become fruitful, having been
planted in a good soil; the Lord hath trained them
upon the walls of the sanctuary, and they bring forth
fruit to His glory; but what are they without their
God?   What are they without the continual influence
of the Spirit, begetting fruitfulness in them?   O believer, learn to reject pride, seeing that thou hast no
ground for it.   Whatever thou art, thou hast nothing to
make thee proud.   The more thou hast, the more thou
art in debt to God; and thou shouldst not be proud
of that which renders thee a debtor.   Consider thine
origin; look back to what thou wast.   Consider what
thou wouldst have been but for divine grace.   Look
upon thyself as thou art now.   Doth not thy conscience reproach thee?   Do not thy thousand wanderings stand before thee, and tell thee that thou art unworthy to be called His son?   And if He hath made
thee anything, art thou not taught thereby that it is
grace which hath made thee to differ?   Great believer,
thou wouldst have been a great sinner if God had
not made thee to differ.   O thou who art valiant for
truth, thou wouldst have been as valiant for error
if grace had not laid hold upon thee.   Therefore,
be not proud, though thou hast a large estate—a
wide domain of grace, thou hadst not once a single
thing to call thine own except thy sin and misery,
Oh! strange infatuation, that thou, who hast borrowed
everything, shouldst think of exalting thyself; a poor
dependent pensioner upon the bounty of thy Saviour,
one who hath a life which dies without fresh streams
of life from Jesus, and yet proud!   Fie on thee, O
silly heart!

"Doth Job fear God for nought?"—Job i. 9.

THIS was the wicked question of Satan concerning that upright man of old, but there are many in the present day concerning whom it might be asked with justice, for they love God after a fashion because He prospers them; but if things went ill with them, they would give up all their boasted faith in God. If they can clearly see that since the time of their supposed conversion the world has gone prosperously with them, then they will love God in their poor carnal way; but if they endure adversity, they rebel against the Lord. Their love is the love of the table, not of the host; a love to the cupboard, not to the master of the house. As for the true Christian, he expects to have his reward in the next life, and to endure hardness in this. The promise of the old covenant was prosperity, but the promise of the new covenant is adversity. Remember Christ's words—"Every branch in Me that beareth not fruit He taketh away, and every branch that beareth fruit"—What? *"He purgeth it, that it may bring forth more fruit."* If you bring forth fruit, you will have to endure affliction. "Alas!" you say, "that is a terrible prospect." But this affliction works out such precious results, that the Christian who is the subject of it must learn to rejoice in tribulations, because as his tribulations abound, so his consolations abound by Christ Jesus. Rest assured, if you are a child of God, you will be no stranger to the rod. Sooner or later every bar of gold must pass through the fire. Fear not, but rather rejoice that such fruitful times are in store for you, for in them you will be weaned from earth and made meet for heaven; you will be delivered from clinging to the present, and made to long for those eternal things which are so soon to be revealed to you. When you feel that as regards the present you do serve God for nought, you will then rejoice in the infinite reward of the future.

" I have exalted one chosen out of the people."—Ps. lxxxix. 19.

WHY was Christ chosen out of the people? Speak, my heart, for heart-thoughts are best. Was it not that He might be able to be *our brother* in the blest tie of kindred blood? Oh, what relationship there is between Christ and the believer! The believer can say, " I have a Brother in heaven; I may be poor, but I have a Brother who is rich, and is a King, and will He suffer me to want while He is on His throne? Oh, no! He loves me; He is my brother." Believer, wear this blessed thought, like a necklace of diamonds, around the neck of thy memory; put it, as a golden ring, on the finger of recollection, and use it as the King's own seal, stamping the petitions of thy faith with confidence of success. He is a brother born for adversity, treat him as such.

Christ was also chosen out of the people that He might know our wants and sympathize with us. " He was tempted in all points like as we are, yet without sin." In all our sorrows we have His sympathy. Temptation, pain, disappointment, weakness, weariness, poverty—He knows them all, for He has felt all. Remember this, Christian, and let it comfort thee. However difficult and painful thy road, it is marked by the footsteps of thy Saviour; and even when thou reachest the dark valley of the shadow of death, and the deep waters of the swelling Jordan, thou wilt find His footprints there. In all places whithersoever we go, He has been our forerunner; each burden we have to carry, has once been laid on the shoulders of Immanuel.

> " His way was much rougher and darker than mine ;
> Did Christ, my Lord, suffer, and shall I repine ? "

Take courage! Royal feet have left a blood-red track upon the road, and consecrated the thorny path for ever.

" We will remember Thy love more than wine."—Sol. Song i. 4.

ESUS will not let His people forget His love. If all the love they have enjoyed should be forgotten, He will visit them with fresh love. "Do you forget My cross?" says He, "I will cause you to remember it; for at My table I will manifest Myself anew to you. Do you forget what I did for you in the council-chamber of eternity? I will remind you of it, for you shall need a counsellor, and shall find Me ready at your call." Mothers do not let their children forget them. If the boy has gone to Australia, and does not write home, his mother writes—"Has John forgotten his mother?" Then there comes back a sweet epistle, which proves that the gentle reminder was not in vain. So is it with Jesus, He says to us, "Remember Me," and our response is, "We will remember Thy love." We *will* remember Thy love and its matchless history. It is ancient as the glory which Thou hadst with the Father before the world was. We remember, O Jesus, Thine eternal love when Thou didst become our Surety, and espouse us as Thy betrothed. We remember the love which suggested the sacrifice of Thyself, the love which, until the fulness of time, mused over that sacrifice, and long for the hour whereof in the volume of the book it was written of Thee, "Lo, I come." We remember Thy love, O Jesus! as it was manifest to us in Thy holy life, from the manger of Bethlehem to the garden of Gethsemane. We track Thee from the cradle to the grave—for every word and deed of Thine was love—and we rejoice in Thy love, which death did not exhaust; Thy love which shone resplendent in Thy resurrection. We remember that burning fire of love which will never let Thee hold Thy peace until Thy chosen ones be all safely housed, until Zion be glorified, and Jerusalem settled on her everlasting foundations of light and love in heaven.

" Surely he shall deliver thee from the snare of the fowler."
Psalm xci 3.

GOD delivers His people from the snare of the
fowler in two senses. *From,* and *out of.*
First, He delivers them *from* the snare—does
not let them enter it; and secondly, if they should be
caught therein, He delivers them *out of* it. The
first promise is the most precious to some; the
second is the best to others.

"He shall deliver thee *from* the snare." How?
Trouble is often the means whereby God delivers us.
God knows that our backsliding will soon end in our
destruction, and He in mercy sends the rod. We
say, "Lord, why is this?" not knowing that our
trouble has been the means of delivering us from
far greater evil. Many have been thus saved from
ruin by their sorrows and their crosses; these have
frightened the birds from the net. At other
times, God keeps His people *from* the snare of the
fowler by giving them great spiritual strength, so that
when they are tempted to do evil they say, "How can
I do this great wickedness, and sin against God?"
But what a blessed thing it is that if the believer
shall, in an evil hour, come into the net, yet God will
bring him *out of* it! O backslider, be cast down,
but do not despair. Wanderer though thou hast been,
hear what thy Redeemer saith—"Return, O backsliding children; I will have mercy upon you." But
you say you cannot return, for you are a captive.
Then listen to the promise—"Surely He shall
deliver thee out of the snare of the fowler." Thou
shalt yet be brought out of all evil into which thou
hast fallen, and though thou shalt never cease to
repent of thy ways, yet He that hath loved thee
will not cast thee away; He will receive thee, and
give thee joy and gladness, that the bones which He
has broken may rejoice. No bird of paradise shall
die in the fowler's net

" Martha was cumbered about much serving."—Luke x. 40.

HER fault was not that she *served:* the condition of a servant well becomes every Christian. "I serve," should be the motto of all the princes of the royal family of heaven. Nor was it her fault that she had *"much* serving." We cannot do too much. Let us do all that we possibly can; let head, and heart, and hands, be engaged in the Master's service. It was no fault of hers that she was busy preparing a feast for the Master. Happy Martha, to have an opportunity of entertaining so blessed a guest; and happy, too, to have the spirit to throw her whole soul so heartily into the engagement. Her fault was that she grew *"cumbered* with much serving," so that she forgot *Him,* and only remembered the service. She allowed service to override communion, and so presented one duty stained with the blood of another. We ought to be Martha and Mary in one: we should do much service, and have much communion at the same time. For this we need great grace. It is easier to serve than to commune. Joshua never grew weary in fighting with the Amalekites; but Moses, on the top of the mountain in prayer, needed two helpers to sustain his hands. The more spiritual the exercise, the sooner we tire in it. The choicest fruits are the hardest to rear: the most heavenly graces are the most difficult to cultivate. Beloved, while we do not neglect external things, which are good enough in themselves, we ought also to see to it that we enjoy living, personal fellowship with Jesus. See to it that sitting at the Saviour's feet is not neglected, even though it be under the specious pretext of doing Him service. The first thing for our soul's health, the first thing for His glory, and the first thing for our own usefulness, is to keep ourselves in perpetual communion with the Lord Jesus, and to see that the vital spirituality of our religion is maintained over and above everything else in the world.

" I will mention the lovingkindnesses of the Lord, and the praises of the Lord, according to all that the Lord hath bestowed on us."—Isaiah lxiii. 7.

AND canst *thou* not do this? Are there no mercies which thou *hast experienced?* What though thou art gloomy now, canst thou forget that blessed hour when Jesus met thee, and said, "Come unto me"? Canst thou not remember that rapturous moment when He snapped thy fetters, dashed thy chains to the earth, and said, " I came to break thy bonds and set thee free "? Or if the love of thine espousals be forgotten, there must surely be some precious milestone along the road of life not quite grown over with moss, on which thou canst read a happy memorial of His mercy towards thee? What, didst thou never have a sickness like that which thou art suffering now, and did he not restore thee? Wert thou never poor before, and did he not supply thy wants? Wast thou never in straits before, and did He not deliver thee? Arise, go to the river of thine experience, and pull up a few bulrushes, and plait them into an ark, wherein thine infant-faith may float safely on the stream. Forget not what thy God has done for thee; turn over the book of thy remembrance, and consider the days of old. Canst thou not remember the hill Mizar? Did the Lord never meet with thee at Hermon? Hast thou never climbed the Delectable Mountains? Hast thou never been helped in time of need? Nay, I know thou hast. Go back, then, a little way to the choice mercies of yesterday, and though all may be dark *now*, light up the lamps of the past, they shall glitter through the darkness, and thou shalt trust in the Lord till the day break and the shadows flee away. "Remember, O Lord, thy tender mercies and thy lovingkindnesses, for they have been ever of old."

"Do we then make void the law through faith? God forbid: yea, we establish the law."—Romans iii. 31.

WHEN the believer is adopted into the Lord's family, his relationship to old Adam and the law ceases at once; but then he is under a new rule, and a new covenant. Believer, you are God's child; it is your first duty to obey your heavenly Father. A servile spirit you have nothing to do with: you are not a slave, but a child; and now, inasmuch as you are a beloved child, you are bound to obey your Father's faintest wish, the least intimation of His will. Does He bid you fulfil a sacred ordinance? It is at your peril that you neglect it, for you will be disobeying your Father. Does He command you to seek the image of Jesus? It is not your joy to do so? Does Jesus tell you, "Be ye perfect, even as your Father which is in heaven is perfect"? Then not because the law commands, but because your Saviour enjoins, you will labour to be perfect in holiness. Does He bid his saints love one another? Do it, not because the law says, "Love thy neighbour," but because Jesus says, "If ye love Me, keep My commandments;" and this is the commandment that He has given unto you, "that ye love one another." Are you told to distribute to the poor? Do it, not because charity is a burden which you dare not shirk, but because Jesus teaches, "Give to him that asketh of thee." Does the Word say, "Love God with all your heart"? Look at the commandment and reply, "Ah! commandment, Christ hath fulfiled thee already—I have no need, therefore, to fulfil thee for my salvation, but I rejoice to yield obedience to thee because God is my Father now and He has a claim upon me, which I would not dispute." May the Holy Ghost make your heart obedient to the constraining power of Christ's love, that your prayer may be, "Make me to go in the path of Thy commandments; for therein do I delight." Grace is the mother and nurse of holiness, and not the apologist of sin.

" Your heavenly Father."—Matthew vi. 26.

GOD'S people are doubly His children, they are His offspring by creation, and they are his sons by adoption in Christ. Hence they are privileged to call Him, " Our Father which art in heaven." Father! Oh, what a precious word is that, Here is *authority* : "If I be a Father, where is mine honour ? " If ye be sons, where is your obedience ? Here is *affection* mingled with authority; an authority which does not provoke rebellion ; an obedience demanded which is most cheerfully rendered—which would not be withheld even if it might. The obedience which God's children yield to Him must be *loving* obedience. Do not go about the service of God as slaves to their taskmaster's toil, but run in the way of His commands because it is your *Father's* way. Yield your bodies as instruments of righteousness, because righteousness is your Father's will, and *His* will should be the will of His child. *Father!*—Here is a kingly attribute so sweetly veiled in love, that the King's crown is forgotten in the King's face, and His sceptre becomes, not a rod of iron, but a silver sceptre of mercy—the sceptre indeed seems to be forgotten in the tender hand of Him who wields it. Father!—Here is honour and love. How great is a Father's love to his children ! That which friendship cannot do, and mere benevolence will not attempt, a father's heart and hand must do for his sons. They are his offspring, he must bless them ; they are his children, he must show himself strong in their defence. If an earthly father watches over his children with unceasing love and care, how much more does our heavenly Father? Abba, Father ! He who can say this, hath uttered better music than cherubim or seraphim can reach. There is heaven in the depth of that word—Father ! There is all I can ask ; all my necessities can demand ; all my wishes can desire. I have all in all to all eternity when I can say, " Father."

"All they that heard it wondered at those things."—Luke ii. 18.

WE must not cease to wonder at the great marvels of our God. It would be very difficult to draw a line between holy wonder and *real worship;* for when the soul is overwhelmed with the majesty of God's glory, though it may not express itself in song, or even utter its voice with bowed head in humble prayer, yet it silently adores. Our incarnate God is to be worshipped as "the Wonderful." That God should consider His fallen creature, man, and instead of sweeping him away with the besom of destruction, should Himself undertake to be man's Redeemer, and to pay his ransom price, is, indeed, marvellous! But to each believer redemption is most marvellous as he views it in relation to himself. It is a miracle of grace indeed, that Jesus should forsake the thrones and royalties above, to suffer ignominiously below *for you.* Let your soul lose itself in wonder, for wonder is in this way a very practical emotion. Holy wonder will lead you to *grateful worship* and *heartfelt thanksgiving.* It will cause within you *godly watchfulness;* you will be afraid to sin against such a love as this. Feeling the presence of the mighty God in the gift of His dear Son, you will put off your shoes from off your feet, because the place whereon you stand is holy ground. You will be moved at the same time to *glorious hope.* If Jesus has done such marvellous things on your behalf, you will feel that heaven itself is not too great for your expectation. Who can be astonished at anything, when he has once been astonished at the manger and the cross? What is there wonderful left after one has seen the Saviour? Dear reader, it may be that from the quietness and solitariness of your life, you are scarcely able to imitate the shepherds of Bethlehem, who told what they had seen and heard, but you can, at least, fill up the circle of the worshippers before the throne, by wondering at what God has done.

" And of his fulness have all we received."—John i. 16.

THESE words tell us that there is a fulness in Christ. There is a fulness of essential Deity, for "in Him dwelleth all the fulness of the Godhead." There is a fulness of perfect manhood, for in Him, bodily, that Godhead was revealed. There is a fulness of atoning efficacy in His blood, for "the blood of Jesus Christ, His Son, cleanseth us from all sin." There is a fulness of justifying righteousness in His life, for "there is therefore now no condemnation to them that are in Christ Jesus." There is a fulness of divine prevalence in his plea, for "He is able to save to the uttermost them that come unto God by Him; seeing He ever liveth to make intercession for them." There is a fulness of victory in His death, for through death He destroyed him that had the power of death, that is the devil. There is a fulness of efficacy in His resurrection from the dead, for by it "we are begotten again unto a lively hope." There is a fulness of triumph in His ascension, for "when He ascended up on high, He led captivity captive, and received gifts for men." There is a fulness of blessings of every sort and shape; a fulness of grace to pardon, of grace to regenerate, of grace to sanctify, of grace to preserve, and of grace to perfect. There is a fulness at all times; a fulness of comfort in affliction; a fulness of guidance in prosperity. A fulness of every divine attribute, of wisdom, of power, of love; a fulness which it were impossible to survey, much less to explore. "It pleased the Father that in Him should *all* fulness dwell." Oh, what a fulness must this be of which *all* receive! Fulness, indeed, must there be when the stream is always flowing, and yet the well springs up as free, as rich, as full as ever. Come, believer, and get all thy need supplied; ask largely, and thou shalt receive largely, for this "fulness" is inexhaustible, and is treasured up where all the needy may reach it, even in Jesus, Immanuel—God with us.

"But Mary kept all these things, and pondered them in her heart."—Luke ii. 19.

THERE was an exercise, on the part of this blessed woman, of three powers of her being: her *memory*—she kept all these things; her *affections*—she kept them in her heart; her *intellect* —she pondered them; so that memory, affection, and understanding, were all exercised about the things which she had heard. Beloved, remember what you have heard of your Lord Jesus, and what He has done for you; make your heart the golden pot of manna to preserve the memorial of the heavenly bread whereon you have fed in days gone by. Let your memory treasure up everything about Christ which you have either felt, or known, or believed, and then let your fond affections hold *Him* fast for evermore. Love the person of your Lord! Bring forth the alabaster box of your heart, even though it be broken, and let all the precious ointment of your affection come streaming on His pierced feet. Let your intellect be exercised concerning the Lord Jesus. Meditate upon what you read: stop not at the surface; dive into the depths. Be not as the swallow which toucheth the brook with her wing, but as the fish which penetrates the lowest wave. Abide with your Lord: let Him not be to you as a wayfaring man, that tarrieth for a night, but constrain Him, saying, "Abide with us, for the day is far spent." Hold Him, and do not let Him go. The word "ponder," means to weigh. Make ready the balances of judgment. Oh, but where are the scales that can weigh the Lord Christ? "He taketh up the isles as a very little thing"—who shall take *Him* up? "He weigheth the mountains in scales"—in what scales shall we weigh *Him?* Be it so, if your understanding cannot comprehend, let your affections apprehend; and if your spirit cannot compass the Lord Jesus in the grasp of understanding, let it embrace Him in the arms of affection.

" Perfect in Christ Jesus."—Colossians i. 28.

DO you not feel in your own soul that perfection is not in you ?   Does not every day teach you that ? Every tear which trickles from your eye, weeps " imperfection ; " every sigh which bursts from your heart, cries " imperfection ; " every harsh word which proceeds from your lip, mutters "imperfection." You have too frequently had a view of your own heart to dream for a moment of any perfection *in yourself.* But amidst this sad consciousness of imperfection, here is comfort for you—you are "perfect *in Christ Jesus.*" In God's sight, you are " complete in Him ; " *even now* you are " accepted in the beloved." But there is a second perfection, yet to be realised, which is sure to all the seed.   Is it not delightful to look forward to the time when every stain of sin shall be removed from the believer, and he shall be presented faultless before the throne, without spot, or wrinkle, or any such thing ? The Church of Christ then will be so pure, that not even the eye of Omniscience will see a spot or blemish in her ; so holy and so glorious, that Hart did not go beyond the truth when he said—

" With my Saviour's garments on,
   Holy as the Holy One."

Then shall we know, and taste, and feel the happiness of this vast but short sentence, " Complete in Christ." Not till then shall we fully comprehend the heights and depths of the salvation of Jesus.   Doth not thy heart leap for joy at the thought of it ? Black as thou art, thou shalt be white one day ; filthy as thou art, thou shalt be clean.   Oh, it is a marvellous salvation this ! Christ takes a worm and transforms it into an angel ; Christ takes a black and deformed thing and makes it clean and matchless in His glory, peerless in His beauty, and fit to be the companion of seraphs. O my soul, stand and admire this blessed truth of perfection in Christ.

"And the shepherds returned, glorifying and praising God for all the things that they had heard and seen, as it was told unto them."—Luke ii. 20.

HAT was the subject of their praise? They *praised God for what they had heard*—for the good tidings of great joy that a Saviour was born unto them. Let us copy them; let us also raise a song of thanksgiving that we have heard of Jesus and His salvation. They also *praised God for what they had seen.* There is the sweetest music—what we have experienced, what we have felt within, what we have made our own—"the things which we have made touching the King." It is not enough to *hear* about Jesus: mere hearing may tune the harp, but the fingers of living faith must create the music. If you have seen Jesus with the God-giving sight of faith, suffer no cobwebs to linger among the harpstrings, but loud to the praise of sovereign grace, awake your psaltery and harp. One point for which they praised God was *the agreement between what they had heard and what they had seen.* Observe the last sentence—"As it was told unto them." Have you not found the gospel to be in yourselves just what the Bible said it would be? Jesus said He would give you rest—have you not enjoyed the sweetest peace in Him? He said you should have joy, and comfort, and life through believing in Him—have you not received all these? Are not His ways ways of pleasantness, and His paths paths of peace? Surely you can say with the queen of Sheba, "The half has not been told me." I have found Christ more sweet than His servants ever said He was. I looked upon His likeness as they painted it, but it was a mere daub compared with Himself; for the King in His beauty outshines all imaginable loveliness. Surely what we have "*seen*" keeps pace with, nay, far exceeds, what we have "*heard.*" Let us, then, glorify and praise God for a Saviour so precious, and so satisfying.

" The things which are not seen."—2 Corinthians iv. 18.

IN our Christian pilgrimage it is well, for the most part, to be looking forward. Forward lies the crown, and onward is the goal. Whether it be for hope, for joy, for consolation, or for the inspiring of our love, the future must, after all, be the grand object of the eye of faith. Looking into the future we see sin cast out, the body of sin and death destroyed, the soul made perfect, and fit to be a partaker of the inheritance of the saints in light. Looking further yet, the believer's enlightened eye can see death's river passed, the gloomy stream forded, and the hills of light attained on which standeth the celestial city ; he seeth himself enter within the pearly gates, hailed as more than conqueror, crowned by the hand of Christ, embraced in the arms of Jesus, glorified with Him, and made to sit together with Him on His throne, even as *He* has overcome and has sat down with the Father on His throne. The thought of this future may well relieve the darkness of the past and the gloom of the present. The joys of heaven will surely compensate for the sorrows of earth. Hush, my fears! this world is but a narrow span, and thou shalt soon have passed it. Hush, hush, my doubts! death is but a narrow stream, and thou shalt soon have forded it. Time, how short—eternity, how long! Death, how brief—immortality, how endless! Methinks I even now eat of Eshcol's clusters, and sip of the well which is within the gate. The road is so, so short! I shall soon be there.

> " When the world my heart is rending
>   With its heaviest storm of care,
> My glad thoughts to heaven ascending,
>   Find a refuge from despair.
> Faith's bright vision shall sustain me
>   Till life's pilgrimage is past;
> Fears may vex and troubles pain me,
>   I shall reach my home at last."

" The dove came in to him in the evening."—Genesis viii. 11.

BLESSED be the Lord for another day of mercy, even though I am now weary with its toils. Unto the preserver of men lift I my song of gratitude. The dove found no rest out of the ark, and therefore returned to it; and my soul has learned yet more fully than ever, this day, that there is no satisfaction to be found in earthly things—God alone can give rest to my spirit. As to my buisness, my possessions, my family, my attainments, these are all well enough in their way, but they cannot fulfil the desires of my immortal nature. "Return unto thy rest, O my soul, for the Lord hath dealt bountifully with thee." It was at the still hour, when the gates of the day were closing, that with weary wing the dove came back to the master: O Lord, enable me this evening thus to return to Jesus. She could not endure to spend a night hovering over the restless waste, nor can I bear to be even for another hour away from Jesus, the rest of my heart, the home of my spirit. She did not merely alight upon the roof of the ark, she "came in to him;" even so would my longing spirit look into the secret of the Lord, pierce to the interior of truth, enter into that which is within the veil, and reach to my Beloved in very deed. To Jesus must I come: short of the nearest and dearest intercourse with Him my panting spirit cannot stay. Blessed Lord Jesus, be with me, reveal Thyself, and abide with me all night, so that when I awake, I may be still with thee. I note that the dove brought in her mouth an olive branch plucked off, the memorial of the past day, and a prophecy of the future. Have I no pleasing record to bring home? No pledge and earnest of lovingkindness yet to come? Yes, my Lord, I present Thee my grateful acknowledgments for tender mercies which have been new every morning and fresh every evening; and now, I pray Thee, put forth Thy hand and take Thy dove into Thy bosom.

" *When thou hearest the sound of a going in the tops of the mulberry trees, then thou shalt bestir thyself.*"—2 Sam. v. 24.

THE members of Christ's Church should be very prayerful, always seeking the unction of the Holy One to rest upon their hearts, that the kingdom of Christ may come, and that His "will be done on earth, even as it is in heaven;" but there are times when God seems especially to favour Zion, such seasons ought to be to them like " the sound of a going in the tops of the mulberry trees." We ought then to be doubly prayerful, doubly earnest, wrestling more at the throne than we have been wont to do. Action should then be prompt and vigorous. The tide is flowing—now let us pull manfully for the shore. O for Pentecostal outpourings and Pentecostal labours. Christian, in *yourself* there are times "when thou hearest the sound of a going in the tops of the mulberry trees." You have a peculiar power in prayer; the Spirit of God gives you joy and gladness; the Scripture is open to you; the promises are applied; you walk in the light of God's countenance; you have peculiar freedom and liberty in devotion, and more closeness of communion with Christ than was your wont. Now, at such joyous periods when you hear the "sound of a going in the tops of the mulberry trees," is the time to bestir yourself; now is the time to get rid of any evil habit, while God the Spirit helpeth your infirmities. Spread your sail; but remember what you sometimes sing—

" I can only spread the sail ;
Thou ! Thou ! must breathe the auspicious gale."

Only be sure you have the sail up. Do not miss the gale for want of preparation for it. Seek help of God, that you may be more earnest in duty when made more strong in faith; that you may be more constant in prayer when you have more liberty at the throne; that you may be more holy in your conversation whilst you live more closely with Christ.

" In whom also we have obtained an inheritance."—Eph. i. 11.

HEN Jesus gave Himself for us, He gave us all the rights and privileges which went with Himself; so that now, although as eternal God, He has essential rights to which no creature may venture to pretend, yet as Jesus, the Mediator, the federal Head of the covenant of grace, He has no heritage apart from us. All the glorious consequences of His obedience unto death are the joint riches of all who are in Him, and on whose behalf He accomplished the divine will. See, He enters into glory, but not for Himself alone, for it it written, "Whither the Forerunner is *for us* entered." Heb. vi. 20. Does He stand in the presence of God?—"He appears in the presence of God *for us.*" Heb. ix. 24. Consider this, believer. You have no right to heaven in yourself: your right lies in Christ. If you are pardoned, it is through *His* blood; if you are justified, it is through *His* righteousness; if you sanctified, it is because *He* is made of God unto you sanctification; if you shall be kept from falling, it will be because you are preserved in Christ Jesus; and if you are perfected at the last, it will be because you are complete in *Him.* Thus Jesus is magnified—for all is in Him and by Him; thus the inheritance is made certain to us— for it is obtained in Him; thus each blessing is the sweeter, and even heaven itself the brighter, because it is Jesus our Beloved "in whom" we have obtained all. Where is the man who shall estimate our divine portion? Weigh the riches of Christ in scales, and His treasures in balances, and then think to count the treasures which belong to the saints. Reach the bottom of Christ's sea of joy, and then hope to understand the bliss which God hath prepared for them that love Him. Overleap the boundaries of Christ's possessions, and then dream of a limit to the fair inheritance of the elect. "All things are yours, for ye are Christ's and Christ is God's."

" The Lord our Righteousness."—Jeremiah xxiii. 6.

IT will always give a Christian the greatest calm, quiet, ease, and peace, to think of the perfect righteousness of Christ. How often are the saints of God downcast and sad! I do not think they ought to be. I do not think they would if they could always see their perfection in Christ. There are some who are always talking about corruption, and the depravity of the heart, and the innate evil of the soul. This is quite true, but why not go a little further, and remember that we are " perfect in Christ Jesus." It is no wonder that those who are dwelling upon their own corruption should wear such downcast looks ; but surely if we call to mind that " Christ is made unto us righteousness," we shall be of good cheer. What though distresses afflict me, though Satan assault me, though there may be many things to be experienced before I get to heaven, those are done for me in the covenant of divine grace ; there is nothing wanting in my Lord, Christ hath done it all. On the cross He said, " It is finished! " and if it be finished, then am I complete in Him, and can rejoice with joy unspeakable and full of glory, " Not having mine own righteousness, which is of the law, but that which is through the faith of Christ, the righteousness which is of God by faith." You will not find on this side heaven a holier people than those who receive into their hearts the doctrine of Christ's righteousness. When the believer says, " I live on Christ alone; I rest on him solely for salvation; and I believe that, however unworthy, I am still saved in Jesus;" then there rises up as a motive of gratitude this thought—" Shall I not live to Christ? Shall I not love Him and serve Him, seeing that I am saved by His merits?" " The love of Christ constraineth us," " that they which live should not henceforth live unto themselves, but unto Him which died for them." If saved by imputed righteousness, we shall greatly value imparted righteousness.

" Then Ahimaaz ran by the way of the plain, and overran Cushi."—2 Samuel xviii. 23.

RUNNING is not everything, there is much in the way which we select: a swift foot over hill and down dale will not keep pace with a slower traveller upon level ground. How is it with my spiritual journey, am I labouring up the hill of my own works and down into the ravines of my own humiliations and resolutions, or do I run by the plain way of "Believe and live"? How blessed is it to wait upon the Lord by faith! The soul runs without weariness, and walks without fainting, in the way of believing. Christ Jesus is the way of life, and He is a plain way, a pleasant way, a way suitable for the tottering feet and feeble knees of trembling sinners: am I found in this way, or am I hunting after another track such as priestcraft or metaphysics may promise me? I read of the way of holiness, that the wayfaring man, though a fool, shall not err therein: have I been delivered from proud reason and been brought as a little child to rest in Jesus' love and blood? If so, by God's grace, I shall outrun the strongest runner who chooses any other path. This truth I may remember to my profit in my daily cares and needs. It will be my wisest course to go at once to my God, and not to wander in a roundabout manner to this friend and that. He knows my wants and can relieve them, to whom should I repair but to Himself by the direct appeal of prayer, and the plain argument of the promise. "Straightforward makes the best runner." I will not parley with the servants, but hasten to their Master.

In reading this passage, it strikes me that if men vie with each other in common matters, and one outruns the other, I ought to be in solemn earnestness so to run that I may obtain. Lord, help me to gird up the loins of my mind, and may I press forward towards the mark for the prize of my high calling of God in Christ Jesus.

" They shall sing in the ways of the Lord."—Ps. cxxxviii. 5.

THE time when Christians begin to sing in the ways of the Lord is when they first lose their burden at the foot of the Cross.   Not even the songs of the angels seem so sweet as the first song of rapture which gushes from the inmost soul of the forgiven child of God.   You know how John Bunyan describes it.   He says, when poor Pilgrim lost his burden at the Cross, he gave three great leaps, and went on his way singing—

> "Blest Cross! blest Sepulchre! blest rather be
> The Man that there was put to shame for me!"

Believer, do you recollect the day when *your* fetters fell off?   Do you remember the place when Jesus met you, and said, "I have loved thee with an everlasting love; I have blotted out as a cloud thy transgressions, and as a thick cloud thy sins; they shall not be mentioned against thee any more for ever." Oh! what a sweet season is that when Jesus takes away the pain of sin.   When the Lord first pardoned my sin, I was so joyous that I could scarce refrain from dancing.   I thought on my road home from the house where I had been set at liberty, that I must tell the stones in the street the story of my deliverance.   So full was my soul of joy, that I wanted to tell every snow-flake that was falling from heaven of the wondrous love of Jesus, who had blotted out the sins of one of the chief of rebels.   But it is not only at the commencement of the Christian life that believers have reason for song; as long as they live they discover cause to sing in the ways of the Lord, and their experience of his constant lovingkindness leads them to say, "I will bless the Lord at all times: His praise shall continually be in my mouth."   See to it, brother, that thou magnifiest the Lord *this day.*

> "Long as we tread this desert land,
> New mercies shall new songs demand."

"Thy love to me was wonderful."—2 Samuel i. 26.

COME, dear readers, let each one of us speak for himself of the wonderful love, not of Jonathan, but of Jesus. We will not relate what we have been told, but the things which we have tasted and handled—of the love of Christ. Thy love to me, O Jesus, was wonderful when I was a stranger wandering far from Thee, fulfilling the desires of the flesh and of the mind. Thy love restrained me from committing the sin which is unto death, and withheld me from self-destruction. Thy love held back the axe when Justice said, "Cut it down! why cumbereth it the ground?" Thy love drew me into the wilderness, stripped me there, and made me feel the guilt of my sin, and the burden of mine iniquity. Thy love spake thus comfortably to me when I was sore dismayed— "Come unto Me, and I will give thee rest." Oh, how matchless Thy love when, in a moment, Thou didst wash my sins away, and make my polluted soul, which was crimson with the blood of my nativity, and black with the grime of my transgressions, to be white as the driven snow, and pure as the finest wool. How Thou didst commend Thy love when Thou didst whisper in my ears, "I am thine and thou art Mine." Kind were those accents when Thou saidst, "The Father Himself loveth you." And sweet the moments, passing sweet, when Thou declaredst to me "the love of the Spirit." Never shall my soul forget those chambers of fellowship where Thou hast unveiled Thyself to me. Had Moses his cleft in the rock, where he saw the train, the back parts of his God? We, too, have had our clefts in the rock, where we have seen the full splendours of the Godhead in the person of Christ. Did David remember the tracks of the wild goat, the land of Jordan and the Hermonites? We, too, can remember spots to memory dear, equal to these in blessedness. Precious Lord Jesus, give us a fresh draught of Thy wondrous love to begin the month with. Amen.

C

" Without shedding of blood is no remission."—Heb. ix. 22.

THIS is the voice of unalterable truth. In none of the Jewish ceremonies were sins, even typically, removed without blood-shedding. In no case, by no means can sin be pardoned without atonement. It is clear, then, that there is no hope for me out of Christ; for there is no other blood-shedding which is worth a thought as an atonement for sin. Am I, then, believing in Him? Is the blood of His atonement truly applied to my soul? All men are on a level as to their need of Him. If we be never so moral, generous, amiable, or patriotic, the rule will not be altered to make an exception for us. Sin will yield to nothing less potent than the blood of Him whom God hath set forth as a propitiation. What a blessing that there is the one way of pardon! Why should we seek another?

Persons of merely formal religion cannot understand how we can rejoice that all our sins are forgiven us for Christ's sake. Their works, and prayers, and ceremonies, give them very poor comfort; and well may they be uneasy, for they are neglecting the one great salvation, and endeavouring to get remission without blood. My soul, sit down, and behold the justice of God as bound to punish sin; see that punishment all executed upon thy Lord Jesus, and fall down in humble joy, and kiss the dear feet of Him whose blood has made atonement for thee. It is in vain when conscience is aroused to fly to feelings and evidences for comfort: this is a habit which we learned in the Egypt of our legal bondage. The only restorative for a guilty conscience is a sight of Jesus suffering on the cross. " The blood is the life thereof," says the Levitical law, and let us rest assured that it is the life of faith and joy and every other holy grace.

> " Oh! how sweet to view the flowing
> Of my Saviour's precious blood;
> With divine assurance knowing
> He has made my peace with God."

"And these are ancient things."—1 Chronicles iv. 22.

ET not so ancient as those precious things which are the delight of our souls. Let us for a moment recount them, telling them over as misers count their gold. *The sovereign choice* of the Father, by which He elected us unto eternal life, or ever the earth was, is a matter of vast antiquity, since no date can be conceived for it by the mind of man. We were chosen from before the foundations of the world. *Everlasting love* went with the choice, for it was not a bare act of divine will by which we were set apart, but the divine affections were concerned. The Father loved us in and from the beginning. Here is a theme for daily contemplation. *The eternal purpose* to redeem us from our foreseen ruin, to cleanse and sanctify us, and at last to glorify us, was of infinite antiquity, and runs side by side with immutable love and absolute sovereignty. *The covenant* is always described as being everlasting, and Jesus, the second party in it, had His goings forth of old; He struck hands in sacred suretyship long ere the first of the stars began to shine, and it was in Him that the elect were ordained unto eternal life. Thus in the divine purpose a most blessed covenant union was established between the Son of God and His elect people, which will remain as the foundation of their safety when time shall be no more. Is it not well to be conversant with these ancient things? Is it not shameful that they should be so much neglected and even rejected by the bulk of professors? If they knew more of their own sin, would they not be more ready to adore distinguishing grace? Let us both admire and adore to-night, as we sing—

> "A monument of grace,
>   A sinner saved by blood;
> The streams of love I trace
>   Up to the Fountain, God;
> And in His sacred bosom see
> Eternal thoughts of love to me."

" Therefore, brethren, we are debtors."—Romans viii. 12.

S God's creatures, we are all debtors to Him: to obey Him with all our body, and soul, and strength. Having broken His commandments, as we all have, we are debtors to His justice, and we owe to Him a vast amount which we are not able to pay. But of the *Christian* it can be said that he does not owe God's *justice* anything, for Christ has paid the debt His people owed; for this reason the believer owes the more to *love*. I am a debtor to God's grace and forgiving mercy; but I am no debtor to His justice, for He will never accuse me of a debt already paid. Christ said, "It is finished!" and by that He meant, that whatever His people owed was wiped away for ever from the book of remembrance. Christ, to the uttermost, has satisfied divine justice; the account is settled; the handwriting is nailed to the cross; the receipt is given, and we are debtors to God's justice no longer. But then, because we are not debtors to our Lord in that sense, we become ten times more debtors to God than we should have been otherwise. Christian, pause and ponder for a moment. What a debtor thou art to divine *sovereignty!* How much thou owest to His disinterested *love*, for He gave His own Son that He might die for thee. Consider how much you owe to His forgiving *grace*, that after ten thousand affronts He loves you as infinitely as ever. Consider what you owe to His *power;* how He has raised you from your death in sin; how He has preserved your spiritual life; how He has kept you from falling; and how, though a thousand enemies have beset your path, you have been able to hold on your way. Consider what you owe to His *immutability*. Though you have changed a thousand times, He has not changed once. Thou art as deep in debt as thou canst be to every attribute of God. To God thou owest thyself, and all thou hast—yield thyself as a living sacrifice, it is but thy reasonable service.

"Tell me . . . where Thou feedest, where Thou makest Thy flock to rest at noon."—Canticles i. 7.

THESE words express the desire of the believer after Christ, and his longing for *present* communion with Him. Where dost Thou feed Thy flock? In *Thy house?* I will go, if I may find Thee there. In private *prayer?* Then I will pray without ceasing. In the *Word?* Then I will read it diligently. In Thine *ordinances?* Then I will walk in them with all my heart. Tell me where Thou feedest, for wherever Thou standest as the Shepherd, there will I lie down as a sheep; for none but Thyself can supply my need. I cannot be satisfied to be apart from Thee. My soul hungers and thirsts for the refreshment of Thy presence. "Where dost Thou make Thy flock to rest at noon?" for whether at dawn or noon, my only rest must be where Thou art and Thy beloved flock. My soul's rest must be a grace-given rest, and can only be found in Thee. Where is the shadow of that rock? Why should I not repose beneath it? "Why should I be as one that turneth aside by the flocks of thy companions?" Thou hast companions—why should I not be one? Satan tells me I am unworthy; but I always was unworthy, and yet Thou hast long loved me; and therefore my unworthiness cannot be a bar to my having fellowship with Thee now. It is true I am weak in faith, and prone to fall, but my very feebleness is the reason why I should always be where Thou feedest Thy flock, that I may be strengthened, and preserved in safety beside the still waters. Why should I turn aside? There is no reason why I should, but there are a thousand reasons why I should not, for Jesus beckons me to come. If He withdraw Himself a little, it is but to make me prize His presence more. Now that I am grieved and distressed at being away from Him, He will lead me yet again to that sheltered nook where the lambs of His fold are sheltered from the burning sun.

" The love of the Lord."—Hosea iii. 1.

BELIEVER, *look back* through all thine experience, and think of the way whereby the Lord thy God has led thee in the wilderness, and how He hath fed and clothed thee every day—how He hath borne with thine ill manners—how He hath put up with all thy murmurings, and all thy longings after the flesh-pots of Egypt—how He has opened the rock to supply thee, and fed thee with manna that came down from heaven. Think of how His grace has been sufficient for thee in all thy troubles—how His blood has been a pardon to thee in all thy sins—how His rod and His staff have comforted thee. When thou hast thus looked back upon the love of the Lord, then let faith survey His love *in the future,* for remember that Christ's covenant and blood have something more in them than the *past.* He who has loved thee and pardoned thee, shall never cease to love and pardon. He is Alpha, and He shall be Omega also : He is first, and He shall be *last.* Therefore, bethink thee, when thou shalt pass through the valley of the shadow of death, thou needest fear no evil, for He is with thee. When thou shalt stand in the cold floods of Jordan, thou needest not fear, for death cannot separate thee from His love ; and when thou shalt come into the mysteries of eternity thou needest not tremble, " For I am persuaded, that neither death; nor life, nor angels, nor principalities, nor powers, nor things present, nor things to come, nor height, nor depth, nor any other creature, shall be able to separate us from the love of God, which is in Christ Jesus our Lord." Now, soul, is not thy love refreshed ? Does not this make thee love Jesus ? Doth not a flight through illimitable plains of the ether of love inflame thy heart and compel thee to delight thyself in the Lord thy God ? Surely as we meditate on " the love of the Lord," our hearts burn within us, and we long to love Him more.

" Your refuge from the avenger of blood."—Joshua xx. 3.

IT is said that in the land of Canaan, cities of refuge were so arranged, that any man might reach one of them within half a day at the utmost. Even so the word of our salvation is near to us; Jesus is a present Saviour, and the way to him is short; it is but a simple renunciation of our own merit, and a laying hold of Jesus, to be our all in all. With regard to the roads to the city of refuge, we are told that they were strictly preserved, every river was bridged, and every obstruction removed, so that the man who fled might find an easy passage to the city. Once a year the elders went along the roads and saw to their order, so that nothing might impede the flight of any one, and cause him, through delay, to be overtaken and slain. How graciously do the promises of the gospel remove stumbling blocks from the way ! Wherever there were by-roads and turnings, there were fixed up hand-posts, with this inscription upon them—"To the city of refuge!" This is a picture of the road to Christ Jesus. It is no roundabout road of the law; it is no obeying this, that, and the other; it is a straight road : "Believe, and live." It is a road so hard, that no self-righteous man can ever tread it, but so easy, that every sinner, who knows himself to be a sinner may by it find his way to heaven. No sooner did the man-slayer reach the outworks of the city than he was safe ; it was not necessary for him to pass far within the walls, but the suburbs themselves were sufficient protection. Learn hence, that if you do but touch the hem of Christ's garment, you shall be made whole ; if you do but lay hold upon him with " faith as a grain of mustard seed," you are safe.

> "A little genuine grace ensures
> The death of all our sins."

Only waste no time, loiter not by the way, for the avenger of blood is swift of foot ; and it may be he is at your heels at this still hour of eventide.

" *The Father sent the Son to be the Saviour of the world.*"
1 John iv. 14.

IT is a sweet thought that Jesus Christ did not
come forth without His Father's permission,
authority, consent, and assistance. He was
sent of the Father, that He might be the Saviour of
men. We are too apt to forget that, while there are
distinctions as to the *persons* in the Trinity, there are
no distinctions of *honour*. We too frequently ascribe the honour of our salvation, or at least the
depths of its benevolence, more to Jesus Christ than
we do the Father. This is a very great mistake.
What if Jesus came? Did not His Father send
Him? If He spake wondrously, did not His Father
pour grace into His lips, that He might be an able
minister of the new covenant? He who knoweth the
Father, and the Son, and the Holy Ghost as he should
know them, never setteth one before another in his
love; he sees them at Bethlehem, at Gethsemane,
and on Calvary, all equally engaged in the work of
salvation. O Christian, hast thou put thy confidence in the Man Christ Jesus? Hast thou placed
thy reliance solely on Him? And art thou united
with Him? Then believe that thou art united unto
the God of heaven Since to the Man Christ Jesus
thou art brother, and holdest closest fellowship, thou
art linked thereby with God the Eternal, and "the
Ancient of days" is thy Father and thy friend.
Didst thou ever consider the depth of love in the
heart of Jehovah, when God the Father equipped
His Son for the great enterprise of mercy? If not,
be this thy day's meditation. The *Father* sent
Him! Contemplate that subject. Think how Jesus
works what the *Father* wills. In the wounds of the
dying Saviour see the love of the great I AM.
Let every thought of Jesus be also connected with the
Eternal, ever-blessed God, for " It pleased the Lord
to bruise Him; He hath put Him to grief."

"At that time Jesus answered."—Matthew xi. 25.

THIS is a singular way in which to commence a verse—"At that time Jesus answered." If you will look at the context you will not perceive that any person had asked Him a question, or that He was in conversation with any human being. Yet it is written, "Jesus answered and said, I thank Thee, O Father." When a man answers, he answers a person who has been speaking to him. Who, then, had spoken to Christ? His Father. Yet there is no record of it; and this should teach us that Jesus had constant fellowship with His Father, and that God spake into His heart so often, so continually, that it was not a circumstance singular enough to be recorded. It was the habit and life of Jesus to talk with God. Even as Jesus was, in this world, so are we; let us therefore learn the lesson which this simple statement concerning Him teaches us. May *we* likewise have silent fellowship with the Father, so that often we may answer Him, and though the world wotteth not to whom we speak, may we be responding to that secret voice unheard of any other ear, which our own ear, opened by the Spirit of God, recognises with joy. God has spoken to us, let us speak to God—either to set to our seal that God is true and faithful to His promise, or to confess the sin of which the Spirit of God has convinced us, or to acknowledge the mercy which God's providence has given, or to express assent to the great truths which God the Holy Ghost has opened to our understanding. What a privilege is intimate communion with the Father of our spirits! It is a secret hidden from the world, a joy with which even the nearest friend intermeddleth not. If we would hear the whispers of God's love, our ear must be purged and fitted to listen to His voice. This very evening may our hearts be in such a state, that when God speaks to us, we, like Jesus, may be prepared at once to *answer* Him.

" *Praying always.*"—Ephesians vi. 18.

WHAT multitudes of prayers we have put up from the first moment when we learned to pray. Our first prayer was a prayer for ourselves; we asked that God would have mercy upon us, and blot out our sin. He heard us. But when He had blotted out our sins like a cloud, then we had more prayers for ourselves. We have had to pray for sanctifying grace, for constraining and restraining grace; we have been led to crave for a fresh assurance of faith, for the comfortable application of the promise, for deliverance in the hour of temptation, for help in the time of duty, and for succour in the day of trial. We have been compelled to go to God for our souls, as constant beggars asking for everything. Bear witness, children of God, you have never been able to get anything for your souls elsewhere. All the bread your soul has eaten has come down from heaven, and all the water of which it has drank has flowed from the living rock—Christ Jesus the Lord. Your soul has never grown rich in itself; it has always been a pensioner upon the daily bounty of God; and hence your prayers have ascended to heaven for a range of spiritual mercies all but infinite. Your wants were innumerable, and therefore the supplies have been infinitely great, and your prayers have been as varied as the mercies have been countless. Then have you not cause to say, " I love the Lord, because He hath heard the voice of my supplication " ? For as your prayers have been many, so also have been God's answers to them. He has heard you in the day of trouble, has strengthened you, and helped you, even when you dishonoured Him by trembling and doubting at the mercy-seat. Remember this, and let it fill your heart with gratitude to God, who has thus graciously heard your poor weak prayers. " Bless the Lord, O my soul, and forget not all His benefits."

" Pray one for another."—James v. 16.

AS an encouragement cheerfully to offer intercessory prayer, remember that *such prayer is
the sweetest God ever hears,* for the prayer of
Christ is of this character. In all the incense which
our Great High Priest now puts into the golden censer, there is not a single grain for Himself. His intercession must be the most acceptable of all supplications—and the more like our prayer is to Christ's,
the sweeter it will be ; thus while petitions for ourselves will be accepted, our pleadings for others,
having in them more of the fruits of the Spirit, more
love, more faith, more brotherly kindness, will be,
through the precious merits of Jesus, the sweetest
oblation that we can offer to God, the very fat of our
sacrifice. Remember, again, that *intercessory prayer is
exceedingly prevalent.* What wonders it has wrought !
The Word of God teems with its marvellous deeds.
Believer, thou hast a mighty engine in thy hand, use
it well, use it constantly, use it with faith, and thou
shalt surely be a benefactor to thy brethren. When
thou hast the King's ear, speak to Him for the
suffering members of His body. When thou art
favoured to draw very near to His throne, and the
King saith to thee, "Ask, and I will give thee what
thou wilt," let thy petitions be, not for thyself alone,
but for the many who need His aid. If thou hast
grace at all, and art not an intercessor, that grace
must be small as a grain of mustard seed. Thou hast
just enough grace to float thy soul clear from the
quicksand, but thou hast no deep floods of grace, or
else thou wouldst carry in thy joyous bark a weighty
cargo of the wants of others, and thou wouldst bring
back from thy Lord, for them, rich blessings which
but for thee they might not have obtained :—

> "Oh, let my hands forget their skill,
> My tongue be silent, cold, and still,
> This bounding heart forget to beat,
> If I forget the mercy-seat!"

"Arise ye, and depart."—Micah ii. 10.

HE hour is approaching when the message will come to us, as it comes to all—" Arise, and go forth from the home in which thou hast dwelt, from the city in which thou hast done thy business, from thy family, from thy friends. Arise, and take thy last journey." And what know we of the journey ? And what know we of the country to which we are bound ? A little we have read thereof, and somewhat has been revealed to us by the Spirit ; but how little do we know of the realms of the future ! We know that there is a black and stormy river called " Death." God bids us cross it, promising to be with us. And, after death, what cometh ? What wonder-world will open upon our astonished sight ? What scene of glory will be unfolded to our view ? No traveller has ever returned to tell. But we know enough of the heavenly land to make us welcome our summons thither with joy and gladness. The journey of death may be dark, but we may go forth on it fearlessly, knowing that God is with us as we walk through the gloomy valley, and therefore we need fear no evil. We shall be departing from all we have known and loved here, but we shall be going to our Father's house—to our Father's home, where Jesus is—to that royal " city which hath foundations, whose builder and maker is God." This shall be our *last* removal, to dwell for ever with Him we love, in the midst of His people, in the presence of God. Christian, meditate much on heaven, it will help thee to press on, and to forget the toil of the way. This vale of tears is but the pathway to the better country : this world of woe is but the stepping-stone to a world of bliss.

> " Prepare us, Lord, by grace divine,
> For Thy bright courts on high ;
> Then bid our spirits rise, and join
> The chorus of the sky."

"And they heard a great voice from heaven saying unto them, Come up hither."— Revelation xi. 12.

WITHOUT considering these words in their prophetical connection, let us regard them as the invitation of our great Forerunner to His sanctified people. In due time there shall be heard "a great voice from heaven" to every believer, saying, "Come up hither." This should be to the saints *the subject of joyful anticipation.* Instead of dreading the time when we shall leave this world to go unto the Father, we should be panting for the hour of our emancipation. Our song should be—

> "My heart is with Him on His throne,
> And ill can brook delay;
> Each moment listening for the voice,
> 'Rise up, and come away.'"

We are not called *down* to the grave, but *up* to the skies. Our heaven-born spirits should long for their native air. Yet should the celestial summons be *the object of patient waiting.* Our God knows best when to bid us "Come up hither." We must not wish to antedate the period of our departure. I know that strong love will make us cry,

> "O Lord of Hosts, the waves divide,
> And land us all in heaven;"

but patience must have her perfect work. God ordains with accurate wisdom the most fitting time for the redeemed to abide below. Surely, if there could be regrets in heaven, the saints might mourn that they did not live longer here to do more good. Oh, for more sheaves for my Lord's garner! more jewels for His crown! But how, unless there be more work? True, there is the other side of it, that, living so briefly, our sins are the fewer; but oh! when we are fully serving God, and He is giving us to scatter precious seed, and reap a hundredfold, we would even say it is well for us to abide where we are. Whether our Master shall say "go," or "stay," let us be equally well pleased. so long as He indulges us with His presence.

" Thou shalt call his name Jesus."—Matthew i. 21.

WHEN a person is dear, everything connected with him becomes dear for his sake. Thus, so precious is the person of the Lord Jesus in the estimation of all true believers, that everything about Him they consider to be inestimable beyond all price. " All Thy garments smell of myrrh, and aloes, and cassia," said David, as if the very vestments of the Saviour were so sweetened by His person that he could not but love them. Certain it is, that there is not a spot where that hallowed foot hath trodden—there is not a word which those blessed lips have uttered—nor a thought which His loving Word has revealed—which is not to us precious beyond all price. And this is true of the *names* of Christ—they are all sweet in the believer's ear. Whether He be called the Husband of the Church, her Bridegroom, her Friend ; whether He be styled the Lamb slain from the foundation of the world—the King, the Prophet, or the Priest—every title of our Master—Shiloh, Emmanuel, Wonderful, the Mighty Counsellor—every name is like the honey-comb dropping with honey, and luscious are the drops that distil from it. But if there be one name sweeter than another in the believer's ear, it is the name of *Jesus*. Jesus ! it is the name which moves the harps of heaven to melody. Jesus ! the life of all our joys. If there be one name more charming, more precious than another, it is this name. It is woven into the very warp and woof of our psalmody. Many of our hymns begin with it, and scarcely any, that are good for anything, end without it. It is the sum total of all delights. It is the music with which the bells of heaven ring ; a song in a word ; an ocean for comprehension, although a drop for brevity : a matchless oratorio in two syllables ; a gathering up of the hallelujahs of eternity in five letters.

> " Jesus, I love Thy charming name,
>   'Tis music to mine ear."

"He shall save His people from their sins."—Matthew i. 21.

MANY persons, if they are asked what they understand by salvation, will reply, "Being saved
from hell and taken to heaven." This is one
result of salvation, but it is not one tithe of what is
contained in that boon. It is true our Lord Jesus
Christ does redeem all His people from the wrath to
come; He saves them from the fearful condemnation
which their sins had brought upon them; but His
triumph is far more complete than this. He saves His
people "from their sins." Oh! sweet deliverance from
our worst foes. Where Christ works a saving work,
He casts Satan from his throne, and will not let him
be master any longer. No man is a true Christian if
sin reigns in his mortal body. Sin will be *in* us—it
will never be utterly expelled till the spirit enters
glory; but it will never have *dominion*. There will
be a striving for dominion—a lusting against the new
law and the new spirit which God has implanted—
but sin will never get the upper hand so as to be
absolute monarch of our nature. Christ will be Master
of the heart, and sin must be mortified. The Lion of
the tribe of Judah shall prevail, and the dragon shall
be cast out. Professor! is sin subdued in you? If
your *life* is unholy your *heart* is unchanged, and if
your heart is unchanged you are an unsaved person.
If the Saviour has not sanctified you, renewed
you, given you a hatred of sin and a love of
holiness, He has done nothing in you of a saving
character. The grace which does not make a man
better than others is a worthless counterfeit. Christ
saves His people, not *in* their sins, but *from* them.
"Without holiness no man shall see the Lord."
"Let every one that nameth the name of Christ
depart from iniquity." If not saved from sin, how
shall we hope to be counted among His people. Lord,
save me even now from all evil, and enable me to
honour my Saviour.

"And David enquired of the Lord."—2 Samuel v. 23.

WHEN David made this enquiry he had just fought the Philistines, and gained a signal victory. The Philistines came up in great hosts, but, by the help of God, David had easily put them to flight. Note, however, that when they came a second time, David did not go up to fight them without enquiring of the Lord. Once he had been victorious, and he might have said, as many have in other cases, " I shall be victorious again ; I may rest quite sure that if I have conquered once I shall triumph yet again. Wherefore should I tarry to seek at the Lord's hands ? " Not so, David. He had gained one battle by the strength of the Lord ; he would not venture upon another until he had ensured the same. He enquired, "Shall I go up against them ? " He waited until God's sign was given. Learn from David to take no step without God. Christian, if thou wouldst know the path of duty, take God for thy compass ; if thou wouldst steer thy ship through the dark billows, put the tiller into the hand of the Almighty. Many a rock might be escaped, if we would let our Father take the helm ; many a shoal or quicksand we might well avoid, if we would leave to His sovereign will to choose and to command. The Puritan said, " As sure as ever a Christian carves for himself, he'll cut his own fingers ; " this is a great truth. Said another old divine, " He that goes before the cloud of God's providence goes on a fool's errand ;" and so he does. We must mark God's providence leading us ; and if providence tarries, tarry till providence comes. He who goes before providence, will be very glad to run back again. "I will instruct thee and teach thee in the way which thou shalt go," is God's promise to His people. Let us, then, take all our perplexities to Him, and say, "Lord, what wilt thou have me to do ? " Leave not thy chamber this morning without enquiring of the Lord.

"Lead us not into temptation; but deliver us from evil [or the evil one]."—Luke xi. 4.

WHAT we are taught to seek or shun in prayer, we should equally pursue or avoid in action. Very earnestly, therefore, should we avoid temptation, seeking to walk so guardedly in the path of obedience, that we may never tempt the devil to tempt us. We are not to enter the thicket in search of the lion. Dearly might we pay for such presumption. This lion may cross our path or leap upon us from the thicket, but we have nothing to do with hunting him. He that meeteth with him, even though he winneth the day, will find it a stern struggle. Let the Christian pray that he may be spared the encounter. Our Saviour, who had experience of what temptation meant, thus earnestly admonished His disciples—"Pray that ye enter not into temptation."

But let us do as we will, we shall be tempted; hence the prayer "deliver us from evil." God had one Son without sin; but He has no son without temptation. The natural man is born to trouble as the sparks fly upwards, and the Christian man is born to temptation just as certainly. We must be always on our watch against Satan, because, like a thief, he gives no intimation of his approach. Believers who have had experience of the ways of Satan, know that there are certain seasons when he will most probably make an attack, just as at certain seasons bleak winds may be expected; thus the Christian is put on a double guard by fear of danger, and the danger is averted by preparing to meet it. Prevention is better than cure: it is better to be so well armed that the devil will not attack you, than to endure the perils of the fight, even though you come off a conqueror. Pray this evening first that you may not be tempted, and next that if temptation be permitted, you may be delivered from the evil one.

" I know how to abound." –Philippians iv. 12.

HERE are many who know "how to be abased " who have not learned "how to abound." When they are set upon the top of a pinnacle their heads grow dizzy, and they are ready to fall. The Christian far oftener disgraces his profession in prosperity than in adversity. It is a dangerous thing to be prosperous. The crucible of adversity is a less severe trial to the Christian than the fining-pot of prosperity. Oh, what leanness of soul and neglect of spiritual things have been brought on through the very mercies and bounties of God ! Yet this is not a matter of necessity, for the apostle tells us that he knew how to abound. When he had much he knew how to use it. Abundant grace enabled him to bear abundant prosperity. When he had a full sail he was loaded with much ballast, and so floated safely. It needs more than human skill to carry the brimming cup of mortal joy with a steady hand, yet Paul had learned that skill, for he declares, " In all things I am instructed both to be full and to be hungry." It is a divine lesson to know how to be full, for the Israelites were full once, but while the flesh was yet in their mouth, the wrath of God came upon them. Many have asked for mercies that they might satisfy their own hearts' lust. Fulness of bread has often made fulness of blood, and that has brought on wantonness of spirit. When we have much of God's providential mercies, it often happens that we have but little of God's grace, and little gratitude for the bounties we have received. We are full and we forget God: satisfied with earth, we are content to do without heaven. Rest assured it is harder to know how to be full than it is to know how to be hungry—so desperate is the tendency of human nature to pride and forgetfulness of God. Take care that you ask in your prayers that God would teach you " how to be full."

> " Let not the gifts Thy love bestows
> Estrange our hearts from Thee."

"I have blotted out, as a thick cloud, thy transgressions, and, as a cloud, thy sins: return unto Me; for I have redeemed thee."—Isaiah xliv. 22.

ATTENTIVELY observe THE INSTRUCTIVE SIMILITUDE: our sins are like *a cloud*. As clouds are of many shapes and shades, so are our transgressions. As clouds obscure the light of the sun, and darken the landscape beneath, so do our sins hide from us the light of Jehovah's face, and cause us to sit in the shadow of death. They are earth-born things, and rise from the miry places of our nature; and when so collected that their measure is full, they threaten us with storm and tempest. Alas! that, unlike clouds, our sins yield us no genial showers, but rather threaten to deluge us with a fiery flood of destruction. O ye black clouds of sin, how can it be fair weather with our souls while ye remain?

Let our joyful eye dwell upon THE NOTABLE ACT of divine mercy—"blotting out." God Himself appears upon the scene, and in divine benignity, instead of manifesting His anger, reveals His grace: He at once and for ever effectually removes the mischief, not by blowing away the cloud, but by blotting it out from existence once for all. Against the justified man no sin remains, the great transaction of the cross has eternally removed His transgressions from him. On Calvary's summit the great deed, by which the sin of all the chosen was for ever put away, was completely and effectually performed.

Practically let us obey THE GRACIOUS COMMAND, *"return unto me."* Why should pardoned sinners live at a distance from their God? If we have been forgiven all our sins, let no legal fear withhold us from the boldest access to our Lord. Let backslidings be bemoaned, but let us not persevere in them. To the greatest possible nearness of communion with the Lord, let us, in the power of the Holy Spirit, strive mightily to return. O Lord, this night restore us!

" And they took knowledge of them, that they had been with Jesus."—Acts. iv. 13.

CHRISTIAN should be a striking likeness of Jesus Christ. You have read lives of Christ, beautifully and eloquently written, but the best life of Christ is His living biography, written out in the words and actions of His people. If we were what we profess to be, and what we should be, we should be pictures of Christ; yea, such striking likenesses of Him, that the world would not have to hold us up by the hour together, and say, " Well, it seems somewhat of a likeness; " but they would, when they once beheld us, exclaim, "He has been with Jesus; he has been taught of Him; he is like Him; he has caught the very idea of the holy Man of Nazareth, and he works it out in his life and every-day actions." A Christian should be like Christ in his *boldness.* Never blush to own your religion; your profession will never disgrace you: take care you never disgrace *that.* Be like Jesus, very valiant for your God. Imitate Him in your *loving* spirit; think kindly, speak kindly, and do kindly, that men may say of you, " He has been with Jesus." Imitate Jesus in His *holiness.* Was He zealous for His Master? So be you ; ever go about doing good. Let not time be wasted : it is too precious. Was He self-denying, never looking to His own interest? Be the same. Was He devout ? Be you fervent in your prayers. Had He deference to His Father's will? So submit yourselves to Him. Was He patient? So learn to endure. And best of all, as the highest portraiture of Jesus, try to forgive your enemies, as He did; and let those sublime words of your Master, " Father, forgive them; for they know not what they do," always ring in your ears. Forgive, as you hope to be forgiven. Heap coals of fire on the head of your foe by your kindness to him. Good for evil, recollect, is godlike. Be godlike, then; and in all ways and by all means, so live that all may say of you, " He has been with Jesus."

"*Thou hast left thy first love.*"—Revelation ii. 4.

EVER to be remembered is that best and brightest of hours, when first we saw the Lord, lost our burden, received the roll of promise, rejoiced in full salvation, and went on our way in peace. It was spring time in the soul; the winter was past; the mutterings of Sinai's thunders were hushed; the flashings of its lightnings were no more perceived; God was beheld as reconciled; the law threatened no vengeance, justice demanded no punishment. Then the flowers appeared in our heart; hope, love, peace, and patience sprung from the sod; the hyacinth of repentance, the snowdrop of pure holiness, the crocus of golden faith, the daffodil of early love, all decked the garden of the soul. The time of the singing of birds was come, and we rejoiced with thanksgiving; we magnified the holy name of our forgiving God, and our resolve was, "Lord, I am Thine, wholly Thine; all I am, and all I have, I would devote to Thee. Thou hast bought me with Thy blood—let me spend myself and be spent in Thy service. In life and in death let me be consecrated to Thee." *How have we kept this resolve?* Our espousal love burned with a holy flame of devotedness to Jesus—is it the same *now*? Might not Jesus well say to us, "I have somewhat against thee, because thou hast left thy first love"? Alas! it is but little we have done for our Master's glory. Our winter has lasted all too long. We are as cold as ice when we should feel a summer's glow and bloom with sacred flowers. We give to God pence when He deserveth pounds, nay, deserveth our heart's blood to be coined in the service of His church and of His truth. But shall we continue thus? O Lord, after Thou hast so richly blessed us, shall we be ungrateful and become indifferent to Thy good cause and work? O quicken us that we may return to our first love, and do our first works! Send us a genial spring, O Sun of Righteousness.

" For as the sufferings of Christ abound in us, so our consolation also aboundeth by Christ."—2 Corinthians i. 5.

HERE is a blessed proportion. The Ruler of Providence bears a pair of scales—in this side He puts His people's trials, and in that He puts their consolations. When the scale of trial is nearly empty, you will always find the scale of consolation in nearly the same condition; and when the scale of trials is full, you will find the scale of consolation just as heavy. When the black clouds gather most, the light is the more brightly revealed to us. When the night lowers and the tempest is coming on, the Heavenly Captain is always closest to His crew. It is a blessed thing, that when we are most cast down, then it is that we are most lifted up by the consolations of the Spirit. One reason is, because *trials make more room for consolation.* Great hearts can only be made by great troubles. The spade of trouble digs the reservoir of comfort deeper, and makes more room for consolation. God comes into our heart—He finds it full—He begins to break our comforts and to make it empty; then there is more room for grace. The humbler a man lies, the more comfort he will always have, because he will be more fitted to receive it. Another reason why we are often most happy in our troubles, is this—*then we have the closest dealings with God.* When the barn is full, man can live without God: when the purse is bursting with gold, we try to do without so much prayer. But once take our *gourds* away, and we want our *God;* once cleanse the idols out of the house, then we are compelled to honour Jehovah. "Out of the depths have I cried unto thee, O Lord." There is no cry so good as that which comes from the bottom of the mountains; no prayer half so hearty as that which comes up from the depths of the soul, through deep trials and afflictions. Hence they bring us to God, and we are happier; for nearness to God is happiness. Come, troubled believer, fret not over your heavy troubles, for they are the heralds of weighty mercies.

" He shall give you another Comforter, that He may abide with you for ever."—John xiv. 16.

THE Great Father revealed Himself to believers of old before the coming of His Son, and was known to Abraham, Isaac, and Jacob as the God Almighty. Then Jesus came, and the ever-blessed Son in His own proper person, was the delight of His people's eyes. At the time of the Redeemer's ascension, the Holy Spirit became the head of the present dispensation, and His power was gloriously manifested on and after Pentecost. He remains at this hour the present Immanuel—God with us, dwelling in and with His people, quickening, guiding, and ruling in their midst. Is His presence recognised as it ought to be? We cannot control His working; He is most sovereign in all His operations, but are we sufficiently anxious to obtain His help, or sufficiently watchful lest we provoke Him to withdraw His aid? Without Him we can do nothing, but by His almighty energy the most extraordinary results can be produced : everything depends upon His manifesting or concealing His power. Do we always look up to Him both for our inner life and our outward service with the respectful dependence which is fitting? Do we not too often run before His call and act independently of His aid? Let us humble ourselves this evening for past neglects, and now entreat the heavenly dew to rest upon us, the sacred oil to anoint us, the celestial flame to burn within us. The Holy Ghost is no temporary gift, He abides with the saints. We have but to seek Him aright, and He will be found of us. He is jealous, but He is pitiful ; if He leaves in anger, He returns in mercy. Condescending and tender, He does not weary of us, but waits to be gracious still.

> Sin has been hammering my heart
> Unto a hardness, void of love,
> Let suppling grace to cross his art
> Drop from above.

*" Behold, what manner of love the Father hath bestowed upon us, that we should be called the sons of God: therefore the world knoweth us not, because it knew Him not.   Beloved, now are we the sons of God."—*1 John iii. 1, 2.

" BEHOLD, what manner of love the Father hath bestowed upon *us*." Consider who we were, and what *we* feel ourselves to be even now when corruption is powerful in us, and you will wonder at our adoption. Yet *we* are called *" the sons of God."* What a high relationship is that of a son, and what privileges it brings ! What care and tenderness the son expects from his father, and what love the father feels towards the son ! But all *that*, and more than *that*, we now have through Christ. As for the temporary drawback of suffering with the elder brother, this we accept as an honour : "Therefore the world knoweth us not, because it knew Him not." We are content to be unknown with Him in His humiliation, for we are to be exalted with Him. *" Beloved, now are we the sons of God."* That is easy to read, but it is not so easy to feel. How is it with your heart this morning ? Are you in the lowest depths of sorrow ? Does corruption rise within your spirit, and grace seem like a poor spark trampled under foot ? Does your faith almost fail you ? Fear not, it is neither your graces nor feelings on which you are to live : you must live simply by faith on Christ. With all these things against us, *now*—in the very depths of our sorrow, wherever we may be—*now*, as much in the valley as on the mountain, " Beloved, *now* are we the sons of God." " Ah, but," you say, "see how I am arrayed ! my graces are not bright ; my righteousness does not shine with apparent glory." But read the next : " *It doth not yet appear what we shall be : but we know that, when He shall appear, we shall be like Him."* The Holy Spirit shall purify our minds, and divine power shall refine our bodies, then shall *we see Him as He is.*

"There is therefore now no condemnation."—Romans viii. 1.

COME, my soul, think thou of this. Believing in Jesus, thou art actually and effectually cleared from guilt; thou art led out of thy prison. Thou art no more in fetters as a bond-slave; thou art delivered *now* from the bondage of the law; thou art freed from sin, and canst walk at large as a freeman, thy Saviour's blood has procured thy full discharge. Thou hast a right now to approach thy Father's throne. No flames of vengeance are there to scare thee now; no fiery sword; justice cannot smite the innocent. Thy disabilities are taken away: thou wast once unable to see thy Father's face: thou canst see it now. Thou couldst not speak with Him; but now thou hast access with boldness. Once there was a fear of hell upon thee; but thou hast no fear of it now, for how can there be punishment for the guiltless? He who believeth is not condemned, and cannot be punished. And more than all, the privileges thou mightst have enjoyed, if thou hadst never sinned, are thine now thou art justified. All the blessings which thou wouldst have had if thou hadst kept the law, and more, are thine, because Christ has kept it for thee. All the love and the acceptance which perfect obedience could have obtained of God, belong to thee, because Christ was perfectly obedient on thy behalf, and hath imputed all His merits to thy account, that thou mightst be exceeding rich through Him, who for thy sake became exceeding poor. Oh! how great the debt of love and gratitude thou owest to thy Saviour!

> "A debtor to mercy alone,
>   Of covenant mercy I sing;
> Nor fear with Thy righteousness on,
>   My person and offerings to bring:
> The terrors of law and of God,
>   With me can have nothing to do;
> My Saviour's obedience and blood
>   Hide all my transgressions from view."

" And his allowance was a continual allowance given him of the king, a daily rate for every day, all the days of his life."—2 Kings xxv. 30.

EHOIACHIN was not sent away from the king's palace with a store to last him for months, but his provision was given him as a daily pension. Herein he well pictures the happy position of all the Lord's people. A daily portion is *all that a man really wants.* We do not need to-morrow's supplies ; that day has not yet dawned, and its wants are as yet unborn. The thirst which we may suffer in the month of June does not need to be quenched in February, for we do not feel it yet ; if we have enough for each day as the days arrive we shall never know want. Sufficient for the day is *all that we can enjoy.* We cannot eat or drink or wear more than the day's supply of food and raiment ; the surplus gives us the care of storing it, and the anxiety of watching against a thief. One staff aids a traveller, but a bundle of staves is a heavy burden. Enough is not only as good as a feast, but is all that the veriest glutton can truly enjoy. This is *all that we should expect;* a craving for more than this is ungrateful. When our Father does not give us more, we should be content with his daily allowance. Jehoiachin's case is ours, we have a *sure* portion, a portion *given us of the king,* a *gracious* portion, and a *perpetual* portion. Here is surely ground for thankfulness.

Beloved Christian reader, in matters of grace *you need a daily supply.* You have no store of strength. Day by day must you seek help from above. It is a very sweet assurance that *a daily portion is provided for you.* In the word, through the ministry, by meditation, in prayer, and waiting upon God you shall receive renewed strength. In Jesus all needful things are laid up for you. Then *enjoy your continual allowance.* Never go hungry while the daily bread of grace is on the table of mercy.

"*She was healed immediately.*"—Luke viii. 47.

ONE of the most touching and teaching of the Saviour's miracles is before us to-night. The woman was very ignorant. She imagined that virtue came out of Christ by a law of necessity, without His knowledge or direct will. Moreover, she was a stranger to the generosity of Jesus' character, or she would not have gone behind to steal the cure which He was so ready to bestow. Misery should always place itself right in the face of mercy. Had she known the love of Jesus' heart, she would have said, "I have but to put myself where He can see me—His omniscience will teach Him my case, and His love at once will work my cure." We admire her faith, but we marvel at her ignorance. After she had obtained the cure, she rejoiced with trembling: glad was she that the divine virtue had wrought a marvel in her: but she feared lest Christ should retract the blessing, and put a negative upon the grant of His grace: little did she comprehend the fulness of His love! We have not so clear a view of Him as we could wish; we know not the heights and depths of His love; but we know of a surety that He is too good to withdraw from a trembling soul the gift which it has been able to obtain. But here is the marvel of it: little as was her knowledge, her faith, because it was real faith, saved her, and saved her at once. There was no tedious delay—faith's miracle was instantaneous. If we have faith as a grain of mustard seed, salvation is our present and eternal possession. If in the list of the Lord's children we are written as the feeblest of the family, yet, being heirs through faith, no power, human or devilish, can eject us from salvation. If we cannot clasp the Lord in our hands with Simeon, if we dare not lean our heads upon His bosom with John, yet if we can venture in the press behind Him, and touch the hem of His garment, we are made whole. Courage, timid one! thy faith hath saved thee; go in peace. "*Being* justified by faith, *we have* peace with God."

HEAVEN will be full of the ceaseless praises of
Jesus. Eternity! thine unnumbered years
shall speed their everlasting course, but for
ever and for ever, "to Him be glory." Is He not a
"Priest for ever after the order of Melchisedek"?
"To Him be glory." Is He not king for ever?—King
of kings and Lord of lords, the everlasting Father?
"To Him be glory *for ever.*" Never shall His praises
cease. That which was bought with blood deserves to
last while immortality endures. The glory of the
cross must never be eclipsed; the lustre of the grave
and of the resurrection must never be dimmed. O
Jesus! thou shalt be praised for ever. Long as
immortal spirits live—long as the Father's throne
endures—for ever, for ever, unto Thee shall be glory.
Believer, you are anticipating the time when you shall
join the saints above in ascribing all glory to Jesus;
but are you glorifying Him *now*? The apostle's words
are, "To Him be glory both *now* and for ever." Will
you not this day make it your prayer? "Lord, help me
to glorify Thee; I am poor, help me to glorify Thee
by contentment; I am sick, help me to give Thee
honour by patience; I have talents, help me to extol
Thee by spending them for Thee; I have time, Lord,
help me to redeem it, that I may serve thee; I have a
heart to feel, Lord, let that heart feel no love but
Thine, and glow with no flame but affection for
Thee; I have a head to think, Lord, help me to
think *of* Thee and *for* Thee; Thou hast put me in
this world for something, Lord, show me what that
is, and help me to work out my life-purpose: I
cannot do much; but as the widow put in her two
mites, which were all her living, so, Lord, I cast my
time and eternity too into Thy treasury; I am all
Thine; take me, and enable me to glorify Thee *now*.
in all that I say, in all that I do, and with all that
I have."

"Whereby they have made Thee glad."—Psalm xlv. 8.

AND who are thus privileged to make the Saviour glad? His church—His people. But is it possible? He makes *us* glad, but how can *we make Him glad?* By *our love.* Ah! we think it so cold, so faint; and so, indeed, we must sorrowfully confess it to be, but it is very sweet to Christ. Hear His own eulogy of that love in the golden Canticle: "How fair is thy love, my sister, my spouse! how much better is thy love than wine!" See, loving heart, how He delights in you. When you lean your head on His bosom, you not only receive, but you give Him joy; when you gaze with love upon His all-glorious face, you not only obtain comfort, but impart delight. Our *praise*, too, gives Him joy—not the song of the lips alone, but the melody of the heart's deep gratitude. Our *gifts*, too, are very pleasant to Him; He loves to see us lay our time, our talents, our substance upon His altar, not for the value of what we give, but for the sake of the motive from which the gift springs. To Him the lowly offerings of His saints are more acceptable than thousands of gold and silver. *Holiness* is like frankincense and myrrh to Him. Forgive your enemy, and you make Christ glad; distribute of your substance to the poor, and He rejoices; be the means of saving souls, and you give Him to see of the travail of His soul; proclaim His gospel, and you are a sweet savour unto Him; go among the ignorant and lift us the cross, and you have given Him honour. It is in your power even now to break the alabaster box, and pour the precious oil of joy upon His head, as did the woman of old, whose memorial is to this day set forth wherever the gospel is preached. Will you be backward then? Will you not perfume your beloved Lord with the myrrh and aloes, and cassia, of your heart's praise? Yes, ye ivory palaces, ye shall hear the songs of the saints!

" I have learned, in whatsoever state I am, therewith to be content."—Philippians iv. 11.

THESE words show us that contentment is not a natural propensity of man. " Ill weeds grow apace." Covetousness, discontent, and murmuring are as natural to man as thorns are to the soil. We need not sow thistles and brambles; they come up naturally enough, because they are indigenous to earth: and so, we need not teach men to complain; they complain fast enough without any education. But the precious things of the earth must be cultivated. If we would have wheat, we must plough and sow; if we want flowers, there must be the garden, and all the gardener's care. Now, contentment is one of the flowers of heaven, and if we would have it, it must be cultivated; it will not grow in us by nature; it is the new nature alone that can produce it, and even then we must be specially careful and watchful that we maintain and cultivate the grace which God has sown in us. Paul says, " I have *learned* . . to be content;" as much as to say, he did not know how at one time. It cost him some pains to attain to the mystery of that great truth. No doubt he sometimes thought he had learned, and then broke down. And when at last he had attained unto it, and could say, "I have learned in whatsoever state I am, therewith to be content," he was an old, grey-headed man, upon the borders of the grave—a poor prisoner shut up in Nero's dungeon at Rome. We might well be willing to endure Paul's infirmities, and share the cold dungeon with him, if we too might by any means attain unto his good degree. Do not indulge the notion that you can be contented without *learning*, or learn without discipline. It is not a power that may be exercised naturally, but a science to be acquired gradually. We know this from experience. Brother, hush that murmur, natural though it be, and continue a diligent pupil in the College of Content.

" Thy good Spirit."—Nehemiah ix. 20.

COMMON, too common is the sin of forgetting the Holy Spirit. This is folly and ingratitude. He deserves well at our hands, for He is good, supremely good. As God, He is *good essentially.* He shares in the threefold ascription of Holy, holy, holy, which ascends to the Triune Jehovah. Unmixed purity, and truth, and grace is He. He is *good benevolently,* tenderly bearing with our waywardness, striving with our rebellious wills; quickening us from our death in sin, and then training us for the skies as a loving nurse fosters her child. How generous, forgiving, and tender is this patient Spirit of God. He is *good operatively.* All His works are good in the most eminent degree: He suggests good thoughts, prompts good actions, reveals good truths, applies good promises, assists in good attainments, and leads to good results. There is no spiritual good in all the world of which He is not the author and sustainer, and heaven itself will owe the perfect character of its redeemed inhabitants to His work. He is *good officially;* whether as Comforter, Instructor, Guide, Sanctifier, Quickener, or Intercessor, He fulfils His office well, and each work is fraught with the highest good to the church of God. They who yield to His influences become good, they who obey His impulses do good, they who live under His power receive good. Let us then act towards so good a person according to the dictates of gratitude. Let us revere His person, and adore Him as God over all, blessed for ever ; let us own His power, and our need of Him by waiting upon Him in all our holy enterprises ; let us hourly seek His aid, and never grieve Him ; and let us speak to His praise whenever occasion occurs. The church will never prosper until more reverently it believes in the Holy Ghost. He is so good and kind, that it is sad indeed that He should be grieved by slights and negligences.

" Isaac dwelt by the well Lahai-roi."—Genesis xxv. 11.

AGAR had once found deliverance there and
Ishmael had drank from the water so graciously revealed by the God who liveth and
seeth the sons of men; but this was a merely casual
visit, such as worldlings pay to the Lord in times
of need, when it serves their turn. They cry to
Him in trouble, but forsake Him in prosperity. Isaac
dwelt there, and made the well of the living and all-
seeing God his constant source of supply. The usual
tenor of a man's life, the *dwelling* of his soul, is the
true test of his state. Perhaps the providential
visitation experienced by Hagar struck Isaac's mind,
and led him to revere the place; its mystical name
endeared it to him; his frequent musings by its brim
at eventide made him familiar with the well; his
meeting Rebecca there had made his spirit feel at
home near the spot; but best of all, the fact that he there
enjoyed fellowship with the living God, had made him
select that hallowed ground for his dwelling. Let us
learn to live in the presence of the living God; let us
pray the Holy Spirit that this day, and every other
day, we may feel, " Thou God seest me." May the
Lord Jehovah be as a well to us, delightful, comforting, unfailing, springing up unto eternal life. The
bottle of the creature cracks and dries up, but the well
of the Creator never fails; happy is he who dwells at
the well, and so has abundant and constant supplies
near at hand. The Lord has been a sure helper to
others: His name is Shaddai, God All-sufficient; our
hearts have often had most delightful intercourse with
Him; through Him our soul has found her glorious
Husband, the Lord Jesus; and in Him this day we
live, and move, and have our being; let us, then, dwell
in closest fellowship with Him. Glorious Lord,
constrain us that we may never leave Thee, but dwell
by the well of the living God.

" Whereas the Lord was there."—Ezekiel xxxv. 10.

EDOM'S princes saw the whole country left desolate, and counted upon its easy conquest ; but there was one great difficulty in their way—quite unknown to them—*" The Lord was there;"* and in His presence lay the special security of the chosen land.   Whatever may be the machinations and devices of the enemies of God's people, there is still the same effectual barrier to thwart their design.   *The saints* are God's heritage, and He is in the midst of them, and will protect His own.   What comfort this assurance yields us in our troubles and spiritual conflicts !   We are constantly opposed, and yet perpetually preserved !   How often Satan shoots his arrows against our *faith*, but our faith defies the power of hell's fiery darts ; they are not only turned aside, but they are quenched upon its shield, for "the Lord is there."   *Our good works* are the subjects of Satan's attacks.   A saint never yet had a virtue or a grace which was not the target for hellish bullets : whether it was hope bright and sparkling, or love warm and fervent, or patience all-enduring, or zeal flaming like coals of fire, the old enemy of everything that is good has tried to destroy it.   The only reason why anything virtuous or lovely survives in us is this, "the Lord is there."

If the Lord be with us through life, we need not fear for our dying confidence ; for *when we come to die,* we shall find that "the Lord is *there;"* where the billows are most tempestuous, and the water is most chill, we shall feel the bottom, and know that it is good : our feet shall stand upon the Rock of Ages when time is passing away.   Beloved, from the first of a Christian's life to the last, the only reason why he does not perish is because *" the Lord is there."* When the God of everlasting love shall change and leave His elect to perish, then may the Church of God be destroyed ; but not till then, because it is written, JEHOVAH SHAMMAH, *"the Lord is there."*

" Shew me wherefore thou contendest with me."—Job x. 2.

PERHAPS, O tried soul, the Lord is doing this to develop thy graces. There are some of thy graces which would never be *discovered* if it were not for thy trials. Dost thou not know that thy faith never looks so grand in summer weather as it does in winter? Love is too often like a glow-worm, showing but little light except it be in the midst of surrounding darkness. Hope itself is like a star—not to be seen in the sunshine of prosperity, and only to be discovered in the night of adversity. Afflictions are often the black foils in which God doth set the jewels of His children's graces, to make them shine the better. It was but a little while ago that on thy knees thou wast saying, "Lord, I fear I have no faith : let me know that I have faith." Was not this really, though perhaps unconsciously, praying for trials?—for how canst thou know that thou hast faith until thy faith is exercised? Depend upon it, God often sends us trials that our graces may be discovered, and that we may be certified of their existence. Besides, it is not merely discovery, *real growth* in grace is the result of sanctified trials. God often takes away our comforts and our privileges in order to make us better Christians. He trains His soldiers, not in tents of ease and luxury, but by turning them out and using them to forced marches and hard service. He makes them ford through streams, and swim through rivers, and climb mountains, and walk many a long mile with heavy knapsacks of sorrow on their backs. Well, Christian, may not this account for the troubles through which thou art passing? Is not the Lord bringing out your graces, and making them grow? Is not this the reason why He is contending with you?

> " Trials make the promise sweet ;
>   Trials give new life to prayer ;
> Trials bring me to His feet,
>   Lay me low, and keep me there."

"Father, I have sinned."—Luke xv. 18.

IT is quite certain that those whom Christ has washed in His precious blood need not make a confession of sin, as culprits or criminals, before God the Judge, for Christ has for ever taken away all their sins in a legal sense, so that they no longer stand where they can be condemned, but are once for all accepted in the Beloved ; but having become children, and offending as children, ought they not every day to go before their heavenly Father and confess their sin, and acknowledge their iniquity in that character ? Nature teaches that it is the duty of erring children to make a confession to their earthly father, and the grace of God in the heart teaches us that we, as Christians, owe the same duty to our heavenly Father. We daily offend, and ought not to rest without daily pardon. For, supposing that my trespasses against my Father are not at once taken to Him to be washed away by the cleansing power of the Lord Jesus, what will be the consequence ? If I have not sought forgiveness and been washed from these offences against my Father, I shall feel at a distance from Him ; I shall doubt His love to me ; I shall tremble at Him ; I shall be afraid to pray to Him : I shall grow like the prodigal, who, although still a child, was yet far off from his father. But if, with a child's sorrow at offending so gracious and loving a Parent, I go to Him and tell Him all, and rest not till I realise that I am forgiven, then I shall feel a holy love to my Father, and shall go through my Christian career, not only as saved, but as one enjoying present peace in God through Jesus Christ my Lord. There is a wide distinction between confessing sin *as a culprit,* and confessing sin *as a child.* The Father's bosom is the place for penitent confessions. We have been cleansed once for all, but our feet still need to be washed from the defilement of our daily walk as children of God.

" Thus saith the Lord God ; I will yet for this be enquired of by the house of Israel, to do it for them."—Ezek. xxxvi. 37.

PRAYER is the forerunner of mercy. Turn to sacred history, and you will find that scarcely ever did a great mercy come to this world unheralded by supplication. You have found this true in your own personal experience. God has given you many an unsolicited favour, but still great prayer has always been the prelude of great mercy with you. When you first found peace through the blood of the cross, you had been praying much, and earnestly interceding with God that He would remove your doubts, and deliver you from your distresses. Your assurance was the result of prayer. When at any time you have had high and rapturous joys, you have been obliged to look upon them as answers to your prayers. When you have had great deliverances out of sore troubles, and mighty helps in great dangers, you have been able to say, " I sought the Lord, and He heard me, and delivered me from all my fears." Prayer is always the preface to blessing. It goes before the blessing *as the blessing's shadow.* When the sunlight of God's mercies rises upon our necessities, it casts the shadow of prayer far down upon the plain. Or, to use another illustration, when God piles up a hill of mercies, He Himself shines behind them, and He casts on our spirits the shadow of prayer, so that we may rest certain, if we are much in prayer, our pleadings are the shadows of mercy. Prayer is thus connected with the blessing *to show us the value of it.* If we had the blessings without asking for them, we should think them common things ; but prayer makes our mercies more precious than diamonds. The things we ask for are precious, but we do not realise their preciousness until we have sought for them earnestly.

> " Prayer makes the darken'd cloud withdraw ;
> Prayer climbs the ladder Jacob saw ;
> Gives exercise to faith and love ;
> Brings every blessing from above."

" He first findeth his own brother Simon."—John i. 41.

HIS case is an excellent pattern of all cases where spiritual life is vigorous. *As soon as a man has found Christ, he begins to find others.* I will not believe that thou hast tasted of the honey of the gospel if thou canst eat it all thyself. True grace puts an end to all spiritual monopoly. Andrew *first* found his own brother Simon, and then others. *Relationship has a very strong demand upon our first individual efforts.* Andrew, thou didst well to begin with Simon. I doubt whether there are not some Christians giving away tracts at other people's houses who would do well to give away a tract at their own— whether there are not some engaged in works of usefulness abroad who are neglecting their special sphere of usefulness at home. Thou mayst or thou mayst not be called to evangelise the people in any particular locality, but certainly thou art called to see after thine own servants, thine own kinsfolk and acquaintance. Let thy religion begin at home. Many tradesmen export their best commodities—the Christian should not. He should have all his conversation everywhere of the best savour ; but let him have a care to put forth the sweetest fruit of spiritual life and testimony in his own family. When Andrew went to find his brother, he little imagined how eminent Simon would become. *Simon Peter was worth ten Andrews* so far as we can gather from sacred history, and yet Andrew was instrumental in bringing him to Jesus. You may be very deficient in talent yourself, and yet you may be the means of drawing to Christ one who shall become eminent in grace and service. Ah! dear friend, you little know the possibilities which are in you. You may but speak a word to a child, and in that child there may be slumbering a noble heart which shall stir the Christian church in years to come. Andrew has only two talents, but he finds Peter. Go thou and do likewise.

" God, that comforteth those that are cast down."—2 Cor. vii. 6.

AND who comforteth like Him? Go to some poor, melancholy, distressed child of God; tell him sweet promises, and whisper in his ear choice words of comfort; he is like the deaf adder, he listens not to the voice of the charmer, charm he never so wisely. He is drinking gall and wormwood, and comfort him as you may, it will be only a note or two of mournful resignation that you will get from him; you will bring forth no psalms of praise, no hallelujahs, no joyful sonnets. But let *God* come to His child, let Him lift up his countenance, and the mourner's eyes glisten with hope. Do you not hear him sing—

> "'Tis paradise, if thou art here;
> If thou depart, 'tis hell"?

You could not have cheered him: but the Lord has done it; "He is the God of all comfort." There is no balm in Gilead, but there is balm in God. There is no physician among the creatures, but the Creator is Jehovah-rophi. It is marvellous how one sweet word of God will make whole songs for Christians. One word of God is like a piece of gold, and the Christian is the goldbeater, and can hammer that promise out for whole weeks. So, then, poor Christian, thou needest not sit down in despair. Go to the Comforter, and ask Him to give thee consolation. Thou art a poor dry well. You have heard it said, that when a pump is dry, you must pour water down it first of all, and then you will get water and so, Christian, when thou art dry, go to God, ask Him to shed abroad His joy in thy heart, and then thy joy shall be full. Do not go to earthly acquaintances, for you will find them Job's comforters after all; but go first and foremost to thy "God, that comforteth those that are cast down," and you will soon say, " In the multitude of my thoughts within me Thy comforts delight my soul."

*" Then was Jesus led up of the Spirit into the wilderness to
be tempted of the devil."*—Matthew iv. 1.

HOLY character does not avert temptation—
Jesus was tempted. When Satan tempts us,
his sparks fall upon tinder ; but in Christ's
case, it was like striking sparks on water ; yet the
enemy continued his evil work. Now, if the devil
goes on striking when there is no result, how much
more will he do it when he knows what inflammable
stuff our hearts are made of ! Though you become
greatly sanctified by the Holy Ghost, expect that the
great dog of hell will bark at you still. In the haunts
of men we expect to be tempted, but even seclusion will
not guard us from the same trial. Jesus Christ was
led away from human society into the wilderness, and
was tempted of the devil. Solitude has its charms and
its benefits, and may be useful in checking the lust of
the eye and the pride of life ; but the devil will follow
us into the most lovely retreats. Do not suppose that
it is only the worldly-minded who have dreadful
thoughts and blasphemous temptations, for even
spiritual-minded persons endure the same ; and in the
holiest position we may suffer the darkest temptation.
The utmost consecration of spirit will not insure you
against Satanic temptation. Christ was consecrated
through and through. It was His meat and drink
to do the will of Him that sent Him : and yet He was
tempted ! Your hearts may glow with a seraphic flame
of love to Jesus, and yet the devil will try to bring
you down to Laodicean lukewarmness. If you will
tell me when God permits a Christian to lay aside his
armour, I will tell you when Satan has left off temptation. Like the old knights in war time, we must sleep
with helmet and breastplate buckled on, for the arch-
deceiver will seize our first unguarded hour to make
us his prey. The Lord keep us watchful in all seasons,
and give us a final escape from the jaw of the lion
and the paw of the bear.

" He hath said."—Hebrews xiii. 5.

IF we can only grasp these words by faith, we have an all-conquering weapon in our hand. What doubt will not be slain by this two-edged sword? What fear is there which shall not fall smitten with a deadly wound before this arrow from the bow of God's covenant? Will not the distresses of life and the pangs of death; will not the corruptions within, and the snares without; will not the trials from above, and the temptations from beneath, all seem but light afflictions, when we can hide ourselves beneath the bulwark of "He hath said"? Yes; whether for delight in our quietude, or for strength in our conflict, " He hath said " must be our daily resort. And this may teach us the extreme value of *searching* the Scriptures. There may be a promise in the Word which would exactly fit your case, but you may not know of it, and therefore you miss its comfort. You are like prisoners in a dungeon, and there may be one key in the bunch which would unlock the door, and you might be free ; but if you will not look for it, you may remain a prisoner still, though liberty is so near at hand. There may be a potent medicine in the great pharmacopœia of Scripture, and you may yet continue sick unless you will examine and search the Scriptures to discover what "He hath said." Should you not, besides reading the Bible, store your memories richly with the promises of God? You can recollect the sayings of great men; you treasure up the verses of renowned poets ; ought you not to be profound in your knowledge of the words of God, so that you may be able to quote them readily when you would solve a difficulty, or overthrow a doubt? Since " He hath said " is the source of all wisdom, and the fountain of all comfort, let it dwell in you richly, as "A well of water, springing up unto everlasting life." So shall you grow healthy, strong, and happy in the divine life.

" Understandest thou what thou readest ? "—Acts viii. 30.

WE should be abler teachers of others, and less liable to be carried about by every wind of doctrine, if we sought to have a more intelligent understanding of the Word of God. As the Holy Ghost, the Author of the Scriptures, is He who alone can enlighten us rightly to understand them, we should constantly ask His teaching, and His guidance into all truth. When the prophet Daniel would interpret Nebuchadnezzar's dream, what did he do? He set himself to earnest prayer that God would open up the vision. The apostle John, in his vision at Patmos, saw a book sealed with seven seals which none was found worthy to open, or so much as to look upon. The book was afterwards opened by the Lion of the tribe of Judah, who had prevailed to open it; but it is written first—" I wept much." The tears of John, which were his liquid prayers, were, so far as he was concerned, the sacred keys by which the folded book was opened. Therefore if, for your own and others' profiting, you desire to be " filled with the knowledge of God's will in all wisdom and spiritual understanding," remember that prayer is your best means of study : like Daniel, you shall understand the dream, and the interpretation thereof, when you have sought unto God ; and like John you shall see the seven seals of precious truth unloosed, after you have wept much. Stones are not broken, except by an earnest use of the hammer ; and the stone-breaker must go down on his knees. Use the hammer of diligence, and let the knee of prayer be exercised, and there is not a stony doctrine in revelation which is useful for you to understand, which will not fly into shivers under the exercise of prayer and faith. You may force your way through anything with the leverage of prayer. Thoughts and reasonings are like the steel wedges which give a hold upon truth ; but prayer is the lever, the prise which forces open the iron chest of sacred mystery, that we may get the treasure hidden within.

" *His bow abode in strength, and the arms of his hands were made strong by the hands of the mighty God of Jacob.*"
Genesis xlix. 24.

WHAT strength which God gives to His Josephs is *real* strength ; it is not a boasted valour, a fiction, a thing of which men talk, but which ends in smoke ; it is true—*divine strength.* Why does Joseph stand against temptation ? Because God gives him aid. There is nought that we can do without the power of God. All true strength comes from " the mighty God of Jacob." Notice in what a *blessedly familiar way* God gives this strength to Joseph—"The arms of his hands were made strong by the hands of the mighty God of Jacob." Thus God is represented as putting His hands on Joseph's hands, placing His arms on Joseph's arms. Like as a father teaches his children, so the Lord teaches them that fear Him. He puts His arms upon them. Marvellous condescension ! God Almighty, Eternal, Omnipotent, stoops from His throne and lays His hand upon the child's hand, stretching His arm upon the arm of Joseph, that he may be made strong ! This strength was also *covenant strength*, for it is ascribed to "the mighty *God of Jacob.*" Now, wherever you read of the God of Jacob in the Bible, you should remember the covenant with Jacob. Christians love to think of God's covenant. All the power, all the grace, all the blessings, all the mercies, all the comforts, all the things we have, flow to us from the well-head, through the covenant. If there were no covenant, then we should fail indeed ; for all grace proceeds from it, as light and heat from the sun. No angels ascend or descend, save upon that ladder which Jacob saw, at the top of which stood a covenant God. Christian, it may be that the archers have sorely grieved you, and shot at you, and wounded you, but still your bow abides in strength ; be sure, then, to ascribe all the glory to Jacob's God.

"The Lord is slow to anger, and great in power."—Nahum i. 3

JEHOVAH *"is slow to anger."* When mercy cometh into the world she driveth winged steeds; the axles of her chariot-wheels are red hot with speed; but when wrath goeth forth, it toileth on with tardy footsteps, for God taketh no pleasure in the sinner's death. God's rod of mercy is ever in His hands outstretched; His sword of justice is in its scabbard, held down by that pierced hand of love which bled for the sins of men. "The Lord is slow to anger," because He is GREAT IN POWER. He is truly great in power who hath power over himself. When God's power doth restrain Himself, then it is power indeed: the power that binds omnipotence is omnipotence surpassed. A man who has a strong mind can bear to be insulted long, and only resents the wrong when a sense of right demands his action. The weak mind is irritated at a little: the strong mind bears it like a rock which moveth not, though a thousand breakers dash upon it, and cast their pitiful malice in spray upon its summit. God marketh His enemies, and yet He bestirs not Himself, but holdeth in His anger. If He were less divine than He is, He would long ere this have sent forth the whole of His thunders, and emptied the magazines of heaven; He would long ere this have blasted the earth with the wondrous fires of its lower regions, and man would have been utterly destroyed; but the greatness of his power brings us mercy. Dear reader, what is your state this evening? Can you by humble faith look to Jesus, and say, "My substitute, Thou art my rock, my trust"? Then, beloved, be not afraid of God's power; for now that you are forgiven and accepted, now that by faith you have fled to Christ for refuge, the power of God need no more terrify you, than the shield and sword of the warrior need terrify those whom he loves. Rather rejoice that He who is "great in power" is your Father and Friend.

" I will never leave thee."—Hebrews xiii. 5.

NO promise is of private interpretation. Whatever God has said to any one saint, He has said to all. When He opens a well for one, it is that all may drink. When He openeth a granary-door to give out food, there may be some one starving man who is the occasion of its being opened, but all hungry saints may come and feed too. Whether He gave the word to Abraham or to Moses, matters not, O believer; He has given it to thee as one of the covenanted seed. There is not a high blessing too lofty for thee, nor a wide mercy too extensive for thee. Lift up now thine eyes to the north and to the south, to the east and to the west, for all this is thine. Climb to Pisgah's top, and view the utmost limit of the divine promise, for the land is all thine own. There is not a brook of living water of which thou mayst not drink. If the land floweth with milk and honey, eat the honey and drink the milk, for both are thine. Be thou bold to believe, for He hath said, "I will never leave *thee*, nor forsake *thee*." In this promise, God gives to His people everything. "*I* will never leave thee." Then no attribute of God can cease to be engaged for us. Is He mighty? He will show Himself strong on the behalf of them that trust Him. Is HE love? Then with lovingkindness will He have mercy upon us. Whatever attributes may compose the character of Deity, every one of them to its fullest extent shall be engaged on our side. To put everything in one, there is nothing you can want, there is nothing you can ask for, there is nothing you can need in time or in eternity, there is nothing living, nothing dying, there is nothing in this world, nothing in the next world, there is nothing now, nothing at the resurrection-morning, nothing in heaven which is not contained in this text—"I will never leave thee, nor forsake thee."

" Take up the cross, and follow Me."—Mark x. 21.

OU have not the making of your own cross, although unbelief is a master carpenter at cross-making; neither are you permitted to choose your own cross, although self-will would fain be lord and master; but your cross is prepared and appointed for you by divine love, and you are cheerfully to accept it; you are to *take up* the cross as your chosen badge and burden, and not to stand cavilling at it. This night Jesus bids you submit your shoulder to His easy yoke. Do not kick at it in petulance, or trample on it in vain-glory, or fall under it in despair, or run away from it in fear, but take it up like a true follower of Jesus. Jesus was a cross-bearer; He leads the way in the path of sorrow. Surely you could not desire a better guide! And if He carries a cross, what nobler burden would you desire? The *Via Crucis* is the way of safety; fear not to tread its thorny paths.

Beloved, the cross is not made of feathers, or lined with velvet, it is heavy and galling to disobedient shoulders; but it is not an iron cross, though your fears have painted it with iron colours, it is a wooden cross, and a man can carry it, for the Man of Sorrows tried the load. Take up your cross, and by the power of the Spirit of God, you will soon be so in love with it, that like Moses, you would not exchange the reproach of Christ for all the treasures of Egypt. Remember that Jesus carried it, and it will smell sweetly; remember that it will soon be followed by the crown, and the thought of the coming weight of glory will greatly lighten the present heaviness of trouble. The Lord help you to bow your spirit in submission to the divine will ere you fall asleep this night, that waking with to-morrow's sun, you may go forth to the day's cross with the holy and submissive spirit which becomes a follower of the Crucified.

" I will cause the shower to come down in his season; there shall be showers of blessing."—Ezekiel xxxiv. 26.

HERE is *sovereign mercy*—"I will give them the shower in its season." Is it not sovereign, *divine* mercy?—for who can say, " I will give them showers," except God? There is only one voice which can speak to the clouds, and bid them beget the rain. Who sendeth down the rain upon the earth? Who scattereth the showers upon the green herb? Do not I, the Lord? So grace is the gift of God, and is not to be created by man. It is also *needed* grace. What would the ground do without showers? You may break the clods, you may sow your seeds, but what can you do without the rain? As absolutely needful is the divine blessing. In vain you labour, until God the plenteous shower bestows, and sends salvation down. Then, it is *plenteous grace.* "I will send them showers." It does not say," I will send them drops,"but "showers." So it is with grace. If God gives a blessing, He usually gives it in such a measure that there is not room enough to receive it. Plenteous grace! Ah! we want plenteous grace to keep us humble, to make us prayerful, to make us holy; plenteous grace to make us zealous, to preserve us through this life, and at last to land us in heaven. We cannot do without saturating showers of grace. Again, it is *seasonable grace.* " I will cause the shower to come down *in his season."* What is thy season this morning? Is it the season of drought? Then that is the season for showers. Is it a season of great heaviness and black clouds? Then that is the season for showers. "As thy days so shall thy strength be." And here is a *varied* blessing. " I will give thee *showers* of blessing." The word is in the plural. All kinds of blessings God will send. All God's blessings go together, like links in a golden chain. If He gives converting grace, He will also give comforting grace. He will send "showers of blessing." Look up to-day, O parched plant, and open thy leaves and flowers for a heavenly watering.

"O Lord of hosts, how long wilt thou not have mercy upon Jerusalem? ... And the Lord answered the angel ... with good words and comfortable words."—Zechariah i. 12, 13.

WHAT a sweet answer to an anxious enquiry! This night let us rejoice in it. O Zion, there are good things in store for thee; thy time of travail shall soon be over; thy children shall be brought forth; thy captivity shall end. Bear patiently the rod for a season, and under the darkness still trust in God, for His love burneth towards thee. God loves the church with a love too deep for human imagination: He loves her with all His infinite heart. Therefore let her sons be of good courage; she cannot be far from prosperity to whom God speaketh "good words and comfortable words." What these comfortable words are the prophet goes on to tell us: "I am jealous for Jerusalem and for Zion with a great jealousy." The Lord loves His church so much that He cannot bear that she should go astray to others; and when she has done so, He cannot endure that she should suffer too much or too heavily. He will not have his enemies afflict her: He is displeased with them because they increase her misery. When God seems most to leave His church, His heart is warm towards her. History shows us that whenever God uses a rod to chasten His servants, He always breaks it afterwards, as if He loathed the rod which gave his children pain. He feels the smart far more than His people. "Like as a father pitieth his children, so the Lord pitieth them that fear Him." God hath not forgotten us because He smites —His blows are no evidences of want of love. If this is true of His church *collectively*, it is of necessity true also of *each individual member*. You may fear that the Lord has passed you by, but it is not so: He who counts the stars, and calls them by their names, is in no danger of forgetting His own children. He knows your case as thoroughly as if you were the only creature He ever made, or the only saint He ever loved. Approach Him and be at peace.

" The wrath to come."—Matthew iii. 7.

T is pleasant to pass over a country after a storm has spent itself; to smell the freshness of the herbs after the rain has passed away, and to note the drops while they glisten like purest diamonds in the sunlight. That is the position of a Christian. He is going through a land where the storm has spent itself upon His Saviour's head, and if there be a few drops of sorrow falling, they distil from clouds of mercy, and Jesus cheers him by the assurance that they are not for his destruction. But how terrible is it to witness the approach of a tempest: to note the forewarnings of the storm; to mark the birds of heaven as they droop their wings; to see the cattle as they lay their heads low in terror; to discern the face of the sky as it groweth black, and look to the sun which shineth not, and the heavens which are angry and frowning ! How terrible to await the dread advance of a hurricane—such as occurs, sometimes, in the tropics—to wait in terrible apprehension till the wind shall rush forth in fury, tearing up trees from their roots, forcing rocks from their pedestals, and hurling down all the dwelling-places of man ! And yet, sinner, this is your present position. No hot drops have as yet fallen, but a shower of fire is coming. No terrible winds howl around you, but God's tempest is gathering its dread artillery. As yet the water-floods are dammed up by mercy, but the flood-gates shall soon be opened : the thunderbolts of God are yet in His storehouse, but lo ! the tempest hastens, and how awful shall that moment be when God, robed in vengeance, shall march forth in fury ! Where, where, where, O sinner, wilt thou hide thy head, or whither wilt thou flee ? O that the hand of mercy may now lead you to Christ ! He is freely set before you in the gospel : His riven side is the rock of shelter. Thou knowest thy need of Him ; believe in Him, cast thyself upon Him, and then the fury shall be overpast for ever.

*" But Jonah rose up to flee unto Tarshish from the presence
of the Lord, and went down to Joppa."*—Jonah i. 3.

INSTEAD of going to Nineveh to preach the Word, as God bade him, Jonah disliked the work, and went down to Joppa to escape from it. There are occasions when God's servants shrink from duty. But what is the consequence? What did Jonah lose by his conduct? *He lost the presence and comfortable enjoyment of God's love.* When *we* serve our Lord Jesus as believers should do, our God is with us; and though we have the whole world against us, if we have God with us, what does it matter? But the moment we start back, and seek our own inventions, we are at sea without a pilot. Then may we bitterly lament and groan out, "O my God, where hast Thou gone? How could I have been so foolish as to shun Thy service, and in this way to lose all the bright shinings of Thy face? This is a price too high. Let me return to my allegiance, that I may rejoice in Thy presence." In the next place, Jonah *lost all peace of mind.* Sin soon destroys a believer's comfort. It is the poisonous upas tree, from whose leaves distil deadly drops which destroy the life of joy and peace. Jonah *lost everything upon which he might have drawn for comfort in any other case.* He could not plead the promise of divine protection, for he was not in God's ways; he could not say, "Lord, I meet with these difficulties in the discharge of my duty, therefore help me through them." He was reaping his own deeds; he was filled with his own ways. Christian, do not play the Jonah, unless you wish to have all the waves and the billows rolling over your head. You will find in the long run that it is far harder to shun the work and will of God than to at once yield yourself to it. *Jonah lost his time,* for he had to go to Tarshish after all. It is hard to contend with God; let us yield ourselves at once.

" Salvation is of the Lord."—Jonah ii. 9.

SALVATION is the work of God. It is He alone who quickens the soul " dead in trespasses and sins," and it is He also who maintains the soul in its spiritual life. He is both " Alpha and Omega." " Salvation is of the Lord." If I am prayerful, God makes me prayerful; if I have graces, they are God's gifts to me ; if I hold on in a consistent life, it is because He upholds me with His hand. I do nothing whatever towards my own preservation, except what God himself first does in me. Whatever I have, all my goodness is of the Lord alone. Wherein I sin, that is my own ; but wherein I act rightly, that is of God, wholly and completely. If I have repulsed a spiritual enemy, the Lord's strength nerved my arm. Do I live before men a consecrated life ? It is not I, but Christ who liveth in me. Am I sanctified ? I did not cleanse myself : God's Holy Spirit sanctifies me. Am I weaned from the world ? I am weaned by *God's* chastisements sanctified to my good. Do I grow in knowledge ? The great Instructor teaches me. All my jewels were fashioned by heavenly art. I find in God all that I want ; but I find in myself nothing but sin and misery. " He only is my rock and my salvation." Do I feed on the Word ? That Word would be no food for me unless the Lord made it food for my soul, and helped me to feed upon it. Do I live on the manna which comes down from heaven ? What is that manna but Jesus Christ himself incarnate, whose body and whose blood I eat and drink ? Am I continually receiving fresh increase of strength ? Where do I gather my might ? My help cometh from heaven's hills : without Jesus I can do nothing. As a branch cannot bring forth fruit except it abide in the vine, no more can I, except I abide in Him. What Jonah learned in the great deep, let me learn this morning in my closet : " Salvation is of the Lord."

"Behold, if the leprosy have covered all his flesh, he shall pronounce him clean that hath the plague."—Lev. xiii. 13.

STRANGE enough this regulation appears, yet there was wisdom in it, for the throwing out of the disease proved that the constitution was sound. This evening it may be well for us to see the typical teaching of so singular a rule. We, too, are lepers, and may read the law of the leper as applicable to ourselves. When a man sees himself to be altogether lost and ruined, covered all over with the defilement of sin, and in no part free from pollution; when he disclaims all righteousness of his own, and pleads guilty before the Lord, then he is clean through the blood of Jesus, and the grace of God. Hidden, unfelt, unconfessed iniquity is the true leprosy; but when sin is seen and felt, it has received its deathblow, and the Lord looks with eyes of mercy upon the soul afflicted with it. Nothing is more deadly than self-righteousness, or more hopeful than contrition. We must confess that we are "nothing else but sin," for no confession short of this will be the whole truth; and if the Holy Spirit be at work with us, convincing us of sin, there will be no difficulty about making such an acknowledgment — it will spring spontaneously from our lips. What comfort does the text afford to truly awakened sinners: the very circumstance which so grievously discouraged them is here turned into a sign and symptom of a hopeful state! Stripping comes before clothing; digging out the foundation is the first thing in building—and a thorough sense of sin is one of the earliest works of grace in the heart. O thou poor leprous sinner, utterly destitute of a sound spot, take heart from the text, and come as thou art to Jesus—

"For let our debts be what they may, however great or small,
As soon as we have nought to pay, our Lord forgives us all.
'Tis perfect poverty alone that sets the soul at large:
While we can call one mite our own, we have no full discharge."

" Thou hast made the Lord, which is my refuge, even the Most High, thy habitation."—Psalm xci. 9.

THE Israelites in the wilderness *were continually exposed to change.* Whenever the pillar stayed its motion, the tents were pitched ; but to-morrow, ere the morning sun had risen, the trumpet sounded, the ark was in motion, and the fiery, cloudy pillar was leading the way through the narrow defiles of the mountain, up the hill-side, or along the arid waste of the wilderness. They had scarcely time to rest a little before they heard the sound of " Away ! this is not your rest ; you must still be onward journeying towards Canaan ! " They were never long in one place.   Even wells and palm trees could not detain them.   Yet they had an abiding home in their God, His cloudy pillar was their roof-tree, and its flame by night their household fire.   They must go onward from place to place, continually changing, never having time to settle, and to say, " Now we are secure ; in this place we shall dwell."   " Yet," says Moses, " though we are always changing, Lord, thou hast been our dwelling-place throughout all generations."   The Christian knows no change with regard to God.   He may be rich to-day and poor to-morrow ; he may be sickly to day and well to-morrow ; he may be in happiness to-day, to-morrow he may be distressed—but there is no change with regard to his relationship to God.   If He loved me yesterday, He loves me to-day.   My unmoving mansion of rest is my blessed Lord.   Let prospects be blighted ; let hopes be blasted ; let joy be withered ; let mildews destroy everything ; I have lost nothing of what I have in God.   He is "my strong habitation whereunto I can continually resort."   I am a pilgrim in the world, but at home in my God.   In the earth I wander, but in God I dwell in a quiet habitation.

" Whose goings forth have been from of old, from everlasting."
M..ah v. 2.

HE Lord Jesus had goings forth for His people *as their representative before the throne, long before they appeared upon the stage of time.* It was " from everlasting" that He signed the compact with His Father, that He would pay blood for blood, suffering for suffering, agony for agony, and death for death, in the behalf of His people ; it was " from everlasting" that He gave Himself up without a murmuring word. that from the crown of His head to the sole of His foot He might sweat great drops of blood, that He might be spit upon, pierced, mocked, rent asunder, and crushed beneath the pains of death. His goings forth as our Surety were from everlasting. Pause, my soul, and wonder ! Thou hadst goings forth in the person of Jesus " from everlasting." Not only when thou wast born into the world did Christ love thee, but His delights were with the sons of men before there were any sons of men. Often did He think of them ; from everlasting to everlasting He had set His affection upon them. What ! my soul, has He been so long about thy salvation, and will not He accomplish it ? Has he from everlasting been going forth to save me, and will He lose me now ? What ! has He carried me in His hand, as His precious jewel, and will He now let me slip from between His fingers ? Did He choose me before the mountains were brought forth, or the channels of the deep were digged, and will He reject me now ? Impossible ! I am sure He would not have loved me so long if He had not been a changeless Lover. If He could grow weary of me, He would have been tired of me long before now. If He had not loved me with a love as deep as hell, and as strong as death, He would have turned from me long ago. Oh, joy above all joys, to know that I am His everlasting and inalienable inheritance, given to Him by His Father or ever the earth was ! Everlasting love shall be the pillow for my head this night.

" My expectation is from Him."—Psalm lxii. 5.

T is the believer's privilege to use this language. If he is looking for aught from the world, it is a poor "expectation" indeed. But if he looks to God for the supply of his wants, whether in temporal or spiritual blessings, his "expectation" will not be a vain one. Constantly he may draw from the bank of faith, and get his need supplied out of the riches of God's lovingkindness. This I know, I had rather have God for my banker than all the Rothschilds. My Lord never fails to honour his promises; and when we bring them to His throne, He never sends them back unanswered. Therefore I will wait only at His door, for He ever opens it with the hand of munificent grace. At this hour I will try him anew. But we have "expectations" beyond this life. We shall die soon; and then our "expectation is from Him." Do we not expect that when we lie upon the bed of sickness He will send angels to carry us to His bosom? We believe that when the pulse is faint, and the heart heaves heavily, some angelic messenger shall stand and look with loving eyes upon us, and whisper, "Sister spirit, come away!" As we approach the heavenly gate, we expect to hear the welcome invitation, "Come, ye blessed of my Father, inherit the kingdom prepared for you from the foundation of the world." We are expecting harps of gold and crowns of glory; we are hoping soon to be amongst the multitude of shining ones before the throne; we are looking forward and longing for the time when we shall be like our glorious Lord— for "We shall see Him as He is." Then if these be thine "expectations," O my soul, live for God; live with the desire and resolve to glorify Him from whom cometh all thy supplies, and of whose grace in thy election, redemption, and calling, it is that thou hast any "expectation" of coming glory.

" The barrel of meal wasted not, neither did the cruse of oil fail, according to the word of the Lord, which He spake by Elijah."—1 Kings xvii. 16.

SEE the faithfulness of divine love. You observe that this woman had *daily necessities.* She had herself and her son to feed in a time of famine ; and now, in addition, the prophet Elijah was to be fed too. But though the need was threefold, yet the supply of meal wasted not, for she had *a constant supply.* Each day she made calls upon the barrel, but yet each day it remained the same. You, dear reader, have daily necessities, and because they come so frequently, you are apt to fear that the barrel of meal will one day be empty, and the cruse of oil will fail you. Rest assured that, according to the Word of God, this shall not be the case. Each day, though it bring its trouble, shall bring its help; and though you should live to outnumber the years of Methuselah, and though your needs should be as many as the sands of the seashore, yet shall God's grace and mercy last through all your necessities, and you shall never know a real lack. For three long years, in this widow's days, the heavens never saw a cloud, and the stars never wept a holy tear of dew upon the wicked earth : famine, and desolation, and death, made the land a howling wilderness, but this woman never was hungry, but always joyful in abundance. So shall it be with you. You shall see the sinner's hope perish, for he trusts his native strength ; you shall see the proud Pharisee's confidence totter . for he builds his hope upon the sand ; you shall see even your own schemes blasted and withered, but you yourself shall find that your place of defence shall be the munition of rocks : "Your bread shall be given you, and your water shall be sure." Better have God for your guardian, than the Bank of England for your possession. You might spend the wealth of the Indies, but the infinite riches of God you can never exhaust.

" With lovingkindness have I drawn thee."—Jer. xxxi. 3.

THE thunders of the law and the terrors of judgment are all used to bring us to Christ ; but the final victory is effected by lovingkindness. The prodigal set out to his father's house from a sense of need ; but his father saw him a great way off, and ran to meet him ; so that the last steps he took towards his father's house were with the kiss still warm upon his cheek, and the welcome still musical in his ears.

> "Law and terrors do but harden
> All the while they work alone ;
> But a sense of blood-bought pardon
> Will dissolve a heart of stone."

The Master came one night to the door, and knocked with the iron hand of the law ; the door shook and trembled upon its hinges ; but the man piled every piece of furniture which he could find against the door, for he said, "I will not admit the man." The Master turned away, but by-and-bye He came back, and with His own soft hand, using most that part where the nail had penetrated, he knocked again—oh, so softly and tenderly. This time the door did not shake, but, strange to say, it opened, and there upon his knees the once unwilling host was found rejoicing to receive his guest. "Come in, come in ; thou hast so knocked that my bowels are moved for thee. I could not think of thy pierced hand leaving its blood-mark on my door, and of thy going away houseless, 'Thy head filled with dew, and thy locks with the drops of the night.' I yield, I yield, Thy love has won my heart." So in every case : lovingkindness wins the day. What Moses with the tablets of stone could never do, Christ does with His pierced hand. Such is the doctrine of effectual calling. Do I understand it experimentally? Can I say, "He drew me, and I followed on, glad to confess the voice divine ?" If so, may He continue to draw me. till at last I shall sit down at the marriage supper of the Lamb.

" Now we have received . . . the spirit which is of God; that we might know the things that are freely given to us of God." 1 Corinthians ii. 12.

DEAR reader, have you received the spirit which is of God, wrought by the Holy Ghost in your soul? The necessity of the work of the Holy Spirit in the heart may be clearly seen from this fact, that *all which has been done by God the Father, and by God the Son, must be ineffectual to us, unless the Spirit shall reveal these things to our souls.* What effect does the doctrine of election have upon any man until the Spirit of God enters into him? Election is a dead letter in my consciousness until the Spirit of God calls me out of darkness into marvellous light. *Then* through my calling, I see my election, and knowing myself to be called of God, I know myself to have been chosen in the eternal purpose. A covenant was made with the Lord Jesus Christ, by His Father; but what avails that covenant to us until the Holy Spirit brings us its blessings, and opens our hearts to receive them? There hang the blessings on the nail—Christ Jesus; but being short of stature, we cannot reach them; the Spirit of God takes them down and hands them to us, and thus they become actually ours. Covenant blessings in themselves are like the manna in the skies, far out of mortal reach, but the Spirit of God opens the windows of heaven and scatters the living bread around the camp of the spiritual Israel. Christ's finished work is like wine stored in the wine-vat; through unbelief we can neither draw nor drink. The Holy Spirit dips our vessel into this precious wine, and then we drink; but without the Spirit we are as truly dead in sin as though the Father never had elected, and though the Son had never bought us with His blood. The Holy Spirit is absolutely necessary to our well-being. Let us walk lovingly towards Him and tremble at the thought of grieving Him.

"Awake, O north wind; and come, thou south; blow upon my garden, that the spices thereof may flow out."—Canticles iv. 16.

NYTHING is better than the dead calm of indifference. Our souls may wisely desire the north wind of trouble if that alone can be sanctified to the drawing forth of the perfume of our graces. So long as it cannot be said, "The Lord was not in the wind," we will not shrink from the most wintry blast that ever blew upon plants of grace. Did not the spouse in this verse humbly submit herself to the reproofs of her Beloved ; only entreating Him to send forth His grace in some form, and making no stipulation as to the peculiar manner in which it should come ?   Did she not, like ourselves, become so utterly weary of deadness and unholy calm that she sighed for any visitation which would brace her to action ?   Yet she desires the warm south wind of comfort too, the smiles of divine love, the joy of the Redeemer's presence; these are often mightily effectual to arouse our sluggish life.   She desires either one or the other, or both ; so that she may but be able to delight her Beloved with the spices of her garden. She cannot endure to be unprofitable, nor can we. How cheering a thought that Jesus can find comfort in our poor feeble graces.   Can it be ?   It seems far too good to be true.   Well may we court trial or even death itself if we shall thereby be aided to make glad Immanuel's heart.   O that our heart were crushed to atoms if only by such bruising our sweet Lord Jesus could be glorified.   Graces unexercised are as sweet perfumes slumbering in the cups of the flowers: the wisdom of the great Husbandman overrules diverse and opposite causes to produce the one desired result, and makes both affliction and consolation draw forth the grateful odours of faith, love, patience, hope, resignation, joy, and the other fair flowers of the garden. May we know by sweet experience, what this means.

" He is precious."—1 Peter ii. 7.

AS all the rivers run into the sea, so all delights centre in our Beloved. The glances of His eyes outshine the sun : the beauties of His face are fairer than the choicest flowers : no fragrance is like the breath of His mouth. Gems of the mine, and pearls from the sea, are worthless things when measured by His preciousness. Peter tells us that Jesus is precious, but he did not and could not tell us *how* precious, nor could any of us compute the value of God's unspeakable gift. Words cannot set forth the preciousness of the Lord Jesus to His people, nor fully tell how essential He is to their satisfaction and happiness. Believer, have you not found in the midst of plenty a sore famine if your Lord has been absent? The sun was shining, but Christ had hidden Himself, and all the world was black to you; or it was night, and since the bright and morning star was gone, no other star could yield you so much as a ray of light. What a howling wilderness is this world without our Lord! If once He hideth Himself from us, withered are the flowers of our garden; our pleasant fruits decay; the birds suspend their songs, and a tempest overturns our hopes. All earth's candles cannot make daylight if the Sun of Righteousness be eclipsed. He is the soul of our soul, the light of our light, the life of our life. Dear reader, what wouldst thou do in the world without Him, in the midst of its temptations and its cares? What wouldst thou do in the morning without Him, when thou wakest up and lookest forward to the day's battle? What wouldst thou do at night, when thou comest home jaded and weary, if there were no door of fellowship between thee and Christ? Blessed be His name, He will not suffer us to try our lot without Him, for Jesus never forsakes His own. Yet, let the thought of *what life would be without Him* enhance His preciousness.

" *But all the Israelites went down to the Philistines, to sharpen every man his share, and his coulter, and his ax, and his mattock.*" –1 Samuel xiii. 20.

WE are engaged in a great war with the Philistines of evil. *Every weapon within our reach must be used.* Preaching, teaching, praying, giving, all must be brought into action, and talents which have been thought too mean for service, must now be employed. Coulter, and axe, and mattock, may all be useful in slaying Philistines ; rough tools may deal hard blows, and killing need not be elegantly done, so long as it is done effectually. Each moment of time, in season or out of season ; each fragment of ability, educated or untutored ; each opportunity, favourable or unfavourable, must be used, for our foes are many and our force but slender.

Most of our tools want sharpening; we need quickness of perception, tact, energy, promptness, in a word, complete adaptation for the Lord's work. Practical common sense is a very scarce thing among the conductors of Christian enterprises. We might learn from our enemies if we would, and so *make the Philistines sharpen our weapons.* This morning let us note enough to sharpen our zeal during this day by the aid of the Holy Spirit. See the energy of the Papists, how they compass sea and land to make one proselyte, are they to monopolize all the earnestness ? Mark the heathen devotees, what tortures they endure in the service of their idols ! are they alone to exhibit patience and self-sacrifice ? Observe the prince of darkness, how persevering in his endeavours, how unabashed in his attempts, how daring in his plans, how thoughtful in his plots, how energetic in all ! The devils are united as one man in their infamous rebellion, while we believers in Jesus are divided in our service of God, and scarcely ever work with unanimity. O that from Satan's infernal industry we may learn to go about like good Samaritans, seeking whom we may bless !

"Unto me, who am less than the least of all saints, is this grace given, that I should preach among the Gentiles the unsearchable riches of Christ."—Ephesians iii. 8.

THE apostle Paul felt it a great privilege to be allowed to preach the gospel. He did not look upon his calling as a drudgery, but he entered upon it with intense delight. Yet while Paul was thus thankful for his office, his success in it greatly humbled him. The fuller a vessel becomes, the deeper it sinks in the water. Idlers may indulge a fond conceit of their abilities, because they are untried; but the earnest worker soon learns his own weakness. If you seek humility, *try hard work;* if you would know your nothingness, attempt some great thing for Jesus. If you would feel how utterly powerless you are apart from the living God, attempt especially the great work of proclaiming the unsearchable riches of Christ, and you will know, as you never knew before, what a weak unworthy thing you are. Although the apostle thus knew and confessed his weakness, he was never perplexed as to the *subject* of his ministry. From his first sermon to his last, Paul preached Christ, and nothing but Christ. He lifted up the cross, and extolled the Son of God who bled thereon. Follow his example in all your personal efforts to spread the glad tidings of salvation, and let " Christ and Him crucified" be your ever recurring theme. The Christian should be like those lovely spring flowers which, when the sun is shining, open their golden cups, as if saying, " Fill us with thy beams!" but when the sun is hidden behind a cloud, they close their cups and droop their heads. So should the Christian feel the sweet influence of Jesus; Jesus must be his sun, and he must be the flower which yields itself to the Sun of Righteousness. Oh! to speak of Christ alone, this is the subject which is both " seed for the sower, and bread for the eater." This is the live coal for the lip of the speaker, and the master-key to the heart of the hearer.

"I have chosen thee in the furnace of affliction."—Is. xlviii. 10.

COMFORT thyself, tried believer, with this thought : God saith, " I have chosen thee in the furnace of affliction." Does not the word come like a soft shower, assuaging the fury of the flame? Yea, is it not an asbestos armour, against which the heat hath no power ? Let affliction come—God has chosen me. Poverty, thou mayst stride in at my door, but God is in the house already, and He has chosen me. Sickness, thou mayst intrude, but I have a balsam ready—God has chosen me. Whatever befalls me in this vale of tears, I know that He has " chosen " me. If, believer, thou requirest still greater comfort, remember *that you have the Son of Man with you in the furnace.* In that silent chamber of yours, there sitteth by your side One whom thou hast not seen, but whom thou lovest ; and ofttimes when thou knowest it not, He makes all thy bed in thy affliction, and smooths thy pillow for thee. Thou art in poverty ; but in that lonely house of thine the Lord of life and glory is a frequent visitor. He loves to come into these desolate places, that He may visit thee. Thy friend sticks closely to thee. Thou canst not see Him, but thou mayst feel the pressure of His hands. Dost thou not hear His voice ? Even in the valley of the shadow of death He says, " Fear not, I am with thee ; be not dismayed, for I am thy God." Remember that noble speech of Cæsar : " Fear not, thou carriest Cæsar and all his fortune." Fear not, Christian ; Jesus is with thee. In all thy fiery trials, His presence is both thy comfort and safety. He will never leave one whom He has chosen for His own. " Fear not, for I am with thee," is His sure word of promise to His chosen ones in the " furnace of affliction." Wilt thou not, then, take fast hold of Christ, and say—

" Through floods and flames, if Jesus lead,
I'll follow where he goes."

"He saw the Spirit of God descending like a dove."
Matthew iii. 16.

AS the Spirit of God descended upon the Lord Jesus, the head, so He also, in measure, descends upon the members of the mystical body. His descent is to us after the same fashion as that in which it fell upon our Lord. There is often a singular *rapidity* about it; or ever we are aware, we are impelled onward and heavenward beyond all expectation. Yet is there none of the hurry of earthly haste, for the wings of the dove are as soft as they are swift. *Quietness* seems essential to many spiritual operations; the Lord is in the still small voice, and like the dew, His grace is distilled in silence. The dove has ever been the chosen type of *purity*, and the Holy Spirit is holiness itself. Where He cometh, everything that is pure and lovely, and of good report, is made to abound, and sin and uncleanness depart. *Peace* reigns also where the Holy Dove comes with power; He bears the olive branch which shows that the waters of divine wrath are assuaged. *Gentleness* is a sure result of the Sacred Dove's transforming power: hearts touched by His benign influence are meek and lowly henceforth and for ever. *Harmlessness* follows, as a matter of course; eagles and ravens may hunt their prey—the turtledove can endure wrong, but cannot inflict it. We must be harmless as doves. The dove is an apt picture of *love*, the voice of the turtle is full of affection; and so, the soul visited by the blessed Spirit, abounds in love to God, in love to the brethren, and in love to sinners; and above all, in love to Jesus. The brooding of the Spirit of God upon the face of the deep, first produced *order and life*, and in our hearts, He causes and fosters new life and light. Blessed Spirit, as Thou didst rest upon our dear Redeemer, even so rest thou upon us from this time forward and for ever.

" My grace is sufficient for thee."—2 Corinthians xii. 9.

IF none of God's saints were poor and tried, we should not know half so well the consolations of divine grace. When we find the wanderer who has not where to lay his head, who yet can say, " Still will I trust in the Lord;"when we see the pauper starving on bread and water, who still glories in Jesus; when we see the bereaved widow overwhelmed in affliction, and yet having faith in Christ, oh! what honour it reflects on the gospel. God's grace is illustrated and magnified in the poverty and trials of believers. Saints bear up under every discouragement, believing that all things work together for their good, and that out of apparent evils a real blessing shall ultimately spring—that their God will either work a deliverance for them speedily, or most assuredly support them in the trouble, as long as He is pleased to keep them in it. This patience of the saints proves the power of divine grace. There is a lighthouse out at sea : it is a calm night—I cannot tell whether the edifice is firm ; the tempest must rage about it, and then I shall know whether it will stand. So with the Spirit's work : if it were not on many occasions surrounded with tempestuous waters, we should not know that it was true and strong ; if the winds did not blow upon it, we should not know how firm and secure it was. The master-works of God are those men who stand in the midst of difficulties, stedfast, unmoveable,—

" Calm mid the bewildering cry,
  Confident of victory."

He who would glorify his God must set his account upon meeting with many trials. No man can be illustrious before the Lord unless his conflicts be many. If then, yours be a much-tried path, rejoice in it, because you will the better show forth the all-sufficient grace of God. As for His failing you. never dream of it—hate the thought. The God who has been sufficient until now, should be trusted to the end.

"They shall be abundantly satisfied with the fatness of Thy house."—Psalm xxxvi. 8.

SHEBA'S queen was amazed at the sumptuousness of Solomon's table. She lost all heart when she saw the provision of a single day; and she marvelled equally at the company of servants who were feasted at the royal board. But what is this to the hospitalities of the God of grace? Ten thousand thousand of his people are daily fed; hungry and thirsty, they bring large appetites with them to the banquet, but not one of them returns unsatisfied; there is enough for each, enough for all, enough for evermore. Though the host that feed at Jehovah's table is countless as the stars of heaven, yet each one has his portion of meat. Think how much grace one saint requires, so much that nothing but the Infinite could supply him for one day; and yet the Lord spreads His table, not for one, but many saints, not for one day, but for many years; not for many years only, but for generation after generation. Observe the full feasting spoken of in the text, the guests at mercy's banquet are satisfied, nay, more "abundantly satisfied;" and that not with ordinary fare, but with fatness, the peculiar fatness of God's own house; and such feasting is guaranteed by a faithful promise to all those children of men who put their trust under the shadow of Jehovah's wings. I once thought if I might but get the broken meat at God's back door of grace I should be satisfied; like the woman who said, "The dogs eat of the crumbs that fall from the master's table;" but no child of God is ever served with scraps and leavings; like Mephibosheth, they all eat from the king's own table. In matters of grace, we all have Benjamin's mess—we all have ten times more than we could have expected, and though our necessities are great, yet are we often amazed at the marvellous plenty of grace which God gives us experimentally to enjoy.

" Let us not sleep, as do others."—1 Thessalonians v. 6.

HERE are many ways of promoting Christian wakefulness. Among the rest, let me strongly advise Christians to converse together concerning the ways of the Lord. Christian and Hopeful, as they journeyed towards the Celestial City, said to themselves, " To prevent drowsiness in this place, let us fall into good discourse." Christian enquired, " Brother, where shall we begin?" And Hopeful answered,"Where God began with us." Then Christian sang this song—

" When saints do sleepy grow, let them come hither,
    And hear how these two pilgrims talk together ;
    Yea, let them learn of them, in any wise,
    Thus to keep ope their drowsy slumb'ring eyes.
    Saints' fellowship, if it be managed well,
    Keeps them awake, and that in spite of hell."

Christians who isolate themselves and walk alone, are very liable to grow drowsy. Hold Christian company, and you will be kept wakeful by it, and refreshed and encouraged to make quicker progress in the road to heaven. But as you thus take " sweet counsel " with others in the ways of God, take care that the theme of your converse is the Lord Jesus. Let the eye of faith be constantly looking unto Him ; let your heart be full of Him ; let your lips speak of His worth. Friend, live near to the cross, and thou wilt not sleep. *Labour to impress thyself with a deep sense of the value of the place to which thou art going.* If thou rememberest that thou art going to heaven, thou wilt not sleep on the road. If thou thinkest that hell is behind thee, and the devil pursuing thee, thou wilt not loiter. Would the manslayer sleep with the avenger of blood behind him, and the city of refuge before him ? Christian, wilt thou sleep whilst the pearly gates are open—the songs of angels waiting for thee to join them—a crown of gold ready for thy brow ? Ah! no ; in holy fellowship continue to watch and pray that ye enter not into temptation.

" Say unto my soul, I am thy salvation."—Psalm. xxxv. 3.

HAT does this sweet prayer teach me ? It shall be my evening's petition ; but first let it yield me an instructive meditation. The text informs me first of all that *David had his doubts;* for why should he pray, " Say unto my soul, I am thy salvation," if he were not sometimes exercised with doubts and fears ? Let me, then, be of good cheer, for I am not the only saint who has to complain of weakness of faith. If David doubted, I need not conclude that *I* am no Christian, because I have doubts. The text reminds me that *David was not content while he had doubts and fears,* but he repaired at once to the mercy-seat to pray for assurance ; for he valued it as much fine gold. I too must labour after an abiding sense of my acceptance in the Beloved, and must have no joy when His love is not shed abroad in my soul. When my Bridegroom is gone from me, my soul must and will fast. I learn also that *David knew where to obtain full assurance.* He went to his God in prayer, crying, " Say unto my soul, I am thy salvation." I must be much alone with God if I would have a clear sense of Jesus' love. Let my prayers cease, and my eye of faith will grow dim. Much in prayer, much in heaven ; slow in prayer, slow in progress. I notice that *David would not be satisfied unless his assurance had a divine source.* " *Say* unto my soul." Lord, do *Thou* say it ! Nothing short of a divine testimony in the soul will ever content the true Christian. Moreover, David could not rest unless his assurance had *a vivid personality* about it. " Say unto *my* soul, I am *thy* salvation." Lord, if Thou shouldst say this to all the saints, it were nothing, unless Thou shouldst say it to me. Lord, I have sinned ; I deserve not Thy smile ; I scarcely dare to ask it ; but oh ! say to *my* soul, even to *my* soul, " I am *thy* salvation." Let me have a present, personal, infallible, indisputable sense that I am Thine, and that Thou art mine.

" Ye must be born again."—John iii. 7.

REGENERATION is a subject which lies at the very basis of salvation, and we should be very diligent to take heed that we really are " born again," for there are many who fancy they are, who are not. Be assured that the name of a Christian is not the nature of a Christian ; and that being born in a Christian land, and being recognised as professing the Christian religion is of no avail whatever, unless there be something more added to it—the being " born again " by the power of the Holy Spirit. To be " born again," is a matter so *mysterious,* that human words cannot describe it. " The wind bloweth where it listeth, and thou hearest the sound thereof, but canst not tell whence it cometh, and whither it goeth : so is every one that is born of the Spirit." Nevertheless, it is a change which is *known and felt:* known by works of holiness, and felt by a gracious experience. This great work is *supernatural.* It is not an operation which a man performs for himself : a new principle is infused, which works in the heart, renews the soul, and affects the entire man. It is not a change of my name, but a renewal of my nature, so that I am not the man I used to be, but a new man in Christ Jesus. To wash and dress a corpse is a far different thing from making it alive : man can do the one, God alone can do the other. If you have then, been " born again," your acknowledgment will be, " O Lord Jesus, the everlasting Father, Thou art my spiritual Parent; unless Thy Spirit had breathed into me the breath of a new, holy, and spiritual life, I had been to this day ' dead in trespasses and sins.' My heavenly life is wholly derived from Thee, to Thee I ascribe it. ' My life is hid with Christ in God.' It is no longer I who live, but Christ who liveth in me." May the Lord enable us to be well assured on this vital point, for to be unregenerate is to be unsaved, unpardoned, without God, and without hope.

" Before destruction the heart of man is haughty."
Proverbs xviii. 12.

IT is an old and common saying, that "coming events cast their shadows before them;" the wise man teaches us that a haughty heart is the prophetic prelude of evil. Pride is as safely the sign of destruction as the change of mercury in the weather-glass is the sign of rain; and far more infallibly so than that. When men have ridden the high horse, destruction *has* always overtaken them. Let David's aching heart show that there is an eclipse of a man's glory when he doats upon his own greatness. 2 Sam. xxiv. 10. See Nebuchadnezzar, the mighty builder of Babylon, creeping on the earth, devouring grass like oxen, until his nails had grown like bird's claws, and his hair like eagle's feathers. Dan. iv. 33. Pride made the boaster a beast, as once before it made an angel a devil. God hates high looks, and never fails to bring them down. All the arrows of God are aimed at proud hearts. O Christian, is thine heart haughty this evening? For pride can get into the Christian's heart as well as into the sinner's; it can delude him into dreaming that he is "rich and increased in goods, and hath need of nothing." Art thou glorying in thy graces or thy talents? Art thou proud of thyself, that thou hast had holy frames and sweet experiences? Mark thee, reader, there is a destruction coming to thee also. Thy flaunting poppies of self-conceit will be pulled up by the roots, thy mushroom graces will wither in the burning heat, and thy self-sufficiency shall become as straw for the dunghill. If we forget to live at the foot of the cross in deepest lowliness of spirit, God will not forget to make us smart under His rod. A destruction will come to thee, O unduly exalted believer, the destruction of thy joys and of thy comforts, though there can be no destruction of thy soul. Wherefore, "He that glorieth, let him glory *in the Lord.*"

"Have faith in God."—Mark xi. 22.

FAITH is the foot of the soul by which it can march along the road of the commandments. Love can make the feet move more swiftly; but faith *is* the foot which carries the soul. Faith is the oil enabling the wheels of holy devotion and of earnest piety to move well; and without faith the wheels are taken from the chariot, and we drag heavily. With faith I can do all things; without faith I shall neither have the inclination nor the power to do anything in the service of God. If you would find the men who serve God the best, you must look for the men of the most faith. Little faith will save a man, but little faith cannot do great things for God. Poor Little-faith could not have fought " Apollyon ;" it needed " Christian " to do that. Poor Little-faith could not have slain " Giant Despair ;" it required " Great-heart's " arm to knock that monster down. Little faith will go to heaven most certainly, but it often has to hide itself in a nut-shell, and it frequently loses all but its jewels. Little-faith says, " It is a rough road, beset with sharp thorns, and full of dangers ; I am afraid to go ;" but Great-faith remembers the promise, " Thy shoes shall be iron and brass ; as thy days, so shall thy strength be :" and so she boldly ventures. Little-faith stands desponding, mingling her tears with the flood ; but great faith sings, " When thou passest through the waters, I will be with thee ; and through the rivers, they shall not overflow thee:" and she fords the stream at once. Would you be comfortable and happy ? Would you enjoy religion ? Would you have the religion of cheerfulness and not that of gloom ? Then " have faith in God." If you love darkness, and are satisfied to dwell in gloom and misery, then be content with little faith ; but if you love the sunshine, and would sing songs of rejoicing, covet earnestly this best gift, " great faith."

" It is better to trust in the Lord, than to put confidence in man."—Psalm cxviii. 8.

DOUBTLESS the reader has been tried with the temptation to rely upon the things which are seen, instead of resting alone upon the invisible God. Christians often look to man for help and counsel, and mar the noble simplicity of their reliance upon their God. Does this evening's portion meet the eye of a child of God anxious about temporals, then would we reason with him awhile. You trust in Jesus, and only in Jesus, for your salvation, then why are you troubled ? *" Because of my great care."* Is it not written, " Cast thy burden upon the Lord "? " Be careful for nothing, but in everything by prayer and supplication make known your wants unto God." Cannot you trust God for temporals ? *" Ah ! I wish I could."* If you cannot trust God for temporals, how dare you trust Him for spirituals ? Can you trust Him for your soul's redemption, and not rely upon Him for a few lesser mercies ? Is not God enough for thy need, or is His all-sufficiency too narrow for thy wants ? Dost thou want another eye beside that of Him who sees every secret thing ? Is His heart faint ? Is His arm weary ? If so, seek another God ; but if He be infinite, omnipotent, faithful, true, and all-wise, why gaddest thou abroad so much to seek another confidence ? Why dost thou rake the earth to find another foundation, when this is strong enough to bear all the weight which thou canst ever build thereon ? Christian, mix not thy wine with water, do not alloy thy gold of faith with the dross of human confidence. Wait thou only upon God, and let thine expectation be from Him. Covet not Jonah's gourd, but rest in Jonah's God. Let the sandy foundations of terrestrial trust be the choice of fools , but do thou, like one who foresees the storm, build for thyself an abiding place upon the Rock of Ages.

" We must through much tribulation enter into the kingdom of God."—Acts xiv. 22.

GOD'S people have their trials. It was never designed by God, when He chose His people, that they should be an untried people. They were chosen in the furnace of affliction; they were never chosen to worldly peace and earthly joy. Freedom from sickness and the pains of mortality was never promised them; but when their Lord drew up the charter of privileges, He included chastisements amongst the things to which they should inevitably be heirs. Trials are a part of our lot; they were predestinated for us in God's solemn decrees, and bequeathed us in Christ's last legacy. So surely as the stars are fashioned by his hands, and their orbits fixed by Him, so surely are our trials allotted to us: He has ordained their season and their place, their intensity and the effect they shall have upon us. Good men must never expect to escape troubles; if they do, they will be disappointed, for none of their predecessors have been without them. Mark the patience of Job; remember Abraham, for he had his trials, and by his faith under them, he became the " Father of the faithful." Note well the biographies of all the patriarchs, prophets, apostles, and martyrs, and you shall discover none of those whom God made vessels of mercy, who were not made to pass through the fire of affliction. It is ordained of old that the cross of trouble should be engraven on every vessel of mercy, as the royal mark whereby the King's vessels of honour are distinguished. But although tribulation is thus the path of God's children, they have the comfort of knowing that their Master has traversed it before them; they have His presence and sympathy to cheer them, His grace to support them, and His example to teach them how to endure; and when they reach "the kingdom," it will more than make amends for the " much tribulation " through which they passed to enter it.

" She called his name Ben-oni (son of sorrow), but his father called him Benjamin (son of my right hand)."—Gen. xxxv. 18.

TO every matter there is a bright as well as a dark side. Rachel was overwhelmed with the sorrow of her own travail and death ; Jacob, though weeping the mother's loss, could see the mercy of the child's birth. It is well for us if, while the flesh mourns over trials, our faith triumphs in divine faithfulness. Samson's lion yielded honey, and so will our adversities, if rightly considered. The stormy sea feeds multitudes with its fishes ; the wild wood blooms with beauteous flowerets ; the stormy wind sweeps away the pestilence, and the biting frost loosens the soil. Dark clouds distil bright drops, and black earth grows gay flowers. A vein of good is to be found in every mine of evil. Sad hearts have peculiar skill in discovering the most disadvantageous point of view from which to gaze upon a trial ; if there were only one slough in the world, they would soon be up to their necks in it, and if there were only one lion in the desert they would hear it roar. About us all there is a tinge of this wretched folly, and we are apt, at times, like Jacob, to cry, " All these things are against me." Faith's way of walking is to cast all care upon the Lord, and then to anticipate good results from the worst calamities. Like Gideon's men, she does not fret over the broken pitcher, but rejoices that the lamp blazes forth the more. Out of the rough oyster-shell of difficulty she extracts the rare pearl of honour, and from the deep ocean-caves of distress she uplifts the priceless coral of experience. When her flood of prosperity ebbs, she finds treasures hid in the sands ; and when her sun of delight goes down, she turns her telescope of hope to the starry promises of heaven. When death itself appears, faith points to the light of resurrection beyond the grave, thus making our dying Ben-oni to be our living Benjamin.

" *Yea, He is altogether lovely.*"—Solomon's Song v. 16.

THE superlative beauty of Jesus is all-attracting; it is not so much to be admired as to be loved. He is more than pleasant and fair, He is LOVELY. Surely the people of God can fully justify the use of this golden word, for He is the object of their warmest love, a love founded on the intrinsic excellence of His person, the complete perfection of His charms. Look, O disciples of Jesus, to your Master's lips, and say, "Are they not most sweet?" Do not His words cause your hearts to burn within you as He talks with you by the way? Ye worshippers of Immanuel, look up to His head of much fine gold, and tell me, are not His thoughts precious unto you? Is not your adoration sweetened with affection as ye humbly bow before that countenance which is as Lebanon, excellent as the cedars? Is there not a charm in His every feature, and is not His whole person fragrant with such a savour of His good ointments, that therefore the virgins love Him? Is there one member of His glorious body which is not attractive?—one portion of His person which is not a fresh loadstone to our souls?—one office which is not a strong cord to bind your heart? Our love is not as a seal set upon His heart of love alone; it is fastened upon His arm of power also; nor is there a single part of Him upon which it does not fix itself. We anoint His whole person with the sweet spikenard of our fervent love. His whole life we would imitate; His whole character we would transcribe. In all other beings we see some lack, in Him there is all perfection. The best even of His favoured saints have had blots upon their garments and wrinkles upon their brows; he is nothing but loveliness. All earthly suns have their spots : the fair world itself hath its wilderness ; we cannot love the whole of the most lovely thing ; but Christ Jesus is gold without alloy—light without darkness—glory without cloud— " Yea, He is *altogether* lovely."

" Abide in Me."—John xv. 4.

COMMUNION with Christ is a certain cure for every ill. Whether it be the wormwood of woe, or the cloying surfeit of earthly delight, close fellowship with the Lord Jesus will take bitterness from the one, and satiety from the other. Live near to Jesus, Christian, and it is matter of secondary importance whether thou livest on the mountain of honour or in the valley of humiliation. Living near to Jesus, thou art covered with the wings of God, and underneath thee are the everlasting arms. Let nothing keep thee from that hallowed intercourse, which is the choice privilege of a soul wedded to THE WELL-BELOVED. Be not content with an interview now and then, but seek always to retain His company, for only in His presence hast thou either comfort or safety. Jesus should not be unto us a friend who calls upon us now and then, but one with whom we walk evermore. Thou hast a difficult road before thee : see, O traveller to heaven, that thou go not without thy guide. Thou hast to pass through the fiery furnace . enter it not unless, like Shadrach, Meshach, and Abednego, thou hast the Son of God to be thy companion. Thou hast to storm the Jericho of thine own corruptions : attempt not the warfare until, like Joshua, thou hast seen the Captain of the Lord's host, with His sword drawn in His hand. Thou art to meet the Esau of thy many temptations : meet him not until at Jabbok's brook thou hast laid hold upon the angel, and prevailed. In every case, in every condition, thou wilt need Jesus ; but most of all, when the iron gates of death shall open to thee. Keep thou close to thy soul's Husband, lean thy head upon His bosom, ask to be refreshed with the spiced wine of His pomegranate, and thou shalt be found of Him at the last, without spot, or wrinkle, or any such thing. Seeing thou hast lived with Him, and lived in Him here, thou shalt abide with Him for ever.

" In my prosperity I said I shall never be moved."
Psalm xxx. 6.

" MOAB is settled on his lees, he hath not been emptied from vessel to vessel " Give a man wealth ; let his ships bring home continually rich freights ; let the winds and waves appear to be his servants to bear his vessels across the bosom of the mighty deep ; let his lands yield abundantly : let the weather be propitious to his crops ; let uninterrupted success attend him ; let him stand among men as a successful merchant ; let him enjoy continued health ; allow him with braced nerve and brilliant eye to march through the world, and live happily ; give him the buoyant spirit ; let him have the song perpetually on his lips ; let his eye be ever sparkling with joy—and the natural consequence of such an easy state to any man, let him be the best Christian who ever breathed, will be *presumption ;* even David said, " I shall never be moved ;" and we are not better than David, nor half so good. Brother, beware of the smooth places of the way ; if you are treading them, or if the way be rough, thank God for it. If God should always rock us in the cradle of prosperity ; if we were always dandled on the knees of fortune ; if we had not some stain on the alabaster pillar ; if there were not a few clouds in the sky ; if we had not some bitter drops in the wine of this life, we should become intoxicated with pleasure, we should dream " we stand ;" and stand we should, but it would be upon a pinnacle ; like the man asleep upon the mast, each moment we should be in jeopardy.

We bless God, then, for our afflictions ; we thank Him for our changes ; we extol his name for losses of property ; for we feel that had He not chastened us thus, we might have become too secure. Continued worldly prosperity is a fiery trial.

> " Afflictions, though they seem severe,
> In mercy oft are sent."

" Man . . . is of few days, and full of trouble."—Job xiv. 1.

IT may be of great service to us, before we fall asleep, to remember this mournful fact, for it may lead us to set loose by earthly things. There is nothing very pleasant in the recollection that we are not above the shafts of adversity, but it may humble us and prevent our boasting like the Psalmist in our morning's portion. " My mountain standeth firm : I shall never be moved." It may stay us from taking too deep root in this soil from which we are so soon to be transplanted into the heavenly garden. Let us recollect the frail tenure upon which we hold our *temporal mercies.* If we would remember that all the trees of earth are marked for the woodman's axe, we should not be so ready to build our nests in them. We should love, but we should love with the love which expects death, and which reckons upon separations. Our dear relations are but loaned to us, and the hour when we must return them to the lender's hand may be even at the door. The like is certainly true of our *worldly goods.* Do not riches take to themselves wings and fly away? Our *health* is equally precarious. Frail flowers of the field, we must not reckon upon blooming for ever. There is a time appointed for weakness and sickness, when we shall have to glorify God by suffering, and not by earnest activity. There is no single point in which we can hope to escape from the sharp arrows of affliction ; out of our few days there is not one secure from sorrow. Man's life is a cask full of bitter wine ; he who looks for joy in it had better seek for honey in an ocean of brine. Beloved reader, set not your affections upon things of earth : but seek those things which are above, for *here* the moth devoureth, and the thief breaketh through, but *there* all joys are perpetual and eternal. The path of trouble is the way home. Lord, make this thought a pillow for many a weary head !

" Sin . . . exceeding sinful."—Romans vii. 13.

BEWARE of light thoughts of sin. At the time of conversion, the conscience is so tender, that we are afraid of the slightest sin. Young converts have a holy timidity, a godly fear lest they should offend against God. But alas! very soon the fine bloom upon these first ripe fruits is removed by the rough handling of the surrounding world: the sensitive plant of young piety turns into a willow in after life, too pliant, too easily yielding. It is sadly true, that even a Christian may grow by degrees so callous, that the sin which once startled him does not alarm him in the least. By degrees men get familiar with sin. The ear in which the cannon has been booming will not notice slight sounds. At first a little sin startles us ; but soon we say, " Is it not a little one ?" Then there comes another, larger, and then another, until by degrees we begin to regard sin as but a little ill; and then follows an unholy presumption: " We have not fallen into open sin. True, we tripped a little, but we stood upright in the main. We may have uttered one unholy word, but as for the most of our conversation, it has been consistent." So we palliate sin ; we throw a cloak over it ; we call it by dainty names. Christian, beware how thou thinkest lightly of sin. Take heed lest thou fall by little and little. Sin, a *little* thing? Is it not a poison? Who knows its deadliness? Sin, a little thing? Do not the little foxes spoil the grapes? Doth not the tiny coral insect build a rock which wrecks a navy? Do not little strokes fell lofty oaks? Will not continual droppings wear away stones? Sin, a little thing? It girded the Redeemer's head with thorns, and pierced His heart! It made *Him* suffer anguish, bitterness, and woe. Could you weigh the least sin in the scales of eternity, you would fly from it as from a serpent, and abhor *the least appearance of evil.* Look upon all sin as that which crucified the Saviour, and you will see it to be " exceeding sinful."

" Thou shalt be called, Sought out."—Isaiah lxii. 12.

THE surpassing grace of God is seen very clearly in that we were not only sought, but sought *out.* Men *seek* for a thing which is lost upon the floor of the house, but in such a case there is only seeking, not seeking *out.* The loss is more perplexing and the search more persevering when a thing is sought *out.* We were mingled with the mire : we were as when some precious piece of gold falls into the sewer, and men gather out and carefully inspect a mass of abominable filth, and continue to stir and rake, and search among the heap until the treasure is found. Or, to use another figure, we were lost in a labyrinth ; we wandered hither and thither, and when mercy came after us with the gospel, it did not find us at the first coming, it had to search for us and seek us out ; for we as lost sheep were so desperately lost, and had wandered into such a strange country, that it did not seem possible that even the Good Shepherd should track our devious roamings. Glory be to unconquerable grace, we were sought *out !* No gloom could hide us, no filthiness could conceal us, we were found and brought home. Glory be to infinite love, God the Holy Spirit restored us !

The lives of some of God's people, if they could be written would fill us with holy astonishment. Strange and marvellous are the ways which God used in their case to find His own. Blessed be His name, He never relinquishes the search until the chosen are sought out effectually. They are not a people sought to-day and cast away to-morrow. Almightiness and wisdom combined will make no failures, they shall be called, *" Sought out !"* That *any* should be sought out is matchless grace, but that *we* should be sought out is grace beyond degree ! We can find no reason for it but God's own sovereign love, and can only lift up our heart in wonder, and praise the Lord that this night *we* wear the name of *" Sought out."*

" Thou shalt love thy neighbour."—Matthew v. 43.

" OVE thy neighbour." Perhaps he rolls in riches, and thou art poor, and living in thy little cot side-by-side with his lordly mansion; thou seest every day his estates, his fine linen, and his sumptuous banquets; God has given him these gifts, covet not his wealth, and think no hard thoughts concerning him. Be content with thine own lot, if thou canst not better it, but do not look upon thy neighbour, and wish that he were as thyself. Love him, and then thou wilt not envy him.

Mayhap, on the other hand, thou art rich, and near thee reside the poor. Do not scorn to call them neighbours. Own that thou art bound to love them. The world calls them thy inferiors. In what are they inferior? They are far more thine equals than thine inferiors, for " God hath made of one blood all people that dwell upon the face of the earth." It is thy coat which is better than theirs, but thou art by no means better than they. They are men, and what art thou more than that? Take heed that thou love thy neighbour even though he be in rags, or sunken in the depths of poverty.

But, perhaps, you say, " I cannot love my neighbours, because for all I do they return ingratitude and contempt. " So much the more room for the heroism of love. Wouldst thou be a feather-bed warrior, instead of bearing the rough fight of love? He who dares the most, shall win the most; and if rough be thy path of love, tread it boldly, still loving thy neighbours through thick and thin. Heap coals of fire on their heads, and if they be hard to please, seek not to please *them*, but to please *thy Master;* and remember if *they* spurn thy love, thy Master hath not spurned it, and thy deed is as acceptable to Him as if it had been acceptable to them. Love thy neighbour, for in so doing thou art following the footsteps of Christ.

" To whom belongest thou ?"—1 Samuel xxx. 13.

O neutralities can exist in religion. We are either ranked under the banner of Prince Immanuel, to serve and fight His battles, or we are vassals of the black prince, Satan. " To whom belongest thou ?"

Reader, let me assist you in your response. *Have you been " born again"?* If you have, you belong to Christ, but without the new birth you cannot be His. *In whom do you trust ?* For those who believe in Jesus are the sons of God. *Whose work are you doing ?* You are sure to serve your master, for he whom you serve is thereby owned to be your lord. *What company do you keep ?* If you belong to Jesus, you will fraternise with those who wear the livery of the cross. " Birds of a feather flock together." *What is your conversation ?* Is it heavenly or is it earthly ? *What have you learned of your Master ?*—for servants learn much from their masters to whom they are apprenticed. If you have served your time with Jesus, it will be said of you, as it was of Peter and John, " They took knowledge of them, that they had been with Jesus."

We press the question, " To whom belongest thou ?" Answer honestly before you give sleep to your eyes. If you are not Christ's you are in a hard service— *Run away from your cruel master !* Enter into the service of the Lord of Love, and you shall enjoy a life of blessedness. If you *are* Christ's, let me advise you to do four things. You belong to Jesus—*obey Him ;* let His word be your law ; let His wish be your will. You belong to the Beloved, then *love Him ;* let your heart embrace Him ; let your whole soul be filled with Him. You belong to the Son of God, then *trust Him ;* rest nowhere but on him. You belong to the King of kings, then *be decided for Him.* Thus, without your being branded upon the brow, all will know to whom you belong.

" Why sit we here until we die ? " —2 Kings vii. 3.

EAR reader, this little book was mainly intended for the edification of believers, but if
you are yet unsaved, our heart yearns over
you : and we would fain say a word which may
be blessed to you. Open your Bible, and read
the story of the lepers, and mark their position,
which was much the same as yours. If you remain
where you are you must perish; if you go to Jesus
you can but die. "Nothing venture, nothing win,"
is the old proverb, and in your case the venture is
no great one. If you sit still in sullen despair,
no one can pity you when your ruin comes; but
if you die with mercy sought, if such a thing were
possible, you would be the object of universal sympathy. None escape who refuse to look to Jesus; but
you know that, at any rate, some are saved who believe
in Him, for certain of your own acquaintances have
received mercy: then why not you? The Ninevites
said, "Who can tell?" Act upon the same hope,
and try the Lord's mercy. To perish is so awful,
that if there were but a straw to catch at, the instinct of self-preservation should lead you to stretch
out your hand. We have thus been talking to you
on your own unbelieving ground, we would now assure
you, as from the Lord, that if you seek Him He will
be found of you. Jesus casts out none who come
unto Him. You shall not perish if you trust Him;
on the contrary, you shall find treasure far richer than
the poor lepers gathered in Syria's deserted camp.
May the Holy Spirit embolden you to go at once,
and you shall not believe in vain. When you are
saved yourself, publish the good news to others.
Hold not your peace; tell the King's household first,
and unite with them in fellowship; let the porter of
the city, the minister, be informed of your discovery,
and then proclaim the good news in every place. The
Lord save thee ere the sun goes down this day.

" Then he put forth his hand, and took her, and pulled her in unto him into the ark."—Genesis viii. 9.

EARIED out with her wanderings, the dove returns at length to the ark as her only resting place. How heavily she flies—she will drop—she will never reach the ark! But she struggles on. Noah has been looking out for his dove all day long, and is ready to receive her. She has just strength to reach the edge of the ark, she can hardly alight upon it, and is ready to drop, when Noah puts forth his hand and pulls her in unto him. Mark that: *"pulled her in unto him."* She did not fly right in herself, but was too fearful, or too weary to do so. She flew as far as she could, and then he put forth his hand and pulled her in unto him. This act of mercy was shown to the wandering dove, and she was not chidden for her wanderings. Just as she was she was pulled into the ark. So you, seeking sinner, with all your sin, will be received. "Only return"—those are God's two gracious words —"only return." What! nothing else? No, "only return." She had no olive branch in her mouth this time, nothing at all but just herself and her wanderings; but it is "only return," and she does return, and Noah pulls her in. Fly, thou wanderer; fly thou fainting one, dove as thou art, though thou thinkest thyself to be black as the raven with the mire of sin, back, back to the Saviour. Every moment thou waitest does but increase thy misery; thine attempts to plume thyself and make thyself fit for Jesus are all vanity. Come thou to Him just as thou art "Return, thou backsliding Israel." He does not say, "Return, thou *repenting* Israel" (there is such an invitation doubtless), but "thou *backsliding* one," as a backslider with all thy backslidings about thee, Return, return, return! Jesus is waiting for thee! He will stretch forth His hand and "pull thee in"— in to Himself, thy heart's true home.

" Let him that thinketh he standeth take heed lest he fall."
1 Corinthians x. 12.

T is a curious fact, that there is such a thing as being proud of grace. A man says, "I have great faith, I shall not fall; poor little faith may, but I never shall." "I have fervent love," says another, "I can stand, there is no danger of my going astray." He who boasts of grace has little grace to boast of. Some who do this imagine that their graces can keep them, knowing not that the stream must flow constantly from the fountain head, or else the brook will soon be dry. If a continuous stream of oil comes not to the lamp, though it burn brightly to-day, it will smoke to-morrow, and noxious will be its scent. Take heed that thou gloriest not in thy graces, but let all thy glorying and confidence be in Christ and His strength, for only so canst thou be kept from falling. Be much more in prayer. Spend longer time in holy adoration. Read the Scriptures more earnestly and constantly. Watch your lives more carefully. Live nearer to God. Take the best examples for your pattern. Let your conversation be redolent of heaven. Let your hearts be perfumed with affection for men's souls. So live that men may take knowledge of you that you have been with Jesus, and have learned of Him; and when that happy day shall come, when He whom you love shall say, "Come up higher," may it be your happiness to hear Him say, "Thou hast fought a good fight, thou hast finished thy course, and henceforth there is laid up for thee a crown of righteousness which fadeth not away." On, Christian, with care and caution! On, with holy fear and trembling! On, with faith and confidence in Jesus alone, and let your constant petition be, "Uphold me according to Thy word." He is able, and He alone, "To keep you from falling, and to present you faultless before the presence of His glory with exceeding joy."

"I will take heed to my ways."—Psalm xxxix. 1.

ELLOW-PILGRIM, say not in your heart,
"I will go hither and thither, and I shall not
sin;" for you are never so out of danger of
sinning as to boast of security. The road is very miry,
it will be hard to pick your path so as not to soil
your garments. This is a world of pitch; you will
need to watch often, if in handling it you are to keep
your hands clean. There is a robber at every turn of
the road to rob you of your jewels; there is a temptation in every mercy; there is a snare in every joy;
and if you ever reach heaven, it will be a miracle
of divine grace to be ascribed entirely to your
Father's power. Be on your guard. When a man
carries a bomb-shell in his hand, he should mind
that he does not go near a candle; and you too must
take care that you enter not into temptation. Even
your common actions are edged tools; you must mind
how you handle them. There is nothing in this
world to foster a Christian's piety, but everything to
destroy it. How anxious should you be to look up to
God, that *He* may keep you! Your prayer should be,
"Hold thou me up, and I shall be safe." Having
prayed, you must also watch; guarding every thought,
word, and action, with holy jealousy. Do not expose
yourselves unnecessarily; but if called to exposure,
if you are bidden to go where the darts are flying,
never venture forth without your shield; for if once
the devil finds you without your buckler, he will rejoice
that his hour of triumph is come, and will soon make
you fall down wounded by his arrows. Though slain
you cannot be; wounded you may be. "Be sober;
be vigilant, danger may be in an hour when all
seemeth securest to thee." Therefore, take heed to
thy ways, and watch unto prayer. No man ever fell
into error through being too watchful. May the
Holy Spirit guide us in all our ways, so shall they
always please the Lord.

" Be strong in the grace that is in Christ Jesus."—2 Tim. ii. 1.

CHRIST has grace without measure in Himself, but He hath not retained it for Himself. As the reservoir empties itself into the pipes, so hath Christ emptied out His grace for His people. "Of His fulness have all we received, and grace for grace." He seems only to have in order to dispense to us. He stands like the fountain, always flowing, but only running in order to supply the empty pitchers and the thirsty lips which draw nigh unto it. Like a tree, He bears sweet fruit, not to hang on boughs, but to be gathered by those who need. Grace, whether its work be to pardon, to cleanse, to preserve, to strengthen, to enlighten, to quicken, or to restore, is ever to be had from Him freely and without price; nor is there one form of the work of grace which He has not bestowed upon His people. As the blood of the body, though flowing from the heart, belongs equally to every member, so the influences of grace are the inheritance of every saint united to the Lamb; and herein there is a sweet communion between Christ and His Church, inasmuch as they both receive the same grace. Christ is the head upon which the oil is first poured; but the same oil runs to the very skirts of the garments, so that the meanest saint has an unction of the same costly moisture as that which fell upon the head. This is true communion when the sap of grace flows from the stem to the branch, and when it is perceived that the stem itself is sustained by the very nourishment which feeds the branch. As we day by day receive grace from Jesus, and more constantly recognise it as coming from Him, we shall behold Him in communion with us, and enjoy the felicity of communion with Him. Let us make daily use of our riches, and ever repair to Him as to our own Lord in covenant, taking from Him the supply of all we need with as much boldness as men take money from their own purse.

"He did it with all his heart and prospered."—2 Chron. xxxi. 21.

THIS is no unusual occurrence ; it is the general rule of the moral universe that those men prosper who do their work with all their hearts, while those are almost certain to fail who go to their labour leaving half their hearts behind them. God does not give harvests to idle men except harvests of thistles, nor is He pleased to send wealth to those who will not dig in the field to find its hid treasure. It is universally confessed that if a man would prosper, he must be diligent in business. It is the same in religion as it is in other things. If you would prosper in your work for Jesus, let it be *heart* work, and let it be done with *all* your heart. Put as much force, energy, heartiness, and earnestness into religion as ever you do into business, for it deserves far more. The Holy Spirit helps our infirmities, but He does not encourage our idleness ; He loves active believers. Who are the most useful men in the Christian church ? The men who do what they undertake for God *with all their hearts.* Who are the most successful Sabbath-school teachers ? The most talented ? No ; the most zealous ; the men whose hearts are on fire, those are the men who see their Lord riding forth prosperously in the majesty of His salvation. Whole-heartedness shows itself in *perseverance;* there may be failure at first, but the earnest worker will say, "It is the Lord's work, and it must be done ; my Lord has bidden me do it, and in His strength I will accomplish it." Christian, art thou thus "with all thine heart" serving thy Master ? Remember the earnestness of Jesus ! Think what heart-work was His ! He could say, " *The zeal of Thine house hath eaten Me up.*" When He sweat great drops of blood, it was no light burden He had to carry upon those blessed shoulders ; and when He poured out His heart, it was no weak effort He was making for the salvation of His people. Was Jesus in earnest, and are we lukewarm ?

" I am a stranger with thee."—Psalm xxxix. 12.

ES, O Lord, *with* Thee, but not *to* Thee. All my natural alienation from Thee, Thy grace has effectually removed; and now, in fellowship with Thyself, I walk through this sinful world as a pilgrim in a foreign country. *Thou* art a stranger in Thine own world. Man forgets Thee, dishonours Thee, sets up new laws and alien customs, and knows Thee not. When Thy dear Son came unto His own, His own received Him not. He was in the world, and the world was made by Him, and the world knew Him not. Never was foreigner so speckled a bird among the denizens of any land as Thy beloved Son among His mother's brethren. It is no marvel, then, if I who live the life of Jesus, should be unknown and a stranger here below. Lord, I would not be a citizen where Jesus was an alien. His pierced hand has loosened the cords which once bound my soul to earth, and now I find myself a stranger in the land. My speech seems to these Babylonians among whom I dwell an outlandish tongue, my manners are singular, and my actions are strange. A Tartar would be more at home in Cheapside than I could ever be in the haunts of sinners. But here is the sweetness of my lot: I am a stranger *with Thee.* Thou art my fellow-sufferer, my fellow-pilgrim. Oh, what joy to wander in such blessed society! My heart burns within me by the way when thou dost speak to me, and though I be a sojourner, I am far more blest than those who sit on thrones, and far more at home than those who dwell in their ceiled houses.

> " To me remains nor place, nor time :
> My country is in every clime ;
> I can be calm and free from care
> On any shore, since God is there.
>
> While place we seek, or place we shun,
> The soul finds happiness in none :
> But with a God to guide our way,
> 'Tis equal joy to go or stay."

"Keep back Thy servant also from presumptuous sins."
Psalm xix. 13.

SUCH was the *prayer of the "man after God's own heart."* Did holy David need to pray thus? How needful, then, must such a prayer be for *us* babes in grace! It is as if he said, "Keep me back, or I shall rush headlong over the precipice of sin." Our evil nature, like an ill-tempered horse, is apt to run away. May the grace of God put the bridle upon it, and hold it in, that it rush not into mischief. What might not the best of us do if it were not for the checks which the Lord sets upon us both in providence and in grace! The psalmist's prayer is directed against the worst form of sin—that which is done with deliberation and wilfulness. Even the holiest need to be "kept back" from the vilest transgressions. It is a solemn thing to find the apostle Paul warning saints against the most loathsome sins. "Mortify therefore your members which are upon the earth; fornication, uncleanness, inordinate affection, evil concupiscence, and covetousness, which is idolatry." What! do saints want warning against such sins as these? Yes, they do. The whitest robes, unless their purity be preserved by divine grace, will be defiled by the blackest spots. Experienced Christian, boast not in your experience; you will trip yet if you look away from Him who is able to keep you from falling. Ye whose love is fervent, whose faith is constant, whose hopes are bright, say not, "We shall never sin," but rather cry, "Lead us not into temptation." There is enough tinder in the heart of the best of men to light a fire that shall burn to the lowest hell, unless God shall quench the sparks as they fall. Who would have dreamed that righteous Lot could be found drunken, and committing uncleanness? Hazael said, "Is Thy servant a dog, that he should do this thing?" and we are very apt to use the same self-righteous question. May infinite wisdom cure us of the madness of self-confidence.

" *Remember the poor.*"—Galatians ii. 10.

HY does God allow so many of His children to be poor? He could make them all rich if He pleased; He could lay bags of gold at their doors; He could send them a large annual income; or He could scatter round their houses abundance of provisions, as once he made the quails lie in heaps round the camp of Israel, and rained bread out of heaven to feed them. There is no necessity that they should be poor, except that He sees it to be best. "The cattle upon a thousand hills are His"—He could supply them; He could make the richest, the greatest, and the mightiest bring all their power and riches to the feet of His children, for the hearts of all men are in His control. But He does not chose to do so; He allows them to suffer want, He allows them to pine in penury and obscurity. Why is this? There are many reasons: one is, *to give us, who are favoured with enough, an opportunity of showing our love to Jesus.* We show our love to Christ when we sing of Him and when we pray to Him; but if there were no sons of need in the world we should lose the sweet privilege of evidencing our love, by ministering in almsgiving to His poorer brethren; He has ordained that thus we should prove that our love standeth not in word only, but in deed and in truth. If we truly love Christ, we shall care for those who are loved by Him. Those who are dear to Him will be dear to us. Let us then look upon it not as a duty but as a privilege to relieve the poor of the Lord's flock—remembering the words of the Lord Jesus, "Inasmuch as ye have done it unto one of the least of these my brethren, ye have done it unto me." Surely this assurance is sweet enough, and this motive strong enough to lead us to help others with a willing hand and a loving heart—recollecting that all we do for His people is graciously accepted by Christ as done to Himself.

"Blessed are the peacemakers: for they shall be called the children of God."—Matthew v. 9.

THIS is the seventh of the beatitudes: and seven was the number of perfection among the Hebrews. It may be that the Saviour placed the peacemaker the seventh upon the list because he most nearly approaches the perfect man in Christ Jesus. He who would have perfect blessedness, so far as it can be enjoyed on earth, must attain to this seventh benediction, and become a peacemaker. There is a significance also in the position of the text. The verse which precedes it speaks of the blessedness of " the pure in heart : for they shall see God." It is well to understand that we are to be " first pure, then peaceable." Our peaceableness is never to be a compact with sin, or toleration of evil. We must set our faces like flints against everything which is contrary to God and His holiness : purity being in our souls a settled matter, we can go on to peaceableness. Not less does the verse that follows seem to have been put there on purpose. However peaceable we may be in this world, yet we shall be misrepresented and misunderstood : and no marvel, for even the Prince of Peace, by His very peacefulness, brought fire upon the earth. He Himself, though He loved mankind, and did no ill, was "despised and rejected of men, a man of sorrows and acquainted with grief." Lest, therefore, the peaceable in heart should be surprised when they meet with enemies, it is added in the following verse, " Blessed are they which are persecuted for righteousness' sake : for theirs is the kingdom of heaven." Thus the peacemakers are not only pronounced to be blessed, but they are compassed about with blessings. Lord, give us grace to climb to this seventh beatitude ! Purify our minds that we may be " first pure, then peaceable," and fortify our souls, that our peaceableness may not lead us into cowardice and despair, when for Thy sake we are persecuted.

" Ye are all the children of God by faith in Christ Jesus."
Gal. iii. 26.

THE *fatherhood of God is common to all his children.* Ah! Little-faith, you have often said, " Oh that I had the courage of Great-heart, that I could wield his sword and be as valiant as he! But, alas, I stumble at every straw, and a shadow makes me afraid." List thee, Little-faith. Great-heart is God's child, and you are God's child too ; and Great-heart is not one whit more God's child than you are. Peter and Paul, the highly-favoured apostles, were of the family of the Most High ; and so are you also ; the weak Christian is as much a child of God as the strong one.

> " This cov'nant stands secure,
>   Though earth's old pillars bow ;
> The strong, the feeble, and the weak,
>   Are one in Jesus now."

All the names are in the same family register. One may have more grace than another, but God our heavenly Father has the same tender heart towards all. One may do more mighty works, and may bring more glory to his Father, but he whose name is the least in the kingdom of heaven is as much the child of God as he who stands among the King's mighty men. Let this cheer and comfort us, when we draw near to God and say, " Our Father."

Yet, while we are comforted by knowing this, let us not rest contented with weak faith, but ask, like the Apostles, to have it increased. However feeble our faith may be, if it be real faith in Christ, we shall reach heaven at last, but we shall not honour our Master much on our pilgrimage, neither shall we abound in joy and peace. If then you would live to Christ's glory, and be happy in His service, seek to be filled with the spirit of adoption more and more completely, till perfect love shall cast out fear.

" As the Father hath loved Me, so have I loved you."
John xv. 9.

S the Father loves the Son, in the same manner Jesus loves His people. What is that divine method ? He loved Him *without beginning*, and thus Jesus loves His members. *" I have loved thee with an everlasting love."* You can trace the beginning of human affection ; you can easily find the beginning of your love to Christ, but His love to us is a stream whose source is hidden in eternity. God the Father loves Jesus *without any change*. Christian, take this for your comfort, that there is no change in Jesus Christ's love to those who rest in Him. Yesterday you were on Tabor's top, and you said, " He loves me :" to-day you are in the valley of humiliation, but He loves you still the same. On the hill Mizar, and among the Hermons, you heard His voice, which spake so sweetly with the turtle-notes of love ; and now on the sea, or even *in* the sea, when all His waves and billows go over you, His heart is faithful to His ancient choice. The Father loves the Son *without any end,* and thus does the Son love His people. Saint, thou needest not fear the loosing of the silver cord, for His love for thee will never cease. Rest confident that even down to the grave Christ will go with you, and that up again from it He will be your guide to the celestial hills. Moreover, the Father loves the Son *without any measure,* and the same immeasurable love the Son bestows upon His chosen ones. The whole heart of Christ is dedicated to His people. He " loved us and gave Himself for us." His is a love which passeth knowledge. Ah ! we have indeed an immutable Saviour, a precious Saviour, one who loves without measure, without change, without beginning, and without end, even as the Father loves Him ! There is much food here for those who know how to digest it. May the Holy Ghost lead us into its marrow and fatness !

"Strong in faith."—Romans iv. 20.

CHRISTIAN, take good care of thy faith; for recollect *faith is the only way whereby thou canst obtain blessings.* If we want blessings from God, nothing can fetch them down but faith. Prayer cannot draw down answers from God's throne except it be the earnest prayer of the man who believes. Faith is the angelic messenger between the soul and the Lord Jesus in glory. Let that angel be withdrawn, we can neither send up prayer, nor receive the answers. Faith is the telegraphic wire which links earth and heaven—on which God's messages of love fly so fast, that before we call He answers, and while we are yet speaking He hears us. But if that telegraphic wire of faith be snapped, how can we receive the promise? Am I in trouble?—I can obtain help for trouble by faith. Am I beaten about by the enemy?—my soul on her dear Refuge leans by faith. But take faith away—in vain I call to God. There is no road betwixt my soul and heaven. In the deepest wintertime faith is a road on which the horses of prayer may travel—ay, and all the better for the biting frost; but blockade the road, and how can we communicate with the Great King? Faith links me with divinity. Faith clothes me with the power of God. Faith engages on my side the omnipotence of Jehovah. Faith ensures every attribute of God in my defence. It helps me to defy the hosts of hell. It makes me march triumphant over the necks of my enemies. But without faith how can I receive anything of the Lord? Let not him that wavereth—who is like a wave of the Sea—expect that he will receive anything of God! O, then. Christian, watch well thy faith; for with it thou canst win all things, however poor thou art, but without it thou canst obtain nothing. "If thou canst believe, all things are possible to him that believeth."

" And she did eat, and was sufficed, and left."—Ruth ii. 14.

WHENEVER we are privileged to eat of the bread which Jesus gives, we are, like Ruth, satisfied with the full and sweet repast. When Jesus is the host no guest goes empty from the table. Our *head* is satisfied with the precious truth which Christ reveals ; our *heart* is content with Jesus, as the altogether lovely object of affection ; our *hope* is satisfied, for whom have we in heaven but Jesus ? and our *desire* is satiated, for what can we wish for more than " to know Christ and to be found in Him " ? Jesus fills our *conscience* till it is at perfect peace ; our *judgment* with persuasion of the certainty of His teachings ; our *memory* with recollections of what He has done, and our *imagination* with the prospects of what He is yet to do. As Ruth was " sufficed, *and left,*" so is it with us. We have had deep draughts ; we have thought that we could take in all of Christ ; but when we have done our best we have had to leave a vast remainder. We have sat at the table of the Lord's love, and said, " Nothing but the infinite can ever satisfy me ; I am such a great sinner that I must have infinite merit to wash my sin away ;" but we have had our sin removed, and found that there was merit to spare ; we have had our hunger relieved at the feast of sacred love, and found that there was a redundance of spiritual meat remaining. There are certain sweet things in the Word of God which we have not enjoyed yet, and which we are obliged to leave for awhile ; for we are like the disciples to whom Jesus said, " I have yet many things to say unto you, but ye cannot bear them now." Yes, there are graces to which we have not attained ; places of fellowship nearer to Christ which we have not reached ; and heights of communion which our feet have not climbed. At every banquet of love there are many baskets of fragments left. Let us magnify the liberality of our glorious Boaz.

" My beloved."—Cant. ii. 8.

HIS was a golden name which the ancient Church in her most joyous moments was wont to give to the Anointed of the Lord. When the time of the singing of birds was come, and the voice of the turtle was heard in her land, *her* love-note was sweeter than either, as she sung, "*My beloved* is mine and I am His : He feedeth among the lilies." Ever in her song of songs doth she call Him by that delightful name, "My beloved!" Even in the long winter, when idolatry had withered the garden of the Lord, her prophets found space to lay aside the burden of the Lord for a little season, and to say, as Esaias did, "Now will I sing to my well-beloved a song of my beloved touching His vineyard." Though the saints had never seen His face, though as yet He was not made flesh, nor had dwelt among us, nor had man beheld His glory, yet He was the consolation of Israel, the hope and joy of all the chosen, the "beloved" of all those who were upright before the Most High. We, in the summer days of the Church, are also wont to speak of Christ as the best beloved of our soul, and to feel that He is very precious, the "chiefest among ten thousand, and the altogether lovely." So true is it that the Church loves Jesus, and claims Him as her beloved, that the apostle dares to defy the whole universe to separate her from the love of Christ, and declares that neither persecutions, distress, affliction, peril, or the sword have been able to do it ; nay, he joyously boasts, "In all these things we are more than conquerors through Him that loved us."

O that we knew more of Thee, Thou ever precious one !

> My sole possession is Thy love;
> In earth beneath, or heaven above,
> I have no other store ;
> And though with fervent suit I pray,
> And importune Thee day by day,
> I ask Thee nothing more.

---

*" Husbands, love your wives, even as Christ also loved
the church."*—Ephesians v. 25.

WHAT a golden example Christ gives to His
disciples! Few masters could venture to say,
"If you would practise my teaching, imitate
my life;" but as the life of Jesus is the exact tran-
script of perfect virtue, He can point to Himself as the
paragon of holiness, as well as the teacher of it. The
Christian should take nothing short of Christ for his
model. Under no circumstances ought we to be content unless we reflect the grace which was in Him.
As a husband, the Christian is to look upon the portrait of Christ Jesus, and he is to paint according to
that copy. The true Christian is to be such a husband
as Christ was to His church. The love of a husband
is *special.* The Lord Jesus cherishes for the church a
peculiar affection, which is set upon her above the
rest of mankind: "I pray for them, I pray not for
the world." The elect church is the favourite of
heaven, the treasure of Christ, the crown of His head,
the bracelet of His arm, the breastplate of His heart,
the very centre and core of His love. A husband
should love his wife with a *constant* love, for thus
Jesus loves His church. He does not vary in His
affection. He may change in His display of affection,
but the affection itself is still the same. A husband
should love his wife with an *enduring* love, for nothing
"shall be able to separate us from the love of God,
which is in Christ Jesus our Lord." A true husband
loves his wife with a *hearty* love, fervent and intense.
It is not mere lip-service. Ah! beloved, what more
could Christ have done in proof of His love than He
has done? Jesus has a *delighted love* towards His
spouse : He prizes her affection, and delights in her
with sweet complacence. Believer, you wonder at
Jesus' love ; you admire it—*are you imitating it?*
In your domestic relationships is the rule and measure
of your love—*" even as Christ loved the church "?*

F

" Ye shall be scattered, every man to his own, and shall leave me alone."—John xvi. 32.

FEW had fellowship with the sorrows of Gethsemane. The majority of the disciples were not sufficiently advanced in grace to be admitted to behold the mysteries of "the agony." Occupied with the passover feast at their own houses, they represent the many who live upon the letter, but are mere babes as to the spirit of the gospel. To twelve, nay, to eleven only was the privilege given to enter Gethsemane and see "this great sight." Out of the eleven, eight were left at a distance ; they had fellowship, but not of that intimate sort to which men greatly beloved are admitted. Only three highly favoured ones could approach the veil of our Lord's mysterious sorrow : within that veil even these must not intrude ; a stone's-cast distance must be left between. He must tread the wine-press *alone*, and of the people there must be none with him. Peter and the two sons of Zebedee, represent the few eminent, experienced saints, who may be written down as "Fathers;" these having done business on great waters, can in some degree measure the huge Atlantic waves of their Redeemer's passion. To some selected spirits it is given, for the good of others, and to strengthen them for future, special, and tremendous conflict, to enter the inner circle and hear the pleadings of the suffering High Priest ; they have fellowship with him in his sufferings, and are made conformable unto his death. Yet even these cannot penetrate the secret places of the Saviour's woe. "Thine unknown sufferings" is the remarkable expression of the Greek liturgy : there was an inner chamber in our Master's grief, shut out from human knowledge and fellowship. There Jesus is *"left alone."* Here Jesus was more than ever an "Unspeakable gift"! Is not Watts right when he sings—

"And all the unknown joys he gives,
Were bought with agonies unknown."

" Canst thou bind the sweet influences of Pleiades, or loose the bands of Orion ?"—Job xxxviii. 31.

F inclined to boast of our abilities, the grandeur of nature may soon show us how puny we are. We cannot move the least of all the twinkling stars, or quench so much as one of the beams of the morning. We speak of power, but the heavens laugh us to scorn. When the Pleiades shine forth in spring with vernal joy we cannot restrain their influences, and when Orion reigns aloft, and the year is bound in winter's fetters, we cannot relax the icy bands. The seasons revolve according to the divine appointment, neither can the whole race of men effect a change therein. Lord, what is man ?

In the spiritual, as in the natural world, man's power is limited on all hands. When the Holy Spirit sheds abroad His delights in the soul, none can disturb ; all the cunning and malice of men are ineffectual to stay the genial quickening power of the Comforter. When he deigns to visit a church and revive it, the most inveterate enemies cannot resist the good work ; they may ridicule it, but they can no more restrain it than they can push back the spring when the Pleiades rule the hour. God wills it, and so it must be. On the other hand, if the Lord in sovereignty, or in justice, bind up a man so that he is in soul bondage, who can give him liberty ? He alone can remove the winter of spiritual death from an individual or a people. He looses the bands of Orion, and none but He. What a blessing it is that He can do it. O that He would perform the wonder to-night. Lord, end my winter, and let my spring begin. I cannot with all my longings raise my soul out of her death and dulness, but all things are possible with Thee. I need celestial influences, the clear shinings of Thy love, the beams of Thy grace, the light of Thy countenance, these are the Pleiades to me. I suffer much from sin and temptation, these are my wintry signs, my terrible Orion. Lord, work wonders in me, and for me. Amen.

" And He went a little farther, and fell on His face, and prayed."—Matt. xxvi. 39.

THERE are several instructive features in our Saviour's prayer in His hour of trial. It was *lonely prayer.* He withdrew even from His three favoured disciples. Believer, be much in solitary prayer, especially in times of trial. Family prayer, social prayer, prayer in the Church, will not suffice, these are very precious, but the best beaten spice will smoke in your censer in your private devotions, where no ear hears but God's.

It was *humble prayer.* Luke says He knelt, but another evangelist says He " fell on His face." Where, then, must be THY place, thou humble servant of the great Master ? What dust and ashes should cover *thy* head ! Humility gives us good foot-hold in prayer. There is no hope of prevalence with God unless we abase ourselves that He may exalt us in due time.

It was *filial prayer.* " Abba, Father." You will find it a stronghold in the day of trial to plead your adoption. You have no rights as a subject, you have forfeited them by your treason ; but nothing can forfeit a child's right to a father's protection. Be not afraid to say, " My Father, hear my cry."

Observe that it was *persevering prayer.* He prayed three times. Cease not until you prevail. Be as the importunate widow, whose continual coming earned what her first supplication could not win. Continue in prayer, and watch in the same with thanksgiving.

Lastly, *it was the prayer of resignation.* "Nevertheless, not as I will, but as thou wilt." Yield, and God yields. Let it be as God wills, and God will determine for the best. Be thou content to leave thy prayer in his hands, who knows when to give, and how to give, and what to give, and what to withhold. So pleading, earnestly, importunately, yet with humility and resignation, thou shalt surely prevail.

" Father, I will that they also, whom Thou hast given Me, be with Me where I am."—John xvii. 24.

DEATH! why dost thou touch the tree beneath whose spreading branches weariness hath rest? Why dost thou snatch away the excellent of the earth, in whom is all our delight? If thou must use thine axe, use it upon the trees which yield no fruit; thou mightst be thanked then. But why wilt thou fell the goodly cedars of Lebanon? O stay thine axe, and spare the righteous. But no, it must not be; death smites the goodliest of our friends; the most generous, the most prayerful, the most holy, the most devoted must die. And why? It is through Jesus' prevailing prayer—" Father, I will that they also, whom Thou hast given Me, be with Me where I am." It is *that* which bears them on eagle's wings to heaven. Every time a believer mounts from this earth to paradise, it is an answer to Christ's prayer. A good old divine remarks, "Many times Jesus and His people pull against one another in prayer. You bend your knee in prayer and say, ' Father, I will that Thy saints be with me where *I* am ;' Christ says, ' Father, I will that they also, whom Thou hast given Me, be with Me where *I* am.' " Thus the disciple is at crosspurposes with his Lord. The soul cannot be in both places : the beloved one cannot be with Christ and with you too. Now, which pleader shall win the day? If you had your choice ; if the King should step from His throne, and say, " Here are two supplicants praying in opposition to one another, which shall be answered?" Oh! I am sure, though it were agony, you would start from your feet, and say, " Jesus, not my will, but Thine be done." You would give up your prayer for your loved one's life, if you could realise the thought that Christ is praying in the opposite direction—" Father, I will that they also, whom Thou hast given Me, be with Me where I am." Lord, Thou shalt have them. By faith we let them go.

*" His sweat was as it were great drops of blood falling down
to the ground."*—Luke xxii. 44.

THE mental pressure arising from our Lord's
struggle with temptation, so forced his frame
to an unnatural excitement, that his pores sent
forth great drops of blood which fell down to the ground.
This proves *how tremendous must have been the weight
of sin* when it was able to crush the Saviour so that
he distilled great drops of blood ! This demonstrates
the mighty power of his love. It is a very pretty observation of old Isaac Ambrose that the gum which
exudes from the tree without cutting is always the
best. This precious camphire-tree yielded most sweet
spices when it was wounded under the knotty whips,
and when it was pierced by the nails on the cross ;
but see, it giveth forth its best spice when there is
no whip, no nail, no wound. This sets forth *the
voluntariness of Christ's sufferings,* since without a
lance the blood flowed freely. No need to put on the
leech, or apply the knife ; it flows spontaneously. No
need for the rulers to cry, " Spring up, O well ; " of
itself it flows in crimson torrents. If men suffer
great pain of mind apparently the blood rushes *to*
the heart. The cheeks are pale ; a fainting fit comes
on ; the blood has gone inward as if to nourish the
inner man while passing through its trial. But see
our Saviour in His agony ; he is so utterly oblivious
of self, that instead of his agony driving his blood to
the heart to nourish himself, it drives it outward to
bedew the earth. The agony of Christ, inasmuch as
it pours him out upon the ground, pictures the fulness
of the offering which he made for men.

Do we not perceive how intense must have been the
wrestling through which he passed, and will we not
hear its voice *to us* ? " Ye have not yet resisted unto
blood, striving against sin." Behold the great Apostle
and High Priest of our profession, and sweat even to
blood rather than yield to the great tempter of your souls.

" I tell you that, if these should hold their peace, the stones would immediately cry out."—Luke xix. 40.

BUT could the stones cry out? Assuredly they could if He who opens the mouth of the dumb should bid them lift up their voice. Certainly if they were to speak, they would have much to testify in praise of Him who created them by the word of His power; they could extol the wisdom and power of their *Maker* who called them into being. Shall not *we* speak well of Him who made us anew, and out of stones raised up children unto Abraham? The old rocks could tell of chaos and order, and the handiwork of God in successive stages of creation's drama; and cannot *we* talk of God's decrees, of God's great work in ancient times, in all that He did for His church in the days of old? If the stones were to speak, they could tell of their *breaker*, how he took them from the quarry, and made them fit for the temple, and cannot we tell of our glorious Breaker, who broke our hearts with the hammer of His word, that He might build us into His temple? If the stones should cry out they would magnify their *builder*, who polished them and fashioned them after the similitude of a palace; and shall not we talk of our Architect and Builder, who has put us in our place in the temple of the living God? If the stones could cry out, they might have a long, long story to tell by way of *memorial*, for many a time hath a great stone been rolled as a memorial before the Lord; and we too can testify of Ebenezers, stones of help, pillars of remembrance. The broken stones of the law cry out against us, but Christ Himself, who has rolled away the stone from the door of the sepulchre, speaks for us. Stones might well cry out, but we will not let them: we will hush their noise with ours; we will break forth into sacred song, and bless the majesty of the Most High, all our days glorifying Him who is called by Jacob the Shepherd and Stone of Israel.

" He was heard in that he feared." Heb. v. 7.

DID this fear arise from the infernal suggestion *that he was utterly forsaken.* There may be sterner trials than this, but surely it is *one* of the worst to be utterly forsaken? "See," said Satan, "thou hast a friend nowhere! Thy Father hath shut up the bowels of his compassion against thee. Not an angel in His courts will stretch out his hand to help thee. All heaven is alienated from Thee; Thou art left alone. See the companions with whom Thou hast taken sweet counsel, what are they worth? Son of Mary, see there thy brother James, see there Thy loved disciple John, and Thy bold apostle Peter, how the cowards sleep when Thou art in Thy sufferings! Lo! Thou hast no friend left in heaven or earth. All hell is against Thee. I have stirred up mine infernal den. I have sent my missives throughout all regions summoning every prince of darkness to set upon Thee this night, and we will spare no arrows, we will use all our infernal might to overwhelm Thee: and what wilt Thou do, Thou solitary one?" It may be, this was the temptation; we think it was, because the appearance of an angel unto Him strengthening Him removed that fear. He was heard in that He feared; He was no more alone, but heaven was with Him. It may be that this is the reason of His coming three times to His disciples—as Hart puts it—

> " Backwards and forwards thrice He ran,
> As if He sought some help from man."

He would see for Himself whether it were really true that all men had forsaken Him; He found them all asleep; but perhaps he gained some faint comfort from the thought that they were sleeping, not from treachery, but from sorrow, the spirit indeed was willing, but the flesh was weak. At any rate He was heard in that he feared. Jesus was heard in His deepest woe; my soul, thou shalt be heard also.

" In that hour Jesus rejoiced in spirit."—Luke x. 21.

HE Saviour was " a man of sorrows," but every thoughtful mind has discovered the fact that down deep in His innermost soul He carried an inexhaustible treasury of refined and heavenly joy. Of all the human race, there was never a man who had a deeper, purer, or more abiding peace than our Lord Jesus Christ. " He was anointed with the oil of gladness above His fellows." His vast benevolence must, from the very nature of things, have afforded Him the deepest possible delight, for benevolence is joy. There were a few remarkable seasons when this joy manifested itself. "At that hour Jesus rejoiced in spirit, and said, I thank thee, O Father, Lord of heaven and earth." Christ had His songs, though it was night with Him; though His face was marred, and His countenance had lost the lustre of earthly happiness, yet sometimes it was lit up with a matchless splendour of unparalleled satisfaction, as He thought upon the recompense of the reward, and in the midst of the congregation sang His praise unto God. In this, the Lord Jesus is a blessed picture of His church on earth. At this hour the church expects to walk in sympathy with her Lord along a thorny road ; through much tribulation she is forcing her way to the crown. To bear the cross is her office, and to be scorned and counted an alien by her mother's children is her lot; and yet the church has a deep well of joy, of which none can drink but her own children. There are stores of wine, and oil, and corn, hidden in the midst of our Jerusalem, upon which the saints of God are evermore sustained and nurtured ; and sometimes, as in our Saviour's case, we have our seasons of intense delight, for "There is a river, the streams whereof shall make glad the city of our God." Exiles though we be, we rejoice in our King; yea, in Him we exceedingly rejoice, while in His name we set up our banners.

" Betrayest thou the Son of Man with a kiss?"
Luke xxii. 48.

" " HE kisses of an enemy are deceitful." Let
me be on my guard when the world puts
on a loving face, for it will, if possible, betray me as it did my Master, with a kiss.   Whenever
a man is about to stab religion, he usually professes
very great reverence for it.   Let me beware of the
sleek-faced hypocrisy which is armour-bearer to heresy
and infidelity.   Knowing the deceivableness of unrighteousness, let me be wise as a serpent to detect
and avoid the designs of the enemy.   The young man,
void of understanding, was led astray by the kiss of
the strange woman : may my soul be so graciously instructed all this day, that "the much fair speech" of
the world may have no effect upon me.   Holy Spirit,
let me not, a poor frail son of man, be betrayed with
a kiss !
     But what if I should be guilty of the same accursed
sin as Judas, that son of perdition ?   I have been baptized into the name of the Lord Jesus ; I am a member of His visible Church ; I sit at the communion
table : all these are so many kisses of my lips.   Am I
sincere in them ?   If not, I am a base traitor.   Do I
live in the world as carelessly as others do, and yet
make a profession of being a follower of Jesus ?   Then
I must expose religion to ridicule, and lead men to
speak evil of the holy name by which I am called.
Surely if I act thus inconsistently I am a Judas, and
it were better for me that I had never been born.   Dare
I hope that I am clear in this matter ?   Then, O Lord,
keep me so.   O Lord, make me sincere and true.   Preserve me from every false way.   Never let me betray
my Saviour.   I do love Thee, Jesus, and though I
often grieve Thee, yet I would desire to abide faithful
even unto death.   O God, forbid that I should be a
high-soaring professor, and then fall at last into the
lake of fire, because I betrayed my Master with a kiss.

"The Son of man."—John iii. 13.

HOW constantly our Master used the title, the "Son of man!" If He had chosen, He might always have spoken of Himself as the Son of God, the Everlasting Father, the Wonderful, the Counsellor, the Prince of Peace ; but behold the lowliness of Jesus! He prefers to call Himself the Son of man. Let us learn a lesson of humility from our Saviour ; let us never court great titles nor proud degrees. There is here, however, a far sweeter thought. Jesus loved manhood so much, that He delighted to honour it ; and since it is a high honour, and indeed, the greatest dignity of manhood, that Jesus is the Son of man, He is wont to display this name, that He may as it were hang royal stars upon the breast of manhood, and show forth the love of God to Abraham's seed. *Son of man*—whenever He said that word, He shed a halo round the head of Adam's children. Yet there is perhaps a more precious thought still. Jesus Christ called Himself the Son of man to express His oneness and sympathy with His people. He thus reminds us that He is one whom we may approach without fear. As a man, we may take to Him all our griefs and troubles, for He knows them by experience ; in that He Himself hath suffered as the "Son of man," He is able to succour and comfort us. All hail, Thou blessed Jesus! inasmuch as Thou art evermore using the sweet name which acknowledges that Thou art a brother and a near kinsman, it is to us a dear token of Thy grace, Thy humility, Thy love.

> " Oh see how Jesus trusts Himself
> 　Unto our childish love,
> As though by His free ways with us
> 　Our earnestness to prove!
>
> His sacred name a common word
> 　On earth He loves to hear ;
> There is no majesty in Him
> 　Which love may not come near."

" Jesus said unto them, If ye seek Me, let these go their way."
John xviii. 8.

ARK, my soul, the care which Jesus manifested even in His hour of trial, towards the sheep of His hand! The ruling passion is strong in death. He resigns himself to the enemy, but He interposes a word of power to set His disciples free. As to himself, like a sheep before her shearers He is dumb and opened not his mouth, but for His disciples' sake He speaks with Almighty energy. Herein is love, constant, self-forgetting, faithful love. But is there not far more here than is to be found upon the surface? Have we not the very soul and spirit of the atonement in these words? The Good Shepherd lays down His life for the sheep, and pleads that they must therefore go free. The Surety is bound, and justice demands that those for whom He stands a substitute should go their way. In the midst of Egypt's bondage, that voice rings as a word of power, *" Let these go their way."* Out of the slavery of sin and Satan the redeemed must come. In every cell of the dungeons of Despair, the sound is echoed, *" Let these go their way,"* and forth come Despondency and Much-afraid. Satan hears the well-known voice, and lifts his foot from the neck of the fallen; and Death hears it, and the grave opens her gates to let the dead arise. *Their way* is one of progress, holiness, triumph, glory, and none shall dare to stay them in it. No lion shall be on their way, neither shall any ravenous beast go up thereon. "The hind of the morning" has drawn the cruel hunters upon himself, and now the most timid roes and hinds of the field may graze at perfect peace among the lilies of his loves. The thundercloud has burst over the Cross of Calvary, and the pilgrims of Zion shall never be smitten by the bolts of vengeance. Come, my heart, rejoice in the immunity which thy Redeemer has secured thee, and bless His name all the day, and every day.

" When He cometh in the glory of His Father with the holy angels."—Mark viii. 38.

IF we have been partakers with Jesus in His shame, we shall be sharers with Him in the lustre which shall surround Him when He appears again in glory. Art thou, beloved one, with Christ Jesus? Does a vital union knit thee to Him? Then thou art to-day with Him in His shame; thou hast taken up His cross, and gone with Him without the camp bearing His reproach; thou shalt doubtless be with Him when the cross is exchanged for the crown. But judge thyself this evening; for if thou art not with Him in the regeneration, neither shalt thou be with Him when He shall come in His glory. If thou start back from the black side of communion, thou shalt not understand its bright, its happy period, when the King shall come, and *all His holy angels with Him.* What! are *angels with Him?* And yet He took not up angels—He took up the seed of Abraham. Are the holy angels *with Him?* Come, my soul, if thou art indeed His own beloved, thou canst not be far from Him. If His friends and His neighbours are called together to see His glory, what thinkest thou if thou art married to Him? Shalt thou be distant? Though it be a day of judgment, yet thou canst not be far from that heart which, having admitted angels into intimacy, has admitted thee into union. Has He not said to thee, O my soul, "I will betroth thee unto Me in righteousness, and in judgment, and in lovingkindness"? Have not His own lips said it, "I am married unto thee, and My delight is in thee"? If the angels, who are but friends and neighbours, shall be with Him, it is abundantly certain that His own beloved Hephzibah, in whom is all His delight, shall be near to Him, and sit at His right hand. Here is a morning star of hope for thee, of such exceeding brilliance, that it may well light up the darkest and most desolate experience.

" Then all the disciples forsook Him and fled."
Matt. xxvi. 56.

HE never deserted them, but they in cowardly fear of their lives, fled from Him in the very beginning of His sufferings. This is but one instructive instance of the frailty of all believers if left to themselves; they are but sheep at the best, and they flee when the wolf cometh. They had all been warned of the danger, and had promised to die rather than leave their Master; and yet they were seized with sudden panic, and took to their heels. It may be, that I, at the opening of this day, have braced up my mind to bear a trial for the Lord's sake, and I imagine myself to be certain to exhibit perfect fidelity; but let me be very jealous of myself, lest having the same evil heart of unbelief, I should depart from my Lord as the apostles did. It is one thing to promise, and quite another to perform. It would have been to their eternal honour to have stood at Jesus' side right manfully; they fled from honour; may I be kept from imitating them! Where else could they have been so safe as near their Master, who could presently call for twelve legions of angels? they fled from their true safety. O God, let me not play the fool also. Divine grace can make the coward brave. The smoking flax can flame forth like fire on the altar when the Lord wills it. These very apostles who were timid as hares, grew to be bold as lions after the Spirit had descended upon them, and even so the Holy Spirit can make my recreant spirit brave to confess my Lord and witness for His truth.

What anguish must have filled the Saviour as He saw His friends so faithless! This was one bitter ingredient in His cup; but that cup is drained dry; let me not put another drop in it. If I forsake my Lord, I shall crucify Him afresh, and put Him to an open shame. Keep me, O blessed Spirit, from an end so shameful.

" And she said, Truth, Lord : yet the dogs eat of the crumbs which fall from their masters' table."—Matthew xv. 27.

THIS woman gained comfort in her misery by thinking GREAT THOUGHTS OF CHRIST. The Master had talked about the children's bread : "Now," argued she, "since Thou art the Master of the table of grace, I know that Thou art a generous housekeeper, and there is sure to be abundance of bread on Thy table ; there will be such an abundance for the children that there will be crumbs to throw on the floor for the dogs, and the children will fare none the worse because the dogs are fed." She thought Him one who kept so good a table that all that she needed would only be a crumb in comparison ; yet remember, what she wanted was to have the devil cast out of her daughter. It was a very great thing to her, but she had such a high esteem of Christ, that she said, "It is nothing to Him, it is but a crumb for Christ to give." This is the royal road to comfort. Great thoughts of your sin alone will drive you to despair ; but great thoughts of Christ will pilot you into the haven of peace. ·· My sins are many, but oh! it is nothing to Jesus to take them all away. The weight of my guilt presses me down as a giant's foot would crush a worm, but it is no more than a grain of dust to Him, because He has already borne its curse in His own body on the tree. It will be but a small thing *for Him* to give me full remission, although it will be an infinite blessing *for me* to receive it." The woman opens her soul's mouth very wide, expecting great things of Jesus, and He fills it with His love. Dear reader, do the same. She confessed what Christ laid at her door, but she laid fast hold upon Him, and drew arguments even out of His hard words ; she believed great things of Him, and she thus overcame Him. SHE WON THE VICTORY BY BELIEVING IN HIM. Her case is an instance of prevailing faith ; and if we would conquer like her, we must imitate her tactics.

" The love of Christ which passeth knowledge."—Eph. iii. 19.

THE love of Christ in its sweetness, its fulness, its greatness, its faithfulness, passeth all human comprehension. Where shall language be found which shall describe His matchless, His unparalleled love towards the children of men ? It is so vast and boundless that, as the swallow but skimmeth the water, and diveth not into its depths, so all descriptive words but touch the surface, while depths immeasurable lie beneath. Well might the poet say,

" O love, thou fathomless abyss ! "

for this love of Christ is indeed measureless and fathomless ; none can attain unto it. Before we can have any right idea of the love of Jesus, we must understand His previous glory in its height of majesty, and His incarnation upon the earth in all its depths of shame. But who can tell us the majesty of Christ ? When He was enthroned in the highest heavens He was very God of very God ; by Him were the heavens made, and all the hosts thereof. His own almighty arm upheld the spheres ; the praises of cherubim and seraphim perpetually surrounded Him; the full chorus of the hallelujahs of the universe unceasingly flowed to the foot of his throne : He reigned supreme above all His creatures, God over all, blessed for ever. Who can tell His height of glory then ? And who, on the other hand, can tell now low He descended ? To be a man was something, to be a man of sorrows was far more ; to bleed, and die, and suffer, these were much for him who was the Son of God ; but to suffer such unparalleled agony—to endure a death of shame and desertion by His Father, this is a depth of condescending love which the most inspired mind must utterly fail to fathom. Herein is love ! and truly it is love that "passeth knowledge." O let this love fill our hearts with adoring gratitude, and lead us to practical manifestations of its power.

" I will accept you with your sweet savour."—Ezekiel xx. 41.

THE merits of our great Redeemer are as sweet savour to the Most High. Whether we speak of the active or passive righteousness of Christ, there is an equal fragrance. There was a sweet savour in His active life by which He honoured the law of God, and made every precept to glitter like a precious jewel in the pure setting of His own person. Such, too, was His passive obedience, when He endured with unmurmuring submission, hunger and thirst, cold and nakedness, and at length sweat great drops of blood in Gethsemane, gave His back to the smiters, and His cheeks to them that plucked out the hair, and was fastened to the cruel wood, that He might suffer the wrath of God in our behalf. These two things are sweet before the Most High; and for the sake of His doing and His dying, His substitutionary sufferings and His vicarious obedience, the Lord our God accepts us. What a preciousness must there be in Him to overcome our want of preciousness! What a sweet savour to put away our ill savour! What a cleansing power in His blood to take away sin such as ours! and what glory in His righteousness to make such unacceptable creatures to be accepted in the Beloved! Mark, believer, how sure and unchanging must be our acceptance, since it is *in Him!* Take care that you never doubt your acceptance in Jesus. You cannot be accepted without Christ; but, when you have received His merit, you cannot be unaccepted. Notwithstanding all your doubts, and fears, and sins, Jehovah's gracious eye never looks upon you in anger; though He sees sin in you, in yourself, yet when He looks at you through Christ, He sees no sin. You are always accepted in Christ, are always blessed and dear to the Father's heart. Therefore lift up a song, and as you see the smoking incense of the merit of the Saviour coming up, this evening, before the sapphire throne, let the incense of your praise go up also.

" Though He were a Son, yet learned He obedience by the things which He suffered."—Hebrews v. 8.

WE are told that the Captain of our salvation was made perfect through suffering, therefore we who are sinful, and who are far from being perfect, must not wonder if we are called to pass through suffering too. Shall the head be crowned with thorns, and shall the other members of the body be rocked upon the dainty lap of ease? Must Christ pass through seas of His own blood to win the crown, and are we to walk to heaven dryshod in silver slippers? No, our Master's experience teaches us that suffering is necessary, and the true-born child of God must not, would not, escape it if he might. But there is one very comforting thought in the fact of Christ's "being made perfect through suffering"—it is, that He can have complete sympathy with us. "He is not an high priest that cannot be touched with the feeling of our infirmities." In this sympathy of Christ we find a sustaining power. One of the early martyrs said, "I can bear it all, for Jesus suffered, and He suffers in me now; He sympathizes with me, and this makes me strong." Believer, lay hold of this thought in all times of agony. Let the thought of Jesus strengthen you as you follow in His steps. Find a sweet support in His sympathy; and remember that, to suffer is an honourable thing—to suffer for Christ is glory. The apostles rejoiced that they were counted worthy to do this. Just so far as the Lord shall give us grace to suffer *for* Christ, to suffer *with* Christ, just so far. does he honour us. The jewels of a Christian are his afflictions. The regalia of the kings whom God hath anointed are their troubles, their sorrows, and their griefs. Let us not, therefore, shun being honoured. Let us not turn aside from being exalted. Griefs exalt us, and troubles lift us up. "If we suffer, we shall also reign with Him."

" I called Him, but He gave me no answer."—Canticles v. 6.

PRAYER sometimes tarrieth, like a petitioner at the gate, until the King cometh forth to fill her bosom with the blessings which she seeketh. The Lord, when He hath given great faith, has been known to try it by long delayings. He has suffered his servants' voices to echo in their ears as from a brazen sky. They have knocked at the golden gate, but it has remained immovable, as though it were rusted upon its hinges. Like Jeremiah, they have cried, " Thou hast covered Thyself with a cloud, that our prayer should not pass through." Thus have true saints continued long in patient waiting without reply, not because their prayers were not vehement, nor because they were unaccepted, but because it so pleased Him who is a Sovereign, and who gives according to His own pleasure. If it pleases Him to bid our patience exercise itself, shall He not do as He wills with His own ! Beggars must not be choosers either as to time, place, or form. But we must be careful not to take delays in prayer for denials : God's long-dated bills will be punctually honoured ; we must not suffer Satan to shake our confidence in the God of truth by pointing to our unanswered prayers. Unanswered petitions are not unheard. God keeps a file for our prayers—they are not blown away by the wind, they are treasured in the King's archives. This is a registry in the court of heaven wherein every prayer is recorded. Tried believer, thy Lord hath a tear-bottle in which the costly drops of sacred grief are put away, and a book in which thy holy groanings are numbered. By-and-by, thy suit shall prevail. Canst thou not be content to wait a little ? Will not thy Lord's time be better than thy time ? By-and-by He will comfortably appear, to thy soul's joy, and make thee put away the sackcloth and ashes of long waiting, and put on the scarlet and fine linen of full fruition.

" He was numbered with the transgressors."—Isaiah liii. 12.

HY did Jesus suffer Himself to be enrolled amongst sinners? This wonderful condescension was justified by many powerful reasons. *In such a character He could the better become their advocate.* In some trials there is an identification of the counsellor with the client, nor can they be looked upon in the eye of the law as apart from one another. Now, when the sinner is brought to the bar, Jesus appears there Himself. *He* stands to answer the accusation. He points to His side, His hands, His feet, and challenges Justice to bring anything against the sinners whom He represents; He pleads His blood, and pleads so triumphantly, being numbered with them and having a part with them, that the Judge proclaims, "Let them go their way; deliver them from going down into the pit, for He hath found a ransom." Our Lord Jesus was numbered with the transgressors in order that they might *feel their hearts drawn towards Him.* Who can be afraid of one who is written in the same list with us? Surely we may come boldly to Him, and confess our guilt. He who is numbered with us cannot condemn us. Was he not put down in the transgressor's list *that we might be written in the red roll of the saints?* He was holy, and written among the holy; we were guilty, and numbered among the guilty; He transfers His name from yonder list to this black indictment, and our names are taken from the indictment and written in the roll of acceptance, for there is a complete transfer made between Jesus and His people. All our estate of misery and sin Jesus has taken; and all that Jesus has comes to us. His righteousness, His blood, and everything that He hath He gives us as our dowry. Rejoice, believer, in your union to Him who was numbered among the transgressors; and prove that you are truly saved by being manifestly numbered with those who are new creatures in Him.

" Let us search and try our ways, and turn again to the Lord.'
Lamentations iii. 40.

THE spouse who fondly loves her absent husband longs for his return ; a long protracted separation from her lord is a semi-death to her spirit : and so with souls who love the Saviour much, they *must* see His face, they cannot bear that He should be away upon the mountains of Bether, and no more hold communion with them. A reproaching glance, an uplifted finger will be grievous to loving children, who fear to offend their tender father, and are only happy in his smile. Beloved, it was so once with you. A text of Scripture, a threatening, a touch of the rod of affliction, and you went to your Father's feet, crying, "Show me wherefore Thou contendest with me?" Is it so now? Are you content to follow Jesus afar off? Can you contemplate suspended communion with Christ without alarm? Can you bear to have your Beloved walking contrary to you, because you walk contrary to Him? Have your sins separated between you and your God, and is your heart at rest? O let me affectionately warn you, for it is a grievous thing when we can live contentedly without the present enjoyment of the Saviour's face. *Let us labour to feel what an evil thing this is*—little love to our own dying Saviour, little joy in our precious Jesus, little fellowship with the Beloved ! Hold a true Lent in your souls, while you sorrow over your hardness of heart. Do not stop at sorrow ! Remember where you first received salvation. *Go at once to the cross.* There, and there only, can you get your spirit quickened. No matter how hard, how insensible, how dead we may have become, let us go again in all the rags and poverty, and defilement of our natural condition. Let us clasp that cross, let us look into those languid eyes, let us bathe in that fountain filled with blood—this will bring back to us our first love ; this will restore the simplicity of our faith, and the tenderness of our heart.

" With His stripes we are healed."—Isaiah liii. 5.

PILATE delivered our Lord to the lictors to be scourged. The Roman scourge was a most dreadful instrument of torture. It was made of the sinews of oxen, and sharp bones were inter-twisted every here and there among the sinews ; so that every time the lash came down these pieces of bone inflicted fearful laceration, and tore off the flesh from the bone. The Saviour was, no doubt, bound to the column, and thus beaten. He had been beaten before ; but this of the Roman lictors was probably the most severe of His flagellations. My soul, stand here and weep over His poor stricken body.

Believer in Jesus, can you gaze upon Him without tears, as He stands before you the mirror of agonizing love ? He is at once fair as the lily for innocence, and red as the rose with the crimson of His own blood. As we feel the sure and blessed healing which His stripes have wrought in us, does not our heart melt at once with love and grief ? If ever we have loved our Lord Jesus, surely we must feel that affection glowing now within our bosoms.

> " See how the patient Jesus stands,
>   Insulted in His lowest case !
>   Sinners have bound the Almig'.ty's hands,
>   And spit in their Creator's face.
>
>   With thorns His temples gor'd and gash'd
>   Send streams of blood from every part ;
>   His back's with knotted scourges lash'd,
>   But sharper scourges tear His heart."

We would fain go to our chambers and weep ; but since our business calls us away, we will first pray our Beloved to print the image of His bleeding self upon the tablets of our hearts all the day, and at nightfall we will return to commune with Him, and sorrow that our sin should have cost Him so dear.

*" And Rizpah the daughter of Aiah took sackcloth, and spread
it for her upon the rock, from the beginning of harvest until
water dropped upon them out of heaven, and suffered neither
the birds of the air to rest on them by day, nor the beasts of
the field by night."*—2 Samuel xxi. 10.

IF the love of a woman to her slain sons could
make her prolong her mournful vigil for so
long a period, shall we weary of considering
the sufferings of our blessed Lord ?   She drove away
the birds of prey, and shall not we chase from our
meditations those worldly and sinful thoughts which
defile both our minds and the sacred themes upon
which we are occupied ?   Away, ye birds of evil wing!
Leave ye the sacrifice alone !   She bore the heats of
summer, the night dews and the rains, unsheltered
and alone.   Sleep was chased from her weeping eyes :
her heart was too full for slumber.   Behold how she
loved her children !   Shall Rizpah thus endure, and
shall we start at the first little inconvenience or trial ?
Are we such cowards that we cannot bear to suffer
with our Lord ?   She chased away even the wild
beasts, with courage unusual in her sex, and will not
we be ready to encounter every foe for Jesus' sake ?
These her children were slain by other hands than
hers, and yet she wept and watched : what ought we
to do who have by our sins crucified our Lord ?
Our obligations are boundless, our love should be
fervent and our repentance thorough.   To watch with
Jesus should be our business, to protect His honour
our occupation, to abide by His cross our solace.
Those ghastly corpses might well have affrighted
Rizpah, especially by night, but in our Lord, at whose
cross-foot we are sitting, there is nothing revolting,
but everything attractive.   Never was living beauty
so enchanting as a dying Saviour.   Jesus, we will
watch with Thee yet awhile, and do Thou graciously
unveil Thyself to us ; then shall we not sit beneath
sackcloth, but in a royal pavilion.

" Let Him kiss me with the kisses of His mouth."—Cant. i. 2.

FOR several days we have been dwelling upon the Saviour's passion, and for some little time to come we shall linger there. In beginning a new month, let us seek the same desires after our Lord as those which glowed in the heart of the elect spouse. See how she leaps at once to *Him;* there are no prefatory words ; she does not even mention His name ; she is in the heart of her theme at once, for she speaks of *Him* who was the only Him in the world to her. How bold is her love ! it was much condescension which permitted the weeping penitent to anoint His feet with spikenard—it was rich love which allowed the gentle Mary to sit at His feet and learn of Him—but here, love, strong, fervent love, aspires to higher tokens of regard, and closer signs of fellowship. Esther trembled in the presence of Ahasuerus, but the spouse in joyful liberty of perfect love knows no fear. If we have received the same free spirit, we also may ask the like. By kisses we suppose to be intended those varied manifestations of affection by which the believer is made to enjoy the love of Jesus. The kiss of *reconciliation* we enjoyed at our conversion, and it was sweet as honey dropping from the comb. The kiss of *acceptance* is still warm on our brow, as we know that He hath accepted our persons and our works through rich grace. The kiss of daily, present *communion,* is that which we pant after to be repeated day after day, till it is changed into the kiss of *reception,* which removes the soul from earth, and the kiss of *consummation* which fills it with the joy of heaven. Faith is our walk, but fellowship sensibly felt is our rest. Faith is the road, but communion with Jesus is the well from which the pilgrim drinks. O lover of our souls, be not strange to us ; let the lips of Thy blessing meet the lips of our asking ; let the lips of Thy fulness touch the lips of our need and straightway the kiss will be effected.

" It is time to seek the Lord."—Hosea x. 12.

THIS month of April is said to derive its name from the Latin verb *aperio*, which signifies *to open*, because all the buds and blossoms are now opening, and we have arrived at the gates of the flowery year. Reader, if you are yet unsaved, may your heart, in accord with the universal awakening of nature, be opened to receive the Lord. Every blossoming flower warns you that *it is time to seek the Lord ;* be not out of tune with nature, but let your heart bud and bloom with holy desires. Do you tell me that the warm blood of youth leaps in your veins ? then, I entreat you, give your vigour to the Lord. It was my unspeakable happiness to be called in early youth, and I could fain praise the Lord every day for it. Salvation is priceless, let it come when it may, but oh ! an early salvation has a double value in it. Young men and maidens, since you may perish ere you reach your prime, *" It is time to seek the Lord."* Ye who feel the first signs of decay, quicken your pace : that hollow cough, that hectic flush, are warnings which you must not trifle with ; with you *it is indeed time to seek the Lord.* Did I observe a little grey mingled with your once luxurious tresses ? Years are stealing on apace, and death is drawing nearer by hasty marches, let each return of spring arouse you to set your house in order, Dear reader, if you are now advanced in life, let me entreat and implore you to delay no longer. There is a day of grace for you now—be thankful for that, but it is a limited season and grows shorter every time that clock ticks. Here in this silent chamber, on this first night of another month, I speak to you as best I can by paper and ink, and from my inmost soul, as God's servant, I lay before you this warning, *" It is time to seek the Lord."* Slight not that word, it may be your last call from destruction, the final syllable from the lip of grace.

" He answered him to never a word."—Matthew xxvii. 14.

E had never been slow of speech when He could
bless the sons of men, but He would not say a
single word for Himself. "Never man spake
like this Man," and never man was silent like Him.
Was this singular silence *the index of His perfect self-
sacrifice?* Did it show that He would not utter a
word to stay the slaughter of His sacred person,
which He had dedicated as an offering for us? Had
He so entirely surrendered Himself that He would
not interfere in His own behalf, even in the minutest
degree, but be bound and slain an unstruggling, uncom-
plaining victim? Was this silence *a type of the defence-
lessness of sin?* Nothing can be said in palliation or
excuse of human guilt ; and, therefore, He who bore its
whole weight stood speechless before His judge. Is
not patient silence *the best reply to a gainsaying world?*
Calm endurance answers some questions infinitely
more conclusively than the loftiest eloquence. The
best apologists for Christianity in the early days were
its martyrs. The anvil breaks a host of hammers by
quietly bearing their blows. Did not the silent Lamb
of God furnish us with *a grand example of wisdom?*
Where every word was occasion for new blasphemy,
it was the line of duty to afford no fuel for the flame
of sin. The ambiguous and the false, the unworthy
and mean, will ere long overthrow and confute themselves, and therefore the true can afford to be quiet,
and finds silence to be its wisdom. Evidently our
Lord, by His silence, furnished *a remarkable fulfilment of prophecy.* A long defence of Himself would
have been contrary to Isaiah's prediction. "He is led
as a lamb to the slaughter, and as a sheep before her
shearers is dumb, so He openeth not His mouth." By
His quiet He conclusively proved Himself to be the
true Lamb of God. As such we salute Him this
morning. Be with us, Jesus, and in the silence of
our heart, let us hear the voice of Thy love.

" He shall see His seed; He shall prolong His days, and the pleasure of the Lord shall prosper in His hand."—
Isaiah liii. 10.

PLEAD for the speedy fulfilment of this promise, all ye who love the Lord. It is easy work to pray when we are grounded and bottomed, as to our desires, upon God's own promise. How can He that gave the word refuse to keep it? Immutable veracity cannot demean itself by a lie, and eternal faithfulness cannot degrade itself by neglect. God must bless His Son, His covenant binds Him to it. That which the Spirit prompts us to ask for Jesus, is that which God decrees to give Him. Whenever you are praying for the kingdom of Christ, let your eyes behold the dawning of the blessed day which draweth near, when the Crucified shall receive His coronation in the place where men rejected Him. Courage, you that prayerfully work and toil for Christ with success of the very smallest kind, it shall not be so always; better times are before you. Your eyes cannot see the blissful future: borrow the telescope of faith; wipe the misty breath of your doubts from the glass; look through it and behold the coming glory. Reader, let us ask, *do you* make this your constant prayer? Remember that the same Christ who tells us to say, " Give us this day our daily bread," had first given us this petition, " Hallowed be Thy name; Thy kingdom come; Thy will be done in earth as it is in heaven." Let not your prayers be all concerning your own sins, your own wants, your own imperfections, your own trials, but let them climb the starry ladder, and get up to Christ Himself, and then, as you draw nigh to the blood-besprinkled mercy-seat, offer this prayer continually, " Lord, extend the kingdom of Thy dear Son." Such a petition, fervently presented, will elevate the spirit of all your devotions. Mind that you prove the sincerity of your prayer by labouring to promote the Lord's glory.

" They took Jesus, and led Him away."—John xix. 16.

E had been all night in agony, He had spent the early morning at the hall of Caiaphas, He had been hurried from Caiaphas to Pilate, from Pilate to Herod, and from Herod back again to Pilate; He had, therefore, but little strength left, and yet neither refreshment nor rest were permitted Him. They were eager for His blood, and therefore led Him out to die, loaded with the cross. O dolorous procession! Well may Salem's daughters weep. My soul, do thou weep also.

What learn we here as we see our blessed Lord led forth? Do we not perceive that truth which was set forth in shadow by *the scapegoat?* Did not the high-priest bring the scapegoat, and put both his hands upon its head, confessing the sins of the people, that thus those sins might be laid upon the goat, and cease from the people? Then the goat was led away by a fit man into the wilderness, and it carried away the sins of the people, so that if they were sought for they could not be found. Now we see Jesus brought before the priests and rulers, who pronounce Him guilty; God Himself imputes our sins *to Him,* "the Lord hath laid on Him the iniquity of us all;" "He was made sin for us;" and, as the substitute for our guilt, bearing our sin upon His shoulders, represented by the cross; we see the great Scapegoat led away by the appointed officers of justice. Beloved, can you feel assured that He carried *your* sin? As you look at the cross upon His shoulders, does it represent *your* sin? There is one way by which you can tell whether he carried your sin or not. Have you laid your hand upon His head, confessed your sin, and trusted in Him? Then your sin lies not on you; it has all been transferred by blessed imputation to Christ, and He bears it on His shoulder as a load heavier than the cross.

Let not the picture vanish till you have rejoiced in your own deliverance, and adored the loving Redeemer upon whom your iniquities were laid.

" All we like sheep have gone astray ; we have turned every one to his own way ; and the Lord hath laid on Him the iniquity of us all."—Isaiah liii. 6.

HERE is a confession of sin *common* to all the elect people of God. They have all fallen, and therefore, in common chorus, they all say, from the first who entered heaven to the last who shall enter there, "All we like sheep have gone astray." The confession, while thus unanimous, is also *special* and particular : " We have turned every one to his own way." There is a peculiar sinfulness about every one of the individuals ; all are sinful, but each one with some special aggravation not found in his fellow. It is the mark of genuine repentance that while it naturally associates itself with other penitents, it also takes up a position of loneliness. " We have turned every one to his own way," is a confession that each man had sinned against light peculiar to himself, or sinned with an aggravation which he could not perceive in others. This confession is *unreserved;* there is not a word to detract from its force, nor a syllable by way of excuse. The confession is *a giving up of all pleas of self-righteousness.* It is the declaration of men who are consciously guilty—guilty with aggravations, guilty without excuse : they stand with their weapons of rebellion broken in pieces, and cry, " All we like sheep have gone astray ; we have turned every one to his own way." Yet we hear no dolorous wailings attending this confession of sin ; for the next sentence makes it almost a song. " The Lord hath laid on Him the iniquity of us all." It is the most grievous sentence of the three, but it overflows with comfort. Strange is it that where misery was concentrated mercy reigned ; where sorrow reached her climax weary souls find rest. The Saviour bruised is the healing of bruised hearts. See how the lowliest penitence gives place to assured confidence through simply gazing at Christ on the cross !

" For He hath made Him to be sin for us, who knew no sin;
that we might be made the righteousness of God in Him."
2 Corinthians v. 21.

OURNING Christian! why weepest thou? Art
thou mourning over thine own corruptions?
Look to thy perfect Lord, and remember,
thou are complete in Him; thou art in God's
sight as perfect as if thou hadst never sinned; nay,
more than that, the Lord our Righteousness hath
put a divine garment upon thee, so that thou hast
more than the righteousness of man—thou hast the
righteousness of God. O thou who art mourning
by reason of inbred sin and depravity, remember,
none of thy sins can condemn thee. Thou hast
learned to hate sin; but thou hast learned also to
know that sin is not thine—it was laid upon Christ's
head. Thy standing is not in thyself—it is in Christ;
thine acceptance is not in thyself, but in thy Lord; thou
art as much accepted of God to-day, with all thy sinfulness, as thou wilt be when thou standest before His
throne, free from all corruption. O, I beseech thee,
lay hold on this precious thought, *perfection in Christ!*
For thou art "complete in Him." With thy Saviour's
garment on, thou art holy as the Holy one. "Who
is he that condemneth? It is Christ that died, yea
rather, that is risen again, who is even at the right
hand of God, who also maketh intercession for us."
Christian, let thy heart rejoice, for thou art "accepted
in the beloved"—what hast thou to fear? Let thy
face ever wear a smile; live near thy Master; live
in the suburbs of the Celestial City; for soon, when
thy time has come, thou shalt rise up where thy Jesus
sits, and reign at His right hand, even as He has overcome and has sat down at His Father's right hand;
and all this because the divine Lord "was made to be
sin for us, who knew no sin; that we might be made
the righteousness of God in Him."

" Come ye, and let us go up to the mountain of the Lord."
Isaiah ii. 3.

IT is exceedingly beneficial to our souls to mount above this present evil world to something nobler and better. The cares of this world and the deceitfulness of riches are apt to choke everything good within us, and we grow fretful, desponding, perhaps proud and carnal. It is well for us to cut down these thorns and briers, for heavenly seed sown among them is not likely to yield a harvest ; and where shall we find a better sickle with which to cut them down than communion with God an the things of the kingdom ? In the valleys oι Switzerland many of the inhabitants are deformed, and all wear a sickly appearance, for the atmosphere is charged with miasma, and is close and stagnant ; but up yonder, on the mountain, you find a hardy race, who breathe the clear fresh air as it blows from the virgin snows of the Alpine summits. It would be well if the dwellers in the valley could frequently leave their abodes among the marshes and the fever mists, and inhale the bracing element upon the hills. It is to such an exploit of climbing that I invite you this evening. May the Spirit of God assist us to leave the mists of fear and the fevers of anxiety, and all the ills which gather in this valley of earth, and to ascend the mountains of anticipated joy and blessedness. May God the Holy Spirit cut the cords that keep us here below, and assist us to mount ! We sit too often like chained eagles fastened to the rock, only that, unlike the eagle, we begin to love our chain, and would, perhaps, if it came really to the test, be loath to have it snapped. May God now grant us grace, if we cannot escape from the chain as to our flesh, yet to do so as to our spirits ; and leaving the body, like a servant, at the foot of the hill, may our soul, like Abraham, attain the top of the mountain, there to indulge in communion with the Most High.

" On Him they laid the cross, that He might bear it after Jesus."
Luke xxiii. 26.

E see in Simon's carrying the cross a picture of the work of the Church throughout all generations; she is the cross-bearer after Jesus. Mark then, Christian, Jesus does not suffer so as to exclude your suffering. He bears a cross, not that you may escape it, but that you may endure it. Christ exempts you from sin, but not from sorrow. Remember that, and expect to suffer.

But let us comfort ourselves with this thought, that in our case, as in Simon's, *it is not our cross, but Christ's cross which we carry.* When you are molested for your piety; when your religion brings the trial of cruel mockings upon you, then remember it is not *your* cross, it is *Christ's* cross; and how delightful is it to carry the cross of our Lord Jesus!

You carry the cross after Him. You have blessed company; your path is marked with the footprints of your Lord. The mark of His blood-red shoulder is upon that heavy burden. 'Tis *His* cross, and He goes before you as a shepherd goes before his sheep. Take up your cross daily, and follow Him.

Do not forget, also, *that you bear this cross in partnership.* It is the opinion of some that Simon only carried one end of the cross, and not the whole of it. That is very possible; Christ may have carried the heavier part, against the transverse beam, and Simon may have borne the lighter end. Certainly it is so with you; you do but carry the light end of the cross, Christ bore the heavier end.

And remember, *though Simon had to bear the cross for a very little while, it gave him lasting honour.* Even so the cross *we* carry is only for a little while at most, and then we shall receive the crown, the glory. Surely we should love the cross, and, instead of shrinking from it, *count it very dear,* when it works out for us "a far more exceeding and eternal weight of glory."

" Before honour is humility."—Proverbs xv. 33.

HUMILIATION of soul always *brings a positive blessing with it.* If we empty our hearts of self God will fill them with His love. He who desires close communion with Christ should remember the word of the Lord, " To this man will I look, even to him that is poor and of a contrite spirit, and trembleth at My word." Stoop if you would climb to heaven. Do we not say of Jesus, " He descended that He might ascend"? so must you. You must grow downwards, that you may grow upwards; for the sweetest fellowship with heaven is to be had by humble souls, and by them alone. God will deny no blessing to a thoroughly humbled spirit. " Blessed are the poor in spirit : for theirs is the kingdom of heaven," with all its riches and treasures. The whole exchequer of God shall be made over by deed of gift to the soul which is humble enough to be able to receive it without growing proud because of it. God blesses us all up to the full measure and extremity of what it is safe for Him to do. If you do not get a blessing, it is because it is not safe for you to have one. If our heavenly Father were to let your unhumbled spirit win a victory in His holy war, you would pilfer the crown for yourself, and meeting with a fresh enemy you would fall a victim ; so that you are kept low for your own safety. When a man is sincerely humble, and never ventures to touch so much as a grain of the praise, there is scarcely any limit to what God will do for him. Humility makes us ready to be blessed by the God of all grace, and fits us to deal efficiently with our fellow men. True humility is a flower which will adorn any garden. This is a sauce with which you may season every dish of life, and you will find an improvement in every case. Whether it be prayer or praise, whether it be work or suffering, the genuine salt of humility cannot be used in excess.

G

" Let us go forth therefore unto Him without the camp."
Hebrews xiii. 13.

JESUS, bearing His cross, went forth to suffer without the gate. The Christian's reason for leaving the camp of the world's sin and religion is not because he loves to be singular, but because *Jesus did so ;* and the disciple must follow his Master. Christ was "not of the world :" His life and His testimony were a constant protest against conformity with the world. Never was such overflowing affection for men as you find in Him ; but still He was separate from sinners. In like manner Christ's people must "go forth unto Him." They must take their position "without the camp," as witness-bearers for the truth. They must be prepared to tread the straight and narrow path. They must have bold,· unflinching, lion-like hearts, loving Christ first, and His truth next, and Christ and His truth beyond all the world. Jesus would have His people "go forth without the camp" *for their own sanctification.* You cannot grow in grace to any high degree while you are conformed to the world. The life of separation may be a path of sorrow, but it is the highway of safety ; and though the separated life may cost you many pangs, and make every day a battle, yet it is a happy life after all. No joy can excel that of the soldier of Christ : Jesus reveals Himself so graciously, and gives such sweet refreshment, that the warrior feels more calm and peace in his daily strife than others in their hours of rest. The highway of holiness is the highway of communion. It is thus we shall hope *to win the crown* if we are enabled by divine grace faithfully to follow Christ "without the camp." The crown of glory will follow the cross of separation. A moment's shame will be well recompensed by eternal honour ; a little while of witness-bearing will seem nothing when we are "for ever with the Lord."

"In the name of the Lord I will destroy them."—Ps. cxviii. 12.

OUR Lord Jesus, by His death, did not purchase a right to a *part* of us only, but to the *entire* man. He contemplated in His passion the sanctification of us wholly, spirit, soul, and body; that in this triple kingdom He Himself might reign supreme without a rival. It is the business of the newborn nature which God has given to the regenerate to assert the rights of the Lord Jesus Christ. My soul, so far as thou art a child of God, thou must conquer all the rest of thyself which yet remains unblest; thou must subdue all thy powers and passions to the silver sceptre of Jesus' gracious reign, and thou must never be satisfied till He who is King by purchase becomes also King by gracious coronation, and reigns in thee supreme. Seeing, then, that sin has no right to any part of us, we go about a good and lawful warfare when we seek, in the name of God, to drive it out. O my body, thou art a member of Christ: shall I tolerate thy subjection to the prince of darkness? O my soul, Christ has suffered for thy sins, and redeemed thee with His most precious blood: shall I suffer thy memory to become a storehouse of evil, or thy passions to be firebrands of iniquity? Shall I surrender my judgment to be perverted by error, or my will to be led in fetters of iniquity? No, my soul, thou art Christ's, and sin hath no right to thee.

Be courageous concerning this, O Christian! be not dispirited, as though your spiritual enemies could never be destroyed. You are able to overcome them —not in your own strength—the weakest of them would be too much for you in that; but you can and shall overcome them through the blood of the Lamb. Do not ask, "How shall I dispossess them, for they are greater and mightier than I?" but go to the strong for strength, wait humbly upon God, and the mighty God of Jacob will surely come to the rescue, and you shall sing of victory through His grace.

"O ye sons of men, how long will ye turn my glory into shame?"
Psalm iv. 2.

AN instructive writer has made a mournful list of the honours which the blinded people of Israel awarded to their long-expected King. (1.) They gave Him *a procession of honour*, in which Roman legionaries, Jewish priests, men and women, took a part, He Himself bearing His cross. This is the triumph which the world awards to Him who comes to overthrow man's direst foes. Derisive shouts are His only acclamations, and cruel taunts His only pæans of praise. (2.) They presented Him with *the wine of honour*. Instead of a golden cup of generous wine they offered Him the criminal's stupifying death-draught, which He refused because He would preserve an uninjured taste wherewith to taste of death; and afterwards when He cried, "I thirst," they gave Him vinegar mixed with gall, thrust to His mouth upon a sponge. Oh! wretched, detestable inhospitality to the King's Son. (3.) He was provided with *a guard of honour*, who showed their esteem of Him by gambling over His garments, which they had seized as their booty. Such was the body-guard of the adored of heaven; a quaternion of brutal gamblers. (4.) A *throne of honour* was found for Him upon the bloody tree; no easier place of rest would rebel men yield to their liege Lord. The cross was, in fact, the full expression of the world's feeling towards Him; "There," they seemed to say, "Thou Son of God, this is the manner in which God Himself should be treated, could we reach Him." (5.) *The title of honour* was nominally "King of the Jews," but that the blinded nation distinctly repudiated, and really called Him "King of thieves," by preferring Barabbas, and by placing Jesus in the place of highest shame between two thieves. His glory was thus in all things turned into shame by the sons of men, but it shall yet gladden the eyes of saints and angels, world without end.

"Deliver me from bloodguiltiness, O God, Thou God of my salvation; and my tongue shall sing aloud of Thy righteousness."—Psalm li. 14.

IN this SOLEMN CONFESSION, it is pleasing to observe that David plainly names his sin. He does not call it manslaughter, nor speak of it as an imprudence by which an unfortunate accident occurred to a worthy man, but he calls it by its true name, bloodguiltiness. He did not actually kill the husband of Bathsheba; but still it was planned in David's heart that Uriah should be slain, and he was before the Lord his murderer. Learn in confession to be honest with God. Do not give fair names to foul sins; call them what you will, they will smell no sweeter. What God sees them to be, that do you labour to feel them to be; and with all openness of heart acknowledge their real character. Observe, that David was evidently oppressed with the heinousness of his sin. It is easy to use words, but it is difficult to feel their meaning. The fifty-first Psalm is the photograph of a contrite spirit. Let us seek after the like brokenness of heart; for however excellent our words may be, if our heart is not conscious of the hell-deservingness of sin, we cannot expect to find forgiveness.

Our text has in it AN EARNEST PRAYER—it is addressed to the God of *salvation*. It is His prerogative to forgive; it is His very name and office to save those who seek His face. Better still, the text calls Him the God of *my* salvation. Yes, blessed be His name, while I am yet going to Him through Jesus' blood, I can rejoice in the God of *my* salvation.

The psalmist ends with A COMMENDABLE VOW: if God will deliver him he will *sing*—nay, more, he will "sing *aloud*." Who can sing in any other style of such a mercy as this! But note the subject of the song—"THY RIGHTEOUSNESS." We must sing of the finished work of a precious Saviour; and he who knows most of forgiving love will sing the loudest.

" If they do these things in a green tree, what shall be done in the dry ? "—Luke xxiii. 31.

MONG other interpretations of this suggestive question, the following is full of teaching : " If I, the innocent substitute for sinners, suffer thus, what will be done when the sinner himself— the dry tree—shall fall into the hands of an angry God?" When God saw Jesus in the sinner's place, He did not spare Him ; and when He finds the unregenerate without Christ, He will not spare *them.* O sinner, Jesus was led away by His enemies : so shall you be dragged away by fiends to the place appointed for you. Jesus was deserted of God ; and if He, who was only imputedly a sinner, was deserted, how much more shall you be ? *" Eloi, Eloi, lama sabachthani ? "* what an awful shriek ! But what shall be your cry when you shall say, " O God ! O God ! why hast Thou forsaken me ? " and the answer shall come back, " Because ye have set at nought all My counsel, and would none of My reproof : I also will laugh at your calamity ; I will mock when your fear cometh." If God spared not His own Son, how much less will He spare you ! What whips of burning wire will be yours when conscience shall smite you with all its terrors. Ye richest, ye merriest, ye most self-righteous sinners—who would stand in your place when God shall say, "Awake, O sword, against the man that rejected Me ; smite him, and let him feel the smart for ever " ? Jesus was spit upon : sinner, what shame will be yours ! We cannot sum up in one word all the mass of sorrows which met upon the head of Jesus who died for us, therefore it is impossible for us to tell you what streams, what oceans of grief must roll over *your* spirit if you die as you now are. You may die so, you may die now. By the agonies of Christ, by His wounds and by His blood, do not bring upon yourselves the wrath to come ! Trust in the Son of God, and you shall never die.

"I will fear no evil: for Thou art with me."—Psalm xxiii. 4.

BEHOLD, how independent of outward circumstances the Holy Ghost can make the Christian! What a bright light may shine within us when it is all dark without! How firm, how happy, how calm, how peaceful we may be, when the word shakes to and fro, and the pillars of the earth are removed! Even death itself, with all its terrible influences, has no power to suspend the music of a Christian's heart, but rather makes that music become more sweet, more clear, more heavenly, till the last kind act which death can do is to let the earthly strain melt into the heavenly chorus, the temporal joy into the eternal bliss! Let us have confidence, then, in the blessed Spirit's power to comfort us. Dear reader, are you looking forward to poverty? Fear not; the divine Spirit can give you, in your want, a greater plenty than the rich have in their abundance. You know not what joys may be stored up for you in the cottage around which grace will plant the roses of content. Are you conscious of a growing failure of your bodily powers? Do you expect to suffer long nights of languishing and days of pain? O be not sad! That bed may become a throne to you. You little know how every pang that shoots through your body may be a refining fire to consume your dross—a beam of glory to light up the secret parts of your soul. Are the eyes growing dim? Jesus will be your light. Do the ears fail you? Jesus' name will be your soul's best music, and His person your dear delight. Socrates used to say, "Philosophers can be happy without music;" and Christians can be happier than philosophers when all outward causes of rejoicing are withdrawn. In Thee, my God, my heart shall triumph, come what may of ills without! By thy power, O blessed Spirit, my heart shall be exceeding glad, though all things should fail me here below.

*" And there followed Him a great company of people, and of
women, which also bewailed and lamented Him."*
Luke xxiii. 27.

AMID the rabble rout which hounded the Redeemer to His doom, there were some gracious souls whose bitter anguish sought vent in wailing and lamentations—fit music to accompany that march of woe. When my soul can, in imagination, see the Saviour bearing His cross to Calvary, she joins the godly women and weeps with them ; for, indeed, there is true cause for grief—cause lying deeper than those mourning women thought. They bewailed innocence maltreated, goodness persecuted, love bleeding, meekness about to die ; but my heart has a deeper and more bitter cause to mourn. My sins were the scourges which lacerated those blessed shoulders, and crowned with thorn those bleeding brows : my sins cried " Crucify Him ! crucify Him ! " and laid the cross upon His gracious shoulders. His being led forth to die is sorrow enough for one eternity : but my having been His murderer, is more, infinitely more, grief than one poor fountain of tears can express.

Why those women loved and wept it were not hard to guess : but they could not have had greater reasons for love and grief than my heart has. Nain's widow saw her son restored—but I myself have been raised to newness of life. Peter's wife's mother was cured of the fever—but I of the greater plague of sin. Out of Magdalene seven devils were cast—but a whole legion out of me. Mary and Martha were favoured with visits—but He dwells with me. His mother bare His body—but He is formed in me the hope of glory. In nothing behind the holy women in debt, let me not be behind them in gratitude or sorrow.

> " Love and grief my heart dividing,
>   With my tears His feet I'll lave—
> Constant still in heart abiding,
>   Weep for Him who died to save."

"Thy gentleness hath made me great."—Psalm xviii. 35.

HE words are capable of being translated, "Thy *goodness* hath made me great." David gratefully ascribed all his greatness not to his own goodness, but to the goodness of God. "Thy *providence;*" is another reading; and providence is nothing more than goodness in action. Goodness is the bud of which providence is the flower, or goodness is the seed of which providence is the harvest. Some render it, "Thy *help,*" which is but another word for providence; providence being the firm ally of the saints, aiding them in the service of their Lord. Or again, "Thy *humility* hath made me great." "Thy *condescension*" may, perhaps, serve as a comprehensive reading, combining the ideas mentioned, including that of *humility.* It is God's making Himself little which is the cause of our being made great. We are so little, that if God should manifest His greatness without condescension, we should be trampled under His feet; but God, who must stoop to view the skies, and bow to see what angels do, turns His eye yet lower, and looks to the lowly and contrite, and makes them great. There are yet other readings, as for instance, the Septuagint, which reads, "Thy discipline"—Thy fatherly correction—"hath made me great;" while the Chaldee paraphrase reads, "Thy word hath increased me." Still the idea is the same. David ascribes all his own greatness to the condescending goodness of his Father in heaven. May this sentiment be echoed in our hearts this evening while we cast our crowns at Jesus' feet, and cry, "Thy gentleness hath made me great." How marvellous has been our experience of God's gentleness! How gentle have been His corrections! How gentle His forbearance! How gentle His teachings! How gentle His drawings! Meditate upon this theme, O believer. Let gratitude be awakened; let humility be deepened; let love be quickened ere thou fallest asleep to-night.

" The place which is called Calvary."—Luke xxiii. 33.

THE hill of comfort is the hill of Calvary; the house of consolation is built with the wood of the cross; the temple of heavenly blessing is founded upon the riven rock—riven by the spear which pierced His side. No scene in sacred history ever gladdens the soul like Calvary's tragedy.

> " Is it not strange, the darkest hour
>   That ever dawned on sinful earth,
>   Should touch the heart with softer power,
>   For comfort, than an angel's mirth?
>   That to the Cross the mourner's eye should turn,
>   Sooner than where the stars of Bethlehem burn?"

Light springs from the midday-midnight of Golgotha, and every herb of the field blooms sweetly beneath the shadow of the once accursed tree. In that place of thirst, grace hath dug a fountain which ever gusheth with waters pure as crystal, each drop capable of alleviating the woes of mankind. You who have had your seasons of conflict, will confess that it was not at Olivet that you ever found comfort, not on the hill of Sinai, nor on Tabor; but Gethsemane, Gabbatha, and Golgotha have been a means of comfort to you. The bitter herbs of Gethsemane have often taken away the bitters of your life; the scourge of Gabbatha has often scourged away your cares, and the groans of Calvary have put all other groans to flight. Thus Calvary yields us comfort rare and rich. We never should have known Christ's love in all its heights and depths if He had not died; nor could we guess the Father's deep affection if He had not given His Son to die. The common mercies we enjoy all sing of love, just as the sea-shell, when we put it to our ears, whispers of the deep sea whence it came; but if we desire to hear the ocean itself, we must not look at every-day blessings, but at the transactions of the crucifixion. He who would know love, let him retire to Calvary and see the Man of sorrows die.

"For there stood by me this night the angel of God."
Acts xxvii. 23.

TEMPEST and long darkness, coupled with imminent risk of shipwreck, had brought the crew of the vessel into a sad case; one man alone among them remained perfectly calm, and by his word the rest were reassured. Paul was the only man who had heart enough to say, "Sirs, be of good cheer." There were veteran Roman legionaries on board, and brave old mariners, and yet their poor Jewish prisoner had more spirit than they all. He had a secret Friend who kept his courage up. The Lord Jesus despatched a heavenly messenger to whisper words of consolation in the ear of His faithful servant, therefore he wore a shining countenance and spake like a man at ease.

If we fear the Lord, we may look for timely interpositions when our case is at its worst. Angels are not kept from us by storms, or hindered by darkness. Seraphs think it no humiliation to visit the poorest of the heavenly family. If angel's visits are few and far between at ordinary times, they shall be frequent in our nights of tempest and tossing. Friends may drop from us when we are under pressure, but our intercourse with the inhabitants of the angelic world shall be more abundant; and in the strength of love-words, brought to us from the throne by the way of Jacob's ladder, we shall be strong to do exploits. Dear reader, is this an hour of distress with you? then ask for peculiar help. Jesus is the angel of the covenant, and if His presence be now earnestly sought, it will not be denied. What that presence brings in heart-cheer those remember who, like Paul, have had the angel of God standing by them in a night of storm, when anchors would no longer hold, and rocks were nigh.

> "O angel of my God, be near,
>   Amid the darkness hush my fear :
> Loud roars the wild tempestuous sea,
>   Thy presence, Lord, shall comfort me."

" I am poured out like water, and all my bones are out of joint."—Psalm xxii. 14.

DID earth or heaven ever behold a sadder spectacle of woe! In soul and body, our Lord felt Himself to be weak as water poured upon the ground. The placing of the cross in its socket had shaken Him with great violence, had strained all the ligaments, pained every nerve, and more or less dislocated all His bones. Burdened with His own weight, the august sufferer felt the strain increasing every moment of those six long hours. His sense of faintness and general weakness were overpowering; while to His own consciousness He became nothing but a mass of misery and swooning sickness. When Daniel saw the great vision, he thus describes his sensations, "There remained no strength in me, for my vigour was turned into corruption, and I retained no strength :" how much more faint must have been our greater Prophet when He saw the dread vision of the wrath of God, and felt it in His own soul! To us, sensations such as our Lord endured would have been insupportable, and kind unconsciousness would have come to our rescue; but in His case, He was wounded, and *felt* the sword; He drained the cup and *tasted* every drop.

> " O King of Grief ! (a title strange, yet true
> To Thee of all kings only due)
> O King of Wounds ! how shall I grieve for Thee,
> Who in all grief preventest me ! "

As we kneel before our now ascended Saviour's throne, let us remember well the way by which He prepared it as a throne of grace for us ; let us in spirit drink of His cup, that we may be strengthened for our hour of heaviness whenever it may come. In His natural body every member suffered, and so must it be in the spiritual; but as out of all His griefs and woes His body came forth uninjured to glory and power, even so shall His mystical body come through the furnace with not so much as the smell of fire upon it.

"Look upon mine affliction and my pain; and forgive all my sins."—Psalm xxv. 18.

IT is well for us when prayers about our sorrows are linked with pleas concerning our sins— when, being under God's hand, we are not wholly taken up with our pain, but remember our offences against God. It is well, also, to take both sorrow and sin to the same place. It was to God that David carried his sorrow : it was to God that David confessed his sin. Observe, then, *we must take our sorrows to God.* Even your little sorrows you may roll upon God, for He counteth the hairs of your head ; and your great sorrows you may commit to Him, for He holdeth the ocean in the hollow of His hand. Go to Him, whatever your present trouble may be, and you shall find Him able and willing to relieve you. *But we must take our sins to God too.* We must carry them to the cross, that the blood may fall upon them, to purge away their guilt, and to destroy their defiling power.

The special lesson of the text is this :—that *we are to go to the Lord with sorrows and with sins in the right spirit.* Note that all David asks concerning his sorrow is, "*Look upon* mine affliction and my pain ;" but the next petition is vastly more express, definite, decided, plain—"*Forgive* all my sins." Many sufferers would have put it, "Remove my affliction and my pain, and look at my sins." But David does not say so ; he cries, "Lord, as for my affliction and my pain, I will not dictate to Thy wisdom. Lord, look at them, I will leave them to Thee, I should be glad to have my pain removed, but do as Thou wilt ; but as for my sins, Lord, I know what I want with them ; I must have them forgiven ; I cannot endure to lie under their curse for a moment." A Christian counts sorrow lighter in the scale than sin ; he can bear that his troubles should continue, but he cannot support the burden of his transgressions.

" My heart is like wax; it is melted in the midst of my bowels."—Psalm xxii. 14.

OUR blessed Lord experienced a terrible sinking and melting of soul. "The spirit of a man will sustain his infirmity, but a wounded spirit who can bear?" Deep depression of spirit is the most grievous of all trials; all besides is as nothing. Well might the suffering Saviour cry to His God, " Be not far from me," for above all other seasons a man needs his God when his heart is melted within him because of heaviness. Believer, come near the cross this morning, and humbly adore the King of glory as having once been brought far lower, in mental distress and inward anguish, than any one among us; and mark His fitness to become a faithful High Priest, who can be touched with a feeling of our infirmities. Especially let those of us whose sadness springs directly from the withdrawal of a present sense of our Father's love, enter into near and intimate communion with Jesus. Let us not give way to despair, since through this dark room the Master has passed before us. Our souls may sometimes long and faint, and thirst even to anguish, to behold the light of the Lord's countenance : at such times let us stay ourselves with the sweet fact of the sympathy of our great High Priest. Our drops of sorrow may well be forgotten in the ocean of His griefs; but how high ought our love to rise ! Come in, O strong and deep love of Jesus, like the sea at the flood in spring tides, cover all my powers, drown all my sins, wash out all my cares, lift up my earth-bound soul, and float it right up to my Lord's feet, and there let me lie, a poor broken shell, washed up by His love, having no virtue or value ; and only venturing to whisper to Him that if He will put His ear to me, He will hear within my heart faint echoes of the vast waves of His own love which have brought me where it is my delight to lie, even at His feet for ever.

"The king's garden."—Nehemiah iii. 15.

MENTION of the king's garden by Nehemiah brings to mind the *paradise* which the King of kings prepared for Adam. Sin has utterly ruined that fair abode of all delights, and driven forth the children of men to till the ground, which yields thorns and briers unto them. My soul, remember the fall, for it was *thy* fall. Weep much because the Lord of love was so shamefully ill-treated by the head of the human race, of which thou art a member, as undeserving as any. Behold how dragons and demons dwell on this fair earth, which once was a garden of delights.

See yonder another King's garden, which the King waters with His bloody sweat—*Gethsemane*, whose bitter herbs are sweeter far to renewed souls than even Eden's luscious fruits. There the mischief of the serpent in the first garden was undone: there the curse was lifted from earth, and borne by the woman's promised seed. My soul, bethink thee much of the agony and the passion; resort to the garden of the olive-press, and view thy great Redeemer rescuing thee from thy lost estate. This is the garden of gardens indeed, wherein the soul may see the guilt of sin and the power of love, two sights which surpass all others.

Is there no other King's garden? Yes, *my heart,* thou art, or shouldst be such. How do the flowers flourish? Do any choice fruits appear? Does the King walk within, and rest in the bowers of my spirit? Let me see that the plants are trimmed and watered, and the mischievous foxes hunted out. Come, Lord, and let the heavenly wind blow at Thy coming, that the spices of Thy garden may flow abroad. Nor must I forget the King's garden of *the church.* O Lord, send prosperity unto it. Rebuild her walls, nourish her plants, ripen her fruits, and from the huge wilderness, reclaim the barren waste, and make thereof "a King's garden."

"A bundle of myrrh is my well-beloved unto me."—Can. i. 13.

MYRRH may well be chosen as the type of Jesus on account of its *preciousness*, its *perfume*, its *pleasantness, its healing, preserving, disinfecting qualities, and its connection with sacrifice.* But why is He compared to "a *bundle* of myrrh"? First, for *plenty.* He is not a drop of it, He is a casket full. He is not a sprig or flower of it, but a whole bundle. There is enough in Christ for all my necessities; let me not be slow to avail myself of Him. Our well-beloved is compared to a "bundle" again, for *variety:* for there is in Christ not only the one thing needful, but in "Him dwelleth all the fulness of the Godhead bodily," everything needful is in Him. Take Jesus in His different characters, and you will see a marvellous variety—Prophet, Priest, King, Husband, Friend, Shepherd. Consider Him in His life, death, resurrection, ascension, second advent; view Him in His virtue, gentleness, courage, self-denial, love, faithfulness, truth, righteousness—everywhere He is a bundle of preciousness. He is a "bundle of myrrh" for *preservation*—not loose myrrh to be dropped on the floor or trodden on, but myrrh tied up, myrrh to be stored in a casket. We must value Him as our best treasure; we must prize His words and His ordinances; and we must keep our thoughts of Him and knowledge of Him as under lock and key, lest the devil should steal anything from us. Moreover Jesus is a "bundle of myrrh" *for speciality.* the emblem suggests the idea of distinguishing, discriminating grace. From before the foundation of the world, He was set apart for His people; and He gives forth His perfume only to those who understand how to enter into communion with Him, to have close dealings with Him. Oh! blessed people whom the Lord hath admitted into His secrets, and for whom He sets Himself apart. Oh! choice and happy who are thus made to say, "A bundle of myrrh is my well-beloved unto me."

"And he shall put his hand upon the head of the burnt-offering; and it shall be accepted for him to make atonement for him."—Leviticus i. 4.

OUR Lord's being made "sin for us" is set forth here by the very significant transfer of sin to the bullock, which was made by the elders of the people. The laying of the hand was not a mere touch of contact, for in some other places of Scripture the original word has the meaning of leaning heavily, as in the expression, "Thy wrath lieth hard upon me." (Psalm lxxxviii. 7.) Surely this is the very essence and nature of faith, which doth not only bring us into contact with the great Substitute, but teaches us to lean upon Him with all the burden of our guilt. Jehovah made to meet upon the head of the Substitute all the offences of His covenant people, but each one of the chosen is brought personally to ratify this solemn covenant act, when by grace he is enabled by faith to lay his hand upon the head of the "Lamb slain from before the foundation of the world." Believer, do you remember that rapturous day when you first realised pardon through Jesus the sin-bearer? Can you not make glad confession, and join with the writer in saying, "My soul recalls her day of deliverance with delight. Laden with guilt and full of fears, I saw my Saviour as my Substitute, and I laid my hand upon Him; oh! how timidly at first, but courage grew and confidence was confirmed until I leaned my soul entirely upon Him; and now it is my unceasing joy to know that my sins are no longer imputed to me, but laid on Him, and like the debts of the wounded traveller, Jesus, like the good Samaritan, has said of all my future sinfulness, 'Set that to My account.' " Blessed discovery! Eternal solace of a grateful heart!

"My numerous sins transferr'd to Him,
Shall never more be found,
Lost in His blood's atoning stream,
Where every crime is drown'd!"

" All they that see me laugh me to scorn: they shoot out the lip, they shake the head."—Psalm xxii. 7.

MOCKERY was a great ingredient in our Lord's woe. Judas mocked Him in the garden ; the chief priests and scribes laughed Him to scorn ; Herod set Him at nought ; the servants and the soldiers jeered at Him, and brutally insulted Him ; Pilate and his guards ridiculed His royalty ; and on the tree all sorts of horrid jests and hideous taunts were hurled at Him. Ridicule is always hard to bear, but when we are in intense pain it is so heartless, so cruel, that it cuts us to the quick. Imagine the Saviour crucified, racked with anguish far beyond all mortal guess, and then picture that motley multitude, all wagging their heads or thrusting out the lip in bitterest contempt of one poor suffering victim! Surely there must have been something more in the crucified One than they could see, or else such a great and mingled crowd would not unanimously have honoured Him with such contempt. Was it not evil confessing, in the very moment of its greatest apparent triumph, that after all it could do no more than mock at that victorious goodness which was then reigning on the cross ? O Jesus, " despised and rejected of men," how couldst Thou die for men who treated Thee so ill ? Herein is love amazing, love divine, yea, love beyond degree. We, too, have despised Thee in the days of our unregeneracy, and even since our new birth we have set the world on high in our hearts, and yet Thou bleedest to heal our wounds, and diest to give us life. O that we could set Thee on a glorious high throne in all men's hearts ! We would ring out thy praises over land and sea till men should as universally adore as once they did unanimously reject.

Thy creatures wrong Thee, O Thou sovereign Good !
Thou art not loved, because not understood :
This grieves me most, that vain pursuits beguile
Ungrateful men, regardless of Thy smile.

"Say ye to the righteous, that it shall be well with him."
Isaiah iii. 10.

IT *is well with the righteous* ALWAYS. If it had said, "Say ye to the righteous, that it is well with him in his prosperity," we must have been thankful for so great a boon, for prosperity is an hour of peril, and it is a gift from heaven to be secured from its snares : or if it had been written, "It is well with him when under persecution," we must have been thankful for so sustaining an assurance, for persecution is hard to bear ; but when no time is mentioned, all time is included. God's "shalls" must be understood always in their largest sense. From the beginning of the year to the end of the year, from the first gathering of evening shadows until the day-star shines, in all conditions and under all circumstances, it shall be well with the righteous. It is so well with him that we could not imagine it to be better, for he is *well fed*, he feeds upon the flesh and blood of Jesus ; he is *well clothed*, he wears the imputed righteousness of Christ ; he is *well housed*, he dwells in God ; he is *well married*, his soul is knit in bonds of marriage union to Christ ; he is *well provided for*, for the Lord is his Shepherd ; he is well endowed, for heaven is his inheritance. It is well with the righteous—*well upon divine authority;* the mouth of God speaks the comforting assurance. O beloved, if God declares that all is well, ten thousand devils may declare it to be ill, but we laugh them all to scorn. Blessed be God for a faith which enables us to believe God when the creatures contradict Him. It is, says the Word, at all times well with thee, thou righteous one ; then, beloved, if thou canst not see it, let God's word stand thee in stead of sight ; yea, believe it on divine authority more confidently than if thine eyes and thy feelings told it to thee. Whom God blesses is blest indeed, and what His lip declares is truth most sure and steadfast.

" My God, my God, why hast Thou forsaken me ?"
Psalm xxii. 1.

WE here behold the Saviour in the depth of His
sorrows. No other place so well shows the
griefs of Christ as Calvary, and no other moment at Calvary is so full of agony as that in which
His cry rends the air—"My God, my God, why
hast thou forsaken me ?" At this moment physical
weakness was united with acute mental torture from
the shame and ignominy through which He had to
pass ; and to make His grief culminate with emphasis,
He suffered spiritual agony surpassing all expression,
resulting from the departure of His Father's presence.
This was the black midnight of His horror ; then it
was that He descended the abyss of suffering. No
man can enter into the full meaning of these words.
Some of us think at times that *we* could cry, "My God,
my God, why hast thou forsaken me ?" There are
seasons when the brightness of our Father's smile is
eclipsed by clouds and darkness ; but let us remember
that God never does really forsake us. It is only a
seeming forsaking with us, but in Christ's case it was
a *real* forsaking. We grieve at a little withdrawal of
our Father's love ; but the real turning away of God's
face from His Son, who shall calculate how deep the
agony which it caused Him ?

In our case, our cry is often dictated by unbelief : in
His case, it was the utterance of a dreadful fact, for God
had really turned away from Him for a season. O thou
poor, distressed soul, who once lived in the sunshine
of God's face, but art now in darkness, remember that
He has not really forsaken thee. God in the clouds
is as much our God as when He shines forth in all
the lustre of His grace ; but since even the *thought*
that He has forsaken us gives us agony, what must
the woe of the Saviour have been when He exclaimed,
" My God, my God, why hast thou forsaken me ?"

"Lift them up for ever."—Psalm xxviii. 9.

OD'S *people need lifting up.* They are very heavy by nature. They have no wings, or, if they have, they are like the dove of old which lay among the pots; and they need divine grace to make them mount on wings covered with silver, and with feathers of yellow gold. By nature sparks fly upward, but the sinful souls of men fall downward. O Lord, "lift them up for ever!" David himself said, "Unto Thee, O God, do I lift up my soul," and he here feels the necessity that other men's souls should be lifted up as well as his own. When you ask this blessing for yourself, forget not to seek it for others also. There are three ways in which God's people require to be lifted up. *They require to be elevated in character.* Lift them up, O Lord; do not suffer Thy people to be like the world's people! The world lieth in the wicked one; lift them out of it! The world's people are looking after silver and gold, seeking their own pleasures, and the gratification of their lusts; but, Lord, lift Thy people up above all this; keep them from being "muck-rakers," as John Bunyan calls the man who was always scraping after gold! Set thou their hearts upon their risen Lord and the heavenly heritage! Moreover, *believers need to be prospered in conflict.* In the battle, if they seem to fall, O Lord, be pleased to give them the victory. If the foot of the foe be upon their necks for a moment, help them to grasp the sword of the Spirit, and eventually to win the battle. Lord, lift up Thy children's spirits in the day of conflict; let them not sit in the dust, mourning for ever. Suffer not the adversary to vex them sore, and make them fret; but if they have been, like Hannah, persecuted, let them sing of the mercy of a delivering God.

We may also ask our Lord to *lift them up at the last!* Lift them up by taking them home; lift their bodies from the tomb, and raise their souls to Thine eternal kingdom in glory.

" The precious blood of Christ."—1 Peter i. 19.

STANDING at the foot of the cross, we see hands, and feet, and side, all distilling crimson streams of precious blood. It is "precious" because of its *redeeming* and *atoning efficacy.* By it the sins of Christ's people are atoned for; they are redeemed from under the law; they are reconciled to God, made one with Him. Christ's blood is also "precious" in its *cleansing power*; it "cleanseth from all sin." "Though your sins be as scarlet, they shall be as white as snow." Through Jesus' blood there is not a spot left upon any believer, no wrinkle nor any such thing remains. O precious blood, which makes us clean, removing the stains of abundant iniquity, and permitting us to stand accepted in the Beloved, notwithstanding the many ways in which we have rebelled against our God. The blood of Christ is likewise "precious" in its *preserving power*. We are safe from the destroying angel under the sprinkled blood. Remember it is *God's seeing* the blood which is the true reason for our being spared. Here is comfort for us when the eye of faith is dim, for God's eye is still the same. The blood of Christ is "precious" also in its *sanctifying influence*. The same blood which justifies by taking away sin, does in its afteraction, quicken the new nature and lead it onward to subdue sin and to follow out the commands of God. There is no motive for holiness so great as that which streams from the veins of Jesus. And "precious," unspeakably precious, is this blood, because it has *an overcoming power*. It is written, "They overcame through the blood of the Lamb." How could they do otherwise? He who fights with the precious blood of Jesus, fights with a weapon which cannot know defeat. The blood of Jesus! sin dies at its presence, death ceases to be death: heaven's gates are opened. The blood of Jesus! we shall march on, conquering and to conquer, so long as we can trust its power!

"And his hands were steady until the going down of the sun."
Exodus xvii. 12.

SO mighty was the prayer of Moses, that all depended upon it. The petitions of Moses discomfited the enemy more than the fighting of Joshua. Yet both were needed. So, in the soul's conflict, force and fervour, decision and devotion, valour and vehemence, must join their forces, and all will be well. You must wrestle with your sin, but the major part of the wrestling must be done alone in private with God. Prayer, like Moses', holds up the token of the covenant before the Lord. The rod was the emblem of God's working with Moses, the symbol of God's government in Israel. Learn, O pleading saint, to hold up the promise and the oath of God before Him. The Lord cannot deny His own declarations. Hold up the rod of promise, and have what you will.

Moses grew weary, and then his friends assisted him. When at any time your prayer flags, let faith support one hand, and let holy hope uplift the other, and prayer seating itself upon the stone of Israel, the rock of our salvation, will persevere and prevail. Beware of faintness in devotion ; if Moses felt it, who can escape ? It is far easier to fight with sin in public, than to pray against it in private. It is remarked that Joshua never grew weary in the fighting, but Moses did grow weary in the praying ; the more spiritual an exercise, the more difficult it is for flesh and blood to maintain it. Let us cry, then, for special strength, and may the Spirit of God, who helpeth our infirmities, as He allowed help to Moses, enable us like him to continue with our hands steady "until the going down of the sun." Intermittent supplication avails but little, we must wrestle all night, and hold up our hands, *"until the going down of the sun;"* till the evening of life is over ; till we shall come to the rising of a better sun in the land where prayer is swallowed up in praise.

*" We are come to the blood of sprinkling, that speaketh better
things than that of Abel."*—Hebrews xii. 24.

READER, have *you* come to the blood of sprinkling ? The question is not whether you have
come to a knowledge of doctrine, or an obser-
vance of ceremonies, or to a certain form of experience,
but *have you come to the blood of Jesus ?* The blood of
Jesus is the life of all vital godliness. If you have
truly come to Jesus, we know how you came—the Holy
Spirit sweetly brought you there. You came to the blood
of sprinkling with no merits of your own. Guilty, lost,
and helpless, you came to take that blood, and that
blood alone, as your everlasting hope. You came to the
cross of Christ, with a trembling and an aching heart ;
and oh ! what a precious sound it was to you to hear
the voice of the blood of Jesus ! The dropping of His
blood is as the music of heaven to the penitent sons of
earth. We are full of sin, but the Saviour bids us lift
our eyes to Him, and as we gaze upon His streaming
wounds, each drop of blood, as it falls, cries, " It is
finished ; I have made an end of sin ; I have brought
in everlasting righteousness." Oh ! sweet language
of the precious blood of Jesus ! If you have come to
that blood once, you will come to it constantly. Your
life will be "Looking unto Jesus." Your whole
conduct will be epitomized in this—"To whom coming." Not to whom I *have* come, but to whom I am
always coming. If thou hast ever come to the blood of
sprinkling, thou wilt feel thy need of coming to it every
day. He who does not desire to wash in that *every
day*, has never washed in it at all. The believer ever
feels it to be his joy and privilege that there is still
a fountain opened. Past experiences are doubtful
food for Christians ; a present coming to Christ alone
can give us joy and comfort. This morning let us
sprinkle our door-post fresh with blood, and then feast
upon the Lamb, assured that the destroying angel
must pass us by.

" We would see Jesus."—John xii. 21.

EVERMORE the worldling's cry is, "Who will show us any good?" He seeks satisfaction in earthly comforts, enjoyments, and riches. But the quickened sinner knows of only one good. "O that I knew where I might find HIM!" When he is truly awakened to feel his guilt, if you could pour the gold of India at his feet, he would say, "Take it away: I want to find HIM." It is a blessed thing for a man, when he has brought his desires into a focus, so that they all centre in one object. When he has fifty different desires, his heart resembles a mere of stagnant water, spread out into a marsh, breeding miasma and pestilence; but when all his desires are brought into one channel, his heart becomes like a river of pure water, running swiftly to fertilise the fields. Happy is he who hath one desire, if that one desire be set on Christ, though it may not yet have been realised. If Jesus be a soul's desire, it is a blessed sign of divine work within. Such a man will never be content with mere ordinances. He will say, "I want Christ; I *must* have Him—mere ordinances are of no use to me; I want *Himself;* do not offer me these; you offer me the empty pitcher, while I am dying of thirst; give me water, or I die. Jesus is my soul's desire. I would see Jesus!"

Is this thy condition, my reader, at this moment? Hast thou but one desire, and is that after Christ? Then thou art not far from the kingdom of heaven. Hast thou but one wish in thy heart, and that one wish that thou mayst be washed from all thy sins in Jesus' blood? Canst thou really say, "I would give all I have to be a Christian; I would give up everything I have and hope for, if I might but feel that I have an interest in Christ"? Then, despite all thy fears, be of good cheer, the Lord loveth thee, and thou shalt come out into daylight soon, and rejoice in the liberty wherewith Christ makes men free.

" She bound the scarlet line in the window."—Joshua ii. 21.

RAHAB depended for her preservation upon the promise of the spies, whom she looked upon as the representatives of the God of Israel. Her faith was simple and firm, but it was very obedient. To tie the scarlet line in the window was a very trivial act in itself, but she dared not run the risk of omitting it. Come, my soul, is there not here a lesson for thee? Hast thou been attentive to all thy Lord's will, even though some of His commands should seem non-essential? Hast thou observed in his own way the two ordinances of believers' baptism and the Lord's Supper? These neglected, argue much unloving disobedience in thy heart. Be henceforth in all things blameless, even to the tying of a thread, if that be matter of command.

This act of Rahab sets forth a yet more solemn lesson. Have I implicitly trusted in the precious blood of Jesus? Have I tied the scarlet cord, as with a Gordian knot in my window, so that my trust can never be removed? Or can I look out towards the Dead Sea of my sins, or the Jerusalem of my hopes, without seeing the blood, and seeing all things in connection with its blessed power? The passer-by can see a cord of so conspicuous a colour, if it hangs from the window: it will be well for me if my life makes the efficacy of the atonement conspicuous to all onlookers. What is there to be ashamed of? Let men or devils gaze if they will, the blood is my boast and my song. My soul, there is One who will see that scarlet line, even when from weakness of faith thou canst not see it thyself; Jehovah, the Avenger, will see it and pass over thee. Jericho's walls fell flat: Rahab's house was on the wall, and yet it stood unmoved; my nature is built into the wall of humanity, and yet when destruction smites the race, I shall be secure. My soul, tie the scarlet thread in the window afresh, and rest in peace.

"And Thou saidst, I will surely do thee good."—Gen. xxxii. 12.

WHEN Jacob was on the other side of the brook Jabbok, and Esau was coming with armed men, he earnestly sought God's protection, and as a master reason he pleaded, "And Thou saidst, I will surely do thee good." Oh, the force of that plea! He was holding God to His word—"Thou saidst." The attribute of God's faithfulness is a splendid horn of the altar to lay hold upon; but the promise, which has in it the attribute and something more, is a yet mightier holdfast—"Thou saidst, I will surely do thee good." And has *He* said, and shall He not do it? "Let God be true, and every man a liar." Shall not *He* be true? Shall *He* not keep His word? Shall not every word that cometh out of His lips stand fast and be fulfilled? Solomon, at the opening of the temple, used this same mighty plea. He pleaded with God to remember the word which He had spoken to his father David, and to bless that place. When a man gives a promissory note, his honour is engaged; he signs his hand, and he must discharge it when the due time comes, or else he loses credit. It shall never be said that God dishonours His bills. The credit of the Most High never was impeached, and never shall be. He is punctual to the moment: He never is before His time, but He never is behind it. Search God's word through, and compare it with the experience of God's people, and you shall find the two tally from the first to the last. Many a hoary patriarch has said with Joshua, "Not one thing hath failed of all the good things which the Lord your God spake concerning you; all are come to pass." If you have a divine promise, you need not plead it with an "if," you may urge it with certainty. The Lord meant to fulfil the promise, or He would not have given it. God does not give His words merely to quiet us, and to keep us hopeful for awhile with the intention of putting us off at last; but when He speaks, it is because He means to do as He has said.

*" Behold, the veil of the temple was rent in twain from the top
to the bottom."*—Matthew xxvii, 51.

NO mean miracle was wrought in the rending of so strong and thick a veil ; but it was not intended merely as a display of power—many lessons were herein taught us. *The old law of ordinances was put away,* and like a worn-out vesture, rent and laid aside. When Jesus died, the sacrifices were all finished, because all fulfilled in him, and therefore the place of their presentation was marked with an evident token of decay. That rent also *revealed all the hidden things of the old dispensation :* the mercy-seat could now be seen, and the glory of God gleamed forth above it. By the death of our Lord Jesus we have a clear revelation of God, for He was " not as Moses, who put a veil over his face." Life and immortality are now brought to light, and things which have been hidden since the foundation of the world are manifest in Him. *The annual ceremony of atonement was thus abolished.* *The atoning blood* which was once every year sprinkled within the veil, *was now offered once* for all by the great High Priest, and therefore the place of the symbolical rite was broken up. No blood of bullocks or of lambs is needed now, for Jesus has entered within the veil with his own blood. Hence *access to God is now permitted,* and is the privilege of every believer in Christ Jesus. There is no small space laid open through which we may peer at the mercy-seat, but the rent reaches from the top to the bottom. We may come with boldness to the throne of the heavenly grace. Shall we err if we say that the opening of the Holy of Holies in this marvellous manner by our Lord's expiring cry was *the type of the opening of the gates of paradise* to all the saints by virtue of the Passion ? Our bleeding Lord hath the key of heaven ; He openeth and no man shutteth ; let us enter in with him into the heavenly places, and sit with Him there till our common enemies shall be made His footstool.

" The Amen."—Revelation iii. 14.

THE word AMEN solemnly confirms that which went before ; and Jesus is the great Confirmer ; immutable, for ever is " the Amen " in all *His promises.* *Sinner,* I would comfort thee with this reflection. Jesus Christ said, " Come unto me all ye that labour and are heavy laden, and I will give you rest." If you come to Him, He will say " Amen " in your soul; His promise shall be true *to you.* He said in the days of His flesh, " The bruised reed I will not break." O thou poor, broken, bruised heart, if thou comest to Him, He will say " Amen " to thee, and that shall be true in *thy* soul as in hundreds of cases in bygone years. *Christian,* is not this very comforting to thee also, that there is not a word which has gone out of the Saviour's lips which he has ever retracted? The words of Jesus shall stand when heaven and earth shall pass away. If thou gettest a hold of but half a promise, thou shalt find it true. Beware of him who is called " Clip-promise," who will destroy much of the comfort of God's word.

Jesus is Yea and Amen in all *His offices.* He was a Priest to pardon and cleanse once, He is Amen as Priest still. He was a King to rule and reign for His people, and to defend them with His mighty arm, He is an Amen King, the same still. He was a Prophet of old, to foretell good things to come, His lips are most sweet, and drop with honey still—He is an Amen Prophet. He is Amen as to the merit of His blood ; He is Amen as to His righteousness. That sacred robe shall remain most fair and glorious when nature shall decay. He is Amen in every single title which He bears ; your Husband, never seeking a divorce ; your Friend, sticking closer than a brother ; your Shepherd, with you in death's dark vale ; your Help and your Deliverer ; your Castle and your High Tower ; the Horn of your strength, your confidence, your joy, your all in all, and your Yea and Amen in all.

" That through death He might destroy him that had the power of death."—Hebrews ii, 14.

CHILD of God, death hath lost its sting, because the devil's power over it is destroyed. Then cease to fear dying. Ask grace from God the Holy Ghost, that by an intimate knowledge and a firm belief of thy Redeemer's death, thou mayst be strengthened for that dread hour. Living near the cross of Calvary thou mayst think of death with pleasure, and welcome it when it comes with intense delight. It is sweet to die in the Lord : it is a covenant-blessing to sleep in Jesus. Death is no longer banishment, it is a return from exile, a going home to the many mansions where the loved ones already dwell. The distance between glorified spirits in heaven and militant saints on earth seems great ; but it is not so. We are not far from home—a moment will bring us there. The sail is spread : the soul is launched upon the deep. How long will be its voyage ? How many wearying winds must beat upon the sail ere it shall be reefed in the port of 'peace ? How long shall that soul be tossed upon the waves before it comes to that sea which knows no storm ? Listen to the answer, " Absent from the body, present with the Lord." Yon ship has just departed, but it is already at its haven. It did but spread its sail and it was there. Like that ship of old, upon the Lake of Galilee, a storm had tossed it, but Jesus said, " Peace, be still," and *immediately* it came to land. Think not that a long period intervenes between the instant of death and the eternity of glory. When the eyes close on earth they open in heaven. The horses of fire are not an instant on the road. Then, O child of God, what is there for thee to fear in death, seeing that through the death of thy Lord its curse and sting are destroyed ? and now it is but a Jacob's ladder whose foot is in the dark grave, but its top reaches to glory everlasting.

"*Fight the Lord's battles.*"—1 Samuel xviii. 17.

THE sacramental host of God's elect is warring still on earth, Jesus Christ being the Captain of their salvation. He has said, "Lo! I am with you alway, even unto the end of the world." Hark to the shouts of war! Now let the people of God stand fast in their ranks, and let no man's heart fail him. It is true that just now in England the battle is turned against us, and unless the Lord Jesus shall lift His sword, we know not what may become of the church of God in this land; but let us be of good courage, and play the man. There never was a day when Protestantism seemed to tremble more in the scales than now that a fierce effort is making to restore the Romish antichrist to his ancient seat. We greatly want a bold voice and a strong hand to preach and publish the old gospel for which martyrs bled and confessors died. The Saviour is, by His Spirit, still on earth; let this cheer us. He is ever in the midst of the fight, and therefore the battle is not doubtful. And as the conflict rages, what a sweet satisfaction it is to know that the Lord Jesus, in His office as our great Intercessor, is prevalently pleading for His people! O anxious gazer, look not so much at the battle below, for there thou shalt be enshrouded in smoke, and amazed with garments rolled in blood; but lift thine eyes yonder where the Saviour lives and pleads, for while He intercedes, the cause of God is safe. Let us fight as if it all depended upon us, but let us look up and know that all depends upon Him.

Now, by the lilies of Christian purity, and by the roses of the Saviour's atonement, by the roes and by the hinds of the field, we charge you who are lovers of Jesus, to do valiantly in the Holy War, for truth and righteousness, for the kingdom and crown jewels of your Master. Onward! "for the battle is not yours but God's"

" I know that my Redeemer liveth."—Job xix. 25.

THE marrow of Job's comfort lies in that little word "My"—"My Redeemer," and in the fact that the Redeemer lives. Oh! to get hold of a living Christ. We must get a property in Him before we can enjoy Him. What is gold in the mine to me? Men are beggars in Peru, and beg their bread in California. It is gold in my purse which will satisfy my necessities, by purchasing the bread I need. So a Redeemer who does not redeem *me*, an avenger who will never stand up for *my* blood, of what avail were such? Rest not content until by faith you can say, "Yes, I cast myself upon my living Lord ; and He is mine." It may be you hold Him with a feeble hand ; you half think it presumption to say, " He lives as *my* Redeemer ;" yet, remember if you have but faith as a grain of mustard seed, that little faith *entitles* you to say it. But there is also another word here, expressive of Job's strong confidence, " *I know.*" To say, " I hope so, I trust so," is comfortable ; and there are thousands in the fold of Jesus who hardly ever get much further. But to reach the essence of consolation you *must* say, " I know." Ifs, buts, and perhapses, are sure murderers of peace and comfort. Doubts are dreary things in times of sorrow. Like wasps they sting the soul ! If I have any suspicion that Christ is not mine, then there is vinegar mingled with the gall of death ; but if I know that Jesus lives for me, then darkness is not dark : even the night is light about me. Surely if Job, in those ages before the coming and advent of Christ, could say, " I know," *we* should not speak less positively. God forbid that our positiveness should be presumption. Let us see that our evidences are right, lest we build upon an ungrounded hope ; and then let us not be satisfied with the mere foundation, for it is from the upper rooms that we get the widest prospect. A living Redeemer, truly mine, is joy unspeakable.

" Who is even at the right hand of God."—Romans viii. 34.

HE who was once despised and rejected of men, now occupies the honourable position of a beloved and honoured Son. The right hand of God is the *place of majesty and favour.* Our Lord Jesus is His people's representative. When He died for them, they had rest; when he rose again for them, they had liberty; when he sat down at His Father's right hand, they had favour, and honour, and dignity. The raising and elevation of Christ is the elevation, the acceptance, the enshrinement, the glorifying of all His people, for He is their head and representative. This sitting at the right hand of God, then, is to be viewed as the acceptance of the person of the Surety, the reception of the Representative, and therefore, the acceptance of *our* souls. O saint, see in this thy sure freedom from condemnation. "Who is he that condemneth?" Who shall condemn the men who are in Jesus at the right hand of God?

The right hand is *the place of power.* Christ at the right hand of God hath all power in heaven and in earth. Who shall fight against the people who have such power vested in their Captain? O my soul, what can destroy thee if Omnipotence be thy helper? If the ægis of the Almighty cover thee, what sword can smite thee? Rest thou secure. If Jesus is thine all-prevailing King, and hath trodden thine enemies beneath His feet; if sin, death, and hell are all vanquished by Him, and thou art represented in Him, by no possibility canst thou be destroyed.

> " Jesu's tremendous name
> Puts all our foes to flight :
> Jesus, the meek, the angry Lamb,
> A Lion is in fight.
>
> " By all hell's host withstood ;
> We all hell's host o'erthrow ;
> And conquering them, through Jesu's blood
> We still to conquer go."

H

" Him hath God exalted."—Acts v. 31.

JESUS, our Lord, once crucified, dead and buried, now sits upon the throne of glory. The highest place that heaven affords is His by undisputed right. It is sweet to remember that the exaltation of Christ in heaven is a *representative exaltation*. He is exalted at the Father's right hand, and though as Jehovah he has eminent glories, in which finite creatures cannot share, yet as the Mediator, the honours which Jesus wears in heaven are the heritage of all the saints. It is delightful to reflect how close is Christ's union with His people. We are actually one with Him ; we are members of His body ; and His exaltation is *our* exaltation. He will give us to sit upon His throne, even as He has overcome, and is set down with His Father on His throne ; He has a crown, and He gives us crowns too ; He has a throne, but He is not content with having a throne to himself, on His right hand there must be His queen, arrayed in " gold of Ophir." He cannot be glorified without His bride. Look up, believer, to Jesus now ; let the eye of your faith behold Him with many crowns upon His head ; and remember that you will one day be like Him, when you shall see Him as He is ; you shall not be so great as He is, you shall not be so divine, but still you shall, in a measure, share the same honours, and enjoy the same happiness and the same dignity which He possesses. Be content to live unknown for a little while, and to walk your weary way through the fields of poverty, or up the hills of affliction ; for by-and-by you shall reign with Christ, for He has " made us kings and priests unto God, and we shall reign for ever and ever." Oh! wonderful thought for the children of God! We have Christ for our glorious representative in heaven's courts *now*, and soon He will come and receive us to Himself, to be with Him there, to behold His glory, and to share His joy.

" Thou shalt not be afraid for the terror by night."
Psalm xci. 5.

WHAT is this terror? It may be the cry of fire, or the noise of thieves, or fancied appearances, or the shriek of sudden sickness or death. We live in the world of death and sorrow, we may therefore look for ills as well in the night-watches as beneath the glare of the broiling sun. Nor should this alarm us, for be the terror what it may, the promise is that the believer shall not be afraid. Why should he? Let us put it more closely, why should *we?* God our Father is here, and will be here all through the lonely hours; He is an almighty Watcher, a sleepless Guardian, a faithful Friend. Nothing can happen without His direction, for even hell itself is under His control. Darkness is not dark to Him. He has promised to be a wall of fire around His people—and who can break through such a barrier? Worldlings may well be afraid, for they have an angry God above them, a guilty conscience within them, and a yawning hell beneath them; but we who rest in Jesus are saved from all these through rich mercy. If we give way to foolish fear we shall dishonour our profession, and lead others to doubt the reality of godliness. We ought to be afraid of being afraid, lest we should vex the Holy Spirit by foolish distrust. Down, then, ye dismal forebodings and groundless apprehensions, God has not forgotten to be gracious, nor shut up His tender mercies; it may be night in the soul, but there need be no terror, for the God of love changes not. Children of light may walk in darkness, but they are not therefore cast away, nay, they are now enabled to prove their adoption by trusting in their heavenly Father as hypocrites cannot do.

"Though the night be dark and dreary,
  Darkness cannot hide from Thee;
Thou art He, who, never weary,
  Watchest where Thy people be."

" Nay, in all these things we are more than conquerors through Him that loved us."—Romans viii. 37.

WE go to Christ for forgiveness, and then too often look to the law for power to fight our sins. Paul thus rebukes us, " O foolish Galatians, who hath bewitched you, that ye should not obey the truth? This only would I learn of you, Received ye the Spirit by the works of the law, or by the hearing of faith? are ye so foolish? having begun in the Spirit, are ye now made perfect by the flesh?" Take your sins to Christ's cross, for the old man can only be crucified there: we are crucified *with Him.* The only weapon to fight sin with is the spear which pierced the side of Jesus. To give an illustration—you want to overcome an angry temper, how do you go to work? It is very possible you have never tried the right way of going to Jesus with it. How did I get salvation? I came to Jesus just as I was, and I trusted Him to save me. I must kill my angry temper in the same way? It is the only way in which I can ever kill it. I must go to the cross with it, and say to Jesus, " Lord, I trust Thee to deliver me from it." This is the only way to give it a death-blow. Are you covetous? Do you feel the world entangle you? You may struggle against this evil so long as you please, but if it be your besetting sin, you will never be delivered from it in any way but by the blood of Jesus. Take it to Christ. Tell Him, " Lord, I have trusted Thee, and Thy name is Jesus, for Thou dost save Thy people from their sins; Lord, this is one of my sins; save me from it!" Ordinances are nothing without Christ as a means of mortification. Your prayers, and your repentances, and your tears—the whole of them put together—are worth nothing apart from Him. " None but Jesus can do helpless sinners good;" or helpless saints either. You must be conquerors through Him who hath loved you, if conquerors at all. Our laurels must grow among His olives in Gethsemane.

" Lo, in the midst of the throne . . . . stood a Lamb as it had been slain."—Revelation v. 6.

HY should our exalted Lord appear in His wounds in glory? The wounds of Jesus are His glories, His jewels, His sacred ornaments. To the eye of the believer, Jesus is passing fair because He is " white and ruddy;" white with innocence, and ruddy with his own blood. We see Him as the lily of matchless purity, and as the rose crimsoned with His own gore. Christ is lovely upon Olivet and Tabor, and by the sea, but oh ! there never was such a matchless Christ as He that did hang upon the cross. There we behold all His beauties in perfection, all His attributes developed, all His love drawn out, all His character expressed. Beloved, the wounds of Jesus are far more fair in our eyes than all the splendour and pomp of kings. The thorny crown is more than an imperial diadem. It is true that He bears not now the sceptre of reed, but there was a glory in it that never flashed from sceptre of gold. Jesus wears the appearance of a slain Lamb as His court dress in which He wooed our souls, and redeemed them by His complete atonement. Nor are these only the ornaments of Christ : they are the *trophies* of His love and of His victory. He has divided the spoil with the strong. He has redeemed for Himself a great multitude whom no man can number, and these scars are the memorials of the fight. Ah ! if *Christ* thus loves to retain the thought of His sufferings for His people, *how precious should his wounds be to us !*

" Behold how every wound of His
    A precious balm distils,
Which heals the scars that sin had made,
    And cures all mortal ills.

" Those wounds are mouths that preach His grace ;
    The ensigns of His love ;
The seals of our expected bliss
    In paradise above."

" And because of all this we make a sure covenant."
Nehemiah ix. 38.

THERE are many occasions in our experience when we may very rightly, and with benefit, renew our covenant with God. After *recovery from sickness* when, like Hezekiah, we have had a new term of years added to our life, we may fitly do it. After any *deliverance from trouble,* when our joys bud forth anew, let us again visit the foot of the cross, and renew our consecration. Especially, let us do this after any *sin which has grieved the Holy Spirit,* or brought dishonour upon the cause of God; let us then look to that blood which can make us whiter than snow, and again offer ourselves unto the Lord. We should not only let our troubles confirm our dedication to God, but *our prosperity* should do the same. If we ever meet with occasions which deserve to be called " crowning mercies," then, surely, if He hath crowned *us,* we ought also to crown our God; let us bring forth anew all the jewels of the divine regalia which have been stored in the jewel-closet of our heart, and let our God sit upon the throne of our love, arrayed in royal apparel. If we would learn to profit by our prosperity, we should not need so much adversity. If we would gather from a kiss all the good it might confer upon us, we should not so often smart under the rod. Have we lately received some blessing which we little expected ? Has the Lord put our feet in a large room ? Can we sing of mercies multiplied ? Then this is the day to put our hand upon the horns of the altar, and say, " Bind me here, my God ; bind me here with cords, even for ever." Inasmuch as we need the fulfilment of new promises from God, let us offer renewed prayers that our old vows may not be dishonoured. Let us this morning make with him a sure covenant, because of the pains of Jesus which for the last month we have been considering with gratitude.

" *The flowers appear on the earth; the time of the singing of birds is come, and the voice of the turtle is heard in our land.*"—Canticles ii. 12.

SWEET is the season of spring : the long and dreary winter helps us to appreciate its genial warmth, and its promise of summer enhances its present delights. After periods of depression of spirit, it is delightful to behold again the light of the Sun of Righteousness ; then our slumbering graces rise from their lethargy, like the crocus and the daffodil from their beds of earth ; then is our heart made merry with delicious notes of gratitude, far more melodious than the warbling of birds—and the comforting assurance of peace, infinitely more delightful than the turtle's note, is heard within the soul. Now is the time for the soul to seek communion with her Beloved ; now must she rise from her native sordidness, and come away from her old associations. If we do not hoist the sail when the breeze is favourable, we shall be blameworthy: times of refreshing ought not to pass over us unimproved. When Jesus Himself visits us in tenderness, and entreats us to arise, can we be so base as to refuse His request? He has Himself risen that He may draw us after Him : He now by His Holy Spirit has revived us, that we may, in newness of life, ascend into the heavenlies, and hold communion with Himself. Let our wintry state suffice-us for coldness and indifference ; when the Lord creates a spring within, let our sap flow with vigour, and our branch blossom with high resolve. O Lord, if it be not spring time in my chilly heart, I pray Thee make it so, for I am heartily weary of living at a distance from Thee. Oh ! the long and dreary winter, when wilt Thou bring it to an end ? Come, Holy Spirit, and renew my soul! quicken Thou me ! restore me, and have mercy upon me ! This very night I would earnestly implore the Lord to take pity upon His servant, and send me a happy revival of spiritual life !

" Rise up my love, my fair one, and come away."
Canticles ii. 10.

O, I hear the voice of my Beloved! He speaks to *me!* Fair weather is smiling upon the face of the earth, and He would not have me spiritually asleep while nature is all around me awaking from her winter's rest. He bids me " Rise up," and well He may, for I have long enough been lying among the pots of worldliness. HE is risen, I am risen in Him, why then should I cleave unto the dust ? From lower loves, desires, pursuits, and aspirations, I would rise towards Him. He calls me by the sweet title of " My love," and counts me fair ; this is a good argument for my rising. If He has thus exalted me, and thinks me thus comely, how can I linger in the tents of Kedar and find congenial associates among the sons of men? He bids me " Come away." Further and further from everything selfish, grovelling, worldly, sinful, He calls me; yea, from the outwardly religious world which knows Him not, and has no sympathy with the mystery of the higher life, He calls me. " Come away " has no harsh sound in it to my ear, for what is there to hold me in this wilderness of vanity and sin ? O my Lord, would that I could come away, but I am taken among the thorns, and cannot escape from them as I would. I would, if it were possible, have neither eyes, nor ears, nor heart for sin. Thou callest me to Thyself by saying " Come away," and this is a melodious call indeed. To come to Thee is to come home from exile, to come to land out of the raging storm, to come to rest after long labour, to come to the goal of my desires and the summit of my wishes. But Lord, how can a stone rise, how can a lump of clay come away from the horrible pit ? O raise me, draw me. Thy grace can do it. Send forth Thy Holy Spirit to kindle sacred flames of love in my heart, and I will continue to rise until I leave life and time behind me, and indeed come away.

" If any man hear My voice, and open the door, I will come in to him."—Revelation iii. 20.

WHAT is your desire this evening? Is it set upon heavenly things. Do you long to enjoy the high doctrine of eternal love? Do you desire liberty in very close communion with God? Do you aspire to know the heights, and depths, and lengths, and breadths? Then you must draw near to Jesus; you must get a clear sight of Him in His preciousness and completeness: you must view Him in His work, in His offices, in His person. He who understands Christ, receives an anointing from the Holy One, by which He knows all things. Christ is the great master-key of all the chambers of God: there is no treasure-house of God which will not open and yield up all its wealth to the soul that lives near to Jesus. Are you saying, " O that He would dwell in my bosom "? " Would that He would make my heart His dwelling-place for ever "? Open the door, beloved, and He will come into your souls. He has long been knocking, and all with this object, that he may sup with you, and you with Him. *He sups with you* because you find the house or the heart, and *you with Him* because He brings the provision. He could not sup with you if it were not in your heart, you finding the house; nor could you sup with Him, for you have a bare cupboard, if He did not bring the provision with Him. Fling wide, then, the portals of your soul. He will come with that love which you long to feel; He will come with that joy into which you cannot work your poor depressed spirit; He will bring the peace which now you have not; He will come with His flagons of wine and sweet apples of love, and cheer you till you have no other sickness but that of " love o'erpowering, love divine." Only open the door to Him, drive out His enemies, give Him the keys of your heart, and He will dwell there for ever. Oh, wondrous love, that brings such a guest to dwell in such a heart!

" This do in remembrance of Me."—1 Corinthians xi. 24.

T seems then, that Christians may forget Christ ! There could be no need for this loving exhortation, if there were not a fearful supposition that our memories might prove treacherous. Nor is this a bare supposition: it is, alas ! too well confirmed in our experience, not as a possibility, but as a lamentable fact. It appears almost impossible that those who have been redeemed by the blood of the dying Lamb, and loved with an everlasting love by the eternal Son of God, should forget that gracious Saviour ; but, if startling to the ear, it is, alas ! too apparent to the eye to allow us to deny the crime. Forget Him who never forgot us ! Forget Him who poured His blood forth for our sins ! Forget Him who loved us even to the death ! Can it be possible ? Yes, it is not only possible, but conscience confesses that it is too sadly a fault with all of us, that we suffer Him to be as a wayfaring man tarrying but for a night. He whom we should make the abiding tenant of our memories is but a visitor therein. The cross where one would think that memory would linger, and unmindfulness would be an unknown intruder, is desecrated by the feet of forgetfulness. Does not your conscience say that this is true ? Do you not find yourselves forgetful of Jesus ? Some creature steals away your heart, and you are unmindful of Him upon whom your affection ought to be set. Some earthly business engrosses your attention when you should fix your eye steadily upon the cross. It is the incessant turmoil of the world, the constant attraction of earthly things which takes away the soul from Christ. While memory too well preserves a poisonous weed, it suffereth the rose of Sharon to wither. Let us charge ourselves to bind a heavenly forget-me-not about our hearts for Jesus our Beloved, and, whatever else we let slip, let us hold fast to Him.

" Blessed is he that watcheth."—Revelation xvi. 15.

"WE die daily," said the apostle. This was the life of the early Christians; they went everywhere with their lives in their hands. We are not in this day called to pass through the same fearful persecutions : if we were, the Lord would give us grace to bear the test ; but the tests of Christian life, at the present moment, though outwardly not so terrible, are yet more likely to overcome us than even those of the fiery age. We have to bear the sneer of the world—that is little ; its blandishments, its soft words, its oily speeches, its fawning, its hypocrisy, are far worse. Our danger is lest we grow rich and become proud, lest we give ourselves up to the fashions of this present evil world, and lose our faith. Or if wealth be not the trial, worldly care is quite as mischievous. If we cannot be torn in pieces by the roaring lion, if we may be hugged to death by the bear, the devil little cares which it is, so long as he destroys our love to Christ, and our confidence in Him. I fear me that the Christian church is far more likely to lose her integrity in these soft and silken days than in those rougher times. We must be awake now, for we traverse the enchanted ground, and are most likely to fall asleep to our own undoing, unless our faith in Jesus be a reality, and our love to Jesus a vehement flame. Many in these days of easy profession are likely to prove tares, and not wheat; hypocrites with fair masks on their faces, but not the true-born children of the living God. Christian, do not think that these are times in which you can dispense with watchfulness or with holy ardour; you need these things more than ever, and may God the eternal Spirit display His omnipotence in you, that you may be able to say, in all these softer things, as well as in the rougher, "We are more than conquerors through Him that loved us."

" God, even our own God."—Psalm lxvii. 6.

T is strange how little use we make of the spiritual blessings which God gives us, but it is stranger still how little use we make of God Himself. Though He is "our own God," we apply ourselves but little to Him, and ask but little of Him. How seldom do we ask counsel at the hands of the Lord! How often do we go about our business, without seeking His guidance! In our troubles how constantly do we strive to bear our burdens ourselves, instead of casting them upon the Lord, that He may sustain us! This is not because we may not, for the Lord seems to say, " I am thine, soul, come and make use of me as thou wilt; thou mayst freely come to my store, and the oftener the more welcome." It is our own fault if we make not free with the riches of our God. Then, since thou hast such a friend, and He invites thee, draw from Him daily. Never want whilst thou hast a God to go to; never fear or faint whilst thou hast God to help thee; go to thy treasure and take whatever thou needest—there is all that thou canst want. Learn the divine skill of making God all things to thee. He can supply thee with all, or, better still, He can be to thee instead of all. Let me urge thee, then, to make use of thy God. Make use of Him *in prayer*. Go to Him often, because He is *thy* God. O, wilt thou fail to use so great a privilege? Fly to Him, tell Him all thy wants. Use Him constantly *by faith* at all times. If some dark providence has beclouded thee, use thy God as a "sun;" if some strong enemy has beset thee, find in Jehovah a "shield," for He is a sun and shield to his people. If thou hast lost thy way in the mazes of life, use Him as a "guide," for He will direct thee. Whatever thou art, and wherever thou art, remember God is just *what* thou wantest, and just *where* thou wantest, and that He can do *all* thou wantest.

" The Lord is King for ever and ever."—Psalm x. 16.

JESUS Christ is no despotic claimant of *divine right*, but He is really and truly the Lord's anointed! "It hath pleased the Father that in Him should all fulness dwell." God hath given to Him all power and all authority. As the Son of man, He is now head over all things to His church, and He reigns over heaven, and earth, and hell, with the keys of life and death at His girdle. Certain princes have delighted to call themselves kings by *the popular will,* and certainly our Lord Jesus Christ is such in His church. If it could be put to the vote whether He should be King in the church, every believing heart would crown Him. O that we could crown Him more gloriously than we do! We would count no expense to be wasted that could glorify Christ. Suffering would be pleasure, and loss would be gain, if thereby we could surround His brow with brighter crowns, and make Him more glorious in the eyes of men and angels. Yes, He shall reign. Long live the King! All hail to Thee, King Jesus! Go forth, ye virgin souls who love your Lord, bow at His feet, strew His way with the lilies of your love, and the roses of your gratitude: "Bring forth the royal diadem, and crown Him Lord of all." Moreover, our Lord Jesus is King in Zion by *right of conquest:* He has taken and carried by storm the hearts of His people, and has slain their enemies who held them in cruel bondage. In the Red Sea of His own blood, our Redeemer has drowned the Pharaoh of our sins: shall He not be King in Jeshurun? He has delivered us from the iron yoke and heavy curse of the law: shall not the Liberator be crowned? We are His portion, whom He has taken out of the hand of the Amorite with His sword and with His bow: who shall snatch His conquest from His hand? All hail, King Jesus! we gladly own Thy gentle sway! Rule in our hearts for ever, Thou lovely Prince of Peace.

" Remember the word unto Thy servant, upon which Thou hast caused me to hope."—Psalm cxix. 49.

WHATEVER your especial need may be, you may readily find some promise in the Bible suited to it.   Are you faint and feeble because your way is rough and you are weary ?   Here is the promise— "He giveth power to the faint."   When you read such a promise, take it back to the great Promiser, and ask Him to fulfil His own word.   Are you seeking after Christ, and thirsting for closer communion with him ? This promise shines like a star upon you—"Blessed are they that hunger and thirst after righteousness, for they shall be filled."   Take that promise to the throne continually ; do not plead anything else, but go to God over and over again with this—" Lord, Thou hast said it ; do as Thou hast said."   Are you distressed because of sin, and burdened with the heavy load of your iniquities ?   Listen to these words—"I, even I, am He that blotteth out thy transgressions, and will no more remember thy sins."   You have no merit of your own to plead why He should pardon you, but plead His written engagements and He will perform them.   Are you afraid lest you should not be able to hold on to the end, lest, after having thought yourself a child of God, you should prove a castaway ?   If that is your state, take this word of grace to the throne and plead it : "The mountains may depart, and the hills may be removed, but the covenant of My love shall not depart from thee."   If you have lost the sweet sense of the Saviour's presence, and are seeking Him with a sorrowful heart, re-member the promises: "Return unto Me, and I will return unto you;" "For a small moment have I forsaken thee, but with great mercies will I gather thee."   Banquet your faith upon God's own word, and whatever your fears or wants, repair to the Bank of Faith with your Father's note of hand, saying, "Remember the word unto Thy servant, upon which Thou hast caused me to hope."

" All the house of Israel are impudent and hardhearted."
Ezekiel iii. 7.

RE there no exceptions? No, not one. Even the favoured race are thus described. Are the best so bad?—then what must the worst be? Come, my heart, consider how far thou hast a share in this universal accusation, and while considering, be ready to take shame unto thyself wherein thou mayst have been guilty. The first charge is *impudence,* or hardness of forehead, a want of holy shame, an unhallowed boldness in evil. Before my conversion, I could sin and feel no compunction, hear of my guilt and yet remain unhumbled, and even confess my iniquity and manifest no inward humiliation on account of it. For a sinner to go to God's house and pretend to pray to Him and praise Him argues a brazen-facedness of the worst kind! Alas! since the day of my new birth I have doubted my Lord to His face, murmured unblushingly in His presence, worshipped before Him in a slovenly manner, and sinned without bewailing myself concerning it. If my forehead were not as an adamant, harder than flint, I should have far more holy fear, and a far deeper contrition of spirit. Woe is me, I am one of the impudent house of Israel. The second charge is *hardheartedness,* and I must not venture to plead innocent here. Once I had nothing but a heart of stone, and although through grace I now have a new and fleshy heart, much of my former obduracy remains. I am not affected by the death of Jesus as I ought to be; neither am I moved by the ruin of my fellow men, the wickedness of the times, the chastisement of my heavenly Father, and my own failures, as I should be. O that my heart would melt at the recital of my Saviour's sufferings and death. Would to God I were rid of this nether millstone within me, this hateful body of death. Blessed be the name of the Lord, the disease is not incurable, the Saviour's precious blood is the universal solvent, and me, even me, it will effectually soften, till my heart melts as wax before the fire.

" Thou art my hope in the day of evil."—Jeremiah xvii. 17.

THE path of the Christian is not always bright with sunshine ; he has his seasons of darkness and of storm. True, it is written in God's Word, " Her ways are ways of pleasantness, and all her paths are peace ;" and it is a great truth, that religion is calculated to give a man happiness below as well as bliss above ; but experience tells us that if the course of the just be "As the shining light that shineth more and more unto the perfect day," yet sometimes *that* light is eclipsed. At certain periods clouds cover the believer's sun, and he walks in darkness and sees no light. There are many who have rejoiced in the presence of God for a season ; they have basked in the sunshine in the earlier stages of their Christian career ; they have walked along the "green pastures" by the side of the "still waters," but suddenly they find the glorious sky is clouded ; instead of the Land of Goshen they have to tread the sandy desert ; in the place of sweet waters, they find troubled streams, bitter to their taste, and they say, "Surely, if I were a child of God, this would not happen." Oh! say not so, thou who art walking in darkness. The best of God's saints must drink the wormwood ; the dearest of His children must bear the cross. No Christian has enjoyed perpetual prosperity ; no believer can always keep his harp from the willows. Perhaps the Lord allotted you at first a smooth and unclouded path, because you were weak and timid. He tempered the wind to the shorn lamb, but now that you are stronger in the spiritual life, you must enter upon the riper and rougher experience of God's full-grown children. We need winds and tempests to exercise our faith, to tear off the rotten bough of self-dependence, and to root us more firmly in Christ. The day of evil reveals to us the value of our glorious hope.

" The Lord taketh pleasure in His people."—Psalm cxlix. 4

OW comprehensive is the love of Jesus! There is no part of His people's interests which He does not consider, and there is nothing which concerns their welfare which is not important to Him. Not merely does He think of you, believer, as an immortal being, but as a mortal being too. Do not deny it or doubt it: "The very hairs of your head are all numbered." "The steps of a good man are ordered by the Lord: and he delighteth in His way." It were a sad thing for us if this mantle of love did not cover all our concerns, for what mischief might be wrought to us in that part of our business which did not come under our gracious Lord's inspection! Believer, rest assured that the heart of Jesus cares about your meaner affairs. The breadth of His tender love is such that you may resort to Him in all matters; for in all your afflictions He is afflicted, and like as a father pitieth his children, so doth He pity you. The meanest interests of all His saints are all borne upon the broad bosom of the Son of God. Oh, what a heart is His, that doth not merely comprehend the persons of His people, but comprehends also the diverse and innumerable concerns of all those persons! Dost thou think, O Christian, that thou canst measure the love of Christ? Think of what His love has brought thee —justification, adoption, sanctification, eternal life! The riches of His goodness are unsearchable; thou shalt never be able to tell them out or even conceive them. Oh, the breadth of the love of Christ! Shall such a love as this have half our hearts? Shall it have a cold love in return? Shall Jesus' marvellous lovingkindness and tender care meet with but faint response and tardy acknowledgment? O my soul, tune thy harp to a glad song of thanksgiving! Go to thy rest rejoicing, for thou art no desolate wanderer, but a beloved child, watched over, cared for, supplied, and defended by thy Lord.

" And all the children of Israel murmured."—Num. xiv. 2.

HERE are murmurers amongst Christians now, as there were in the camp of Israel of old. There are those who, when the rod falls, cry out against the afflictive dispensation. They ask, " Why am I thus afflicted ? What have I done to be chastened in this manner ?" A word with thee, O murmurer ! Why shouldst thou murmur against the dispensations of thy heavenly Father ? Can He treat thee more hardly than thou deservest ? Consider what a rebel thou wast once, but he has pardoned thee ! Surely, if He in His wisdom sees fit now to chasten thee, thou shouldst not complain. After all, art thou smitten as hardly as thy sins deserve ? Consider the corruption which is in thy breast, and then wilt thou wonder that there needs so much of the rod to fetch it out ? Weigh thyself, and discern how much dross is mingled with thy gold ; and dost thou think the fire too hot to purge away so much dross as thou hast ? Does not that proud rebellious spirit of thine prove that thy heart is not thoroughly sanctified ? Are not those murmuring words contrary to the holy submissive nature of God's children ? Is not the correction needed ? But if thou *wilt* murmur against the chastening, take heed, for it will go hard with murmurers. God always chastises His children twice, if they do not bear the first stroke patiently. But know one thing— " He doth not afflict willingly, nor grieve the children of men." All His corrections are sent in love, to purify thee, and to draw thee nearer to Himself. Surely it must help thee to bear the chastening with resignation if thou art able to recognise thy *Father's* hand. For "whom the Lord loveth He chasteneth, and scourgeth every son whom He receiveth. If ye endure chastening, God dealeth with you as with sons." " Murmur not as some of them also murmured and were destroyed of the destroyer."

" How precious also are Thy thoughts unto me, O God."
Psalm cxxxix. 17.

DIVINE omniscience affords no comfort to the
ungodly mind, but to the child of God it overflows with consolation. God is always thinking
upon us, never turns aside His mind from us, has us
always before His eyes ; and this is precisely as we
would have it, for it would be dreadful to exist for
a moment beyond the observation of our heavenly
Father. His thoughts are always tender, loving, wise,
prudent, far-reaching, and they bring to us countless
benefits : hence it is a choice delight to remember
them. The Lord always did think upon His people :
hence their election and the covenant of grace by which
their salvation is secured ; He always will think upon
them : hence their final perseverance by which they
shall be brought safely to their final rest. In all our
wanderings the watchful glance of the Eternal Watcher
is evermore fixed upon us,—we never roam beyond the
Shepherd's eye. In our sorrows He observes us in-
cessantly, and not a pang escapes Him ; in our toils He
marks all our weariness, and writes in His book all the
struggles of His faithful ones. These thoughts of the
Lord encompass us in all our paths, and penetrate the
innermost region of our being. Not a nerve or tissue,
valve or vessel, of our bodily organization is uncared
for ; all the littles of our little world are thought upon
by the great God.

Dear reader, is this precious to you ? then hold to
it. Never be led astray by those philosophic fools
who preach up an impersonal God, and talk of self-
existent, self-governing matter. The Lord liveth and
thinketh upon us, this is a truth far too precious for
us to be lightly robbed of it. The notice of a noble-
man is valued so highly that he who has it counts his
fortune made ; but what is it to be thought of by the
King of kings ! If the Lord thinketh upon us, all is
well, and we may rejoice evermore.

" His cheeks are as a bed of spices, as sweet flowers."
Cant. v. 13.

LO, the flowery month is come ! March winds and April showers have done their work, and the earth is all bedecked with beauty. Come my soul, put on thine holiday attire and go forth to gather garlands of heavenly thoughts. Thou knowest whither to betake thyself, for to thee " the beds of spices " are well known, and thou hast so often smelt the perfume of " the sweet flowers," that thou wilt go at once to thy well-beloved and find all loveliness, all joy in Him. That cheek once so rudely smitten with a rod, oft bedewed with tears of sympathy and then defiled with spittle—that cheek as it smiles with mercy is as fragrant aromatic to my heart. Thou didst not hide thy face from shame and spitting, O Lord Jesus, and therefore I will find my dearest delight in praising thee. Those cheeks were furrowed by the plough of grief, and crimsoned with red lines of blood from thy thorn-crowned temples ; such marks of love unbounded cannot but charm my soul far more than "pillars of perfume." If I may not see the whole of his face I would behold his cheeks, for the least glimpse of him is exceedingly refreshing to my spiritual sense and yields a variety of delights. In Jesus I find not only fragrance, but a bed of spices ; not one flower, but all manner of sweet flowers. He is to me my rose and my lily, my heartsease and my cluster of camphire. When he is with me, it is May all the year round, and my soul goes forth to wash her happy face in the morning-dew of his grace, and to solace herself with the singing of the birds of his promises. Precious Lord Jesus, let me in very deed know the blessedness which dwells in abiding, unbroken fellowship with thee. I am a poor worthless one, whose cheek thou hast deigned to kiss ! O let me kiss thee in return with the kisses of my lips.

" I am the rose of Sharon."—Solomon's Song ii. 1.

WHATEVER there may be of beauty in the material world, Jesus Christ possesses all that in the spiritual world in a tenfold degree. Amongst flowers the rose is deemed the sweetest, but Jesus is infinitely more beautiful in the garden of the soul than the rose can be in the gardens of earth. He takes the first place as the fairest among ten thousand. He is the sun, and all others are the stars ; the heavens and the day are dark in comparison with Him, for *the King in His beauty transcends all.* " I am the rose *of Sharon."* This was the best and rarest of roses. Jesus is not " the rose " alone, He is "the rose of Sharon," just as He calls His righteousness "gold," and then adds, " the gold of Ophir "—the best of the best. He is positively lovely, and superlatively the loveliest. *There is variety in His charms.* The rose is delightful to the eye, and its scent is pleasant and refreshing ; so each of the senses of the soul, whether it be the taste or feeling, the hearing, the sight, or the spiritual smell, finds appropriate gratification in Jesus. *Even the recollection of His love is sweet.* Take the rose of Sharon, and pull it leaf from leaf, and lay by the leaves in the jar of memory, and you shall find each leaf fragrant long afterwards, filling the house with perfume. Christ *satisfies the highest taste* of the most educated spirit to the very full. The greatest amateur in perfumes is quite satisfied with the rose : and when the soul has arrived at her highest pitch of true taste, she shall still be content with Christ, nay, she shall be the better able to appreciate Him. Heaven itself possesses nothing which excels the rose of Sharon. What emblem can fully set forth His beauty ? Human speech and earth-born things fail to tell of Him. Earth's choicest charms commingled, feebly picture His abounding preciousness. Blessed rose, bloom in my heart for ever !

" I pray not that Thou shouldst take them out of the world."
John xvii. 15.

IT is a sweet and blessed event which will occur to all believers in God's own time—the going home to be with Jesus. In a few more years the Lord's soldiers, who are now fighting " the good fight of faith," will have done with conflict, and have entered into the joy of their Lord. But although Christ prays that His people may eventually be with Him where He is, He does not ask that they may be taken at once away from this world to heaven. He wishes them to stay here. Yet how frequently does the wearied pilgrim put up the prayer, " O that I had wings like a dove ! for then would I fly away and be at rest ;" but Christ does not pray like that, He leaves us in His Father's hands, until, like shocks of corn fully ripe, we shall each be gathered into our Master's garner. Jesus does not plead for our instant removal by death, for to abide in the flesh is needful for others if not profitable for ourselves. He asks that we may be kept from evil, but he never asks for us to be admitted to the inheritance in glory till we are of full age. Christians often want to die when they have any trouble. Ask them why, and they tell you, " Because we would be with the Lord." We fear it is not so much because they are longing to be with the Lord, as because they desire to get rid of their troubles ; else they would feel the same wish to die at other times when not under the pressure of trial. They want to go home, not so much for the Saviour's company, as to be at rest. Now it is quite right to desire to depart if we can do it in the same spirit that Paul did, because to be with Christ is far better, but the wish to escape from trouble is a selfish one. Rather let your care and wish be to glorify God by your life here as long as He pleases, even though it be in the midst of toil, and conflict, and suffering, and leave Him to say when " it is enough."

" These all died in faith."—Hebrews xi. 13.

BEHOLD the epitaph of all those blessed saints who fell asleep before the coming of our Lord ! It matters nothing how else they died, whether of old age, or by violent means ; this one point, in which they all agree, is the most worthy of record, " they all died in faith." In faith they lived—it was their comfort, their guide, their motive and their support ; and in the same spiritual grace they died, ending their life-song in the sweet strain in which they had so long continued. They did not die resting in the flesh or upon their own attainments ; they made no advance from their first way of acceptance with God, but held to the way of faith to the end. Faith is as precious to die by as to live by.

Dying in faith has distinct reference to *the past.* They believed the promises which had gone before, and were assured that their sins were blotted out through the mercy of God. Dying in faith has to do with *the present.* These saints were confident of their acceptance with God, they enjoyed the beams of His love, and rested in His faithfulness. Dying in faith looks into *the future.* They fell asleep, affirming that the Messiah would surely come, and hat when He should in the last days appear upon the earth, they would rise from their graves to behold Him. To them the pains of death were but the birth-pangs of a better state. Take courage, my soul, as thou readest this epitaph. Thy course, through grace, is one of faith, and sight seldom cheers thee : this has also been the pathway of the brightest and the best. Faith was the orbit in which these stars of the first magnitude moved all the time of their shining here ; and happy art thou that it is thine. Look anew to-night to Jesus, the author and finisher of thy faith, and thank Him for giving thee like precious faith with souls now in glory.

"In the world ye shall have tribulation."—John xvi. 33.

ART thou asking the reason of this, believer?
Look *upward* to thy heavenly Father, and
behold Him pure and holy.   Dost thou know
that thou art one day to be like Him ?   Wilt thou
easily be conformed to his image ?   Wilt thou not
require much refining in the furnace of affliction to
purify thee ?   Will it be an easy thing to get rid of
thy corruptions, and make thee perfect even as thy
Father which is in heaven is perfect ?   Next, Christian, turn thine eye *downward.*   Dost thou know what
foes thou hast beneath thy feet ?   Thou wast once a
servant of Satan, and no king will willingly lose his
subjects.   Dost thou think that Satan will let thee
alone ?   No, he will be always at thee, for he "goeth
about like a roaring lion, seeking whom he may
devour."   Expect trouble, therefore, Christian, when
thou lookest beneath thee.   Then look *around thee.*
Where art thou ?   Thou art in an enemy's country,
a stranger and a sojourner. The world is not thy friend.
If it be, then thou art not God's friend, for he who is
the friend of the world is the enemy of God.   Be
assured that thou shalt find foemen everywhere.   When
thou sleepest, think that thou art resting on the battle-
field ; when thou walkest, suspect an ambush in every
hedge.   As mosquitoes are said to bite strangers more
than natives, so will the trials of earth be sharpest
to you.   Lastly, look *within thee,* into thine own heart
and observe what is there.   *Sin* and *self* are still within.
Ah ! if thou hadst no devil to tempt thee, no enemies
to fight thee, and no world to ensnare thee, thou wouldst
still find in thyself evil enough to be a sore trouble to
thee, for "the heart is deceitful above all things, and
desperately wicked."   Expect trouble then, but despond not on account of it, for God is with thee to help
and to strengthen thee.   He hath said, "I will be with
thee in trouble ; I will deliver thee and honour thee."

" A very present help."—Psalm xlvi. 1.

COVENANT blessings are not meant to be looked at only, but to be appropriated. Even our Lord Jesus is given to us for our present use. Believer, thou dost not make use of Christ as thou oughtest to do. When thou art in trouble, why dost thou not tell Him all thy grief? Has He not a sympathising heart, and can He not comfort and relieve thee? No, thou art going about to all thy friends, save thy best Friend, and telling thy tale everywhere except into the bosom of thy Lord. Art thou burdened with this day's sins? Here is a fountain filled with blood : use it, saint, use it. Has a sense of guilt returned upon thee? The pardoning grace of Jesus may be proved again and again. Come to Him at once for cleansing. Dost thou deplore thy weakness? He is thy strength : why not lean upon Him? Dost thou feel naked? Come hither, soul ; put on the robe of Jesus' righteousness. Stand not looking at it, but wear it. Strip off thine own righteousness, and thine own fears too : put on the fair white linen, for it was meant to *wear*. Dost thou feel thyself sick? Pull the night-bell of prayer, and call up the Beloved Physician! He will give the cordial that will revive thee. Thou art poor, but then thou hast " a kinsman, a mighty man of wealth." What! wilt thou not go to Him, and ask Him to give thee of His abundance, when He has given thee this promise, that thou shalt be joint heir with Him, and has made over all that He is and all that He has to be thine? There is nothing Christ dislikes more than for His people to make a show-thing of Him, and not to use Him. He loves to be employed by us. The more burdens we put on His shoulders, the more precious will He be to us.

> " Let us be simple with Him, then,
>   Not backward, stiff, or cold,
> As though our Bethlehem could be
>   What Sinai was of old."

" Shall a man make gods unto himself, and they are no gods ?"
Jer. xvi. 20.

ONE great besetting sin of ancient Israel was idolatry, and the spiritual Israel are vexed with a tendency to the same folly. Remphan's star shines no longer, and the women weep no more for Tammuz, but Mammon still intrudes his golden calf, and the shrines of pride are not forsaken. Self in various forms struggles to subdue the chosen ones under its dominion, and the flesh sets up its altars wherever it can find space for them. Favourite children are often the cause of much sin in believers ; the Lord is grieved when he sees us doting upon them above measure ; they will live to be as great a curse to us as Absalom was to David, or they will be taken from us to leave our homes desolate. If Christians desire to grow thorns to stuff their sleepless pillows, let them dote upon their dear ones.

It is truly said that " they are no gods," for the objects of our foolish love are very doubtful blessings, the solace which they yield us now is dangerous, and the help which they can give us in the hour of trouble is little indeed. Why, then, are we so bewitched with vanities ? We pity the poor heathen who adore a god of stone, and yet worship a god of gold. Where is the vast superiority between a god of flesh and one of wood ? The principle, the sin, the folly is the same in either case, only that in ours the crime is more aggravated because we have more light, and sin in the face of it. The heathen bows to a false deity, but the true God he has never known ; we commit two evils, inasmuch as we forsake the living God and turn unto idols. May the Lord purge us all from this grievous iniquity !

> " The dearest idol I have known,
> Whate'er that idol be ;
> Help me to tear it from thy throne,
> And worship only thee."

---

*" Being born again, not of corruptible seed, but of
incorruptible."*—1 Peter i. 23.

PETER most earnestly exhorted the scattered
saints to love each other " with a pure heart
fervently," and he wisely fetched his argument, not from the law, from nature, or from philosophy, but from that high and divine nature which
God hath implanted in His people. Just as some
judicious tutor of princes might labour to beget and
foster in them a kingly spirit and dignified behaviour,
finding arguments in their position and descent, so,
looking upon God's people as heirs of glory, princes
of the blood royal, descendants of the King of kings,
earth's truest and oldest aristocracy, Peter saith to
them, " See that ye love one another, because of your
noble birth, being born of incorruptible seed ; because
of your pedigree, being descended from God, the
Creator of all things ; and because of your immortal
destiny, for you shall never pass away, though the
glory of the flesh shall fade, and even its existence
shall cease." It would be well if, in the spirit of
humility, we recognised the true dignity of our regenerated nature, and lived up to it. What is a
Christian ? If you compare him with a king, he adds
priestly sanctity to royal dignity. The king's royalty
often lieth only in his crown, but with a Christian it
is infused into his inmost nature. He is as much
above his fellows through his new birth, as a man is
above the beast that perisheth. Surely he ought to
carry himself, in all his dealings, as one who is not of
the multitude, but chosen out of the world, distinguished by sovereign grace, written among " the
peculiar people " and who therefore cannot grovel in
the dust as others, nor live after the manner of the
world's citizens. Let the dignity of your nature, and
the brightness of your prospects, O believers in Christ,
constrain you to cleave unto holiness, and to avoid the
very appearance of evil.

" I will be their God, and they shall be my people."
2 Corinthians vi. 16.

WHAT a sweet title : "My people !" What a cheering revelation : "Their God !" How much of meaning is couched in those two words, "My people ! " Here is *speciality.* The whole world is God's ; the heaven, even the heaven of heavens is the Lord's, and He reigneth among the children of men ; but of those whom he hath chosen, whom He hath purchased to himself, He saith what He saith not of others—"My people." In this word there is the idea of *proprietorship.* In a special manner the " Lord's portion is His people ; Jacob is the lot of His inheritance." All the nations upon earth are His ; the whole world is in His power ; yet are His people, His chosen, more especially His possession ; for He has done more for them than others ; He has bought them with His blood ; He has brought them nigh to Himself ; He has set His great heart upon them ; He has loved them with an everlasting love, a love which many waters cannot quench, and which the revolutions of time shall never suffice in the least degree to diminish. Dear friends, can you, by faith, see yourselves in that number ? Can you look up to heaven and say, " My Lord and my God : mine by that sweet *relationship* which entitles me to call Thee Father ; mine by that hallowed *fellowship* which I delight to hold with Thee when Thou art pleased to manifest Thyself unto me as Thou dost not unto the world ?" Canst thou read the Book of Inspiration, and find there the indentures of thy salvation ? Canst thou read thy title writ in precious blood ? Canst thou, by humble faith, lay hold of Jesus' garments, and say, " My Christ "? If thou canst, then God saith of thee, and of others like thee, " My people ;" for, if God be your God, and Christ your Christ, the Lord has a special, peculiar favour to you ; you are the object of His choice, accepted in His beloved Son.

" He that handleth a matter wisely shall find good : and whoso trusteth in the Lord, happy is he."—Proverbs xvi. 20.

ISDOM is man's true strength ; and, under its guidance, he best accomplishes the ends of his being. Wisely handling the matter of life gives to man the richest enjoyment, and presents the noblest occupation for his powers ; hence by it he finds good in the fullest sense. Without wisdom, man is as the wild ass's colt, running hither and thither, wasting strength which might be profitably employed. Wisdom is the compass by which man is to steer across the trackless waste of life ; without it he is a derelict vessel, the sport of winds and waves. A man must be prudent in such a world as this, or he will find no good, but be betrayed into unnumbered ills. The pilgrim will sorely wound his feet among the briers of the wood of life if he do not pick his steps with the utmost caution. He who is in a wilderness infested with robber bands must handle matters wisely if he would journey safely. If, trained by the Great Teacher, we follow where He leads, we shall find good, even while in this dark abode ; there are celestial fruits to be gathered this side of Eden's bowers, and songs of paradise to be sung amid the groves of earth. But where shall this wisdom be found ? Many have dreamed of it, but have not possessed it. Where shall we learn it ? Let us listen to the voice of the Lord, for He hath declared the secret ; He hath revealed to the sons of men wherein true wisdom lieth, and we have it in the text, " Whoso trusteth in the Lord, happy is he." *The true way to handle a matter wisely is to trust in the Lord.* This is the sure clue to the most intricate labyrinths of life, follow it and find eternal bliss. He who trusts in the Lord has a diploma for wisdom granted by inspiration : happy is he now, and happier shall he be above. Lord, in this sweet eventide walk with me in the garden, and teach me the wisdom of faith.

"We dwell in Him."—1 John iv. 13.

O you want a house for your soul? Do you ask, "What is the purchase?" It is something less than proud human nature will like to give. It is without money and without price. Ah! you would like to pay a respectable rent! You would love to do something to win Christ? Then you cannot have the house, for it is "without price." Will you take my Master's house on a lease for all eternity, with nothing to pay for it, nothing but the ground-rent of loving and serving Him for ever? Will you take Jesus and "dwell in Him?" See, this house is furnished with all you want; it is filled with riches more than you will spend as long as you live. Here you can have intimate communion with Christ and feast on His love; here are tables well-stored with food for you to live on for ever; in it, when weary, you can find rest with Jesus; and from it you can look out and see heaven itself. Will you have the house? Ah! if you are houseless, you will say, "I should like to have the house; but may I have it?" Yes; there is the key—the key is, "Come to Jesus." "But," you say, "I am too shabby for such a house." Never mind; there are garments inside. If you feel guilty and condemned, come; and though the house is too good for you, Christ will make you good enough for the house by-and-by. He will wash you and cleanse you, and you will yet be able to sing, "We dwell in Him." Believer: thrice happy art thou to have such a dwelling-place! Greatly privileged thou art, for thou hast a "strong habitation" in which thou art ever safe. And "dwelling in Him," thou hast not only a perfect and secure house, but an *everlasting* one. When this world shall have melted like a dream, our house shall live, and stand more imperishable than marble, more solid than granite, self-existent as God, for it is God Himself—"We dwell in Him."

"All the days of my appointed time will I wait."—Job. xiv. 14.

LITTLE stay on earth will make heaven more heavenly. Nothing makes rest so sweet as toil; nothing renders security so pleasant as exposure to alarms. The bitter quassia cups of earth will give a relish to the new wine which sparkles in the golden bowls of glory. Our battered armour and scarred countenances will render more illustrious our victory above, when we are welcomed to the seats of those who have overcome the world. We should not have full *fellowship with Christ* if we did not for awhile sojourn below, for He was baptized with a baptism of suffering among men, and we must be baptized with the same if we would share his kingdom. Fellowship with Christ is so honourable that the sorest sorrow is a light price by which to procure it. Another reason for our lingering here is *for the good of others.* We would not wish to enter heaven till our work is done, and it may be that we are yet ordained to minister light to souls benighted in the wilderness of sin. Our prolonged stay here is doubtless *for God's glory.* A tried saint, like a well-cut diamond, glitters much in the King's crown. Nothing reflects so much honour on a workman as a protracted and severe trial of his work, and its triumphant endurance of the ordeal without giving way in any part. We are God's workmanship, in whom he will be glorified by our afflictions. It is for the honour of Jesus that we endure the trial of our faith with sacred joy. Let each man surrender his own longings to the glory of Jesus, and feel, "If my lying in the dust would elevate my Lord by so much as an inch, let me still lie among the pots of earth. If to live on earth for ever would make my Lord more glorious, it should be my heaven to be shut out of heaven." Our time is fixed and settled by eternal decree. Let us not be anxious about it, but wait with patience till the gates of pearl shall open.

" Great multitudes followed Him, and He healed them all."
Matthew xii. 15.

WHAT a mass of hideous sickness must have thrust itself under the eye of Jesus! Yet we read not that He was disgusted, but patiently waited on every case. What a singular variety of evils must have met at His feet! What sickening ulcers and putrefying sores! Yet He was ready for every new shape of the monster evil, and was victor over it in every form. Let the arrow fly from what quarter it might, he quenched its fiery power. The heat of fever, or the cold of dropsy ; the lethargy of palsy, or the rage of madness ; the filth of leprosy, or the darkness of ophthalmia—all knew the power of His word, and fled at His command. In every corner of the field He was triumphant over evil, and received the homage of delivered captives. He came, He saw, He conquered everywhere. It is even so this morning. Whatever my own case may be, the beloved Physician can heal me; and whatever may be the state of others whom I may remember at this moment in prayer, I may have hope in Jesus that He will be able to heal them of their sins. My child, my friend, my dearest one, I can have hope for each, for all, when I remember the healing power of my Lord ; and on my own account, however severe my struggle with sins and infirmities, I may yet be of good cheer. He who on earth walked the hospitals, still dispenses his grace, and works wonders among the sons of men : let me go to Him at once in right earnest.

Let me praise Him, this morning, as I remember *how* he wrought His spiritual cures, which bring Him most renown. It was by taking upon Himself our sicknesses. " By His stripes we are healed." The Church on earth is full of souls healed by our beloved Physician ; and the inhabitants of heaven itself confess that " He healed them all." Come, then, my soul, publish abroad the virtue of His grace, and let it be " to the Lord for a name, for an everlasting sign which shall not be cut off."

"Jesus saith unto him, Rise, take up thy bed, and walk."
John v. 8.

IKE many others, the impotent man had been waiting for a wonder to be wrought, and a sign to be given. Wearily did he watch the pool, but no angel came, or came not for him ; yet, thinking it to be his only chance, he waited still, and knew not that there was One near him whose word could heal him in a moment. Many are in the same plight : they are waiting for some singular emotion, remarkable impression, or celestial vision ; they wait in vain and watch for nought. Even supposing that, in a few cases, remarkable signs are seen, yet these are rare, and no man has a right to look for them in his own case ; no man especially who feels his impotency to avail himself of the moving of the water even if it came. It is a very sad reflection that tens of thousands are now waiting in the use of means, and ordinances, and vows, and resolutions, and have so waited time out of mind, in vain, utterly in vain. Meanwhile these poor souls forget the present Saviour, who bids them look unto Him and be saved. *He* could heal them at once, but they prefer to wait for an angel and a wonder. To trust Him is the sure way to every blessing, and He is worthy of the most implicit confidence ; but unbelief makes them prefer the cold porches of Bethesda to the warm bosom of His love. O that the Lord may turn His eye upon the multitudes who are in this case to-night ; may He forgive the slights which they put upon His divine power, and call them by that sweet constraining voice, to rise from the bed of despair, and in the energy of faith take up their bed and walk. O Lord, hear our prayer for all such at this calm hour of sunset, and ere the day breaketh may they look and live.

Courteous reader, is there anything in this portion for you?

" He that was healed wist not who it was."—John v. 13.

YEARS are short to the happy and healthy ; but thirty-eight years of disease must have dragged a very weary length along the life of the poor impotent man. When Jesus, therefore, healed him by a word, while he lay at the pool of Bethesda, he was delightfully *sensible of a change.* Even so the sinner who has for weeks and months been paralysed with despair, and has wearily sighed for salvation, is very conscious of the change when the Lord Jesus speaks the word of power, and gives joy and peace in believing. The evil removed is too great to be removed without our discerning it; the life imparted is too remarkable to be possessed and remain inoperative; and the change wrought is too marvellous not to be perceived. Yet the poor man was *ignorant of the author* of his cure; he knew not the sacredness of His person, the offices which he sustained, or the errand which brought Him among men. Much ignorance of Jesus may remain in hearts which yet feel the power of His blood. We must not hastily condemn men for lack of knowledge; but where we can see the faith which saves the soul, we must believe that salvation has been bestowed. The Holy Spirit makes men penitents long before He makes them divines; and he who believes what he knows, shall soon know more clearly what he believes. Ignorance is, however, an evil ; for this poor man was much *tantalized by the Pharisees,* and was quite unable to cope with them. It is good to be able to answer gainsayers ; but we cannot do so if we know not the Lord Jesus clearly and with understanding. The cure of his ignorance, however, soon followed the cure of his infirmity, for he was *visited by the Lord in the temple ;* and after that gracious manifestation, he was *found testifying* that " it was Jesus who had made him whole." Lord, if Thou hast saved me, show me Thyself, that I may declare Thee to the sons of men.

" Acquaint now thyself with Him."—Job xxii. 21.

F we would rightly " acquaint ourselves with God, and be at peace," we must know Him as He has revealed Himself, not only in *the unity of His essence and subsistence,* but also in *the plurality of His persons.* God said, " Let *us* make man in our *own* image ;" let not man be content until he knows something of the " us " from whom his being was derived. Endeavour to know *the Father ;* bury your head in His bosom in deep repentance, and confess that you are not worthy to be called His son ; receive the kiss of His love ; let the ring which is the token of His eternal faithfulness be on your finger ; sit at His table and let your heart make merry in His grace. Then press forward and seek to know much of *the Son* of God who is the brightness of His Father's glory, and yet in unspeakable condescension of grace became man for our sakes ; know Him in the singular complexity of His nature : eternal God, and yet suffering, finite man ; follow Him as He walks the waters with the tread of deity, and as He sits upon the well in the weariness of humanity. Be not satisfied unless you know much of Jesus Christ as your Friend, your Brother, your Husband, your all. Forget not *the Holy Spirit ;* endeavour to obtain a clear view of His nature and character, His attributes, and His works. Behold that Spirit of the Lord, who first of all moved upon chaos, and brought forth order ; who now visits the chaos of your soul, and creates the order of holiness. Behold Him as the Lord and giver of spiritual life, the Illuminator, the Instructor, the Comforter, and the Sanctifier. Behold Him as, like holy unction, He descends upon the head of Jesus, and then afterwards rests upon *you* who are as the skirts of His garments. Such an intelligent, scriptural, and experimental belief in the Trinity in Unity is yours if you truly know God ; and such knowledge *brings peace indeed.*

" Who hath blessed us with all spiritual blessings."—Eph. i. 3.

ALL the goodness of the past, the present, and the future, Christ bestows upon His people. In the mysterious ages of the past the Lord Jesus was His Father's first elect, and in His *election* He gave us an interest, for we were chosen in Him from before the foundation of the world. He had from all eternity the prerogatives of *Sonship*, as His Father's only-begotten and well-beloved Son, and He has, in the riches of His grace, by adoption and regeneration, elevated us to sonship also, so that to us He has given " power to become the sons of God." The *eternal covenant,* based upon suretiship and confirmed by oath, is ours, for our strong consolation and security. In the *everlasting settlements of predestinating wisdom* and omnipotent decree, the eye of the Lord Jesus was ever fixed on us ; and we may rest assured that in the whole roll of destiny there is not a line which militates against the interests of His redeemed. The *great betrothal* of the Prince of Glory is ours, for it is to us that He is affianced, as the sacred nuptials shall ere long declare to an assembled universe. The *marvellous incarnation* of the God of heaven, with all the amazing condescension and humiliation which attended it, is ours. The bloody sweat, the scourge, the cross, are ours for ever. Whatever blissful consequences flow from *perfect obedience, finished atonement, resurrection, ascension, or intercession,* all are ours by His own gift. Upon His breastplate he is now bearing our names ; and in His authoritative pleadings at the throne He remembers our persons and pleads our cause. His *dominion* over principalities and powers, and His absolute majesty in heaven, He employs for the benefit of them who trust in Him. His high estate is as much at our service as was His condition of abasement. He who gave Himself for us in the depths of woe and death, doth not withdraw the grant now that He is enthroned in the highest heavens.

" Come, my beloved, let us go forth into the field . . . let us see if the vine flourish."—Canticles vii. 11, 12.

THE church was about to engage in earnest labour, and desired her Lord's company in it. She does not say, " I will go," but " let us go." It is blessed working when Jesus is at our side ! It is the business of God's people to be trimmers of God's vines. Like our first parents, we are put into the garden of the Lord for usefulness; let us therefore go forth into the field. Observe that the church, when she is in her right mind, in all her many labours desires to enjoy communion with Christ. Some imagine that they cannot serve Christ actively, and yet have fellowship with Him : they are mistaken. Doubtless it is very easy to fritter away our inward life in outward exercises, and come to complain with the spouse, " They made me keeper of the vineyards ; but mine own vineyard have I not kept :" but there is no reason why this should be the case except our own folly and neglect. Certain is it that a professor may do nothing, and yet grow quite as lifeless in spiritual things as those who are most busy. Mary was not praised for sitting still ; but for her sitting at Jesus' feet. Even so, Christians are not to be praised for neglecting duties under the pretence of having secret fellowship with Jesus : it is not sitting, but *sitting at Jesus' feet* which is commendable. Do not think that activity is in itself an evil : it is a great blessing, and a means of grace to us. Paul called it a grace given to him to be allowed to preach ; and every form of Christian service may become a personal blessing to those engaged in it. Those who have most fellowship with Christ are not recluses or hermits, who have much time to spare, but indefatigable labourers who are toiling for Jesus, and who, in their toil, have Him side by side with them, so that they are workers together with God. Let us remember then, in anything we have to do for Jesus, that we car do it, and should do it in close communion with Him

" But now is Christ risen from the dead."—1 Cor. xv. 20.

THE whole system of Christianity rests upon the fact that "Christ is risen from the dead;" for, "If Christ be not risen, then is our preaching vain, and your faith is also vain: ye are yet in your sins." The *divinity* of Christ finds its surest proof in His resurrection, since He was "Declared to be the Son of God with power, according to the spirit of holiness, by the resurrection from the dead." It would not be unreasonable to doubt His Deity if He had not risen. Moreover, Christ's *sovereignty* depends upon His resurrection, "For to this end Christ both died, and rose, and revived, that He might be Lord both of the dead and living." Again, our *justification*, that choice blessing of the covenant, is linked with Christ's triumphant victory over death and the grave; for "He was delivered for our offences, and was raised again for our justification." Nay, more, our very *regeneration* is connected with His resurrection, for we are "Begotten again unto a lively hope by the resurrection of Jesus Christ from the dead." And most certainly our *ultimate resurrection* rests here, for, "If the Spirit of Him that raised up Jesus from the dead dwell in you, He that raised up Christ from the dead shall also quicken your mortal bodies by His Spirit that dwelleth in you." If Christ be not risen, then shall we not rise; but if He be risen then they who are asleep in Christ have not perished, but in their flesh shall surely behold their God. Thus, the silver thread of resurrection runs through all the believer's blessings, from his regeneration onwards to his eternal glory, and binds them together. How important then will this glorious fact be in his estimation, and how will he rejoice that beyond a doubt it is established, that "now is Christ risen from the dead."

> " The promise is fulfill'd,
> Redemption's work is done,
> Justice with mercy's reconciled,
> For God has raised His Son."

" The only begotten of the Father, full of grace and truth."
John i. 14.

BELIEVER, you can bear your testimony that Christ *is the only begotten of the Father,* as well as the first begotten from the dead. You can say, "He is divine to me, if He be human to all the world beside. He has done that for me which none but a God could do. He has subdued my stubborn will, melted a heart of adamant, opened gates of brass, and snapped bars of iron. He hath turned for me my mourning into laughter, and my desolation into joy; He hath led my captivity captive, and made my heart rejoice with joy unspeakable and full of glory. Let others think as they will of Him, to me He must be the only begotten of the Father : blessed be His name. And He is *full of grace.* Ah! had He not been I should never have been saved. He drew me when I struggled to escape from His grace ; and when at last I came all trembling like a condemned culprit to His mercy-seat He said, ' Thy sins which are many are all forgiven thee : be of good cheer.' And He is *full of truth.* True have His promises been, not one has failed. I bear witness that never servant had such a master as I have ; never brother such a kinsman as He has been to me ; never spouse such a husband as Christ has been to my soul ; never sinner a better Saviour ; never mourner a better comforter than Christ hath been to my spirit. I want none beside Him. In life He is my life, and in death He shall be the death of death ; in poverty Christ is my riches ; in sickness he makes my bed ; in darkness He is my star, and in brightness He is my sun ; He is the manna of the camp in the wilderness, and He shall be the new corn of the host when they come to Canaan. Jesus is to me all grace and no wrath, all truth and no falsehood : and of truth and grace He is *full,* infinitely full. My soul, this night, bless with all thy might ' the only Begotten.' "

" I am with you alway."—Matthew xxviii. 20.

IT is well there is One who is ever the same, and who is ever with us. It is well there is one stable rock amidst the billows of the sea of life. O my soul, set not thine affections upon rusting, moth-eaten, decaying treasures, but set thine heart upon Him who abides for ever faithful to thee. Build not thine house upon the moving quicksands of a deceitful world, but found thy hopes upon this rock, which, amid descending rain and roaring floods, shall stand immovably secure. My soul, I charge thee, lay up thy treasure in the only secure cabinet; store thy jewels where thou canst never lose them. Put thine all in Christ; set all thine affections on His person, all thy hope in His merit, all thy trust in His efficacious blood, all thy joy in His presence, and so thou mayest laugh at loss, and defy destruction. Remember that all the flowers in the world's garden fade by turns, and the day cometh when nothing will be left but the black, cold earth. Death's black extinguisher must soon put out thy candle. Oh! how sweet to have sunlight when the candle is gone! The dark flood must soon roll between thee and all thou hast; then wed thine heart to Him who will never leave thee; trust thyself with Him who will go with thee through the black and surging current of death's stream, and who will land thee safely on the celestial shore, and make thee sit with Him in heavenly places for ever. Go, sorrowing son of affliction, tell thy secrets to the Friend who sticketh closer than a brother. Trust all thy concerns with Him who never can be taken from thee, who will never leave thee, and who will never let thee leave Him, even " Jesus Christ, the same yesterday, and to-day, and for ever." " Lo, I am with you alway," is enough for my soul to live upon, let who will forsake me.

" Only be thou strong and very courageous."—Joshua i. 7.

OUR God's tender love for His servants makes Him concerned for the state of their inward feelings. He desires them to be of good courage. Some esteem it a small thing for a believer to be vexed with doubts and fears, but God thinks not so. From this text it is plain that our Master would not have us entangled with fears. He would have us without carefulness, without doubt, without cowardice. Our Master does not think so lightly of our unbelief as we do. When we are desponding we are subject to a grievous malady, not to be trifled with, but to be carried at once to the beloved Physician. Our Lord loveth not to see our countenance sad. It was a law of Ahasuerus that no one should come into the king's court dressed in mourning : this is not the law of the King of kings, for we may come mourning as we are ; but still He would have us put off the spirit of heaviness, and put on the garment of praise, for there is much reason to rejoice. The Christian man ought to be of a courageous spirit, in order that he may glorify the Lord by enduring trials in an heroic manner. If he be fearful and fainthearted, *it will dishonour his God.* Besides, *what a bad example it is.* This disease of doubtfulness and discouragement is an epidemic which soon spreads amongst the Lord's flock. One downcast believer makes twenty souls sad. Moreover, unless your courage is kept up *Satan will be too much for you.* Let your spirit be joyful in God your Saviour, the joy of the Lord shall be your strength, and no fiend of hell shall make headway against you : but cowardice throws down the banner. Moreover, *labour is light* to a man of cheerful spirit ; and *success waits upon cheerfulness.* The man who toils, rejoicing in his God, believing with all his heart, has success guaranteed. He who sows in hope shall reap in joy ; therefore, dear reader, " be thou strong, and very courageous."

" And will manifest myself to him."—John xiv. 21.

THE Lord Jesus gives special revelations of Himself to his people. Even if Scripture did not declare this, there are many of the children of God who could testify the truth of it from their own experience. They have had manifestations of their Lord and Saviour Jesus Christ in a peculiar manner, such as no mere reading or hearing could afford. In the biographies of eminent saints, you will find many instances recorded in which Jesus has been pleased, in a very special manner to speak to their souls, and to unfold the wonders of His person ; yea, so have their souls been steeped in happiness that they have thought themselves to be in heaven, whereas they were not there, though they were well nigh on the threshold of it—for when Jesus manifests Himself to his people, it is heaven on earth ; it is paradise in embryo; it is bliss begun. Especial manifestations of Christ exercise a holy influence on the believer's heart. One effect will be *humility.* If a man says, " I have had such-and-such spiritual communications, I am a great man," he has never had any communion with Jesus at all; for " God hath respect unto the lowly : but the proud He knoweth *afar off."* He does not need to come near them to know them, and will never give them any visits of love. Another effect will be *happiness ;* for in God's presence there are pleasures for evermore. *Holiness* will be sure to follow. A man who has no holiness has never had this manifestation. Some men profess a great deal ; but we must not believe any one unless we see that his deeds answer to what he says. " Be not deceived ; God is not mocked." He will not bestow his favours upon the wicked : for while he will not cast away a perfect man, neither will he respect an evil doer. Thus there will be three effects of nearness to Jesus— humility, happiness, and holiness. May God give them to thee, Christian !

"Fear not to go down into Egypt; for I will there make of thee a great nation: I will go down with thee into Egypt; and I will also surely bring thee up again."—Gen. xlvi. 3, 4.

JACOB must have shuddered at the thought of leaving the land of his father's sojourning, and dwelling among heathen strangers. It was *a new scene, and likely to be a trying one:* who shall venture among courtiers of a foreign monarch without anxiety? Yet the way was *evidently appointed* for him, and therefore he resolved to go. This is frequently the position of believers now—they are called to perils and temptations altogether untried: at such seasons *let them imitate Jacob's example* by offering sacrifices of prayer unto God, and seeking His direction; let them not take a step until they have waited upon the Lord for His blessing: then they *will have Jacob's companion* to be their friend and helper. How blessed to feel assured that the Lord is with us in all our ways, and condescends to go down into our humiliations and banishments with us! Even beyond the ocean our Father's love beams like the sun in its strength. We cannot hesitate to go where Jehovah promises His presence; even the valley of deathshade grows bright with the radiance of this assurance. Marching onwards with faith in their God, believers *shall have Jacob's promise.* They shall be brought up again, whether it be from the troubles of life or the chambers of death. Jacob's seed came out of Egypt in due time, and so shall all the faithful pass unscathed through the tribulation of life, and the terror of death. Let us *exercise Jacob's confidence.* *"Fear not,"* is the Lord's command and His divine encouragement to those who at His bidding are launching upon new seas; the divine presence and preservation forbid so much as one unbelieving fear. Without our God we should fear to move; but when He bids us go, it would be dangerous to tarry. Reader, go forward. and fear not.

" Weeping may endure for a night, but joy cometh in the morning."—Psalm xxx. 5.

CHRISTIAN ! If thou art in a night of trial, think of the morrow : cheer up thy heart with the thought of the coming of thy Lord.   Be patient, for

"Lo! He comes with clouds descending."

Be patient! The Husbandman waits until He reaps His harvest.   Be patient; for you know who has said, "Behold, I come quickly ; and my reward is with me, to give to every man according as his work shall be."   If you are never so wretched now, remember

"A few more rolling suns, at most,
Will land thee on fair Canaan's coast."

Thy head may be crowned with thorny troubles now, but it shall wear a starry crown ere long ; thy hand may be filled with cares—it shall sweep the strings of the harp of heaven soon.   Thy garments may be soiled with dust now; they shall be white by-and-by.   Wait a little longer.   Ah! how despicable our troubles and trials will seem when we look back upon them !   Looking at them here in the prospect, they seem immense ; but when we get to heaven we shall then

"With transporting joys recount,
The labours of our feet."

Our trials will then seem light and momentary afflictions.   Let us go on boldly ; if the night be never so dark, the morning cometh, which is more than they can say who are shut up in the darkness of hell.   Do you know what it is thus to live on the future—to live on expectation—to antedate heaven ?   Happy believer, to have so sure, so comforting a hope.   It may be all dark now, but it will soon be light ; it may be all trial now, but it will soon be all happiness.   What matters it though "weeping may endure for a night," when "joy cometh in the morning ?"

"Thou art my portion, O Lord."—Psalm cxix. 57.

OOK at thy possessions, O believer, and compare thy portion with the lot of thy fellow-men. Some of them have their portion in the field; they are rich, and their harvests yield them a golden increase; but what are harvests compared with thy God, who is the God of harvests? What are bursting granaries compared with Him, who is the Husbandman, and feeds thee with the bread of heaven? Some have their portion in the city; their wealth is abundant, and flows to them in constant streams, until they become a very reservoir of gold; but what is gold compared with thy God? Thou couldst not live on it; thy spiritual life could not be sustained by it. Put it on a troubled conscience, and could it allay its pangs? Apply it to a desponding heart, and see if it could stay a solitary groan, or give one grief the less? But thou hast God, and in Him thou hast more than gold or riches ever could buy. Some have their portion in that which most men love—applause and fame; but ask thyself, is not thy God more to thee than that? What if a myriad clarions should be loud in thine applause, would this prepare thee to pass the Jordan, or cheer thee in prospect of judgment? No, there are griefs in life which wealth cannot alleviate; and there is the deep need of a dying hour, for which no riches can provide. But when thou hast *God* for thy portion, thou hast more than all else put together. In Him every want is met, whether in life or in death. With God for thy portion thou art rich indeed, for He will supply thy need, comfort thy heart, assuage thy grief, guide thy steps, be with thee in the dark valley, and then take thee home, to enjoy Him as thy portion for ever. "I have enough," said Esau; this is the best thing a worldly man can say, but Jacob replies, "I have all things," which is a note too high for carnal minds.

" Joint heirs with Christ."—Romans viii. 17.

THE boundless realms of His Father's universe are Christ's by prescriptive right. As " heir of all things," He is the sole proprietor of the vast creation of God, and He has admitted us to claim the whole as ours, by virtue of that deed of joint-heirship which the Lord hath ratified with His chosen people. The golden streets of paradise, the pearly gates, the river of life, the transcendent bliss, and the unutterable glory, are, by our blessed Lord, made over to us for our everlasting possession. All that He has He shares with His people. The crown royal He has placed upon the head of His Church, appointing her a kingdom, and calling her sons a royal priesthood, a generation of priests and kings. He uncrowned Himself that we might have a coronation of glory ; He would not sit upon his own throne until he had procured a place upon it for all who overcome by His blood. Crown the head and the whole body shares the honour. Behold here the reward of every Christian conqueror ! Christ's throne, crown, sceptre, palace, treasure, robes, heritage, are yours. Far superior to the jealousy, selfishness, and greed, which admit of no participation of their advantages, Christ deems His happiness completed by his people sharing it. " The glory which thou gavest me have I given them." " These things have I spoken unto you, that My joy might remain in you, and that your joy might be full." The smiles of His Father are all the sweeter to Him, because His people share them. The honours of His kingdom are more pleasing, because His people appear with Him in glory. More valuable to Him are His conquests, since they have taught His people to overcome. He delights in His throne, because on it there is a place for them. He rejoices in His royal robes, since over them His skirts are spread. He delights the more in His joy, because He calls them to enter into it.

" He shall gather the lambs with His arm, and carry them in His bosom."—Isaiah xl. 11.

HO is He of whom such gracious words are spoken? He is THE GOOD SHEPHERD. *Why* doth He carry the lambs in His bosom? Because *He hath a tender heart, and any weakness at once melts His heart.* The sighs, the ignorance, the feebleness of the little ones of His flock draw forth His compassion. *It is His office,* as a faithful High Priest, to consider the weak. Besides, *He purchased them with blood, they are His property:* He must and will care for *that* which cost Him so dear. Then He is *responsible for each lamb,* bound by covenant engagements not to lose one. Moreover, *they are all a part of His glory and reward.*

But how may we understand the expression, "He will *carry* them"? Sometimes He carries them by *not permitting them to endure much trial.* Providence deals tenderly with them. Often they are "carried" by being filled with *an unusual degree of love,* so that they bear up and stand fast. Though their knowledge may not be deep, they have great sweetness in what they do know. Frequently He "carries" them by giving them *a very simple faith,* which takes the promise just as it stands, and believingly runs with every trouble straight to Jesus. The simplicity of their faith gives them an unusual degree of confidence, which carries them above the world.

"He carries the lambs *in His bosom.*" Here is *boundless affection.* Would He put them in His bosom if He did not love them much? Here is *tender nearness:* so near are they, that they could not possibly be nearer. Here is *hallowed familiarity:* there are precious love-passages between Christ and His weak ones. Here is *perfect safety:* in His bosom who can hurt them? They must hurt the Shepherd first. Here is *perfect rest and sweetest comfort.* Surely we are not sufficiently sensible of the infinite tenderness of Jesus!

" All that believe are justified."—Acts xiii. 39.

THE believer in Christ receives a *present* justification. Faith does not produce this fruit by-and-by, but *now*. So far as justification is the result of faith, it is given to the soul in the moment when it closes with Christ, and accepts Him as its all in all. Are they who stand before the throne of God justified now?—so are we, as truly and as clearly justified as they who walk in white and sing melodious praises to celestial harps. The thief upon the cross was justified the moment that he turned the eye of faith to Jesus ; and Paul, the aged, after years of service, was not more justified than was the thief with no service at all. We are *to-day* accepted in the Beloved, *to-day* absolved from sin, *to-day* acquitted at the bar of God. Oh! soul-transporting thought! There are some clusters of Eshcol's vine which we shall not be able to gather till we enter heaven ; but this is a bough which runneth over the wall. This is not as the corn of the land, which we can never eat till we cross the Jordan ; but this is part of the manna in the wilderness, a portion of our daily nutriment with which God supplies us in our journeying to and fro. We are *now*—even *now* pardoned ; even *now* are our sins put away ; even *now* we stand in the sight of God accepted, as though we had never been guilty. "There is therefore *now* no condemnation to them which are in Christ Jesus." There is not a sin in the Book of God, even *now*, against one of His people. Who dareth to lay anything to their charge? There is neither speck, nor spot, nor wrinkle, nor any such thing remaining upon any one believer in the matter of justification in the sight of the Judge of all the earth. Let present privilege awaken us to present duty, and now, while life lasts, let us spend and be spent for our sweet Lord Jesus.

"Made perfect."—Hebrews xii. 23.

RECOLLECT that there are two kinds of perfection which the Christian needs—the perfection of justification in the person of Jesus, and the perfection of sanctification wrought in him by the Holy Spirit. At present, corruption yet remains even in the breasts of the regenerate—experience soon teaches us this. Within us are still lusts and evil imaginations. But I rejoice to know that the day is coming when God shall finish the work which He has begun ; and He shall present my soul, not only perfect in Christ, but perfect through the Spirit, without spot or blemish, or any such thing. Can it be true that this poor sinful heart of mine is to become holy even as God is holy ? Can it be that this spirit, which often cries, "O wretched man that I am ! who shall deliver me from the body of this sin and death ?" shall get rid of sin and death—that I shall have no evil things to vex my ears, and no unholy thoughts to disturb my peace ? Oh, happy hour ! may it be hastened ! When I cross the Jordan, the work of sanctification will be finished ; but not till that moment shall I even claim perfection in myself. Then my spirit shall have its last baptism in the Holy Spirit's fire. Methinks I long to die to receive that last and final purification which shall usher me into heaven. Not an angel more pure than I shall be, for I shall be able to say, in a double sense, "I am clean," through Jesus' blood, and through the Spirit's work. Oh, how should we extol the power of the Holy Ghost in thus making us fit to stand before our Father in heaven ! Yet let not the hope of perfection hereafter make us content with imperfection now. If it does this, our hope cannot be genuine ; for a good hope is a purifying thing, even now. The work of grace must be *abiding in us now* or it cannot be *perfected then.* Let us pray to "be filled with the Spirit," that we may bring forth *increasingly* the fruits of righteousness.

"Who giveth us richly all things to enjoy."—1 Timothy vi. 17.

OUR Lord Jesus is ever giving, and does not for a solitary instant withdraw his hand. As long as there is a vessel of grace not yet full to the brim, the oil shall not be stayed. He is a sun ever-shining; He is manna always falling round the camp; He is a rock in the desert, ever sending out streams of life from His smitten side; the rain of His grace is always dropping; the river of His bounty is ever-flowing, and the well-spring of his love is constantly overflowing. As the King can never die, so His grace can never fail. Daily we pluck His fruit, and daily His branches bend down to our hand with a fresh store of mercy. There are seven feast-days in His weeks, and as many as are the days, so many are the banquets in His years. Who has ever returned from His door unblessed? Who has ever risen from His table unsatisfied, or from His bosom un-emparadised? His mercies are new every morning and fresh every evening. Who can know the number of His benefits, or recount the list of His bounties? Every sand which drops from the glass of time is but the tardy follower of a myriad of mercies. The wings of our hours are covered with the silver of His kindness, and with the yellow gold of His affection. The river of time bears from the mountains of eternity the golden sands of His favour. The countless stars are but as the standard bearers of a more innumerable host of blessings. Who can count the dust of the benefits which He bestows on Jacob, or tell the number of the fourth part of His mercies towards Israel? How shall my soul extol Him who daily loadeth us with benefits, and who crowneth us with loving-kindness? O that my praise could be as ceaseless as His bounty! O miserable tongue, how canst thou be silent? Wake up, I pray thee, lest I call thee no more my glory, but my shame. "Awake, psaltery and harp: I myself will awake right early."

" And he said, Thus saith the Lord, Make this valley full of ditches. For thus saith the Lord, Ye shall not see wind, neither shall ye see rain ; yet that valley shall be filled with water, that ye may drink, both ye and your cattle, and your beasts."—2 Kings iii. 16, 17.

THE armies of the three kings were famishing for want of water : God was about to send it, and in these words the prophet announced the coming blessing. Here was *a case of human helplessness :* not a drop of water could all the valiant men procure from the skies or find in the wells of earth. Thus often the people of the Lord are at their wits' end ; they see the vanity of the creature, and learn experimentally where their help is to be found. Still the people were to make *a believing preparation for the divine blessing ;* they were to dig the trenches in which the precious liquid would be held. The church must by her varied agencies, efforts, and prayers, make herself ready to be blessed ; she must make the pools, and the Lord will fill them. This must be done in faith, in the full assurance that the blessing is about to descend. By-and-by there was *a singular bestowal of the needed boon.* Not as in Elijah's case did the shower pour from the clouds, but in a silent and mysterious manner the pools were filled. The Lord has His own sovereign modes of action : He is not tied to manner and time as we are, but doeth as He pleases among the sons of men. It is ours thankfully to receive from Him, and not to dictate to Him. We must also notice *the remarkable abundance of the supply*—there was enough for the need of all. And so it is in the gospel blessing ; all the wants of the congregation and of the entire church shall be met by the divine power in answer to prayer ; and above all this, victory shall be speedily given to the armies of the Lord.

What am I doing for Jesus ? What trenches am I digging ? O Lord, make me ready to receive the blessing which Thou art so willing to bestow.

" So to walk even as He walked."—1 John ii. 6.

WHY should Christians imitate Christ? They should do it for *their own sakes.* If they desire to be in a healthy state of soul—if they would escape the sickness of sin, and enjoy the vigour of growing grace, let Jesus be their model. For their own happiness' sake, if they would drink wine on the lees, well refined; if they would enjoy holy and happy communion with Jesus; if they would be lifted up above the cares and troubles of this world, let them walk even as He walked. There is nothing which can so assist you to walk towards heaven with good speed, as wearing the image of Jesus on your heart to rule all its motions. It is when, by the power of the Holy Spirit, you are enabled to walk with Jesus in His very footsteps, that you are most happy, and most known to be the sons of God. Peter afar off is both unsafe and uneasy. Next, for *religion's sake,* strive to be like Jesus. Ah! poor religion, thou hast been sorely shot at by cruel foes, but thou hast not been wounded one-half so dangerously by thy foes as by thy friends. Who made those wounds in the fair hand of Godliness? The professor who used the dagger of hypocrisy. The man who with pretences, enters the fold, being nought but a wolf in sheep's clothing, worries the flock more than the lion outside. There is no weapon half so deadly as a Judas-kiss. Inconsistent professors injure the gospel more than the sneering critic or the infidel. But, especially for *Christ's own sake,* imitate His example. Christian, lovest thou thy Saviour? Is His name precious to thee? Is His cause dear to thee? Wouldst thou see the kingdoms of the world become His? Is it thy desire that He should be glorified? Art thou longing that souls should be won to Him? If so, *imitate* Jesus; be an "epistle of Christ, known and read of all men."

"Thou art My servant; I have chosen thee."—Isaiah xli. 9.

IF we have received the grace of God in our hearts, its practical effect has been to make us God's *servants*. We may be unfaithful servants, we certainly are unprofitable ones, but yet, blessed be His name, we *are* His servants, wearing His livery, feeding at His table, and obeying His commands. We were once the servants of sin, but He who made us free has now taken us into His family and taught us obedience to His will. We do not serve our Master perfectly, but we would if we could. As we hear God's voice saying unto us, "Thou art My servant," we can answer with David, "I am thy servant; Thou hast loosed my bonds." But the Lord calls us not only His *servants*, but His *chosen* ones—"I have chosen thee." We have not chosen Him first, but He hath chosen us. If we be God's servants, we were not always so; to sovereign grace the change must be ascribed. The eye of sovereignty singled us out, and the voice of unchanging grace declared, "I have loved thee with an everlasting love." Long ere time began or space was created God had written upon His heart the names of His elect people, had predestinated them to be conformed unto the image of His Son, and ordained them heirs of all the fulness of His love, His grace, and His glory. What comfort is here! Has the Lord loved us so long, and will He yet cast us away? He knew how stiffnecked we should be; He understood that our hearts were evil, and yet He made the choice. Ah! our Saviour is no fickle lover. He doth not feel enchanted for awhile with some gleams of beauty from His church's eye, and then afterwards cast her off because of her unfaithfulness. Nay, He married her in old eternity; and it is written of Jehovah, "He hateth putting away." The eternal choice is a bond upon *our* gratitude and upon *His* faithfulness which neither can disown.

*" In Him dwelleth all the fulness of the Godhead bodily.
And ye are complete in Him."*—Colossians ii. 9, 10.

ALL the attributes of Christ, as God and man,
are at our disposal. All the fulness of the
Godhead, whatever that marvellous term may
comprehend, is ours to make us complete. He cannot
endow us with the attributes of Deity ; but He has
done all that can be done, for He has made even
His divine power and Godhead subservient to our
salvation. His omnipotence, omniscience, omnipre-
sence, immutability and infallibility, are all combined
for our defence. Arise, believer, and behold the Lord
Jesus yoking the whole of His divine Godhead to the
chariot of salvation! How vast his grace, how firm
His faithfulness, how unswerving His immutability,
how infinite His power, how limitless His knowledge!
All these are by the Lord Jesus made the pillars
of the temple of salvation; and all, without diminution
of their infinity, are covenanted to us as our perpetual
inheritance. The fathomless love of the Saviour's
heart is every drop of it ours; every sinew in the arm
of might, every jewel in the crown of majesty, the
immensity of divine knowledge, and the sternness of
divine justice, all are ours, and shall be employed for us.
The whole of Christ, in His adorable character as the
Son of God, is by Himself made over to us most richly
to enjoy. His wisdom is our direction, His knowledge
our instruction, His power our protection, His justice
our surety, His love our comfort, His mercy our
solace, and His immutability our trust. He makes no
reserve, but opens the recesses of the Mount of God
and bids us dig in its mines for the hidden treasures.
"All, all, all are yours," saith He, " be ye satisfied
with favour and full of the goodness of the Lord." Oh!
how sweet thus to behold Jesus, and to call upon Him
with the certain confidence that in seeking the interposition of His love or power, we are but asking for
that which He has already faithfully promised.

"Afterward."—Hebrews xii. 11.

OW happy are tried Christians, *afterwards*. No calm more deep than that which succeeds a storm. Who has not rejoiced in clear shinings after rain? Victorious banquets are for well-exercised soldiers. After killing the lion, we eat the honey; after climbing the Hill Difficulty, we sit down in the arbour to rest; after traversing the Valley of Humiliation, after fighting with Apollyon, the shining one appears, with the healing branch from the tree of life. Our sorrows, like the passing keels of the vessels upon the sea, leave a silver line of holy light behind them "afterwards." It is peace, sweet, deep peace, which follows the horrible turmoil which once reigned in our tormented, guilty souls. See, then, the happy estate of a Christian! He has his best things last, and he therefore in this world receives his worst things first. But even his worst things are "afterward" good things, harsh ploughings yielding joyful harvests. Even now he grows rich by his losses, he rises by his falls, he lives by dying, and becomes full by being emptied; if, then, his grievous afflictions yield him so much peaceable fruit in this life, what shall be the full vintage of joy "afterwards" in heaven? If his dark nights are as bright as the world's days, what shall his days be? If even his starlight is more splendid than the sun, what must his sunlight be? If he can sing in a dungeon, how sweetly will he sing in heaven! If he can praise the Lord in the fires, how will he extol Him before the eternal throne! If evil be good to him *now*, what will the overflowing goodness of God be to him *then?* Oh, blessed "afterward!" Who would not be a Christian? Who would not bear the present cross for the crown which cometh afterwards? But herein is work for patience, for the rest is not for to-day, nor the triumph for the present, but "afterward." Wait, O soul, and let patience have her perfect work.

"I have seen servants upon horses, and princes walking as servants upon the earth."—Ecclesiastes x. 7.

UPSTARTS frequently usurp the highest places, while the truly great pine in obscurity. This is a riddle in providence whose solution will one day gladden the hearts of the upright; but it is so common a fact, that none of us should murmur if it should fall to our own lot. When our Lord was upon earth, although He is the Prince of the kings of the earth, yet He walked the footpath of weariness and service as the Servant of servants: what wonder is it if His followers, who are princes of the blood, should also be looked down upon as inferior and contemptible persons? The world is upside down, and therefore, the first are last and the last first. See how the servile sons of Satan lord it in the earth! What a high horse they ride! How they lift up their horn on high! Haman is in the court, while Mordecai sits in the gate; David wanders on the mountains, while Saul reigns in state; Elijah is complaining in the cave while Jezebel is boasting in the palace; yet who would wish to take the places of the proud rebels? and who, on the other hand, might not envy the despised saints? When the wheel turns, those who are lowest rise, and the highest sink. Patience, then, believer, eternity will right the wrongs of time.

Let us not fall into the error of letting our passions and carnal appetites ride in triumph, while our nobler powers walk in the dust. Grace must reign as a prince, and make the members of the body instruments of righteousness. The Holy Spirit loves order, and He therefore sets our powers and faculties in due rank and place, giving the highest room to those spiritual faculties which link us with the great King; let us not disturb the divine arrangement, but ask for grace that we may keep under our body and bring it into subjection. We were not new created to allow our passions to rule over us, but that we, as kings, may reign in Christ Jesus over the triple kingdom of our spirit, soul, and body, to the glory of God the Father.

" And he requested for himself that he might die."
1 Kings xix. 4.

IT was a remarkable thing that the man who was never to die, for whom God had ordained an infinitely better lot, the man who should be carried to heaven in a chariot of fire, and be translated, that he should not see death—should thus pray, " Let me die ; I am no better than my fathers." We have here a memorable proof that God does not always answer prayer in kind, though He always does in effect. He gave Elias something better than that which he asked for, and thus really heard and answered him. Strange was it that the lion-hearted Elijah should be so depressed by Jezebel's threat as to ask to die, and blessedly kind was it on the part of our heavenly Father that he did not take his desponding servant at his word. There is a limit to the doctrine of the prayer of faith. We are not to expect that God will give us everything we choose to ask for. We know that we sometimes ask, and do not receive, because we ask amiss. If we ask for that which is not promised—if we run counter to the spirit which the Lord would have us cultivate—if we ask contrary to His will, or to the decrees of His providence—if we ask merely for the gratification of our own ease, and without an eye to His glory, we must not expect that we shall receive. Yet, when we ask in faith, nothing doubting, if we receive not the precise thing asked for, we shall receive an equivalent, and more than an equivalent, for it. As one remarks, "If the Lord does not pay in silver, He will in gold ; and if He does not pay in gold, He will in diamonds." If He does not give you precisely what you ask for, He will give you that which is tantamount to it, and that which you will greatly rejoice to receive in lieu thereof. Be then, dear reader, much in prayer, and make this evening a season of earnest intercession, but take heed what you ask.

" Marvellous lovingkindness."—Psalm xvii. 7.

WHEN we give our hearts with our alms, we give well, but we must often plead to a failure in this respect. Not so our Master and our Lord. His favours are always performed with the love of His heart. He does not send to us the cold meat and the broken pieces from the table of His luxury, but He dips our morsel in His own dish, and seasons our provisions with the spices of His fragrant affections. When he puts the golden tokens of His grace into our palms, he accompanies the gift with such a warm pressure of our hand, that the manner of His giving is as precious as the boon itself. He will come into our houses upon His errands of kindness, and He will not act as some austere visitors do in the poor man's cottage, but He sits by our side, not despising our poverty, nor blaming our weakness. Beloved, with what smiles does he speak ! What golden sentences drop from His gracious lips ! What embraces of affection does He bestow upon us ! If He had but given us farthings, the way of His giving would have gilded them ; but as it is, the costly alms are set in a golden basket by His pleasant carriage. It is impossible to doubt the sincerity of His chârity, for there is a bleeding heart stamped upon the face of all His benefactions. He giveth liberally and upbraideth not. Not one hint that we are burdensome to Him ; not one cold look for His poor pensioners ; but He rejoices in His mercy, and presses us to His bosom while He is pouring out His life for us. There is a fragrance in His spikenard which nothing but His heart could produce ; there is a sweetness in His honey-comb which could not be in it unless the very essence of His soul's affection had been mingled with it. Oh! the rare communion which such singular heartiness effecteth ! May we continually taste and know the blessedness of it !

" I drew them with cords of a man, with bands of love."
Hosea xi. 4.

OUR heavenly Father often draws us with the cords of love ; but ah ! how backward we are to run towards Him ! How slowly do we respond to His gentle impulses ! *He draws us to exercise a more simple faith in Him;* but we have not yet attained to Abraham's confidence ; we do not leave our worldly cares with God, but, like Martha, we cumber ourselves with much serving. Our meagre faith brings leanness into our souls ; we do not open our mouths wide, though God has promised to fill them. Does He not this evening draw us to trust Him ? Can we not hear Him say, " Come, My child, and trust Me. The veil is rent; enter into My presence, and approach boldly to the throne of My grace. I am worthy of thy fullest confidence, cast thy cares on Me. Shake thyself from the dust of thy cares, and put on thy beautiful garments of joy." But, alas ! though called with tones of love to the blessed exercise of this comforting grace, we will not come. At another time *He draws us to closer communion with Himself.* We have been sitting on the doorstep of God's house, and He bids us advance into the banqueting hall and sup with Him, but we decline the honour. There are secret rooms not yet opened to us ; Jesus invites us to enter them, but we hold back. Shame on our cold hearts ! We are but poor lovers of our sweet Lord Jesus, not fit to be His servants, much less to be His brides, and yet He hath exalted us to be bone of His bone and flesh of His flesh, married to Him by a glorious marriage-covenant. Herein is love ! But it is love which *takes no denial.* If we obey not the gentle drawings of His love, He will send affliction to drive us into closer intimacy with Himself. Have us nearer He will. What foolish children we are to refuse those bands of love, and so bring upon our backs that scourge of small cords, which Jesus knows how to use!

" If so be ye have tasted that the Lord is gracious."
1 Peter ii. 3.

F :—then, this is not a matter to be taken for granted concerning every one of the human race. " If :"—then there is a possibility and a probability that some may not have tasted that the Lord is gracious. " If :"—then this is not a general but a special mercy ; and it is needful to enquire whether we know the grace of God by inward experience. There is no spiritual favour which may not be a matter for heart-searching.

But while this should be a matter of earnest and prayerful inquiry, no one ought to be content whilst there is any such thing as an " if " about his having tasted that the Lord is gracious. A jealous and holy distrust of self may give rise to the question even in the believer's heart, but the *continuance* of such a doubt would be an evil indeed. We must not rest without a desperate struggle to clasp the Saviour in the arms of faith, and say, " I know whom I have believed, and I am persuaded that he is able to keep that which I have committed unto him." Do not rest, O believer, till thou hast a full assurance of thine interest in Jesus. Let nothing satisfy thee till, by the infallible witness of the Holy Spirit bearing witness with thy spirit, thou art certified that thou art a child of God. Oh, trifle not here ; let no "perhaps" and "peradventure," and " if," and " may be," satisfy thy soul. Build on eternal verities, and verily build upon them. Get the sure mercies of David, and surely get them. Let thine anchor be cast into that which is within the veil, and see to it that thy soul be linked to the anchor by a cable that will not break. Advance beyond these dreary " ifs ;" abide no more in the wilderness of doubts and fears ; cross the Jordan of distrust, and enter the Canaan of peace, where the Canaanite still lingers, but where the land ceaseth not to flow with milk and honey.

" There is corn in Egypt."—Genesis xlii. 2.

FAMINE pinched all the nations, and it seemed inevitable that Jacob and his family should suffer great want ; but the God of providence, who never forgets the objects of electing love, had stored a granary for His people by giving the Egyptians warning of the scarcity, and leading them to treasure up the grain of the years of plenty. Little did Jacob expect deliverance from Egypt, but there was the corn in store for him. Believer, though all things are apparently against thee, rest assured that God has made a reservation on thy behalf ; in the roll of thy griefs there is a saving clause. Somehow He will deliver thee, and somewhere He will provide for thee. The quarter from which thy rescue shall arise may be a very unexpected one, but help will assuredly come in thine extremity, and thou shalt magnify the name of the Lord. If men do not feed thee, ravens shall ; and if earth yield not wheat, heaven shall drop with manna. Therefore be of good courage, and rest quietly in the Lord. God can make the sun rise in the west if He pleases, and make the source of distress the channel of delight. The corn in Egypt was all in the hands of the beloved Joseph; he opened or closed the granaries at will. And so the riches of providence are all in the absolute power of our Lord Jesus, who will dispense them liberally to His people. Joseph was abundantly ready to succour his own family ; and Jesus is unceasing in His faithful care for His brethren. Our business is to go after the help which is provided for us : we must not sit still in despondency, but bestir ourselves. Prayer will bear us soon into the presence of our royal Brother : once before His throne we have only to ask and have : His stores are not exhausted ; there is corn still : His heart is not hard, He will give the corn to us. Lord, forgive our unbelief, and this evening constrain us to draw largely from Thy fulness and receive grace for grace.

"He led them forth by the right way."—Psalm cvii. 7.

CHANGEFUL experience often leads the anxious believer to enquire "Why is it thus with me?" I looked for light, but lo, darkness came; for peace, but behold trouble. I said in my heart, my mountain standeth firm, I shall never be moved. Lord, thou dost hide Thy face, and I am troubled. It was but yesterday that I could read my title clear; to-day my evidences are bedimmed, and my hopes are clouded. Yesterday I could climb to Pisgah's top, and view the landscape o'er, and rejoice with confidence in my future inheritance; to-day, my spirit has no hopes, but many fears; no joys, but much distress. Is this part of God's plan with me? Can this be the way in which God would bring me to heaven? Yes, it is even so. The eclipse of your faith, the darkness of your mind, the fainting of your hope, all these things are but parts of God's method of making you ripe for the great inheritance upon which you shall soon enter. These trials are for the testing and strengthening of your faith—they are waves that wash you further upon the rock—they are winds which waft your ship the more swiftly towards the desired haven. According to David's words, so it might be said of you, "so He bringeth them to their desired haven." By honour and dishonour, by evil report and by good report, by plenty and by poverty, by joy and by distress, by persecution and by peace, by all these things is the life of your soul maintained, and by each of these are you helped on your way. Oh, think not, believer, that your sorrows are out of God's plan; they are necessary parts of it. "We must, through much tribulation, enter the kingdom." Learn, then, even to "count it all joy when ye fall into divers temptations."

> "O let my trembling soul be still,
> And wait Thy wise, Thy holy will!
> I cannot, Lord, Thy purpose see,
> Yet all is well since ruled by Thee."

" Behold, Thou art fair, my Beloved."—Canticles i. 16.

FROM every point our Well-beloved is most fair. Our various experiences are meant by our heavenly Father to furnish fresh standpoints from which we may view the loveliness of Jesus; how amiable are our trials when they carry us aloft where we may gain clearer views of Jesus than ordinary life could afford us! We have seen Him from the top of Amana, from the top of Shenir and Hermon, and He has shone upon us as the sun in his strength; but we have seen Him also " from the lions' dens, from the mountains of the leopards," and He has lost none of His loveliness. From the languishing of a sick bed, from the borders of the grave, have we turned our eyes to our soul's spouse, and He has never been otherwise than " all fair." Many of His saints have looked upon Him from the gloom of dungeons, and from the red flames of the stake, yet have they never uttered an ill word of Him, but have died extolling His surpassing charms. Oh, noble and pleasant employment to be for ever gazing at our sweet Lord Jesus! Is it not unspeakably delightful to view the Saviour in all His offices, and to perceive Him matchless in each?—to shift the kaleidoscope, as it were, and to find fresh combinations of peerless graces? In the manger and in eternity, on the cross and on His throne, in the garden and in His kingdom, among thieves or in the midst of cherubim, He is everywhere "altogether lovely." Examine carefully every little act of His life, and every trait of His character, and He is as lovely in the minute as in the majestic. Judge Him as you will, you cannot censure; weigh Him as you please, and He will not be found wanting. Eternity shall not discover the shadow of a spot in our Beloved, but rather, as ages revolve, His hidden glories shall shine forth with yet more inconceivable splendour, and His unutterable loveliness shall more and more ravish all celestial minds.

" The Lord will perfect that which concerneth me."—
Psalm cxxxviii. 8.

MOST manifestly the confidence which the Psalmist here expressed was a *divine confidence.* He
did not say, " *I* have grace enough to perfect
that which concerneth me—my faith is so steady that
it will not stagger—my love is so warm that it will
never grow cold—my resolution is so firm that nothing can move it; no, his dependence was on the
Lord alone. If we indulge in any confidence which is
not grounded on the Rock of ages, our confidence is
worse than a dream, it will fall upon us, and cover us
with its ruins, to our sorrow and confusion. All that
Nature spins time will unravel, to the eternal confusion of all who are clothed therein. The Psalmist was
wise, he rested upon nothing short of the *Lord's* work.
It is the Lord who has begun the good work within
us; it is He who has carried it on; and if he does not
finish it, it never will be complete. If there be one
stitch in the celestial garment of our righteousness
which we are to insert ourselves, then we are lost; but
this is our confidence, the Lord who began will perfect. He *has* done it all, *must* do it all, and *will* do
it all. Our confidence must not be in what we have
done, nor in what we have resolved to do, but entirely
in what *the Lord* will do. Unbelief insinuates—" You
will never be able to stand. Look at the evil of your
heart, you can never conquer sin; remember the sinful pleasures and temptations of the world that beset
you, you will be certainly allured by them and led
astray." Ah! yes, we should indeed perish if left to
our own strength. If we had alone to navigate our
frail vessels over so rough a sea, we might well give
up the voyage in despair; but, thanks be to God, He
will perfect that which concerneth us, and bring us to
the desired haven. We can never be too confident
when we confide in Him alone, and never too much
concerned to *have such* a trust.

" Thou hast bought me no sweet cane with money."
Isaiah xliii. 24.

ORSHIPPERS at the temple were wont to bring presents of sweet perfumes to be burned upon the altar of God : but Israel, in the time of her backsliding, became ungenerous, and made but few votive offerings to her Lord : this was an evidence of coldness of heart towards God and His house. Reader, does this never occur with you ? Might not the complaint of the text be occasionally, if not frequently, brought against you ? Those who are poor in pocket, if rich in faith, will be accepted none the less because their gifts are small ; but, poor reader, do you give in fair proportion to the Lord, or is the widow's mite kept back from the sacred treasury ? The rich believer should be thankful for the talent entrusted to him, but should not forget his large responsibility, for where much is given much will be required ; but, rich reader, are you mindful of your obligations, and rendering to the Lord according to the benefit received ? Jesus gave His blood for us, what shall we give to Him ? We are His, and all that we have, for He has purchased us unto Himself—can we act as if we were our own ? O for more consecration ! and to this end, O for more love ! Blessed Jesus, how good it is of Thee to accept our sweet cane bought with money ! nothing is too costly as a tribute to Thine unrivalled love, and yet Thou dost receive with favour the smallest sincere token of affection ! Thou dost receive our poor forget-me-nots and love-tokens as though they were intrinsically precious, though indeed they are but as the bunch of wild flowers which the child brings to its mother. Never may we grow niggardly towards Thee, and from this hour never may we hear Thee complain of us again for withholding the gifts of our love. We will give Thee the first fruits of our increase, and pay Thee tithes of all, and then we will confess "of Thine own have we given Thee."

" Blessed be God, which hath not turned away my prayer."
Psalm lxvi. 20.

IN looking back upon the character of our prayers, if we do it honestly, we shall be filled with wonder that God has ever answered them. There may be some who think their prayers worthy of acceptance—as the Pharisee did ; but the true Christian, in a more enlightened retrospect, weeps over his prayers, and if he could retrace his steps he would desire to pray more earnestly. Remember, Christian, how *cold* thy prayers have been. When in thy closet thou shouldst have wrestled as Jacob did ; but instead thereof, thy petitions have been faint and few—far removed from that humble, believing, persevering faith, which cries, " I will not let Thee go except Thou bless me." Yet, wonderful to say, God has heard these cold prayers of thine, and not only heard, but answered them. Reflect also, how *unfrequent* have been thy prayers, unless thou hast been in trouble, and *then* thou hast gone often to the mercy-seat : but when deliverance has come, where has been thy constant supplication ? Yet, notwithstanding thou hast ceased to pray as once thou didst, God has not ceased to bless. When thou hast neglected the mercy-seat, God has not deserted it, but the bright light of the Shekinah has always been visible between the wings of the cherubim. Oh ! it is marvellous that the Lord should regard those intermittent spasms of importunity which come and go with our necessities. What a God is He thus to hear the prayers of those who come to Him when they have pressing wants, but neglect Him when they have received a mercy ; who approach Him when they are forced to come, but who almost forget to address Him when mercies are plentiful and sorrows are few. Let His gracious kindness in hearing such prayers touch our hearts, so that we may henceforth be found " Praying always with all prayer and supplication in the Spirit."

"Only let your conversation be as it becometh the gospel of Christ."—Philippians i. 27.

THE word "conversation" does not merely mean our talk and converse with one another, but the whole course of our life and behaviour in the world. The Greek word signifies the actions and the privileges of citizenship: and thus we are commanded to let our actions, as citizens of the New Jerusalem, be such as becometh the gospel of Christ. What sort of conversation is this? In the first place, *the gospel is very simple.* So Christians should be simple and plain in their habits. There should be about our manner, our speech, our dress, our whole behaviour, that simplicity which is the very soul of beauty. The gospel is *pre-eminently true,* it is gold without dross; and the Christian's life will be lustreless and valueless without the jewel of truth. The gospel is a very *fearless gospel,* it boldly proclaims the truth, whether men like it or not: we must be equally faithful and unflinching. But the gospel is also *very gentle.* Mark this spirit in its Founder: "a bruised reed He will not break." Some professors are sharper than a thorn-hedge; such men are not like Jesus. Let us seek to win others by the gentleness of our words and acts. The gospel is *very loving.* It is the message of the God of love to a lost and fallen race. Christ's last command to His disciples was, "Love one another." O for more real, hearty union and love to all the saints; for more tender compassion towards the souls of the worst and vilest of men! We must not forget that the gospel of Christ is *holy.* It never excuses sin: it pardons it, but only through an atonement. If our life is to resemble the gospel, we must shun, not merely the grosser vices, but everything that would hinder our perfect conformity to Christ. For His sake, for our own sakes, and for the sake of others, we must strive day by day to let our conversation be more in accordance with His gospel.

" Forsake me not, O Lord."—Psalm xxxviii. 21.

FREQUENTLY we pray that God would not forsake us in the hour of trial and temptation, but we too much forget that we have need to use this prayer *at all times.* There is no moment of our life, however holy, in which we can do without His constant upholding. Whether in light or in darkness, in communion or in temptation, we alike need the prayer, " Forsake me not, O Lord." "Hold Thou me up, and I shall be safe." A little child, while learning to walk, always needs the nurse's aid. The ship left by the pilot drifts at once from her course. We cannot do without continued aid from above ; let it then be your prayer to-day, "Forsake me not. Father, forsake not Thy child, lest he fall by the hand of the enemy. Shepherd, forsake not Thy lamb, lest he wander from the safety of the fold. Great Husbandman, forsake not Thy plant, lest it wither and die. 'Forsake me not, O Lord,' now ; and forsake me not at any moment of my life. Forsake me not in my joys, lest they absorb my heart. Forsake me not in my sorrows, lest I murmur against Thee. Forsake me not in the day of my repentance, lest I lose the hope of pardon, and fall into despair ; and forsake me not in the day of my strongest faith, lest faith degenerate into presumption. Forsake me not, for without Thee I am weak, but with Thee I am strong. Forsake me not, for my path is dangerous, and full of snares, and I cannot do without thy guidance. The hen forsakes not her brood, do Thou then evermore cover me with Thy feathers, and permit me under Thy wings to find my refuge. 'Be not far from me, O Lord, for trouble is near, for there is none to help.' 'Leave me not, neither forsake me, O God of my salvation !' "

> "O ever in our cleansed breast,
> Bid Thine Eternal Spirit rest;
> And make our secret soul to be
> A temple pure and worthy Thee."

" And they rose up the same hour, and returned to Jerusalem. . . and they told what things were done in the way, and how He was known of them."—Luke xxiv. 33, 35.

WHEN the two disciples had reached Emmaus, and were refreshing themselves at the evening meal, the mysterious stranger who had so enchanted them upon the road, took bread and brake it, made Himself known to them, and then vanished out of their sight. They had constrained Him to abide with them, because the day was far spent; but now, although it was much later, their love was a lamp to their feet, yea, wings also; they forgot the darkness, their weariness was all gone, and forthwith they journeyed back the threescore furlongs to tell the gladsome news of a risen Lord, who had appeared to them by the way. They reached the Christians in Jerusalem, and were received by a burst of joyful news before they could tell their own tale. These early Christians were all on fire to speak of Christ's resurrection, and to proclaim what they knew of the Lord; they made common property of their experiences. This evening let their example impress us deeply. We too must bear our witness concerning Jesus. John's account of the sepulchre needed to be supplemented by Peter; and Mary could speak of something further still; combined, we have a full testimony from which nothing can be spared. We have each of us peculiar gifts and special manifestations; but the one object God has in view is the perfecting of the whole body of Christ. We must, therefore, bring our spiritual possessions and lay them at the apostle's feet, and make distribution unto all of what God has given to us. Keep back no part of the precious truth, but speak what you know, and testify what you have seen. Let not the toil or darkness, or possible unbelief of your friends, weigh one moment in the scale. Up, and be marching to the place of duty, and there tell what great things God has shown to your soul.

" Cast thy burden upon the Lord, and He shall sustain thee."
Psalm lv. 22.

CARE, even though exercised upon legitimate objects, if carried to excess, has in it the nature of sin. The precept to avoid anxious care is earnestly inculcated by our Saviour, again and again ; it is reiterated by the apostles ; and it is one which cannot be neglected without involving transgression: for the very essence of anxious care is the imagining that we are wiser than God, and the thrusting ourselves into His place to do for Him that which He has undertaken to do for us. We attempt to think of that which we fancy He will forget ; we labour to take upon ourselves our weary burden, as if He were unable or unwilling to take it for us. Now this disobedience to His plain precept, this unbelief in His Word, this presumption in intruding upon His province, is all sinful. Yet more than this, anxious care often leads to acts of sin. He who cannot calmly leave his affairs in God's hand, but will carry his own burden, is very likely to be tempted to use wrong means to help himself. This sin leads to a forsaking of God as our counsellor, and resorting instead to human wisdom. This is going to the "broken cistern" instead of to the "fountain ;" a sin which was laid against Israel of old. Anxiety makes us doubt God's lovingkindness, and thus our love to Him grows cold ; we feel mistrust, aud thus grieve the Spirit of God, so that our prayers become hindered, our consistent example marred, and our life one of self-seeking. Thus want of confidence in God leads us to wander far from Him ; but if through simple faith in His promise, we cast each burden as it comes upon Him, and are "careful for nothing" because He undertakes to care for us, it will keep us close to Him, and strengthen us against much temptation. "Thou wilt keep him in perfect peace whose mind is stayed on Thee, because he trusteth in Thee."

" *Continue in the faith.*"—Acts xiv. 22.

PERSEVERANCE is the badge of true saints. The Christian life is not a *beginning* only in the ways of God, but also a *continuance* in the same as long as life lasts. It is with a Christian as it was with the great Napoleon: he said, " Conquest has made me what I am, and conquest must maintain me." So, under God, dear brother in the Lord, conquest has made you what you are, and conquest must sustain you. Your motto must be, " Excelsior." He only is a true conqueror, and shall be crowned at the last, who continueth till war's trumpet is blown no more. Perseverance is, therefore, the target of all our spiritual enemies. The *world* does not object to your being a Christian for a time, if she can but tempt you to cease your pilgrimage, and settle down to buy and sell with her in Vanity Fair. The *flesh* will seek to ensnare you, and to prevent your pressing on to glory. " It is weary work being a pilgrim; come, give it up. Am I always to be mortified? Am I never to be indulged? Give me at least a furlough from this constant warfare." *Satan* will make many a fierce attack on your perseverance; it will be the mark for all his arrows. He will strive to hinder you *in service:* he will insinuate that you are doing no good; and that you want rest. He will endeavour to make you weary of *suffering*, He will whisper, " Curse God, and die." Or he will attack your *steadfastness:* " What is the good of being so zealous? Be quiet like the rest; sleep as do others, and let your lamp go out as the other virgins do." Or he will assail your *doctrinal sentiments:* " Why do you hold to these denominational creeds? Sensible men are getting more liberal; they are removing the old landmarks: fall in with the times." Wear your shield. Christian, therefore, close upon your armour, and cry mightily unto God, that by His Spirit you may endure to the end.

" So Mephibosheth dwelt in Jerusalem: for he did eat con-
tinually at the king's table; and was lame on both his feet."
2 Samuel ix. 13.

EPHIBOSHETH was no great ornament to a
royal table, yet he had a continual place at
David's board, because the king could see in
his face the features of the beloved Jonathan. Like
Mephibosheth, we may cry unto the King of Glory,
"What is Thy servant, that Thou shouldst look upon
such a dead dog as I am ?" but still the Lord indulges
as with most familiar intercourse with Himself, because
He sees in our countenances the remembrance of His
dearly-beloved Jesus. The Lord's people are *dear for
another's sake.* Such is the love which the Father bears
to His only begotten, that for His sake He raises His
lowly brethren from poverty and banishment, to courtly
companionship, noble rank, and royal provision. Their
deformity shall not rob them of their privileges. Lameness
is no bar to sonship ; the cripple is as much the heir as
if he could run like Asahel. Our right does not limp,
though our might may. A king's table is a noble hiding-
place for lame legs, and at the gospel feast we learn to
glory in infirmities, because the power of Christ resteth
upon us. Yet grievous *disability may mar the persons
of the best-loved saints.* Here is one feasted by David,
and yet so lame in both his feet that he could not go
up with the king when he fled from the city, and was
therefore maligned and injured by his servant Ziba.
Saints whose faith is weak, and whose knowledge is
slender, are great losers ; they are exposed to many
enemies, and cannot follow the king whithersoever he
goeth. This *disease frequently arises from falls.*
Bad nursing in their spiritual infancy often causes
converts to fall into a despondency from which
they never recover, and sin in other cases brings
broken bones. Lord, help the lame to leap like an
hart, and satisfy all Thy people with the bread of Thy
table !

*" What is thy servant, that thou shouldest look upon such a dead
dog as I am?"*—2 Samuel ix. 8.

F Mephibosheth was thus humbled by David's
kindness, what shall *we* be in the presence of
our gracious Lord? The more grace we have,
the less we shall think of ourselves, for grace, like
light, reveals our impurity. Eminent saints have
scarcely known to what to compare themselves, their
sense of unworthiness has been so clear and keen. " I
am," says holy Rutherford, " a dry and withered
branch, a piece of dead carcass, dry bones, and not
able to step over a straw." In another place he writes,
" Except as to open outbreakings, I want nothing of
what Judas and Cain had." The meanest objects in
nature appear to the humbled mind to have a preference
above itself, because they have never contracted sin :
a dog may be greedy, fierce, or filthy, but it has no
conscience to violate, no Holy Spirit to resist. A dog
may be a worthless animal, and yet by a little kindness it is soon won to love its master, and is faithful
unto death ; but we forget the goodness of the Lord,
and follow not at His call. The term " dead dog " is
the most expressive of all terms of contempt, but it is
none too strong to express the self-abhorrence of instructed believers. They do not affect mock modesty,
they mean what they say, they have weighed themselves
in the balances of the sanctuary, and found out the
vanity of their nature. At best, we are but clay, animated dust, mere walking hillocks ; but viewed as sinners, we are monsters indeed. Let it be published in
heaven as a wonder, that the Lord Jesus should set
His heart's love upon such as we are. Dust and ashes
though we be, we must and will " magnify the exceeding greatness of His grace." Could not His heart find
rest in heaven ? Must He needs come to these tents of
Kedar for a spouse, and choose a bride upon whom the
sun had looked ? O heavens and earth, break forth into
a song, and give all glory to our sweet Lord Jesus.

"*Whom He justified, them He also glorified.*"—Romans viii.30.

HERE is a precious truth for thee, believer. Thou mayest be poor, or in suffering, or unknown, but for thine encouragement take a review of thy "calling" and the consequences that flow from it, and especially that blessed result here spoken of. As surely as thou art God's child to-day, so surely shall all thy trials soon be at an end, and thou shalt be rich to all the intents of bliss. Wait awhile, and that weary head shall wear the crown of glory, and that hand of labour shall grasp the palm-branch of victory. Lament not thy troubles, but rather rejoice that ere long thou wilt be where "there shall be neither sorrow, nor crying, neither shall there be any more pain." The chariots of fire are at thy door, and a moment will suffice to bear thee to the glorified. The everlasting song is almost on thy lip. The portals of heaven stand open for thee. Think not that thou canst fail of entering into rest. If He hath called thee, nothing can divide thee from His love. Distress cannot sever the bond ; the fire of persecution cannot burn the link ; the hammer of hell cannot break the chain. Thou art secure ; that voice which called thee at first, shall call thee yet again from earth to heaven, from death's dark gloom to immortality's unuttered splendours. Rest assured, the heart of Him who has justified thee beats with infinite love towards thee. Thou shalt soon be with the glorified, where thy portion is ; thou art only waiting here to be made meet for the inheritance, and that done, the wings of angels shall waft thee far away, to the mount of peace, and joy, and blessedness, where,

> " Far from a world of grief and sin,
>   With God eternally shut in,"

thou shalt rest for ever and ever.

" This I recall to my mind, therefore have I hope."—Lam.iii.21.

EMORY is frequently the bondslave of despondency. Despairing minds call to remembrance every dark foreboding in the past, and dilate upon every gloomy feature in the present; thus memory, clothed in sackcloth, presents to the mind a cup of mingled gall and wormwood. There is, however, no necessity for this. Wisdom can readily transform memory into an angel of comfort. That same recollection which in its left hand brings so many gloomy omens, may be trained to bear in its right a wealth of hopeful signs. She need not wear a crown of iron, she may encircle her brow with a fillet of gold, all spangled with stars. Thus it was in Jeremiah's experience: in the previous verse memory had brought him to deep humiliation of soul: "My soul hath them still in remembrance, and is humbled in me;" and now this same memory restored him to life and comfort. "This I recall to my mind, therefore have I hope." Like a two-edged sword, his memory first killed his pride with one edge, and then slew his despair with the other. As a general principle, if we would exercise our memories more wisely, we might, in our very darkest distress, strike a match which would instantaneously kindle the lamp of comfort. There is no need for God to create a new thing upon the earth in order to restore believers to joy; if they would prayerfully rake the ashes of the past, they would find light for the present; and if they would turn to the book of truth and the throne of grace, their candle would soon shine as aforetime. Be it ours to remember the lovingkindness of the Lord, and to rehearse His deeds of grace. Let us open the volume of recollection which is so richly illuminated with memorials of mercy, and we shall soon be happy. Thus memory may be, as Coleridge calls it, "the bosom-spring of joy," and when the Divine Comforter bends it to His service, it may be chief among earthly comforters.

" Thou hatest wickedness."—Ps. xlv. 7.

"BE ye angry, and sin not." There can hardly be goodness in a man if he be not angry at sin; he who loves truth must hate every false way. How our Lord Jesus hated it when the temptation came! Thrice it assailed Him in different forms, but ever He met it with, "Get thee behind me, Satan." He hated it in others; none the less fervently because He showed His hate oftener in tears of pity than in words of rebuke; yet what language could be more stern, more Elijah-like, than the words, "Woe unto you, scribes and Pharisees, hypocrites! for ye devour widows' houses, and for a pretence make long prayer." He hated wickedness, so much that He bled to wound it to the heart; He died that it might die; He was buried that He might bury it in his tomb; and He rose that He might for ever trample it beneath His feet. Christ is in the Gospel, and that Gospel is opposed to wickedness in every shape. Wickedness arrays itself in fair garments, and imitates the language of holiness; but the precepts of Jesus, like His famous scourge of small cords, chase it out of the temple, and will not tolerate it in the Church. So, too, in the heart where Jesus reigns, what war there is between Christ and Belial! And when our Redeemer shall come to be our Judge, those thundering words, "Depart, ye cursed," which are, indeed, but a prolongation of His life-teaching concerning sin, shall manifest His abhorrence of iniquity. As warm as is His love to sinners, so hot is His hatred of sin; as perfect as is His righteousness, so complete shall be the destruction of every form of wickedness. O thou glorious champion of right, and destroyer of wrong, for this cause hath God, even Thy God, anointed thee with the oil of gladness above Thy fellows.

*" Cursed be the man before the Lord, that riseth up and
buildeth this city Jericho."*—Joshua vi. 26.

SINCE he was cursed who rebuilt Jericho, much
more the man who labours to restore Popery
among us. In our fathers' days the gigantic
walls of Popery fell by the power of their faith,
the perseverance of their efforts, and the blast of
their gospel trumpets ; and now there are some who
would rebuild that accursed system upon its old
foundations. O Lord, be pleased to thwart their
unrighteous endeavours, and pull down every stone
which they build. It should be a serious business
with us to be thoroughly purged of every error which
may have a tendency to foster the spirit of Popery, and
when we have made a clean sweep at home we should
seek in every way to oppose its all too rapid spread
abroad in the church and in the world. This last can
be done in secret by fervent prayer, and in public by
decided testimony. We must warn with judicious
boldness those who are inclined towards the errors of
Rome; we must instruct the young in gospel truth,
and tell them of the black doings of Popery in the
olden times. We must aid in spreading the light
more thoroughly through the land, for priests, like
owls, hate daylight. Are we doing all we can for
Jesus and the gospel? If not, our negligence
plays into the hands of priestcraft. What are we
doing to spread the Bible, which is the Pope's bane
and poison? Are we casting abroad good, sound
gospel writings? Luther once said, " The devil hates
goose quills," and, doubtless, he has good reason, for
ready writers, by the Holy Spirit's blessing, have
done his kingdom much damage. If the thousands
who will read this short word this night will do all
they can to hinder the rebuilding of this accursed
Jericho, the Lord's glory shall speed among the
sons of men. Reader, what can you do? What
will you do?

" Take us the foxes, the little foxes that spoil the vines."
Canticles ii. 15.

A LITTLE thorn may cause much suffering. A little cloud may hide the sun. Little foxes spoil the vines ; and little sins do mischief to the tender heart. These little sins burrow in the soul, and make it so full of that which is hateful to Christ, that He will hold no comfortable fellowship and communion with us. A great sin cannot destroy a Christian, but a little sin can make him miserable. Jesus will not walk with his people unless they drive out every known sin. He says, " If ye keep My commandments, ye shall abide in My love, even as I have kept My father's commandments and abide in His love." Some Christians very seldom enjoy their Saviour's presence. How is this ? Surely it must be an affliction for a tender child to be separated from his father. Art thou a child of God, and yet satisfied to go on without seeing thy Father's face ? What ! thou the spouse of Christ, and yet content without His company ! Surely, thou hast fallen into a sad state, for the chaste spouse of Christ mourns like a dove without her mate, when he has left her. Ask, then, the question, what has driven Christ from thee? He hides His face behind the wall of thy sins. That wall may be built up of *little* pebbles, as easily as of great stones. The sea is made of drops ; the rocks are made of grains : and the sea which divides thee from Christ may be filled with the drops of thy little sins ; and the rock which has well nigh wrecked thy barque, may have been made by the daily working of the coral insects of thy little sins. If thou wouldst live with Christ, and walk with Christ, and see Christ, and have fellowship with Christ, take heed of " the little foxes that spoil the vines, for our vines have tender grapes." Jesus invites you to go *with Him* and take them. He will surely, like Samson, take the foxes at once and easily. Go with Him to the hunting.

" That henceforth we should not serve sin."—Romans vi. 6.

CHRISTIAN, what hast thou to do with sin?
Hath it not cost thee enough already? Burnt
child, wilt thou play with the fire? What!
when thou hast already been between the jaws of the
lion, wilt thou step a second time into his den? Hast
thou not had enough of the old serpent? Did he not
poison all thy veins once, and wilt thou play upon the
hole of the asp, and put thy hand upon the cockatrice's
den a second time? Oh, be not so mad! so foolish!
Did sin ever yield thee real pleasure? Didst thou find
solid satisfaction in it? If so, go back to thine old
drudgery, and wear the chain again, if it delight thee.
But inasmuch as sin did never give thee what it
promised to bestow, but deluded thee with lies, be not
a second time snared by the old fowler—be free, and
let the remembrance of thy ancient bondage forbid
thee to enter the net again! *It is contrary to the
designs of eternal love,* which all have an eye to thy
purity and holiness; therefore run not counter to the
purposes of thy Lord. Another thought should restrain thee from sin. *Christians can never sin cheaply;*
they pay a heavy price for iniquity. Transgression
destroys peace of mind, obscures fellowship with
Jesus, hinders prayer, brings darkness over the
soul; therefore be not the serf and bondman of sin.
There is yet a higher argument: each time you " serve
sin," you have " *Crucified the Lord afresh, and put Him
to an open shame.*" Can you bear *that* thought? Oh!
if you have fallen into any special sin during this
day, it may be my Master has sent this admonition
this evening, to bring you back before you have back-
slidden very far. Turn thee to Jesus anew; He has
not forgotten His love to thee; His grace is still the
same. With weeping and repentance, come thou to
His footstool, and thou shalt be once more received
into His heart; thou shalt be set upon a rock again,
and thy goings shall be established.

" The king also himself passed over the brook Kidron."
2 Samuel xv. 23.

DAVID passed that gloomy brook when flying
with his mourning company from his traitor
son. The man after God's own heart was not
exempt from trouble, nay, his life was full of it. He
was both the Lord's Anointed, and the Lord's Afflicted.
Why then should we expect to escape ? At sorrow's
gates the noblest of our race have waited with ashes
on their heads, wherefore then should we complain as
though some strange thing had happened unto us ?

THE KING of kings himself was not favoured with a
more cheerful or royal road. He passed over the filthy
ditch of Kidron, through which the filth of Jerusalem
flowed. God had one Son without sin, but not a single
child without the rod. It is a great joy to believe that
Jesus has been tempted in all points like as we are.
What is our Kidron this morning ? Is it a faithless
friend, a sad bereavement, a slanderous reproach, a
dark foreboding ? The King has passed over all these.
Is it bodily pain, poverty, persecution, or contempt ?
Over each of these Kidrons the King has gone before
us. " In all our afflictions He was afflicted." The idea
of strangeness in our trials must be banished at once and
for ever, for He who is the Head of all saints, knows by
experience the grief which we think so peculiar. All
the citizens of Zion must be free of the Honourable
Company of Mourners, of which the Prince Immanuel
is Head and Captain.

Notwithstanding the abasement of David, he yet
returned in triumph to his city, and David's Lord
arose victorious from the grave ; let us then be of
good courage, for we also shall win the day. We shall
yet with joy draw water out of the wells of salvation,
though now for a season we have to pass by the
noxious streams of sin and sorrow. Courage, soldiers
of the Cross, the King himself triumphed after going
over Kidron, and so shall you.

" Who healeth all thy diseases."—Psalm ciii. 3.

HUMBLING as is the statement, yet the fact is certain, that we are all more or less suffering under the disease of sin. What a comfort to know that we have a great ´Physician who is both able and willing to heal us! Let us think of Him awhile to-night. His cures are very *speedy*—there is life in a look at Him; His cures are *radical*—He strikes at the centre of the disease; and hence, His cures are *sure* and certain. He never fails, and *the disease never returns.* There is no relapse where Christ heals; no fear that His patients should be merely patched up for a season, He makes new men of them: a new heart also does he give them, and a right spirit does He put within them. He is well skilled in *all* diseases. Physicians generally have some *specialité.* Although they may know a little about almost all our pains and ills, there is usually one disease which they have studied above all others; but Jesus Christ is thoroughly acquainted with the whole of human nature. He is as much at home with one sinner as with another, and never yet did He meet with an out-of-the-way case that was difficult to Him. He has had extraordinary complications of strange diseases to deal with, but He has known exactly with one glance of His eye how to treat the patient. He is the only universal doctor; and the medicine He gives is the only true catholicon, healing in every instance. Whatever our spiritual malady may be, we should apply at once to this Divine Physician. There is no brokenness of heart which Jesus cannot bind up. " His blood cleanseth from all sin." We have but to think of the myriads who have been delivered from all sorts of diseases through the power and virtue of His touch, and we shall joyfully put ourselves in His hands. We trust Him, and sin dies; we love Him, and grace lives; we wait for Him, and grace is strengthened; we see Him as He is, and grace is perfected for ever.

" The evening and the morning were the first day."
Genesis i. 5.

AS it so even in the beginning ? Did light and darkness divide the realm of time in the first day ? Then little wonder is it if I have also changes in my circumstances from the sunshine of prosperity to the midnight of adversity. It will not always be the blaze of noon even in my soul concerns, I must expect at seasons to mourn the absence of my former joys, and seek my Beloved in the night. Nor am I alone in this, for all the Lord's beloved ones have had to sing the mingled song of judgment and of mercy, of trial and deliverance, of mourning and of delight. It is one of the arrangements of Divine providence that day and night shall not cease either in the spiritual or natural creation till we reach the land of which it is written, " there is no night there." What our heavenly Father ordains is wise and good.

What, then, my soul, is it best for thee to do ? Learn first *to be content* with this divine order, and be willing, with Job, to receive evil from the hand of the Lord as well as good. Study next, to *make the outgoings of the morning and the evening to rejoice.* Praise the Lord for the sun of joy when it rises, and for the gloom of evening as it falls. There is beauty both in sunrise and sunset, sing of it, and glorify the Lord. Like the nightingale, pour forth thy notes at all hours. *Believe that the night is as useful as the day.* The dews of grace fall heavily in the night of sorrow. The stars of promise shine forth gloriously amid the darkness of grief. *Continue thy service* under all changes. If in the day thy watchword be *labour*, at night exchange it for *watch.* Every hour has its duty, do thou continue in thy calling as the Lord's servant until He shall suddenly appear in His glory. My soul, thine evening of old age and death is drawing near, dread it not, for it is part of the day ; and the Lord has said, " I will cover him all the day long."

" He will make her wilderness like Eden."—Isaiah li. 3.

METHINKS I see in vision a howling wilderness, a great and terrible desert, like to the Sahara. I perceive nothing in it to relieve the eye, all around I am wearied with a vision of hot and arid sand, strewn with ten thousand bleaching skeletons of wretched men who have expired in anguish, having lost their way in the pitiless waste. What an appalling sight! How horrible! a sea of sand without a bound, and without an oasis, a cheerless graveyard for a race forlorn! But behold and wonder! Upon a sudden, upspringing from the scorching sand I see a plant of renown; and as it grows it buds, the bud expands—it is a rose, and at its side a lily bows its modest head; and, miracle of miracles! as the fragrance of those flowers is diffused the wilderness is transformed into a fruitful field, and all around it blossoms exceedingly, the glory of Lebanon is given unto it, the excellency of Carmel and Sharon. Call it not Sahara, call it Paradise. Speak not of it any longer as the valley of deathshade, for where the skeletons lay bleaching in the sun, behold a resurrection is proclaimed, and up spring the dead, a mighty army, full of life immortal. Jesus is that plant of renown, and His presence makes all things new. Nor is the wonder less in each individual's salvation. Yonder I behold you, dear reader, cast out, an infant, unswathed, unwashed, defiled with your own blood, left to be food for beasts of prey. But lo, a jewel has been thrown into your bosom by a divine hand, and for its sake you have been pitied and tended by divine providence, you are washed and cleansed from your defilement, you are adopted into heaven's family, the fair seal of love is upon your forehead, and the ring of faithfulness is on your hand —you are now a prince unto God, though once an orphan, cast away. O prize exceedingly the matchless power and grace which changes deserts into gardens, and makes the barren heart to sing for joy.

*" For the flesh lusteth against the Spirit, and the Spirit
against the flesh."*—Gal. v. 17.

N every believer's heart there is a constant
struggle between the old nature and the new.
The old nature is very active, and loses no
opportunity of plying all the weapons of its deadly
armoury against newborn grace ; while on the other
hand, the new nature is ever on the watch to resist
and destroy its enemy. Grace within us will employ prayer, and faith, and hope, and love, to cast
out the evil ; it takes unto it the " whole armour of
God," and wrestles earnestly. These two opposing
natures will never cease to struggle so long as we
are in this world. The battle of " Christian " with
" Apollyon " lasted three hours, but the battle of
Christian with himself lasted all the way from the
Wicket Gate to the river Jordan. The enemy is so
securely entrenched within us that he can never
be driven out while we are in this body : but
although we are closely beset, and often in sore conflict, we have an Almighty helper, even Jesus, the
Captain of our salvation, who is ever with us, and
who assures us that we shall eventually come off more
than conquerors through Him. With such assistance
the new-born nature is more than a match for its
foes. Are you fighting with the adversary to-day ?
Are Satan, the world, and the flesh, all against you ?
Be not discouraged nor dismayed. Fight on ! For
God Himself is with you ; *Jehovah Nissi* is your
banner, and *Jehovah Rophi* is the healer of your
wounds. Fear not, you shall overcome, for who can
defeat Omnipotence ? Fight on, "looking unto Jesus ;"
and though long and stern be the conflict, sweet will
be the victory, and glorious the promised reward.

> " From strength to strength go on ;
>   Wrestle, and fight, and pray,
>   Tread all the powers of darkness down,
>   And win the well-fought day."

"*Good Master.*"—Matthew xix. 16.

IF the young man in the gospel used this title in speaking to our Lord, how much more fitly may I thus address Him! He is indeed my Master in both senses, a ruling Master and a teaching Master. I delight to run upon His errands, and to sit at His feet. I am both His servant and His disciple, and count it my highest honour to own the double character. If He should ask me why I call Him "*good*," I should have a ready answer. It is true that "there is none good but one, that is, God," but then He is God, and all the goodness of Deity shines forth in Him. In my experience, I have found Him good, so good, indeed, that all the good I have has come to me through Him. He was good to me when I was dead in sin, for He raised me by His Spirit's power; He has been good to me in all my needs, trials, struggles, and sorrows. Never could there be a better Master, for His service is freedom, His rule is love: I wish I were one thousandth part as good a servant. When He teaches me as my Rabbi, He is unspeakably good, His doctrine is divine, His manner is condescending, His spirit is gentleness itself. No error mingles with His instruction—pure is the golden truth which He brings forth, and all His teachings lead to goodness, sanctifying as well as edifying the disciple. Angels find Him a good Master and delight to pay their homage at His footstool. The ancient saints proved Him to be a good Master, and each of them rejoiced to sing, "I am Thy servant, O Lord!" My own humble testimony must certainly be to the same effect. I will bear this witness before my friends and neighbours, for possibly they may be led by my testimony to seek my Lord Jesus as their Master. O that they would do so! They would never repent so wise a deed. If they would but take His easy yoke, they would find themselves in so royal a service that they would enlist in it for ever.

" These were potters, and those that dwelt among plants and hedges : there they dwelt with the king for his work."— 1 Chron iv. 23.

POTTERS were not the very highest grade of workers, but " the king " needed potters, and therefore they were in *royal service,* although the material upon which they worked was nothing but clay. We, too, may be engaged in the most menial part of the Lord's work, but it is a great privilege to do anything for " the king ;" and therefore we will abide in our calling, hoping that, " although we have lien among the pots, yet shall we be as the wings of a dove covered with silver, and her feathers with yellow gold." The text tells us of those who *dwelt among plants and hedges,* having rough, rustic, hedging and ditching work to do. They may have desired to live in the city, amid its life, society, and refinement, but they kept their appointed places, for they also were doing the king's work. The place of our habitation is fixed, and we are not to remove from it out of whim and caprice, but seek to serve the Lord in it, by being a blessing to those among whom we reside. These potters and gardeners had *royal company,* for they dwelt " with the king," and although among hedges and plants, they dwelt with the king *there.* No lawful place, or gracious occupation, however mean, can debar us from communion with our divine Lord. In visiting hovels, swarming lodging-houses, workhouses, or gaols, we may go *with the king.* In all works of faith we may count upon Jesu's fellowship. It is when we are in His work that we may reckon upon his smile. Ye unknown workers who are occupied for your Lord amid the dirt and wretchedness of the lowest of the low, be of good cheer, for jewels have been found upon dunghills ere now, earthen pots have been filled with heavenly treasure, and ill weeds have been transformed into precious flowers. Dwell ye with the king for his work, and when He writes His chronicles your name shall be recorded

"He humbled Himself."—Philippians ii. 8.

JESUS is the great teacher of lowliness of heart. We need daily to learn of Him. See the Master taking a towel and washing His disciples' feet! Follower of Christ, wilt thou not humble thyself? See Him as the Servant of servants, and surely thou canst not be proud! Is not this sentence the compendium of His biography, "He humbled Himself"? Was He not on earth always stripping off first one robe of honour and then another, till, naked, He was fastened to the cross, and there did He not empty out His inmost self, pouring out His life-blood, giving up for all of us, till they laid Him penniless in a borrowed grave? How low was our dear Redeemer brought! How then can we be proud? Stand at the foot of the cross, and count the purple drops by which you have been cleansed; see the thorn-crown; mark His scourged shoulders, still gushing with encrimsoned rills; see hands and feet given up to the rough iron, and His whole self to mockery and scorn; see the bitterness, and the pangs, and the throes of inward grief, showing themselves in His outward frame; hear the thrilling shriek, "My God, my God, why hast Thou forsaken Me?" And if you do not lie prostrate on the ground before that cross, you have never seen it: if you are not humbled in the presence of Jesus, you do not know Him. You were so lost that nothing could save you but the sacrifice of God's only begotten. Think of that, and as Jesus stooped for you, bow yourself in lowliness at His feet. A sense of Christ's amazing love to us has a greater tendency to humble us than even a consciousness of our own guilt. May the Lord bring us in contemplation to Calvary, then our position will no longer be that of the pompous man of pride, but we shall take the humble place of one who loves much because much has been forgiven him. Pride cannot live beneath the cross. Let us sit there and learn our lesson, and then rise and carry it into practice.

" The kindness and love of God our Saviour."
Titus iii. 4.

HOW sweet it is to behold the Saviour communing with His own beloved people! There can be nothing more delightful than, by the Divine Spirit, to be led into this fertile field of delight. Let the mind for an instant consider the history of the Redeemer's love, and a thousand enchanting acts of affection will suggest themselves, all of which have had for their design the weaving of the heart into Christ, and the intertwisting of the thoughts and emotions of the renewed soul with the mind of Jesus. When we meditate upon this amazing love, and behold the all-glorious Kinsman of the Church endowing her with all His ancient wealth, our souls may well faint for joy. Who is he that can endure such a weight of love? That partial sense of it which the Holy Spirit is sometimes pleased to afford, is more than the soul can contain; how transporting must be a complete view of it! When the soul shall have understanding to discern all the Saviour's gifts, wisdom wherewith to estimate them, and time in which to meditate upon them, such as the world to come will afford us, we shall then commune with Jesus in a nearer manner than at present. But who can imagine the sweetness of such fellowship? It must be one of the things which have not entered into the heart of man, but which God hath prepared for them that love Him. Oh, to burst open the door of our Joseph's granaries, and see the plenty which he hath stored up for us! This will overwhelm us with love. By faith we see, as in a glass darkly, the reflected image of his unbounded treasures, but when we shall actually see the heavenly things themselves, with our own eyes, how deep will be the stream of fellowship in which our soul shall bathe itself! Till then our loudest sonnets shall be reserved for our loving benefactor, Jesus Christ our Lord, whose love to us is wonderful, passing the love of women.

" Received up into glory."—1 Timothy iii. 16.

WE have seen our well-beloved Lord in the days of His flesh, humiliated and sore vexed; for He was "despised and rejected of men, a man of sorrows, and acquainted with grief." He whose brightness is as the morning, wore the sackcloth of sorrow as His daily dress: shame was His mantle, and reproach was His vesture. Yet now, inasmuch as He has triumphed over all the powers of darkness upon the bloody tree, our faith beholds our King returning with dyed garments from Edom, robed in the splendour of victory. How glorious must He have been in the eyes of seraphs, when a cloud received Him out of mortal sight, and He ascended up to heaven! Now He wears the glory which He had with God or ever the earth was, and yet another glory above all— that which He has well earned in the fight against sin, death, and hell. As victor He wears the illustrious crown. Hark how the song swells high! It is a new and sweeter song: "Worthy is the Lamb that was slain, for He hath redeemed us unto God by His blood!" He wears the glory of an Intercessor who can never fail, of a Prince who can never be defeated, of a Conqueror who has vanquished every foe, of a Lord who has the heart's allegiance of every subject. Jesus wears all the glory which the pomp of heaven can bestow upon Him, which ten thousand times ten thousand angels can minister to Him. You cannot with your utmost stretch of imagination conceive His exceeding greatness; yet there will be a further revelation of it when He shall descend from heaven in great power, with all the holy angels—"Then shall He sit upon the throne of His glory." Oh, the splendour of that glory! It will ravish His people's hearts. Nor is this the close, for eternity shall sound His praise, "Thy throne, O God, is for ever and ever!" Reader, if you would joy in Christ's glory hereafter, He must be glorious in your sight now. *Is He so?*

" The Lord shut him in."—Gen. vii. 16.

NOAH was shut in *away from all the world* by the hand of divine love. The door of electing purpose interposes between us and the world which lieth in the wicked one. We are not of the world even as our Lord Jesus was not of the world. Into the sin, the gaiety, the pursuits of the multitude we cannot enter; we cannot play in the streets of Vanity Fair with the children of darkness, for our heavenly Father has shut us in. Noah was shut in *with his God.* "*Come* thou into the ark," was the Lord's invitation, by which He clearly showed that He Himself intended to dwell in the ark with His servant and his family. Thus all the chosen dwell in God and God in them. Happy people to be enclosed in the same circle which contains God in the Trinity of His persons, Father, Son, and Spirit. Let us never be inattentive to that gracious call, "Come, my people, enter thou into thy chambers, and shut thy doors about thee, and hide thyself as it were for a little moment until the indignation be overpast." Noah was so shut in that *no evil could reach him.* Floods did but lift him heavenward, and winds did but waft him on his way. Outside of the ark all was ruin, but inside all was rest and peace. Without Christ we perish, but in Christ Jesus there is perfect safety. Noah was so shut in that *he could not even desire to come out,* and those who are in Christ Jesus are in Him for ever. They shall go no more out for ever, for eternal faithfulness has shut them in, and infernal malice cannot drag them out. The Prince of the house of David shutteth and no man openeth; and when once in the last days as Master of the house He shall rise up and shut to the door, it will be in vain for mere professors to knock, and cry Lord, Lord open unto us, for that same door which shuts in the wise virgins will shut out the foolish for ever. Lord, shut me in by Thy grace.

" He that loveth not knoweth not God."—1 John iv. 8.

HE distinguishing mark of a Christian is his confidence in the love of Christ, and the yielding of his affections to Christ in return. First, faith sets her seal upon the man by enabling the soul to say with the apostle, " Christ loved me and gave Himself for me." Then love gives the countersign, and stamps upon the heart gratitude and love to Jesus in return. " We love Him because He first loved us." In those grand old ages, which are the heroic period of the Christian religion, this double mark was clearly to be seen in all believers in Jesus ; they were men who knew the love of Christ, and rested upon it as a man leaneth upon a staff whose trustiness he has tried. The love which they felt towards the Lord was not a quiet emotion which they hid within themselves in the secret chamber of their souls, and which they only spake of in their private assemblies when they met on the first day of the week, and sang hymns in honour of Christ Jesus the crucified, but it was a passion with them of such a vehement and all-consuming energy, that it was visible in all their actions, spoke in their common talk, and looked out of their eyes even in their commonest glances. Love to Jesus was a flame which fed upon the core and heart of their being ; and, therefore, from its own force burned its way into the outer man, and shone there. Zeal for the glory of King Jesus was the seal and mark of all genuine Christians. Because of their dependence upon Christ's love they *dared* much, and because of their love to Christ they *did* much, and it is the same now. The children of God are ruled in their inmost powers by love—the love of Christ constraineth them ; they rejoice that divine love is set upon them, they feel it shed abroad in their hearts by the Holy Ghost, which is given unto them, and then by force of gratitude they love the Saviour with a pure heart, fervently. My reader, do *you* love Him ? Ere you sleep give an honest answer to a weighty question !

"Behold, I am Vile."—Job xl. 4.

ONE cheering word, poor lost sinner, for thee! You think you must not come to God because you are vile. Now, there is not a saint living on earth but has been made to feel that he is vile. If Job, and Isaiah, and Paul were all obliged to say I am vile, oh, poor sinner, wilt thou be ashamed to join in the same confession? If divine grace does not eradicate all sin from the believer, how dost thou hope to do it thyself? and if God loves His people while they are yet vile, dost thou think thy vileness will prevent His loving thee? Believe on Jesus, thou outcast of the world's society! Jesus calls *thee*, and such as thou art.

> "Not the righteous, not the righteous;
> Sinners, Jesus came to call."

Even now say, "Thou hast died for sinners; I am a sinner, Lord Jesus sprinkle Thy blood on me;" if thou wilt confess thy sin thou shalt find pardon. If, now, with all thy heart, thou wilt say, "I am vile, wash me," thou shalt be washed *now*. If the Holy Spirit shall enable thee from thy heart to cry

> "Just as I am, without one plea
> But that Thy blood was shed for me,
> And that Thou bidd'st me come to Thee,
> O Lamb of God, I come!"

thou shalt rise from reading this morning's portion with all thy sins pardoned; and though thou didst wake this morning with every sin that man hath ever committed on thy head, thou shalt rest to-night accepted in the Beloved; though once degraded with the rags of sin, thou shalt be adorned with a robe of righteousness, and appear white as the angels are. For "now," mark it, "*Now* is the accepted time." If thou "believest on Him who justifieth the ungodly thou art saved." Oh! may the Holy Spirit give thee saving faith in Him who receives the vilest.

" Are they Israelites ? so am I."—2 Corinthians xi. 22.

E have here A PERSONAL CLAIM, and one that *needs proof.* The apostle knew that *His* claim was indisputable, but there are many persons who have no right to the title who yet claim to belong to the Israel of God. If we are with confidence declaring, " So am I also an Israelite," let us only say it after having searched our heart as in the presence of God. But if we can give proof that we are following Jesus, if we can from the heart say, " I trust Him wholly, trust Him only, trust Him simply, trust Him now, and trust Him ever," then the position which the saints of God hold belongs to us—all their enjoyments are our possessions ; we may be the very least in Israel, " less than the least of all saints," yet since the mercies of God belong to the saints AS SAINTS, and not as advanced saints, or well-taught saints, we may put in our plea, and say, " Are they Israelites ? so am I ; therefore the promises are mine, grace is mine, glory will be mine." The claim, rightfully made, is one which will yield untold comfort. When God's people are rejoicing that they are His, what a happiness if they can say, " So AM I !" When they speak of being pardoned, and justified, and accepted in the Beloved, how joyful to respond, " *Through the grace of God,* so AM I." But this claim not only has its enjoyments and privileges, but also its conditions and duties. We must share with God's people in cloud as well as in sunshine. When we hear them spoken of with contempt and ridicule for being Christians, we must come boldly forward and say, " So am I." When we see them working for Christ, giving their time, their talent, their whole heart to Jesus, we must be able to say, " So do I." O let us prove our gratitude by our devotion, and live as those who, having claimed a privilege, are willing to take the responsibility connected with it.

" Ye that love the Lord hate evil."—Psalm xcvii. 10.

THOU hast good reason to "hate evil," for only consider what harm it has already wrought thee. Oh, what a world of mischief sin has brought into thy heart! Sin blinded thee so that thou couldst not see the beauty of the Saviour; it made thee deaf so that thou couldst not hear the Redeemer's tender invitations. Sin turned thy feet into the way of death, and poured poison into the very fountain of thy being; it tainted thy heart, and made it "deceitful above all things, and desperately wicked." Oh, what a creature thou wast when evil had done its utmost with thee, before divine grace interposed! Thou wast an heir of wrath even as others; thou didst "run with the multitude to do evil." Such were all of us; but Paul reminds us, "but ye are washed, but ye are sanctified, but ye are justified in the name of the Lord Jesus, and by the Spirit of our God." We have good reason, indeed, for hating evil when we look back and trace its deadly workings. Such mischief did evil do us, that our souls would have been lost had not omnipotent love interfered to redeem us. Even now it is an active enemy, ever watching to do us hurt, and to drag us to perdition. Therefore "hate evil," O Christians, unless you desire trouble. If you would strew your path with thorns, and plant nettles in your death-pillow, then neglect to "hate evil:" but if you would live a happy life, and die a peaceful death, then walk in all the ways of holiness, hating evil, even unto the end. If you truly love your Saviour, and would honour Him, then "hate evil." We know of no cure for the love of evil in a Christian like abundant intercourse with the Lord Jesus. Dwell much with Him, and it is impossible for you to be at peace with sin.

"Order my footsteps by Thy Word,
And make my heart sincere;
Let sin have no dominion, Lord,
But keep my conscience clear."

" Be zealous."—Revelation iii. 19.

IF you would see souls converted, if you would hear the cry that "the kingdoms of this world have become the kingdoms of our Lord ;" if you would place crowns upon the head of the Saviour, and His throne lifted high, then be filled with zeal. For, under God, the way of the world's conversion must be by the zeal of the church. Every grace shall do exploits, but this shall be first; prudence, knowledge, patience, and courage will follow in their places, but zeal must lead the van. It is not the extent of your knowledge, though that is useful ; it is not the extent of your talent, though that is not to be despised ; it is your zeal that shall do great exploits. This zeal is the fruit of the Holy Spirit : it draws its vital force from *the continued operations of the Holy Ghost* in the soul. If our inner life dwindles, if our heart beats slowly before God, we shall not know zeal; but if all be strong and vigorous within, then we cannot but feel a loving anxiety to see the kingdom of Christ come, and His will done on earth, even as it is in heaven. A deep *sense of gratitude* will nourish Christian zeal. Looking to the hole of the pit whence we were digged, we find abundant reason why we should spend and be spent for God. And zeal is also stimulated by *the thought of the eternal future.* It looks with tearful eyes down to the flames of hell, and it cannot slumber : it looks up with anxious gaze to the glories of heaven, and it cannot but bestir itself. It feels that time is short compared with the work to be done, and therefore it devotes all that it has to the cause of its Lord. And it is ever strengthened by *the remembrance of Christ's example.* He was clothed with zeal as with a cloak. How swift the chariot-wheels of duty went with Him ! He knew no loitering by the way. Let us prove that we are His disciples by manifesting the same spirit of zeal.

"There fell down many slain, because the war was of God."—
1 Chron. v. 22.

ARRIOR, fighting under the banner of the
Lord Jesus, observe this verse with holy joy,
for as it was in the days of old so is it now, if
the war be of God the victory is sure. The sons of
Reuben, and the Gadites, and the half tribe of
Manasseh could barely muster five and forty thousand
fighting men, and yet in their war with the Hagarites,
they slew "men, an hundred thousand," "for they
cried to God in the battle, and He was entreated of
them, because they put their trust in Him." The
Lord saveth not by many nor by few; it is ours to go
forth in Jehovah's name if we be but a handful of
men, for the Lord of Hosts is with us for our Captain.
They did not neglect buckler, and sword, and bow,
neither did they place their trust in these weapons;
we must use all fitting means, but our confidence must
rest in the Lord alone, for He is the sword and the
shield of His people. The great reason of their extraordinary success lay in the fact that "the war
was of God." Beloved, in fighting with sin without
and within, with error doctrinal or practical, with
spiritual wickedness in high places or low places, with
devils and the devil's allies, you are waging Jehovah's
war, and unless He himself can be worsted, you need
not fear defeat. Quail not before superior numbers,
shrink not from difficulties or impossibilities, flinch not
at wounds or death, smite with the two-edged sword of
the Spirit, and the slain shall lie in heaps. The battle
is the Lord's and He will deliver His enemies into
our hands. With steadfast foot, strong hand, dauntless
heart, and flaming zeal, rush to the conflict, and the
hosts of evil shall fly like chaff before the gale.

Stand up! stand up for Jesus!
The strife will not be long;
This day the noise of battle,
The next the victor's song:

To him that overcometh,
A crown of life shall be;
He with the King of glory
Shall reign eternally.

" Thou shalt see now whether My word shall come to pass unto thee or not."—Numbers xi. 23.

GOD had made a positive promise to Moses that for the space of a whole month He would feed the vast host in the wilderness with flesh. Moses, being overtaken by a fit of unbelief, looks to the outward means, and is at a loss to know how the promise can be fulfilled. He looked to the creature instead of the Creator. But doth the Creator expect the creature to fulfil his promise for Him? No; He who makes the promise ever fulfils it by His own unaided omnipotence. If He speaks, it is done—done by Himself. His promises do not depend for their fulfilment upon the co-operation of the puny strength of man. We can at once perceive the mistake which Moses made. And yet how commonly we do the same! God has promised to supply our needs, and we look to the creature to do what God has promised to do; and then, because we perceive the creature to be weak and feeble, we indulge in unbelief. Why look we to that quarter at all? Will you look to the top of the Alps for summer heat? will you journey to the north pole to gather fruits ripened in the sun? Verily, you would act no more foolishly if ye did this than when you look to the weak for strength, and to the creature to do the Creator's work. Let us, then, put the question on the right footing. The ground of faith is not the sufficiency of the visible means for the performance of the promise, but the all-sufficiency of the invisible God, who will most surely do as He hath said. If after clearly seeing that the onus lies with the Lord and not with the creature, we dare to indulge in mistrust, the question of God comes home mightily to us: "Has the Lord's hand waxed short?" May it happen, too, in His mercy, that with the question there may flash upon our souls that blessed declaration, "Thou shalt see now whether My word shall come to pass unto thee or not."

" *The Lord hath done great things for us, whereof we are glad.*"—Psalm cxxvi. 3.

SOME Christians are sadly prone to *look* on the *dark* side of everything, and to dwell more upon what they have gone through than upon what God has done for them. Ask for their impression of the Christian life, and they will describe their continual conflicts, their deep afflictions, their sad adversities, and the sinfulness of their hearts, yet with scarcely any allusion to the mercy and help which God has vouchsafed them. But a Christian whose soul is in a *healthy* state, will come forward joyously, and say, " I will speak, not about myself, but to the honour of my God. He hath brought me up out of an horrible pit, and out of the miry clay, and set my feet upon a rock, and established my goings : and He hath put a new song in my mouth, even praise unto our God. The Lord hath done great things for me, whereof I am glad." Such an abstract of experience as this is the very best that any child of God can present. It *is* true that we endure trials, but it is just as true that we are delivered out of them. It *is* true that we have our corruptions, and mournfully do we know this, but it is quite as true that we have an all-sufficient Saviour, who overcomes these corruptions, and delivers us from their dominion. In looking back, it would be wrong to deny that we have been in the Slough of Despond, and have crept along the Valley of Humiliation, but it would be equally wicked to forget that we have been *through* them safely and profitably ; we have not remained in them, thanks to our Almighty Helper and Leader, who has brought us " out into a wealthy place." the deeper our troubles, the louder our thanks to God, who has led us through all, and preserved us until now. Our griefs cannot mar the melody of our praise, we reckon them to be the bass part of our life's song, " He hath done great things for us, whereof we are glad."

" Search the Scriptures."—John v. 39.

HE Greek word here rendered *search* signifies a strict, close, diligent, curious search, such as men make when they are seeking gold, or hunters when they are in earnest after game. We must not rest content with having given a superficial reading to a chapter or two, but with the candle of the Spirit we must deliberately seek out the hidden meaning of the word. Holy Scripture *requires searching*—much of it can only be learned by careful study. There is milk for babes, but also meat for strong men. The rabbis wisely say that a mountain of matter hangs upon every word, yea, upon every title of Scripture. Tertullian exclaims, "I adore the fulness of the Scriptures." No man who merely skims the book of God can profit thereby ; we must dig and mine until we obtain the hid treasure. The door of the word only opens to the key of diligence. The Scriptures *claim searching.* They are the writings of God, bearing the divine stamp and imprimatur—who shall dare to treat them with levity ? He who despises them despises the God who wrote them. God forbid that any of us should leave our Bibles to become swift witnesses against us in the great day of account. The word of God *will repay searching.* God does not bid us sift a mountain of chaff with here and there a grain of wheat in it, but the Bible is winnowed corn—we have but to open the granary door and find it. Scripture grows upon the student. It is full of surprises. Under the teaching of the Holy Spirit, to the searching eye it glows with splendour of revelation, like a vast temple paved with wrought gold, and roofed with rubies, emeralds, and all manner of gems. No merchandise like the merchandise of Scripture truth. Lastly, *the Scriptures reveal Jesus :* " They are they which testify of Me." No more powerful motive can be urged upon Bible readers than this : he who finds Jesus finds life, heaven, all things. Happy **he** who, searching his Bible, discovers his Saviour.

"We live unto the Lord."—Romans xiv. 8.

IF God had willed it, each of us might have entered heaven at the moment of conversion. It was not absolutely necessary for our preparation for immortality that we should tarry here. It is possible for a man to be taken to heaven, and to be found meet to be a partaker of the inheritance of the saints in light, though he has but just believed in Jesus. It is true that our sanctification is a long and continued process, and we shall not be perfected till we lay aside our bodies and enter within the veil; but nevertheless, had the Lord so willed it, He might have changed us from imperfection to perfection, and have taken us to heaven at once. Why then are we here? Would God keep His children out of paradise a single moment longer than was necessary ? Why is the army of the living God still on the battle-field when one charge might give them the victory? Why are his children still wandering hither and thither through a maze, when a solitary word from His lips would bring them into the centre of their hopes in heaven? The answer is—they are here that they may *"live unto the Lord,"* and may bring others to know His love. We remain on earth as sowers to scatter good seed; as ploughmen to break up the fallow ground; as heralds publishing salvation. We are here as the "salt of the earth," to be a blessing to the world. We are here to glorify Christ in our daily life. We are here as workers for Him, and as "workers together with him." Let us see that our life answereth its end. Let us live earnest, useful, holy lives, to "the praise of the glory of His grace." Meanwhile we long to be with Him, and daily sing—

> "My heart is with Him on His throne,
>   And ill can brook delay;
> Each moment listening for the voice,
>   'Rise up, and come away.'"

"They are they which testify of Me."—John v. 39.

JESUS Christ is the Alpha and Omega of the Bible. He is the constant theme of its sacred pages; from first to last they testify of Him. At the creation we at once discern Him as one of the sacred Trinity; we catch a glimpse of Him in the promise of the woman's seed; we see Him typified in the ark of Noah; we walk with Abraham, as He sees Messiah's day; we dwell in the tents of Isaac and Jacob, feeding upon the gracious promise; we hear the venerable Israel talking of Shiloh; and in the numerous types of the law, we find the Redeemer abundantly foreshadowed. Prophets and kings, priests and preachers, all look one way—they all stand as the cherubs did over the ark, desiring to look within, and to read the mystery of God's great propitiation. Still more manifestly in the New Testament we find our Lord the one pervading subject. It is not an ingot here and there, or dust of gold thinly scattered, but here you stand upon a solid floor of gold; for the whole substance of the New Testament is Jesus crucified, and even its closing sentence is bejewelled with the Redeemer's name. We should always read Scripture in this light; we should consider the word to be as a mirror into which Christ looks down from heaven; and then we, looking into it, see His face reflected as in a glass—darkly, it is true, but still in such a way as to be a blessed preparation for seeing Him as we shall see Him face to face. This volume contains Jesus Christ's letters to us, perfumed by his love. These pages are the garments of our King, and they all smell of myrrh, and aloes, and cassia. Scripture is the royal chariot in which Jesus rides, and it is paved with love for the daughters of Jerusalem. The Scriptures are the swaddling bands of the holy child Jesus; unroll them and you find your Saviour. The quintessence of the word of God is Christ.

" We love Him because He first loved us."—1 John iv. 19.

THERE is no light in the planet but that which proceedeth from the sun; and there is no true love to Jesus in the heart but that which cometh from the Lord Jesus himself. From this overflowing fountain of the infinite love of God, all our love to God must spring. This must ever be a great and certain truth, that we love Him for no other reason than because He first loved us. Our love to Him is *the fair offspring* of His love to us. Cold admiration, when studying the works of God, anyone may have, but the warmth of love can only be kindled in the heart by God's Spirit. How great the wonder that such as we should ever have been brought to love Jesus at all! How marvellous that when we had rebelled against Him, he should, by a display of such amazing love, seek to draw us back. No! never should we have had a grain of love towards God unless it had been sown in us by the sweet seed of His love to us. Love, then, has for its parent the love of God shed abroad in the heart: but after it is thus divinely born, it must be *divinely nourished.* Love is an exotic; it is not a plant which will flourish naturally in human soil, it must be watered from above. Love to Jesus is a flower of a delicate nature, and if it received no nourishment but that which could be drawn from the rock of our hearts it would soon wither. As love comes from heaven, so it must feed on heavenly bread. It cannot exist in the wilderness unless it be fed by manna from on high. Love must feed on love. The very soul and life of our love to God is His love to us.

> "I love thee, Lord, but with no love of mine,
>   For I have none to give;
> I love thee, Lord; but all the love is thine,
>   *For by thy love I live.*
> I am as nothing, and rejoice to be
> Emptied, and lost, and swallowed up in thee."

"There brake He the arrows of the bow, the shield, and the sword, and the battle."—Psalm lxxvi. 3.

OUR Redeemer's glorious cry of "It is finished," was the death-knell of all the adversaries of His people, the breaking of "the arrows of the bow, the shield, and the sword, and the battle." Behold the hero of Golgotha using His cross as an anvil, and His woes as a hammer, dashing to shivers bundle after bundle of our sins, those poisoned "arrows of the bow;" trampling on every indictment, and destroying every accusation. What glorious blows the mighty Breaker gives with a hammer far more ponderous than the fabled weapon of Thor! How the diabolical darts fly to fragments, and the infernal bucklers are broken like potters' vessels! Behold, He draws from its sheath of hellish workmanship the dread sword of Satanic power! He snaps it across His knee, as a man breaks the dry wood of a fagot, and casts it into the fire. Beloved, no sin of a believer can now be an arrow mortally to wound him, no condemnation can now be a sword to kill him, for the punishment of our sin was borne by Christ, a full atonement was made for all our iniquities by our blessed Substitute and Surety. Who now accuseth? Who now condemneth? Christ hath died, yea rather, hath risen again. Jesus has emptied the quivers of hell, has quenched every fiery dart, and broken off the head of every arrow of wrath; the ground is strewn with the splinters and relics of the weapons of hell's warfare, which are only visible to us to remind us of our former danger, and of our great deliverance. Sin hath no more dominion over us. Jesus has made an end of it, and put it away for ever. O thou enemy, destructions are come to a perpetual end. Talk ye of all the wondrous works of the Lord, ye who make mention of His name, keep not silence, neither by day, nor when the sun goeth to his rest. Bless the Lord, O my soul.

" Thou art weighed in the balances and art found wanting."
Daniel v. 27.

IT is well frequently to weigh ourselves in the scale of God's Word. You will find it a holy exercise to read some psalm of David, and, as you meditate upon each verse, to ask yourself, " Can I say this? Have I felt as David felt? Has my heart ever been broken on account of sin, as his was when he penned his penitential psalms? Has my soul been full of true confidence in the hour of difficulty as his was when he sang of God's mercies in the cave of Adullam, or in the holds of Engedi? Do I take the cup of salvation and call upon the name of the Lord?" Then turn to the life of Christ, and as you read, ask yourselves how far you are conformed to His likeness. Endeavour to discover whether you have the meekness, the humility, the lovely spirit which He constantly inculcated and displayed. Take, then, the epistles, and see whether you can go with the apostle in what he said of his experience. Have you ever cried out as he did—" O wretched man that I am! who shall deliver me from the body of this death "? Have you ever felt his self-abasement? Have you seemed to yourself the chief of sinners, and less than the least of all saints? Have you known anything of his devotion? Could you join with him and say, " For me to live is Christ, and to die is gain"? If we thus read God's Word as a test of our spiritual condition, we shall have good reason to stop many a time and say, " Lord, I feel I have never yet been here, O bring me here! give me true penitence, such as this I read of. Give me real faith; give me warmer zeal; inflame me with more fervent love; grant me the grace of meekness; make me more like Jesus. Let me no longer be ' found wanting,' when weighed in the balances of the sanctuary, lest I be found wanting in the scales of judgment." " Judge yourselves that ye be not judged."

" Who hath saved us, and called us with an holy calling."
2 Timothy i. 9.

HE apostle uses the perfect tense and says, "Who *hath* saved us." Believers in Christ Jesus *are* saved. They are not looked upon as persons who are in a hopeful state, and may ultimately be saved, but they *are* already saved. Salvation is not a blessing to be enjoyed upon the dying bed, and to be sung of in a future state above, but a matter to be obtained, received, promised, and enjoyed now. The Christian is perfectly saved *in God's purpose;* God has ordained him unto salvation, and that purpose is complete. He is saved also as to the *price which has been paid for him:* " It is finished " was the cry of the Saviour ere He died. The believer is also perfectly saved *in His covenant head,* for as he fell in Adam, so he lives in Christ. This complete salvation is accompanied by a *holy calling.* Those whom the Saviour saved upon the cross are in due time effectually called by the power of God the Holy Spirit unto holiness ; they leave their sins ; they endeavour to be like Christ ; they choose holiness, not out of any compulsion, but from the stress of a new nature, which leads them to rejoice in holiness just as naturally as aforetime they delighted in sin. God neither chose them nor called them because they were holy, but He called them that they might be holy, and holiness is the beauty produced by His workmanship in them. The excellencies which we see in a believer are as much the work of God as the atonement itself. Thus is brought out very sweetly the fulness of the grace of God. Salvation must be of grace, because the Lord is the author of it : and what motive but grace could move Him to save the guilty ? Salvation must be of grace, because the Lord works in such a manner that our righteousness is for ever excluded. Such is the believer's privilege—*a present salvation;* such is the evidence that he is called to it—*a holy life.*

" Whosoever will, let him take the water of life freely."—
Rev. xxii. 17.

JESUS says, "take freely." He wants no payment or preparation. He seeks no recommendation from our virtuous emotions. If you have no good feelings, if you be but willing, you are invited ; therefore come ! You have no belief and no repentance,—come to Him, and He will give them to you. Come just as you are, and take "Freely," without money and without price. He gives Himself to needy ones. The drinking fountains at the corners of our streets are valuable institutions ; and we can hardly imagine any one so foolish as to feel for his purse, when he stands before one of them, and to cry, "I cannot drink because I have not five pounds in my pocket." However poor the man is, there is the fountain, and just as he is he may drink of it. Thirsty passengers, as they go by, whether they are dressed in fustian or in broadcloth, do not look for any warrant for drinking ; its being there is their warrant for taking its water freely. The liberality of some good friends has put the refreshing crystal there and we take it, and ask no questions. Perhaps the only persons who need go thirsty through the street where there is a drinking fountain, are the fine ladies and gentlemen who are in their carriages. They are very thirsty, but cannot think of being so vulgar as to get out to drink. It would bemean them, they think, to drink at a common drinking fountain : so they ride by with parched lips. Oh, how many there are who are rich in their own good works and cannot therefore come to Christ ! "I will not be saved," they say, "in the same way as the harlot or the swearer." What ! go to heaven in the same way as a chimney sweep. Is there no pathway to glory but the path which led the thief there ? I will not be saved that way. Such proud boasters must remain without the living water ; but, "WHOSOEVER WILL, LET HIM TAKE THE WATER OF LIFE FREELY."

" Remove far from me vanity and lies."—Proverbs xxx. 8.
" O my God, be not far from me."—Psalm xxxviii. 21.

HERE we have two great lessons—what to deprecate and what to supplicate. The happiest state of a Christian is the holiest state. As there is the most heat nearest to the sun, so there is the most happiness nearest to Christ. No Christian enjoys comfort when his eyes are fixed on vanity—he finds no satisfaction unless his soul is quickened in the ways of God. The world may win happiness elsewhere, but he cannot. I do not blame ungodly men for rushing to their pleasures. Why should I? Let them have their fill. That is all they have to enjoy. A converted wife who despaired of her husband was always very kind to him, for she said, " I fear that this is the only world in which he will be happy, and therefore I have made up my mind to make him as happy as I can in it." Christians must seek their delights in a higher sphere than the insipid frivolities or sinful enjoyments of the world. Vain pursuits are dangerous to renewed souls. We have heard of a philosopher who, while he looked *up* to the stars, fell into a pit ; but how deeply do they fall who look *down*. Their fall is fatal. No Christian is safe when his soul is slothful, and his God is far from him. Every Christian is always safe as to the great matter of his standing in Christ, but he is not safe as regards his experience in holiness, and communion with Jesus in this life. Satan does not often attack a Christian who is living near to God. It is when the Christian departs from his God, becomes spiritually starved, and endeavours to feed on vanities, that the devil discovers his vantage hour. He may sometimes stand foot to foot with the child of God who is active in his Master's service, but the battle is generally short : he who slips as he goes down into the Valley of Humiliation, every time he takes a false step invites Apollyon to assail him. O for grace to walk humbly with our God !

" Delight thyself also in the Lord."—Ps. xxxvii. 4.

THE teaching of these words must seem very surprising to those who are strangers to vital godliness, but to the sincere believer it is only the inculcation of a recognised truth. The life of the believer is here described as a *delight* in God, and we are thus certified of the great fact that true religion overflows with happiness and joy. Ungodly persons and mere professors never look upon religion as a joyful thing ; to them it is service, duty, or necessity, but never pleasure or delight. If they attend to religion at all, it is either that they may gain thereby, or else because they dare not do otherwise. The thought of *delight* in religion is so strange to most men, that no two words in their language stand further apart than " holiness " and " delight." But believers who know Christ, understand that delight and faith are so blessedly united, that the gates of hell cannot prevail to separate them. They who love God with all their hearts, find that his ways are ways of pleasantness, and all His paths are peace. Such joys, such brimful delights, such overflowing blessednesses, do the saints discover in their Lord, that so far from serving Him from custom, they would follow Him though all the world cast out His name as evil. We fear not God because of any compulsion ; our faith is no fetter, our profession is no bondage, we are not dragged to holiness, nor driven to duty. No, our piety is our pleasure, our hope is our happiness, our duty is our delight.

Delight and true religion are as allied as root and flower ; as indivisible as truth and certainty ; they are, in fact, two precious jewels glittering side by side in a setting of gold.

> " 'Tis when we taste Thy love,
> Our joys divinely grow,
> Unspeakable like those above,
> And heaven begins below."

*" O Lord, to us belongeth confusion of face . . . because we
have sinned against Thee."*—Daniel ix. 8.

DEEP sense and clear sight of sin, its heinousness, and the punishment which it deserves,
should make us lie low before the throne.
We have sinned as Christians. Alas! that it should
be so. Favoured as we have been, we have yet been
ungrateful: privileged beyond most, we have not
brought forth fruit in proportion. Who is there,
although he may long have been engaged in the
Christian warfare, that will not blush when he looks
back upon the past? As for our days before we were
regenerate, may they be forgiven and forgotten; but
since then, though we have not sinned as before, yet
we have sinned against light and against love—light
which has really penetrated our minds, and love in
which we have rejoiced. Oh, the atrocity of the sin of
a pardoned soul! An unpardoned sinner sins cheaply
compared with the sin of one of God's own elect ones,
who has had communion with Christ and leaned his
head upon Jesus' bosom. Look at David! Many will
talk of his sin, but I pray you look at his repentance,
and hear his broken bones, as each one of them moans
out its dolorous confession! Mark his tears, as they
fall upon the ground, and the deep sighs with which he
accompanies the softened music of his harp! We
have erred: let us, therefore, seek the spirit of penitence. Look, again, at Peter! We speak much of
Peter's denying his Master. Remember, it is written,
" He wept bitterly." Have *we* no denials of our Lord
to be lamented with tears? Alas! these sins of ours,
before and after conversion, would consign us to the
place of inextinguishable fire if it were not for the sovereign mercy which has made us to differ, snatching us
like brands from the burning. My soul, bow down
under a sense of thy natural sinfulness, and worship
thy God. Admire the grace which saves thee—the
mercy which spares thee—the love which pardons thee!

---

*" And Sarah said, God hath made me to laugh, so that all
that hear will laugh with me."*—Genesis xxi. 6.

IT was far above the power of nature, and even
contrary to its laws, that the aged Sarah
should be honoured with a son ; and even so
it is beyond all ordinary rules that I, a poor, helpless,
undone sinner, should find grace to bear about in my
soul the indwelling Spirit of the Lord Jesus.   I, who
once despaired, as well I might, for my nature was as
dry, and withered, and barren, and accursed as a
howling wilderness, even I have been made to bring
forth fruit unto holiness.   Well may my mouth be
filled with joyous laughter, because of the singular,
surprising grace which I have received of the Lord,
for I have found Jesus, the promised seed, and He is
mine for ever.   This day will I lift up psalms of
triumph unto the Lord who has remembered my low
estate, for " my heart rejoiceth in the Lord ; mine horn
is exalted in the Lord ; my mouth is enlarged over
mine enemies, because I rejoice in Thy salvation."
  I would have all those that hear of my great deliverance from hell, and my most blessed visitation
from on high, laugh for joy with me.   I would surprise my family with my abundant peace ; I would
delight my friends with my ever-increasing happiness ;
I would edify the Church with my grateful confessions ;
and even impress the world with the cheerfulness of
my daily conversation.   Bunyan tells us that Mercy
laughed in her sleep, and no wonder when she dreamed
of Jesus ; my joy shall not stop short of hers while
my Beloved is the theme of my daily thoughts.   The
Lord Jesus is a deep sea of joy : my soul shall dive
therein, shall be swallowed up in the delights of His
society.   Sarah looked on her Isaac, and laughed with
excess of rapture, and all her friends laughed with
her ; and thou, my soul, look on thy Jesus, and bid
heaven and earth unite in thy joy unspeakable.

" He openeth, and no man shutteth."—Revelation iii. 7.

JESUS is the keeper of the gates of paradise and before every believing soul He setteth an open door, which no man or devil shall be able to close against it. What joy it will be to find that faith in Him is the golden key to the everlasting doors. My soul, dost though carry this key in thy bosom, or art thou trusting to some deceitful pick-lock, which will fail thee at last? Hear this parable of the preacher, and remember it. The great King has made a banquet, and He has proclaimed to all the world that none shall enter but those who bring with them the fairest flower that blooms. The spirits of men advance to the gate by thousands, and they bring each one the flower which he esteems the queen of the garden ; but in crowds they are driven from the royal presence, and enter not into the festive halls. Some bear in their hand the deadly nightshade of superstition, or the flaunting poppies of Rome, or the hemlock of self-righteousness, but these are not dear to the King, the bearers are shut out of the pearly gates. My soul, hast thou gathered the rose of Sharon ? Dost thou wear the lily of the valley in thy bosom constantly ? If so, when thou comest up to the gates of heaven thou wilt know its value, for thou hast only to show this choicest of flowers, and the Porter will open : not for a moment will He deny thee an mission, for to that rose the Porter openeth ever. Thou shalt find thy way with the rose of Sharon in thy hand up to the throne of God Himself, for heaven itself possesses nothing that excels its radiant beauty, and of all the flowers that bloom in paradise there is none that can rival the lily of the valleys. My soul, get Calvary's blood-red rose into thy hand by faith, by love wear it, by communion preserve it, by daily watchfulness make it thine all in all, and thou shalt be blessed beyond all bliss, happy beyond a dream. Jesus, be mine for ever, my God, my heaven, my all.

"And I give unto them eternal life, and they shall never perish."—John x. 28.

THE Christian should never think or speak lightly of unbelief. For a child of God to mistrust His love, His truth, His faithfulness, must be greatly displeasing to Him. How can we ever grieve Him by doubting His upholding grace? Christian! it is contrary to every promise of God's precious Word that thou shouldst ever be forgotten or left to perish. If it could be so, how could He be true who has said, " Can a woman forget her sucking child, that she should not have compassion on the son of her womb ? Yea, they may forget, yet will I never forget thee." What were the value of that promise— " The mountains shall depart, and the hills be removed ; but My kindness shall not depart from thee, neither shall the covenant of My peace be removed, saith the Lord that hath mercy on thee "? Where were the truth of Christ's words—" I give unto My sheep eternal life ; and they shall never perish, neither shall any man pluck them out of My hand. My Father, which gave them Me, is greater than all; and no man is able to pluck them out of My Father's hand"? Where were the doctrines of grace ? They would be all disproved if one child of God should perish. Where were the veracity of God, His honour, His power, His grace, His covenant, His oath, if any of those for whom Christ has died, and who have put their trust in Him, should nevertheless be cast away ? Banish those unbelieving fears which so dishonour God. Arise, shake thyself from the dust, and put on thy beautiful garments. Remember it is sinful to doubt His Word wherein He has promised thee that thou shalt never perish. Let the eternal life within thee express itself in confident rejoicing.

> " The gospel bears my spirit up:
>   A faithful and unchanging God
>   Lays the foundation for my hope,
>   In oaths, and promises, and blood."

"The Lord is my light and my salvation; whom shall I fear? the Lord is the strength of my life; of whom shall I be afraid?"—Psalm xxvii. 1.

"THE Lord is my light and my salvation." Here is personal interest, *"my light," "my salvation;"* the soul is assured of it, and therefore declares it boldly. Into the soul at the new birth divine light is poured as the precursor of salvation; where there is not enough light to reveal our own darkness and to make us long for the Lord Jesus, there is no evidence of salvation. After conversion our God is our joy, comfort, guide, teacher, and in every sense our light: He is light within, light around, light reflected from us, and light to be revealed to us. Note, it is not said merely that the Lord gives light, but that He *is* light; nor that He gives salvation, but that He *is* salvation; he, then, who by faith has laid hold upon God, has all covenant blessings in his possession. This being made sure as a fact, the argument drawn from it is put in the form of a question, *"Whom shall I fear?"* A question which is its own answer. The powers of darkness are not to be feared, for the Lord, our light, destroys them; and the damnation of hell is not to be dreaded by us, for the Lord is our salvation. This is a very different challenge from that of boastful Goliath, for it rests, not upon the conceited vigour of an arm of flesh, but upon the real power of the omnipotent I AM. *"The Lord is the strength of my life."* Here is a third glowing epithet, to show that the writer's hope was fastened with a threefold cord which could not be broken. We may well accumulate terms of praise where the Lord lavishes deeds of grace. Our life derives all its strength from God; and if He deigns to make us strong, we cannot be weakened by all the machinations of the adversary. *"Of whom shall I be afraid?"* The bold question looks into the future as well as the present. "If God be for us," who can be against us, either now or in time to come?

"Help, Lord."—Psalm xii. 1.

THE prayer itself is remarkable, for it is *short*, but *seasonable*, *sententious*, and *suggestive*. David mourned the fewness of faithful men, and therefore lifted up his heart in supplication ; when the creature failed, he flew to the Creator. He evidently felt his own weakness, or he would not have cried for help ; but at the same time he intended honestly to exert himself for the cause of truth, for the word "help" is inapplicable where we ourselves do nothing. There is much of *directness, clearness of perception,* and *distinctness of utterance* in this petition of two words ; much more, indeed, than in the long rambling outpourings of certain professors. The Psalmist runs straightforward to his God, with a well-considered prayer ; he knows what he is seeking, and where to seek it. Lord, teach us to pray in the same blessed manner.

The occasions for the use of this prayer are frequent. In *providential afflictions* how suitable it is for tried believers who find all helpers failing them. Students, in *doctrinal difficulties,* may often obtain aid by lifting up this cry of "Help, Lord," to the Holy Spirit, the great Teacher. Spiritual warriors in *inward conflicts* may send to the throne for reinforcements, and this will be a model for their request. Workers in *heavenly labour* may thus obtain grace in time of need. Seeking sinners, in *doubts and alarms,* may offer up the same weighty supplication ; in fact, in all cases, times, and places, this will serve the turn of needy souls. "Help, Lord," will suit us living and dying, suffering or labouring, rejoicing or sorrowing. In Him our help is found, let us not be slack to cry to Him.

The answer to the prayer is certain, if it be sincerely offered through Jesus. The Lord's character assures us that He will not leave His people ; His relationship as Father and Husband guarantee us His aid ; His gift of Jesus is a pledge of every good thing ; and His sure promise stands, "Fear not, I WILL HELP THEE."

" Then Israel sang this song, Spring up, O well; sing ye unto it."—Numbers xxi. 17.

AMOUS was the well of Beer in the wilderness, because it was *the subject of a promise :* "That is the well whereof the Lord spake unto Moses, Gather the people together, and I will give them water." The people needed water, and it was promised by their gracious God. We need fresh supplies of heavenly grace, and in the covenant the Lord has pledged Himself to give all we require. The well next became *the cause of a song.* Before the water gushed forth, cheerful faith prompted the people to sing ; and as they saw the crystal fount bubbling up, the music grew yet more joyous. In like manner, we who believe the promise of God should rejoice in the prospect of divine revivals in our souls, and as we experience them our holy joy should overflow. Are we thirsting ? Let us not murmur, but sing. Spiritual thirst is bitter to bear, but we need not bear it—the promise indicates a well ; let us be of good heart, and look for it. Moreover, the well was *the centre of prayer.* "Spring up, O well." What God has engaged to give, we must enquire after, or we manifest that we have neither desire nor faith. This evening let us ask that the Scripture we have read, and our devotional exercises, may not be an empty formality, but a channel of grace to our souls. O that God the Holy Spirit would work in us with all His mighty power, filling us with all the fulness of God. Lastly, the well was *the object of effort.* "The nobles of the people digged it with their staves." The Lord would have us active in obtaining grace. Our staves are ill adapted for digging in the sand, but we must use them to the utmost of our ability. Prayer must not be neglected ; the assembling of ourselves together must not be forsaken : ordinances must not be slighted. The Lord will give us His grace most plenteously, but not in a way of idleness. Let us, then, bestir ourselves to seek Him in whom are all our fresh springs.

" Thy Redeemer."—Is. liv. 5.

JESUS, the Redeemer, is altogether ours and ours for ever. All the *offices* of Christ are held on our behalf. He is king for us, priest for us, and prophet for us. Whenever we read a new title of the Redeemer, let us appropriate Him as ours under that name as much as under any other. The shepherd's staff, the father's rod, the captain's sword, the priest's mitre, the prince's sceptre, the prophet's mantle, all are ours. Jesus hath no dignity which he will not employ for our exaltation, and no prerogative which he will not exercise for our defence. His fulness of *Godhead* is our unfailing, inexhaustible treasure-house.

His *manhood* also, which he took upon him for us, is ours in all its perfection. To us our gracious Lord communicates the spotless virtue of a stainless character; to us he gives the meritorious efficacy of a devoted life; on us he bestows the reward procured by obedient submission and incessant service. He makes the unsullied garment of his life our covering beauty; the glittering virtues of his character our ornaments and jewels; and the superhuman meekness of his death our boast and glory. He bequeaths us his manger, from which to learn how God came down to man; and his Cross to teach us how man may go up to God. All his thoughts, emotions, actions, utterances, miracles, and intercessions, were for us. He trod the road of sorrow on our behalf, and hath made over to us as his heavenly legacy the full results of all the labours of his life. He is now as much ours as heretofore; and he blushes not to acknowledge himself "*our* Lord Jesus Christ," though he is the blessed and only Potentate, the King of kings, and Lord of lords. Christ everywhere and every way is our Christ, for ever and ever most richly to enjoy. O my soul, by the power of the Holy Spirit! call him this morning, "thy Redeemer."

"I am come into my garden, my sister, my spouse."—Cant. v. 1.

THE heart of the believer is Christ's garden. He bought it with His precious blood, and He enters it and claims it as His own. A garden *implies separation*. It is not the open common; it is not a wilderness; it is walled around, or hedged in. Would that we could see the wall of separation between the church and the world made broader and stronger. It makes one sad to hear Christians saying, "Well, there is no harm in this; there is no harm in that," thus getting as near to the world as possible. Grace is at a low ebb in that soul which can even raise the question of how far it may go in worldly conformity. A garden is *a place of beauty*, it far surpasses the wild uncultivated lands. The genuine Christian must seek to be more excellent in his life than the best moralist, because Christ's garden ought to produce the best flowers in all the world. Even the best is poor compared with Christ's deservings: let us not put Him off with withering and dwarf plants. The rarest, richest, choicest lilies and roses ought to bloom in the place which Jesus calls His own. The garden is *a place of growth*. The saints are not to remain undeveloped, always mere buds and blossoms. We should grow in grace, and in the knowledge of our Lord and Saviour Jesus Christ. Growth should be rapid where Jesus is the Husbandman, and the Holy Spirit the dew from above. A garden is *a place of retirement*. So the Lord Jesus Christ would have us reserve our souls as a place in which He can manifest Himself, as He doth not unto the world. O that Christians were more retired, that they kept their hearts more closely shut up for Christ! We often worry and trouble ourselves, like Martha, with much serving, so that we have not the room for Christ that Mary had, and do not sit at His feet as we should. The Lord grant the sweet showers of His grace to water His garden this day.

"And they were all filled with the Holy Ghost."—Acts ii. 4.

RICH were the blessings of this day if all of us were filled with the Holy Ghost. The consequences of this sacred filling of the soul it would be impossible to overestimate. Life, comfort, light, purity, power, peace ; and many other precious blessings are inseparable from the Spirit's benign presence. As sacred *oil*, he anoints the head of the believer, sets him apart to the priesthood of saints, and gives him grace to execute his office aright. As the only truly purifying *water* He cleanses us from the power of sin and sanctifies us unto holiness, working in us to will and to do of the Lord's good pleasure. As the *light*, he manifested to us at first our lost estate, and now He reveals the Lord Jesus to us and in us, and guides us in the way of righteousness. Enlightened by his pure celestial ray, we are no more darkness but light in the Lord. *As fire*, he both purges us from dross, and sets our consecrated nature on a blaze. He is the sacrificial flame by which we are enabled to offer our whole souls as a living sacrifice unto God. As heavenly *dew*, He removes our barrenness and fertilizes our lives. O that He would drop from above upon us at this early hour! Such morning dew would be a sweet commencement for the day. As the *dove*, with wings of peaceful love He broods over His Church and over the souls of believers, and as a Comforter He dispels the cares and doubts which mar the peace of His beloved. He descends upon the chosen as upon the Lord in Jordan, and bears witness to their sonship by working in them a filial spirit by which they cry Abba, Father. As the *wind*, He brings the breath of life to men ; blowing where He listeth He performs the quickening operations by which the spiritual creation is animated and sustained. Would to God, that we might feel His presence this day and every day.

*" My Beloved is mine, and I am His : He feedeth among
the lilies.   Until the day break, and the shadows flee away,
turn, my Beloved, and be Thou like a roe or a young hart
upon the mountains of Bether."*—Solomon's Song ii. 16, 17.

SURELY if there be a happy verse in the Bible
it is this—" My Beloved is mine, and I am
His." So peaceful, so full of assurance, so
overrunning with happiness and contentment is it,
that it might well have been written by the same
hand which penned the twenty-third Psalm. Yet
though the prospect is exceeding fair and lovely—
earth cannot show its superior—it is not entirely a
sunlit landscape. There is a cloud in the sky which
casts a shadow over the scene. Listen, " Until the
day break, and the shadows flee away."

There is a word, too, about the " mountains of
Bether," or, " the mountains of division," and to
our love, anything like division is bitterness.
Beloved, this may be your present state of mind;
you do not doubt your salvation; you know
that Christ is yours, but you are not feasting
with Him. You understand your vital interest in
Him, so that you have no shadow of a doubt of your
being His, and of His being yours, but still His left
hand is not under your head, nor doth His right
hand embrace you. A shade of sadness is cast over
your heart, perhaps by affliction, certainly by the
temporary absence of your Lord, so even while ex-
claiming, " I am His," you are forced to take to your
knees, and to pray, " Until the day break, and the
shadows flee away, turn, my Beloved."

" Where is He?" asks the soul. And the answer
comes, " He feedeth among the lilies." If we would
find Christ, we must get into communion with His
people, we must come to the ordinances with His
saints. Oh, for an evening glimpse of Him! Oh,
to sup with him to-night!

"For, lo, I will command, and I will sift the house Israel among all nations, like as corn is sifted in a sieve, yet shall not the least grain fall upon the earth."—Amos ix. 9.

EVERY sifting comes by *divine command and permission.* Satan must ask leave before he can lay a finger upon Job. Nay, more, in some sense our siftings are *directly the work of heaven,* for the text says, "I will sift the house of Israel." Satan, like a drudge, may hold the sieve, hoping to destroy the corn ; but the overruling hand of the Master is accomplishing the purity of the grain by the very process which the enemy intended to be destructive. Precious, but much sifted corn of the Lord's floor, be comforted by the blessed fact that the Lord directeth both flail and sieve to His own glory, and to thine eternal profit.

The Lord Jesus will surely use the fan which is in His hand, and will *divide the precious from the vile.* All are not Israel that are of Israel ; the heap on the barn floor is not clean provender, and hence the winnowing process must be performed. In the sieve true weight alone has power. Husks and chaff being devoid of substance must fly before the wind, and only solid corn will remain.

Observe the *complete safety of the Lord's wheat ;* even the least grain has a promise of preservation. God Himself sifts, and therefore it is stern and terrible work ; He sifts them in all places, "among all nations ;" He sifts them in the most effectual manner, "like as corn is sifted in a sieve ;" and yet for all this, not the smallest, lightest, or most shrivelled grain, is permitted to fall to the ground. Every individual believer is precious in the sight of the Lord ; a shepherd would not lose one sheep, nor a jeweller one diamond, nor a mother one child, nor a man one limb of his body, nor will the Lord lose one of his redeemed people. However little we may be, if we are the Lord's, we may rejoice that we are preserved in Christ Jesus.

" Straightway they forsook their nets, and followed Him."
Mark i. 18.

WHEN they heard the call of Jesus, Simon and Andrew obeyed at once without demur. If we would always, punctually and with resolute zeal, put in practice what we hear upon the spot, or at the first fit occasion, our attendance at the means of grace, and our reading of good books, could not fail to enrich us spiritually. He will not lose his loaf who has taken care at once to eat it, neither can he be deprived of the benefit of the doctrine who has already acted upon it. Most readers and hearers become moved so far as to purpose to amend; but, alas! the proposal is a blossom which has not been knit, and therefore no fruit comes of it; they wait, they waver, and then they forget, till, like the ponds in nights of frost, when the sun shines by day, they are only thawed in time to be frozen again. That fatal *to-morrow* is blood-red with the murder of fair resolutions; it is the slaughter-house of the innocents. We are very concerned that our little book of " Evening Readings " should not be fruitless, and therefore we pray that readers may not be readers only, but doers, of the word. *The practice of truth is the most profitable reading of it.* Should the reader be impressed with any duty while perusing these pages, let him hasten to fulfil it before the holy glow has departed from his soul, and let him leave his nets, and all that he has, sooner than be found rebellious to the Master's call. Do not give place to the devil by delay! Haste while opportunity and quickening are in happy conjunction. Do not be caught in your own nets, but break the meshes of worldliness, and away where glory calls you. Happy is the writer who shall meet with readers resolved to carry out his teachings : his harvest shall be a hundredfold, and his Master shall have great honour. Would to God that such might be our reward upon these brief meditations and hurried hints. Grant it, O Lord, unto thy servant!

" Thou art fairer than the children of men."—Ps. xlv. 2.

THE entire person of Jesus is but as one gem,
and His life is all along but one impression of
the seal. He is altogether complete ; not only
in His several parts, but as a gracious all-glorious
whole. His character is not a mass of fair colours
mixed confusedly, nor a heap of precious stones laid
carelessly one upon another; He is a picture of beauty
and a breastplate of glory. In Him, all the "things
of good repute" are in their proper places, and assist
in adorning each other. Not one feature in His glorious person attracts attention at the expense of others;
but he is perfectly and altogether lovely.

Oh, Jesus ! Thy power, Thy grace, Thy justice, Thy
tenderness, Thy truth, Thy majesty, and Thine immutability make up such a man, or rather such a God-
man, as neither heaven nor earth hath seen elsewhere.
Thy infancy,Thy eternity,Thy sufferings,Thy triumphs,
Thy death, and Thine immortality, are all woven in one
gorgeous tapestry, without seam or rent. Thou art
music without discord ; Thou art many, and yet not
divided ; Thou art all things, and yet not diverse. As
all the colours blend into one resplendent rainbow, so
all the glories of heaven and earth meet in Thee, and
unite so wondrously, that there is none like Thee in
all things ; nay, if all the virtues of the most excellent
were bound in one bundle, they could not rival Thee,
Thou mirror of all perfection. Thou hast been anointed
with the holy oil of myrrh and cassia, which Thy God
hath reserved for Thee alone ; and as for Thy fragrance,
it is as the holy perfume, the like of which none other
can ever mingle, even with the art of the apothecary;
each spice is fragrant, but the compound is divine.

> " Oh, sacred symmetry ! oh, rare connection
> Of many perfects, to make one perfection !
> Oh, heavenly music, where all parts do meet
> In one sweet strain, to make one perfect sweet !"

" The foundation of God standeth sure."—2 Timothy ii. 19

HE foundation upon which our faith rests is
this, that "God was in Christ reconciling the
world unto himself, not imputing their trespasses unto them." The great fact on which genuine
faith relies is, that "the Word was made flesh and
dwelt among us," and that " Christ also hath suffered
for sin, the just for the unjust, that He might bring
us to God;" "Who Himself bare our sins in His
own body on the tree;" "For the chastisement of
our peace was upon Him, and by His stripes we
are healed." In one word, the great pillar of the
Christian's hope is *substitution.* The vicarious sacrifice
of Christ for the guilty, Christ being made sin for us
that we might be made the righteousness of God in
Him, Christ offering up a true and proper expiatory
and substitutionary sacrifice in the room, place, and
stead of as many as the Father gave Him, who are
known to God by name, and are recognised in their
own hearts by their trusting in Jesus—this is the
cardinal fact of the gospel. If this foundation were
removed, what could we do ?   But it standeth firm as
the throne of God.   We know it ; we rest on it ; we
rejoice in it ; and our delight is to hold it, to meditate upon it, and to proclaim it, while we desire to be
actuated and moved by gratitude for it in every part
of our life and conversation.   In these days a direct
attack is made upon the doctrine of the atonement.
Men cannot bear substitution.   They gnash their
teeth at the thought of the Lamb of God bearing the
sin of man.   But we, who know by experience the
preciousness of this truth, will proclaim it in defiance
of them confidently and unceasingly.   We will neither
dilute it nor change it, nor fritter it away in any shape
or fashion.   It shall still be Christ, a *positive substitute,* bearing human guilt and suffering in the stead
of men.   We cannot, dare not, give it up, for it is our
life, and despite every controversy we feel that " Nevertheless the foundation of God standeth sure."

" He shall build the temple of the Lord; and He shall bear the glory."—Zech. vi. 13.

CHRIST Himself is the builder of His spiritual temple, and He has built it on the mountains of His unchangeable affection, His omnipotent grace, and His infallible truthfulness. But as it was in Solomon's temple, so in this; the materials need making ready. There are the " Cedars of Lebanon," but they are not framed for the building; they are not cut down, and shaped, and made into those planks of cedar, whose odoriferous beauty shall make glad the courts of the Lord's house in Paradise. There are also the rough stones still in the quarry, they must be hewn thence, and squared. All this is Christ's own work. Each individual believer is being prepared, and polished, and made ready for his place in the temple; but Christ's own hand performs the preparation-work. Afflictions cannot sanctify, excepting as they are used by Him to this end. Our prayers and efforts cannot make us ready for heaven, apart from the hand of Jesus, who fashioneth our hearts aright.

As in the building of Solomon's temple, " there was neither hammer, nor axe, nor any tool of iron, heard in the house," because all was brought perfectly ready for the exact spot it was to occupy—so is it with the temple which Jesus builds ; the making ready is all done on earth. When we reach heaven, there will be no sanctifying us there, no squaring us with affliction, no planing us with suffering. No, we must be made meet here—all *that* Christ will do beforehand ; and when He has done it, we shall be ferried by a loving hand across the stream of death, and brought to the heavenly Jerusalem, to abide as eternal pillars in the temple of our Lord.

> " Beneath His eye and care,
> The edifice shall rise,
> Majestic, strong, and fair,
> And shine above the skies."

" That those things which cannot be shaken may remain."
Hebrews xii. 27.

E have many things in our possession at the present moment which *can* be shaken, and it ill becomes a Christian man to set much store by them, for there is nothing stable beneath these rolling skies; change is written upon all things. Yet, we have certain " things which *cannot* be shaken," and I invite you this evening to think of them, that if the things which can be shaken should all be taken away, you may derive real comfort from the things that cannot be shaken, which will remain. Whatever your losses have been, or may be, you enjoy *present salvation.* You are standing at the foot of His cross, trusting alone in the merit of Jesus' preeious blood, and no rise or fall of the markets can interfere with your salvation in Him; no breaking of banks, no failures and bankruptcies can touch that. Then you are *a child of God* this evening. God is your Father. No change of circumstances can ever rob you of *that.* Although by losses brought to poverty, and stripped bare, you can say, " He is my Father still. In my Father's house are many mansions; therefore will I not be troubled." You have another permanent blessing, namely, *the love of Jesus Christ.* He who is God and Man loves you with all the strength of His affectionate nature—nothing can affect *that.* The fig tree may not blossom, and the flocks may cease from the field, it matters not to the man who can sing, " My Beloved is mine, and I am His." Our best portion and richest heritage we cannot lose. Whatever troubles come, let us play the man; let us show that we are not such little children as to be cast down by what may happen in this poor fleeting state of time. Our country is Immanuel's land, our hope is above the sky, and, therefore, calm as the summer's ocean; we will see the wreck of everything earthborn, and yet rejoice in the God of our salvation.

" Ephraim is a cake not turned."—Hosea vii. 8.

A CAKE not turned is *uncooked on one side ;* and so Ephraim was, in many respects, untouched by divine grace : though there was some partial obedience, there was very much rebellion left. My soul, I charge thee, see whether this be thy case. Art thou thorough in the things of God ? Has grace gone through the very centre of thy being so as to be felt in its divine operations in all thy powers, thy actions, thy words, and thy thoughts ? To be sanctified, spirit, soul, and body, should be thine aim and prayer ; and although sanctification may not be perfect in thee anywhere in degree, yet it must be universal in its action ; there must not be the appearance of holiness in one place and reigning sin in another, else thou, too, wilt be a cake not turned.

A cake not turned *is soon burnt on the side nearest the fire,* and although no man can have too much religion, there are some who seem burnt black with bigoted zeal for that part of truth which they have received, or are charred to a cinder with a vain-glorious Pharisaic ostentation of those religious performances which suit their humour. The assumed appearance of superior sanctity frequently accompanies a total absence of all vital godliness. The saint in public is a devil in private. He deals in flour by day and in soot by night. The cake which is burned on one side, is dough on the other.

If it be so with me, O Lord, turn me ! Turn my unsanctified nature to the fire of Thy love and let it feel the sacred glow, and let my burnt side cool a little while I learn my own weakness and want of heat when I am removed from thy heavenly flame. Let me not be found a double-minded man, but one entirely under the powerful influence of reigning grace ; for well I know if I am left like a cake unturned, and am not on both sides the subject of Thy grace, I must be consumed for ever amid everlasting burnings.

" *Waiting for the adoption*."—Romans viii. 23.

EVEN in this world saints are God's children, but men cannot discover them to be so, except by certain moral characteristics. The adoption is not manifested, the children are not yet openly declared. Among the Romans a man might adopt a child, and keep it private for a long time : but there was a second adoption in public ; when the child was brought before the constituted authorities its former garments were taken off, and the father who took it to be his child gave it raiment suitable to its new condition of life. " Beloved, now are we the sons of God, and it doth not yet appear what we shall be." We are not yet arrayed in the apparel which befits the royal family of heaven; we are wearing in this flesh and blood just what we wore as the sons of Adam ; but we know that " when *He* shall appear " who is the " first-born among many brethren," we shall be like Him, we shall see Him as He is. Cannot you imagine that a child taken from the lowest ranks of society, and adopted by a Roman senator, would say to himself, " I long for the day when I shall be publicly adopted. Then I shall leave off these plebeian garments, and be robed as becomes my senatorial rank "? Happy in what he has received, for that very reason he groans to get the fulness of what is promised him. So it is with us to-day. We are waiting till we shall put on our proper garments, and shall be manifested as the children of God. We are young nobles, and have not yet worn our coronets. We are young brides, and the marriage day is not yet come, and by the love our Spouse bears us, we are led to long and sigh for the bridal morning. Our very happiness makes us groan after more ; our joy, like a swollen spring, longs to well up like an Iceland geyser, leaping to the skies, and it heaves and groans within our spirit for want of space and room by which to manifest itself to men.

" A certain woman of the company lifted up her voice, and said unto Him, Blessed is the womb that bare Thee, and the paps which thou hast sucked.   But He said, Yea rather, blessed are they that hear the word of God, and keep it."— Luke xi. 27, 28.

IT is fondly imagined by some that it must have involved very special privileges to have been the mother of our Lord, because they supposed that she had the benefit of looking into His very heart in a way in which we cannot hope to do. There may be an appearance of plausibility in the supposition, but not much. We do not know that Mary knew more than others ; what she did know she did well to lay up in her heart ; but she does not appear from anything we read in the Evangelists to have been a better-instructed believer than any other of Christ's disciples. All that she knew we also may discover. Do you wonder that we should say so ? Here is a text to prove it : "The secret of the Lord is with them that fear Him, and He will show them His covenant."   Remember the Master's words—" Henceforth I call you not serv ants ; for the servant knoweth not what his Lord doeth : but I have called you friends; for all things that I have heard of my Father I have made known unto you." So blessedly does this Divine Revealer of secrets tell us His heart, that He keepeth back nothing which is profitable to us ; His own assurance is, " If it were not so, I would have told you."   Doth He not this day manifest Himself unto us as He doth not unto the world ? It is even so ; and therefore we will not ignorantly cry out, " Blessed is the womb that bare thee," but we will intelligently bless God that, having heard the Word and kept it, we have first of all as true a communion with the Saviour as the Virgin had, and in the second place as true an acquaintance with the secrets of His heart as she can be supposed to have obtained. Happy soul to be thus privileged !

*" Shadrach, Meshach, and Abed-nego, answered and said . . .
Be it known unto thee, O king, that we will not serve thy
gods."*—Daniel iii. 16. 18.

THE narrative of the manly courage and marvellous deliverance of the three holy children,
or rather champions, is well calculated to
excite in the minds of believers firmness and steadfastness in upholding the truth in the teeth of tyranny
and in the very jaws of death. Let young Christians
especially learn from their example, both in matters
of faith in religion, and matters of uprightness in
business, never to sacrifice their consciences. Lose
all rather than lose your integrity, and when all else
is gone, still hold fast a clear conscience as the rarest
jewel which can adorn the bosom of a mortal. Be not
guided by the will-o'-the-wisp of policy, but by the
pole-star of divine authority. Follow the right at all
hazards. When you see no present advantage, walk
by faith and not by sight. Do God the honour to
trust Him when it comes to matters of loss for the
sake of principle. See whether He will be your debtor!
See if He doth not even in this life prove His word
that "Godliness, with contentment, is great gain,"
and that they who " seek first the kingdom of God
and His righteousness, shall have all these things
added unto them." Should it happen that, in the
providence of God, you are a loser by conscience, you
shall find that if the Lord pays you not back in the
silver of earthly prosperity, He will discharge His
promise in the gold of spiritual joy. Remember that
a man's life consisteth not in the abundance of that
which he possesseth. To wear a guileless spirit, to
have a heart void of offence, to have the favour and
smile of God, is greater riches than the mines of
Ophir could yield, or the traffic of Tyre could win.
" Better is a dinner of herbs where love is, than a
stalled ox and inward contention therewith." An
ounce of heart's-ease is worth a ton of gold.

" Get thee up into the high mountain."—Isaiah xl. 9.

OUR knowledge of Christ is somewhat like climbing one of our Welsh mountains. When you are at the base you see but little : the mountain itself appears to be but one-half as high as it really is. Confined in a little valley, you discover scarcely anything but the rippling brooks as they descend into the stream at the foot of the mountain. Climb the first rising knoll, and the valley lengthens and widens beneath your feet. Go higher, and you see the country for four or five miles round, and you are delighted with the widening prospect. Mount still, and the scene enlarges ; till at last, when you are on the summit, and look east, west, north, and south, you see almost all England lying before you. Yonder is a forest in some distant county, perhaps two hundred miles away, and here the sea, and there a shining river and the smoking chimneys of a manufacturing town, or the masts of the ships in a busy port. All these things please and delight you, and you say, " I could not have imagined that so much could be seen at this elevation." Now, the Christian life is of the same order. When we first believe in Christ we see but little of Him. The higher we climb the more we discover of His beauties. But who has ever gained the summit ? Who has known all the heights and depths of the love of Christ which passes knowledge ? Paul, when grown old, sitting greyhaired, shivering in a dungeon in Rome, could say with greater emphasis than we can, " I know whom I have believed," for each experience had been like the climbing of a hill, each trial had been like ascending another summit, and his death seemed like gaining the top of the mountain, from which he could see the whole of the faithfulness and the love of Him to whom he had committed his soul. Get thee up, dear friend, into the high mountain.

" The dove found no rest for the sole of her foot."—Gen. viii. 9.

READER, can you find rest apart from the ark, Christ Jesus? Then be assured that your religion is vain. Are you satisfied with anything short of a conscious knowledge of your union and interest in Christ? Then woe unto you. If you profess to be a Christian, yet find full satisfaction in worldly pleasures and pursuits, your profession is false. If your soul can stretch herself at rest, and find the bed long enough, and the coverlet broad enough to cover her in the chambers of sin, then you are a hypocrite, and far enough from any right thoughts of Christ or perception of His preciousness. But if, on the other hand, you feel that if you could indulge in sin without punishment, yet it would be a punishment of itself; and that if you could have the whole world, and abide in it for ever, it would be quite enough misery not to be parted from it; for your God—your God—is what your soul craves after; then be of good courage, thou art a child of God. With all thy sins and imperfections, take this to thy comfort : if thy soul has no rest in sin, thou are not as the sinner is! If thou art still crying after and craving after something better, Christ has not forgotten thee, for thou hast not quite forgotten Him. The believer cannot do without his Lord ; words are inadequate to express his thoughts of Him. We cannot live on the sands of the wilderness, we want the manna which drops from on high ; our skin bottles of creature confidence cannot yield us a drop of moisture, but we drink of the rock which follows us, and that rock is Christ. When you feed on Him your soul can sing, " He hath satisfied my mouth with good things, so that my youth is renewed like the eagle's," but if you have Him not, your bursting wine vat and well-filled barn can give you no sort of satisfaction : rather lament over them in the words of wisdom, " Vanity of vanities, all is vanity !"

" Art thou become like unto us ? "—Isaiah xiv. 10.

WHAT must be the apostate professor's doom when his naked soul appears before God? How will he bear that voice, " Depart, ye cursed ; thou hast rejected me, and I reject thee ; thou hast played the harlot, and departed from Me : I also have banished thee for ever from my presence, and will will not have mercy upon thee." What will be this wretch's shame at the last great day when, before assembled multitudes, the apostate shall be unmasked ? See the profane, and sinners who never professed religion, lifting themselves up from their beds of fire to point at him. " There he is," says one, "will he preach the gospel in hell ?" " There he is," says another, " he rebuked me for cursing, and was a hypocrite himself ! " " Aha !" says another, " here comes a psalm-singing Methodist—one who was always at his meeting ; he is the man who boasted of his being sure of everlasting life ; and here he is ! " No greater eagerness will ever be seen among Satanic tormentors, than in that day when devils drag the hypocrite's soul down to perdition. Bunyan pictures this with massive but awful grandeur of poetry when he speaks of the back-way to hell. Seven devils bound the wretch with nine cords, and dragged him from the road to heaven, in which he had professed to walk, and thrust him through the back-door into hell. Mind that back-way to hell, professors ! " Examine yourselves, whether ye be in the faith." Look well to your state ; see whether you be in Christ or not. It is the easiest thing in the world to give a lenient verdict when oneself is to be tried ; but O, be just and true here. Be just to all, but be rigorous to yourself. Remember if it be not a rock on which you build, when the house shall fall, great will be the fall of it. O may the Lord give you sincerity, constancy, and firmness ; and in no day, however evil, may you be led to turn aside.

" Having escaped the corruption that is in the world through lust."—2 Peter i. 4.

BANISH for ever all thought of indulging the flesh if you would live in the power of your risen Lord. It were ill that a man who is alive in Christ should dwell in the corruption of sin. " Why seek ye the living among the dead ?" said the angel to Magdalene. Should the living dwell in the sepulchre ? Should divine life be immured in the charnel house of fleshly lust ? How can we partake of the cup of the Lord and yet drink the cup of Belial ? Surely, believer, from open lusts and sins you are delivered : have you also escaped from the more secret and delusive lime-twigs of the Satanic fowler ? Have you come forth from the lust of pride ? Have you escaped from slothfulness ? Have you clean escaped from carnal security ? Are you seeking day by day to live above worldliness, the pride of life, and the ensnaring vice of avarice ? Remember, it is for this that you have been enriched with the treasures of God. If you be indeed the chosen of God, and beloved by Him, do not suffer all the lavish treasure of grace to be wasted upon you. Follow after holiness; it is the Christian's crown and glory. An unholy church ! it is useless to the world, and of no esteem among men. It is an abomination, hell's laughter, heaven's abhorrence. The worst evils which have ever come upon the world have been brought upon her by an unholy church. O Christian, the vows of God are upon you. You are God's priest : act as such. You are God's king : reign over your lusts. You are God's chosen ; do not associate with Belial. Heaven is your portion : live like a heavenly spirit, so shall you prove that you have true faith in Jesus, for there cannot be faith in the heart unless there be holiness in the life.

> " Lord, I desire to live as one
> Who bears a blood-bought name,
> As one who fears but grieving Thee,
> And knows no other shame."

" Only ye shall not go very far away."—Ex. viii. 28.

THIS is a crafty word from the lip of the arch-tyrant Pharaoh. If the poor bondaged Israel-ites must needs go out of Egypt, then he bargains with them that it shall not be very far away; not too far for them to escape the terror of his arms, and the observation of his spies. After the same fashion, the world loves not the nonconformity of nonconformity, or the dissidence of dissent, it would have us be more charitable and not carry matters with too severe a hand. Death to the world, and burial with Christ, are experiences which carnal minds treat with ridicule, and hence the ordinance which sets them forth is almost universally neglected, and even con-temned. Worldly wisdom recommends the path of compromise, and talks of " moderation." According to this carnal policy, purity is admitted to be very desirable, but we are warned against being too precise; truth is of course to be followed, but error is not to be severely denounced. "Yes," says the world, " be spiritually minded by all means, but do not deny yourself a little gay society, an occasional ball, and a Christmas visit to a theatre. What's the good of crying down a thing when it is so fashionable, and everybody does it ? " Multitudes of professors yield to this cunning advice, to their own eternal ruin. If we would follow the Lord wholly, we must go right away into the wilderness of separation, and leave the Egypt of the carnal world behind us. We must leave its maxims, its pleasures, and its religion too, and go far away to the place where the Lord calls His sanctified ones. When the town is on fire, our house cannot be too far from the flames. When the plague is abroad, a man cannot be too far from its haunts. The further from a viper the better, and the further from worldly conformity the better. To all true believers let the trumpet-call be sounded, " Come ye out from among them, be ye separate."

" Let every man abide in the same calling wherein he was called."—1 Corinthians vii. 20.

SOME persons have the foolish notion that the only way in which they can live for God is by becoming ministers, missionaries, or Bible women. Alas! how many would be shut out from any opportunity of magnifying the Most High if this were the case. Beloved, it is not office, it is earnestness ; it is not position, it is grace which will enable us to glorify God. God is most surely glorified in that cobbler's stall, where the godly worker, as he plies the awl, sings of the Saviour's love, ay, glorified far more than in many a prebendal stall where official *religiousness* performs its scanty duties. The name of Jesus is glorified by the poor unlearned carter as he drives his horse, and blesses his God, or speaks to his fellow labourer by the roadside, as much as by the popular divine who, throughout the country, like Boanerges, is thundering out the gospel. God is glorified by our serving Him in our proper vocations. Take care, dear reader, that you do not forsake the path of duty by leaving your occupation, and take care you do not dishonour your profession while in it. Think little of yourselves, but do not think too little of your callings. Every lawful trade may be sanctified by the gospel to noblest ends. Turn to the Bible, and you will find the most menial forms of labour connected either with most daring deeds of faith, or with persons whose lives have been illustrious for holiness. Therefore be not discontented with your calling. Whatever God has made your position, or your work, abide in that, unless you are *quite sure* that he calls you to something else. Let your first care be to glorify God to the utmost of your power where you are. Fill your present sphere to His praise, and if He needs you in another He will show it you. This evening lay aside vexatious ambition, and embrace peaceful content.

" Looking unto Jesus."--Heb. xii. 2.

T is ever the Holy Spirit's work to turn our
eyes away from self to Jesus; but Satan's
work is just the opposite of this, for he is constantly trying to make us regard ourselves instead of
Christ. He insinuates, " Your sins are too great for
pardon; you have no faith; you do not repent enough;
you will never be able to continue to the end; you
have not the joy of His children; you have such a
wavering hold of Jesus." All these are thoughts
about self, and we shall never find comfort or assurance by looking within. But the Holy Spirit turns our
eyes entirely away from self: He tells us that we are
nothing, but that " Christ is all in all." Remember,
therefore, it is not *thy hold* of Christ that saves thee—
it is Christ; it is not *thy joy* in Christ that saves thee—
it is Christ; it is not even faith in Christ, though that
be the instrument—it is Christ's blood and merits;
therefore, look not so much to thy hand with which
thou art grasping Christ, as to Christ; look not to thy
hope, but to Jesus, the source of thy hope; look not
to thy faith, but to Jesus, the author and finisher of
thy faith. We shall never find happiness by looking
at our prayers, our doings, or our feelings; it is what
Jesus is, not what *we* are, that gives rest to the soul.
If we would at once overcome Satan and have peace
with God, it must be by " looking unto Jesus." Keep
thine eye simply on Him; let His death, His sufferings, His merits, His glories, His intercession, be
fresh upon thy mind; when thou wakest in the morning look to Him; when thou liest down at night look
to Him. Oh! let not thy hopes or fears come between thee and Jesus; follow hard after Him, and
He will never fail thee.

> " My hope is built on nothing less
> Than Jesu's blood and righteousness:
> I dare not trust the sweetest frame,
> But wholly lean on Jesu's name."

"But Aaron's rod swallowed up their rods."—Exodus vii. 12.

THIS incident is an instructive emblem of the sure victory of the divine handiwork over all opposition. Whenever a divine principle is cast into the heart, though the devil may fashion a counterfeit, and produce swarms of opponents, as sure as ever God is in the work, it will swallow up all its foes. If God's grace takes possession of a man, the world's magicians may throw down all their rods; and every rod may be as cunning and poisonous as a serpent, but Aaron's rod will swallow up their rods. The sweet attractions of the cross will woo and win the man's heart, and he who lived only for this deceitful earth will now have an eye for the upper spheres, and a wing to mount into celestial heights. When grace has won the day the worldling seeks the world to come. The same fact is to be observed in the life of the believer. What multitudes of foes has our faith had to meet! Our old sins—the devil threw them down before us, and they turned to serpents. What hosts of them! Ah, but the cross of Jesus destroys them all. Faith in Christ makes short work of all our sins. Then the devil has launched forth another host of serpents in the form of worldly trials, temptations, unbelief; but faith in Jesus is more than a match for them, and overcomes them all. The same absorbing principle shines in the faithful service of God! with an enthusiastic love for Jesus difficulties are surmounted, sacrifices become pleasures, sufferings are honours. But, if religion is thus a consuming passion in the heart, then it follows that there are many persons who profess religion but have it not; for what they have will not bear this test. Examine yourself, my reader, on this point. Aaron's rod *proved* its heaven-given power. Is your religion doing so? If Christ be anything He must be everything. O rest not till love and faith in Jesus be the master passions of your soul!

ET us not imagine that *the soul* sleeps in insen-
sibility. "To-day shalt thou be with me in
paradise," is the whisper of Christ to every
dying saint. They "sleep in Jesus," but their souls
are before the throne of God, praising Him day and
night in His temple, singing hallelujahs to Him who
washed them from their sins in His blood. The body
sleeps in its lonely bed of earth, beneath the coverlet
of grass. But what is this sleep? The idea connected with sleep is "*rest*," and that is the thought
which the Spirit of God would convey to us. Sleep
makes each night a Sabbath for the day. Sleep shuts
fast the door of the soul, and bids all intruders tarry
for a while, that the life within may enter its summer
garden of ease. The toilworn believer quietly sleeps,
as does the weary child when it slumbers on its
mother's breast. Oh! happy they who die in the
Lord; they rest from their labours, and their works do
follow them. Their quiet repose shall never be broken
until God shall rouse them to give them their full
reward. Guarded by angel watchers, curtained by
eternal mysteries, they sleep on, the heritors of glory,
till the fulness of time shall bring the fulness of
redemption. What an awaking shall be theirs! They
were laid in their last resting place, weary and worn,
but such they shall not rise. They went to their
rest with the furrowed brow, and the wasted features,
but they wake up in beauty and glory. The shrivelled
seed, so destitute of form and comeliness, rises from
the dust a beauteous flower. The winter of the
grave gives way to the spring of redemption and
the summer of glory. Blessed is death, since it,
through the divine power, disrobes us of this work-
day garment, to clothe us with the wedding garment
of incorruption. Blessed are those who "sleep in
Jesus."

" *Howbeit, in the business of the ambassadors of the princes of
Babylon, who sent unto him to enquire of the wonder that
was done in the land, God left him, to try him, that He
might know all that was in his heart.*"—2 Chron. xxxii. 31.

HEZEKIAH was growing so inwardly great, and
priding himself so much upon the favour
of God, that self-righteousness crept in, and
through his carnal security, the grace of God was for
a time, in its more active operations, withdrawn. Here
is quite enough to account for his folly with the Babylonians ; for if the grace of God should leave the best
Christian, there is enough of sin in his heart to make
him the worst of transgressors. If left to yourselves,
you who are warmest for Christ would cool down like
Laodicea into sickening lukewarmness : you who are
sound in the faith would be white with the leprosy of
false doctrine ; you who now walk before the Lord in
excellency and integrity would reel to and fro, and
stagger with a drunkenness of evil passion. Like the
moon, we borrow our light; bright as we are when grace
shines on us, we are darkness itself when the Sun of
Righteousness withdraws Himself. *Therefore let us cry
to God never to leave us.* " Lord, take not thy Holy
Spirit from us ! withdraw not from us Thine indwelling grace ! Hast Thou not said, ' I the Lord do keep
it ; I will water it every moment : lest any hurt it, I
will keep it night and day '? Lord, keep us everywhere. Keep us when in the valley, that we murmur
not against Thy humbling hand ; keep us when on
the mountain, that we wax not giddy through being
lifted up ; keep us in youth, when our passions are
strong ; keep us in old age, when becoming conceited
of our wisdom, we may therefore prove greater fools
than the young and giddy ; keep us when we come to
die, lest, at the very last, we should deny Thee ! Keep
us living, keep us dying, keep us labouring, keep us
suffering, keep us fighting, keep us resting, keep us
everywhere, for everywhere we need Thee, O our God !"

" And the glory which Thou gavest me I have given them."
John xvii. 22.

BEHOLD the superlative liberality of the Lord Jesus, for He hath given us His all. Although a tithe of His possessions would have made a universe of angels rich beyond all thought, yet was He not content until He had given us all that He had. It would have been surprising grace if He had allowed us to eat the crumbs of His bounty beneath the table of His mercy ; but He will do nothing by halves, He makes us sit with Him and share the feast. Had He given us some small pension from His royal coffers, we should have had cause to love Him eternally ; but no, He will have His bride as rich as Himself, and He will not have a glory or a grace in which she shall not share. He has not been content with less than making us joint-heirs with Himself, so that we might have equal possessions. He has emptied all His estate into the coffers of the Church, and hath all things common with His redeemed. There is not one room in His house the key of which He will withhold from His people. He gives them full liberty to take all that He hath to be their own ; He loves them to make free with His treasure, and appropriate as much as they can possibly carry. The boundless fulness of His all-sufficiency is as free to the believer as the air he breathes. Christ hath put the flagon of His love and grace to the believer's lip, and bidden him drink on for ever ; for could he drain it, he is welcome to do so, and as he cannot exhaust it, he is bidden to drink abundantly, for it is all his own. What truer proof of fellowship can heaven or earth afford ?

> " When I stand before the throne
> Dressed in beauty not my own ;
> When I see Thee as Thou art,
> Love Thee with unsinning heart ;
> Then, Lord, shall I fully know—
> Not till then—how much I owe."

" Ah Lord God, behold, Thou hast made the heaven and the earth by thy great power and stretched out arm, and there is nothing too hard for Thee."—Jeremiah xxxii. 17.

AT the very time when the Chaldeans surrounded Jerusalem, and when the sword, famine and pestilence had desolated the land, Jeremiah was commanded by God to purchase a field, and have the deed of transfer legally sealed and witnessed. This was a strange purchase for a rational man to make. Prudence could not justify it, for it was buying with scarcely a probability that the person purchasing could ever enjoy the possession. But it was enough for Jeremiah that his God had bidden him, for well he knew that God will be justified of all His children. He reasoned thus. " Ah, Lord God ! Thou canst make this plot of ground of use to me; Thou canst rid this land of these oppressors ; Thou canst make me yet sit under my vine and my fig-tree in the heritage which I have bought ; for Thou didst make the heavens and the earth, and there is nothing too hard for Thee." This gave a majesty to the early saints, that they dared to do at God's command things which carnal reason would condemn. Whether it be a Noah who is to build a ship on dry land, an Abraham who is to offer up his only son, or a Moses who is to despise the treasures of Egypt, or a Joshua who is to besiege Jericho seven days, using no weapons but the blasts of rams' horns, they all act upon God's command, contrary to the dictates of carnal reason ; and the Lord gives them a rich reward as the result of their obedient faith. Would to God we had in the religion of these modern times a more potent infusion of this heroic faith in God. If we would venture more upon the naked promise of God, we should enter a world of wonders to which as yet we are strangers. Let Jeremiah's place of confidence be ours—nothing is too hard for the God that created the heavens and the earth.

" In summer and in winter shall it be."—Zech. xiv. 8.

THE streams of living water which flow from Jerusalem are not dried up by the parching heats of sultry midsummer any more than they were frozen by the cold winds of blustering winter. Rejoice, O my soul, that thou art spared to testify of the faithfulness of the Lord. The seasons change and thou changest, but thy Lord abides evermore the same, and the streams of His love are as deep, as broad and as full as ever. The heats of business cares and scorching trials make me need the cooling influences of the river of His grace; I may go at once and drink to the full from the inexhaustible fountain, for in summer and in winter it pours forth its flood. The upper springs are never scanty, and blessed be the name of the Lord, the nether springs cannot fail either. Elijah found Cherith dry up, but Jehovah was still the same God of providence. Job said his brethren were like deceitful brooks, but he found his God an overflowing river of consolation. The Nile is the great confidence of Egypt, but its floods are variable ; our Lord is evermore the same. By turning the course of the Euphrates, Cyrus took the city of Babylon, but no power, human or infernal, can divert the current of divine grace. The tracks of ancient rivers have been found all dry and desolate, but the streams which take their rise on the mountains of divine sovereignty and infinite love shall ever be full to the brim. Generations melt away, but the course of grace is unaltered. The river of God may sing with greater truth than the brook in the poem—

> " Men may come, and men may go,
> But I go on for ever."

How happy art thou, my soul, to be led beside such still waters! never wander to other streams, lest thou hear the Lord's rebuke, " What hast thou to do in the way of Egypt to drink of the muddy river ? "

" The voice of the Lord God walking in the garden in the cool of the day."—Genesis iii. 8.

MY soul, now that the cool of the day has come, retire awhile and hearken to the voice of thy God. He is always ready to speak with thee when thou art prepared to hear. If there be any slowness to commune it is not on His part, but altogether on thine own, for He stands at the door and knocks, and if His people will but open He rejoices to enter. But in what state is my heart, which is my Lord's garden? May I venture to hope that it is well trimmed and watered, and is bringing forth fruit fit for Him? If not, He will have much to reprove, but still I pray Him to come unto me, for nothing can so certainly bring my heart into a right condition as the presence of the Sun of Righteousness, who brings healing in His wings. Come, therefore, O Lord, my God, my soul invites Thee earnestly, and waits for thee eagerly. Come to me, O Jesus, my well-beloved, and plant fresh flowers in my garden, such as I see blooming in such perfection in Thy matchless character! Come, O my Father, who art the Husbandman, and deal with me in Thy tenderness and prudence! Come, O Holy Spirit, and bedew my whole nature, as the herbs are now moistened with the evening dews. O that God would speak to me. Speak, Lord, for Thy servant heareth! O that He would walk with me ; I am ready to give up my whole heart and mind to Him, and every other thought is hushed. I am only asking what He delights to give. I am sure that He will condescend to have fellowship with me, for He has given me His Holy Spirit to abide with me for ever. Sweet is the cool twilight, when every star seems like the eye of heaven, and the cool wind is as the breath of celestial love. My Father, my elder Brother, my sweet Comforter, speak now in lovingkindness, for Thou hast opened mine ear and I am not rebellious.

" Our heart shall rejoice in Him."—Psalm xxxiii. 21.

BLESSED is the fact that Christians can rejoice even in the deepest distress ; although trouble may surround them, they still sing ; and, like many birds, they sing best in their cages. The waves may roll over them, but their souls soon rise to the surface and see the light of God's countenance ; they have a buoyancy about them which keeps their head always above the water, and helps them to sing amid the tempest, " God is with me still." To whom shall the glory be given ? Oh ! to *Jesus*—it is all by Jesus. Trouble does not necessarily bring consolation with it to the believer, but the presence of the Son of God in the fiery furnace with him fills his heart with joy. He is sick and suffering, but Jesus visits him and makes his bed for him. He is dying, and the cold chilly waters of Jordan are gathering about him up to the neck, but Jesus puts His arms around him, and cries, " Fear not, beloved ; to die is to be blessed ; the waters of death have their fountain-head in heaven ; they are not bitter, they are sweet as nectar, for they flow from the throne of God." As the departing saint wades through the stream, and the billows gather around him, and heart and flesh fail him, the same voice sounds in his ears, " Fear not ; I am with thee ; be not dismayed ; I am thy God." As he nears the borders of the infinite unknown, and is almost affrighted to enter the realm of shades, Jesus says, " Fear not, it is your Father's good pleasure to give you the kingdom." Thus strengthened and consoled, the believer is not afraid to die ; nay, he is even willing to depart, for since he has seen Jesus as the morning star, he longs to gaze upon Him as the sun in his strength. Truly, the presence of Jesus is all the heaven we desire. He is at once

> " The glory of our brightest days ;
> The comfort of our nights."

" Unto Thee will I cry, O Lord my rock; be not silent to me: lest, if Thou be silent to me, I become like them that go down into the pit."—Psalm xxviii. 1.

CRY is the natural expression of sorrow, and a suitable utterance when all other modes of appeal fail us; but the cry must be alone directed to the Lord, for to cry to man is to waste our entreaties upon the air. When we consider the readiness of the Lord to hear, and His ability to aid, we shall see good reason for directing all our appeals at once to the God of our salvation. It will be in vain to call to the rocks in the day of judgment, but our Rock attends to our cries.

" Be not silent to me." Mere formalists may be content without answers to their prayers, but genuine suppliants cannot; they are not satisfied with the results of prayer itself in calming the mind and subduing the will—they must go further, and obtain actual replies from heaven, or they cannot rest; and those replies they long to receive at once, they dread even a little of God's silence. God's voice is often so terrible that it shakes the wilderness; but His silence is equally full of awe to an eager suppliant. When God seems to close His ear, we must not therefore close our mouths, but rather cry with more earnestness; for when our note grows shrill with eagerness and grief, He will not long deny us a hearing. What a dreadful case should we be in if the Lord should become for ever silent to our prayers? *" Lest, if Thou be silent to me, I become like them that go down into the pit."* Deprived of the God who answers prayer, we should be in a more pitiable plight than the dead in the grave, and should soon sink to the same level as the lost in hell. We *must* have answers to prayer: ours is an urgent case of dire necessity; surely the Lord will speak peace to our agitated minds, for He never can find it in His heart to permit His own elect to perish.

" The illfavoured and leanfleshed kine did eat up the seven wellfavoured and fat kine."—Gen. xli. 4.

PHARAOH'S dream has too often been my waking experience. My days of sloth have ruinously destroyed all that I had achieved in times of zealous industry; my seasons of coldness have frozen all the genial glow of my periods of fervency and enthusiasm; and my fits of worldliness have thrown me back from my advances in the divine life. I had need to beware of lean prayers, lean praises, lean duties, and lean experiences, for these will eat up the fat of my comfort and peace. If I neglect prayer for never so short a time, I lose all the spirituality to which I had attained; if I draw no fresh supplies from heaven, the old corn in my granary is soon consumed by the famine which rages in my soul. When the caterpillars of indifference, the cankerworms of worldliness, and the palmerworms of self-indulgence, lay my heart completely desolate, and make my soul to languish, all my former fruitfulness and growth in grace avails me nothing whatever. How anxious should I be to have no lean-fleshed days, no ill-favoured hours! If every day I journeyed towards the goal of my desires I should soon reach it, but backsliding leaves me still far off from the prize of my high calling, and robs me of the advances which I had so laboriously made. The only way in which all my days can be as the "fat kine," is to feed them in the right meadow, to spend them with the Lord, in His service, in His company, in His fear, and in His way. Why should not every year be richer than the past, in love, and usefulness, and joy?—I am nearer the celestial hills, I have had more experience of my Lord, and should be more like Him. O Lord, keep far from me the curse of leanness of soul; let me not have to cry, "My leanness, my leanness, woe unto me!" but may I be well-fed and nourished in Thy house, that I may praise Thy name.

" If we suffer, we shall also reign with Him."—2 Tim. ii. 12.

E *must not imagine that we are suffering for Christ, and with Christ, if we are not in Christ.* Beloved friend, are you trusting to Jesus only? If not, whatever you may have to mourn over on earth, you are not "suffering with Christ," and have no hope of reigning with Him in heaven. Neither are we to conclude that all a Christian's sufferings are sufferings with Christ, for *it is essential that he be called by God to suffer.* If we are rash and imprudent, and run into positions for which neither providence nor grace has fitted us, we ought to question whether we are not rather sinning than communing with Jesus. If we let passion take the place of judgment, and self-will reign instead of Scriptural authority, we shall fight the Lord's battles with the devil's weapons, and if we cut our own fingers we must not be surprised. Again, *in troubles which come upon us as the result of sin, we must not dream that we are suffering with Christ.* When Miriam spoke evil of Moses, and the leprosy polluted her, she was not suffering for God. Moreover, suffering which God accepts *must have God's glory as its end.* If I suffer that I may earn a name, or win applause, I shall get no other reward than that of the Pharisee. It is requisite also *that love to Jesus, and love to his elect, be ever the mainspring of all our patience. We must manifest the Spirit of Christ* in meekness, gentleness, and forgiveness. Let us search and see if we truly *suffer with Jesus.* And if we do thus suffer, what is our "light affliction" compared with *reigning with Him?* Oh it is so blessed to be in the furnace with Christ, and such an honour to stand in the pillory with Him, that if there were no future reward, we might count ourselves happy in present honour; but when the recompense is so eternal, so infinitely more than we had any right to expect, shall we not take up the cross with alacrity, and go on our way rejoicing?

" Sanctify them through Thy truth."—John xvii. 17.

SANCTIFICATION begins in regeneration. The Spirit of God infuses into man that new living principle by which he becomes "a new creature" in Christ Jesus. This work, which begins in the new birth, is carried on in two ways—mortification, whereby the lusts of the flesh are subdued and kept under ; and vivification, by which the life which God has put within us is made to be a well of water springing up unto everlasting life. This is carried on every day in what is called "perseverance," by which the Christian is preserved and continued in a gracious state, and is made to abound in good works unto the praise and glory of God ; and it culminates or comes to perfection, in "glory," when the soul, being thoroughly purged, is caught up to dwell with holy beings at the right hand of the Majesty on high. But while the Spirit of God is thus the author of sanctification, yet there is a visible agency employed which must not be forgotten. "Sanctify them," said Jesus, "through thy *truth:* thy word is truth." The passages of Scripture which prove that the instrument of our sanctification is the Word of God are very many. The Spirit of God brings to our minds the precepts and doctrines of truth, and applies them with power. These are heard in the ear, and being received in the heart, they work in us to will and to do of God's good pleasure. The truth is the sanctifier, and if we do not hear or read the truth, we shall not grow in sanctification. We only progress in sound living as we progress in sound understanding. "Thy word is a lamp unto my feet and a light unto my path." Do not say of any error, "It is a mere matter of opinion." No man indulges an error of judgment, without sooner or later tolerating an error in practice. Hold fast the truth, for by so holding the truth shall you be sanctified by the Spirit of God.

" He that hath clean hands, and a pure heart; who hath not lifted up his soul unto vanity, nor sworn deceitfully."— Psalm xxiv. 4.

OUTWARD practical holiness is a very precious mark of grace. It is to be feared that many professors have perverted the doctrine of justification by faith in such a way as to treat good works with contempt; if so, they will receive everlasting contempt at the last great day. If our hands are not clean, let us wash them in Jesus' precious blood, and so let us lift up pure hands unto God. But *" clean hands "* will not suffice, unless they are connected with *"a pure heart."* True religion is heart-work. We may wash the outside of the cup and the platter as long as we please, but if the inward parts be filthy, we are filthy altogether in the sight of God, for our hearts are more truly ourselves than our hands are ; the very life of our being lies in the inner nature, and hence the imperative need of purity within. The pure in heart shall see God, all others are but blind bats.

The man who is born for heaven *" hath not lifted up his soul unto vanity."* All men have their joys, by which their souls are lifted up; the worldling lifts up his soul in carnal delights, which are mere empty vanities ; but the saint loves more substantial things ; like Jehoshaphat, he is lifted up in the ways of the Lord. He who is content with husks, will be reckoned with the swine. Does the world satisfy thee ? Then thou hast thy reward and portion in this life ; make much of it, for thou shalt know no other joy.

" Nor sworn deceitfully." The saints are men of honour still. The Christian man's word is his only oath ; but that is as good as twenty oaths of other men. False speaking will shut any man out of heaven, for a liar shall not enter into God's house, whatever may be his professions or doings. Reader, does the text before us condemn thee. or dost thou hope to ascend into the hill of the Lord ?

"Called to be saints."—Romans i. 7.

WE are very apt to regard the apostolic saints as if they were "saints" in a more especial manner than the other children of God. All are "saints" whom God has called by His grace, and sanctified by His Spirit; but we are apt to look upon the *apostles* as extraordinary beings, scarcely subject to the same weaknesses and temptations as ourselves. Yet in so doing we are forgetful of this truth, that the nearer a man lives to God the more intensely has he to mourn over his own evil heart; and the more his Master honours him in His service, the more also doth the evil of the flesh vex and tease him day by day. The fact is, if we had seen the apostle Paul, we should have thought him remarkably like the rest of the chosen family: and if we had talked with him, we should have said, "We find that his experience and ours are much the same. He is more faithful, more holy, and more deeply taught than we are, but he has the selfsame trials to endure. Nay, in some respects he is more sorely tried than ourselves." Do not, then, look upon the ancient saints as being exempt either from infirmities or sins; and do not regard them with that mystic reverence which will almost make us idolators. Their holiness is attainable even by us. We are "called to be saints" by that same voice which constrained them to their high vocation. It is a Christian's duty to force his way into the inner circle of saintship; and if these saints were superior to us in their attainments, as they certainly were let us follow them; let us emulate their ardour and holiness. We have the same light that they had, the same grace is accessible to us, and why should we rest satisfied until we have equalled them in heavenly character? They lived *with* Jesus, they lived *for* Jesus, therefore they grew *like* Jesus. Let us live by the same Spirit as they did, "looking unto Jesus," and our saintship will soon be apparent.

" Trust ye in the Lord for ever : for in the Lord Jehovah is everlasting strength."—Isaiah xxvi. 4.

SEEING that we have such a God to trust to, let us rest upon him with all our weight; let us resolutely drive out all unbelief, and endeavour to get rid of doubts and fears, which so much mar our comfort; since there is no excuse for fear where God is the foundation of our trust. A loving parent would be sorely grieved if his child could not trust him; and how ungenerous, how unkind is our conduct when we put so little confidence in our heavenly Father who has never failed us, and who never will. It were well if doubting were banished from the household of God; but it is to be feared that old Unbelief is as nimble nowadays as when the psalmist asked, "Is His mercy clean gone for ever? Will He be favourable no more?" David had not made any very lengthy trial of the mighty sword of the giant Goliath, and yet he said, "There is none like it." He had tried it once in the hour of his youthful victory, and it had proved itself to be of the right metal, and therefore he praised it ever afterwards; even so should we speak well of our God, there is none like unto Him in the heaven above or the earth beneath; "To whom then will ye liken Me, or shall I be equal? saith the Holy One." There is no rock like unto the rock of Jacob, our enemies themselves being judges. So far from suffering doubts to live in our hearts, we will take the whole detestable crew, as Elijah did the prophets of Baal, and slay them over the brook; and for a stream to kill them at, we will select the sacred torrent which wells forth from our Saviour's wounded side. We have been in many trials, but we have never yet been cast where we could not find in our God all that we needed. Let us then be encouraged to trust in the Lord for ever, assured that His ever lasting strength will be, as it has been, our succour and stay.

*" Whoso hearkeneth unto me shall dwell safely, and shall be
quiet from fear of evil."*—Prov. i. 33.

DIVINE love is rendered conspicuous when it
shines in the midst of judgments. Fair is
that lone star which smiles through the rifts
of the thunder clouds ; bright is the oasis which blooms
in the wilderness of sand ; so fair and so bright is love
in the midst of wrath. When the Israelites provoked
the Most High by their continued idolatry, He
punished them by withholding both dew and rain, so
that their land was visited by a sore famine ; but
while He did this, He took care that His own chosen
ones should be secure. If all other brooks are dry, yet
shall there be one reserved for Elijah ; and when that
fails, God shall still preserve for him a place of
sustenance ; nay, not only so, the Lord had not simply
one "Elijah," but He had a remnant according to the
election of grace, who were hidden by fifties in a cave,
and though the whole land was subject to famine, yet
these fifties in the cave were fed, and fed from Ahab's
table too by His faithful, God-fearing steward, Obadiah.
Let us from this draw the inference, that come what
may, God's people are safe. Let convulsions shake
the solid earth, let the skies themselves be rent in
twain, yet amid the wreck of worlds the believer shall
be as secure as in the calmest hour of rest. If God
cannot save His people *under* heaven, He will save
them *in* heaven. If the world becomes too hot to
hold them, then heaven shall be the place of their
reception and their safety. Be ye then confident,
when ye hear of wars, and rumours of wars. Let no
agitation distress you, but be quiet from fear of evil.
Whatsoever cometh upon the earth, you, beneath the
broad wings of Jehovah, shall be secure. Stay yourself
upon His promise ; rest in His faithfulness, and bid
defiance to the blackest future, for there is nothing in
it direful for you. Your sole concern should be to
show forth to the world the blessedness of hearkening
to the voice of wisdom.

"How many are mine iniquities and sins?"—Job xiii. 23.

HAVE you ever really weighed and considered how great the sin of God's people is? Think how heinous is your own transgression, and you will find that not only does a sin here and there tower up like an alp, but that your iniquities are heaped upon each other, as in the old fable of the giants who piled Pelian upon Ossa, mountain upon mountain. What an aggregate of sin there is in the life of one of the most sanctified of God's children! Attempt to multiply this, the sin of one only, by the multitude of the redeemed, " a number which no man can number," and you will have some conception of the great mass of the guilt of the people for whom Jesus shed His blood. But we arrive at a more adequate idea of the magnitude of sin by the greatness of the remedy provided. It is the blood of Jesus Christ, God's only and well-beloved Son. God's Son! Angels cast their crowns before Him! All the choral symphonies of heaven surround his glorious throne. "God over all, blessed for ever. Amen." And yet He takes upon Himself the form of a servant, and is scourged and pierced, bruised and torn, and at last slain; since nothing but the blood of the incarnate Son of God could make atonement for our offences. No human mind can adequately estimate the infinite value of the divine sacrifice, for great as is the sin of God's people, the atonement which takes it away is immeasurably greater. Therefore, the believer, even when sin rolls like a black flood, and the remembrance of the past is bitter, can yet stand before the blazing throne of the great and holy God, and cry, "Who is he that condemneth? It is Christ that died; yea rather, that hath risen again." While the recollection of his sin fills him with shame and sorrow, he at the same time makes it a foil to show the brightness of mercy—guilt is the dark night in which the fair star of divine love shines with serene splendour.

" Brethren, pray for us."—1 Thess. v. 25.

THIS one morning in the year we reserved to refresh the reader's memory upon the subject of prayer for ministers, and we do most earnestly implore every Christian household to grant the fervent request of the text first uttered by an apostle and now repeated by us. Brethren, our work is solemnly momentous, involving weal or woe to thousands; we treat with souls for God on eternal business, and our word is either a savour of life unto life, or of death unto death. A very heavy responsibility rests upon us, and it will be no small mercy if at the last we be found clear of the blood of all men. As officers in Christ's army, we are the especial mark of the enmity of men and devils; they watch for our halting, and labour to take us by the heels. Our sacred calling involves us in temptations from which you are exempt, above all it too often draws us away from our personal enjoyment of truth into a ministerial and official consideration of it. We meet with many knotty cases, and our wits are at a non plus; we observe very sad backslidings, and our hearts are wounded; we see millions perishing, and our spirits sink. We wish to profit you by our preaching; we desire to be blest to your children; we long to be useful both to saints and sinners; therefore, dear friends, intercede for us with our God. Miserable men are we if we miss the aid of your prayers, but happy are we if we live in your supplications. You do not look to us but to our Master for spiritual blessings, and yet how many times has He given those blessings through His ministers; ask then, again and again, that we may be the earthen vessels into which the Lord may put the treasure of the gospel. We, the whole company of missionaries, ministers, city missionaries, and students, do in the name of Jesus beseech you

"BRETHREN, PRAY FOR US."

"When I passed by thee, I said unto thee, Live."—Ezek. xvi. 6.

SAVED one, consider gratefully this mandate of mercy. Note that this fiat of God is *majestic*. In our text, we perceive a sinner with nothing in him but sin, expecting nothing but wrath; but the eternal Lord passes by in His glory; He looks, He pauses, and He pronounces the solitary but royal word, "Live." There speaks a God. Who but He could venture thus to deal with life and dispense it with a single syllable? Again, this fiat is *manifold*. When He saith "Live," it includes many things. Here is judicial life. The sinner is ready to be condemned, but the mighty One saith, "Live," and he rises pardoned and absolved. It is spiritual life. We knew not Jesus—our eyes could not see Christ, our ears could not hear His voice—Jehovah said, "Live," and we were quickened who were dead in trespasses and sins. Moreover, it includes glory-life, which is the perfection of spiritual life. "I said unto thee, Live:" and that word rolls on through all the years of time till death comes, and in the midst of the shadows of death, the Lord's voice is still heard, "Live!" In the morning of the resurrection it is that self-same voice which is echoed by the archangel, "Live," and as holy spirits rise to heaven to be blest for ever in the glory of their God, it is in the power of this same word, "Live." Note again, that it is an *irresistible* mandate. Saul of Tarsus is on the road to Damascus to arrest the saints of the living God. A voice is heard from heaven and a light is seen above the brightness of the sun, and Saul is crying out, "Lord, what wilt thou have me to do?" This mandate is a mandate of *free grace*. When sinners are saved, it is only and solely because God *will* do it to magnify His free, unpurchased, unsought grace. Christians, see your position, debtors to grace; show your gratitude by earnest, Christlike lives, and as God has bidden you live, see to it that you live in earnest.

" Tell me I pray thee wherein thy great strength lieth."—
Judges xvi. 6.

WHERE lies the secret strength of faith ? It lies in the food it feeds on; for faith studies *what the promise is*—an emanation of divine grace, an overflowing of the great heart of God; and faith says, "My God could not have given this promise, except from love and grace; therefore it is quite certain His Word will be fulfilled." Then faith thinketh, " *Who gave* this promise ?" It considereth not so much its greatness, as, "Who is the author of it ?" She remembers that it is God who cannot lie— God omnipotent, God immutable; and therefore concludeth that the promise must be fulfilled; and forward she advances in this firm conviction. She remembereth, *why the promise was given,*—namely, for God's glory, and she feels perfectly sure that God's glory is safe, that He will never stain His own escutcheon, nor mar the lustre of His own crown; and therefore the promise must and will stand. Then faith also considereth the amazing *work of Christ* as being a clear proof of the Father's intention to fulfil His word. "He that spared not His own Son, but freely delivered Him up for us all, how shall He not with Him also freely give us all things ?" Moreover faith looks back upon *the past,* for her battles have strengthened her, and her victories have given her courage. She remembers that God never has failed her; nay, that He never did once fail any of His children. She recollecteth times of great peril, when deliverance came; hours of awful need, when as her day her strength was found, and she cries, " No, I never will be led to think that He can change and leave His servant now. Hitherto the Lord hath helped me, and He will help me still." Thus faith views each promise in its connection with the promise-giver, and, because she does so, can with assurance say, " Surely goodness and mercy shall follow me all the days of my life !"

" Lead me in Thy truth, and teach me: for Thou art the God of my salvation; on Thee do I wait all the day."—Ps. xxv. 5.

WHEN the believer has begun with trembling feet to walk in the way of the Lord, he asks to be still led onward like a little child upheld by its parent's helping hand, and he craves to be further instructed in the alphabet of truth. Experimental teaching is the burden of this prayer. David knew much, but he felt his ignorance, and desired to be still in the Lord's school : four times over in two verses he applies for a scholarship in the college of grace. It were well for many professors if instead of following their own devices, and cutting out new paths of thought for themselves, they would enquire for the good old ways of God's own truth, and beseech the Holy Ghost to give them sanctified understandings and teachable spirits. *" For thou art the God of my salvation."* The Three-One Jehovah is the Author and Perfecter of salvation to His people. Reader, is He the God of *your* salvation ? Do you find in the Father's election, in the Son's atonement, and in the Spirit's quickening, all the grounds of your eternal hopes ? If so, you may use this as an argument for obtaining further blessings ; if the Lord has ordained to save you, surely He will not refuse to instruct you in His ways. It is a happy thing when we can address the Lord with the confidence which David here manifests, it gives us great power in prayer, and comfort in trial. *" On Thee do I wait all the day."* Patience is the fair handmaid and daughter of faith ; we cheerfully wait when we are certain that we shall not wait in vain. It is our duty and our privilege to wait upon the Lord in service, in worship, in expectancy, in trust all the days of our life. Our faith will be tried faith, and if it be of the true kind, it will bear continued trial without yielding. We shall not grow weary of waiting upon God if we remember how long and how graciously He once waited for us.

" Forget not all His benefits."—Psalm ciii. 2.

IT is a delightful and profitable occupation to mark the hand of God in the lives of ancient saints, and to observe His goodness in delivering them, His mercy in pardoning them, and His faithfulness in keeping His covenant with them. But would it not be even more interesting and profitable for us to remark the hand of God in our own lives? Ought we not to look upon our own history as being at least as full of God, as full of His goodness and of His truth, as much a proof of His faithfulness and veracity, as the lives of any of the saints who have gone before? We do our Lord an injustice when we suppose that He wrought all His mighty acts, and showed Himself strong for those in the early time, but doth not perform wonders or lay bare his arm for the saints who are now upon the earth. Let us review our own lives. Surely in these we may discover some happy incidents, refreshing to ourselves and glorifying to our God. Have you had no *deliverances?* Have you passed through no rivers, supported by the divine presence? Have you walked through no fires unharmed? Have you had no *manifestations?* Have you had no *choice favours?* The God who gave Solomon the desire of his heart, hath He never listened to you and answered your requests? That God of lavish bounty of whom David sang, " Who satisfieth thy mouth with good things," hath He never satiated *you* with fatness? Have you never been made to lie down in green pastures? Have you never been led by the still waters? Surely the goodness of God has been the same to us as to the saints of old. Let us, then, weave His mercies into a song. Let us take the pure gold of thankfulness, and the jewels of praise and make them into another crown for the head of Jesus. Let our souls give forth music as sweet and as exhilarating as came from David's harp, while we praise the Lord whose mercy endureth for ever.

"And God divided the light from the darkness."—Gen. i. 4.

BELIEVER has two principles at work within him. In his natural estate he was subject to one principle only, which was darkness ; now light has entered, and the two principles disagree. Mark the apostle Paul's words in the seventh chapter of Romans : " I find then a law, that, when I would do good, evil is present with me. For I delight in the law of God after the inward man : but I see another law in my members, warring against the law of my mind, and bringing me into captivity to the law of sin, which is in my members." How is this state of things occasioned ? " The Lord divided the light from the darkness." Darkness, by itself, is quiet and undisturbed, but when the Lord sends in light, there is a conflict, for the one is in opposition to the other : a conflict which will never cease till the believer is altogether light in the Lord. If there be a division *within* the individual Christian, there is certain to be *a division without.* So soon as the Lord gives to any man light, he proceeds to separate himself from the darkness around ; he secedes from a merely worldly religion of outward ceremonial, for nothing short of the gospel of Christ will now satisfy him, and he withdraws himself from worldly society and frivolous amusements, and seeks the company of the saints, for "We know we have passed from death unto life, because we love the brethren." The light gathers to itself, and the darkness to itself. What God has divided, let us never try to unite, but as Christ went without the camp, bearing His reproach, so let us come out from the ungodly, and be a peculiar people. He was holy, harmless, undefiled, separate from sinners ; and, as He was, so we are to be nonconformists to the world, dissenting from all sin, and distinguished from the rest of mankind by our likeness to our Master.

"Fellow citizens with the saints."—Eph. ii. 19.

WHAT is meant by our being citizens in heaven? It means that *we are under heaven's government.* Christ the king of heaven reigns in our hearts; our daily prayer is, "Thy will be done on earth as it is in heaven." The proclamations issued from the throne of glory are freely received by us : the decrees of the Great King we cheerfully obey. Then as citizens of the New Jerusalem, *we share heaven's honours.* The glory which belongs to beatified saints belongs to us, for we are already sons of God, already princes of the blood imperial ; already we wear the spotless robe of Jesu's righteousness ; already we have angels for our servitors, saints for our companions, Christ for our Brother, God for our Father, and a crown of immortality for our reward. We share the honours of citizenship, for we have come to the general assembly and Church of the first-born whose names are written in heaven. As citizens, we have *common rights to all the property of heaven.* Ours are its gates of pearl and walls of chrysolite ; ours the azure light of the city that needs no candle nor light of the sun ; ours the river of the water of life, and the twelve manner of fruits which grow on the trees planted on the banks thereof ; there is nought in heaven that belongeth not to us. "Things present, or things to come," all are ours. Also as citizens of heaven we *enjoy its delights.* Do they there rejoice over sinners that repent—prodigals that have returned? So do we. Do they chant the glories of triumphant grace? We do the same. Do they cast their crowns at Jesu's feet? Such honours as we have we cast there too. Are they charmed with His smile? It is not less sweet to us who dwell below. Do they look forward, waiting for His second advent? We also look and long for His appearing. If, then, we are thus *citizens of heaven*, let our walk and actions be consistent with our high dignity.

" And the evening and the morning were the first day."
Genesis i. 5.

THE evening was " darkness " and the morning was " light," and yet *the two together are called by the name that is given to the light alone!* This is somewhat remarkable, but it has an exact analogy in spiritual experience. In every believer there is darkness and light, and yet he is not to be named a sinner because there is sin in him, but he is to be named a saint because he possesses some degree of holiness. This will be a most comforting thought to those who are mourning their infirmities, and who ask, " Can I be a child of God while there is so much darkness in me ?" Yes; for you, like the day, take not your name from the evening, but from the morning ; and you are spoken of in the word of God as if you were even now perfectly holy as you will be soon. You are called the child of light, though there is darkness in you still. You are named after what is the predominating quality in the sight of God, which will one day be the only principle remaining. Observe that *the evening comes first.* Naturally we are darkness first in order of time, and the gloom is often first in our mournful apprehension, driving us to cry out in deep humiliation, " God be merciful to me, a sinner." The place of the morning is second, it dawns when grace overcomes nature. It is a blessed aphorism of John Bunyan, " That which is last, lasts for ever." That which is first, yields in due season to the last ; but nothing comes after the last. So that though you are naturally darkness, when once you become light in the Lord, there is no evening to follow; " thy sun shall no more go down." The first day in this life is an evening and a morning ; but the second day, when we shall be with God for ever, shall be a day with no evening, but one, sacred, high, eternal noon.

"After that ye have suffered awhile, make you perfect, stablish, strengthen, settle you."—1 Peter v. 10.

YOU have seen the arch of heaven as it spans the plain : glorious are its colours, and rare its hues. It is beautiful, but, alas, it passes away, and lo, it is not. The fair colours give way to the fleecy clouds, and the sky is no longer brilliant with the tints of heaven. It is not *established.* How can it be ? A glorious show made up of transitory sunbeams and passing rain-drops, how can it abide ? The graces of the Christian character must not resemble the rainbow in its transitory beauty, but, on the contrary, must be stablished, settled, abiding. Seek, O believer, that every good thing you have may be an abiding thing. May your character not be a writing upon the sand, but an inscription upon the rock ! May your faith be no " baseless fabric of a vision," but may it be builded of material able to endure that awful fire which shall consume the wood, hay, and stubble of the hypocrite. May you be rooted and grounded in love. May your convictions be deep, your love real, your desires earnest. May your whole life be so settled and established, that all the blasts of hell, and all the storms of earth shall never be able to remove you. But notice how this blessing of being " stablished in the faith " is gained. The apostle's words point us to *suffering* as the means employed—" *After that ye have suffered awhile.*" It is of no use to hope that we shall be well rooted if no rough winds pass over us. Those old gnarlings on the root of the oak tree, and those strange twistings of the branches, all tell of the many storms that have swept over it, and they are also indicators of the depth into which the roots have forced their way. So the Christian is made strong, and firmly rooted by all the trials and storms of life. Shrink not then from the tempestuous winds of trial, but take comfort, believing that by their rough discipline God is fulfilling this benediction to you.

" Tell ye your children of it, and let your children tell their children, and their children another generation."—Joel i. 3.

IN this simple way, by God's grace, a living testimony for truth is always to be kept alive in the land—the beloved of the Lord are to hand down their witness for the gospel, and the covenant to their heirs, and these again to their next descendants. This is our *first* duty, we are to begin at the family hearth : he is a bad preacher who does not commence his ministry at home. The heathen are to be sought by all means, and the highways and hedges are to be searched, but home has a prior claim, and woe unto those who reverse the order of the Lord's arrangements. To teach our children is a *personal* duty ; we cannot delegate it to Sunday School Teachers, or other friendly aids, these can assist us, but cannot deliver us from the sacred obligation ; proxies and sponsors are wicked devices in this case : mothers and fathers must, like Abraham, command their households in the fear of God, and talk with their offspring concerning the wondrous works of the Most High. Parental teaching is a *natural* duty—who so fit to look to the child's well-being as those who are the authors of his actual being ? To neglect the instruction of our offspring is worse than brutish. Family religion is *necessary* for the nation, for the family itself, and for the church of God. By a thousand plots Popery is covertly advancing in our land, and one of the most effectual means for resisting its inroads is left almost neglected, namely, the instruction of children in the faith. Would that parents would awaken to a sense of the importance of this matter. It is a *pleasant* duty to talk of Jesus to our sons and daughters, and the more so because it has often proved to be an *accepted* work, for God has saved the children through the parents' prayers and admonitions. May every house into which this volume shall come honour the Lord and receive His smile.

" Sanctified by God the Father."—Jude 1.   *" Sanctified in Christ Jesus."*—1 Corinthians i. 2.   *" Through sanctification of the Spirit."*—1 Peter i. 2.

MARK the union of the Three Divine Persons in all their gracious acts. How unwisely do those believers talk who make preferences in the Persons of the Trinity ; who think of Jesus as if He were the embodiment of everything lovely and gracious, while the Father they regard as severely just, but destitute of kindness. Equally wrong are those who magnify the decree of the Father, and the atonement of the Son, so as to depreciate the work of the Spirit. In deeds of grace none of the Persons of the Trinity act apart from the rest. They are as united in their deeds as in their essence. In their love towards the chosen they are one, and in the actions which flow from that great central source they are still undivided. Specially notice this in the matter of sanctification. While we may without mistake speak of sanctification as the work of the Spirit, yet we must take heed that we do not view it as if the Father and the Son had no part therein. It is correct to speak of sanctification as the work of the Father, of the Son, and of the Spirit. Still doth Jehovah say, " Let *us* make man in our own image after our likeness," and thus we are " *his* workmanship, created in Christ Jesus unto good works, which God hath before ordained that we should walk in them." See the value which God sets upon real holiness, since the Three Persons in the Trinity are represented as co-working to produce a Church without " spot, or wrinkle, or any such thing." And you, believer, as the follower of Christ, must also set a high value on holiness—upon purity of life and godliness of conversation. Value the blood of Christ as the foundation of your hope, but never speak disparagingly of the work of the Spirit which is your meetness for the inheritance of the saints in light. This day let us so live as to manifest the work of the Triune God in us.

" His heavenly kingdom."—2 Timothy iv. 18.

YONDER city of the great King is a place of *active service.* Ransomed spirits serve Him day and night in His temple. They never cease to fulfil the good pleasure of their King. They always " rest," so far as ease and freedom from care is concerned ; and never " rest," in the sense of indolence or inactivity. Jerusalem the golden is the place of *communion* with all the people of God. We shall sit with Abraham, Isaac, and Jacob, in eternal fellowship. We shall hold high converse with the noble host of the elect, all reigning with Him who by His love and His potent arm has brought them safely home. We shall not sing solos, but in chorus shall we praise our King. Heaven is a place of *victory realised.* Whenever, Christian, thou hast achieved a victory over thy lusts—whenever after hard struggling, thou hast laid a temptation dead at thy feet —thou hast in that hour a foretaste of the joy that awaits thee when the Lord shall shortly tread Satan under thy feet, and thou shalt find thyself more than conqueror through Him who hath loved thee. Paradise is a place of *security.* When you enjoy the full assurance of faith, you have the pledge of that glorious security which shall be yours when you are a perfect citizen of the heavenly Jerusalem. O my sweet home, Jerusalem, thou happy harbour of my soul! Thanks, even now, to Him whose love hath taught me to long for Thee ; but louder thanks in eternity, when I shall possess thee.

> " My soul has tasted of the grapes,
>   And now it longs to go
> Where my dear Lord His vineyard keeps
>   And all the clusters grow.

> " Upon the true and living vine
>   My famish'd soul would feast,
> And banquet on the fruit divine,
>   An everlasting guest."

390 MORNING July 13

"God said to Jonah, Doest thou well to be angry?"—Jon. iv. 9.

NGER is not always or necessarily sinful, but it has such a tendency to run wild that whenever it displays itself, we should be quick to question its character, with this enquiry, " Doest thou well to be angry ? " It may be that we can answer, " YES." Very frequently anger is the madman's firebrand, but sometimes it is Elijah's fire from heaven. We do well when we are angry with sin, because of the wrong which it commits against our good and gracious God ; or with ourselves because we remain so foolish after so much divine instruction ; or with others when the sole cause of anger is the evil which they do. He who is not angry at transgression becomes a partaker in it. Sin is a loathsome and hateful thing, and no renewed heart can patiently endure it. God himself is angry with the wicked every day, and it is written in His Word, " Ye that love the Lord, hate evil."

Far more frequently it is to be feared that our anger is not commendable or even justifiable, and then we must answer, " NO." Why should we be fretful with children, passionate with servants, and wrathful with companions ? Is such anger honourable to our Christian profession, or glorifying to God ? Is it not the old evil heart seeking to gain dominion, and should we not resist it with all the might of our newborn nature. Many professors give way to temper as though it were useless to attempt resistance ; but let the believer remember that he must be a conqueror in every point, or else he cannot be crowned. If we cannot control our tempers, what has grace done for us? Some one told Mr. Jay that grace was often grafted on a crab-stump. " Yes," said he, " but the fruit will not be crabs." We must not make natural infirmity an excuse for sin, but we must fly to the cross and pray the Lord to crucify our tempers, and renew us in gentleness and meekness after his own image.

*" When I cry unto Thee, then shall mine enemies turn back:
this I know; for God is for me."*—Psalm lvi. 9.

IT is impossible for any human speech to
express the full meaning of this delightful
phrase, *" God is for me."* He was " for us "
before the worlds were made ; He was " for us," or
He would not have given His well-beloved Son ; He
was " for us " when He smote the Only-begotten, and
laid the full weight of His wrath upon Him—He
was "for *us*," though He was against *Him;* He was
" for us," when we were ruined in the fall—He loved
us notwithstanding all ; He was " for us," when we
were rebels against Him, and with a high hand were
bidding Him defiance ; He was " for us," or He
would not have brought us humbly to seek His
face. He has been " for us " in many struggles ; we
have been summoned to encounter hosts of dangers ;
we have been assailed by temptations from without
and within—how could we have remained unharmed
to this hour if He had not been "for us"? He is
"for us," with all the infinity of His being ; with
all the omnipotence of His love ; with all the infallibility of His wisdom ; arrayed in all His divine
attributes, He is " for us,"—eternally and immutably
" for us ;" " for us " when yon blue skies shall be
rolled up like a worn out vesture ; " for us " throughout
eternity. And because He is " for us," the voice of
prayer will always ensure His help. *" When I cry
unto Thee, then shall mine enemies be turned back."*
This is no uncertain hope, but a well grounded assurance—*" this I know."* I will direct my prayer
unto Thee, and will look up for the answer, assured
that it will come, and that mine enemies shall be defeated, " for God is for me." O believer, how happy
art thou with the King of kings on thy side ! How
safe with such a Protector ! How sure thy cause
pleaded by such an Advocate ! If God be for thee,
who can be against thee ?

" If thou lift up thy tool upon it, thou hast polluted it."—
Ex. xx. 25.

GOD'S altar was to be built of unhewn stones, that no trace of human skill or labour might be seen upon it. Human wisdom delights to trim and arrange the doctrines of the cross into a system more artificial and more congenial with the depraved tastes of fallen nature ; instead, however, of improving the gospel carnal wisdom pollutes it, until it becomes another gospel, and not the truth of God at all. All alterations and amendments of the Lord's own Word are defilements and pollutions. The proud heart of man is very anxious to have a hand in the justification of the soul before God ; preparations for Christ are dreamed of, humblings and repentings are trusted in, good works are cried up, natural ability is much vaunted, and by all means the attempt is made to lift up human tools upon the divine altar. It were well if sinners would remember that so far from perfecting the Saviour's work, their carnal confidences only pollute and dishonour it. The Lord alone must be exalted in the work of atonement, and not a single mark of man's chisel or hammer will be endured. There is an inherent blasphemy in seeking to add to what Christ Jesus in His dying moments declared to be finished, or to improve that in which the Lord Jehovah finds perfect satisfaction. Trembling sinner, away with thy tools, and fall upon thy knees in humble supplication ; and accept the Lord Jesus to be the altar of thine atonement, and rest in Him alone.

Many professors may take warning from this morning's text as to the doctrines which they believe. There is among Christians far too much inclination to square and reconcile the truths of revelation; this is a form of irreverence and unbelief, let us strive against it, and receive truth as we find it ; rejoicing that the doctrines of the Word are unhewn stones, and so are all the more fit to build an altar for the Lord.

"As it began to dawn, came Magdalene, to see the sepulchre."
Matthew xxviii. 1.

ET us learn from Mary Magdalene how to obtain fellowship with the Lord Jesus. Notice how she sought. She sought the Saviour *very early* in the morning. If thou canst wait for Christ, and be patient in the hope of having fellowship with Him at some distant season, thou wilt never have fellowship at all ; for the heart that is fitted for communion is a hungering and a thirsting heart. She sought Him also with *very great boldness.* Other disciples fled from the sepulchre, for they trembled and were amazed ; but Mary, it is said, " stood " at the sepulchre. If you would have Christ with you, seek Him boldly. Let nothing hold you back. Defy the world. Press on where others flee. She sought Christ *faithfully*—she stood *at the sepulchre.* Some find it hard to stand by a living Saviour, but she stood by a dead one. Let us seek Christ after this mode, cleaving to the very least thing that has to do with Him, remaining faithful though all others should forsake Him. Note further, she sought Jesus *earnestly* —she stood " *weeping.*" Those tear-droppings were as spells that led the Saviour captive, and made Him come forth and show Himself to her. If you desire Jesus' presence, weep after it ! If you cannot be happy unless He come and say to you, " Thou art My beloved," you will soon hear His voice. Lastly, she sought the Saviour *only.* What cared she for angels, she turned herself back from them ; her search was only for her Lord. If Christ be your one and only love, if your heart has cast out all rivals, you will not long lack the comfort of His presence. Mary Magdalene sought thus *because she loved much.* Let us arouse ourselves to the same intensity of affection ; let our heart, like Mary's, be full of Christ, and our love, like hers, will be satisfied with nothing short of Himself. O Lord, reveal Thyself to us this evening !

" The fire shall ever be burning upon the altar; it shall never go out."—Lev. vi. 13.

KEEP the altar of *private prayer* burning. This is the very life of all piety. The sanctuary and family altars borrow their fires here, therefore let this burn well. Secret devotion is the very essence, evidence, and barometer, of vital and experimental religion.

Burn here the fat of your sacrifices. Let your closet seasons be, if possible, regular, frequent, and undisturbed. Effectual prayer availeth much. Have you nothing to pray for? Let us suggest the Church, the ministry, your own soul, your children, your relations, your neighbours, your country, and the cause of God and truth throughout the world. Let us examine ourselves on this important matter. Do we engage with lukewarmness in private devotion? Is the fire of devotion burning dimly in our hearts? Do the chariot wheels drag heavily? If so, let us be alarmed at this sign of decay. Let us go with weeping, and ask for the Spirit of grace and of supplications. Let us set apart special seasons for extraordinary prayer. For if this fire should be smothered beneath the ashes of a worldly conformity, it will dim the fire on the family altar, and lessen our influence both in the Church and in the world.

The text will also apply to *the altar of the heart.* This is a golden altar indeed. God loves to see the hearts of His people glowing towards Himself. Let us give to God our hearts, all blazing with love, and seek His grace, that the fire may never be quenched; for it will not burn if the Lord does not keep it burning. Many foes will attempt to extinguish it; but if the unseen hand behind the wall pour thereon the sacred oil, it will blaze higher and higher. Let us use texts of Scripture as fuel for our heart's fire, they are live coals; let us attend sermons, but above all, let us be much alone with Jesus.

" He appeared first to Mary Magdalene."—Mark xvi. 9.

JESUS " appeared first to Mary Magdalene," probably not only on account of her great love and persevering seeking, but because, as the context intimates, *she had been a special trophy of Christ's delivering power.* Learn from this, that the greatness of our sin before conversion should not make us imagine that we may not be specially favoured with the very highest grade of fellowship. She was one who had left all to become *a constant attendant on the Saviour.* He was her first, her chief object. Many who were on Christ's side did not take up Christ's cross ; *she* did. *She spent her substance in relieving His wants.* If we would see much of Christ, let us *serve* Him. Tell me who they are that sit oftenest under the banner of His love, and drink deepest draughts from the cup of communion, and I am sure they will be those who give most, who serve best, and who abide closest to the bleeding heart of their dear Lord. But notice *how* Christ revealed Himself to this sorrowing one—by *a word*, " Mary." It needed but one word *in His voice*, and at once she knew Him, and *her heart owned allegiance by another word*, her heart was too full to say more. That one word would naturally be the most fitting for the occasion. It implies obedience. She said, *" Master."* There is no state of mind in which this confession of allegiance will be too cold. No, when your spirit glows most with the heavenly fire, then you will say, " I am Thy servant, Thou hast loosed my bonds." If you can say, " Master," if you feel that His will is your will, then you stand in a happy, holy place. He must have said, " Mary," or else you could not have said, " Rabboni." See, then, from all this, how Christ honours those who honour Him, how love draws our Beloved, how it needs but one word of His to turn our weeping to rejoicing, how His presence makes the heart's sunshine.

" They gathered manna every morning."—Ex. xvi. 21.

LABOUR *to maintain a sense of thine entire de-pendence upon the Lord's good will and pleasure for the continuance of thy richest enjoyments.* Never try to live on the old manna, nor seek to find help in Egypt. All must come from Jesus, or thou art undone for ever. Old anointings will not suffice to impart unction to thy spirit; thine head must have fresh oil poured upon it from the golden horn of the sanctuary, or it will cease from its glory. To-day thou mayest be upon the summit of the mount of God, but He who has put thee there must keep thee there, or thou wilt sink far more speedily than thou dreamest. Thy mountain only stands firm when He settles it in its place; if He hide His face, thou wilt soon be troubled. If the Saviour should see fit, there is not a window through which thou seest the light of heaven which He could not darken in an instant. Joshua bade the sun stand still, but Jesus can shroud it in total darkness. He can withdraw the joy of thine heart, the light of thine eyes, and the strength of thy life; in His hand thy comforts lie, and at His will they can depart from thee. This hourly dependence our Lord is determined that we shall feel and recognise, for He only permits us to pray for "daily bread," and only promises that "as our days our strength shall be." Is it not best for us that it should be so, that we may often repair to His throne, and constantly be reminded of His love? Oh! how rich the grace which supplies us so continu-ally, and doth not refrain itself because of our ingrati-tude! The golden shower never ceases, the cloud of blessing tarries evermore above our habitation. O Lord Jesus, we would bow at Thy feet, conscious of our utter inability to do anything without Thee, and in every favour which we are privileged to receive, we would adore Thy blessed name and acknowledge Thine unexhausted love.

*" Thou shalt arise, and have mercy upon Zion : for the time
to favour her, yea, the set time is come. For Thy servants
take pleasure in her stones, and favour the dust thereof."*
Psalm cii. 13, 14.

SELFISH man in trouble is exceedingly hard
to comfort, because the springs of his comfort
lie entirely within himself, and when he is sad
all his springs are dry. But a large-hearted man
full of Christian philanthropy, has other springs
from which to supply himself with comfort beside
those which lie within. He can go to his God first of
all, and there find abundant help; and he can discover arguments for consolation in things relating to
the world at large, to his country, and, above all, to
the church. David in this Psalm was exceedingly
sorrowful ; he wrote, " I am like an owl of the desert.
I watch, and am as a sparrow alone upon the house
top." The only way in which he could comfort himself, was in the reflection that God would arise, and
have mercy upon Zion : though *he* was sad, yet Zion
should prosper; however low his own estate, yet Zion
should arise. Christian man ! learn to comfort thyself in God's gracious dealing towards the church.
That which is so dear to thy Master, should it not
be dear above all else to thee ? What though thy
way be dark, canst thou not gladden thine heart with
the triumphs of His cross and the spread of His truth ?
Our own personal troubles are forgotten while we
look, not only upon what God *has* done, and *is* doing
for Zion, but on the glorious things He *will yet do*
for His church. Try this receipt, O believer, whenever thou art sad of heart and in heaviness of spirit :
forget thyself and thy little concerns, and seek the
welfare and prosperity of Zion. When thou bendest
thy knee in prayer to God, limit not thy petition to
the narrow circle of thine own life, tried though it be,
but send out thy longing prayers for the church's
prosperity, " Pray for the peace of Jerusalem," and
thine own soul shall be refreshed.

" Knowing, brethren beloved, your election of God."
1 Thess. i. 4.

MANY persons want to know their election before
they look to Christ, but they cannot learn it
thus, it is only to be discovered by "looking
unto Jesus." If you desire to ascertain your own
election ;—after the following manner, shall you assure
your heart before God. Do you feel yourself to be a lost,
guilty sinner ? go straightway to the cross of Christ,
and tell Jesus so, and tell Him that you have read
in the Bible, "Him that cometh unto me, I will in
no wise cast out." Tell Him that He has said, "This
is a faithful saying, and worthy of all acceptation,
that Christ Jesus came into the world to save sinners."
Look to Jesus and believe on Him, and you shall
make proof of your election directly, for so surely as
thou believest, thou art elect. If you will give yourself wholly up to Christ and trust Him, then you
are one of God's chosen ones ; but if you stop and
say, "I want to know first whether I am elect," you
ask you know not what. Go to Jesus, be you never
so guilty, just as you are. Leave all curious inquiry
about election alone. Go straight to Christ and
hide in His wounds, and you shall know your election.
The assurance of the Holy Spirit shall be given to
you, so that you shall be able to say, "I know whom
I have believed, and I am persuaded that he is able
to keep that which I have committed to Him." Christ
was at the everlasting council : He can tell you whether
you were chosen or not ; but you cannot find it out in
any other way. Go and put your trust in Him, and His
answer will be—"I have loved thee with an everlasting love, therefore with lovingkindness have I drawn
thee." There will be no doubt about His having
chosen *you*, when you have chosen *Him*.

"Sons we are through God's election,
  Who in Jesus Christ believe."

" Let not one of them escape."—1 Kings xviii. 40.

WHEN the prophet Elijah had received the answer to his prayer, and the fire from heaven had consumed the sacrifice in the presence of all the people, he called upon the assembled Israelites to take the priests of Baal, and sternly cried, " Let not one of them escape." He took them all down to the brook Kishon, and slew them there. So must it be with our sins—they are all doomed, not one must be preserved. Our darling sin must die. Spare it not for its much crying. Strike, though it be as dear as an Isaac. Strike, for God struck at sin when it was laid upon His own Son. With stern unflinching purpose must you condemn to death that sin which was once the idol of your heart. Do you ask how you are to accomplish this? Jesus will be your power. You have grace to overcome sin given you in the covenant of grace ; you have strength to win the victory in the crusade against inward lusts, because Christ Jesus has promised to be with you even unto the end. If you would triumph over darkness, set yourself in the presence of the Sun of Righteousness. There is no place so well adapted for the discovery of sin, and recovery from its power and guilt, as the immediate presence of God. Job never knew how to get rid of sin half so well as he did when his eye of faith rested upon God, and then he abhorred himself, and repented in dust and ashes. The fine gold of the Christian is oft becoming dim. We need the sacred fire to consume the dross. Let us fly to our God, He is a consuming fire ; He will not consume our spirit, but our sins. Let the goodness of God excite us to a sacred jealousy, and to a holy revenge against those iniquities which are hateful in His sight. Go forth to battle with Amalek in His strength, and utterly destroy the accursed crew : let not one of them escape.

" They shall go hindmost with their standards."—Num. ii. 31.

THE camp of Dan brought up the rear when the armies of Israel were on the march. The Danites occupied *the hindmost place*, but what mattered the position, since they were as truly part of the host as were the foremost tribes ; they followed the same fiery cloudy pillar, they ate of the same manna, drank of the same spiritual rock, and journeyed to the same inheritance. Come, my heart, cheer up, though last and least ; it is thy privilege to be in the army, and to fare as they fare who lead the van. Some one must be hindmost in honour and esteem, some one must do menial work for Jesus, and why should not I ? In a poor village, among an ignorant peasantry ; or in a back street, among degraded sinners, I will work on, and "go hindmost with my standard."

The Danites occupied *a very useful place*. Stragglers have to be picked up upon the march, and lost property has to be gathered from the field. Fiery spirits may dash forward over untrodden paths to learn fresh truth, and win more souls to Jesus ; but some of a more conservative spirit may be well engaged in reminding the Church of her ancient faith, and restoring her fainting sons. Every position has its duties, and the slowly moving children of God will find their peculiar state one in which they may be eminently a blessing to the whole host.

The rear guard is a *place of danger*. There are foes behind us as well as before us. Attacks may come from any quarter. We read that Amalek fell upon Israel, and slew some of the hindmost of them. The experienced Christian will find much work for his weapons in aiding those poor doubting, desponding, wavering, souls, who are hindmost in faith, knowledge, and joy. These must not be left unaided, and therefore be it the business of well-taught saints to bear their standards among the hindmost. My soul, do thou tenderly watch to help the hindmost this day.

" Neither shall one thrust another ; they shall walk every one in his path."—Joel ii. 8.

LOCUSTS always keep their rank, and although their number is legion, they do not crowd upon each other, so as to throw their columns into confusion. This remarkable fact in natural history shows how thoroughly the Lord has infused the spirit of order into His universe, since the smallest animate creatures are as much controlled by it as are the rolling spheres or the seraphic messengers. It would be wise for believers to be ruled by the same influence in all their spiritual life. *In their Christian graces* no one virtue should usurp the sphere of another, or eat out the vitals of the rest for its own support. Affection must not smother honesty, courage must not elbow weakness out of the field, modesty must not jostle energy, and patience must not slaughter resolution. So also with *our duties*, one must not interfere with another ; public usefulness must not injure private piety ; church work must not push family worship into a corner. It is ill to offer God one duty stained with the blood of another. Each thing is beautiful in its season, but not otherwise. It was to the Pharisee that Jesus said, " This ought ye to have done, and not to have left the other undone." The same rule applies to *our personal position*, we must take care to know our place, take it, and keep to it. We must minister as the Spirit has given us ability, and not intrude upon our fellow servant's domain. Our Lord Jesus taught us not to covet the high places, but to be willing to be the least among the brethren. Far from us be an envious, ambitious spirit, let us feel the force of the Master's command, and do as He bids us, keeping rank with the rest of the host. To-night let us see whether we are keeping the unity of the Spirit in the bonds of peace, and let our prayer be that, in all the churches of the Lord Jesus, peace and order may prevail.

" The Lord our God hath shewed us His glory."—Deut. v. 24

OD'S great design in all His works is the manifestation of His own glory. Any aim less than this were unworthy of Himself. But how shall the glory of God be manifested to such fallen creatures as we are? Man's eye is not single, he has ever a side glance towards his own honour, has too high an estimate of his own powers, and so is not qualified to behold the glory of the Lord. It is clear, then, that self must stand out of the way, that there may be room for God to be exalted ; and this is the reason why He bringeth His people ofttimes into straits and difficulties, that, being made conscious of their own folly and weakness, they may be fitted to behold the majesty of God when He comes forth to work their deliverance. He whose life is one even and smooth path, will see but little of the glory of the Lord, for he has few occasions of self-emptying, and hence, but little fitness for being filled with the revelation of God. They who navigate little streams and shallow creeks, know but little of the God of tempests ; but they who " do business in great waters," these see His " wonders in the deep." Among the huge Atlantic-waves of bereavement, poverty, temptation, and reproach, we learn the power of Jehovah, because we feel the littleness of man. Thank God, then, if you have béen led by a rough road : it is this which has given you your experience of God's greatness and lovingkindness. Your troubles have enriched you with a wealth of knowledge to be gained by no other means : your trials have been the cleft of the rock in which Jehovah has set you, as He did His servant Moses, that you might behold His glory as it passed by. Praise God that you have not been left to the darkness and ignorance which continued prosperity might have involved, but that in the great fight of affliction, you have been capacitated for the outshinings of His glory in His wonderful dealings with you.

" A bruised reed shall He not break, and smoking flax shall He not quench."—Matthew xii. 20.

WHAT is weaker than the bruised reed or the smoking flax ? *A reed* that groweth in the fen or marsh, let but the wild duck light upon it, and it snaps ; let but the foot of man brush against it, and it is bruised and broken ; every wind that flits across the river moves it to and fro. You can conceive of nothing more frail or brittle, or whose existence is more in jeopardy, than a bruised reed. Then look at the smoking flax—what is it ? It has a spark within it, it is true, but it is almost smothered ; an infant's breath might blow it out ; nothing has a more precarious existence than its flame. *Weak things* are here described, yet Jesus says of them, " The smoking flax I will not quench ; the bruised reed I will not break." Some of God's children are made strong to do mighty works for Him ; God has His Samsons here and there who can pull up Gaza's gates, and carry them to the top of the hill ; He has a few mighties who are lion-like men, but the majority of His people are a timid, trembling race. They are like starlings, frightened at every passer by ; a little fearful flock. If temptation comes, they are taken like birds in a snare ; if trial threatens, they are ready to faint ; their frail skiff is tossed up and down by every wave, they are drifted along like a sea bird on the crest of the billows—weak things, without strength, without wisdom, without foresight. Yet, weak as they are, and *because* they are so weak, they have this promise made specially to them. Herein is grace and graciousness ! Herein is love and lovingkindness ! How it opens to us the compassion of Jesus—so gentle, tender, considerate ! We need never shrink back from *His* touch. We need never fear a harsh word from *Him;* though He might well chide us for our weakness, He rebuketh not. Bruised reeds shall have no blows from Him, and the smoking flax no damping frowns.

" The earnest of our inheritance."—Eph. i. 14.

OH ! what enlightenment, what joys, what consolation, what delight of heart is experienced by that man who has learned to feed on Jesus, and on Jesus alone. Yet the realization which we have of Christ's preciousness is, in this life, imperfect at the best. As an old writer says, " 'Tis but a taste ! " We have tasted " that the Lord is gracious," but we do not yet know *how* good and gracious He is, although what we know of His sweetness makes us long for more. We have enjoyed the firstfruits of the Spirit, and they have set us hungering and thirsting for the fulness of the heavenly vintage. We groan within ourselves, waiting for the adoption. *Here* we are like Israel in the wilderness, who had but one cluster from Eshcol, *there* we shall be in the vineyard. Here we see the manna falling small, like coriander seed, but there shall we eat the bread of heaven and the old corn of the kingdom. We are but beginners now in spiritual education ; for although we have learned the first letters of the alphabet, we cannot read words yet, much less can we put sentences together ; but as one says, " He that has been in heaven but five minutes, knows more than the general assembly of divines on earth." We have many ungratified desires at present, but soon every wish shall be satisfied ; and all our powers shall find the sweetest employment in that eternal world of joy. O Christian, antedate heaven for a few years. Within a very little time thou shalt be rid of all thy trials and thy troubles. Thine eyes now suffused with tears shall weep no longer. Thou shalt gaze in ineffable rapture upon the splendour of Him who sits upon the throne. Nay, more, upon His throne shalt thou sit. The triumph of His glory shall be shared by thee ; His crown, His joy, His paradise, these shall be thine, and thou shalt be co-heir with Him who is the heir of all things.

" And now what hast thou to do in the way of Egypt, to drink the waters of Sihor ?"—Jeremiah ii. 18.

BY sundry miracles, by divers mercies, by strange deliverances Jehovah had proved Himself to be worthy of Israel's trust. Yet they broke down the hedges with which God had enclosed them as a sacred garden ; they forsook their own true and living God, and followed after false gods. Constantly did the Lord reprove them for this infatuation, and our text contains one instance of God's expostulating with them, " What hast thou to do in the way of Egypt, to drink the waters of the muddy river?"—for so it may be translated. " Why dost thou wander afar and leave thine own cool stream from Lebanon ? Why dost thou forsake Jerusalem to turn aside to Noph and to Tahapanes ? Why art thou so strangely set on mischief, that thou canst not be content with the good and healthful, but wouldst follow after that which is evil and deceitful ?" Is there not here a word of expostulation and warning to the Christian ? O true believer, called by grace and washed in the precious blood of Jesus, thou hast tasted of better drink than the muddy river of this world's pleasure can give thee ; thou hast had fellowship with Christ ; thou hast obtained the joy of seeing Jesus, and leaning thine head upon His bosom. Do the trifles, the songs, the honours, the merriment of this earth content thee after that ? Hast thou eaten the bread of angels, and canst thou live on husks ? Good Rutherford once said, " I have tasted of Christ's own manna, and it hath put my mouth out of taste for the brown bread of this world's joys." Methinks it should be so with thee. If thou art wandering after the waters of Egypt, O return quickly to the one living fountain : the waters of Sihor may be sweet to the Egyptians, but they will prove only bitterness to thee. What hast *thou* to do with them ? *Jesus asks thee this question* this evening— what wilt thou answer Him ?

" The daughter of Jerusalem hath shaken her head at thee."
Is. xxxvii. 22.

EASSURED by the Word of the Lord, the
poor trembling citizens of Zion grew bold,
and shook their heads at Sennacherib's boastful threats. Strong faith enables the servants of God
to look with calm contempt upon their most haughty
foes. *We know that our enemies are attempting impossibilities.* They seek to destroy the eternal life,
which cannot die while Jesus lives ; to overthrow
the citadel, against which the gates of hell shall not
prevail. They kick against the pricks to their own
wounding, and rush upon the bosses of Jehovah's
buckler to their own hurt.

We know their weakness. What are they but men ?
And what is man but a worm ? They roar and swell
like waves of the sea, foaming out their own shame.
When the Lord ariseth, they shall fly as chaff before
the wind, and be consumed as crackling thorns.
Their utter powerlessness to do damage to the cause
of God and His truth, may make the weakest soldiers
in Zion's ranks laugh them to scorn.

Above all, *we know that the Most High is with us,*
and when He dresses Himself in arms, where are His
enemies ? If He cometh forth from His place, the
potsherds of the earth will not long contend with
their Maker. His rod of iron shall dash them in
pieces like a potter's vessel, and their very remembrance shall perish from the earth. Away, then, all
fears, the kingdom is safe in the King's hands. Let
us shout for joy, for the Lord reigneth, and His foes
shall be as straw for the dunghill.

> " As true as God's own word is true ;
> Nor earth, nor hell, with all their crew,
>   Against us shall prevail.
> A jest, and by-word, are they grown ;
> God *is* with us, we *are* his own,
>   Our victory cannot fail."

" Why go I mourning ?"—Psalm xlii. 9.

CANST thou answer this, believer ? Canst thou find any reason why thou art so often mourning instead of rejoicing ? Why yield to gloomy anticipations ? Who told thee that the night would never end in day ? Who told thee that the sea of circumstances would ebb out till there should be nothing left but long leagues of the mud of horrible poverty ? Who told thee that the winter of thy discontent would proceed from frost to frost, from snow, and ice, and hail, to deeper snow, and yet more heavy tempest of despair ? Knowest thou not that day follows night, that flood comes after ebb, that spring and summer succeed to winter ? Hope thou then ! Hope thou ever ! for God fails thee not. Dost thou not know that thy God loves thee in the midst of all this ? Mountains, when in darkness hidden, are as real as in day, and God's love is as true to thee now as it was in thy brightest moments. No father chastens always : thy Lord hates the rod as much as thou dost ; He only cares to use it for that reason which should make thee willing to receive it, namely, that it works thy lasting good. Thou shalt yet climb Jacob's ladder with the angels, and behold Him who sits at the top of it—thy covenant God. Thou shalt yet, amidst the splendours of eternity, forget the trials of time, or only remember them to bless the God who led thee through them, and wrought thy lasting good by them. Come, sing in the midst of tribulation. Rejoice even while passing through the furnace. Make the wilderness to blossom like the rose ! Cause the desert to ring with thine exulting joys, for these light afflictions will soon be over, and then " for ever with the Lord," thy bliss shall never wane.

> " Faint not nor fear, His arms are near,
> He changeth not, and thou art dear ;
> Only believe and thou shalt see,
> That Christ is all in all to thee."

" I am married unto you."—Jer. iii. 14.

CHRIST Jesus is joined unto His people in marriage-union. In love He espoused His Church as a chaste virgin, long before she fell under the yoke of bondage. Full of burning affection He toiled, like Jacob for Rachel, until the whole of her purchase-money had been paid, and now, having sought her by His Spirit, and brought her to know and love Him, He awaits the glorious hour when their mutual bliss shall be consummated at the marriage-supper of the Lamb. Not yet hath the glorious Bridegroom presented His betrothed, perfected and complete, before the Majesty of heaven; not yet hath she actually entered upon the enjoyment of her dignities as His wife and queen : she is as yet a wanderer in a world of woe, a dweller in the tents of Kedar ; but she is even now the bride, the spouse of Jesus, dear to His heart, precious in His sight, written on His hands, and united with His person. On earth he exercises towards her all the affectionate offices of Husband. He makes rich provision for her wants, pays all her debts, allows her to assume His name, and to share in all His wealth. Nor will He ever act otherwise to her. The word divorce He will never mention, for " He hateth putting away." Death must sever the conjugal tie between the most loving mortals, but it cannot divide the links of this immortal marriage. In heaven they marry not, but are as the angels of God ; yet there is this one marvellous exception to the rule, for in Heaven Christ and His Church shall celebrate their joyous nuptials. This affinity as it is more lasting, so is it more near than earthly wedlock. Let the love of husband be never so pure and fervent, it is but a faint picture of the flame which burns in the heart of Jesus. Passing all human union is that mystical cleaving unto the Church, for which Christ left His Father, and became one flesh with her.

" Behold the Man!"—John xix. 5.

IF there be one place where our Lord Jesus most fully becomes the joy and comfort of His people, it is where he plunged deepest into the depths of woe. Come hither, gracious souls, and behold the Man in the garden of Gethsemane; behold His heart so brimming with love that He cannot hold it in—so full of sorrow that it must find a vent. Behold the bloody sweat as it distils from every pore of His body, and falls upon the ground. Behold the Man as they drive the nails into His hands and feet. Look up, repenting sinners, and see the sorrowful image of your suffering Lord. Mark Him, as the ruby drops stand on the thorn-crown, and adorn with priceless gems the diadem of the King of Misery. Behold Man when all His bones are out of joint, and He is poured out like water and brought into the dust of death; God hath forsaken Him, and hell compasseth Him about. Behold and see, was there ever sorrow like unto His sorrow that is done unto Him? All ye that pass by draw near and look upon this spectacle of grief, unique, unparalleled, a wonder to men and angels, a prodigy unmatched. Behold the Emperor of Woe who had no equal or rival in His agonies! Gaze upon Him, ye mourners, for if there be not consolation in a crucified Christ there is no joy in earth or heaven. If in the ransom price of His blood there be not hope, ye harps of heaven, there is no joy in you, and the right hand of God shall know no pleasures for evermore. We have only to sit more continually at the cross foot to be less troubled with our doubts and woes. We have but to see *His* sorrows, and *our* sorrows we shall be ashamed to mention; we have but to gaze into His wounds and heal our own. If we would live aright it must be by the contemplation of His death; if we would rise to dignity, it must be by considering His humiliation and His sorrow.

" Even thou wast as one of them."—Obadiah i. 11.

BROTHERLY kindness was due from Edom to Israel in the time of need, but instead thereof, the men of Esau made common cause with Israel's foes. Special stress in the sentence before us is laid upon the word *thou;* as when Cæsar cried to Brutus, "and *thou* Brutus ;" a bad action may be all the worse, because of the person who has committed it. When *we* sin, who are the chosen favorites of heaven, we sin with an emphasis ; ours is a crying offence, because we are so peculiarly indulged. If an angel should lay his hand upon us when we are doing evil, he need not use any other rebuke than the question, "What *thou?* What dost *thou* here ?" Much forgiven, much delivered, much instructed, much enriched, much blessed, shall we dare to put forth our hand unto evil ? God forbid !

A few minutes of confession may be beneficial to thee, gentle reader, this morning. Hast thou never been as the wicked ? At an evening party certain men laughed at uncleanness, and the joke was not altogether offensive to thine ear, *even thou wast as one of them.* When hard things were spoken concerning the ways of God, thou wast bashfully silent ; and so, to on-lookers, *thou wast as one of them.* When worldlings were bartering in the market, and driving hard bargains, wast thou not as one of them ? When they were pursuing vanity with a hunter's foot, wert thou not as greedy for gain as they were ? Could any difference be discerned between thee and them ? *Is there any difference?* Here we come to close quarters. Be honest with thine own soul, and make sure that thou art a new creature in Christ Jesus ; but when this is sure, walk jealously, lest any should again be able to say, "Even thou wast as one of them." Thou wouldst not desire to share their eternal doom, why then be like them here ? Come not thou into their secret, lest thou come into their ruin. Side with the afflicted people of God, and not with the world.

" The blood of Jesus Christ His Son cleanseth us from all sin."—1 John i. 7.

" CLEANSETH," says the text — not "*shall cleanse.*" There are multitudes who think thas as a dying hope they may look forward to pardon. Oh! how infinitely better to have cleansing now than to depend on the bare possibility of forgiveness when I come to die. Some imagine that a sense of pardon is an attainment only obtainable after many years of Christian experience. But forgiveness of sin is a *present* thing—a privilege for this day, a joy for this very hour. The moment a sinner trusts Jesus he is fully forgiven. The text, being written in the present tense, also indicates *continuance;* it was " cleanseth " yesterday, it is " cleanseth " to-day, it will be " cleanseth" to-morrow: it will be always so with you, Christian, until you cross the river; every hour you may come to this fountain, for it cleanseth still. Notice, likewise, *the completeness* of the cleansing, " The blood of Jesus Christ His Son cleanseth us from *all sin*"—not only from sin, but "from *all* sin." Reader, I cannot tell you the exceeding sweetness of this word, but I pray God the Holy Ghost to give you a taste of it. Manifold are our sins against God. Whether the bill be little or great, the same receipt can discharge one as the other. The blood of Jesus Christ is as blessed and divine a payment for the transgressions of blaspheming Peter as for the shortcomings of loving John; our iniquity is gone, all gone at once, and all gone for ever. Blessed completeness! What a sweet theme to dwell upon as one gives himself to sleep.

> " Sins against a holy God ;
> Sins against His righteous laws ;
> Sins against His love, His blood ;
> Sins against His name and cause ;
> Sins immense as is the sea—
> From them all He cleanseth me."

" Stand still, and see the salvation of the Lord."—Ex. xiv. 13.

THESE words contain God's command to the believer when he is reduced to great straits and brought into extraordinary difficulties. He cannot retreat ; he cannot go forward ; he is shut up on the right hand and on the left ; what is he now to do? The Master's word to him is, "Stand still." It will be well for him if at such times he listens only to his Master's word, for other and evil advisers come with their suggestions. *Despair* whispers, " Lie down and die ; give it all up." But God would have us put on a cheerful courage, and even in our worst times, rejoice in His love and faithfulness. *Cowardice* says, "Retreat ; go back to the worldling's way of action ; you cannot play the Christian's part, it is too difficult. Relinquish your principles." But, however much Satan may urge this course upon you, you cannot follow it if you are a child of God. His divine fiat has bid thee go from strength to strength, and so thou shalt, and neither death nor hell shall turn thee from thy course. What, if for a while thou art called to stand still, yet this is but to renew thy strength for some greater advance in due time. *Precipitancy* cries, "do something. Stir yourself ; to stand still and wait, is sheer idleness." We *must* be doing something at once—*we* must do it so we think—instead of looking to the Lord, who will not only do something but will do everything. *Presumption* boasts, "If the sea be before you, march into it and expect a miracle." But Faith listens neither to Presumption, nor to Despair, nor to Cowardice, nor to Precipitancy, but it hears God say, "Stand still," and immoveable as a rock it stands. "*Stand* still ;"—keep the posture of an upright man, ready for action, expecting further orders, cheerfully and patiently awaiting the directing voice ; and it will not be long ere God shall say to you, as distinctly as Moses said it to the people of Israel, "Go forward."

" His camp is very great."—Joel ii. 11.

CONSIDER, my soul, the mightiness of the Lord who is thy glory and defence. He is a man of war, Jehovah is His name. All *the forces of heaven* are at His beck, legions wait at his door, cherubim and seraphim, watchers and holy ones, principalities and powers, are all attentive to His will. If our eyes were not blinded by the ophthalmia of the flesh, we should see horses of fire and chariots of fire round about the Lord's beloved. *The powers of nature* are all subject to the absolute control of the Creator : stormy wind and tempest, lightning and rain, and snow, and hail, and the soft dews and cheering sunshine, come and go at His decree. The bands of Orion He looseth, and bindeth the sweet influences of the Pleiades. Earth, sea, and air, and the places under the earth, are the barracks for Jehovah's great armies ; space is His camping ground, light is His banner, and flame is His sword. When He goeth forth to war, famine ravages the land, pestilence smites the nations, hurricane sweeps the sea, tornado shakes the mountains, and earthquake makes the solid world to tremble. As for *animate creatures,* they all own His dominion, and from the great fish which swallowed the prophet, down to " all manner of flies," which plagued the field of Zoan, all are His servants, and like the palmer-worm, the caterpillar, and the cankerworm, are squadrons of His great army, for His camp is very great. My soul, see to it that thou be at peace with this mighty King, yea, more, be sure to enlist under His banner, for to war against Him is madness, and to serve Him is glory. Jesus, Immanuel, God with us, is ready to receive recruits for the army of the Lord : if I am not already enlisted let me go to Him ere I sleep, and beg to be accepted through His merits ; and if I be already, as I hope I am, a soldier of the cross, let me be of good courage ; for the enemy is powerless compared with my Lord, whose camp is very great.

" He left his garment in her hand, and fled, and got him out."
Gen. xxxix. 12.

IN contending with certain sins there remains no mode of victory but by flight. The ancient naturalists wrote much of basilisks, whose eyes fascinated their victims and rendered them easy victims ; so the mere gaze of wickedness puts us in solemn danger. He who would be safe from acts of evil must haste away from occasions of it. A covenant must be made with our eyes not even to look upon the cause of temptation, for such sins only need a spark to begin with and a blaze follows in an instant. Who would wantonly enter the leper's prison and sleep amid its horrible corruption ? He only who desires to be leprous himself would thus court contagion. If the mariner knew how to avoid a storm, he would do anything rather than run the risk of weathering it. Cautious pilots have no desire to try how near the quicksand they can sail, or how often they may touch a rock without springing a leak ; their aim is to keep as nearly as possible in the midst of a safe channel.

This day I may be exposed to great peril, let me have the serpent's wisdom to keep out of it and avoid it. The wings of a dove may be of more use to me to-day than the jaws of a lion. It is true I may be an apparent loser by declining evil company, but I had better leave my cloak than lose my character ; it is not needful that I should be rich, but it is imperative upon me to be pure. No ties of friendship, no chains of beauty, no flashings of talent, no shafts of ridicule must turn me from the wise resolve to flee from sin. The devil I am to resist and he will flee from me, but the lusts of the flesh, *I* must flee, or they will surely overcome me. O God of holiness preserve thy Josephs, that Madam Bubble bewitch them not with her vile suggestions. May the horrible trinity of the world, the flesh, and the devil, never overcome us !

" In their affliction they will seek Me early."—Hosea v. 15.

LOSSES and adversities are frequently the means which the great Shepherd uses to fetch home His wandering sheep; like fierce dogs they worry the wanderers back to the fold. There is no making lions tame if they are too well fed; they must be brought down from their great strength, and their stomachs must be lowered, and then they will submit to the tamer's hand; and often have we seen the Christian rendered obedient to the Lord's will by straitness of bread and hard labour. When rich and increased in goods many professors carry their heads much too loftily, and speak exceeding boastfully. Like David, they flatter themselves, " My mountain standeth fast; I shall never be moved." When the Christian groweth wealthy, is in good repute, hath good health, and a happy family, he too often admits Mr. Carnal Security to feast at his table, and then if he be a true child of God there is a rod preparing for him. Wait awhile, and it may be you will see his substance melt away as a dream. There goes a portion of his estate—how soon the acres change hands. That debt, that dishonoured bill—how fast his losses roll in, where will they end? It is a blessed sign of divine life if when these embarrassments occur one after another he begins to be distressed about his backslidings, and betakes himself to his God. Blessed are the waves that wash the mariner upon the rock of salvation ! Losses in business are often sanctified to our soul's enriching. If the chosen soul will not come to the Lord full-handed, it shall come empty. If God, in His grace, findeth no other means of making us honour Him among men, He will cast us into the deep; if we fail to honour Him on the pinnacle of riches, He will bring us into the valley of poverty. Yet faint not, heir of sorrow, when thou art thus rebuked, rather recognise the loving hand which chastens, and say, " I will arise, and go unto my Father."

*" Giving all diligence, add to your faith virtue; and to
virtue knowledge, &c."*—2 Peter i. 5, 6.

F thou wouldest enjoy the eminent grace of
the full assurance of faith, under the blessed
Spirit's influence, and assistance, do what the
Scripture tells thee, *" Give diligence."* Take care
that thy *faith* is of the right kind—that it is not a
mere belief of doctrine, but a simple faith, depending
on Christ, and on Christ alone. Give diligent heed to
thy *courage*. Plead with God that He would give
thee the face of a lion, that thou mayest, with a consciousness of right, go on boldly. Study well the
Scriptures, and get *knowledge;* for a knowledge of
doctrine will tend very much to confirm faith. Try to
understand God's Word; let it dwell in thy heart
richly.

When thou hast done this, " Add to thy knowledge
temperance." Take heed to thy body : be temperate
without. Take heed to thy soul : be temperate within.
Get temperance of lip, life, heart, and thought. Add
to this, by God's Holy Spirit, *patience;* ask Him to
give thee that patience which endureth affliction,
which, when it is tried, shall come forth as gold.
Array yourself with patience, that you may not
murmur nor be depressed in your afflictions. When
that grace is won look to *godliness.* Godliness is
something more than religion. Make God's glory
your object in life ; live in His sight ; dwell close to
Him ; seek for fellowship with Him ; and thou hast
"godliness ;" and to that add *brotherly love.* Have a
love to all the saints : and add to that a *charity,* which
openeth its arms to all men, and loves their souls.
When you are adorned with these jewels, and just in
proportion as you practise these heavenly virtues,
will you come to know by clearest evidence "your
calling and election." " Give diligence," if you would
get assurance, for lukewarmness and doubting very
naturally go hand in hand.

" That He may set him with princes."—Psalm cxiii. 8.

OUR spiritual privileges are of the highest order. "Among princes" *is the place of select society.* "Truly our fellowship is with the Father, and with His Son Jesus Christ." Speak of select society, there is none like this! "We are a chosen generation, a peculiar people, a royal priesthood." "We are come unto the general assembly and church of the first-born, whose names are written in heaven." The saints *have courtly audience:* princes have admittance to royalty when common people must stand afar off. The child of God has free access to the inner courts of heaven. "For through Him we both have access by one Spirit unto the Father." "Let us come boldly," says the apostle, "*to the throne* of the heavenly grace." Among princes there is *abundant wealth,* but what is the abundance of princes compared with the riches of believers? for "all things are yours, and ye are Christ's, and Christ is God's." "He that spared not his own Son, but delivered Him up for us all, how shall He not with Him also freely give us all things?" Princes have *peculiar power.* A prince of heaven's empire has great influence : he wields a sceptre in his own domain ; he sits upon Jesus' throne, for "He hath made us kings and priests unto God, and we shall reign for ever and ever." We reign over the united kingdom of time and eternity. Princes, again, have *special honour.* We may look down upon all earth-born dignity from the eminence upon which grace has placed us. For what is human grandeur to this, "He hath raised us up together, and made us sit together in heavenly places in Christ Jesus"? We share the honour of Christ, and compared with this, earthly splendours are not worth a thought. Communion with Jesus is a richer gem than ever glittered in imperial diadem. Union with the Lord is a coronet of beauty outshining all the blaze of imperial pomp.

" Exceeding great and precious promises."—2 Peter i. 4.

F you would know experimentally the preciousness of the promises, and enjoy them in your
own heart, *meditate much upon them.* There
are promises which are like grapes in the wine-press;
if you will tread them the juice will flow. Thinking
over the hallowed words will often be the prelude to
their fulfilment. While you are musing upon them,
the boon which you are seeking will insensibly come
to you. Many a Christian who has thirsted for the
promise has found the favour which it ensured gently
distilling into his soul even while he has been considering the divine record ; and he has rejoiced that
ever he was led to lay the promise near his heart.

But besides *meditating* upon the promises, *seek in
thy soul to receive them as being the very words of God.*
Speak to thy soul thus, " If I were dealing with a
man's promise, I should carefully consider the ability
and the character of the man who had covenanted with
me. So with the promise of God ; my eye must not
be so much fixed upon the greatness of the mercy—
that may stagger me ; as upon the greatness of the
promiser—that will cheer me. My soul, it is God,
even thy God, God that cannot lie, who speaks to thee.
This word of His which thou art now considering is
as true as His own existence. He is a God unchangeable. He has not altered the thing which has gone
out of His mouth, nor called back one single con-
solatory sentence. Nor doth he lack any power ; it
is the God that made the heavens and the earth who
has spoken thus. Nor can he fail in wisdom as to the
time when he will bestow the favours, for He knoweth
when it is best to give and when better to withhold.
Therefore, seeing that it is the word of a God so
true, so immutable, so powerful, so wise, I will and
must believe the promise." If we thus meditate upon
the promises, and consider the Promiser, we shall
experience their sweetness, and obtain their fulfilment.

" Who shall lay anything to the charge of God's elect?"
Romans viii. 33.

MOST blessed challenge ! How unanswerable it is ! Every sin of the elect was laid upon the great Champion of our salvation, and by the atonement carried away. There is no sin in God's book against His people : He seeth no sin in Jacob, neither iniquity in Israel ; they are justified in Christ for ever. When the guilt of sin was taken away, the punishment of sin was removed. For the Christian there is no stroke from God's angry hand—nay, not so much as a single frown of punitive justice. The believer may be chastised by his Father, but God the Judge has nothing to say to the Christian, except " I have absolved thee : thou art acquitted." For the Christian there is no penal death in this world, much less any second death. He is completely freed from all the punishment as well as the guilt of sin, and the power of sin is removed too. It may stand in our way, and agitate us with perpetual warfare ; but sin is a conquered foe to every soul in union with Jesus. There is no sin which a Christian cannot overcome if he will only rely upon his God to do it. They who wear the white robe in heaven overcame through the blood of the Lamb, and we may do the same. No lust is too mighty, no besetting sin too strongly entrenched ; we can overcome through the power of Christ. Do believe it, Christian, that thy sin is a condemned thing. It may kick and struggle, but it is doomed to die. God has written condemnation across its brow. Christ has crucified it, " nailing it to His cross." Go now and mortify it, and the Lord help you to live to His praise, for sin with all its guilt, shame, and fear, is gone.

> " Here's pardon for transgressions past,
> It matters not how black their cast ;
> And, O my soul, with wonder view,
> For sins to come here's pardon too."

" *So foolish was I, and ignorant; I was as a beast before
Thee.*"—Psalm lxxiii. 22.

REMEMBER this is the confession of the man after God's own heart ; and in telling us his inner life, he writes, " So foolish was I, and ignorant." The word "*foolish*," here, means more than it signifies in ordinary language. David, in a former verse of the Psalm, writes, " I was envious at *the foolish* when I saw the prosperity of the wicked," which shows that the folly he intended had *sin* in it. He puts himself down as being thus " foolish," and adds a word which is to give intensity to it ; " so foolish was I." *How foolish* he could not tell. It was a sinful folly, a folly which was not to be excused by frailty, but to be condemned because of its perverseness and wilful ignorance, for he had been envious of the present prosperity of the ungodly, forgetful of the dreadful end awaiting all such. And are we better than David that *we* should call ourselves wise ! Do we profess that we have attained perfection, or to have been so chastened that the rod has taken all our wilfulness out of us ? Ah, this were pride indeed ! If *David* was foolish, how foolish should *we* be in our own esteem if we could but see ourselves! Look back, believer : think of your doubting God when he has been so faithful to you—think of your foolish outcry of " Not so, my Father," when he crossed his hands in affliction to give you the larger blessing ; think of the many times when you have read His providences in the dark, misinterpreted His dispensations, and groaned out, " All these things are against me," when they are all working together for your good ! Think how often you have chosen sin because of its pleasure, when indeed, that pleasure was a root of bitterness to you ! Surely if we know our own heart we must plead guilty to the indictment of a sinful folly ; and conscious of this " foolishness," we must make David's consequent resolve our own—" *Thou shalt guide me with Thy counsel.*"

" Who went about doing good."—Acts x. 38.

EW words, but yet an exquisite miniature of the Lord Jesus Christ. There are not many touches, but they are the strokes of a master's pencil. Of the Saviour and only of the Saviour is it true in the fullest, broadest, and most unqualified sense. " He went about doing good." From this description it is evident that He did good *personally*. The evangelists constantly tell us that He touched the leper with His own finger, that He anointed the eyes of the blind, and that in cases where He was asked to speak the word only at a distance, He did not usually comply, but went Himself to the sick bed, and there personally wrought the cure. A lesson to us, if we would do good, to do it ourselves. Give alms with your own hand ; a kind look, or word, will enhance the value of the gift. Speak to a friend about his soul ; your loving appeal will have more influence than a whole library of tracts. Our Lord's mode of doing good sets forth His *incessant activity !* He did not only the good which came close to hand, but He " went about " on his errands of mercy. Throughout the whole land of Judea there was scarcely a village or a hamlet which was not gladdened by the sight of Him. How this reproves the creeping, loitering manner, in which many professors serve the Lord. Let us gird up the loins of our mind, and be not weary in well doing. Does not the text imply that Jesus Christ *went out of His way to do good?* " He went *about* doing good." He was never deterred by danger or difficulty. He sought out the objects of His gracious intentions. So must we. If old plans will not answer, we must try new ones, for fresh experiments sometimes achieve more than regular methods. Christ's *perseverance*, and the *unity* of His purpose, are also hinted at, and the practical application of the subject may be summed up in the words, " He hath left us an example that we should follow in His steps."

" Nevertheless I am continually with Thee."
Ps. lxxiii. 23.

"NEVERTHELESS,"—As if, notwithstanding all the foolishness and ignorance which David had just been confessing to God, not one atom the less was it true and certain that David was saved and accepted, and that the blessing of being constantly in God's presence was undoubtedly his. Fully conscious of his own lost estate, and of the deceitfulness and vileness of his nature, yet, by a glorious outburst of faith, he sings "nevertheless I am continually with thee." Believer, you are forced to enter into Asaph's confession and acknowledgment, endeavour in like spirit to say " nevertheless, since I belong to Christ I am continually with God !" By this is meant continually upon His *mind,* He is always thinking of me for my good. Continually before His *eye;*—the eye of the Lord never sleepeth, but is perpetually watching over my welfare. Continually in His *hand,* so that none shall be able to pluck me thence. Continually on His *heart,* worn there as a memorial, even as the high priest bore the names of the twelve tribes upon his heart for ever. Thou always thinkest of me, O God. The bowels of Thy love continually yearn towards me. Thou art always making providence work for my good. Thou hast set me as a signet upon thine arm ; thy love is strong as death, many waters cannot quench it ; neither can the floods drown it. Surprising grace ! Thou seest me in Christ, and though in myself abhorred, Thou beholdest me as wearing Christ's garments, and washed in His blood, and thus I stand accepted in Thy presence. I am thus continually in Thy favour—"continually with Thee." Here is comfort for the tried and afflicted soul ; vexed with the tempest within— look at the calm without. " *Nevertheless* "—O say it in thy heart, and take the peace it gives. " Nevertheless I am continually with thee."

"All that the Father giveth Me shall come to Me."—John vi. 37.

THIS declaration involves *the doctrine of election :* there are some whom the Father gave to Christ. It involves *the doctrine of effectual calling :* these who are given must and shall come ; however stoutly they may set themselves against it, yet they shall be brought out of darkness into God's marvellous light. It teaches us *the indispensable necessity of faith ;* for even those who are given to Christ are not saved except they come to Jesus. Even *they* must come, for there is no other way to heaven but by the door, Christ Jesus. All that the Father gives to our Redeemer *must come to Him,* therefore none can come to heaven they come to Christ.

Oh ! the power and majesty which rest in the words *" shall come."* He does not say they have power to come, nor they may come if they will, but they *" shall come."* The Lord Jesus doth by his messengers, His word, and His Spirit, sweetly and graciously compel men to come in that they may eat of His marriage supper ; and this He does, not by any violation of the free agency of man, but by the power of His grace. I may exercise power over another man's will, and yet that other man's will may be perfectly free, because the constraint is exercised in a manner accordant with the laws of the human mind. Jehovah Jesus knows how, by irresistible arguments addressed to the understanding, by mighty reasons appealing to the affections, and by the mysterious influence of His Holy Spirit operating upon all the powers and passions of the soul, so to subdue the whole man, that whereas he was once rebellious, he yields cheerfully to His government, subdued by sovereign love. But how shall those be known whom God hath chosen ? By this result : that they do willingly and joyfully accept Christ, and come to Him with simple and unfeigned faith, resting upon Him as all their salvation and all their desire. Reader, have you thus come to Jesus ?

" And when he thought thereon, he wept."—Mark xiv. 72.

IT has been thought by some that as long as Peter lived, the fountain of his tears began to flow whenever he remembered his denying his Lord. It is not unlikely that it was so, for his sin was very great, and grace in him had afterwards a perfect work. This same experience is common to all the redeemed family according to the degree in which the Spirit of God has removed the natural heart of stone. We, like Peter, remember *our boastful promise:* " Though all men shall forsake Thee, yet will not I." We eat our own words with the bitter herbs of repentance. When we think of what we vowed we would be, and of what we have been, we may weep whole showers of grief. He thought on *his denying his Lord.* The place in which he did it, the little cause which led him into such heinous sin, the oaths and blasphemies with which he sought to confirm his falsehood, and the dreadful hardness of heart which drove him to do so again and yet again. Can we, when we are reminded of our sins, and their exceeding sinfulness, remain stolid and stubborn ? Will we not make our house a Bochim, and cry unto the Lord for renewed assurances of pardoning love ? May we never take a dry-eyed look at sin, lest ere long we have a tongue parched in the flames of hell. Peter also thought upon *his Master's look of love.* The Lord followed up the cock's warning voice with an admonitory look of sorrow, pity, and love. That glance was never out of Peter's mind so long as he lived. It was far more effectual than ten thousand sermons would have been without the Spirit. The penitent apostle would be sure to weep when he recollected the *Saviour's full forgiveness,* which restored him to his former place. To think that we have offended so kind and good a Lord is more than sufficient reason for being constant weepers. Lord, smite our rocky hearts, and make the waters flow.

" Him that cometh to Me I will in no wise cast out."
John vi. 37.

NO limit is set to *the duration* of this promise.
It does not merely say, " I will not cast out a
sinner at his first coming," but, " I will in
no wise cast out." The original reads, " I will *not,
not* cast out," or " I will never, never cast out." The
text means, that Christ will not *at first* reject a believer ; and that as he will not do it at first, so He
will not *to the last*.

But suppose the believer sins after coming ? " If
any man sin we have an advocate with the Father,
Jesus Christ the righteous." But suppose that believers backslide ? " I will heal their backsliding, I
will love them freely : for Mine anger is turned away
from him." But believers may fall under temptation !
" God is faithful, who will not suffer you to be tempted
above that ye are able ; but will with the temptation
also make a way to escape, that ye may be able to bear
it." But the believer may fall into sin as David did !
Yes, but He will " Purge them with hyssop, and they
shall be clean ; He will wash them and they shall be
whiter than snow ;" " From all their iniquities will I
cleanse them."

> " Once in Christ, in Christ for ever,
> Nothing from His love can sever."

" I give unto My sheep," saith He, " eternal life ; and
they shall never perish, neither shall any man pluck
them out of My hand." What sayest thou to this, O
trembling feeble mind ? Is not this a precious mercy,
that coming to Christ, thou dost not come to one who
will treat thee well for a little while, and then send
thee about thy business, but He will receive thee and
make thee His bride, and thou shalt be His for ever ?
Receive no longer the spirit of bondage again to fear,
but the spirit of adoption whereby thou shalt cry,
Abba, Father ! Oh ! the grace of these words : " I
will in no wise cast out."

" I in them."—John xvii. 23.

IF such be the union which subsists between our souls and the person of our Lord, how deep and broad is the channel of our communion! This is no narrow pipe through which a thread-like stream may wind its way, it is a channel of amazing depth and breadth, along whose glorious length a ponderous volume of living water may roll its floods. Behold he hath set before us an open door, let us not be slow to enter. This city of communion hath many pearly gates, every several gate is of one pearl, and each gate is thrown open to the uttermost that we may enter, assured of welcome. If there were but one small loophole through which to talk with Jesus, it would be a high privilege to thrust a word of fellowship through the narrow door ; how much we are blessed in having so large an entrance ! Had the Lord Jesus been far away from us, with many a stormy sea between, we should have longed to send a messenger to Him to carry Him our loves, and bring us tidings from his Father's house ; but see His kindness, He has built His house next door to ours, nay, more, He takes lodging with us, and tabernacles in poor humble hearts, that so He may have perpetual intercourse with us. O how foolish must we be, if we do not live in habitual communion with Him. When the road is long, and dangerous, and difficult, we need not wonder that friends seldom meet each other, but when they live together, shall Jonathan forget his David ? A wife may when her husband is upon a journey, abide many days without holding converse with him, but she could never endure to be separated from him if she knew him to be in one of the chambers of her own house. Why, believer, dost not thou sit at His banquet of wine ? Seek thy Lord, for He is near ; embrace Him, for He is thy Brother. Hold Him fast, for He is thine Husband ; and press Him to thine heart, for He is of thine own flesh.

"And these are the singers . . . . they were employed in that work day and night."—1 Chronicles ix. 33.

WELL was it so ordered in the temple that the sacred chant never ceased : for evermore did the singers praise the Lord, whose mercy endureth for ever. As mercy did not cease to rule either by day or by night, so neither did music hush its holy ministry. My heart, there is a lesson sweetly taught to thee in the ceaseless song of Zion's temple, thou too art a constant debtor, and see thou to it that thy gratitude, like charity, never faileth. God's praise is constant in heaven, which is to be thy final dwelling-place, learn thou to practise the eternal hallelujah. Around the earth as the sun scatters his light, his beams awaken grateful believers to tune their morning hymn, so that by the priesthood of the saints perpetual praise is kept up at all hours. they swathe our globe in a mantle of thanksgiving, and girdle it with a golden belt of song.

The Lord always deserves to be praised for what He is in Himself, for His works of creation and providence, for His goodness towards His creatures, and especially for the transcendant act of redemption, and all the marvellous blessing flowing therefrom. It is always beneficial to praise the Lord ; it cheers the day and brightens the night ; it lightens toil and softens sorrow ; and over earthly gladness it sheds a sanctifying radiance which makes it less liable to blind us with its glare. Have we not something to sing about at this moment ? Can we not weave a song out of our present joys, or our past deliverances, or our future hopes ? Earth yields her summer fruits : the hay is housed, the golden grain invites the sickle, and the sun tarrying long to shine upon a fruitful earth, shortens the interval of shade that we may lengthen the hours of devout worship. By the love of Jesus, let us be stirred up to close the day with a psalm of sanctified gladness.

" Let me now go to the field, and glean ears of corn."
Ruth ii. 2.

DOWNCAST and troubled Christian, come and glean to-day in the broad field of promise. Here are abundance of precious promises, which exactly meet thy wants. Take this one : " He will not break the bruised reed, nor quench the smoking flax." Doth not that suit thy case ?   A reed, helpless, insignificant, and weak ; a bruised reed, out of which no music can come ; weaker than weakness itself ; a reed, and that reed bruised, yet, He will not break thee ; but on the contrary, will restore and strengthen thee. Thou art like the smoking flax : no light, no warmth, can come from thee ; but He will not quench thee ; He will blow with His sweet breath of mercy till He fans thee to a flame.   Wouldst thou glean another ear ? "Come unto Me all ye that labour and are heavy laden, and I will give you rest." What soft words ! Thy heart is tender, and the Master knows it, and therefore He speaketh so gently to thee.   Wilt thou not obey Him, and come to Him even now ?   Take another ear of corn : "Fear not, thou worm Jacob, I will help thee, saith the Lord and thy Redeemer, the Holy One of Israel."   How canst thou fear with such a wonderful assurance as this ?   Thou mayest gather ten thousand such golden ears as these !   "I have blotted out thy sins like a cloud, and like a thick cloud thy transgressions."   Or this, "Though your sins be as scarlet, they shall be as white as snow ; though they be red like crimson, they shall be as wool."   Or this, "The Spirit and the Bride say, Come, and let him that is athirst come, and whosoever will let him take the water of life freely."   Our Master's field is very rich ; behold the handfuls.   See, there they lie before thee, poor timid believer !   Gather them up, make them thine own, for Jesus bids the take them.   Be not afraid, only believe !   Grasp these sweet promises, thresh them out by meditation and feed on them with joy.

" Thou crownest the year with Thy goodness."—Psalm lxv. 11.

ALL the year round, every hour of every day, God is richly blessing us ; both when we sleep and when we wake His mercy waits upon us. The sun may leave us a legacy of darkness, but our God never ceases to shine upon His children with beams of love. Like a river, His lovingkindness is always flowing, with a fulness inexhaustible as His own nature. Like the atmosphere which constantly surrounds the earth, and is always ready to support the life of man, the benevolence of God surrounds all His creatures ; in it, as in their element, they live, and move, and have their being. Yet as the sun on summer days gladdens us with beams more warm and bright than at other times, and as rivers are at certain seasons swollen by the rain, and as the atmosphere itself is sometimes fraught with more fresh, more bracing, or more balmy influences than heretofore, so is it with the mercy of God ; it hath its golden hours ; its days of overflow, when the Lord magnifieth His grace before the sons of men. Amongst the blessings of the nether springs, *the joyous days of harvest* are a special season of excessive favour. It is the glory of autumn that the ripe gifts of providence are then abundantly bestowed ; it is the mellow season of realization, whereas all before was but hope and expectation. Great is the joy of harvest. Happy are the reapers who fill their arms with the liberality of heaven. The Psalmist tells us that the harvest is the crowning of the year. Surely these crowning mercies call for crowning thanksgiving ! Let us render it by the *inward emotions of gratitude.* Let our hearts be warmed ; let our spirits remember, meditate, and think upon this goodness of the Lord. Then let us *praise him with our lips,* and laud and magnify His name from whose bounty all this goodness flows. Let us glorify God by yielding *our gifts* to His cause. A practical proof of our gratitude is a special thankoffering to the Lord of the harvest.

" Who worketh all things after the counsel of His own will."—
Eph. i. 11.

OUR belief in God's wisdom supposes and necessitates that He has a settled purpose and plan in the work of salvation. What would *creation* have been without His design? Is there a fish in the sea, or a fowl in the air, which was left to chance for its formation? Nay, in every bone, joint, and muscle, sinew, gland, and blood-vessel, you mark the presence of a God working everything according to the design of infinite wisdom. And shall God be present in creation, ruling over all, and not in *grace?* Shall the new creation have the fickle genius of free will to preside over it when divine counsel rules the old creation? Look at *Providence!* Who knoweth not that not a sparrow falleth to the ground without your Father? Even the hairs of your head are all numbered. God weighs the mountains of our grief in scales, and the hills of our tribulation in balances. And shall there be a God in providence and not in grace? Shall the shell be ordained by wisdom and the kernel be left to blind chance. No; he knows the end from the beginning. He sees in its appointed place, not merely the corner-stone which He has laid in fair colours, in the blood of His dear Son, but He beholds in their ordained position each of the chosen stones taken out of the quarry of nature, and polished by His grace; He sees the whole from corner to cornice, from base to roof, from foundation to pinnacle. He hath in His mind a clear knowledge of every stone which shall be laid in its prepared space, and how vast the edifice shall be, and when the top-stone shall be brought forth with shoutings of "Grace! Grace! unto it." At the last it shall be clearly seen that in every chosen vessel of mercy, Jehovah did as He willed with His own; and that in every part of the work of grace He accomplished His purpose, and glorified His own name.

" So she gleaned in the field until even."—Ruth ii. 17.

ET me learn from Ruth, the gleaner. As she went out to gather the ears of corn, so must I go forth into the fields of prayer, meditation, the ordinances, and hearing the word to gather spiritual food. *The gleaner gathers her portion ear by ear ;* her gains are little by little : so must I be content to search for single truths, if there be no greater plenty of them. Every ear helps to make a bundle, and every gospel lesson assists in making us wise unto salvation. *The gleaner keeps her eyes open :* if she stumbled among the stubble in a dream, she would have no load to carry home rejoicingly at eventide. I must be watchful in religious exercises lest they become unprofitable to me ; I fear I have lost much already—O that I may rightly estimate my opportunities, and glean with greater diligence. *The gleaner stoops for all she finds,* and so must I. High spirits criticise and object, but lowly minds glean and receive benefit. A humble heart is a great help towards profitably hearing the gospel. The engrafted soul-saving word is not received except with meekness. A stiff back makes a bad gleaner ; down, master pride, thou art a vile robber, not to be endured for a moment. *What the gleaner gathers she holds :* if she dropped one ear to find another, the result of her day's work would be but scant ; she is as careful to retain as to obtain, and so at last her gains are great. How often do I forget all that I hear ; the second truth pushes the first out of my head, and so my reading and hearing end in much ado about nothing ! Do I feel duly the importance of storing up the truth ? A hungry belly makes the gleaner wise ; if there be no corn in her hand, there will be no bread on her table ; she labours under the sense of necessity, and hence her tread is nimble and her grasp is firm; I have even a greater necessity, Lord, help me to feel it, that it may urge me onward to glean in fields which yield so plenteous a reward to diligence.

"The Lamb is the light thereof."—Rev. xxi. 23.

QUIETLY contemplate the Lamb as the light of heaven. Light in Scripture is the emblem of *joy.* The joy of the saints in heaven is comprised in this : *Jesus* chose us, loved us, bought us, cleansed us, robed us, kept us, glorified us : we are here entirely through the Lord Jesus. Each one of these thoughts shall be to them like a cluster of the grapes of Eshcol. Light is also the cause of *beauty.* Nought of beauty is left when light is gone. Without light no radiance flashes from the sapphire, no peaceful ray proceedeth from the pearl ; and thus all the beauty of the saints above comes from Jesus. As planets, they reflect the light of the Sun of Righteousness ; they live as beams proceeding from the central orb. If He withdrew, they must die ; if His glory were veiled, their glory must expire. Light is also the emblem of *knowledge.* In heaven our knowledge will be perfect, but the Lord Jesus Himself will be the fountain of it. Dark providences, never understood before, will then be clearly seen, and all that puzzles us now will become plain to us in the light of the Lamb. Oh! what unfoldings there will be and what glorifying of the God of love! Light also means *manifestation.* Light manifests. In this world it doth not yet appear what we shall be. God's people are a hidden people, but when Christ receives his people into heaven, he will touch them with the wand of his own love, and change them into the image of his manifested glory. They were poor and wretched, but what a transformation! They were stained with sin, but one touch of his finger, and they are bright as the sun, and clear as crystal. Oh! what a manifestation! All this proceeds from the exalted Lamb. Whatever there may be of effulgent splendour, Jesus shall be the centre and soul of it all. Oh! to be present and to see him in his own light, the King of kings, and Lord of lords !

" But as He went."—Luke viii. 42.

ESUS is passing through the throng to the house of Jairus, to raise the ruler's dead daughter; but He is so profuse in goodness that he works another miracle while upon the road. While yet this rod of Aaron bears the blossom of an unaccomplished wonder, it yields the ripe almonds of a perfect work of mercy. It is enough for us, if we have some one purpose, straightway to go and accomplish it; it were imprudent to expend our energies by the way. Hastening to the rescue of a drowning friend, we cannot afford to exhaust our strength upon another in like danger. It is enough for a tree to yield one sort of fruit, and for a man to fulfil his own peculiar calling. But our Master knows no limit of power or boundary of mission. He is so prolific of grace, that like the sun which shines as it rolls onward in its orbit, His path is radiant with lovingkindness. He is a swift arrow of love, which not only reaches its ordained target, but perfumes the air through which it flies. Virtue is evermore going out of Jesus, as sweet odours exhale from flowers; and it always will be emanating from Him, as water from a sparkling fountain. What delightful encouragement this truth affords us! If our Lord is so ready to heal the sick and bless the needy, then, my soul, be not thou slow to put thyself in His way, that He may smile on thee. Be not slack in asking, if He be so abundant in bestowing. Give earnest heed to His word now, and at all times, that Jesus may speak through it to thy heart. Where He is to be found there make thy resort, that thou mayst obtain His blessing. When He is present to heal, may He not heal Thee? But surely He is present even now, for He always comes to hearts which need Him. And dost not thou need Him? Ah, *He* knows how much! Thou Son of David, turn Thine eye and look upon the distress which is now before Thee, and make Thy suppliant whole.

" The people that do know their God shall be strong."
Daniel xi. 32.

EVERY believer understands that to know God
is the highest and best form of knowledge ;
and this spiritual knowledge is a source of
strength to the Christian. It strengthens his *faith.*
Believers are constantly spoken of in the Scriptures as
being persons who are enlightened and taught of the
Lord ; they are said to "have an unction from the
Holy One," and it is the Spirit's peculiar office to lead
them into all truth, and all this for the increase and
the fostering of their faith. Knowledge strengthens
love, as well as faith. Knowledge opens the door, and
then through that door we see our Saviour. Or, to use
another similitude, knowledge paints the portrait of
Jesus, and when we see that portrait then we love Him,
we cannot love a Christ whom we do not know, at least,
in some degree. If we know but little of the excellences of Jesus, what He has done for us, and what
He is doing now, we cannot love Him much ; but the
more we know Him, the more we shall love Him. Knowledge also strengthens *hope.* How can we hope for a
thing if we do not know of its existence ? Hope may
be the telescope, but till we receive instruction, our
ignorance stands in the front of the glass, and we can
see nothing whatever ; knowledge removes the inter-
posing object, and when we look through the bright
optic glass we discern the glory to be revealed, and
anticipate it with joyous confidence. Knowledge supplies us reasons for *patience.* How shall we have patience
unless we know something of the sympathy of Christ,
and understand the good which is to come out
of the correction which our heavenly Father sends
us ? Nor is there one single grace of the Christian
which, under God, will not be fostered and brought to
perfection by holy knowledge. How important, then,
is it that we should grow not only in grace, but in the
"knowledge" of our Lord and Saviour Jesus Christ.

*" I smote you with blasting and with mildew and with hail
in all the labours of your hands."*—Haggai ii. 17.

HOW destructive is the hail to the standing
crops, beating out the precious grain upon the
ground ! How grateful ought we to be when
the corn is spared so terrible a ruin ! Let us offer
unto the Lord thanksgiving. Even more to be
dreaded are those mysterious destroyers—smut, bunt,
rust, and mildew. These turn the ear into a mass of
soot, or render it putrid, or dry up the grain, and all
in a manner so beyond all human control that the
farmer is compelled to cry, " This is the finger of God."
Innumerable minute fungi cause the mischief, and
were it not for the goodness of God, the rider on the
black horse would soon scatter famine over the land.
Infinite mercy spares the food of men, but in view of the
active agents which are ready to destroy the harvest,
right wisely are we taught to pray, " Give us this day
our daily bread." The curse is abroad; we have constant
need of the blessing. When blight and mildew come
they are chastisements from heaven, and men must
learn to hear the rod, and Him that hath appointed it.

Spiritually, mildew is no uncommon evil. When
our work is most promising this blight appears.
We hoped for many conversions, and lo ! a general
apathy, an abounding worldliness, or a cruel hardness
of heart ! There may be no open sin in those for
whom we are labouring, but there is a deficiency of
sincerity and decision sadly disappointing our desires.
We learn from this our dependence upon the Lord,
and the need of prayer that no blight may fall upon
our work. Spiritual pride or sloth will soon bring
upon us the dreadful evil, and only the Lord of the
harvest can remove it. Mildew may even attack our
own hearts, and shrivel our prayers and religious
exercises. May it please the great Husbandman to
avert so serious a calamity. Shine, blessed Sun of
Righteousness, and drive the blights away.

" We know that all things work together for good to them that love God."—Romans viii. 28.

UPON some points a believer is absolutely sure. He knows, for instance, that God sits in the stern-sheets of the vessel when it rocks most. He believes that an invisible hand is always on the world's tiller, and that wherever providence may drift, Jehovah steers it. That re-assuring knowledge prepares him for everything. He looks over the raging waters and sees the spirit of Jesus treading the billows, and he hears a voice saying, "It is I, be not afraid." He knows too that God is always wise, and, knowing this, he is confident that there can be no accidents, no mistakes ; that nothing can occur which ought not to arise. He can say, "If I should lose all I have, it is better that I should lose than have, if God so wills : the worst calamity is the wisest and the kindest thing that could befall to me if God ordains it." "We know that all things work together for good to them that love God." The Christian does not merely hold this as a theory, but *he knows it* as a matter of fact. Everything *has* worked for good as yet ; the poisonous drugs mixed in fit proportions have worked the cure ; the sharp cuts of the lancet have cleansed out the proud flesh and facilitated the healing. Every event as yet has worked out the most divinely blessed results ; and so, believing that God rules all, that He governs wisely, that He brings good out of evil, the believer's heart is assured, and he is enabled calmly to meet each trial as it comes. The believer can in the spirit of true resignation pray, "Send me what thou wilt, my God, so long as it comes from Thee ; never came there an ill portion from Thy table to any of Thy children."

"Say not my soul, 'From whence can God relieve my care ?
Remember that Omnipotence has servants everywhere.
His method is sublime, His heart profoundly kind,
God never is before His time, and never is behind."

" Shall your brethren go to war, and shall ye sit here ?"
Numbers xxxii. 6.

KINDRED has its obligations. The Reubenites and Gadites would have been most unbrotherly if they had claimed the land which had been conquered, and had left the rest of the people to fight for their portions alone. We have received much by means of the efforts and sufferings of the saints in years gone by, and if we do not make some return to the church of Christ by giving her our best energies, we are unworthy to be enrolled in her ranks. Others are combating the errors of the age manfully, or excavating perishing ones from amid the ruins of the fall, and if we fold our hands in idleness we had need be warned, lest the curse of Meroz fall upon us. The Master of the vineyard saith, " Why stand ye here all the day idle ?" What is the idler's excuse ? Personal service of Jesus becomes all the more the duty of all because it is cheerfully and abundantly rendered by some. The toils of devoted missionaries and fervent ministers shame us if we sit still in indolence. Shrinking from trial is the temptation of those who are at ease in Zion : they would fain escape the cross and yet wear the crown ; to them the question for this evening's meditation is very applicable. If the most precious are tried in the fire, are we to escape the crucible ? If the diamond must be vexed upon the wheel, are we to be made perfect without suffering ? Who hath commanded the wind to cease from blowing because our bark is on the deep ? Why and wherefore should we be treated better than our Lord ? The firstborn felt the rod, and why not the younger brethren ? It is a cowardly pride which would choose a downy pillow and a silken couch for a soldier of the cross. Wiser far is he who, being first resigned to the divine will, groweth by the energy of grace to be pleased with it, and so learns to gather lilies at the cross foot, and, like Samson, to find honey in the lion.

" Watchman, what of the night?"—Isaiah xxi. 11.

HAT *enemies are abroad?* Errors are a numerous horde, and new ones appear every hour : against what heresy am I to be on my guard ? Sins creep from their lurking places when the darkness reigns ; I must myself mount the watch-tower, and watch unto prayer. Our heavenly Protector foresees all the attacks which are about to be made upon us, and when as yet the evil designed us is but in the desire of Satan, He prays for us that our faith fail not, when we are sifted as wheat. Continue O gracious Watchman, to forewarn us of our foes, and for Zion's sake hold not Thy peace.

"Watchman, what of the night ?" *What weather is coming* for the Church ? Are the clouds lowering, or is it all clear and fair overhead ? We must care for the Church of God with anxious love ; and now that Popery and infidelity are both threatening, let us observe the signs of the times and prepare for conflict.

"Watchman, what of the night ?" *What stars are visible?* What precious promises suit our present case ? You sound the alarm, give us the consolation also. Christ, the pole-star, is ever fixed in His place, and all the stars are secure in the right hand of their Lord.

But watchman, *when comes the morning?* The Bridegroom tarries. Are there no signs of His coming forth as the Sun of Righteousness ? Has not the morning star arisen as the pledge of day ? When will the day dawn, and the shadows flee away ? O Jesus, if Thou come not in person to thy waiting Church this day, yet come in Spirit to my sighing heart, and make it sing for joy.

> "Now all the earth is bright and glad
>   With the fresh morn ;
> But all my heart is cold, and dark and sad :
> Sun of the soul, let me behold Thy dawn !
>   Come, Jesus, Lord,
> O quickly come, according to Thy word."

*" Let the whole earth be filled with His glory; Amen, and
Amen."*—Psalm lxxii. 19.

THIS is a large petition. To intercede for a
whole city needs a stretch of faith, and there
are times when a prayer for one man is
enough to stagger us. But how far-reaching was the
psalmist's dying intercession! How comprehensive!
How sublime! "Let the whole earth be filled with
His glory." It doth not exempt a single country however crushed by the foot of superstition; it doth not
exclude a single nation however barbarous. For the
cannibal as well as for the civilized, for all climes and
races this prayer is uttered: the whole circle of the
earth it encompasses, and omits no son of Adam. We
must be up and doing for our Master, or we cannot
honestly offer such a prayer. The petition is not
asked with a sincere heart unless we endeavour, as God
shall help us, to extend the kingdom of our Master.
Are there not some who *neglect* both to plead and to
labour? Reader, is it *your* prayer? Turn your eyes
to Calvary. Behold the Lord of Life nailed to a cross,
with the thorn-crown about His brow, with bleeding
head, and hands, and feet. What! can you look upon
this miracle of miracles, the death of the Son of God,
without feeling within your bosom a marvellous adoration that language never can express? And when you
feel the blood applied to your conscience, and know
that He has blotted out your sins, *you are not a man*
unless you start from your knees and cry, "Let the
whole earth be filled with His glory; Amen, and Amen."
Can you bow before the Crucified in loving homage,
and not wish to see your Monarch master of the
world? Out on you if you can pretend to love your
Prince, and desire not to see him the universal ruler
Your piety is worthless unless it leads you to wish
that the same mercy which has been extended to you
may bless the whole world. Lord, it is harvest-time,
put in Thy sickle and reap.

" The upright love Thee."—Canticles i. 4.

BELIEVERS love Jesus with a deeper affection than they dare to give to any other being. They would sooner lose father and mother than part with Christ. They hold all earthly comforts with a loose hand, but they carry him fast locked in their bosoms. They voluntarily deny themselves for His sake, but they are not to be driven to deny *Him*. It is scant love which the fire of persecution can dry up ; the true believer's love is a deeper stream than this. Men have laboured to divide the faithful from their Master, but their attempts have been fruitless in every age. Neither crowns of honour, nor frowns of anger, have untied this more than Gordian knot. This is no every-day attachment which the world's power may at length dissolve. Neither man nor devil have found a key which opens this lock. Never has the craft of Satan been more at fault than when he has exercised it in seeking to rend in sunder this union of two divinely welded hearts. It is written, and nothing can blot out the sentence, *" The upright love Thee."* The intensity of the love of the upright, however, is not so much to be judged by what it appears as by what the upright long for. It is our daily lament that we cannot love enough. Would that our hearts were capable of holding more, and reaching further. Like Samuel Rutherford, we sigh and cry, " Oh, for as much love as would go round about the earth, and over heaven—yea, the heaven of heavens, and ten thousand worlds—that I might let all out upon fair, fair, only fair Christ." Alas ! our longest reach is but a span of love, and our affection is but as a drop of a bucket compared with His deserts. Measure our love by our intentions, and it is high indeed ; 'tis thus, we trust, our Lord doth judge of it. Oh, that we could give all the love in all hearts in one great mass, a gathering together of all loves to Him who is alto-gether lovely !

"Satan hindered us."—1 Thessalonians ii. 18.

SINCE the first hour in which goodness came into conflict with evil, it has never ceased to be true in spiritual experience, that Satan hinders us. From all points of the compass, all along the line of battle, in the vanguard and in the rear, at the dawn of day and in the midnight hour, Satan hinders us. If we toil in the field, he seeks to break the ploughshare; if we build the wall, he labours to cast down the stones; if we would serve God in suffering or in conflict—everywhere Satan hinders us. He hinders us when we are first coming to Jesus Christ. Fierce conflicts we had with Satan when we first looked to the cross and lived. Now that we are saved, he endeavours to hinder the completeness of our personal character. You may be congratulating yourself, "I have hitherto walked consistently; no man can challenge my integrity." Beware of boasting, for your virtue will yet be tried; Satan will direct his engines against that very virtue for which you are the most famous. If you have been hitherto a firm believer, your faith will ere long be attacked; if you have been meek as Moses, expect to be tempted to speak unadvisedly with your lips. The birds will peck at your ripest fruit, and the wild boar will dash his tusks at your choicest vines. Satan is sure to hinder us when we are earnest in prayer. He checks our importunity, and weakens our faith in order that, if possible, we may miss the blessing. Nor is Satan less vigilant in obstructing Christian effort. There was never a revival of religion without a revival of his opposition. As soon as Ezra and Nehemiah begin to labour, Sanballat and Tobiah are stirred up to hinder them. What then? We are not alarmed because Satan hindereth us, for it is a proof that we are on the Lord's side, and are doing the Lord's work, and in His strength we shall win the victory, and triumph over our adversary.

" They weave the spider's web." —Isaiah lix. 5.

SEE the spider's web, and behold in it a most suggestive picture of the hypocrite's religion. *It is meant to catch his prey:* the spider fattens himself on flies, and the Pharisee has his reward. Foolish persons are easily entrapped by the loud professions of pretenders, and even the more judicious cannot always escape.   Philip baptized Simon Magus, whose guileful declaration of faith was so soon exploded by the stern rebuke of Peter. Custom, reputation praise, advancement, and other flies, are the small game which hypocrites take in their nets.   A spider's web is *a marvel of skill:* look at it and admire the cunning hunter's wiles.   Is not a deceiver's religion equally wonderful?   How does he make so barefaced a lie appear to be a truth?   How can he make his tinsel answer so well the purpose of gold?   A spider's web *comes all from the creature's own bowels.* The bee gathers her wax from flowers, the spider sucks no flowers, and yet she spins out her material to any length. Even so hypocrites find their trust and hope within themselves ; their anchor was forged on their own anvil, and their cable twisted by their own hands. They lay their own foundation, and hew out the pillars of their own house, disdaining to be debtors to the sovereign grace of God.   But a spider's web is *very frail.*   It is curiously wrought, but not enduringly manufactured. It is no match for the servant's broom, or the traveller's staff.   The hypocrite needs no battery of Armstrongs to blow his hope to pieces, a mere puff of wind will do it.   Hypocritical cobwebs will soon come down when the besom of destruction begins its purifying work.   Which reminds us of one more thought, viz., that such cobwebs *are not to be endured in the Lord's house:* He will see to it that they and those who spin them shall be destroyed for ever. O my soul, be thou resting on something better than a spider's web. Be the Lord Jesus thine eternal hiding-place.

" All things are possible to him that believeth."—Mark ix. 23.

MANY professed Christians are always doubting and fearing, and they forlornly think that this is the necessary state of believers. This is a mistake, for "all things are possible to him that believeth;" and it is possible for us to mount into a state in which a doubt or a fear shall be but as a bird of passage flitting across the soul, but never lingering there. When you read of the high and sweet communions enjoyed by favoured saints, you sigh and murmur in the chamber of your heart, "Alas! these are not for me." O climber, if thou hast but faith, thou shalt yet stand upon the sunny pinnacle of the temple, for "all things are possible to him that believeth." You hear of exploits which holy men have done for Jesus; what they have enjoyed of Him; how much they have been like Him; how they have been able to endure great persecutions for His sake; and you say, "Ah! as for me, I am but a worm; I can never attain to this." But there is nothing which one saint was, that you may not be. There is no elevation of grace, no attainment of spirituality, no clearness of assurance, no post of duty, which is not open to you if you have but the power to believe. Lay aside your sackcloth and ashes, and rise to the dignity of your true position; you are little in Israel because you will be so, not because there is any necessity for it. It is not meet that thou shouldst grovel in the dust, O child of a King. Ascend! The golden throne of assurance is waiting for you! The crown of communion with Jesus is ready to bedeck your brow. Wrap yourself in scarlet and fine linnen, and fare sumptuously every day; for if thou believest, thou mayst eat the fat of kidneys of wheat; thy land shall flow with milk and honey, and thy soul shall be satisfied as with marrow and fatness. Gather golden sheaves of grace, for they await thee in the fields of faith. "All things are possible to him that believeth."

" The city hath no need of the sun, neither of the moon, to shine in it."—Rev. xxi. 23.

YONDER in the better world, the inhabitants are independent of all creature comforts. They have no need of raiment; their white robes never wear out, neither shall they ever be defiled. They need no medicine to heal diseases, "for the inhabitant shall not say, I am sick." They need no sleep to recruit their frames—they rest not day nor night, but unweariedly praise Him in His temple. They need no social relationship to minister comfort, and whatever happiness they may derive from association with their fellows is not essential to their bliss, for their Lord's society is enough for their largest desires. They need no teachers there; they doubtless commune with one another concerning the things of God, but they do not require this by way of instruction; they shall all be taught of the Lord. Ours are the alms at the king's gate, but they feast at the table itself. Here we lean upon the friendly arm, but there they lean upon their Beloved and upon Him alone. Here we must have the help of our companions, but there they find all they want in Christ Jesus. Here we look to the meat which perisheth, and to the raiment which decays before the moth, but there they find everything in God. We use the bucket to fetch us water from the well, but there they drink from the fountain head, and put their lips down to the living water. Here the angels bring us blessings, but we shall want no messengers from heaven then. They shall need no Gabriels there to bring their love-notes from God, for there they shall see *Him* face to face. Oh! what a blessed time shall that be when we shall have mounted above every second cause and shall rest upon the bare arm of God! What a glorious hour when God, and not His creatures; the Lord, and not His works, shall be our daily joy! Our souls shall then have attained the perfection of bliss.

" He appeared first to Mary Magdalene, out of whom He had cast seven devils."—Mark xvi. 9.

MARY of Magdala was *the victim of a fearful evil.* She was possessed by not one devil only, but seven. These dreadful inmates caused much pain and pollution to the poor frame in which they had found a lodging. Hers was a hopeless, horrible case. She could not help herself, neither could any human succour avail. But Jesus passed that way, and unsought, and probably even resisted by the poor demoniac, He uttered the word of power, and Mary of Magdala became *a trophy of the healing power of Jesus.* All the seven demons left her, left her never to return, forcibly ejected by the Lord of all. What a blessed deliverance! What a happy change! From delirium to delight, from despair to peace, from hell to heaven! Straightway she became *a constant follower of Jesus,* catching His every word, following His devious steps, sharing His toilsome life ; and withal she became *His generous helper,* first among that band of healed and grateful women who ministered unto Him of their substance. When Jesus was lifted up in crucifixion, Mary remained *the sharer of His shame :* we find her first beholding from afar, and then drawing near to the foot of the cross. She could not die on the cross with Jesus, but she stood as near it as she could, and when His blessed body was taken down, she watched to see how and where it was laid. She was *the faithful and watchful believer,* last at the sepulchre where Jesus slept, first at the grave whence He arose. Her holy fidelity made her *a favoured beholder of her beloved Rabboni,* who deigned to call her by her name, and to make her *His messenger of good news* to the trembling disciples and Peter. Thus grace found her a maniac and made her a minister, cast out devils and gave her to behold angels, delivered her from Satan, and united her for ever to the Lord Jesus. May I also be such a miracle of grace !

" Christ, who is our life."—Colossians iii. 4.

AUL'S marvellously rich expression indicates, that Christ is the *source* of our life. "You hath He quickened who were dead in trespasses and sins." That same voice which brought Lazarus out of the tomb raised us to newness of life. He is now the *substance* of our spiritual life. It is by His life that we live; He is in us, the hope of glory, the spring of our actions, the central thought which moves every other thought. *Christ is the sustenance of our life.* What can the Christian feed upon but Jesus' flesh and blood? "This is the bread which cometh down from heaven, that a man may eat thereof, and not die." O wayworn pilgrims in this wilderness of sin, you never get a morsel to satisfy the hunger of your spirits, except ye find it in Him! *Christ is the solace of our life.* All our true joys come from Him; and in times of trouble, His presence is our consolation. There is nothing worth living for but Him; and His lovingkindness is better than life! *Christ is the object of our life.* As speeds the ship towards the port, so hastes the believer towards the haven of his Saviour's bosom. As flies the arrow to its goal, so flies the Christian towards the perfecting of his fellowship with Christ Jesus. As the soldier fights for his captain, and is crowned in his captain's victory, so the believer contends for Christ, and gets his triumph out of the triumphs of his Master. "For him to live is Christ." *Christ is the exemplar of our life.* Where there is the same life within, there will, there must be, to a great extent, the same developments without; and if we live in near fellowship with the Lord Jesus we shall grow like Him. We shall set Him before us as our Divine copy, and we shall seek to tread in His footsteps, until He shall become *the crown of our life* in glory. Oh! how safe, how honoured, how happy is the Christian, since Christ is **our** life!

" The Son of Man hath power on earth to forgive sins."
Matthew ix. 6.

BEHOLD one of the great Physician's mightiest arts : He has power to forgive sin! While here He lived below, before the ransom had been paid, before the blood had been literally sprinkled on the mercy-seat, He had power to forgive sin. Hath He not power to do it now that He hath died ? What power must dwell in Him who to the utmost farthing has faithfully discharged the debts of His people! He has boundless power now that He has finished transgression and made an end of sin. If ye doubt it, see Him rising from the dead! behold Him in ascending splendour raised to the right hand of God ! Hear Him pleading before the eternal Father, pointing to His wounds, urging the merit of His sacred passion! What power to forgive is here ! "He hath ascended on high, and received gifts for men." " He is exalted on high to give repentance and remission of sins." The most crimson sins are removed by the crimson of His blood. At this moment, dear reader, whatever thy sinfulness, Christ has power to pardon, power to pardon *thee*, and millions such as thou art. A word will speak it. He has nothing more to do to win thy pardon ; all the atoning work is done. He can, in answer to thy tears, forgive thy sins to-day, and make thee know it. He can breathe into thy soul at this very moment a peace with God which passeth all understanding, which shall spring from perfect remission of thy manifold iniquities. Dost thou believe that ? I trust thou believest it. Mayst thou experience now the power of Jesus to forgive sin ! Waste no time in applying to the Physician of souls, but hasten to Him with words like these :—

"Jesus! Master! hear my cry ;
Save me, heal me with a word ;
Fainting at Thy feet I lie,
Thou my whisper'd plaint hast heard."

" Oh that I were as in months past."—Job xxix. 2.

NUMBERS of Christians can view the past with pleasure, but regard the present with dissatisfaction; they look back upon the days which they have passed in communing with the Lord as being the sweetest and the best they have ever known, but as to the present, it is clad in a sable garb of gloom and dreariness. Once they lived near to Jesus, but now they feel that they have wandered from Him, and they say, "O that I were as in months past!" They complain that they have lost their evidences, or that they have not present peace of mind, or that they have no enjoyment in the means of grace, or that conscience is not so tender, or that they have not so much zeal for God's glory. The causes of this mournful state of things are manifold. It may arise through a comparative *neglect of prayer*, for a neglected closet is the beginning of all spiritual decline. Or it may be the result of *idolatry*. The heart has been occupied with something else, more than with God; the affections have been set on the things of earth, instead of the things of heaven. A jealous God will not be content with a divided heart; He must be loved first and best. He will withdraw the sunshine of his presence from a cold, wandering heart. Or the cause may be found in *self-confidence* and *self-righteousness*. Pride is busy in the heart, and self is exalted instead of lying low at the foot of the cross. Christian, if you are not now as you "were in months past," do not rest satisfied with *wishing* for a return of former happiness, but go at once to seek your Master, and tell Him your sad state. Ask His grace and strength to help you to walk more closely with Him; humble yourself before Him, and He will lift you up, and give you yet again to enjoy the light of His countenance. Do not sit down to sigh and lament; while the beloved Physician lives there is hope, nay there is a certainty of recovery for the worst cases.

"Everlasting consolation."—2 Thessalonians ii. 16.

"CONSOLATION." There is music in the word: like David's harp, it charms away the evil spirit of melancholy. It was a distinguished honour to Barnabas to be called "the son of consolation;" nay, it is one of the illustrious names of a greater than Barnabas, for the Lord Jesus is "the consolation of Israel." *"Everlasting consolation"*—here is the cream of all, for the eternity of comfort is the crown and glory of it. What is this "everlasting consolation"? It includes a sense of pardoned sin. A Christian man has received in his heart the witness of the Spirit that his iniquities are put away like a cloud, and his transgressions like a thick cloud. If sin be pardoned, is not that an everlasting consolation? Next, the Lord gives His people an abiding sense of acceptance in Christ. The Christian knows that God looks upon him as standing in union with Jesus. Union to the risen Lord is a consolation of the most abiding order; it is, in fact, everlasting. Let sickness prostrate us, have we not seen hundreds of believers as happy in the weakness of disease as they would have been in the strength of hale and blooming health? Let death's arrows pierce us to the heart, our comfort dies not, for have not our ears full often heard the songs of saints as they have rejoiced because the living love of God was shed abroad in their hearts in dying moments? Yes, a sense of acceptance in the Beloved is an everlasting consolation. Moreover, the Christian has a conviction of his security. God has promised to save those who trust in Christ: the Christian does trust in Christ, and he belives that God will be as good as His word, and will save him. He feels that he is safe by virtue of his being bound up with the person and work of Jesus.

"The Lord reigneth, let the earth rejoice."—Psalm xcvii. 1.

AUSES for disquietude there are none so long as this blessed sentence is true. *On earth* the Lord's power as readily controls the rage of the wicked as the rage of the sea; His love as easily refreshes the poor with mercy as the earth with showers. Majesty gleams in flashes of fire amid the tempest's horrors, and the glory of the Lord is seen in its grandeur in the fall of empires, and the crash of thrones. In all our conflicts and tribulations, we may behold the hand of the divine King.

> "God is God; He sees and hears
> All our troubles, all our tears.
> Soul, forget not, 'mid thy pains,
> God o'er all for ever reigns."

In hell, evil spirits own, with misery, His undoubted supremacy. When permitted to roam abroad, it is with a chain at their heel; the bit is in the mouth of behemoth, and the hook in the jaws of leviathan. Death's darts are under the Lord's lock, and the grave's prisons have divine power as their warder. The terrible vengeance of the Judge of all the earth makes fiends cower down and tremble, even as dogs in the kennel fear the hunter's whip.

> "Fear not death, nor Satan's thrusts,
> God defends who in Him trusts;
> Soul, remember, in thy pains,
> God o'er all for ever reigns."

In heaven none doubt the sovereignty of the King Eternal, but all fall on their faces to do Him homage. Angels are His courtiers, the redeemed His favourites, and all delight to serve Him day and night. May we soon reach the city of the great King!

> "For this life's long night of sadness
> He will give us peace and gladness.
> Soul, remember, in thy pains,
> God o'er all for ever reigns."

" The bow shall be seen in the cloud."—Genesis ix. 14.

THE rainbow, the symbol of the covenant with Noah, is typical of our Lord Jesus, who is the Lord's witness to the people. When may we *expect to see the token of the covenant?* The rainbow is only to be seen painted upon a *cloud.* When the sinner's conscience is dark with clouds, when he remembers his past sin, and mourneth and lamenteth before God, Jesus Christ is revealed to him as the covenant Rainbow, displaying all the glorious hues of the divine character and betokening peace. To the believer, when his trials and temptations surround him, it is sweet to behold the person of our Lord Jesus Christ—to see Him bleeding, living, rising, and pleading for us. God's rainbow is hung over the cloud of our sins, our sorrows, and our woes, to prophesy deliverance. Nor does a *cloud* alone give a rainbow, there must be the *crystal drops* to reflect the light of the sun. So, our sorrows must not only threaten, but they must really fall upon us. There had been no Christ for us if the vengeance of God had been merely a threatening cloud: punishment must fall in terrible drops upon the Surety. Until there is a *real* anguish in the sinner's conscience, there is no Christ for him; until the chastisement which he feels becomes grievous, he cannot see Jesus. But there must also be *a sun;* for clouds and drops of rain make not rainbows unless the sun shineth. Beloved, our God, who is as the sun to us, always shines, but we do not always see Him—clouds hide His face; but no matter what drops may be falling, or what clouds may be threatening, if *He* does but shine there will be a rainbow at once. It is said that when we see the rainbow the shower is over. Certain it is, that when Christ comes, our troubles remove; when we behold Jesus, our sins vanish, and our doubts and fears subside. When Jesus walks the waters of the sea, how profound the calm!

" The cedars of Lebanon which He hath planted."—Ps. civ. 16.

EBANON'S cedars are emblematic of the Christian, in that *they owe their planting entirely to the Lord.* This is quite true of every child of God. He is not man-planted, nor self-planted, but God-planted. The mysterious hand of the divine Spirit dropped the living seed into a heart which He had Himself prepared for its reception. Every true heir of heaven owns the great Husbandman as his planter. Moreover, the cedars of Lebanon *are not dependent upon man for their watering;* they stand on the lofty rock, unmoistened by human irrigation; and yet our heavenly Father supplieth them. Thus it is with the Christian who has learned to live by faith. He is independent of man, even in temporal things ; for his continued maintenance he looks to the Lord his God, and to Him alone. The dew of heaven is his portion, and the God of heaven is his fountain. Again, the cedars of Lebanon are *not protected by any mortal power.* They owe nothing to man for their preservation from stormy wind and tempest. They are God's trees, kept and preserved by Him, and by Him alone. It is precisely the same with the Christian. He is not a hot-house plant, sheltered from temptation ; he stands in the most exposed position; he has no shelter, no protection, except this, that the broad wings of the eternal God always cover the cedars which He Himself has planted. Like cedars, believers *are full of sap,* having vitality enough to be ever green, even amid winter's snows. Lastly, the flourishing and majestic condition of the cedar is *to the praise of God only.* The Lord, even the Lord alone hath been everything unto the cedars, and, therefore David very sweetly puts it in one of the psalms, "Praise ye the Lord, fruitful trees and all cedars." In the believer there is nothing that can magnify man ; he is planted, nourished, and protected by the Lord's own hand, and to Him let all the glory be ascribed.

"And I will remember My covenant."—Genesis ix, 15.

MARK the form of the promise. God does not say, "And when *ye* shall look upon the bow, and *ye* shall remember My covenant, *then* I will not destroy the earth," but it is gloriously put, not upon *our* memory, which is fickle and frail, but upon *God's* memory, which is infinite and immutable. "The bow shall be in the cloud; and *I* will look upon it, that *I* may remember the everlasting covenant." Oh! it is not *my* remembering God, it is God's remembering *me* which is the ground of my safety; it is not *my* laying hold of His covenant, but His covenant's laying hold on me. Glory be to God! the whole of the bulwarks of salvation are secured by divine power, and even the minor towers, which we may imagine might have been left to man, are guarded by almighty strength. Even the *remembrance* of the covenant is not left to our memories, for *we* might forget, but our Lord cannot forget the saints whom He has graven on the palms of His hands. It is with us as with Israel in Egypt; the blood was upon the lintel and the two side-posts, but the Lord did not say, "When *you* see the blood I will pass over you," but "When *I* see the blood I will pass over you." My looking to Jesus brings me joy and peace, but it is God's looking to Jesus which secures my salvation and that of all His elect, since it is impossible for our God to look at Christ, our bleeding Surety, and then to be angry with us for sins already punished in Him. No, it is not left with *us* even to be saved by remembering the covenant. There is no linsey-wolsey here—not a single thread of the creature mars the fabric. It is not *of* man, neither *by* man, but of the Lord alone. We *should* remember the covenant, and we *shall* do it, through divine grace; but the hinge of our safety does not hang there—it is God's remembering *us*, not our remembering *him;* and hence the covenant is *an everlasting covenant.*

" Thou, Lord, hast made me glad through Thy work."
Psalm xcii. 4.

DO you believe that your sins are forgiven, and that Christ has made a full atonement for them? Then what a joyful Christian *you ought to be!* How you should live above the common trials and troubles of the world! Since sin is forgiven, can it matter what happens to you now? Luther said, "Smite, Lord, smite, for my sin is forgiven; if Thou hast but forgiven me, smite as hard as Thou wilt;" and in a similar spirit you may say, "Send sickness, poverty, losses, crosses, persecution, what Thou wilt, *Thou hast forgiven me,* and my soul is glad." Christian, if thou art thus saved, whilst thou art glad, *be grateful and loving.* Cling to that cross which took thy sin away; serve thou Him who served thee. "I beseech you therefore, by the mercies of God, that ye present your bodies a living sacrifice, holy, acceptable unto God, which is your reasonable service." Let not your zeal evaporate in some little ebullition of song. Show your love in expressive tokens. Love the brethren of Him who loved you. If there be a Mephibosheth anywhere who is lame or halt, help him for Jonathan's sake. If there be a poor tried believer, weep with him, and bear his cross for the sake of Him who wept for thee and carried thy sins. Since thou art thus forgiven freely for Christ's sake, go and tell to others the joyful news of pardoning mercy. Be not contented with this unspeakable blessing for thyself alone, but publish abroad the story of the cross. Holy gladness and holy boldness will make you a good preacher, and all the world will be a pulpit for you to preach in. Cheerful holiness is the most forcible of sermons, but the Lord must give it you. Seek it this morning before you go into the world. When it is the Lord's work in which we rejoice, we need not be afraid of being too glad.

" I know their sorrows."—Exodus iii. 7.

THE child is cheered as he sings, "This my father knows;" and shall not we be comforted as we discern that our dear Friend and tender soul-husband knows all about us?

1. *He is the Physician*, and if He knows all, there is no need that the patient should know. Hush, thou silly, fluttering heart, prying, peeping, and suspecting! What thou knowest not now, thou shalt know hereafter, and meanwhile Jesus, the beloved Physician, knows thy soul in adversities. Why need the patient analyse all the medicine, or estimate all the symptoms? This is the Physician's work, not mine; it is my business to trust, and his to prescribe. If He shall write His prescription in uncouth characters which I cannot read, I will not be uneasy on that account, but rely upon His unfailing skill to make all plain in the result, however mysterious in the working.

2. *He is the Master*, and His knowledge is to serve us instead of our own; we are to obey, not to judge: "The servant knoweth not what his lord doeth." Shall the architect explain his plans to every hodman on the works? If he knows his own intent, is it not enough? The vessel on the wheel cannot guess to what pattern it shall be conformed, but if the potter understands his art, what matters the ignorance of the clay? My Lord must not be cross-questioned any more by one so ignorant as I am.

3. *He is the Head.* All understanding centres there What judgment has the arm? What comprehension has the foot? All the power to know lies in the head. Why should the member have a brain of its own when the head fulfils for it every intellectual office? Here, then, must the believer rest his comfort in sickness, not that he himself can see the end, but that Jesus knows all. Sweet Lord, be thou for ever eye, and soul, and head for us, and let us be content to know only what Thou choosest to reveal.

" Isaac went out to meditate in the field at the eventide."—
Gen. xxiv. 63.

ERY admirable was his occupation. If those who spend so many hours in idle company, light reading, and useless pastimes, could learn wisdom, they would find more profitable society and more interesting engagements in meditation than in the vanities which now have such charms for them. We should all know more, live nearer to God, and grow in grace, if we were more alone. Meditation chews the cud and extracts the real nutriment from the mental food gathered elsewhere. When Jesus is the theme, meditation is sweet indeed. Isaac found Rebecca while engaged in private musings ; many others have found their best beloved there.

Very admirable was the choice of place. In the field we have a study hung round with texts for thought. From the cedar to the hyssop, from the soaring eagle down to the chirping grasshopper, from the blue expanse of heaven to a drop of dew, all things are full of teaching, and when the eye is divinely opened, that teaching flashes upon the mind far more vividly than from written books. Our little rooms are neither so healthy, so suggestive, so agreeable, or so inspiring as the fields. Let us count nothing common or unclean, but feel that all created things point to their Maker, and the field will at once be hallowed.

Very admirable was the season. The season of sunset as it draws a veil over the day, befits that repose of the soul when earthborn cares yield to the joys of heavenly communion. The glory of the setting sun excites our wonder, and the solemnity of approaching night awakens our awe. If the business of this day will permit it, it will be well, dear reader, if you can spare an hour to walk in the field at eventide, but if not, the Lord is in the town too, and will meet with thee in thy chamber or in the crowded street. Let thy heart go forth to meet Him.

" And I will give you an heart of flesh."—Ezekiel xxxvi. 26.

HEART of flesh is known by its *tenderness concerning sin.* To have indulged a foul imagination, or to have allowed a wild desire to tarry even for a moment, is quite enough to make a heart of flesh grieve before the Lord, The heart of stone calls a great iniquity nothing, but not so the heart of flesh.

> " If to the right or left I stray,
>   That moment, Lord, reprove ;
> And let me weep my life away,
>   For having grieved thy love."

The heart of flesh is *tender of God's will.* My Lord Will-be-will is a great blusterer, and it is hard to subject him to God's will ; but when the heart of flesh is given, the will quivers like an aspen leaf in every breath of heaven, and bows like an osier in every breeze of God's Spirit. The natural will is cold, hard iron, which is not to be hammered into form, but the renewed will, like molten metal, is soon moulded by the hand of grace. In the fleshy heart there is a *tenderness of the affections.* The hard heart does not love the Redeemer, but the renewed heart burns with affection towards Him. The hard heart is selfish and coldly demands, " Why should I weep for sin ? Why should I love the Lord ?" But the heart of flesh says ; " Lord, Thou knowest that I love Thee ; help me to love Thee more !" Many are the privileges of this renewed heart ; " 'Tis here the Spirit dwells, 'tis here that Jesus rests." It is fitted to receive every spiritual blessing, and every blessing comes to it. It is prepared to yield every heavenly fruit to the honour and praise of God, and therefore the Lord delights in it. A tender heart is the best defence against sin, and the best preparation for heaven. A renewed heart stands on its watchtower looking for the coming of the Lord Jesus. Have you this heart of flesh?

" Give unto the Lord the glory due unto His name."
Psalm xxix. 2.

GOD'S glory is the result of His nature and acts.
He is glorious in His character, for there is
such a store of everything that is holy, and
good, and lovely in God, that He must be glorious.
The actions which flow from His character are also
glorious ; but while He intends that they should manifest to His creatures His goodness, and mercy, and
justice, He is equally concerned that the glory associated with them should be given only to Himself. Nor
is there aught in ourselves in which we may glory ;
for who maketh us to differ from another ? And what
have we that we did not receive from the God of all
grace ? Then how careful ought we to be *to walk
humbly before the Lord!* The moment we glorify ourselves, since there is room for one glory only in the
universe, we set ourselves up as rivals to the Most
High. Shall the insect of an hour glorify itself
against the sun which warmed it into life ? Shall the
potsherd exalt itself above the man who fashioned it
upon the wheel ? Shall the dust of the desert strive
with the whirlwind ? Or the drops of the ocean
struggle with the tempest ? Give unto the Lord, all
ye righteous, give unto the Lord glory and strength ;
give unto Him the honour that is due unto His name.
Yet it is, perhaps, one of the hardest struggles of the
Christian life to learn this sentence—"Not unto us,
not unto us, but unto Thy name be glory." It is a
lesson which God is ever teaching us, and teaching us
sometimes by most painful discipline. Let a Christian
begin to boast, " I can do all things," without adding
"through Christ which strengtheneth me," and before
long he will have to groan, "I can do nothing," and
bemoan himself in the dust. When we do anything
for the Lord, and He is pleased to accept of our
doings, let us lay our crown at His feet, and exclaim,
"Not I, but the grace of God which was with me !"

" Ourselves also, which have the firstfruits of the Spirit."
Romans viii. 23.

PRESENT possession is declared. At this present moment we have the firstfruits of the Spirit. We have repentance, that gem of the first water; faith, that priceless pearl; hope, the heavenly emerald; and love, the glorious ruby. We are already made " new creatures in Christ Jesus," by the effectual working of God the Holy Ghost. This is called the firstfruit because *it comes first.* As the wave-sheaf was the first of the harvest, so the spiritual life, and all the graces which adorn that life, are the first operations of the Spirit of God in our souls. *The firstfruits were the pledge of the harvest.* As soon as the Israelite had plucked the first handful of ripe ears, he looked forward with glad anticipation to the time when the wain should creak beneath the sheaves. So, brethren, when God gives us things which are pure, lovely, and of good report, as the work of the Holy Spirit, these are to us the prognostics of the coming glory. *The firstfruits were always holy to the Lord,* and our new nature, with all its powers, is a consecrated thing. The new life is not ours that we should ascribe its excellence to our own merit: it is Christ's image and creation, and is ordained for His glory. But *the firstfruits were not the harvest,* and the works of the Spirit in us at this moment are not the consummation—the perfection is yet to come. We must not boast that we have attained, and so reckon the wave-sheaf to be all the produce of the year: we must hunger and thirst after righteousness, and pant for the day of full redemption. Dear reader, this evening open your mouth wide, and God will fill it. Let the boon in present possession excite in you a sacred avarice for more grace. Groan within yourself for higher degrees of consecration, and your Lord will grant them to you, for He is able to do exceeding abundantly above what we ask or even think.

" The mercy of God."—Psalm lii. 8.

EDITATE a little on this mercy of the Lord.
It is *tender mercy.* With gentle, loving touch,
He healeth the broken in heart, and bindeth
up their wounds. He is as gracious in the manner of
His mercy as in the matter of it. It *is great mercy.*
There is nothing little in God ; His mercy is like
Himself—it is infinite. You cannot measure it. His
mercy is so great that it forgives great sins to great
sinners, after great lengths of time, and then gives
great favours and great privileges, and raises us up to
great enjoyments in the great heaven of the great
God. It is *undeserved* mercy, as indeed all true
mercy must be, for deserved mercy is only a misnomer
for justice. There was no right on the sinner's part
to the kind consideration of the Most High ; had the
rebel been doomed at once to eternal fire he would have
richly merited the doom, and if delivered from wrath,
sovereign love alone has found a cause, for there was
none in the sinner himself. It *is rich mercy.* Some
things are great, but have little efficacy in them, but
this mercy is a cordial to your drooping spirits ; a golden
ointment to your bleeding wounds ; a heavenly bandage
to your broken bones ; a royal chariot for your weary
feet ; a bosom of love for your trembling heart. It *is
manifold mercy.* As Bunyan says, " All the flowers in
God's garden are double." There is no single mercy.
You may think you have but one mercy, but you shall
find it to be a whole cluster of mercies. It *is abounding mercy.* Millions have received it, yet far from its
being exhausted, it is as fresh, as full, and as free as
ever. It *is unfailing mercy.* It will never leave thee.
If mercy be thy friend, mercy will be with thee
in temptation to keep thee from yielding ; with thee
in trouble to prevent thee from sinking ; with thee
living to be the light and life of thy countenance ;
and with thee dying to be the joy of thy soul when
earthly comfort is ebbing fast.

" This sickness is not unto death."—John xi. 4.

FROM our Lord's words we learn that there is a limit to sickness. Here is an " unto " within which its ultimate end is restrained, and beyond which it cannot go. Lazarus might pass through death, but death was not to be the ultimatum of his sickness. In all sickness, the Lord saith to the waves of pain, " Hitherto shall ye go, but no further." His fixed purpose is not the destruction, but the instruction of His people. Wisdom hangs up the thermometer at the furnace mouth, and regulates the heat.

1. *The limit is encouragingly comprehensive.* The God of providence has limited the time, manner, intensity, repetition, and effects of all our sicknesses; each throb is decreed, each sleepless hour predestinated, each relapse ordained, each depression of spirit foreknown, and each sanctifying result eternally purposed. Nothing great or small escapes the ordaining hand of Him who numbers the hairs of our head.

2. *This limit is wisely adjusted* to our strength, to the end designed, and to the grace apportioned. Affliction comes not at haphazard—the weight of every stroke of the rod is accurately measured. He who made no mistakes in balancing the clouds and meting out the heavens, commits no errors in measuring out the ingredients which compose the medicine of souls. We cannot suffer too much nor be relieved too late.

3. *The limit is tenderly appointed.* The knife of the heavenly Surgeon never cuts deeper than is absolutely necessary. " He doth not afflict willingly, nor grieve the children of men." A mother's heart cries, " Spare my child ;" but no mother is more compassionate than our gracious God. When we consider how hardmouthed we are, it is a wonder that we are not driven with a sharper bit. The thought is full of consolation, that He who has fixed the bounds of our habitation, has also fixed the bounds of our tribulation.

" Strangers are come into the sanctuaries of the Lord's house."
Jeremiah li. 51.

ON this account the faces of the Lord's people were covered with shame, for it was a terrible thing that men should intrude into the Holy Place reserved for the priests alone. Everywhere about us we see like cause for sorrow. How many ungodly men are now educating with the view of entering into the ministry! What a crying sin is that solemn lie by which our whole population is nominally comprehended in a National Church! How fearful it is that ordinances should be pressed upon the unconverted, and that among the more enlightened churches of our land there should be such laxity of discipline. If the thousands who will read this portion shall all take this matter before the Lord Jesus this day, He will interfere and avert the evil which else will come upon His Church. To adulterate the Church is to pollute a well, to pour water upon fire, to sow a fertile field with stones. May we all have grace to maintain in our own proper way the purity of the Church, as being an assembly of believers, and not a nation, an unsaved community of unconverted men.

Our zeal must, however, begin at home. Let us examine *ourselves* as to our right to eat at the Lord's table. Let us see to it that we have on our wedding garment, lest we ourselves be intruders in the Lord's sanctuaries. Many are called, but few are chosen; the way is narrow, and the gate is strait. O for grace to come to Jesus aright, with the faith of God's elect. He who smote Uzzah for touching the ark is very jealous of his two ordinances; as a true believer I may approach them freely, as an alien I must not touch them lest I die. Heartsearching is the duty of all who are baptized or come to the Lord's table. "Search me, O God, and know my way, try me and know my heart."

---

*"And they gave Him to drink wine mingled with myrrh :
but He received it not."*—Mark xv. 23.

A GOLDEN truth is couched in the fact that
the Saviour put the myrrhed wine-cup from
His lips. On the heights of heaven the Son
of God stood of old, and as He looked down upon
our globe He measured the long descent to the utmost depths of human misery; He cast up the sum
total of all the agonies which expiation would require,
and abated not a jot. He solemnly determined that
to offer a sufficient atoning sacrifice He must go the
whole way, from the highest to the lowest, from the
throne of highest glory to the cross of deepest woe.
This myrrhed cup, with its soporific influence, would
have stayed Him within a little of the utmost limit
of misery, therefore He refused it. He would not
stop short of all he had undertaken to suffer for His
people. Ah, how many of us have pined after reliefs
to our grief which would have been injurious to us!
Reader, did you never pray for a discharge from hard
service or suffering with a petulant and wilful eagerness? Providence has taken from you the desire of
your eyes with a stroke. Say, Christian, if it had
been said, "If you so desire it, that loved one of
yours shall live, but God will be dishonoured," could
you have put away the temptation, and said, "Thy
will be done"? Oh, it is sweet to be able to say,
"My Lord, if for other reasons I need not suffer, yet
if I can honour Thee more by suffering, and if the
loss of my earthly all will bring Thee glory, then so
let it be. I refuse the comfort, if it comes in the way
of Thine honour." O that we thus walked more in
the footsteps of our Lord, cheerfully enduring trial for
His sake, promptly and willingly putting away the
thought of self and comfort when it would interfere
with our finishing the work which He has given
us to do. Great grace is needed, but great grace is
provided.

" He shall stand and feed in the strength of the Lord."—
Micah v. 4.

CHRIST'S reign in His Church is that of a *shepherd-king.* He has supremacy, but it is the superiority of a wise and tender shepherd over his needy and loving flock ; He commands and receives obedience, but it is the willing obedience of the well-cared-for sheep, rendered joyfully to their beloved Shepherd, whose voice they know so well. He rules by the force of love and the energy of goodness.

His reign is *practical in its character.* It is said, " He shall stand *and feed."* The great Head of the Church is actively engaged in providing for His people. He does not sit down upon the throne in empty state, or hold a sceptre without wielding it in government. No, He stands and feeds. The expression "feed," in the original, is like an analogous one in the Greek, which means to shepherdize, to do everything expected of a shepherd : to guide, to watch, to preserve, to restore, to tend, as well as to feed.

His reign is *continual in its duration.* It is said, *" He shall stand* and feed ;" not " He shall feed now and then, and leave His position ;" not, " He shall one day grant a revival, and then next day leave His Church to barrenness." His eyes never slumber, and His hands never rest ; His heart never ceases to beat with love, and His shoulders are never weary of carrying His people's burdens.

His reign is *effectually powerful in its action;* "He shall feed in the strength of Jehovah." Wherever Christ is, there is God ; and whatever Christ does is the act of the Most High. Oh ! it is a joyful truth to consider that He who stands to-day representing the interests of His people is very God of very God, to whom every knee shall bow. Happy are we who belong to such a shepherd, whose humanity communes with us, and whose divinity protects us. Let us worship and bow down before Him as the people of His pasture.

" Pull me out of the net that they have laid privily for me:
for Thou art my strength."—Psalm xxxi. 4.

OUR spiritual foes are of the serpent's brood, and seek to ensnare us by subtlety. The prayer before us supposes the possibility of the believer being caught like a bird. So deftly does the fowler do his work, that simple ones are soon surrounded by the net. The text asks that even out of Satan's meshes the captive one may be delivered; this is a proper petition, and one which can be granted: from between the jaws of the lion, and out of the belly of hell, can eternal love rescue the saint. It may need a sharp *pull* to save a soul from the net of temptation, and a mighty pull to extricate a man from the snares of malicious cunning, but the Lord is equal to every emergency, and the most skilfully placed nets of the hunter shall never be able to hold His chosen ones. Woe unto those who are so clever at net laying; they who tempt others shall be destroyed themselves.

" For Thou art my strength." What an inexpressible sweetness is to be found in these few words! How joyfully may we encounter toils, and how cheerfully may we endure sufferings, when we can lay hold upon celestial strength. Divine power will rend asunder all the toils of our enemies, confound their politics, and frustrate their knavish tricks; he is a happy man who has such matchless might engaged upon his side. Our own strength would be of little service when embarrassed in the nets of base cunning, but the Lord's strength is ever available; we have but to invoke it, and we shall find it near at hand. If by faith we are depending alone upon the strength of the mighty God of Israel, we may use our holy reliance as a plea in supplication.

> "Lord, evermore Thy face we seek:
> Tempted we are, and poor, and weak;
> Keep us with lowly hearts, and meek.
> Let us not fall. Let us not fall."

" The sweet psalmist of Israel."—2 Samuel xxiii. 1.

AMONG all the saints whose lives are recorded in Holy Writ, David possesses an experience of the most striking, varied, and instructive character. In his history we meet with trials and temptations not to be discovered, as a whole, in other saints of ancient times, and hence he is all the more suggestive a type of our Lord. David knew the trials of all ranks and conditions of men. Kings have their troubles, and David wore a crown : the peasant has his cares, and David handled a shepherd's crook : the wanderer has many hardships, and David abode in the caves of Engedi : the captain has his difficulties, and David found the sons of Zeruiah too hard for him. The psalmist was also tried in his friends, his counsellor Ahithophel forsook him, "He that eateth bread with me, hath lifted up his heel against me." His worst foes were they of his own household : his children were his greatest affliction. The temptations of poverty and wealth, of honour and reproach, of health and weakness, all tried their power upon him. He had temptations from without to disturb his peace, and from within to mar his joy. David no sooner escaped from one trial than he fell into another; no sooner emerged from one season of despondency and alarm, than he was again brought into the lowest depths, and all God's waves and billows rolled over him. It is probably from this cause that David's psalms are so universally the delight of experienced Christians. Whatever our frame of mind, whether ecstacy or depression, David has exactly described our emotions. He was an able master of the human heart, because he had been tutored in the best of all schools—the school of heart-felt, personal experience. As we are instructed in the same school, as we grow matured in grace and in years, we increasingly appreciate David's psalms, and find them to be "green pastures." My soul, let David's experience cheer and counsel thee this day.

" And they fortified Jerusalem unto the broad wall."
Nehemiah iii. 8.

CITIES well fortified have broad walls, and so had Jerusalem in her glory. The New Jerusalem must, in like manner, be surrounded and preserved by a broad wall of nonconformity to the world, and *separation* from its customs and spirit. The tendency of these days is to break down the holy barrier, and make the distinction between the church and the world merely nominal. Professors are no longer strict and Puritanical, questionable literature is read on all hands, frivolous pastimes are currently indulged, and a general laxity threatens to deprive the Lord's peculiar people of those sacred singularities which separate them from sinners. It will be an ill day for the church and the world when the proposed amalgamation shall be complete, and the sons of God and the daughters of men shall be as one : then shall another deluge of wrath be ushered in. Beloved reader, be it your aim in heart, in word, in dress, in action to maintain the broad wall, remembering that the friendship of this world is enmity against God.

The broad wall afforded a pleasant place of *resort* for the inhabitants of Jerusalem, from which they could command prospects of the surrounding country. This reminds us of the Lord's exceeding broad commandments, in which we walk at liberty in communion with Jesus, overlooking the scenes of earth, and looking out towards the glories of heaven. Separated from the world, and denying ourselves all ungodliness and fleshly lusts, we are nevertheless not in prison, nor restricted within narrow bounds ; nay, we walk at liberty, because we keep His precepts. Come, reader, this evening walk with God in His statutes. As friend met friend upon the city wall, so meet thou thy God in the way of holy prayer and meditation. The bulwarks of salvation thou hast a right to traverse, for thou art a freeman of the royal burgh, a citizen of the metropolis of the universe.

" He that watereth shall be watered also himself."—
Proverbs xi. 25.

WE are here taught the great lesson, that to get, we must give ; that to accumulate, we must scatter; that to make ourselves happy, we must make others happy ; and that in order to become spiritually vigorous, we must seek the spiritual good of others.   In watering others, we are ourselves watered.   How ?   Our efforts to be useful, *bring out our powers for usefulness.*   We have latent talents and dormant faculties, which are brought to light by exercise.   Our strength for labour is hidden even from ourselves, until we venture forth to fight the Lord's battles, or to climb the mountains of difficulty.   We do not know what tender sympathies we possess until we try to dry the widow's tears, and soothe the orphan's grief.   We often find in attempting to teach others, that we *gain instruction for ourselves.* Oh, what gracious lessons some of us have learned at sick beds !   We went to teach the Scriptures, we came away blushing that we knew so little of them. In our converse with poor saints, we are taught the way of God more perfectly for ourselves and get a deeper insight into divine truth.   So that watering others *makes us humble.*   We discover how much grace there is where we had not looked for it ; and how much the poor saint may outstrip us in knowledge.   Our own *comfort is also increased* by our working for others.   We endeavour to cheer them, and the consolation gladdens our own heart. Like the two men in the snow ; one chafed the other's limbs to keep him from dying, and in so doing kept his own blood in circulation, and saved his own life. The poor widow of Sarepta gave from her scanty store a supply for the prophet's wants, and from that day she never again knew what want was.   Give then, and it shall be given unto you, good measure, pressed down, and running over.

" I said not unto the seed of Jacob, Seek ye Me in vain."
Isaiah xlv. 19.

E may gain much solace by considering what God has *not* said. What He *has* said is inexpressibly full of comfort and delight; what He has *not* said is scarcely less rich in consolation. It was one of these " *said nots* " which preserved the kingdom of Israel in the days of Jeroboam the son of Joash, for " the Lord said not that He would blot out the name of Israel from under heaven." 2 Kings xiv. 27. In our text we have an assurance that God *will* answer prayer, because He hath " *not* said unto the seed of Israel, Seek ye Me in vain." You who write bitter things against yourselves should remember that, let your doubts and fears say what they will, if *God* has not cut you off from mercy, there is no room for despair: even the voice of conscience is of little weight if it be not seconded by the voice of God. What God *has* said, tremble at! But suffer not your vain imaginings to overwhelm you with despondency and sinful despair. Many timid persons have been vexed by the suspicion that there may be something in God's decree which shuts *them* out from hope, but here is a complete refutation to that troublesome fear, for no true seeker can be decreed to wrath. " I have not spoken in secret, in a dark place of the earth ; I have not said," even in the secret of my unsearchable decree, " Seek ye Me in vain." God has clearly revealed that He *will* hear the prayer of those who call upon Him, and that declaration cannot be contravened. He has so firmly, so truthfully, so righteously spoken, that there can be no room for doubt. He does not reveal His mind in unintelligible words, but He speaks plainly and positively, " Ask, and ye shall receive." Believe, O trembler, this sure truth—that prayer must and shall be heard, and that never, even in the secrets of eternity, has the Lord said unto any living soul, " Seek ye Me in vain."

"I charge you, O daughters of Jerusalem, if ye find my be-loved, that ye tell him, that I am sick of love."—Solomon's Song v. 8.

SUCH is the language of the believer panting after present fellowship with Jesus, *he is sick for his Lord.* Gracious souls are never perfectly at ease except they are in a state of nearness to Christ; for when they are away from him they lose their peace. The nearer to Him, the nearer to the perfect calm of heaven; the nearer to Him, the fuller the heart is, not only of peace, but of life, and vigour, and joy, for these all depend on constant intercourse with Jesus. What the sun is to the day, what the moon is to the night, what the dew is to the flower, such is Jesus Christ to us. What bread is to the hungry, clothing to the naked, the shadow of a great rock to the traveller in a weary land, such is Jesus Christ to us; and, therefore, if we are not consciously one with Him, little marvel if our spirit cries in the words of the Song, "I charge you, O ye daughters of Jerusalem, if ye find my beloved, tell Him that I am sick of love." *This earnest longing after Jesus has a blessing attending it:* "Blessed are they that do hunger and thirst after righteousness;" and therefore, supremely blessed are they who thirst after the Righteous One. Blessed is that hunger, since it comes from God: if I may not have the full-blown blessedness of being filled, I would seek the same blessedness in its sweet bud-pining in emptiness and eagerness till I am filled with Christ. If I may not feed on Jesus, it shall be next door to heaven to hunger and thirst after Him. There is a hallowedness about that hunger, since it sparkles among the beati-tudes of our Lord. But the blessing *involves a promise.* Such hungry ones *"shall be filled"* with what they are desiring. If Christ thus causes us to long after Himself, He will certainly satisfy those longings; and when he does come to us, as come He will, *oh, how sweet it will be!*

" The unsearchable riches of Christ."—Ephesians iii. 8.

MY Master has riches beyond the count of arithmetic, the measurement of reason, the dream of imagination, or the eloquence of words. They are *unsearchable !* You may look, and study, and weigh, but Jesus is a greater Saviour than you think Him to be when your thoughts are at the greatest. My Lord is more ready to pardon than you to sin, more able to forgive than you to transgress. My Master is more willing to supply your wants than you are to confess them. Never tolerate low thoughts of my Lord Jesus. When you put the crown on His head, you will only crown Him with silver when He deserves gold. *My Master has riches of happiness to bestow upon you now.* He can make you to lie down in green pastures, and lead you beside still waters. There is no music like the music of His pipe, when He is the Shepherd and you are the sheep, and you lie down at His feet. There is no love like His, neither earth nor heaven can match it. To know Christ and to be found in Him—oh ! this is life, this is joy, this is marrow and fatness, wine on the lees well refined. My Master does not treat His servants churlishly ; He gives to them as a king giveth to a king ; He gives them two heavens—a heaven below in serving Him here, and a heaven above in delighting in Him for ever. *His unsearchable riches will be best known in eternity.* He will give you on the way to heaven all you need ; your place of defence shall be the munitions of rocks, your bread shall be given you, and your waters shall be sure ; but it is there, THERE, where you shall hear the song of them that triumph, the shout of them that feast, and shall have a face-to-face view of the glorious and beloved One. The unsearchable riches of Christ ! This is the tune for the minstrels of earth, and the song for the harpers of heaven. Lord, teach us more and more of Jesus, and we will tell out the good news to others.

" The voice of weeping shall be no more heard."—Is. lxv. 19.

THE glorified weep no more, for *all outward causes of grief are gone.* There are no broken friendships, nor blighted prospects in heaven. Poverty, famine, peril, persecution, and slander, are unknown there. No pain distresses, no thought of death or bereavement saddens. They weep no more, for *they are perfectly sanctified.* No "evil heart of unbelief" prompts them to depart from the living God ; they are without fault before His throne, and are fully conformed to His image. Well may they cease to mourn who have ceased to sin. They weep no more, because *all fear of change is past.* They know that they are eternally secure. Sin is shut out, and they are shut in. They dwell within a city which shall never be stormed ; they bask in a sun which shall never set ; they drink of a river which shall never dry ; they pluck fruit from a tree which shall never wither. Countless cycles may revolve, but eternity shall not be exhausted, and while eternity endures, their immortality and blessedness shall co-exist with it. They are for ever with the Lord. They weep no more, because *every desire is fulfilled.* They cannot wish for anything which they have not in possession. Eye and ear, heart and hand, judgment, imagination, hope, desire, will, all the faculties, are completely satisfied ; and imperfect as our present ideas are of the things which God hath prepared for them that love him, yet we know enough, by the revelation of the Spirit, that the saints above are supremely blessed. The joy of Christ, which is an infinite fulness of delight, is in them. They bathe themselves in the bottomless, shoreless sea of infinite beatitude. That same joyful rest remains for us. It may not be far distant. Ere long the weeping willow shall be exchanged for the palm-branch of victory, and sorrow's dewdrops will be transformed into the pearls of everlasting bliss. "Wherefore comfort one another with these words."

"That Christ may dwell in your hearts by faith."
Ephesians iii. 17.

EYOND measure it is desirable that we, as believers, should have the person of Jesus constantly before us, to inflame our love towards Him, and to increase our knowledge of Him. I would to God that my readers were all entered as diligent scholars in Jesus' college, students of Corpus Christi, or the body of Christ, resolved to attain unto a good degree in the learning of the cross. But to have Jesus ever near, the heart must be full of Him, welling up with His love, even to overrunning; hence the apostle prays "that Christ may *dwell in your hearts.*" See how near he would have Jesus to be! You cannot get a subject closer to you than to have it in the heart itself. *"That He may dwell;"* not that He may call upon you sometimes, as a casual visitor enters into a house and tarries for a night, but that He may *dwell;* that Jesus may become the Lord and Tenant of your inmost being, never more to go out.

Observe the words—that He may dwell *in your heart,* that best room of the house of manhood; not in your thoughts alone, but in your affections; not merely in the mind's meditations, but in the heart's emotions. We should pant after love to Christ of a most abiding character, not a love that flames up and then dies out into the darkness of a few embers, but a constant flame, fed by sacred fuel, like the fire upon the altar which never went out. This cannot be accomplished except by faith. Faith must be strong, or love will not be fervent; the root of the flower must be healthy, or we cannot expect the bloom to be sweet. Faith is the lily's root, and love is the lily's bloom. Now, reader, Jesus cannot be in your heart's love except you have a firm hold of Him by your heart's faith; and, therefore, pray that you may always trust Christ in order that you may always love Him. If love be cold, be sure that faith is drooping.

" The breaker is come up before them."—Micah ii. 13.

NASMUCH as Jesus has gone before us, things remain not as they would have been had he never passed that way. He has *conquered every foe* that obstructed the way. Cheer up now thou faint-hearted warrior. Not only has Christ travelled the road, but He has slain thine enemies. Dost thou dread sin? He has nailed it to his cross. Dost thou fear death? He has been the death of Death. Art thou afraid of hell? He has barred it against the advent of any of His children; they shall never see the gulf of perdition. Whatever foes may be before the Christian, they are all overcome. There are lions, but their teeth are broken; there are serpents, but their fangs are extracted; there are rivers, but they are bridged or fordable; there are flames, but we wear that matchless garment which renders us invulnerable to fire. The sword that has been forged against us is already blunted; the instruments of war which the enemy is preparing have already lost their point. God has taken away in the person of Christ all the power that anything can have to hurt us. Well then, the army may safely march on, and you may go joyously along your journey, for all your enemies are conquered beforehand. What shall you do but march on to take the prey? They are beaten, they are vanquished; all you have to do is to divide the spoil. You shall, it is true, often engage in combat; but your fight shall be with a vanquished foe. His head is broken; he may attempt to injure you, but his strength shall not be sufficient for his malicious design. Your victory shall be easy, and your treasure shall be beyond all count.

"Proclaim aloud the Saviour's fame,
Who bears *the Breaker's* wond'rous name;
Sweet name; and it becomes him well,
Who breaks down earth, sin, death, and hell."

" If fire break out, and catch in thorns, so that the stacks of corn, or the standing corn, or the field, be consumed therewith; he that kindled the fire shall surely make restitution." Exodus xxii. 6.

BUT what restitution can he make who casts abroad the fire-brands of error, or the coals of lasciviousness, and sets men's souls on a blaze with the fire of hell? The guilt is beyond estimate, and the result is irretrievable. If such an offender be forgiven, what grief it will cause him in the retrospect, since he cannot undo the mischief which he has done! An ill example may kindle a flame which years of amended character cannot quench. To burn the food of man is bad enough, but how much worse to destroy the soul! It may be useful to us to reflect how far we may have been guilty in the past, and to enquire whether, even in the present, there may not be evil in us which has a tendency to bring damage to the souls of our relatives, friends, or neighbours.

The fire of strife is a terrible evil when it breaks out in a Christian church. Where converts were multiplied, and God was glorified, jealousy and envy do the devil's work most effectually. Where the golden grain was being housed, to reward the toil of the great Boaz, the fire of enmity comes in and leaves little else but smoke and a heap of blackness. Woe unto those by whom offences come. May they never come through us, for although we cannot make restitution, we shall certainly be the chief sufferers if we are the chief offenders. Those who feed the fire deserve just censure, but he who first kindles it is most to blame. Discord usually takes first hold upon the thorns; it is nurtured among the hypocrites and base professors in the church, and away it goes among the righteous, blown by the winds of hell, and no one knows where it may end. O Thou Lord and giver of peace, make us peacemakers, and never let us aid and abet the men of strife, or even unintentionally cause the least division among Thy people.

"His fruit was sweet to my taste."—Cant. ii. 3.

FAITH, in the Scripture, is spoken of under the emblem of all the senses. It is *sight:* "Look unto me and be ye saved." It is *hearing:* "Hear, and your soul shall live." Faith is *smelling:* "All thy garments smell of myrrh, and aloes, and cassia;" "thy name is as ointment poured forth." Faith is spiritual *touch*. By this faith the woman came behind and touched the hem of Christ's garment, and by this we handle the things of the good word of life. Faith is equally the spirit's *taste*. "How sweet are Thy words to my taste! yea, sweeter than honey to my lips." "Except a man eat my flesh," saith Christ, "and drink my blood, there is no life in him."

This *"taste"* is faith *in one of its highest operations*. One of the first performances of faith is *hearing*. We hear the voice of God, not with the outward ear alone, but with the inward ear; we hear it as God's Word, and we believe it to be so; that is the "hearing" of faith. Then our mind *looketh* upon the truth as it is presented to us; that is to say, we understand it, we perceive its meaning; that is the "seeing" of faith. Next we discover its preciousness; we begin to admire it, and find how fragrant it is; that is faith in its *"smell."* Then we appropriate the mercies which are prepared for us in Christ; that is faith in its *"touch."* Hence follow the enjoyments, peace, delight, communion; which are faith in its "taste." Any one of these acts of faith is saving. To hear Christ's voice as the sure voice of God in the soul will save us; but that which gives true enjoyment is the aspect of faith wherein Christ, by holy taste, is received into us, and made, by inward and spiritual apprehension of His sweetness and preciousness, to be the food of our souls. It is then we sit "under His shadow with great delight," and find His fruit sweet to our taste.

" If thou believest with all thine heart, thou mayest."
Acts viii. 37.

THESE words may answer your scruples, devout reader, concerning *the ordinances.* Perhaps you say, " I should be afraid to be baptized ; it is such a solemn thing to avow myself to be dead with Christ, and buried with Him. I should not feel at liberty to come to the Master's table ; I should be afraid of eating and drinking damnation unto myself, not discerning the Lord's body." Ah ! poor trembler, Jesus has given you liberty, be not afraid. If a stranger came to your house, he would stand at the door, or wait in the hall ; he would not dream of intruding unbidden into your parlour—he is not at home : but your child makes himself very free about the house ; and so is it with the child of God. A stranger may not intrude where a child may venture. When the Holy Ghost has given you to feel the spirit of adoption, you may come to Christian ordinances without fear. The same rule holds good of the *Christian's inward privileges.* You think, poor seeker, that you are not allowed to rejoice with joy unspeakable and full of glory ; if you are permitted to get inside Christ's door, or sit at the bottom of His table, you will be well content. Ah ! but you shall not have less privileges than the very greatest. God makes no difference in His love to His children. A child is a child to Him ; He will not make him a hired servant ; but he shall feast upon the fatted calf, and shall have the music and the dancing as much as if he had never gone astray. When Jesus comes into the heart, he issues a general licence to be glad in the Lord. No chains are worn in the court of King Jesus. Our admission into full privileges may be gradual, but it is sure. Perhaps our reader is saying, "I wish I could enjoy the promises, and walk at liberty in my Lord's commands." "If thou believest with all thine heart, thou mayest." Loose the chains of thy neck, O captive daughter, for Jesus makes thee free.

" He hath commanded His covenant for ever."—Ps. cxi. 9.

THE Lord's people delight in the covenant it-self. It is an unfailing source of consolation to them so often as the Holy Spirit leads them into its banqueting house and waves its banner of love. They delight to contemplate *the antiquity* of that covenant, remembering that before the day-star knew its place, or planets ran their round, the interests of the saints were made secure in Christ Jesus. It is peculiarly pleasing to them to remember *the sureness* of the covenant, while meditating upon "the sure mercies of David." They delight to cele-brate it as "signed, and sealed, and ratified, in all things ordered well." It often makes their hearts dilate with joy to think of its *immutability*, as a covenant which neither time nor eternity, life nor death, shall ever be able to violate—a covenant as old as eternity and as everlasting as the Rock of ages. They rejoice also to feast upon *the fulness* of this covenant, for they see in it all things provided for them. God is their portion, Christ their companion, the Spirit their Comforter, earth their lodge, and heaven their home. They see in it an inheritance reserved and entailed to every soul possessing an interest in its ancient and eternal deed of gift. Their eyes sparkled when they saw it as a treasure-trove in the Bible; but oh! how their souls were gladdened when they saw in the last will and testament of their divine kinsman, that it was be-queathed to them! More especially it is the pleasure of God's people to contemplate *the graciousness* of this covenant. They see that the law was made void because it was a covenant of works and depended upon merit, but this they perceive to be enduring be-cause grace is the basis, grace the condition, grace the strain, grace the bulwark, grace the foundation, grace the topstone. The covenant is a treasury of wealth, a granary of food, a fountain of life, a store-house of salvation, a charter of peace, and a haven of joy.

"The people, when they beheld Him, were greatly amazed, and running to Him saluted Him."—Mark ix. 15.

HOW great the difference between Moses and Jesus! When the prophet of Horeb had been forty days upon the mountain, he underwent a kind of transfiguration, so that his countenance shone with exceeding brightness, and he put a veil over his face, for the people could not endure to look upon his glory. Not so our Saviour. He had been transfigured with a greater glory than that of Moses, and yet, it is not written that the people were blinded by the blaze of His countenance, but rather they were amazed, and running to Him they saluted Him. The glory of the law repels, but the greater glory of Jesus attracts. Though Jesus is holy and just, yet blended with His purity there is so much of truth and grace, that sinners run to Him amazed at His goodness, fascinated by His love; they salute Him, become His disciples, and take Him to be their Lord and Master. Reader, it may be that just now you are blinded by the dazzling brightness of the law of God. You feel its claims on your conscience, but you cannot keep it in your life. Not that you find fault with the law, on the contrary, it commands your profoundest esteem, still you are in nowise drawn by it to God; you are rather hardened in heart, and are verging towards desperation. Ah, poor heart! turn thine eye from Moses, with all his repelling splendour, and look to Jesus, resplendent with milder glories. Behold His flowing wounds and thorn-crowned head! He is the Son of God, and therein He is greater than Moses, but He is the Lord of love, and therein more tender than the lawgiver. He bore the wrath of God, and in His death revealed more of God's justice than Sinai on a blaze, but that justice is now vindicated, and henceforth it is the guardian of believers in Jesus. Look, sinner to the bleeding Saviour, and as thou feelest the attraction of His love, fly to His arms, and thou shalt be saved.

"How long will it be ere they believe me ?"—Num. xiv. 11.

STRIVE with all diligence to keep out that mon-ster unbelief. It so dishonours Christ, that he will withdraw his visible presence if we insult him by indulging it. It is true it is a weed, the seeds of which we can never entirely extract from the soil, but we must aim at its root with zeal and perseverance. Among hateful things it is the most to be abhorred. Its injurious nature is so venomous that he that exerciseth it and he upon whom it is exercised are both hurt thereby. In thy case, O believer! it is most wicked, for the mercies of thy Lord in the past, increase thy guilt in doubting Him now. When thou dost distrust the Lord Jesus, He may well cry out, "Behold I am pressed under you, as a cart is pressed that is full of sheaves." This is crowning his head with thorns of the sharpest kind. It is very cruel for a well-beloved wife to mistrust a kind and faithful husband. The sin is needless, foolish, and un-warranted. Jesus has never given the slightest ground for suspicion, and it is hard to be doubted by those to whom our conduct is uniformly affectionate and true. Jesus is the Son of the Highest, and has unbounded wealth ; it is shameful to doubt Omni-potence and distrust all-sufficiency. The cattle on a thousand hills will suffice for our most hungry feeding, and the granaries of heaven are not likely to be emptied by our eating. If Christ were only a cistern, we might soon exhaust His fulness, but who can drain a foun-tain ? Myriads of spirits have drawn their supplies from Him, and not one of them has murmured at the scantiness of his resources. Away, then, with this lying traitor unbelief, for his only errand is to cut the bonds of communion and make us mourn an absent Saviour. Bunyan tells us that unbelief has "as many lives as a cat :" if so, let us kill one life now, and continue the work till the whole nine are gone. Down with thee, thou traitor, my heart abhors thee.

"Into Thine hand I commit my spirit: Thou hast redeemed me, O Lord God of truth."—Psalm xxxi. 5.

THESE words have been frequently used by holy men in their hour of departure. We may profitably consider them this evening. The object of the faithful man's solicitude in life and death is not his body or his estate, but his spirit; this is his choice treasure—if this be safe, all is well. What is this mortal state compared with the soul? The believer commits his soul to the hand of his God; it came from him, it is his own, he has aforetime sustained it, he is able to keep it, and it is most fit that he should receive it. All things are safe in Jehovah's hands; what we entrust to the Lord will be secure, both now and in that day of days towards which we are hastening. It is peaceful living, and glorious dying, to repose in the care of heaven. At all times we should commit our all to Jesus' faithful hand; then, though life may hang on a thread, and adversities may multiply as the sands of the sea, our soul shall dwell at ease, and delight itself in quiet resting places.

"Thou hast redeemed me, O Lord God of truth." Redemption is a solid basis for confidence. David had not known Calvary as we have done, but temporal redemption cheered him; and shall not eternal redemption yet more sweetly console us? Past deliverances are strong pleas for present assistance. What the Lord has done He will do again, for He changes not. He is faithful to His promises, and gracious to His saints; He will not turn away from His people.

> " Though Thou slay me I will trust,
> Praise Thee even from the dust,
> Prove, and tell it as I prove,
> Thine unutterable love.
>
> Thou mayst chasten and correct,
> But Thou never canst neglect;
> Since the ransom price is paid,
> On Thy love my hope is stay'd."

" Oil for the light."—Exodus xxv. 6.

MY soul, how much thou needest this, for thy lamp will not long continue to burn without it. Thy snuff will smoke and become an offence if light be gone, and gone it will be if oil be absent. Thou hast no oil well springing up in thy human nature, and therefore thou must go to them that sell and buy for thyself, or like the foolish virgins, thou wilt have to cry, "My lamp is gone out." Even the consecrated lamps could not give light without oil; though they shone in the tabernacle they needed to be fed, though no rough winds blew upon them they required to be trimmed, and thy need is equally as great. Under the most happy circumstances thou canst not give light for another hour unless fresh oil of grace be given thee.

It was not every oil that might be used in the Lord's service; neither the petroleum which exudes so plentifully from the earth, nor the produce of fishes, nor that extracted from nuts would be accepted; one oil only was selected, and that the best olive oil. Pretended grace from natural goodness, fancied grace from priestly hands, or imaginary grace from outward ceremonies will never serve the true saint of God; he knows that the Lord would not be pleased with rivers of such oil. He goes to the olive-press of Gethsemane, and draws his supplies from Him who was crushed therein. The oil of gospel grace is pure and free from lees and dregs, and hence the light which is fed thereon is clear and bright. Our churches are the Saviour's golden candelabra, and if they are to be lights in this dark world, they must have much holy oil. Let us pray for ourselves, our ministers, and our churches, that they may never lack oil for the light. Truth, holiness, joy, knowledge, love, these are all beams of the sacred light, but we cannot give them forth unless in private we receive oil from God the Holy Ghost.

***"Sing, O barren."*—Isaiah liv. 1.**

THOUGH we have brought forth some fruit unto Christ, and have a joyful hope that we are "plants of His own right hand planting," yet there are times when we feel very barren. Prayer is lifeless, love is cold, faith is weak, each grace in the garden of our heart languishes and droops. We are like flowers in the hot sun, requiring the refreshing shower. In such a condition what are we to do? The text is addressed to us in just such a state. *"Sing, O barren, break forth and cry aloud."* But what can I sing about? I cannot talk about the present, and even the past looks full of barrenness. Ah! I *can* sing of *Jesus Christ.* I can talk of visits which the Redeemer has aforetimes paid to me; or if not of these, I can magnify the great love wherewith He loved His people when He came from the heights of heaven for their redemption. I will go to the cross again. Come, my soul, heavy laden thou wast once, and thou didst lose thy burden there. Go to Calvary again. Perhaps that very cross which gave thee life may give thee fruitfulness. What is my barrenness? It is the platform for His fruit-creating power. What is my desolation? It is the black setting for the sapphire of His everlasting love. I will go in poverty, I will go in helplessness, I will go in all my shame and backsliding, I will tell Him that I am still His child, and in confidence in His faithful heart, even I, the barren one, will sing and cry aloud.

Sing, believer, for it will cheer thine own heart, and the hearts of other desolate ones. Sing on, for now that thou art really ashamed of being barren, thou wilt be fruitful soon; now that God makes thee *loath* to be without fruit He will soon cover thee with clusters. The experience of our barrenness is painful, but the Lord's visitations are delightful. A sense of our own poverty drives us to Christ, and that is where we need to be, for in Him is our fruit found.

"Have mercy upon me, O God."—Psalm li. 1.

WHEN Dr. Carey was suffering from a dangerous illness, the enquiry was made, "If this sickness should prove fatal, what passage would you select as the text for your funeral sermon?" He replied, "Oh, I feel that such a poor sinful creature is unworthy to have anything said about him; but if a funeral sermon must be preached, let it be from the words, 'Have mercy upon me, O God, according to Thy lovingkindness; according unto the multitude of Thy tender mercies blot out my transgressions.'" In the same spirit of humility he directed in his will that the following inscription and nothing more should be cut on his gravestone:—

WILLIAM CAREY, BORN AUGUST 17th, 1761:

DIED—

"A wretched, poor, and helpless worm
On Thy kind arms I fall."

Only on the footing of free grace can the most experienced and most honoured of the saints approach their God. The best of men are conscious above all others that they are men at the best. Empty boats float high, but heavily laden vessels are low in the water; mere professors can boast, but true children of God cry for mercy upon their unprofitableness. We have need that the Lord should have mercy upon our good works, our prayers, our preachings, our almsgivings, and our holiest things. The blood was not only sprinkled upon the doorposts of Israel's dwelling houses, but upon the sanctuary, the mercy-seat, and the altar, because as sin intrudes into our holiest things, the blood of Jesus is needed to purify them from defilement. If mercy be needed to be exercised towards our duties, what shall be said of our sins? How sweet the remembrance that inexhaustible mercy is waiting to be gracious to us, to restore our backslidings, and make our broken bones rejoice!

"All the days of his separation shall he eat nothing that is made of the vine tree, from the kernels even to the husk."— Numbers vi. 4.

NAZARITES had taken, among other vows, one which debarred them from the use of wine. In order that they might not violate the obligation, they were forbidden to drink the vinegar of wine or strong liquors, and to make the rule still more clear, they were not to touch the unfermented juice of grapes, nor even to eat the fruit either fresh or dried. In order, altogether, to secure the integrity of the vow, they were not even allowed anything that had to do with the vine ; they were, in fact, to avoid the appearance of evil. Surely this is a lesson to the Lord's separated ones, teaching them to come away from sin in every form, to avoid not merely its grosser shapes, but even its spirit and similitude. Strict walking is much despised in these days, but rest assured, dear reader, it is both the safest and the happiest. He who yields a point or two to the world is in fearful peril ; he who eats the grapes of Sodom will soon drink the wine of Gomorrah. A little crevice in the sea-bank in Holland lets in the sea, and the gap speedily swells till a province is drowned. Worldly conformity, in any degree, is a snare to the soul, and makes it more and more liable to presumptuous sins. Moreover, as the Nazarite who drank grape juice could not be quite sure whether it might not have endured a degree of fermentation, and consequently could not be clear in heart that his vow was intact, so the yielding, temporising Christian cannot wear a conscience void of offence, but must feel that the inward monitor is in doubt of him. Things doubtful we need not doubt about ; they are wrong to us. Things tempting we must not dally with, but flee from them with speed. Better be sneered at as a Puritan than be despised as a hypocrite. Careful walking may involve much self-denial, but it has pleasures of its own which are more than a sufficient recompense.

" Wait on the Lord."—Psalm xxvii. 14.

IT may seem an easy thing to *wait*, but it is one of the postures which a Christian soldier learns not without years of teaching. Marching and quick-marching are much easier to God's warriors than standing still. There are hours of perplexity when the most willing spirit, anxiously desirous to serve the Lord, knows not what part to take. Then what shall it do? Vex itself by despair? Fly back in cowardice, turn to the right hand in fear, or rush forward in presumption? No, but simply wait. *Wait in prayer*, however. Call upon God, and spread the case before Him ; tell Him your difficulty, and plead His promise of aid. In dilemmas between one duty and another, it is sweet to be humble as a child, and *wait with simplicity of soul* upon the Lord. It is sure to be well with us when we feel and know our own folly, and are heartily willing to be guided by the will of God. But *wait in faith*. Express your unstaggering confidence in Him; for unfaithful, untrusting waiting, is but an insult to the Lord. Believe that if He keep you tarrying even till midnight, yet He will come at the right time ; the vision shall come and shall not tarry. *Wait in quiet patience*, not rebelling because you are under the affliction, but blessing your God for it. Never murmur against the second cause, as the children of Israel did against Moses ; never wish you could go back to the world again, but accept the case as it is, and put it as it stands, simply and with your whole heart, without any self-will, into the hand of your covenant God, saying, "Now, Lord, not my will, but Thine be done. I know not what to do; I am brought to extremities, but I will wait until Thou shalt cleave the floods, or drive back my foes. I will wait, if Thou keep me many a day, for my heart is fixed upon thee alone, O God, and my spirit waiteth for thee in the full conviction that Thou wilt yet be my joy and my salvation, my refuge and my strong tower."

" Heal me, O Lord, and I shall be healed."—Jer. xvii. 14.
" I have seen His ways, and will heal him."—Isa. lvii. 18.

IT is the sole prerogative of God to remove spiritual disease. Natural disease may be instrumentally healed by men, but even then the honour is to be given to God who giveth virtue unto medicine, and bestoweth power unto the human frame to cast off disease. As for spiritual sicknesses, these remain with the great Physician alone; He claims it as His prerogative, " I kill and I make alive, I wound and I heal;" and one of the Lord's choice titles is Jehovah-Rophi, the Lord that healeth thee. " I will heal thee of thy wounds," is a promise which could not come from the lip of man, but only from the mouth of the eternal God. On this account the psalmist cried unto the Lord, " O Lord, heal me, for my bones are sore vexed," and again, " Heal my soul, for I have sinned against thee." For this, also, the godly praise the name of the Lord, saying, " He healeth all our diseases." He who made man can restore man; He who was at first the creator of our nature can new create it. What a transcendent comfort it is that in the person of Jesus " dwelleth all the fulness of the Godhead bodily! " My soul, whatever thy disease may be, this great Physician can heal thee. If He be God, there can be no limit to His power. Come then with the blind eye of darkened understanding, come with the limping foot of wasted energy, come with the maimed hand of weak faith, the fever of an angry temper, or the ague of shivering despondency, come just as thou art, for He who is God can certainly restore thee of thy plague. None shall restrain the healing virtue which proceeds from Jesus our Lord. Legions of devils have been made to own the power of the beloved Physician, and never once has He been baffled. All His patients have been cured in the past and shall be in the future, and thou shalt be one among them, my friend, if thou wilt but rest thyself in Him this night.

" On mine arm shall they trust."—Isaiah li. 5.

IN seasons of severe trial, the Christian has nothing on earth that he can trust to, and is therefore compelled to cast himself on his God alone. When his vessel is on its beam-ends, and no human deliverance can avail, he must simply and entirely trust himself to the providence and care of God. Happy storm that wrecks a man on such a rock as this! O blessed hurricane that drives the soul to God and God alone! There is no getting at our God sometimes because of the multitude of our friends; but when a man is so poor, so friendless, so helpless that he has nowhere else to turn, he flies into his Father's arms, and is blessedly clasped therein! When he is burdened with troubles so pressing and so peculiar, that he cannot tell them to any but his God, he may be thankful for them; for he will learn more of his Lord then than at any other time. Oh, tempest-tossed believer, it is a happy trouble that drives thee to thy Father! Now that thou hast only thy God to trust to, see that thou puttest thy full confidence in Him. Dishonour not thy Lord and Master by unworthy doubts and fears; but be strong in faith, giving glory to God. Show the world that thy God is worth ten thousand worlds to thee. Show rich men how rich thou art in thy poverty when the Lord God is thy helper. Show the strong man how strong thou art in thy weakness when underneath thee are the everlasting arms. Now is the time for feats of faith and valiant exploits. Be strong and very courageous, and the Lord thy God shall certainly, as surely as He built the heavens and the earth, glorify Himself in thy weakness, and magnify his might in the midst of thy distress. The grandeur of the arch of heaven would be spoiled if the sky were supported by a single visible column, and your faith would lose its glory if it rested on anything discernible by the carnal eye. May the Holy Spirit give you to rest in Jesus this closing day of the month.

" If we walk in the light, as He is in the light."—1 John i. 7.

S He is in the light! Can we ever attain to this? Shall we ever be able to walk as clearly in the light as He is whom we call " Our Father," of whom it is written, " God is light, and in Him is no darkness at all"? Certainly, this is the model which it set before us, for the Saviour Himself said, " Be ye perfect, even as your Father who is in heaven is perfect;" and although we may feel that we can never rival the perfection of God, yet we are to seek after it, and never to be satisfied until we attain to it. The youthful artist, as he grasps his early pencil, can hardly hope to equal Raphael or Michael Angelo, but still, if he did not have a noble *beau ideal* before his mind, he would only attain to something very mean and ordinary. But what is meant by the expression that the Christian is to walk in light as God is in the light? We conceive it to import *likeness,* but not *degree.* We are as truly in the light, we are as heartily in the light, we are as sincerely in the light, as honestly in the light, though we cannot be there in the same measure. I cannot dwell in the sun, it is too bright a place for my residence, but I can *walk* in the light of the sun; and so, though I cannot attain to that perfection of purity and truth which belongs to the Lord of hosts by nature as the infinitely good, yet I can set the Lord always before me, and strive, by the help of the indwelling Spirit, after conformity to his image. That famous old commentator, John Trapp, says, " We may be in the light as God is in the light for *quality,* but not for *equality.*" We are to have the same light, and are as truly to have it and walk in it as God does, though, as for equality with God in his holiness and purity, that must be left until we cross the Jordan and enter into the perfection of the Most High. Mark that the blessings of sacred fellowship and perfect cleansing are bound up with walking in the light.

" Thou shalt guide me with Thy counsel, and afterward receive me to glory."—Psalm lxxiii. 24.

THE Psalmist felt his need of divine guidance. He had just been discovering the foolishness of his own heart, and lest he should be constantly led astray by it, he resolved that God's counsel should henceforth guide him. A sense of our own folly is a great step towards being wise, when it leads us to rely on the wisdom of the Lord. The blind man leans on his friend's arm and reaches home in safety, and so would we give ourselves up implicitly to divine guidance, nothing doubting; assured that though we cannot see, it is always safe to trust the All-seeing God. *" Thou shalt,"* is a blessed expression of confidence. He was sure that the Lord would not decline the condescending task. There is a word for thee, O believer; rest thou in it. Be assured that thy God will be thy counsellor and friend; He shall guide thee; He will direct all thy ways. In His written Word thou hast this assurance in part fulfilled, for holy Scripture is His counsel to thee. Happy are we to have God's Word always to guide us! What were the mariner without his compass? And what were the Christian without the Bible? This is the unerring chart, the map in which every shoal is described, and all the channels from the quicksands of destruction to the haven of salvation mapped and marked by one who knows all the way. Blessed be Thou, O God, that we may trust Thee to guide us now, and guide us even to the end! After this guidance through life, the Psalmist anticipates a divine reception at last—*" and afterward receive me to glory."* What a thought for thee, believer! *God* Himself will receive *thee* to glory—*thee!* Wandering, erring, straying, yet He will bring thee safe at last *to glory!* This is thy portion; live on it this day, and if perplexities should surround thee, go in the strength of this text straight to the throne.

" Trust in Him at all times."—Psalm lxii. 8.

AITH is as much the rule of temporal as of spiritual life; we ought to have faith in God for our earthly affairs as well as for our heavenly business. It is only as we learn to trust in God for the supply of all our daily need that we shall live above the world. We are not to be idle, *that* would show we did *not* trust in God, who worketh hitherto, but in the devil, who is the father of idleness. We are not to be imprudent or rash; that were to trust chance, and not the living God, who is a God of economy and order. Acting in all prudence and uprightness, we are to rely simply and entirely upon the Lord at all times.

Let me commend to you a life of trust in God in temporal things. Trusting in God, you will not be compelled to mourn because you have used sinful means to grow rich. Serve God with integrity, and if you achieve no success, at least no sin will lie upon your conscience. Trusting God, you will not be guilty of self-contradiction. He who trusts in craft, sails this way to-day, and that way the next, like a vessel tossed about by the fickle wind; but he that trusteth in the Lord is like a vessel propelled by steam, she cuts through the waves, defies the wind, and makes one bright silvery straightforward track to her destined haven. Be you a man with living principles within; never bow to the varying customs of worldly wisdom. Walk in your path of integrity with steadfast steps, and show that you are invincibly strong in the strength which confidence in God alone can confer. Thus you will be delivered from carking care, you will not be troubled with evil tidings, your heart will be fixed, trusting in the Lord. How pleasant to float along the stream of providence! There is no more blessed way of living than a life of dependence upon a covenant-keeping God. We have no care, for He careth for us; we have no troubles, because we cast our burdens upon the Lord.

*" But Simon's wife's mother lay sick of a fever, and anon
they tell Him of her."*—Mark i. 30.

ERY interesting is this little peep into the
house of the Apostolic Fisherman. We see
at once that household joys and cares are no
hindrance to the full exercise of ministry, nay, that
since they furnish an opportunity for personally witnessing the Lord's gracious work upon one's own flesh
and blood, they may even instruct the teacher better
than any other earthly discipline. Papists and other
sectaries may decry marriage, but true Christianity
and household life agree well together. Peter's house
was probably a poor fisherman's hut, but the Lord of
Glory entered it, lodged in it, and wrought a miracle
in it. Should our little book be read this morning in
some very humble cottage, let this fact encourage the
inmates to seek the company of King Jesus. God is
oftener in little huts than in rich palaces. Jesus is
looking round your room now, and is waiting to be
gracious to you. Into Simon's house sickness had
entered, fever in a deadly form had prostrated his
mother-in-law, and as soon as Jesus came they told
Him of the sad affliction, and He hastened to the
patient's bed. Have you any sickness in the house
this morning? You will find Jesus by far the best
physician, go to Him at once and tell him all about
the matter. Immediately lay the case before Him. It
concerns one of His people, and therefore will not be
trivial to Him. Observe, that *at once* the Saviour
restored the sick woman ; none can heal as He does.
We may not make sure that the Lord will at once
remove all disease from those we love, but we may
know that believing prayer for the sick is far more
likely to be followed by restoration than anything else
in the world; and where this avails not, we must
meekly bow to His will by whom life and death are
determined. The tender heart of Jesus waits to hear
our griefs, let us pour them into His patient ear.

" Except ye see signs and wonders, ye will not believe."
John iv. 48.

CRAVING after marvels was a symptom of the sickly state of men's minds in our Lord's day; they refused solid nourishment, and pined after mere wonder. The gospel which they so greatly needed they would not have; the miracles which Jesus did not always choose to give they eagerly demanded. Many nowadays must see signs and wonders, or they will not believe. Some have said in their heart, " I must feel deep horror of soul, or I never will believe in Jesus." But what if you never should feel it, as probably you never may? Will you go to hell out of spite against God, because He will not treat you like another? One has said to himself, "If I had a dream, or if I could feel a sudden shock of I know not what, then I would believe." Thus you undeserving mortals dream that my Lord is to be dictated to by you! You are beggars at His gate, asking for mercy, and you must needs draw up rules and regulations as to how He shall give that mercy. Think you that He will submit to this? My Master is of a generous spirit, but He has a right royal heart, He spurns all dictation, and maintains his sovereignty of action. Why, dear reader, if such be your case, do you crave for signs and wonders? Is not the gospel its own sign and wonder? Is not this a miracle of miracles, that "God so loved the world that he gave His only begotten Son, that whosoever believeth in him might not perish "? Surely that precious word, "Whosoever will, let him come and take the water of life freely" and that solemn promise, " Him that cometh unto Me, I will in no wise cast out," are better than signs and wonders! A truthful Saviour ought to be believed. He is truth itself. Why will you ask proof of the veracity of one who cannot lie? The devils themselves declared Him to be the Son of God; will you mistrust Him?

"Thou whom my soul loveth."—Cant. i. 7.

IT is well to be able, without any " if " or " but,"
to say of the Lord Jesus—" *Thou whom my
soul loveth.*" Many can only say of Jesus
that they *hope* they love Him; they *trust* they love
Him; but only a poor and shallow experience will
be content to stay here. No one ought to give any
rest to his spirit till he feels quite sure about a matter of such vital importance. We ought not to be satisfied with a superficial *hope* that Jesus loves us, and
with a bare trust that we love Him. The old saints
did not generally speak with " buts," and " ifs," and
" hopes," and " trusts," but they spoke positively
and plainly. " I know whom I have believed," saith
Paul. " I know that my Redeemer liveth," saith
Job. Get positive knowledge of your love of Jesus,
and be not satisfied till you can speak of your interest
in Him as a reality, which you have made sure by
having received the witness of the Holy Spirit, and
His seal upon your soul by faith.

True love to Christ is in every case the Holy
Spirit's work, and must be wrought in the heart by
Him. He is the *efficient cause* of it; but the logical
reason why we love Jesus lies in *Himself.* *Why* do
we love Jesus? *Because He first loved us.* *Why* do
we love Jesus? Because He " *gave Himself for us.*"
We have life through His death; we have peace
through His blood. Though He was rich, yet *for our
sakes* He became poor. *Why* do we love Jesus?
Because of the *excellency of His person.* We are filled
with a sense of His beauty! an admiration of His
charms! a consciousness of His infinite perfection!
His greatness, goodness, and loveliness, in one resplendent ray, combine to enchant the soul till it is
so ravished that it exclaims, " Yea, He is altogether
lovely." Blessed love this—a love which binds the
heart with chains more soft than silk, and yet more
firm than adamant!

" The Lord trieth the righteous."—Psalm xi. 5.

ALL events are under the control of Providence; consequently all the trials of our outward life are traceable at once to the great First Cause. Out of the golden gate of God's ordinance the armies of trial march forth in array, clad in their iron armour, and armed with weapons of war. All providences are doors to trial. Even our mercies, like roses, have their thorns. Men may be drowned in seas of prosperity as well as in rivers of affliction. Our mountains are not too high, and our valleys are not too low for temptations: trials lurk on all roads. Everywhere. above and beneath, we are beset and surrounded with dangers. Yet no shower falls unpermitted from the threatening cloud; every drop has its order ere it hastens to the earth. The trials which come from God are sent to prove and strengthen our graces, and so at once to illustrate the power of divine grace, to test the genuineness of our virtues, and to add to their energy. Our Lord in His infinite wisdom and superabundant love, sets so high a value upon His people's faith that He will not screen them from those trials by which faith is strengthened. You would never have possessed the precious faith which now supports you if the trial of your faith had not been like unto fire. You are a tree that never would have rooted so well if the wind had not rocked you to and fro, and made you take firm hold upon the precious truths of the covenant of grace. Worldly ease is a great foe to faith; it loosens the joints of holy valour, and snaps the sinews of sacred courage. The balloon never rises until the cords are cut; affliction doth this sharp service for believing souls. While the wheat sleeps comfortably in the husk it is useless to man, it must be threshed out of its resting place before its value can be known. Thus it is well that Jehovah trieth the righteous, for it causeth them to grow rich towards God.

" I will; be thou clean."—Mark i. 41.

RIMEVAL darkness heard the Almighty fiat, "light be," and straightway light was, and the word of the Lord Jesus is equal in majesty to that ancient word of power. Redemption like Creation has its word of might. Jesus speaks and it is done. Leprosy yielded to no human remedies, but it fled at once at the Lord's " I will." The disease exhibited no hopeful signs or tokens of recovery, nature contributed nothing to its own healing, but the unaided word effected the entire work on the spot and for ever. The sinner is in a plight more miserable than the leper; let him imitate his example and go to Jesus, " beseeching Him and kneeling down to Him." Let him exercise what little faith he has, even though it should go no further than " Lord, if thou wilt, thou canst make me clean ;" and there need be no doubt as to the result of the application. Jesus heals all who come, and casts out none. In reading the narrative in which our morning's text occurs, it is worthy of devout notice that Jesus touched the leper. This unclean person had broken through the regulations of the ceremonial law and pressed into the house, but Jesus so far from chiding him broke through the law himself in order to meet him. He made an interchange with the leper, for while he cleansed him, he contracted by that touch a Levitical defilement. Even so Jesus Christ was made sin for us, although in Himself He knew no sin, that we might be made the righteousness of God in Him. O that poor sinners would go to Jesus, believing in the power of His blessed substitutionary work, and they would soon learn the power of his gracious touch. That hand which multiplied the loaves, which saved sinking Peter, which upholds afflicted saints, which crowns believers, that same hand will touch every seeking sinner, and in a moment make him clean. The love of Jesus is the source of salvation. He loves, He looks, He touches us, WE LIVE.

"Just balances, just weights, a just ephah, and a just hin, shall ye have."—Leviticus xix. 36.

WEIGHTS, and scales, and measures were to be all according to the standard of justice. Surely no Christian man will need to be reminded of this in his business, for if righteousness were banished from all the world beside, it should find a shelter in believing hearts. There are, however, other balances which weigh moral and spiritual things, and these often need examining. We will call in the officer to-night.

The balances in which we weigh our own and other men's characters, are they quite accurate? Do we not turn our own ounces of goodness into pounds, and other persons' bushels of excellence into pecks? See to weights and measures here, Christian. The scales in which we measure our trials and troubles, are they according to standard? Paul, who had more to suffer than we have, called his afflictions light, and yet we often consider ours to be heavy—surely something must be amiss with the weights! We must see to this matter, lest we get reported to the court above for unjust dealing. Those weights with which we measure our doctrinal belief, are they quite fair? The doctrines of grace should have the same weight with us as the precepts of the word, no more and no less; but it is to be feared that with many one scale or the other is unfairly weighted. It is a grand matter to give just measure in truth. Christian, be careful here. Those measures in which we estimate our obligations and responsibilities look rather small. When a rich man gives no more to the cause of God than the poor contribute, is that a just ephah and a just hin? When ministers are half starved, is that honest dealing? When the poor are despised, while ungodly rich men are held in admiration, is that a just balance? Reader, we might lengthen the list, but we prefer to leave it as your evening's work to find out and destroy all unrighteous balances, weights, and measures.

" Woe is me, that I sojourn in Mesech, that I dwell in the tents of Kedar !"—Psalm cxx. 5.

AS a Christian you have to live in the midst of an ungodly world, and it is of little use for you to cry " Woe is me." Jesus did not pray that you should be taken out of the world, and what He did not pray for you need not desire. Better far in the Lord's strength to meet the difficulty, and glorify Him in it. The enemy is ever on the watch to detect inconsistency in your conduct ; be therefore very *holy*. Remember that the eyes of all are upon you, and that more is expected from you than from other men. Strive to give no occasion for blame. Let your goodness be the only fault they can discover in you. Like Daniel, compel them to say of you, " We shall not find any occasion against this Daniel, except we find it against him concerning the law of his God." Seek to be *useful* as well as consistent. Perhaps you think, " If I were in a more favourable position I might serve the Lord's cause, but I cannot do any good where I am :" but the worse the people are among whom you live, the more need have they of your exertions ; if they be crooked, the more necessity that you should set them straight ; and if they be perverse, the more need have you to turn their proud hearts to the truth. Where should the physician be but where there are many sick ? Where is honour to be won by the soldier but in the hottest fire of the battle ? And when weary of the strife and sin that meets you on every hand, consider that all the saints have endured the same trial. They were not carried on beds of down to heaven, and you must not expect to travel more easily than they. They had to hazard their lives unto the death in the high places of the field, and you will not be crowned till you also have endured hardness as a good soldier of Jesus Christ. Therefore, " stand fast in the faith, quit you like men, be strong."

" Hast thou entered into the springs of the sea ? "
Job xxxviii. 16.

SOME things in nature must remain a mystery to the most intelligent and enterprising investigators. Human knowledge has bounds beyond which it cannot pass. Universal knowledge is for God alone. If this be so in the things which are seen and temporal, I may rest assured that it is even more so in matters spiritual and eternal. Why, then, have I been torturing my brain with speculations as to destiny and will, fixed fate, and human responsibility? These deep and dark truths I am no more able to comprehend than to find out the depth which coucheth beneath, from which old ocean draws her watery stores. Why am I so curious to know the reason of my Lord's providences, the motive of His actions, the design of His visitations? Shall I ever be able to clasp the sun in my fist, and hold the universe in my palm? yet these are as a drop of a bucket compared with the Lord my God. Let me not strive to understand the infinite, but spend my strength in love. What I cannot gain by intellect I can possess by affection, and let that suffice me. I cannot penetrate the heart of the sea, but I can enjoy the healthful breezes which sweep over its bosom, and I can sail over its blue waves with propitious winds. If I could enter the springs of the sea, the feat would serve no useful purpose either to myself or others, it would not save the sinking bark, or give back the drowned mariner to his weeping wife and children; neither would my solving deep mysteries avail me a single whit, for the least love to God, and the simplest act of obedience to Him, are better than the profoundest knowledge. My Lord, I leave the infinite to Thee, and pray Thee to put far from me such a love for the tree of knowledge as might keep me from the tree of life.

" In the midst of a crooked and perverse nation, among whom ye shine as lights in the world."—Philippians ii. 15.

E use lights to *make manifest.* A Christian man should so shine in his life, that a person could not live with him a week without knowing the gospel. His conversation should be such that all who are about him should clearly perceive whose he is, and whom he serves ; and should see the image of Jesus reflected in his daily actions. Lights are intended for *guidance.* We are to help those around us who are in the dark. We are to hold forth to them the Word of life. We are to point sinners to the Saviour, and the weary to a divine resting-place. Men sometimes read their Bibles, and fail to understand them ; we should be ready, like Philip, to instruct the inquirer in the meaning of God's Word, the way of salvation, and the life of godliness. Lights are also used for *warning.* On our rocks and shoals a lighthouse is sure to be erected. Christian men should know that there are many false lights shown everywhere in the world, and therefore the right light is needed. The wreckers of Satan are always abroad, tempting the ungodly to sin under the name of pleasure; they hoist the wrong light, be it ours to put up the true light upon every dangerous rock, to point out every sin, and tell what it leads to, that so we may be clear of the blood of all men, shining as lights in the world. Lights also have a very *cheering* influence, and so have Christians. A Christian ought to be a comforter, with kind words on his lips, and sympathy in his heart ; he should carry sunshine wherever he goes, and diffuse happiness around him.

Gracious Spirit dwell with me ;
I myself would gracious be,
And with words that help and heal
Would thy life in mine reveal,
And with actions bold and meek
Would for Christ my Saviour speak.

" If ye be led of the Spirit, ye are not under the law."
Galatians v. 18.

HE who looks at his own character and position from a legal point of view, will not only despair when he comes to the *end* of his reckoning, but if he be a wise man he will despair at the *beginning;* for if we are to be judged on the footing of the law, there shall no flesh living be justified. How blessed to know that we dwell in the domains of grace and not of law! When thinking of my state before God the question is not, "Am I perfect in myself before the law?" but, "Am I perfect in Christ Jesus?" That is a very different matter. We need not enquire, "Am I without sin naturally?" but, " Have I been washed in the fountain opened for sin and for uncleanness?" It is not "Am I in myself well pleasing to God?" but it is "Am I accepted in the Beloved?" The Christian views his evidences from the top of Sinai, and grows alarmed concerning his salvation ; it were better far if he read his title by the light of Calvary. "Why," saith he, "my faith has unbelief in it, it is not able to save me." Suppose he had considered *the object* of his faith instead of his faith, then he would have said, "There is no failure in *Him,* and therefore I am safe." He sighs over his hope: "Ah! my hope is marred and dimmed by an anxious carefulness about present things; how can I be accepted?" Had he regarded *the ground* of his hope, he would have seen that the promise of God standeth sure, and that whatever our doubts may be, the oath and promise never fail. Ah! believer, it is safer always for you to be led of the Spirit into gospel liberty than to wear legal fetters. Judge yourself at what *Christ* is rather than at what *you* are. Satan will try to mar your peace by reminding you of your sinfulness and imperfections: you can only meet his accusations by faithfully adhering to the gospel and refusing to wear the yoke of bondage.

*" And when they could not come nigh unto Him for the press,
they uncovered the roof where he was : and when they had
broken it up, they let down the bed wherein the sick of the
palsy lay."*—Mark ii. 4.

FAITH *is full of inventions.* The house was full,
a crowd blocked up the door, but faith found
a way of getting at the Lord and placing the
palsied man before Him. If we cannot get sinners
where Jesus is by ordinary methods we must use extraordinary ones. It seems, according to Luke v. 19,
that a tiling had to be removed, which would make
dust and cause a measure of danger to those below, but
where the case is very urgent we must not mind running some risks and shocking some proprieties. Jesus
was there to heal, and therefore fall what might, faith
ventured all so that her poor paralysed charge might
have his sins forgiven. O that we had more daring
faith among us ! Cannot we, dear reader, seek it this
morning for ourselves and for our fellow-workers, and
will we not try to-day to perform some gallant act for
the love of souls and the glory of the Lord.

The world is constantly inventing ; genius serves all
the purposes of human desire : cannot faith invent too,
and reach by some new means the outcasts who lie
perishing around us ? It was the presence of Jesus
which excited victorious courage in the four bearers of
the palsied man : is not the Lord among us now ?
Have we seen His face for ourselves this morning ?
Have we felt His healing power in our own souls ? If
so, then through door, through window, or through
roof, let us, breaking through all impediments, labour
to bring poor souls to Jesus. All means are good and
decorous when faith and love are truly set on winning souls. If hunger for bread can break through
stone walls, surely hunger for souls is not to be
hindered in its efforts. O Lord, make us quick to
suggest methods of reaching Thy poor sin-sick ones,
and bold to carry them out at all hazards.

" There is sorrow on the sea; it cannot be quiet."—Jer. xlix. 23.

ITTLE know we what sorrow may be upon the sea at this moment. We are safe in our quiet chamber, but far away on the salt sea the hurricane may be cruelly seeking for the lives of men. Hear how the death fiends howl among the cordage; how every timber starts as the waves beat like battering rams upon the vessel! God help you, poor drenched and wearied ones! My prayer goes up to the great Lord of sea and land, that he will make the storm a calm, and bring you to your desired haven! Nor ought I to offer prayer alone, I should try to benefit those hardy men who risk their lives so constantly. Have I ever done anything for them? What can I do? How often does the boisterous sea swallow up the mariner! Thousands of corpses lie where pearls lie deep. There is death-sorrow on the sea, which is echoed in the long wail of widows and orphans. The salt of the sea is in many eyes of mothers and wives. Remorseless billows, ye have devoured the love of women, and the stay of households. What a resurrection shall there be from the caverns of the deep when the sea gives up her dead! till then there will be sorrow on the sea. As if in sympathy with the woes of earth, the sea is for ever fretting along a thousand shores, wailing with a sorrowful cry like her own birds, booming with a hollow crash of unrest, raving with uproarious discontent, chafing with hoarse wrath, or jangling with the voices of ten thousand murmuring pebbles. The roar of the sea may be joyous to a rejoicing spirit, but to the son of sorrow the wide, wide ocean is even more forlorn than the wide, wide world. This is not our rest, and the restless billows tell us so. There is a land where there is no more sea—our faces are steadfastly set towards it; we are going to the place of which the Lord hath spoken. Till then, we cast our sorrows on the Lord who trod the sea of old, and who maketh a way for His people through the depths thereof.

" From Me is thy fruit found."—Hosea xiv. 8.

OUR fruit is found from our God as to *union.* The fruit of the branch is directly traceable to the root. Sever the connection, the branch dies, and no fruit is produced. By virtue of our union with Christ we bring forth fruit. Every bunch of grapes have been first in the root, it has passed through the stem, and flowed through the sap vessels, and fashioned itself externally into fruit, but it was first in the stem ; so also every good work was first in Christ, and then is brought forth in us. O Christian, prize this precious union to Christ ; for it must be the source of all the fruitfulness which thou canst hope to know. If thou wert not joined to Jesus Christ, thou wouldst be a barren bough indeed.

Our fruit comes from God as to *spiritual providence.* When the dew-drops fall from heaven, when the cloud looks down from on high, and is about to distil its liquid treasure, when the bright sun swells the berries of the cluster, each heavenly boon may whisper to the tree and say, " From me is thy fruit found." The fruit owes much to the root—that is essential to fruitfulness —but it owes very much also to external influences. How much we owe to God's grace-providence ! in which He provides us constantly with quickening, teaching, consolation, strength, or whatever else we want. To this we owe our all of usefulness or virtue.

Our fruit comes from God as to *wise husbandry.* The gardener's sharp-edged knife promotes the fruitfulness of the tree, by thinning the clusters, and by cutting off superfluous shoots. So is it, Christian, with that pruning which the Lord gives to thee. "My Father is the husbandman. Every branch in Me that beareth not fruit He taketh away ; and every branch that beareth fruit He purgeth it, that it may bring forth more fruit." Since our God is the author of our spiritual graces, let us give to Him all the glory of our salvation.

" The exceeding greatness of His power to us-ward who believe according to the working of His mighty power, which He wrought in Christ, when He raised Him from the dead."—Ephesians i. 19, 20.

IN the resurrection of Christ, as in our salvation, there was put forth nothing short of a *divine power*. What shall we say of those who think that conversion is wrought by the free will of man, and is due to his own betterness of disposition ? When we shall see the dead rise from the grave by their own power, then may we expect to see ungodly sinners of their own free will turning to Christ. It is not the word preached, nor the word read in itself; all quickening power proceeds from the Holy Ghost. This power was *irresistible*. All the soldiers and the high priests could not keep the body of Christ in the tomb ; Death himself could not hold Jesus in his bonds : even thus irresistible is the power put forth in the believer when he is raised to newness of life. No sin, no corruption, no devils in hell nor sinners upon earth, can stay the hand of God's grace when it intends to convert a man. If God omnipotently says, " Thou shalt," man shall not say, " I will not." Observe that the power which raised Christ from the dead was *glorious*. It reflected honour upon God and wrought dismay in the hosts of evil. So there is great glory to God in the conversion of every sinner. It was *everlasting power*. " Christ being raised from the dead dieth no more ; death hath no more dominion over Him." So we, being raised from the dead, go not back to our dead works nor to our old corruptions, but we live unto God. " Because He lives we live also." " For we are dead, and our life is hid with Christ in God." "Like as Christ was raised up from the dead by the glory of the Father, even so we also should walk in newness of life." Lastly, in the text mark the *union of the new life to Jesus*. The same power which raised the Head works life in the members. What a blessing to be quickened together with Christ !

"I will answer thee, and shew thee great and mighty things which thou knowest not."—Jeremiah xxxiii. 3.

THERE are different translations of these words. One version renders it, "I will shew thee great and fortified things." Another, "Great and reserved things." Now, there are reserved and special things in Christian experience: all the developments of spiritual life are not alike easy of attainment. There are the common frames and feelings of repentance, and faith, and joy, and hope, which are enjoyed by the entire family; but there is an upper realm of rapture, of communion, and conscious union with Christ, which is far from being the common dwelling-place of believers. We have not all the high privilege of John, to lean upon Jesus' bosom; nor of Paul, to be caught up into the third heaven. There are heights in experimental knowledge of the things of God which the eagle's eye of acumen and philosophic thought hath never seen: God alone can bear us there; but the chariot in which He takes us up, and the fiery steeds with which that chariot is dragged, are prevailing prayers. Prevailing prayer is victorious over the God of mercy, "By his strength he had power with God: yea, he had power over the angel, and prevailed: he wept, and made supplication unto Him: he found Him in Beth-el, and there He spake with us." Prevailing prayer takes the Christian to Carmel, and enables him to cover heaven with clouds of blessing, and earth with floods of mercy. Prevailing prayer bears the Christian aloft to Pisgah, and shows him the inheritance reserved; it elevates us to Tabor and transfigures us, till in the likeness of his Lord, as he is, so are we also in this world. If you would reach to something higher than ordinary grovelling experience, look to the Rock that is higher than you, and gaze with the eye of faith through the window of importunate prayer. When you open the window on your side, it will not be bolted on the other.

*"And round about the throne were four and twenty seats:
and upon the seats I saw four and twenty elders sitting,
clothed in white raiment."*—Revelation iv. 4.

THESE representatives of the saints in heaven
are said to be *around the throne.* In the
passage in Canticles, where Solomon sings of
the King sitting at his table, some render it " a round
table." From this, some expositors, I think, without
straining the text, have said, " There is an equality
among the saints." That idea is conveyed by the
equal nearness of the four and twenty elders. The
condition of glorified spirits in heaven is that of nearness to Christ, clear vision of His glory, constant
access to His court, and familiar fellowship with His
person: nor is there any difference in this respect
between one saint and another, but all the people of
God, apostles, martyrs, ministers, or private and
obscure Christians, shall all be seated *near the throne,*
where they shall for ever gaze upon their exalted
Lord, and be satisfied with His love. They shall all be
near to Christ, all ravished with His love, all eating
and drinking at the same table with Him, all equally
beloved as His favourites and friends even if not all
equally rewarded as servants.

Let believers on earth imitate the saints in heaven
in their nearness to Christ. Let us on earth be as the
elders are in heaven, sitting around the throne. May
Christ be the object of our thoughts, the centre of our
lives. How can we endure to live at such a distance
from our Beloved? Lord Jesu, draw us nearer to
Thyself! Say unto us, " Abide in Me, and I in you;"
and permit us to sing, " His left hand is under my
head, and His right hand doth embrace me."

> O lift me higher, nearer Thee,
> And as I rise more pure and meet,
> O let my soul's humility
> Make me lie lower at Thy feet;
> Less trusting self, the more I prove
> The blessed comfort of Thy love.

"And he goeth up into a mountain, and calleth unto him whom he would: and they came unto him."—Mark iii. 13.

ERE was sovereignty. Impatient spirits may fret and fume, because they are not called to the highest places in the ministry ; but reader be it thine to rejoice that Jesus calleth whom He wills. If He shall leave me to be a doorkeeper in His house, I will cheerfully bless Him for His grace in permitting me to do anything in His service. The call of Christ's servants comes from above. Jesus stands on the mountain, evermore above the world in holiness, earnestness, love and power. Those whom He calls must go up the mountain to Him, they must seek to rise to His level by living in constant communion with Him. They may not be able to mount to classic honours, or attain scholastic eminence, but they must like Moses go up into the mount of God and have familiar intercourse with the unseen God, or they will never be fitted to proclaim the gospel of peace. Jesus went apart to hold high fellowship with the Father, and we must enter into the same divine companionship if we would bless our fellow-men. No wonder that the apostles were clothed with power when they came down fresh from the mountain where Jesus was. This morning we must endeavour to ascend the mount of communion, that there we may be ordained to the life-work for which we are set apart. Let us not see the face of man to-day till we have seen Jesus. Time spent with Him is laid out at blessed interest. We too shall cast out devils and work wonders if we go down into the world girded with that divine energy which Christ alone can give. It is of no use going to the Lord's battle till we are armed with heavenly weapons. We *must* see Jesus, this is essential. At the mercy-seat we will linger till He shall manifest himself unto us as He doth not unto the world, and until we can truthfully say, " We were with Him in the Holy Mount."

" Evening wolves."—Habakkuk i. 8.

WHILE preparing the present volume, this particular expression recurred to me so frequently, that in order to be rid of its constant importunity I determined to give a page to it. The evening wolf, infuriated by a day of hunger, was fiercer and more ravenous than he would have been in the morning. May not the furious creature represent our doubts and fears after a day of distraction of mind, losses in business, and perhaps ungenerous tauntings from our fellow men? How our thoughts howl in our ears, " Where is now thy God ?" How voracious and greedy they are, swallowing up all suggestions of comfort, and remaining as hungry as before. Great Shepherd, slay these evening wolves, and bid Thy sheep lie down in green pastures, undisturbed by insatiable unbelief. How like are the fiends of hell to evening wolves, for when the flock of Christ are in a cloudy and dark day, and their sun seems going down, they hasten to tear and to devour. They will scarcely attack the Christian in the daylight of faith, but in the gloom of soul conflict they fall upon him. O Thou who hast laid down Thy life for the sheep, preserve them from the fangs of the wolf.

False teachers who craftily and industriously hunt for the precious life, devouring men by their falsehoods, are as dangerous and detestable as evening wolves. Darkness is their element, deceit is their character, destruction is their end. We are most in danger from them when they wear the sheep's skin. Blessed is he who is kept from them, for thousands are made the prey of grievous wolves that enter within the fold of the church.

What a wonder of grace it is when fierce persecutors are converted, for then the wolf dwells with the lamb, and men of cruel ungovernable dispositions become gentle and teachable. O Lord, convert many such : for such we will pray to-night.

"Be ye separate."—2 Corinthians vi. 17.

THE Christian, while in the world, is not to be of the world. He should be distinguished from it in *the great object of his life.* To him, "to live," should be " Christ." Whether he eats, or drinks, or whatever he does, he should do all to God's glory. You may lay up treasure ; but lay it up in heaven, where neither moth nor rust doth corrupt, where thieves break not through nor steal. You may strive to be rich ; but be it your ambition to be "rich in faith," and good works. You may have pleasure ; but when you are merry, sing psalms and make melody in your hearts to the Lord. In your *spirit,* as well as in your aim, you should differ from the world. Waiting humbly before God, always conscious of His presence, delighting in communion with Him, and seeking to know His will, you will prove that you are of heavenly race. And you should be separate from the world in your *actions.* If a thing be right, though you lose by it, it must be done ; if it be wrong, though you would gain by it, you must scorn the sin for your Master's sake. You must have no fellowship with the unfruitful works of darkness, but rather reprove them. Walk worthy of your high calling and dignity. Remember, O Christian, that thou art a son of the King of kings. Therefore, keep thyself unspotted from the world. Soil not the fingers which are soon to sweep celestial strings ; let not these eyes become the windows of lust which are soon to see the King in His beauty—let not those feet be defiled in miry places, which are soon to walk the golden streets— let not those hearts be filled with pride and bitterness which are ere long to be filled with heaven, and to overflow with ecstatic joy.

Then rise my soul ! and soar away,
　Above the thoughtless crowd;
Above the pleasures of the gay,
　And splendours of the proud;

Up where eternal beauties bloom,
　And pleasures all divine;
Where wealth, that never can con-
　And endless glories shine. [sume,

" Lead me, O Lord, in Thy righteousness because of mine enemies."—Psalms v. 8.

VERY bitter is the enmity of the world against the people of Christ. Men will forgive a thousand faults in others, but they will magnify the most trivial offence in the followers of Jesus. Instead of vainly regretting this, let us turn it to account, and since so many are watching for our halting, let this be a special motive for walking very carefully before God. If we live carelessly, the lynx-eyed world will soon see it, and with its hundred tongues, it will spread the story, exaggerated and emblazoned by the zeal of slander. They will shout triumphantly. " Aha! So would we have it! See how these Christians act ! They are hypocrites to a man." Thus will much damage be done to the cause of Christ, and much insult offered to His name. The cross of Christ is in itself an offence to the world ; let us take heed that we add no offence of our own. It is " to the Jews a stumblingblock": let us mind that we put no stumblingblocks where there are enough already. " To the Greeks it is foolishness ": let us not add our folly to give point to the scorn with which the worldly-wise deride the gospel. How jealous should we be of ourselves ! How rigid with our consciences ! In the presence of adversaries who will misrepresent our best deeds, and impugn our motives where they cannot censure our actions, how circumspect should we be ! Pilgrims travel as suspected persons through Vanity Fair. Not only are we under surveillance, but there are more spies than we reck of. The espionage is everywhere, at home and abroad. If we fall into the enemies' hands we may sooner expect generosity from a wolf, or mercy from a fiend, than anything like patience with our infirmities from men who spice their infidelity towards God with scandals against His people. O Lord, lead us ever, lest our enemies trip us up !

" *God is jealous.*"—Nahum i. 2.

OUR Lord is very jealous of your love, O believer.
Did He choose you? He cannot bear that
you should choose another. Did He buy you
with His own blood? He cannot endure that you
should think that you are your own, or that you belong
to this world. He loved you with such a love that
He would not stop in heaven without you ; He would
sooner die than you should perish, and He cannot
endure that anything should stand between your
heart's love and Himself. *He is very jealous of your
trust.* He will not permit you to trust in an arm of
flesh. He cannot bear that you should hew out broken
cisterns, when the overflowing fountain is always free
to you When we lean upon Him, He is glad, but
when we transfer our dependence to another, when we
rely upon our own wisdom, or the wisdom of a friend
—worst of all, when we trust in any works of our own,
He is displeased, and will chasten us that He may
bring us to Himself. *He is also very jealous of our
company.* There should be no one with whom we converse so much as with Jesus. To abide in Him only,
this is true love ; but to commune with the world, to
find sufficient solace in our carnal comforts, to prefer
even the society of our fellow Christians to secret intercourse with Him, this is grievous to our jealous Lord.
He would fain have us abide in Him, and enjoy constant
fellowship with Himself ; and many of the trials which
He sends us are for the purpose of weaning our hearts
from the creature, and fixing them more closely upon
Himself. Let this jealousy which should keep us neaɪ
to Christ *be also a comfort* to us, for if He loves us
so much as to care thus about *our* love we may be
sure that He will suffer nothing to harm us, and will
protect us from all our enemies. Oh that we may have
grace this day to keep our hearts in sacred chastity for
our Beloved alone, with sacred jealousy shutting our
eyes to all the fascinations of the world !

" I will sing of mercy and judgment."—Psalm ci. 1.

FAITH triumphs in trial. When reason is thrust into the inner prison, with her feet made fast in the stocks, faith makes the dungeon walls ring with her merry notes as she cries, " I will sing of mercy and of judgment. Unto thee, O Lord, will I sing." Faith pulls the black mask from the face of trouble, and discovers the angel beneath. Faith looks up at the cloud, and sees that

> " 'Tis big with mercy and shall break
> In blessings on her head."

There is a subject for song even in the judgments of God towards us. For, first, the trial is *not so heavy as it might have been;* next, the trouble is *not so severe as we deserved to have borne;* and our affliction is *not so crushing as the burden which others have to carry.* Faith sees that in her worst sorrow there is nothing penal; there is not a drop of God's wrath in it; it is all sent in love. Faith discerns love gleaming like a jewel on the breast of an angry God. Faith says of her grief, " This is a badge of honour, for the child must feel the rod "; and then she sings of the sweet result of her sorrows, because they work her spiritual good. Nay, more, says Faith, " These light afflictions, which are but for a moment, work out for me a far more exceeding and eternal weight of glory." So Faith rides forth on the black horse, conquering and to conquer, trampling down carnal reason and fleshly sense, and chanting notes of victory amid the thickest of the fray.

> " All I meet I find assists me
> In my path to heavenly joy:
> Where, though trials now attend me,
> Trials never more annoy.

> " Blest there with a weight of glory,
> Still the path I'll ne'er forget,
> But, exulting, cry, it led me
> To my blessed Saviour's seat."

" Who passing through the valley of Baca make it a well, the rain also filleth the pools."—Psalm lxxxiv. 6.

THIS teaches us that the *comfort* obtained by one may often prove serviceable to another ; just as wells would be used by the company who came after. We read some book full of consolation, which is like Jonathan's rod, dropping with honey. Ah! we think our brother has been here before us, and digged this well for us as well as for himself. Many a "Night of Weeping," "Midnight Harmonies," an "Eternal Day," "A Crook in the Lot," a "Comfort for Mourners," has been a well digged by a pilgrim for himself, but has proved quite as useful to others. Specially we notice this in the Psalms, such as that beginning, "Why art thou cast down, O my soul?" Travellers have been delighted to see the footprint of man on a barren shore, and we love to see the waymarks of pilgrims while passing through the vale of tears.

The pilgrims dig the well, but, strange enough, it fills from the top instead of the bottom. We use the means, but the blessing does not spring from the means. We dig a well, but heaven fills it with rain. The horse is prepared against the day of battle, but safety is of the Lord. The means are connected with the end, but they do not of themselves produce it. See here the rain fills the pools, so that the wells become useful as reservoirs for the water ; labour is not lost, but yet it does not supersede divine help.

Grace may well be compared to rain for its purity, for its refreshing and vivifying influence, for its coming alone from above, and for the sovereignty with which it is given or withheld. May our readers have showers of blessing, and may the wells they have digged be filled with water! Oh, what are means and ordinances without the smile of heaven! they are as clouds without rain, and pools without water. O God of love, open the windows of heaven and pour us out a blessing !

" This man receiveth sinners."—Luke xv. 2.

OBSERVE *the condescension* of this fact. This Man, who towers above all other men, holy, harmless, undefiled, and separate from sinners—*this* Man receiveth sinners. This man, who is no other than the eternal God, before whom angels veil their faces—*this* Man receiveth sinners. It needs an angel's tongue to describe such a mighty stoop of love. That any of *us* should be willing to seek after the lost is nothing wonderful—they are of our own race; but that He, the offended God, against whom the transgression has been committed, should take upon Himself the form of a servant, and bear the sin of many, and should then be willing to receive the vilest of the vile, this is marvellous.

" This Man receiveth sinners "; not, however, that they may remain sinners, but He receives them that He may pardon their sins, justify their persons, cleanse their hearts by His purifying word, preserve their souls by the indwelling of the Holy Ghost, and enable them to serve him, to show forth His praise, and to have communion with Him. Into His heart's love He receives sinners, takes them from the dunghill, and wears them as jewels in His crown; plucks them as brands from the burning, and preserves them as costly monuments of His mercy. None are so precious in Jesus' sight as the sinners for whom He died. When Jesus receives sinners, He has not some out-of-doors reception place, no casual ward where He charitably entertains them as men do passing beggars, but He opens the golden gates of His royal heart, and receives the sinner right into Himself— yea, He admits the humble penitent into personal union and makes Him a member of His body, of His flesh, and of His bones. There was never such a reception as this! This fact is still most sure this evening, He is still receiving sinners: would to God sinners would receive Him.

" There were also with Him other little ships."—Mark iv. 36.

JESUS was the Lord High Admiral of the sea that night, and His presence preserved the whole convoy. It is well to sail with Jesus, even though it be in a little ship. When we sail in Christ's company, we may not make sure of fair weather, for great storms may toss the vessel which carries the Lord Himself, and we must not expect to find the sea less boisterous around our little boat. If we go with Jesus we must be content to fare as He fares; and when the waves are rough to Him, they will be rough to us. It is by tempest and tossing that we shall come to land, as He did before us.

When the storm swept over Galilee's dark lake all faces gathered blackness, and all hearts dreaded shipwreck. When all creature help was useless, the slumbering Saviour arose, and with a word, transformed the riot of the tempest into the deep quiet of a calm ; then were the little vessels at rest as well as that which carried the Lord. Jesus is the star of the sea ; and though there be sorrow upon the sea, when Jesus is on it there is joy too. May our hearts make Jesus their anchor, their rudder, their lighthouse, their life-boat, and their harbour. His Church is the Admiral's flagship, let us attend her movements, and cheer her officers with our presence. He Himself is the great attraction ; let us follow ever in His wake, mark His signals, steer by His chart, and never fear while He is within hail. Not one ship in the convoy shall suffer wreck ; the great Commodore will steer every barque in safety to the desired haven. By faith we will slip our cable for another day's cruise, and sail forth with Jesus into a sea of tribulation. Winds and waves will not spare us, but they all obey Him ; and, therefore, whatever squalls may occur without, faith shall feel a blessed calm within. He is ever in the centre of the weather-beaten company : let us rejoice in Him. His vessel has reached the haven, and so shall ours.

" *I acknowledged my sin unto Thee, and mine iniquity have I not hid. I said, I will confess my transgressions unto the Lord; and Thou forgavest the iniquity of my sin.*"— Psalm xxxii. 5.

DAVID'S grief for sin was bitter. Its effects were visible upon his outward frame: "his bones waxed old"; "his moisture was turned into the drought of summer." No remedy could he find, until he made a full confession before the throne of the heavenly grace. He tells us that for a time he kept silence, and his heart became more and more filled with grief: like a mountain tarn whose outlet is blocked up, his soul was swollen with torrents of sorrow. He fashioned excuses; he endeavoured to divert his thoughts, but it was all to no purpose; like a festering sore his anguish gathered, and as he would not use the lancet of confession, his spirit was full of torment, and knew no rest. At last it came to this, that he must return unto his God in humble penitence, or die outright; so he hastened to the mercy-seat, and there unrolled the volume of his iniquities before the all-seeing One, acknowledging all the evil of his ways in language such as you read in the fifty-first and other penitential Psalms. Having done this, a work so simple and yet so difficult to pride, he received at once the token of divine forgiveness; the bones which had been broken were made to rejoice, and he came forth from his closet to sing the blessedness of the man whose transgression is forgiven. See the value of a grace-wrought confession of sin! It is to be prized above all price, for in every case where there is a genuine, gracious confession, mercy is freely given, not because the repentance and confession *deserve* mercy, but for *Christ's sake*. Blessed be God, there is always healing for the broken heart; the fountain is ever flowing to cleanse us from our sins. Truly, O Lord, Thou art a God "ready to pardon!" Therefore will we acknowledge our iniquities.

" He shall not be afraid of evil tidings."—Psalm cxii. 7.

CHRISTIAN, you ought not to dread the arrival of evil tidings; because if you are distressed by them, *what do you more than other men?* Other men have not your God to fly to ; they have never proved His faithfulness as you have done, and it is no wonder if they are bowed down with alarm and cowed with fear : but you profess to be of another spirit ; you have been begotten again unto a lively hope, and your heart lives in heaven and not on earthly things ; now, if you are seen to be distracted as other men, what is the value of that grace which you profess to have received ? Where is the dignity of that new nature which you claim to possess ?

Again, if you should be filled with alarm, as others are, *you would, doubtless, be led into the sins so common to others under trying circumstances.* The ungodly, when they are overtaken by evil tidings, rebel against God ; they murmur, and think that God deals hardly with them. Will you fall into that same sin ? Will you provoke the Lord as they do ?

Moreover, unconverted men often run to wrong means in order to escape from difficulties, and you will be sure to do the same if your mind yields to the present pressure. Trust in the Lord, and wait patiently for Him. Your wisest course is to do as Moses did at the Red Sea, "Stand still and see the salvation of God." For if you give way to fear when you hear of evil tidings, you will be unable to meet the trouble with that calm composure which nerves for duty, and sustains under adversity. How can you glorify God if you play the coward ? Saints have often sung God's high praises in the fires, but will your doubting and desponding, as if you had none to help you, magnify the Most High ? Then take courage, and relying in sure confidence upon the faithfulness of your covenant God, "let not your heart be troubled, neither let it be afraid."

" A people near unto him."—Psalm cxlviii. 14.

THE dispensation of the old covenant was that of distance. When God appeared even to His servant Moses, He said, " Draw not nigh hither: put off thy shoes from off thy feet ;" and when He manifested Himself upon Mount Sinai, to His own chosen and separated people, one of the first commands was, " Thou shalt set bounds about the mount." Both in the sacred worship of the tabernacle and the temple, the thought of distance was always prominent. The mass of the people did not even enter the outer court. Into the inner court none but the priests might dare to intrude ; while into the innermost place, or the holy of holies, the high priest entered but once in the year. It was as if the Lord in those early ages would teach man that sin was so utterly loathsome to Him, that He must treat men as lepers put without the camp; and when He came nearest to them, He yet made them feel the width of the separation between a holy God and an impure sinner. When the gospel came, we were placed on quite another footing. The word " Go " was exchanged for " Come ;" distance was made to give place to nearness, and we who aforetime were afar off, were made nigh by the blood of Jesus Christ. Incarnate Deity has no wall of fire about it. " Come unto me, all ye that labour and are heavy laden, and I will give you rest," is the joyful proclamation of God as He appears in human flesh. Not now does He teach the leper his leprosy by setting him at a distance, but by Himself suffering the penalty of His defilement. What a state of safety and privilege is this nearness to God through Jesus ! Do you know it by experience ? If you know it, are you living in the power of it ? Marvellous is this nearness, yet it is to be followed by a dispensation of greater nearness still, when it shall be said, " The tabernacle of God is with men, and He doth dwell among them." Hasten it, O Lord.

"Partakers of the divine nature."—2 Peter i. 4.

O be a partaker of the divine nature is not, of course, to become God. That cannot be. The essence of Deity is not to be participated in by the creature. Between the creature and the Creator there must ever be a gulf fixed in respect of essence : but as the first man Adam was made in the image of God, so we, by the renewal of the Holy Spirit, are in a yet diviner sense made in the image of the Most High, and are partakers of the divine nature. We are, by grace, made like God. "God is love ;" we become love—"He that loveth is born of God." God is truth ; we become true, and we love that which is true : God is good, and He makes us good by His grace, so that we become the pure in heart who shall see God. Moreover, we become partakers of the divine nature in even a higher sense than this—in fact, in as lofty a sense as can be conceived, short of our being absolutely divine. Do we not become members of the body of the divine person of Christ ? Yes, the same blood which flows in the head flows in the hand : and the same life which quickens Christ quickens His people, for "Ye are dead, and your life is hid with Christ in God." Nay, as if this were not enough, we are married unto Christ. He hath betrothed us unto Himself in righteousness and in faithfulness, and he who is joined unto the Lord is one spirit. Oh ! marvellous mystery ! we look into it, but who shall understand it ? One with Jesus—so one with Him that the branch is not more one with the vine than we are a part of the Lord, our Saviour, and our Redeemer ! While we rejoice in this, let us remember that those who are made partakers of the divine nature will manifest their high and holy relationship in their intercourse with others, and make it evident by their daily walk and conversation that they have escaped the corruption that is in the world through lust. O for more divine holiness of life !

" Am I a sea, or a whale, that Thou settest a watch over me?"
Job vii, 12.

THIS was a strange question for Job to ask of the Lord. He felt himself to be too insignificant to be so strictly watched and chastened, and he hoped that he was not so unruly as to need to be so restrained. The enquiry was natural from one surrounded with such insupportable miseries, but after all, it is capable of a very humbling answer. It is true man is not the sea, but he is even more troublesome and unruly. The sea obediently respects its boundary, and though it be but a belt of sand, it does not overleap the limit. Mighty as it is, it hears the divine *hitherto,* and when most raging with tempest it respects the word ; but self-willed man defies heaven and oppresses earth, neither is there any end to his rebellious rage. The sea, obedient to the moon, ebbs and flows with ceaseless regularity, and thus renders an active as well as a passive obedience ; but man, restless beyond his sphere, sleeps within the lines of duty, indolent where he should be active. He will neither come nor go at the divine command, but sullenly prefers to do what he should not, and to leave undone that which is required of him. Every drop in the ocean, every beaded bubble, and every yeasty foam-flake, every shell and pebble, feel the power of law, and yield or move at once. O that our nature were but one thousandth part as much conformed to the will of God ! We call the sea fickle and false, but how constant it is ! Since our fathers' days, and the old time before them, the sea is where it was, beating on the same cliffs to the same tune ; we *know* where to find it, it forsakes not its bed, and changes not in its ceaseless boom ; but where is man— vain, fickle man ? Can the wise man guess by what folly he will next be seduced from his obedience ? We need more watching than the billowy sea, and are far more rebellious. Lord, rule us for Thine own glory. Amen.

" Bring him unto me."—Mark ix. 19.

DESPAIRINGLY the poor disappointed father turned away from the disciples to their Master. His son was in the worst possible condition, and all means had failed, but the miserable child was soon delivered from the evil one when the parent in faith obeyed the Lord Jesus' word, " Bring him unto me." Children are a precious gift from God, but much anxiety comes with them. They may be a great joy or a great bitterness to their parents ; they may be filled with the Spirit of God, or possessed with the spirit of evil. In all cases, the Word of God gives us one receipt for the curing of all their ills, " Bring him unto me." O for more agonizing prayer on their behalf while they are yet babes ! Sin is there, let our prayers begin to attack it. Our cries for our offspring should precede those cries which betoken their actual advent into a world of sin. In the days of their youth we shall see sad tokens of that dumb and deaf spirit which will neither pray aright, nor hear the voice of God in the soul, but Jesus still commands, " Bring them unto me." When they are grown up they may wallow in sin and foam with enmity against God ; then when our hearts are breaking we should remember the great Physician's words, " Bring them unto me." Never must we cease to pray until they cease to breathe. No case is hopeless while Jesus lives.

The Lord sometimes suffers his people to be driven into a corner that they may experimentally know how necessary He is to them. Ungodly children, when they show us our own powerlessness against the depravity of their hearts, drive us to flee to the strong for strength, and this is a great blessing to us. Whatever our morning's need may be, let it like a strong current bear us to the ocean of divine love. Jesus can soon remove our sorrow, he delights to comfort us. Let us hasten to Him while He waits to meet us.

" Encourage him."—Deuteronomy i. 38.

GOD employs His people to encourage one another. He did not say to an angel, "Gabriel, my servant Joshua is about to lead my people into Canaan—go, encourage him." God never works needless miracles ; if his purposes can be accomplished by ordinary means, He will not use miraculous agency. Gabriel would not have been half so well fitted for the work as Moses. A brother's sympathy is more precious than an angel's embassy. The angel, swift of wing, had better known the Master's bidding than the people's temper. An angel had never experienced the hardness of the road, nor seen the fiery serpents, nor had he led the stiff-necked multitude in the wilderness as Moses had done. We should be glad that God usually works for man by man. It forms a bond of brotherhood, and being mutually dependent on one another, we are fused more completely into one family. Brethren, take the text as God's message to you. Labour to help others, and especially strive to *encourage* them. Talk cheerily to the young and anxious enquirer, lovingly try to remove stumbling-blocks out of his way. When you find a spark of grace in the heart, kneel down and blow it into a flame. Leave the young believer to discover the roughness of the road by degrees, but tell him of the strength which dwells in God, of the sureness of the promise, and of the charms of communion with Christ. Aim to comfort the sorrowful, and to animate the desponding. Speak a word in season to him that is weary, and encourage those who are fearful to go on their way with gladness. God encourages you by His promises ; Christ encourages *you* as He points to the heaven He has won for you, and the Spirit encourages *you* as He works in you to will and to do of His own will and pleasure. Imitate divine wisdom, and encourage others, according to the word of this evening.

" If we live in the Spirit, let us also walk in the Spirit."—
Galatians **v.** 25.

THE two most important things in our holy religion are the *life of faith* and the *walk of faith.* He who shall rightly understand these is not far from being a master in experimental theology, for they are vital points to a Christian. You will never find true faith unattended by true godliness; on the other hand, you will never discover a truly holy life which has not for its root a living faith upon the righteousness of Christ. Woe unto those who seek after the one without the other! There are some who cultivate faith and forget holiness; these may be very high in orthodoxy, but they shall be very deep in condemnation, for they hold the truth in unrighteousness: and there are others who have strained after holiness of life, but have denied the faith, like the Pharisees of old, of whom the Master said, they were " whitewashed sepulchres." We must have faith, for this is the foundation; we must have holiness of life, for this is the superstructure. Of what service is the mere foundation of a building to a man in the day of tempest? Can he hide himself therein? He wants a house to cover him, as well as a foundation for that house. Even so we need the superstructure of spiritual life if we would have comfort in the day of doubt. But seek not a holy life without faith, for that would be to erect a house which can afford no permanent shelter, because it has no foundation on a rock. Let faith and life be put together, and, like the two abutments of an arch, they will make our piety enduring. Like light and heat streaming from the same sun, they are alike full of blessing. Like the two pillars of the temple, they are for glory and for beauty. They are two streams from the fountain of grace; two lamps lit with holy fire; two olive trees watered by heavenly care. O Lord, give us this day life within, and it will reveal itself without to thy glory.

" And they follow me."—John x. 27.

E should follow our Lord as unhesitatingly as sheep follow their shepherd, for *He has a right to lead us wherever He pleases.* We are not our own, we are bought with a price—let us recognise the rights of the redeeming blood. The soldier follows his captain, the servant obeys his master, much more must we follow our Redeemer, to whom we are a purchased possession. We are not true to our profession of being Christians, if we question the bidding of our Leader and Commander. Submission is our duty, cavilling is our folly. Often might our Lord say to us as to Peter, " What is that to thee ? follow thou Me." Wherever Jesus may lead us, *He goes before us.* If we know not where we go, we know *with whom* we go. With such a companion, who will dread the perils of the road ? The journey may be long, but His everlasting arms will carry us to the end. The presence of Jesus is the assurance of eternal salvation, because He lives, we shall live also. We should follow Christ in simplicity and faith, because *the paths in which He leads us all end in glory and immortality.* It is true they may not be *smooth* paths—they may be covered with sharp flinty trials, but they lead to the " city which hath foundations, whose builder and maker is God." " All the paths of the Lord are mercy and truth unto such as keep His covenant." Let us put full trust in our Leader, since we know that, come prosperity or adversity, sickness or health, popularity or contempt, his purpose shall be worked out, and that purpose shall be pure, unmingled good to every heir of mercy. We shall find it sweet to go up the bleak side of the hill with Christ ; and when rain and snow blow into our faces, His dear love will make us far more blest than those who sit at home and warm their hands at the world's fire. To the top of Amana, to the dens of lions, or to the hills of leopards, we will follow our Beloved. Precious Jesus, draw us, and we will run after Thee.

" The liberty wherewith Christ hath made us free."—
Galatians v. 1.

THIS " liberty " makes us *free to* heaven's charter—*the Bible.* Here is a choice passage, believer, "When thou passest through the rivers I will be with thee." You are free to that. Here is another : "The mountains shall depart, and the hills be removed, but my kindness shall not depart from thee ;" you are free to that. You are a welcome guest at the table of the promises. Scripture is a never-failing treasury filled with boundless stores of grace. It is the bank of heaven ; you may draw from it as much as you please, without let or hindrance. Come in faith and you are welcome to all *covenant blessings.* There is not a promise in the Word which shall be withheld. In the depths of tribulations let this freedom comfort you ; amidst waves of distress let it cheer you ; when sorrows surround thee let it be thy solace. This is thy Father's love-token ; thou art free to it at all times. Thou art also *free to the throne of grace.* It is the believer's privilege to have access at all times to His heavenly Father. Whatever our desires, our difficulties, our wants, we are at liberty to spread all before Him. It matters not how much we may have sinned, we may ask and expect pardon. It signifies nothing how poor we are, we may plead His promise that He will provide all things needful. We have permission to approach His throne at all times—in midnight's darkest hour, or in noontide's most burning heat. Exercise thy right, O believer, and live up to thy privilege. Thou art free to all that is treasured up *in Christ*—wisdom, righteousness, sanctification, and redemption. It matters not what thy need is, for there is fulness of supply in Christ, and it is there *for thee.* O what a " freedom " is thine ! freedom from condemnation, freedom to the promises, freedom to the throne of grace, and at last freedom to enter heaven !

" For this child I prayed."—1 Samuel i. 27.

EVOUT souls delight to look upon those mercies which they have obtained in answer to supplication, for they can see God's especial love in them. When we can name our blessings Samuel, that is, " asked of God," they will be as dear to us as her child was to Hannah. Peninnah had many children, but they came as common blessings unsought in prayer : Hannah's one heaven-given child was dearer far, because he was the fruit of earnest pleadings. How sweet was that water to Samson which he found at " the well of him that prayed ! " Quassia cups turn all waters bitter, but the cup of prayer puts a sweetness into the draughts it brings. Did we pray for the conversion of our children ? How doubly sweet, when they are saved, to see in them our own petitions fulfilled ! Better to rejoice over them as the fruit of our pleadings than as the fruit of our bodies. Have we sought of the Lord some choice spiritual gift ? When it comes to us it will be wrapped up in the gold cloth of God's faithfulness and truth, and so be doubly precious. Have we petitioned for success in the Lord's work ? How joyful is the prosperity which comes flying upon the wings of prayer ! It is always best to get blessings into our house in the legitimate way, by the door of prayer ; then they are blessings indeed, and not temptations. Even when prayer speeds not, the blessings grow all the richer for the delay ; the child Jesus was all the more lovely in the eyes of Mary when she found Him after having sought Him sorrowing. That which we win by prayer we should dedicate to God, as Hannah dedicated Samuel. The gift came from heaven, let it go to heaven. Prayer brought it, gratitude sang over it, let devotion consecrate it. Here will be a special occasion for saying, " Of Thine own have I given unto Thee." Reader, is prayer your element or your weariness ? Which ?

" *The sword of the Lord, and of Gideon.*"—Judges vii. 20.

GIDEON ordered his men to do two things: covering up a torch in an earthen pitcher, he bade them, at an appointed signal, break the pitcher and let the light shine, and then sound with the trumpet, crying, " The sword of the Lord, and of Gideon ! the sword of the Lord, and of Gideon !" This is precisely what all Christians must do. First, *you must shine;* break the pitcher which conceals your light ; throw aside the bushel which has been hiding your candle, and shine. Let your light shine before men ; let your good works be such, that when men look upon you, they shall know that you have been with Jesus. Then *there must be the sound,* the blowing of the trumpet. There must be active exertions for the ingathering of sinners by proclaiming Christ crucified. Take the gospel to them ; carry it to their door ; put it in their way ; do not suffer them to escape it ; blow the trumpet right against their ears. Remember that the true war-cry of the Church is Gideon's watchword, " *The sword of the Lord,* and of Gideon !" God must do it, it is His own work. But we are not to be idle ; instrumentality is to be used—" The sword of the Lord, *and of Gideon !*" If we only cry, " The sword of the Lord !' we shall be guilty of an idle presumption ; and if we shout, " The sword of Gideon !" alone, we shall manifest idolatrous reliance on an arm of flesh : we must blend the two in practical harmony, " The sword of the Lord, and of Gideon !" We can do nothing of ourselves, but we can do everything by the help of our God ; let us, therefore, in His name determine to go out personally and serve with our flaming torch of holy example, and with our trumpet tones of earnest declaration and testimony, and God shall be with us, and Midian shall be put to confusion, and the Lord of hosts shall reign for ever and ever.

" In the evening withhold not thy hand."—Ecclesiastes xi. 6.

N the evening of the day opportunities are plentiful: men return from their labour, and the zealous soul-winner finds time to tell abroad the love of Jesus. Have I no evening work for Jesus? If I have not, let me no longer withhold my hand from a service which requires abundant labour. Sinners are perishing for lack of knowledge; he who loiters may find his skirts crimson with the blood of souls. Jesus gave both his hands to the nails, how can I keep back one of mine from His blessed work? Night and day he toiled and prayed for me, how can I give a single hour to the pampering of my flesh with luxurious ease? Up, idle heart; stretch out thy hand to work, or uplift it to pray; heaven and hell are in earnest, let me be so, and this evening sow good seed for the Lord my God.

The evening of life has also its calls. Life is so short that a morning of manhood's vigour, and an evening of decay, make the whole of it. To some it seems long, but a fourpence is a great sum of money to a poor man. Life is so brief that no man can afford to lose a day. It has been well said that if a great king should bring us a great heap of gold, and bid us take as much as we could count in a day, we should make a long day of it; we should begin early in the morning, and in the evening we should not withhold our hand; but to win souls is far nobler work, how is it that we so soon withdraw from it? Some are spared to a long evening of green old age; if such be my case, let me use such talents as I still retain, and to the last hour serve my blessed and faithful Lord. By His grace I will die in harness, and lay down my charge only when I lay down my body. Age may instruct the young, cheer the faint, and encourage the desponding; if eventide has less of vigorous heat, it should have more of calm wisdom, therefore in the evening I will not withhold my hand.

" I will rejoice over them to do them good."—Jer. xxxii. 41.

OW heart-cheering to the believer is the delight which God has in His saints! We cannot see any reason in ourselves why the Lord should take pleasure in us ; we cannot take delight in ourselves, for we often have to groan, being burdened ; conscious of our sinfulness, and deploring our unfaithfulness ; and we fear that God's people cannot take much delight in us, for they must perceive so much of our imperfections and our follies, that they may rather lament our infirmities than admire our graces. But we love to dwell upon this transcendent truth, this glorious mystery : that as the bridegroom rejoiceth over the bride, so does the Lord rejoice over us. We do not read anywhere that God delighteth in the cloud-capped mountains, or the sparkling stars, but we do read that He delighteth in the habitable parts of the earth, and that His delights are with the sons of men. We do not find it written that even angels give His soul delight ; nor doth He say, concerning cherubim and seraphim, "Thou shalt be called Hephzibah, for the Lord delighteth in thee ;" but He does say all that to poor fallen creatures like ourselves, debased and depraved by sin, but saved, exalted, and glorified by His grace. In what strong language He expresses His delight in his people ! Who could have conceived of the eternal One as bursting forth into a song ? Yet it is written, "He will rejoice over thee with joy, He will rest in His love, He will joy over thee with singing." As He looked upon the world He had made, He said, "It is very good ;" but when He beheld those who are the purchase of Jesus' blood, His own chosen ones, it seemed as if the great heart of the Infinite could restrain itself no longer, but overflowed in divine exclamations of joy. Should not we utter our grateful response to such a marvellous declaration of His love, and sing, "I will rejoice in the Lord, I will joy in the God of my salvation"?

" Gather not my soul with sinners."—Psalm xxvi. 9.

FEAR made David pray thus, for something whispered, " Perhaps, after all, thou mayst be gathered with the wicked." That fear, although marred by unbelief, springs, in the main, from holy anxiety, arising from the recollection of past sin. Even the pardoned man will enquire, " What if at the end my sins should be remembered, and I should be left out of the catalogue of the saved ?" He recollects his present unfruitfulness— so little grace, so little love, so little holiness, and looking forward to the future, he considers his weakness and the many temptations which beset him, and he fears that he may fall, and become a prey to the enemy. A sense of sin and present evil, and his prevailing corruptions, compel him to pray, in fear and trembling, " Gather not my soul with sinners." Reader, if you have prayed this prayer, and if your character be rightly described in the Psalm from which it is taken, you need not be afraid that you shall be gathered with sinners. Have you the two virtues which David had—the outward walking in integrity, and the inward trusting in the Lord? Are you resting upon Christ's sacrifice, and can you compass the altar of God with humble hope? If so, rest assured, with the wicked you never shall be gathered, for that calamity is impossible. The gathering at the judgment is like to like. "Gather ye together first the tares, and bind them in bundles to burn them : but gather the wheat into my barn." If, then, thou art *like* God's people, thou shalt be *with* God's people. You cannot be gathered with the wicked, for you are too dearly bought. Redeemed by the blood of Christ, you are His for ever, and where He is, there must His people be. You are loved too much to be cast away with reprobates. Shall one dear to Christ perish ? Impossible ! Hell cannot hold thee ! Heaven claims thee ! Trust in thy Surety and fear not !

" Let Israel rejoice in him."—Psalm cxlix. 2.

BE glad of heart, O believer, but take care that
thy gladness has its spring *in the Lord.* Thou
hast much cause for gladness in thy God, for
thou canst sing with David, " God, my exceeding
joy." Be glad that the Lord reigneth, that Jehovah
is King ! Rejoice that He sits upon the throne, and
ruleth all things ! Every attribute of God should become a fresh ray in the sunlight of our gladness.
That He is *wise* should make us glad, knowing as we
do our own foolishness. That He is *mighty,* should
cause us to rejoice who tremble at our weakness. That
He is *everlasting,* should always be a theme of joy
when we know that *we* wither as the grass. That
He is *unchanging,* should perpetually yield us a song,
since *we* change every hour. That He is full of grace,
that He is overflowing with it, and that this grace
in covenant He has given to us; that it is ours to
cleanse us, ours to keep us, ours to sanctify us, ours
to perfect us, ours to bring us to glory—all this
should tend to make us glad in Him. This gladness
in God is as a deep river ; we have only as yet touched
its brink, we know a little of its clear sweet, heavenly
streams, but onward the depth is greater, and the
current more impetuous in its joy. The Christian
feels that he may delight himself not only in what
God *is,* but also in all that God *has done* in the past.
The Psalms show us that God's people in olden times
were wont to think much of God's actions, and to
have a song concerning each of them. So let God's
people now rehearse the deeds of the Lord ! Let
them tell of His mighty acts, and " sing unto the
Lord, for He hath triumphed gloriously." Nor let
them ever cease to sing, for as new mercies flow to
them day by day, so should their gladness in the
Lord's loving acts in providence and in grace show
itself in continued thanksgiving. Be glad ye children
of Zion and rejoice in the Lord your God.

" When my heart is overwhelmed: lead me to the Rock
that is higher than I."—Psalm lxi. 2.

MOST of us know what it is to be overwhelmed
in heart; emptied as when a man wipeth a
dish and turneth it upside down; submerged
and thrown on our beam ends like a vessel mastered
by the storm. Discoveries of inward corruption will
do this, if the Lord permits the great deep of our depravity to become troubled and cast up mire and
dirt. Disappointments and heart-breaks will do this
when billow after billow rolls over us, and we are like
a broken shell hurled to and fro by the surf. Blessed
be God, at such seasons we are not without an all-
sufficient solace, our God is the harbour of weather-
beaten sails, the hospice of forlorn pilgrims. Higher
than we are is He, His mercy higher than our sins,
His love higher than our thoughts. It is pitiful to
see men putting their trust in something lower than
themselves; but our confidence is fixed upon an
exceeding high and glorious Lord. A Rock He is
since He changes not, and a high Rock, because the
tempests which overwhelm us roll far beneath at His
feet; He is not disturbed by them, but rules them
at His will. If we get under the shelter of this
lofty Rock we may defy the hurricane; all is calm
under the lee of that towering cliff. Alas! such is
the confusion in which the troubled mind is often cast,
that we need piloting to this divine shelter. Hence
the prayer of the text. O Lord, our God, by Thy
Holy Spirit, teach us the way of faith, lead us into
Thy rest. The wind blows us out to sea, the helm
answers not to our puny hand; Thou, Thou alone
canst steer us over the bar between yon sunken rocks,
safe into the fair haven. How dependent we are
upon Thee—we need Thee to bring us to Thee. To
be wisely directed and steered into safety and peace is
Thy gift, and Thine alone. This night be pleased to
deal well with Thy servants.

" Accepted in the beloved."—Ephesians i. 6.

HAT a state of privilege ! It includes our *justification* before God, but the term "acceptance" in the Greek means more than that. It signifies that we are the objects of *divine complacency*, nay, even of *divine delight.* How marvellous that we, worms, mortals, sinners, should be the objects of divine love ! But it is only *" in the beloved."* Some Christians seem to be accepted in their own experience, at ｣east, that is their apprehension. When their spirit is lively, and their hopes bright, they think God accepts them, for they feel so high, so heavenly-minded, so drawn above the earth ! But when their souls cleave to the dust, they are the victims of the fear that they are no longer accepted. If they could but see that all their high joys do not exalt them, and all their low despondencies do not really depress them in their Father's sight, but that they stand accepted in one who never alters, in one who is always the beloved of God, always perfect, always without spot or wrinkle, or any such thing, how much happier they would be, and how much more they would honour the Saviour ! Rejoice then, believer, in this : thou art accepted "in the beloved." Thou lookest within, and thou sayest, "There is nothing acceptable *here !* " But look at Christ, and see if there is not everything acceptable *there.* Thy sins trouble thee ; but God has cast thy sins behind His back, and thou art accepted in the Righteous One. Thou hast to fight with corruption, and to wrestle with temptation, but thou art already accepted in Him who has overcome the powers of evil. The devil tempts thee ; be of good cheer, he cannot destroy thee, for thou art accepted in Him who has broken Satan's head. Know by full assurance thy glorious standing. Even glorified souls are not more accepted than thou art. They are only accepted in heaven " in the beloved," and thou art even now accepted in Christ after the same manner.

"Jesus said unto him, If thou canst believe."—Mark ix. 23.

A CERTAIN man had a demoniac son, who was afflicted with a dumb spirit. The father, having seen the futility of the endeavours of the disciples to heal his child, had little or no faith in Christ, and therefore, when he was bidden to bring his son to Him, he said to Jesus, "If Thou canst do anything, have compassion on us, and help us." Now there was an "if" in the question, but the poor trembling father had put the "if" in the wrong place : Jesus Christ, therefore, without commanding him to retract the "if," kindly puts it in its legitimate position. "Nay, verily," He seemed to say, "there should be no 'if' about My power, nor concerning My willingness, the 'if' lies somewhere else." "*If thou canst believe*, all things are possible to him that believeth." The man's trust was strengthened, he offered a humble prayer for an increase of faith, and instantly Jesus spoke the word, and the devil was cast out, with an injunction never to return. There is a lesson here which we need to learn. We, like this man, often see that there is an "if" somewhere, but we are perpetually blundering by putting it in the wrong place. *If* Jesus can help me—*if* He can give me grace to overcome temptation—*if* He can give me pardon—*if* He can make me successful ? Nay, *if* you can believe, He both can and will. You have misplaced your "if." If you can confidently trust, even as all things are possible to Christ, so shall all things be possible to you. Faith standeth in God's power, and is robed in God's majesty ; it weareth the royal apparel, and rideth on the King's horse, for it is the grace which the King delighteth to honour. Girding itself with the glorious might of the all-working Spirit, it becomes, in the omnipotence of God, mighty to do, to dare, and to suffer. All things, without limit, are possible to him that believeth. My soul, canst thou believe thy Lord to-night ?

"For I was ashamed to require of the king a band of soldiers and horsemen to help us against the enemy in the way: because we had spoken unto the king, saying, The hand of our God is upon all them for good that seek Him; but His power and his wrath is against all them that forsake Him."
Ezra viii. 22.

CONVOY on many accounts would have been desirable for the pilgrim band, but a holy shame-facedness would not allow Ezra to seek one. He feared lest the heathen king should think his professions of faith in God to be mere hypocrisy, or imagine that the God of Israel was not able to preserve His own worshippers. He could not bring his mind to lean on an arm of flesh in a matter so evidently of the Lord, and therefore the caravan set out with no visible protection, guarded by Him who is the sword and shield of His people. It is to be feared that few believers feel this holy jealousy for God; even those who in a measure walk by faith, occasionally mar the lustre of their life by craving aid from man. It is a most blessed thing to have no props and no buttresses, but to stand upright on the Rock of Ages, upheld by the Lord alone. Would any believers seek state endowments for their Church, if they remembered that the Lord is dishonoured by their asking Cæsar's aid? as if the Lord could not supply the needs of His own cause! Should we run so hastily to friends and relations for assistance, if we remembered that the Lord is magnified by our implicit reliance upon His solitary arm? My soul, wait thou only upon God. "But," says one, "are not means to be used?" Assuredly they are; but our fault seldom lies in their neglect: far more frequently it springs out of foolishly believing in them instead of believing in God. Few run too far in neglecting the creature's arm; but very many sin greatly in making too much of it. Learn, dear reader, to glorify the Lord by leaving means untried, if by using them thou wouldst dishonour the name of the Lord.

" I sleep, but my heart waketh."—Solomon's Song v. 2.

PARADOXES abound in Christian experience, and here is one—the spouse was asleep, and yet she was awake. He only can read the believer's riddle who has ploughed with the heifer of his experience. The two points in this evening's text are—a mournful sleepiness and a hopeful wakefulness. *I sleep.* Through sin that dwelleth in us we may become lax in holy duties, slothful in religious exercises, dull in spiritual joys, and altogether supine and careless. This is a shameful state for one in whom the quickening Spirit dwells ; and it is dangerous to the highest degree. Even wise virgins sometimes slumber, but it is high time for all to shake off the bands of sloth. It is to be feared that many believers lose their strength as Samson lost his locks, while sleeping on the lap of carnal security. With a perishing world around us, to sleep is cruel ; with eternity so near at hand, it is madness. Yet we are none of us so much awake as we should be ; a few thunder-claps would do us all good, and it may be, unless we soon bestir ourselves, we shall have them in the form of war, or pestilence, or personal bereavements and losses. O that we may leave for ever the couch of fleshly ease, and go forth with flaming torches to meet the coming Bridegroom ! *My heart waketh.* This is a happy sign. Life is not extinct, though sadly smothered. When our renewed heart struggles against our natural heaviness, we should be grateful to sovereign grace for keeping a little vitality within the body of this death. Jesus will hear our hearts, will help our hearts, will visit our hearts ; for the voice of the wakeful heart is really the voice of our Beloved, saying, " Open to me." Holy zeal will surely unbar the door.

> " Oh lovely attitude! He stands
> With melting heart and laden hands ;
> My soul forsakes her every sin,
> And lets the heavenly stranger in."

" Just, and the justifier of him which believeth."—Rom. iii. 26

BEING justified by faith, we have peace with God. Conscience accuses no longer. Judgment now decides for the sinner instead of against him. Memory looks back upon past sins, with deep sorrow for the sin, but yet with no dread of any penalty to come; for Christ has paid the debt of his people to the last jot and tittle, and received the divine receipt; and unless God can be so unjust as to demand double payment for one debt, no soul for whom Jesus died as a substitute can ever be cast into hell. It seems to be one of the very principles of our enlightened nature to believe that God is just; we feel that it must be so, and this gives us our terror at first; but is it not marvellous that this very same belief that God is just, becomes afterwards the pillar of our confidence and peace! If God be just, I, a sinner, alone and without a substitute, must be punished; but Jesus stands in my stead and is punished for me; and now, if God be just, I, a sinner, standing in Christ, can never be punished. God must change His nature before one soul, for whom Jesus was a substitute, can ever by any possibility suffer the lash of the law. Therefore, Jesus having taken the place of the believer—having rendered a full equivalent to divine wrath for all that His people ought to have suffered as the result of sin, the believer can shout with glorious triumph, " Who shall lay anything to the charge of God's elect ? " Not God, for He hath justified; not Christ, for He hath died, " yea rather hath risen again." My hope lives not because I am not a sinner, but because I am a sinner for whom Christ died; my trust is not that I am holy, but that being unholy, *He* is my righteousness. My faith rests not upon what I am, or shall be, or feel, or know, but in what Christ is, in what He has done, and in what He is now doing for me. On the lion of justice the fair maid of hope rides like a queen.

" Who of God is made unto us wisdom."—1 Cor. i. 30.

MAN'S intellect seeks after rest, and by nature seeks it apart from the Lord Jesus Christ. Men of education are apt, even when converted, to look upon the simplicities of the cross of Christ with an eye too little reverent and loving. They are snared in the old net in which the Grecians were taken, and have a hankering to mix philosophy with revelation. The temptation with a man of refined thought and high education is to depart from the simple truth of Christ crucified, and to invent, as the term is, a more *intellectual* doctrine. This led the early Christian churches into Gnosticism, and bewitched them with all sorts of heresies. This is the root of Neology, and the other fine things which in days gone by were so fashionable in Germany, and are now so ensnaring to certain classes of divines. Whoever you are, good reader, and whatever your education may be, if you be the Lord's, be assured you will find no rest in philosophising divinity. You may receive this dogma of one great thinker, or that dream of another profound reasoner, but what the chaff is to the wheat, that will these be to the pure word of God. All that reason, when best guided, can find out is but the A B C of truth, and even that lacks certainty, while in Christ Jesus there is treasured up all the fulness of wisdom and knowledge. All attempts on the part of Christians to be content with systems such as Unitarian and Broad-church thinkers would approve of, must fail; true heirs of heaven must come back to the grandly simple reality which makes the ploughboy's eye flash with joy, and glads the pious pauper's heart—"Jesus Christ came into the world to save sinners." Jesus satisfies the most elevated intellect when He is believingly received, but apart from Him the mind of the regenerate discovers no rest. "The fear of the Lord is the beginning of knowledge." "A good understanding have all they that do His commandments."

" The myrtle trees that were in the bottom."—Zechariah i. 8.

THE vision in this chapter describes the condition of Israel in Zechariah's day ; but being interpreted in its aspect towards *us*, it describes the Church of God as we find it now in the world. The Church is compared to a myrtle grove flourishing in a valley. It is *hidden*, unobserved, secreted ; courting no honour and attracting no observation from the careless gazer. The Church, like her head, has a glory, but it is concealed from carnal eyes, for the time of her breaking forth in all her splendour is not yet come. The idea of *tranquil security* is also suggested to us : for the myrtle grove in the valley is still and calm, while the storm sweeps over the mountain summits. Tempests spend their force upon the craggy peaks of the Alps, but down yonder where flows the stream which maketh glad the city of our God, the myrtles flourish by the still waters, all unshaken by the impetuous wind. How great is the inward tranquility of God's Church ! Even when opposed and persecuted, she has a peace which the world gives not, and which, therefore, it cannot take away : the peace of God which passeth all understanding keeps the hearts and minds of God's people. Does not the metaphor forcibly picture the peaceful, *perpetual growth* of the saints ? The myrtle sheds not her leaves, she is always green ; and the Church in her worst time still hath a blessed verdure of grace about her ; nay, she has sometimes exhibited *most* verdure when her winter has been sharpest. She has prospered most when her adversities have been most severe. Hence the text *hints at victory.* The myrtle is the emblem of peace, and a significant token of *triumph.* The brows of conquerors were bound with myrtle and with laurel ; and is not the Church ever victorious ? Is not every Christian more than a conqueror through Him that loved him ? Living in peace, do not the saints fall asleep in the arms of victory ?

" Howl, fir tree; for the cedar is fallen."—Zech. xi. 2.

WHEN in the forest there is heard the crash of a falling oak, it is a sign that the woodman is abroad, and every tree in the whole company may tremble lest to-morrow the sharp edge of the axe should find it out. We are all like trees marked for the axe, and the fall of one should remind us that for every one, whether great as the cedar, or humble as the fir, the appointed hour is stealing on apace. I trust we do not, by often hearing of death, become callous to it. May we never be like the birds in the steeple, which build their nests when the bells are tolling, and sleep quietly when the solemn funeral peals are startling the air. May we regard death as the most weighty of all events, and be sobered by its approach. It ill behoves us to sport while our eternal destiny hangs on a thread. The sword is out of its scabbard—let us not trifle; it is furbished, and the edge is sharp—let us not play with it. He who does not prepare for death is more than an ordinary fool, he is a madman. When the voice of God is heard among the trees of the garden, let fig tree and sycamore, and elm and cedar, alike hear the sound thereof.

Be ready, servant of Christ, for thy Master comes on a sudden, when an ungodly world least expects Him. See to it that thou be faithful in His work, for the grave shall soon be digged for thee. Be ready, parents, see that your children are brought up in the fear of God, for they must soon be orphans; be ready, men of business, take care that your affairs are correct, and that you serve God with all your hearts, for the days of your terrestrial service will soon be ended, and you will be called to give account for the deeds done in the body, whether they be good or whether they be evil. May we all prepare for the tribunal of the great King with a care which shall be rewarded with the gracious commendation, " Well done, good and faithful servant."

" Happy art thou, O Israel; who is like unto thee, O people saved by the Lord?"—Deuteronomy xxxiii. 29.

HE who affirms that Christianity makes men miserable, is himself an utter stranger to it. It were strange indeed, if it made us wretched, for see *to what a position it exalts us!* It makes us sons of God. Suppose you that God will give all the happiness to His enemies, and reserve all the mourning for His own family? Shall His foes have mirth and joy, and shall His home-born children inherit sorrow and wretchedness? Shall the sinner, who has no part in Christ, call himself rich in happiness, and shall we go mourning as if we were penniless beggars? No, we will rejoice in the Lord always, and glory in our inheritance, for we "have not received the spirit of bondage again to fear; but we have received the spirit of adoption, whereby we cry, Abba, Father." The rod of chastisement must rest upon us in our measure, but it worketh for us the comfortable fruits of righteousness; and therefore by the aid of the divine Comforter, we, the " people saved of the Lord," will joy in the God of our salvation. We are married unto Christ; and shall our great Bridegroom permit His spouse to linger in constant grief? Our hearts are knit unto Him : we are His members, and though for awhile we may suffer as our Head once suffered, yet we are even now blessed with heavenly blessings in Him. We have the earnest of our inheritance in the comforts of the Spirit, which are neither few nor small. Heritors of joy for ever, we have foretastes of our portion. There are streaks of the light of joy to herald our eternal sunrising. Our riches are beyond the sea; our city with firm foundations lies on the other side the river; gleams of glory from the spirit-world cheer our hearts, and urge us onward. Truly is it said of us, " Happy art thou, O Israel; who is like unto thee, O people saved by the Lord ?"

" My Beloved put in His hand by the hole of the door, and my bowels were moved for Him."—Solomon's Song v. 4.

KNOCKING was not enough, for my heart was too full of sleep, too cold and ungrateful to arise and open the door, but the touch of His effectual grace has made my soul bestir itself. Oh, the longsuffering of my Beloved, to tarry when He found Himself shut out, and me asleep upon the bed of sloth! Oh, the greatness of His patience, to knock and knock again, and to add His voice to His knockings, beseeching me to open to Him! How could I have refused Him! Base heart, blush and be confounded! But what greatest kindness of all is this. that He becomes His own porter and unbars the door Himself! Thrice blessed is the hand which condescends to lift the latch and turn the key. Now I see that nothing but my Lord's own power can save such a naughty mass of wickedness as I am; ordinances fail, even the gospel has no effect upon me, till His hand is stretched out. Now, also, I perceive that His hand is good where all else is unsuccessful, He can open when nothing else will. Blessed be His name, I feel His gracious presence even now. Well may my bowels move for Him, when I think of all that He has suffered for me, and of my ungenerous return. I have allowed my affections to wander. I have set up rivals. I have grieved Him. Sweetest and dearest of all beloveds, I have treated Thee as an unfaithful wife treats her husband. Oh, my cruel sins, my cruel self! What can I do? Tears are a poor show of my repentance, my whole heart boils with indignation at myself. Wretch that I am, to treat my Lord, my All in All, my exceeding great joy, as though He were a stranger. Jesus, thou forgivest freely, but this is not enough, prevent my unfaithfulness in the future. Kiss away these tears, and then purge my heart and bind it with sevenfold cords to Thyself, never to wander more.

" The Lord looketh from heaven; He beholdeth all the sons of men."—Psalm xxxiii. 13.

PERHAPS no figure of speech represents God in a more gracious light than when He is spoken of as stooping from His throne, and coming down from heaven to attend to the wants and to behold the woes of mankind. We love Him, who, when Sodom and Gomorrah were full of iniquity, would not destroy those cities until he had made a personal visitation of them. We cannot help pouring out our heart in affection for our Lord who inclines his ear from the highest glory, and puts it to the lip of the dying sinner, whose failing heart longs after reconciliation. How can we but love Him when we know that he numbers the very hairs of our heads, marks our path, and orders our ways ? Specially is this great truth brought near to our heart, when we recollect how attentive He is, not merely to the temporal interests of His creatures, but to their spiritual concerns. Though leagues of distance lie between the finite creature and the infinite Creator, yet there are links uniting both. When a tear is wept by thee, think not that God doth not behold ; for, " Like as a father pitieth his children, so the Lord pitieth them that fear Him." Thy sigh is able to move the heart of Jehovah ; thy whisper can incline His ear unto thee ; thy prayer can stay His hand ; thy faith can move His arm. Think not that God sits on high taking no account of thee. Remember that however poor and needy thou art, yet the Lord thinketh upon thee. For the eyes of the Lord run to and fro throughout the whole earth, to show himself strong in the behalf of them whose heart is perfect towards Him.

> Oh ! then repeat the truth that never tires ;
> No God is like the God my soul desires ;
> He at whose voice heaven trembles, even He,
> *Great as He is, knows how to stoop to me.*

" Go again seven times."—1 Kings xviii. 43.

SUCCESS is certain when the Lord has promised it. Although you may have pleaded month after month without evidence of answer, it is not possible that the Lord should be deaf when His people are earnest in a matter which concerns His glory. The prophet on the top of Carmel continued to wrestle with God, and never for a moment gave way to a fear that he should be non-suited in Jehovah's courts. Six times the servant returned, but on each occasion no word was spoken but " Go again." We must not dream of unbelief, but hold to our faith even to seventy times seven. Faith sends expectant hope to look from Carmel's brow, and if nothing is beheld, she sends again and again. So far from being crushed by repeated disappointment, faith is animated to plead more fervently with her God. She is humbled, but not abashed : her groans are deeper, and her sighings more vehement, but she never relaxes her hold or stays her hand. It would be more agreeable to flesh and blood to have a speedy answer, but believing souls have learned to be submissive, and to find it good to wait *for* as well as *upon* the Lord. Delayed answers often set the heart searching itself, and so lead to contrition and spiritual reformation : deadly blows are thus struck at our corruption, and the chambers of imagery are cleansed. The great danger is lest men should faint, and miss the blessing. Reader, do not fall into that sin, but continue in prayer and watching. At last the little cloud was seen, the sure forerunner of torrents of rain, and even so with you, the token for good shall surely be given, and you shall rise as a prevailing prince to enjoy the mercy you have sought. Elijah was a man of like passions with us : his power with God did not lie in his own merits. If his believing prayer availed so much, why not yours? Plead the precious blood with unceasing importunity, and it shall be with you according to your desire.

" Behold, if the leprosy have covered all his flesh, he shall pronounce him clean that hath the plague."—Lev. xiii. 13.

STRANGE enough this regulation appears, yet there was wisdom in it, for the throwing out of the disease proved that the constitution was sound. This morning it may be well for us to see the typical teaching of so singular a rule. We, too, are lepers, and may read the law of leper as applicable to ourselves. When a man sees himself to be altogether lost and ruined, covered all over with the defilement of sin, and no part free from pollution; when he disclaims all righteousness of his own, and pleads guilty before the Lord, then is he clean through the blood of Jesus, and the grace of God. Hidden, unfelt, unconfessed iniquity is the true leprosy, but when sin is seen and felt it has received its death blow, and the Lord looks with eyes of mercy upon the soul afflicted with it. Nothing is more deadly than self-righteousness, or more hopeful than contrition. We must confess that we are "nothing else but sin," for no confession short of this will be the whole truth, and if the Holy Spirit be at work with us, convincing us of sin, there will be no difficulty about making such an acknowledgment — it will spring spontaneously from our lips. What comfort does the text afford to those under a deep sense of sin! Sin mourned and confessed, however black and foul, shall never shut a man out from the Lord Jesus. Whosoever cometh unto Him, He will in no wise cast out. Though dishonest as the thief, though unchaste as the woman who was a sinner, though fierce as Saul of Tarsus, though cruel as Manasseh, though rebellious as the prodigal, the great heart of love will look upon the man who feels himself to have no soundness in him, and will pronounce him clean, when he trusts in Jesus crucified. Come to Him, then, poor heavy-laden sinner,

Come needy, come guilty, come loathsome and bare;
You can't come too filthy—come just as you are.

" I found Him whom my soul loveth : I held Him, and would not let Him go."—Canticles iii 4.

DOES Christ receive us when we come to Him, notwithstanding all our past sinfulness ? Does He never chide us for having tried all other refuges first ? And is there none on earth like Him ? Is He the best of all the good, the fairest of all the fair ? Oh, then let us praise him! Daughters of Jerusalem, extol Him with timbrel and harp! Down with your idols, up with the Lord Jesus. Now let the standards of pomp and pride be trampled under foot, but let the cross of Jesus, which the world frowns and scoffs at, be lifted on high. O for a throne of ivory for our King Solomon! let Him be set on high for ever, and let my soul sit at His footstool, and kiss His feet, and wash them with my tears. Oh, how precious is Christ ? How can it be that I have thought so little of Him ? How is it I can go abroad for joy or comfort when He is so full, so rich, so satisfying. Fellow believer, make a covenant with thine heart that thou wilt never depart from Him, and ask thy Lord to ratify it. Bid Him set thee as a signet upon His finger, and as a bracelet upon His arm. Ask Him to bind thee about Him, as the bride decketh herself with ornaments, and as the bridegroom putteth on his jewels. I would live in Christ's heart ; in the clefts of that rock my soul would eternally abide. The sparrow hath made a house, and the swallow a nest for herself where she may lay her young, even thine altars, O Lord of hosts, my King and my God ; and so too would I make my nest, my home, in Thee, and never from Thee may the soul of Thy turtle dove go forth again, but may I nestle close to Thee, O Jesus, my true and only rest.

> " When my precious Lord I find,
> All my ardent passions glow ;
> Him with cords of love I bind,
> Hold and will not let Him go."

" Sing forth the honour of His name, make His praise glorious."—Psalm lxvi. 2.

IT is not left to our own option whether we shall praise God or not. Praise is God's most righteous due, and every Christian, as the recipient of His grace, is bound to praise God from day to day. It is true we have no authoritative rubric for daily praise ; we have no commandment prescribing certain hours of song and thanksgiving : but the law written upon the heart teaches us that it is right to praise God ; and the unwritten mandate comes to us with as much force as if it had been recorded on the tables of stone, or handed to us from the top of thundering Sinai. Yes, it is the Christian's *duty* to praise God. It is not only a pleasureable exercise, but it is the absolute obligation of his life. Think not ye who are always mourning, that ye are guiltless in this respect, or imagine that ye can discharge your duty to your God without songs of praise. You are bound by the bonds of his love to bless His name so long as you live, and His praise should continually be in your mouth, for you are blessed, in order that ycu may bless Him ; "this people have I formed for myself, they shall show forth my praise ;" and if you do not praise God, you are not bringing forth the fruit which He, as the Divine Husbandman, has a right to expect at your hands. Let not your harp then hang upon the willows, but take it down, and strive, with a grateful heart, to bring forth its loudest music. Arise and chant His praise. With every morning's dawn, lift up your notes of thanksgiving, and let every setting sun be followed with your song. Girdle the earth with your praises ; surround it with an atmosphere of melody, and God Himself will hearken from heaven and accept your music.

> " E'en so I love Thee, and will love,
> And in Thy praise will sing,
> Because Thou art my loving God,
> And my redeeming King."

" A living dog is better than a dead lion."—Ecc. ix. 4.

IFE is a precious thing, and in its humblest form it is superior to death. This truth is eminently certain in spiritual things. It is better to be the least in the kingdom of heaven than the greatest out of it. The lowest degree of grace is superior to the noblest development of unregenerate nature. Where the Holy Ghost implants divine life in the soul, there is a precious deposit which none of the refinements of education can equal. The thief on the cross excels Cæsar on his throne; Lazarus among the dogs is better than Cicero among the senators; and the most unlettered Christian is in the sight of God superior to Plato. Life is the badge of nobility in the realm of spiritual things, and men without it are only coarser or finer specimens of the same lifeless material, needing to be quickened, for they are dead in trespasses and sins.

A living, loving, gospel sermon, however unlearned in matter and uncouth in style, is better than the finest discourse devoid of unction and power. A living dog keeps better watch than a dead lion, and is of more service to his master; and so the poorest spiritual preacher is infinitely to be preferred to the exquisite orator who has no wisdom but that of words, no energy but that of sound. The like holds good of our prayers and other religious exercises; if we are quickened in them by the Holy Spirit, they are acceptable to God through Jesus Christ, though we may think them to be worthless things; while our grand performances in which our hearts were absent, like dead lions, are mere carrion in the sight of the living God. O for living groans, living sighs, living despondencies, rather than lifeless songs and dead calms. Better anything than death. The snarlings of the dog of hell will at least keep us awake, but dead faith and dead profession, what greater curses can a man have? Quicken us, quicken us, O Lord!

" Pleasant fruits, new and old, which I have laid up for thee,
O my beloved."—Canticles vii. 13.

THE spouse desires to give to Jesus all that she produces. Our heart has " all manner of pleasant fruits," both " new and old," and they are laid up for our Beloved. At this rich autumnal season of fruit, let us survey our stores. We have *new* fruits. We desire to feel new life, new joy, new gratitude ; we wish to make new resolves and carry them out by new labours ; our heart blossoms with new prayers, and our soul is pledging herself to new efforts. But we have some *old* fruits too. There is our first love : a choice fruit that ! and Jesus delights in it. There is our first faith : that simple faith by which, having nothing, we became possessors of all things. There is our joy when first we knew the Lord : let us revive it. We have our old remembrances of the promises. How faithful has God been ! In sickness, how softly did He make our bed ! In deep waters, how placidly did He buoy us up! In the flaming furnace, how graciously did He deliver us. Old fruits, indeed ! we have many of them, for His mercies have been more than the hairs of our head. Old sins we must regret, but then we have had repentances which He has given us, by which we have wept our way to the cross, and learned the merit of His blood. We have fruits, this morning, both new and old ; but here is the point— *they are all laid up for Jesus.* Truly, those are the best and most acceptable services in which Jesus is the solitary aim of the soul, and His glory, without any admixture whatever, the end of all our efforts. Let our many fruits be laid up only for our Beloved ; let us display them when He is with us, and not hold them up before the gaze of men. Jesus, we will turn the key in our garden door, and none shall enter to rob Thee of one good fruit from the soil which Thou hast watered with Thy bloody sweat. Our all shall be Thine, Thine only, O Jesus, our Beloved !

" He will give grace and glory."—Psalm lxxxiv. 11.

BOUNTEOUS is Jehovah in His nature ; to give is His delight. His gifts are beyond measure precious, and are as freely given as the light of the sun. He gives grace to His elect because He wills it, to His redeemed because of His covenant, to the called because of His promise, to believers because they seek it, to sinners because they need it. He gives grace abundantly, seasonably, constantly, readily, sovereignly ; doubly enhancing the value of the boon by the manner of its bestowal. Grace in all its forms He freely renders to His people : comforting, preserving, sanctifying, directing, instructing, assisting grace, He generously pours into their souls without ceasing, and He always will do so, whatever may occur. Sickness may befall, but the Lord will give grace ; poverty may happen to us, but grace will surely be afforded ; death must come, but grace will light a candle at the darkest hour. 'Reader, how blessed it is as years roll round, and the leaves begin again to fall, to enjoy such an unfading promise as this, " The Lord will give grace."

The little conjunction *and* in this verse is a diamond rivet binding the present with the future : grace and glory always go together. God has married them, and none can divorce them. The Lord will never deny a soul glory to whom He has freely given to live upon His grace ; indeed, glory is nothing more than grace in its Sabbath dress, grace in full bloom, grace like autumn fruit, mellow and perfected. How soon we may have glory none can tell ! It may be before this month of October has run out we shall see the Holy City ; but be the interval longer or shorter, we shall be glorified ere long. Glory, the glory of heaven, the glory of eternity, the glory of Jesus, the glory of the Father, the Lord will surely give to His chosen. Oh, rare promise of a faithful God !

> Two golden links of one celestial chain :
> Who owneth grace shall surely glory gain.

" The hope which is laid up for you in heaven."—Col. i. 5.

OUR hope in Christ for the future is the main-spring and the mainstay of our joy here. It will animate our hearts to think often of heaven, for all that we can desire is promised there. Here we are weary and toilworn, but yonder is the land of *rest* where the sweat of labour shall no more bedew the worker's brow, and fatigue shall be for ever banished. To those who are weary and spent, the word " rest " is full of heaven. We are always in the field of battle ; we are so tempted within, and so molested by foes without, that we have little or no peace ; but in heaven we shall enjoy the *victory*, when the banner shall be waved aloft in triumph, and the sword shall be sheathed, and we shall hear our Captain say, " Well done, good and faithful servant." We have suffered bereavement after bereavement, but we are going to the land of the *immortal* where graves are unknown things. Here sin is a constant grief to us, but there we shall be perfectly *holy*, for there shall by no means enter into that kingdom anything which defileth. Hemlock springs not up in the furrows of celestial fields. Oh ! is it not joy, that you are not to be in banishment for ever, that you are not to dwell eternally in this wilderness, but shall soon inherit Canaan ? Nevertheless let it never be said of us, that we are dreaming about the *future* and forgetting the *present*, let the future sanctify the present to highest uses. Through the Spirit of God the hope of heaven is the most potent force for the product of virtue ; it is a fountain of joyous effort, it is the corner stone of cheerful holiness. The man who has this hope in him goes about his work with vigour, for the joy of the Lord is his strength. He fights against temptation with ardour, for the hope of the next world repels the fiery darts of the adversary. He can labour without present reward, for he looks for a reward in the world to come.

"A man greatly beloved."—Daniel x. 11.

CHILD of God, do you hesitate to appropriate this title? Ah! has your unbelief made you forget that *you* are greatly beloved too? Must you not have been greatly beloved, to have been bought with the precious blood of Christ, as of a lamb without blemish and without spot? When God smote His only begotten Son for you, what was this but being greatly beloved? You lived in sin, and rioted in it, must you not have been greatly beloved for God to have borne so patiently with you? You were called by grace and led to a Saviour, and made a child of God and an heir of heaven. All this proves, does it not, a very great and superabounding love? Since that time, whether your path has been rough with troubles, or smooth with mercies, it has been full of proofs that you are a man greatly beloved. If the Lord has chastened you, yet not in anger; if He has made you poor, yet in grace you have been rich. The more unworthy you feel yourself to be, the more evidence have you that nothing but unspeakable love could have led the Lord Jesus to save such a soul as yours. The more demerit you feel, the clearer is the display of the abounding love of God in having chosen you, and called you, and made you an heir of bliss. Now, if there be such love between God and us let us live in the influence and sweetness of it, and use the privilege of our position. Do not let us approach our Lord as though we were strangers, or as though He were unwilling to hear us—for we are greatly beloved by our loving Father. "He that spared not His own Son, but delivered Him up for us all, how shall He not with Him also freely give us all things?" Come boldly, O believer, for despite the whisperings of Satan and the doubtings of thine own heart, thou art greatly beloved. Meditate on the exceeding greatness and faithfulness of divine love this evening, and so go to thy bed in peace.

"Are they not all ministering spirits, sent forth to minister for them who shall be heirs of salvation?"—Heb. i. 14.

ANGELS are the unseen attendants of the saints of God; they bear us up in their hands, lest we dash our foot against a stone. Loyalty to their Lord leads them to take a deep interest in the children of His love; they rejoice over the return of the prodigal to his father's house below, and they welcome the advent of the believer to the King's palace above. In olden times the sons of God were favoured with their visible appearance, and at this day, although unseen by us, heaven is still opened, and the angels of God ascend and descend upon the Son of man, that they may visit the heirs of salvation. Seraphim still fly with live coals from off the altar to touch the lips of men greatly beloved. If our eyes could be opened, we should see horses of fire and chariots of fire about the servants of the Lord; for we have come to an innumerable company of angels, who are all watchers and protectors of the seed-royal. Spenser's line is no poetic fiction, where he sings—

> "How oft do they with golden pinions cleave
> The flitting skies, like flying pursuivant
> Against foul fiends to aid us militant!"

To what dignity are the chosen elevated when the brilliant courtiers of heaven become their willing servitors! Into what communion are we raised since we have intercourse with spotless celestials! How well are we defended since all the twenty-thousand chariots of God are armed for our deliverance! To whom do we owe all this? Let the Lord Jesus Christ be for ever endeared to us, for through Him we are made to sit in heavenly places far above principalities and powers. He it is whose camp is round about them that fear Him; He is the true Michael whose foot is upon the dragon. All hail, Jesus! thou Angel of Jehovah's presence, to Thee this family offers its morning vows.

" He Himself hath suffered being tempted." —Hebrews ii. 18

IT is a common-place thought, and yet it tastes like nectar to the weary heart—Jesus was tempted as I am. You have heard that truth many times : have you grasped it ? He was tempted to the very same sins into which we fall. Do not dissociate Jesus from our common manhood. It is a dark room which you are going through, but Jesus went through it before. It is a sharp fight which you are waging, but Jesus has stood foot to foot with the same enemy. Let us be of good cheer, Christ has borne the load before us, and the blood-stained footsteps of the King of glory may be seen along the road which we traverse at this hour. There is something sweeter yet—Jesus was tempted, but Jesus never sinned. Then, my soul, it is not needful for thee to sin, for Jesus was a man, and if one man endured these temptations and sinned not, then in His power His members may also cease from sin. Some beginners in the divine life think that they cannot be tempted without sinning, but they mistake ; there is no sin in *being tempted,* but there *is* sin in *yielding to temptation.* Herein is comfort for the sorely tempted ones. There is still more to encourage them if they reflect that the Lord Jesus, though tempted, gloriously triumphed, and as He overcame, so surely shall His followers also, for Jesus is the representative man for His people ; the Head has triumphed, and the members share in the victory. Fears are needless, for Christ is with us, armed for our defence. Our place of safety is the bosom of the Saviour. Perhaps we are tempted just now, in order to drive us nearer to Him. Blessed be any wind that blows us into the port of our Saviour's love ! Happy wounds, which make us seek the beloved Physician. Ye tempted ones, come to your tempted Saviour, for He can be touched with a feeling of your infirmities, and will succour every tried and tempted one.

"At evening time it shall be light."—Zech. xiv. 7.

OFTENTIMES we look forward with forebodings to *the time of old age*, forgetful that at eventide it shall be light. To many saints, old age is the choicest season in their lives. A balmier air fans the mariner's cheek as he nears the shore of immortality, fewer waves ruffle his sea, quiet reigns, deep, still and solemn. From the altar of age the flashes of the fire of youth are gone, but the more real flame of earnest feeling remains. The pilgrims have reached the land Beulah, that happy country, whose days are as the days of heaven upon earth. Angels visit it, celestial gales blow over it, flowers of paradise grow in it, and the air is filled with seraphic music. Some dwell here for years, and others come to it but a few hours before their departure, but it is an Eden on earth. We may well long for the time when we shall recline in its shady groves and be satisfied with hope until the time of fruition comes. The setting sun seems larger than when aloft in the sky, and a splendour of glory tinges all the clouds which surround his going down. Pain breaks not the calm of the sweet twilight of age, for strength made perfect in weakness bears up with patience under it all. Ripe fruits of choice experience are gathered as the rare repast of life's evening, and the soul prepares itself for rest.

The Lord's people shall also enjoy light in *the hour of death*. Unbelief laments; the shadows fall, the night is coming, existence is ending. Ah no, crieth faith, the night is far spent, the true day is at hand. Light is come, the light of immortality, the light of a Father's countenance. Gather up thy feet in the bed, see the waiting band of spirits! Angels waft thee away. Farewell, beloved one, thou art gone, thou wavest thine hand. Ah, now it is light. The pearly gates are open, the golden streets shine in the jasper light. We cover our eyes, but thou beholdest the unseen; adieu, brother, thou hast light at even-tide, such as we have not yet.

*" If any man sin, we have an advocate with the Father,
Jesus Christ the righteous."*—1 John ii. 1.

" IF any man sin, we *have* an advocate." Yes,
though we sin; we have Him still. John
does not say, " If any man sin he has forfeited his advocate," but " we *have* an advocate,"
sinners though we are. All the sin that a believer
ever did, or can be allowed to commit, cannot destroy
his interest in the Lord Jesus Christ as his advocate.
The name here given to our Lord is suggestive.
"*Jesus.*" Ah! then He is an advocate such as we
need, for Jesus is the name of one whose business
and delight it is to save. " They shall call His name
Jesus, for *He shall save* His people from their sins."
His sweetest name implies His success. Next, it
is " Jesus *Christ*"—Christos, the anointed. This
shows *His authority* to plead. The Christ has a right
to plead, for He is the Father's own appointed advocate and elected priest. If He were of our choosing
He might fail, but if God hath laid help upon one
that is mighty, we may safely lay our trouble where
God has laid his help. He is Christ, and therefore
authorised; He is Christ, and therefore *qualified*, for
the anointing has fully fitted Him for His work. He
can plead so as to move the heart of God and prevail.
What words of tenderness, what sentences of persuasion will the anointed use when He stands up to
plead for me! One more letter of His name remains,
" Jesus Christ *the righteous.*" This is not only His
character, BUT His plea. It is His character, and if
the Righteous One be my advocate, then my cause is
good, or He would not have espoused it. It is His
plea, for He meets the charge of unrighteousness
against me by the plea that *He* is righteous. He
declares Himself my substitute and puts His obedience
to my account. My soul, thou hast a friend well fitted
to be thine advocate, He cannot but succeed; leave
thyself entirely in His hands.

"He arose, and did eat and drink, and went in the strength of that meat forty days and forty nights."—1 Kings xix. 8.

ALL the strength supplied to us by our gracious God is meant for service, not for wantonness or boasting. When the prophet Elijah found the cake baked on the coals, and the cruse of water placed at his head, as he lay under the juniper tree, he was no gentleman to be gratified with dainty fare that he might stretch himself at his ease ; far otherwise, he was commissioned to go forty days and forty nights in the strength of it, journeying towards Horeb, the mount of God. When the Master invited the disciples to " Come and dine" with Him, after the feast was concluded He said to Peter, " Feed my sheep ;" further adding, " Follow me." Even thus it is with us ; we eat the bread of heaven, that we may expend our strength in the Master's service. We come to the passover, and eat of the paschal lamb with loins girt, and staff in hand, so as to start off at once when we have satisfied our hunger. Some Christians are for living *on* Christ, but are not so anxious to live *for* Christ. Earth should be a preparation for heaven ; and heaven is the place where saints feast most and work most. They sit down at the table of our Lord, and they serve Him day and night in His temple. They eat of heavenly food and render perfect service. Believer, in the strength you daily gain from Christ labour for Him. Some of us have yet to learn much concerning the design of our Lord in giving us His grace. We are not to retain the precious grains of truth as the Egyptian mummy held the wheat for ages, without giving it an opportunity to grow : we must sow it and water it. Why does the Lord send down the rain upon the thirsty earth, and give the genial sunshine ? Is it not that these may all help the fruits of the earth to yield food for man ? Even so the Lord feeds and refreshes our souls that we may afterwards use our renewed strength in the promotion of His glory.

"He that believeth and is baptized shall be saved."
Mark xvi. 16.

MR. MACDONALD asked the inhabitants of the island of St. Kilda how a man must be saved. An old man replied, "We shall be saved if we repent, and forsake our sins, and turn to God." "Yes," said a middle-aged female, "and with a true heart too." "Ay," rejoined a third, "and with prayer;" and, added a fourth, "It must be the prayer of the heart." "And we must be diligent too," said a fifth, "in keeping the commandments." Thus, each having contributed his mite, feeling that a very decent creed had been made up, they all looked and listened for the preacher's approbation, but they had aroused his deepest pity. The carnal mind always maps out for itself a way in which self can work and become great, but the Lord's way is quite the reverse. Believing and being baptized are no matters of merit to be gloried in—they are so simple that boasting is excluded, and free grace bears the palm. It may be that the reader is unsaved—what is the reason? Do you think the way of salvation as laid down in the text to be dubious? How can that be when God has pledged His own word for its certainty? Do you think it too easy? Why, then, do you not attend to it? Its ease leaves those without excuse who neglect it. To believe is simply to trust, to depend, to rely upon Christ Jesus. To be baptized is to submit to the ordinance which our Lord fulfilled at Jordan, to which the converted ones submitted at Pentecost, to which the jailer yielded obedience the very night of his conversion. The outward sign saves not, but it sets forth to us our death, burial, and resurrection with Jesus, and, like the Lord's Supper, is not to be neglected. Reader, do you believe in Jesus? Then, dear friend, dismiss your fears, you shall be saved. Are you still an unbeliever, then remember there is but one door, and if you will not enter by it you will perish in your sins.

" Whosoever drinketh of the water that I shall give him shall never thirst."—John iv. 14.

HE who is a believer in Jesus finds enough in his Lord to satisfy him now, and to content him for evermore. The believer is not the man whose days are weary for want of comfort, and whose nights are long from absence of heart-cheering thought, for he finds in religion such a spring of joy, such a fountain of consolation, that he is content and happy. Put him in a dungeon and he will find good company ; place him in a barren wilderness, he will eat the bread of heaven ; drive him away from friendship, he will meet the "friend that sticketh closer than a brother." Blast all his gourds, and he will find shadow beneath the Rock of Ages ; sap the foundation of his earthly hopes, but his heart will still be fixed, trusting in the Lord. The heart is as insatiable as the grave till Jesus enters it, and then it is a cup full to overflowing. There is such a fulness in Christ that He alone is the believer's all. The true saint is so completely satisfied with the all-sufficiency of Jesus that he thirsts no more—except it be for deeper draughts of the living fountain. In that sweet manner, believer, shalt thou thirst ; is shall not be a thirst of pain, but of loving desire ; thou wilt find it a sweet thing to be panting after a fuller enjoyment of Jesus' love. One in days of yore said, "I have been sinking my bucket down into the well full often, but now my thirst after Jesus has become so insatiable, that I long to put the well itself to my lips, and drink right on." Is this the feeling of thine heart now, believer ? Dost thou feel that all thy desires are satisfied in Jesus, and that thou hast no want now, but to know more of Him, and to have closer fellowship with Him ? Then come continually to the fountain, and take of the water of life freely. Jesus will never think you take too much, but will ever welcome you, saying, " Drink, yea, drink abundantly, O beloved."

" He had married an Ethiopian woman."—Numbers xii 1.

STRANGE choice of Moses, but how much more strange the choice of Him who is a prophet like unto Moses, and greater than he ! Our Lord, who is fair as the lily, has entered into marriage union with one who confesses herself to be black, because the sun has looked upon her. It is the wonder of angels that the love of Jesus should be set upon poor, lost, guilty men. Each believer must, when filled with a sense of Jesus' love, be also over-whelmed with astonishment that such love should be lavished on an object so utterly unworthy of it. Knowing as we do our secret guiltiness, unfaithfulness, and black-heartedness, we are dissolved in grateful admiration of the matchless freeness and sovereignty of grace. Jesus must have found the cause of His love in His own heart, He could not have found it in us, for it is not there. Even since our conversion we have been black, though grace has made us comely. Holy Rutherford said of himself what we must each subscribe to—" His relation to me is, that I am sick, and He is the Physician of whom I stand in need. Alas! how often I play fast and loose with Christ ! He bindeth, I loose ; He buildeth, I cast down ; I quarrel with Christ, and He agreeth with me twenty times a day !" Most tender and faithful Husband of our souls, pursue Thy gracious work of conforming us to Thine image, till Thou shalt present even us poor Ethiops unto Thyself, without spot, or wrinkle, or any such thing. Moses met with opposition be-cause of his marriage, and both himself and his spouse were the subjects of an evil eye. Can we wonder if this vain world opposes Jesus and His spouse, and especially when great sinners are con-verted? for this is ever the Pharisee's ground of objection, " This man receiveth sinners." Still is the old cause of quarrel revived, " Because he had married an Ethiopian woman."

" Wherefore hast Thou afflicted Thy servant?"—Num. xi. 11.

OUR heavenly Father sends us frequent troubles *to try our faith.* If our faith be worth anything, it will stand the test. Gilt is afraid of fire, but gold is not: the *paste* gem dreads to be touched by the diamond, but the true jewel fears no test. It is a poor faith which can only trust God when friends are true, the body full of health, and the business profitable ; but that is true faith which holds by the Lord's faithfulness when friends are gone, when the body is sick, when spirits are depressed, and the light of our Father's countenance is hidden. A faith which can say, in the direst trouble, " Though He slay me, yet will I trust in Him," is heaven-born faith. The Lord afflicts His servants *to glorify himself,* for He is greatly glorified in the graces of His people, which are His own handiwork. When " tribulation worketh patience ; and patience, experience ; and experience, hope," the Lord is honoured by these growing virtues. We should never know the music of the harp if the strings were left untouched ; nor enjoy the juice of the grape if it were not trodden in the wine-press ; nor discover the sweet perfume of cinnamon if it were not pressed and beaten ; nor feel the warmth of fire if the coals were not utterly consumed. The wisdom and power of the great Workman are discovered by the trials through which His vessels of mercy are permitted to pass. Present afflictions *tend also to heighten future joy.* There must be shades in the picture to bring out the beauty of the lights. Could we be so supremely blessed in heaven, if we had not known the curse of sin and the sorrow of earth? Will not peace be sweeter after conflict, and rest more welcome after toil ? Will not the recollection of past sufferings enhance the bliss of the glorified? There are many other comfortable answers to the question with which we opened our brief meditation, let us muse upon it all day long.

" Now on whom dost thou trust ? "—Isaiah xxxvi. 5.

READER, this is an important question. Listen to the Christian's answer, and see if it is yours. "On whom dost thou trust?" "I trust," says the Christian, "in a triune God. I trust *the Father*, believing that He has chosen me from before the foundations of the world ; I trust Him to provide for me in providence, to teach me, to guide me, to correct me if need be, and to bring me home to His own house where the many mansions are. I trust *the Son*. Very God of very God is He—the man Christ Jesus. I trust in Him to take away all my sins by His own sacrifice, and to adorn me with His perfect righteousness. I trust Him to be my Intercessor, to present my prayers and desires before His Father's throne, and I trust Him to be my Advocate at the last great day, to plead my cause, and to justify me. I trust Him for what He is, for what He has done, and for what He has promised yet to do. And I trust *the Holy Spirit*—He has begun to save me from my inbred sins ; I trust Him to drive them all out ; I trust Him to curb my temper, to subdue my will, to enlighten my understanding, to check my passions, to comfort my despondency, to help my weakness, to illuminate my darkness ; I trust Him to dwell in me as my life, to reign in me as my King, to sanctify me wholly, spirit, soul, and body, and then to take me up to dwell with the saints in light for ever."

Oh, blessed trust ! To trust Him whose power will never be exhausted, whose love will never wane, whose kindness will never change, whose faithfulness will never fail, whose wisdom will never be nonplussed, and whose perfect goodness can never know a diminution ! Happy art thou, reader, if this trust is thine ! So trusting, thou shalt enjoy sweet peace now, and glory hereafter, and the foundation of thy trust shall never be removed.

" Launch out into the deep, and let down your nets for a draught."—Luke v. 4.

WE learn from this narrative, the *necessity of human agency.* The draught of fishes was miraculous, yet neither the fisherman nor his boat, nor his fishing tackle were ignored; but all were used to take the fishes. So in the saving of souls, God worketh by means; and while the present economy of grace shall stand, God will be pleased by the foolishness of preaching to save them that believe. When God worketh without instruments, doubtless He is glorified; but He hath Himself selected the plan of instrumentality as being that by which He is most magnified in the earth. *Means of themselves are utterly unavailing.* "Master, we have toiled all the night and have taken nothing." What was the reason of this? Were they not fishermen plying their special calling? Verily, they were no raw hands; they understood the work. Had they gone about the toil unskilfully? No. Had they lacked industry? No, they had *toiled.* Had they lacked perseverance? No, they had toiled *all the night.* Was there a deficiency of fish in the sea? Certainly not, for as soon as the Master came, they swam to the net in shoals. What, then, is the reason? Is it because there is no power in the means of themselves apart from the presence of Jesus? "Without Him we can do nothing." But with Christ we can do all things. *Christ's presence confers success.* Jesus sat in Peter's boat, and His will, by a mysterious influence, drew the fish to the net. When Jesus is lifted up in His Church, His presence is the Church's power—the shout of a king is in the midst of her. "I, if I be lifted up, will draw all men unto me." Let us go out this morning on our work of soul fishing, looking up in faith, and around us in solemn anxiety. Let us toil till night comes, and we shall not labour in vain, for He who bids us let down the net, will fill it with fishes.

" Praying in the Holy Ghost."—Jude 20.

ARK the grand characteristic of true prayer— *" In the Holy Ghost."* The seed of acceptable devotion must come from heaven's storehouse. Only the prayer which comes from God can go to God. We must shoot the Lord's arrows back to Him. That desire which He writes upon our heart will move His heart and bring down a blessing, but the desires of the flesh have no power with Him.

Praying in the Holy Ghost is praying in *fervency.* Cold prayers ask the Lord not to hear them. Those who do not plead with fervency, plead not at all. As well speak of lukewarm fire as of lukewarm prayer— it is essential that it be red hot. It is praying *perseveringly.* The true suppliant gathers force as he proceeds, and grows more fervent when God delays to answer. The longer the gate is closed, the more vehemently does he use the knocker, and the longer the angel lingers the more resolved is he that he will never let him go without the blessing. Beautiful in God's sight is tearful, agonizing, unconquerable importunity. It means praying *humbly,* for the Holy Spirit never puffs us up with pride. It His office to convince of sin, and so to bow us down in contrition and brokenness of spirit. We shall never sing *Gloria in excelsis* except we pray to God *De profundis :* out of the depths must we cry, or we shall never behold glory in the highest. It is *loving* prayer. Prayer should be perfumed with love, saturated with love—love to our fellow saints, and love to Christ. Moreover, it must be a prayer full of *faith.* A man prevails only as he believes. The Holy Spirit is the author of faith, and strengthens it, so that we pray believing God's promise. O that this blessed combination of excellent graces, priceless and sweet as the spices of the merchant, might be fragrant within us because the Holy Ghost is in our hearts! Most blessed Comforter, exert Thy mighty power within us, helping our infirmities in prayer.

" Able to keep you from falling."—Jude 24.

IN some sense the path to heaven is very safe, but in other respects there is *no road so dangerous*. It is beset with difficulties. One false step, (and how easy it is to take that if grace be absent,) and down we go. What a slippery path is that which some of us have to tread! How many times have we to exclaim with the Psalmist, "My feet were almost gone; my steps had well nigh slipped." If we were strong, sure-footed mountaineers, this would not matter so much; but in ourselves, *how weak we are!* In the best roads *we soon falter*, in the smoothest paths we quickly stumble. These feeble knees of ours can scarcely support our tottering weight. A straw may throw us, and a pebble can wound us; we are mere children tremblingly taking our first steps in the walk of faith, our heavenly Father holds us by the arms or we should soon be down. Oh, if we are kept from falling, how must we bless the patient power which watches over us day by day! Think, how prone we are to sin, how apt to choose danger, how strong our tendency to cast ourselves down, and these reflections will make us sing more sweetly than we have ever done, "Glory be to Him, who is able to keep us from falling." *We have many foes* who try to push us down. The road is rough and we are weak, but in addition to this, enemies lurk in ambush, who rush out when we least expect them, and labour to trip us up, or hurl us down the nearest precipice. Only an Almighty arm can preserve us from these unseen foes, who are seeking to destroy us. Such an arm is engaged for our defence. He is faithful that hath promised, and He is able to keep us from falling, so that with a deep sense of our utter weakness, we may cherish a firm belief in our perfect safety, and say, with joyful confidence,

> " Against me earth and hell combine,
> But on my side is power divine;
> Jesus is all, and He is mine!"

" But He answered her not a word."—Matthew xv. 23.

GENUINE seekers who as yet have not obtained the blessing, may take comfort from the story before us. The Saviour did not at once bestow the blessing, even though the woman had great faith in Him. He intended to give it, but He waited awhile. "He answered her not a word." Were not her prayers good? Never better in the world. Was not her case needy? Sorrowfully needy. Did she not *feel* her need sufficiently? She felt it overwhelmingly. Was she not earnest enough? She was intensely so. Had she no faith? She had such a high degree of it that even Jesus wondered, and said, "O woman, great is thy faith." See then, although it is true that faith brings peace, yet it does not always bring it instantaneously. There may be certain reasons calling for the trial of faith, rather than the reward of faith. Genuine faith may be in the soul like a hidden seed, but as yet it may not have budded and blossomed into joy and peace. A painful silence from the Saviour is the grievous trial of many a seeking soul, but heavier still is the affliction of a harsh cutting reply such as this, "It is not meet to take the children's bread, and to cast it to dogs." Many in waiting upon the Lord find immediate delight, but this is not the case with all. Some, like the jailer, are in a moment turned from darkness to light, but others are plants of slower growth. A deeper sense of sin may be given to you instead of a sense of pardon, and in such a case you will have need of patience to bear the heavy blow. Ah! poor heart, though Christ beat and bruise thee, or even slay thee, trust Him; though He should give thee an angry word, believe in the love of His heart. Do not, I beseech thee, give up seeking or trusting my Master, because thou hast not yet obtained the conscious joy which thou longest for. Cast thyself on Him, and perseveringly depend even where thou canst not rejoicingly hope.

" Faultless before the presence of His glory."—Jude 24.

REVOLVE in your mind that wondrous word, *"faultless!"* We are far off from it now ; but as our Lord never stops short of perfection in His work of love, we shall reach it one day. The Saviour who will keep His people to the end, will also present them at last to Himself, as "a glorious church, not having spot, or wrinkle, or any such thing, but holy and without blemish." All the jewels in the Saviour's crown are of the first water and without a single flaw. All the maids of honour who attend the Lamb's wife are pure virgins without spot or stain. But how will Jesus make us faultless ? He will wash us from our sins in His own blood until we are white and fair as God's purest angel ; and we shall be clothed in His righteousness, that righteousness which makes the saint who wears it positively faultless ; yea, perfect in the sight of God. We shall be unblameable and unreproveable even in His eyes. His law will not only have no charge against us, but it will be magnified in us. Moreover, the work of the Holy Spirit within us will be altogether complete. He will make us so perfectly holy, that we shall have no lingering tendency to sin. Judgment, memory, will—every power and passion shall be emancipated from the thraldom of evil. We shall be holy even as God is holy, and in His presence we shall dwell for ever. Saints will not be out of place in heaven, their beauty will be as great as that of the place prepared for them. Oh the rapture of that hour when the everlasting doors shall be lifted up, and we, being made meet for the inheritance, shall dwell with the saints in light. Sin gone, Satan shut out, temptation past for ever, and ourselves "faultless" before God, this will be heaven indeed ! Let us be joyful now as we rehearse the song of eternal praise so soon to roll forth in full chorus from all the bloodwashed host ; let us copy David's exultings before the ark as a prelude to our ecstacies before the throne.

" And I will deliver thee out of the hand of the wicked, and I will redeem thee out of the hand of the terrible."—Jer. xv. 21.

NOTE the glorious personality of the promise. *I* will, *I* will. The Lord Jehovah Himself interposes to deliver and redeem His people. He pledges Himself personally to rescue them. His own arm shall do it, that He may have the glory. Here is not a word said of any effort of our own which may be needed to assist the Lord. Neither our strength nor our weakness is taken into the account, but the lone *I*, like the sun in the heavens, shines out resplendent in all-sufficience. Why then do we calculate our forces, and consult with flesh and blood to our grievous wounding ? Jehovah has power enough without borrowing from our puny arm. Peace, ye unbelieving thoughts, be still, and know that the Lord reigneth. Nor is there a hint concerning secondary means and causes. The Lord says nothing of friends and helpers : He undertakes the work alone, and feels no need of human arms to aid Him. Vain are all our lookings around to companions and relatives ; they are broken reeds if we lean upon them—often unwilling when able, and unable when they are willing. Since the promise comes alone from God, it would be well to wait only upon Him ; and when we do so, our expectation never fails us. Who are the wicked that we should fear them ? The Lord will utterly consume them ; they are to be pitied rather than feared. As for terrible ones, they are only terrors to those who have no God to fly to, for when the Lord is on our side, whom shall we fear ? If we run into sin to please the wicked, we have cause to be alarmed, but if we hold fast our integrity, the rage of tyrants shall be overruled for our good. When the fish swallowed Jonah, he found him a morsel which he could not digest ; and when the world devours the church, it is glad to be rid of it again. In all times of fiery trial, in patience let us possess our souls.

" Let us lift up our heart with our hands unto God in the heavens."—Lam. iii. 41.

HE act of prayer *teaches us our unworthiness*, which is a very salutary lesson for such proud beings as we are. If God gave us favours without constraining us to pray for them we should never know how poor we are, but a true prayer is an inventory of wants, a catalogue of necessities, a revelation of hidden poverty. While it is an application to divine wealth, it is a confession of human emptiness. The most healthy state of a Christian is to be always empty in self and constantly depending upon the Lord for supplies ; to be always poor in self and rich in Jesus ; weak as water personally, but mighty through God to do great exploits ; and hence the use of prayer, because, while it adores God, it lays the creature where it should be, in the very dust. Prayer is in itself, apart from the answer which it brings, a great benefit to the Christian. As the runner gains strength for the race by daily exercise, so for the great race of life we acquire energy by the hallowed labour of prayer. Prayer plumes the wings of God's young eaglets, that they may learn to mount above the clouds. Prayer girds the loins of God's warriors, and sends them forth to combat with their sinews braced and their muscles firm. An earnest pleader cometh out of his closet, even as the sun ariseth from the chambers of the east, rejoicing like a strong man to run his race. Prayer is that uplifted hand of Moses which routs the Amalekites more than the sword of Joshua ; it is the arrow shot from the chamber of the prophet foreboding defeat to the Syrians. Prayer girds human weakness with divine strength, turns human folly into heavenly wisdom, and gives to troubled mortals the peace of God. We know not what prayer cannot do ! We thank thee, great God, for the mercy-seat, a choice proof of thy marvellous lovingkindness. Help us to use it aright throughout this day !

" Whom He did predestinate, them He also called."
Romans viii. 30

IN the second epistle to Timothy, first chapter, and ninth verse, are these words—" Who hath saved us, and called us with an *holy* calling." Now, here is a touchstone by which we may try our calling. It is " an holy calling, not according to our works, but according to his own purpose and grace." This calling forbids all trust in our own doings, and conducts us to Christ alone for salvation, but it afterwards purges us from dead works to serve the living and true God. As He that hath called you is holy, so must you be holy. If you are living in sin, you are not called, but if you are truly Christ's, you can say, " Nothing pains me so much as sin ; I desire to be rid of it; Lord, help me to be holy." Is this the panting of thy heart ? Is this the tenor of thy life towards God, and His divine will ? Again, in Philippians, iii. 13, 14, we are told of " The *high* calling of God in Christ Jesus." Is then your calling a high calling ? Has it ennobled your heart, and set it upon heavenly things ? Has it elevated your hopes, your tastes, your desires ? Has it upraised the constant tenor of your life, so that you spend it with God and for God ? Another test we find in Hebrews iii. 1—" Partakers of the *heavenly* calling." Heavenly calling means a call *from* heaven. If man alone call thee, thou art uncalled. Is thy calling of God ? Is it a call *to* heaven as well as from heaven ? Unless thou art a stranger here, and heaven thy home, thou hast not been called with a heavenly calling ; for those who have been so called, declare that they look for a city which hath foundations, whose builder and maker is God, and they themselves are strangers and pilgrims upon the earth. Is thy calling thus holy, high, heavenly ? Then, beloved, thou hast been called of God, for such is the calling wherewith God doth call His people.

" I will meditate in Thy precepts."—Psalm cxix. 15.

THERE are times when solitude is better than society, and silence is wiser than speech. We should be better Christians if we were more alone, waiting upon God, and gathering through meditation on His Word spiritual strength for labour in His service. We ought to muse *upon the things of God, because we thus get the real nutriment out of them.* Truth is something like the cluster of the vine : if we would have wine from it, we must bruise it ; we must press and squeeze it many times. The bruisers feet must come down joyfully upon the bunches, or else the juice will not flow; and they must well tread the grapes, or else much of the precious liquid will be wasted. So we must, by meditation, tread the clusters of truth, if we would get the wine of consolation therefrom. Our bodies are not supported by merely taking food into the mouth, but the process which really supplies the muscle, and the nerve, and the sinew, and the bone, is the process of digestion. It is by digestion that the outward food becomes assimilated with the inner life. Our souls are not nourished merely by listening awhile to this, and then to that, and then to the other part of divine truth. Hearing, reading, marking, and learning, all require inwardly digesting to complete their usefulness, and the inward digesting of the truth lies for the most part in meditating upon it. Why is it that some Christians, although they hear many sermons, make but slow advances in the divine life ? Because they neglect their closets, and do not thoughtfully meditate on God's Word. They love the wheat, but they do not grind it ; they would have the corn, but they will not go forth into the fields to gather it ; the fruit hangs upon the tree, but they will not pluck it ; the water flows at their feet, but they will not stoop to drink it. From such folly deliver us, O Lord, and be this our resolve this morning, " I will meditate in Thy precepts."

"The Comforter, which is the Holy Ghost."—John xiv. 26.

THIS age is peculiarly the dispensation of the Holy Spirit, in which Jesus cheers us, not by His personal presence, as He shall do by-and-by, but by the indwelling and constant abiding of the Holy Ghost, who is evermore the Comforter of the church. It is His office to console the hearts of God's people. He convinces of sin; He illuminates and instructs; but still the main part of His work lies in making glad the hearts of the renewed, in confirming the weak, and lifting up all those that be bowed down. He does this by revealing Jesus to them. The Holy Spirit consoles, but Christ *is the consolation.* If we may use the figure, the Holy Spirit is the Physician, but Jesus is the medicine. *He* heals the wound, but it is by applying the holy ointment of Christ's name and grace. He takes not of His own things, but of the things of Christ. So if we give to the Holy Spirit the Greek name of *Paraclete,* as we sometimes do, then our heart confers on our blessed Lord Jesus the title of the *Paraclesis.* If the one be the Comforter, the other is the Comfort. Now, with such rich provision for his need, why should the Christian be sad and desponding? The Holy Spirit has graciously engaged to be thy Comforter: dost thou imagine, O thou weak and trembling believer, that He will be negligent of His sacred trust? Canst thou suppose that He has undertaken what he cannot or will not perform? If it be His especial work to strengthen thee, and to comfort thee, dost thou suppose He has forgotten His business, or that He will fail in the loving office which he sustains towards thee? Nay, think not so hardly of the tender and blessed Spirit whose name is "the Comforter." He delights to give the oil of joy for mourning, and the garment of praise for the spirit of heaviness. Trust thou in Him, and He will surely comfort thee till the house of mourning is closed for ever, and the marriage feast has begun.

" Godly sorrow worketh repentance."—2 Corinthians vii. 10.

GENUINE, spiritual mourning for sin is *the work of the Spirit of God.* Repentance is too choice a flower to grow in nature's garden. Pearls grow naturally in oysters, but penitence never shows itself in sinners except divine grace works it in them. If thou hast one particle of real hatred for sin, God must have given it thee, for human nature's thorns never produced a single fig. " That which is born of the flesh is flesh."

True repentance *has a distinct reference to the Saviour.* When we repent of sin, we must have one eye upon sin and another upon the cross, or it will be better still if we fix both our eyes upon Christ and see our transgressions only, in the light of His love.

True sorrow for sin is *eminently practical.* No man may say he hates sin, if he lives in it. Repentance makes us see the evil of sin, not merely as a theory, but experimentally—as a burnt child dreads fire. We shall be as much afraid of it, as a man who has lately been stopped and robbed is afraid of the thief upon the highway ; and we shall shun it—shun it in everything —not in great things only, but in little things, as men shun little vipers as well as great snakes. True mourning for sin will make us very jealous over our tongue, lest it should say a wrong word ; we shall be very watchful over our daily actions, lest in anything we offend, and each night we shall close the day with painful confessions of shortcoming, and each morning awaken with anxious prayers, that this day God would hold us up that we may not sin against Him.

Sincere repentance is *continual.* Believers repent until their dying day. This dropping well is not intermittent. Every other sorrow yields to time, but this dear sorrow grows with our growth, and it is so sweet a bitter, that we thank God we are permitted to enjoy and to suffer it until we enter our eternal rest.

" Love is strong as death."—Solomon's Song viii. 6.

HOSE love can this be which is as mighty as the conqueror of monarchs, the destroyer of the human race? Would it not sound like satire if it were applied to my poor, weak, and scarcely living love to Jesus my Lord? I do love Him, and perhaps by His grace, I could even die for Him, but as for my love in itself, it can scarcely endure a scoffing jest, much less a cruel death. Surely it is my Beloved s love which is here spoken of—the love of Jesus, the matchless lover of souls. His love was indeed stronger than the most terrible death, for it endured the trial of the cross triumphantly. It was a lingering death, but love survived the torment; a shameful death, but love despised the shame; a penal death, but love bore our iniquities; a forsaken, lonely death, from which the eternal Father hid His face, but love endured the curse, and gloried over all. Never such love, never such death. It was a desperate duel, but love bore the palm. What then, my heart? Hast thou no emotions excited within thee at the contemplation of such heavenly affection? Yes, my Lord, I long, I pant to feel Thy love flaming like a furnace within me. Come Thou Thyself and excite the ardour of my spirit.

> " For every drop of crimson blood
> Thus shed to make me live,
> O wherefore, wherefore have not I
> A thousand lives to give?"

Why should I despair of loving Jesus with a love as strong as death? He deserves it: I desire it. The martyrs felt such love, and they were but flesh and blood, then why not I? They mourned their weakness, and yet out of weakness were made strong. Grace gave them all their unflinching constancy—there is the same grace for me. Jesus, lover of my soul, shed abroad such love, even Thy love in my heart, this evening.

*" I count all things but loss for the excellency of the knowledge
of Christ Jesus my Lord."*—Philippians iii. 8.

SPIRITUAL knowledge of Christ will be a *personal* knowledge. I cannot know Jesus through
another person's acquaintance with Him. No,
I must know Him *myself;* I must know Him on my
own account. It will be an *intelligent* knowledge—I
must know *Him,* not as the visionary dreams of Him,
but as the Word reveals Him. I must know His
natures, divine and human. I must know His offices—
His attributes—His works—His shame—His glory. I
must meditate upon Him until I " comprehend with
all saints what is the breadth, and length, and depth,
and height; and know the love of Christ, which
passeth knowledge." It will be an *affectionate* knowledge of Him; indeed, if I know Him at all, I must
love Him. An ounce of heart knowledge is worth a
ton of head learning. Our knowledge of Him will be
a *satisfying* knowledge. When I know my Saviour,
my mind will be full to the brim—I shall feel that
I have that which my spirit panted after. " This
is that bread whereof if a man eat he shall never
hunger." At the same time it will be an *exciting*
knowledge; the more I know of my Beloved, the
more I shall want to know. The higher I climb the
loftier will be the summits which invite my eager
footsteps. I shall want the more as I get the more.
Like the miser's treasure, my gold will make me covet
more. To conclude; this knowledge of Christ Jesus
will be a most *happy* one; in fact, so elevating, that
sometimes it will completely bear me up above all
trials, and doubts, and sorrows; and it will, while I
enjoy it, make me something more than " Man that
is born of woman, who is of few days, and full of
trouble ;" for it will fling about me the immortality
of the everliving Saviour, and gird me with the
golden girdle of His eternal joy. Come, my soul, sit
at Jesus's feet and learn of Him all this day.

" And be not conformed to this world."—Romans xii. 2.

F a Christian can by possibility be saved while he conforms to this world, at any rate it must be so as by fire. Such a bare salvation is almost as much to be dreaded as desired. Reader, would you wish to leave this world in the darkness of a desponding death bed, and enter heaven as a shipwrecked mariner climbs the rocks of his native country? then be worldly; be mixed up with Mammonites, and refuse to go without the camp bearing Christ's reproach. But would you have a heaven below as well as a heaven above? Would you comprehend with all saints what are the heights and depths, and know the love of Christ which passeth knowledge? Would you receive an abundant entrance into the joy of your Lord? Then come ye out from among them, and be ye separate, and touch not the unclean thing. Would you attain the full assurance of faith? you cannot gain it while you commune with sinners. Would you flame with vehement love? your love will be damped by the drenchings of godless society. You cannot become a great Christian—you may be a babe in grace, but you never can be a perfect man in Christ Jesus while you yield yourself to the worldly maxims and modes of business of men of the world. It is ill for an heir of heaven to be a great friend with the heirs of hell. It has a bad look when a courtier is too intimate with his king's enemies. Even small inconsistencies are dangerous. Little thorns make great blisters, little moths destroy fine garments, and little frivolities and little rogueries will rob religion of a thousand joys. O professor, too little separated from sinners, you know not what you lose by your conformity to the world. It cuts the tendons of your strength, and makes you creep where you ought to run. Then, for your own comfort's sake, and for the sake of your growth in grace, if you be a Christian, be a Christian, and be a marked and distinct one.

" But who may abide the day of his coming ?"—Malachi iii. 2.

IS first coming was without external pomp or show of power, and yet in truth there were few who could abide its testing might. Herod and all Jerusalem with him were stirred at the news of the wondrous birth. Those who supposed themselves to be waiting for him, showed the fallacy of their professions by rejecting him when he came. His life on earth was a winnowing fan, which tried the great heap of religious profession, and few enough could abide the process. But what will his second advent be? What sinner can endure to think of it? " He shall smite the earth with the rod of His mouth, and with the breath of His lips shall He slay the wicked." When in His humiliation he did but say to the soldiers, "I am He," they fell backward ; what will be the terror of His enemies when He shall more fully reveal Himself as the " *I am ?*" His death shook earth and darkened heaven, what shall be the dreadful splendour of that day in which as the living Saviour, He shall summon the quick and dead before Him? O that the terrors of the Lord would persuade men to forsake their sins and kiss the Son lest He be angry! Though a lamb, He is yet the lion of the tribe of Judah, rending the prey in pieces ; and though He breaks not the bruised reed, yet will He break His enemies with a rod of iron, and dash them in pieces like a potter's vessel. None of His foes shall bear up before the tempest of His wrath, or hide themselves from the sweeping hail of His indignation ; but His beloved bloodwashed people look for His appearing with joy, and hope to abide it without fear : to them He sits as a refiner even now, and when He has tried them they shall come forth as gold. Let us search ourselves this morning and make our calling and election sure, so that the coming of the Lord may cause no dark forebodings in our mind. O for grace to cast away all hypocrisy, and to be found of Him sincere and without rebuke in the day of His appearing.

---

*" But the firstling of an ass thou shalt redeem with a lamb:
and if thou redeem him not, then shalt thou break his neck."*
Exodus xxxiv. 20.

EVERY firstborn creature must be the Lord's,
but since the ass was unclean, it could not be
presented in sacrifice. What then? Should
it be allowed to go free from the universal law? By
no means. God admits of no exceptions. The ass is
His due, but He will not accept it; He will not abate
the claim, but yet He cannot be pleased with the
victim. No way of escape remained but redemption—
the creature must be saved by the substitution of a
lamb in its place; or if not redeemed, it must die. My
soul, here is a lesson for thee. That unclean animal is
thyself; thou art justly the property of the Lord who
made thee and preserves thee, but thou art so sinful
that God will not, cannot, accept thee; and it has
come to this, the Lamb of God must stand in thy
stead, or thou must die eternally. Let all the world
know of thy gratitude to that spotless Lamb who has
already bled for thee, and so redeemed thee from the
fatal curse of the law. Must it not sometimes have
been a question with the Israelite which should die, the
ass or the lamb? Would not the good man pause to
estimate and compare? Assuredly there was no comparison between the value of the soul of man and the
life of the Lord Jesus, and yet the Lamb dies, and
man the ass is spared. My soul, admire the boundless
love of God to thee and others of the human race.
Worms are bought with the blood of the Son of the
Highest! Dust and ashes redeemed with a price far
above silver and gold! What a doom had been
mine had not plenteous redemption been found! The
breaking of the neck of the ass was but a momentary
penalty, but who shall measure the wrath to come
to which no limit can be imagined? Inestimably dear
is the glorious Lamb who has redeemed us from such
a doom.

" Jesus saith unto them, Come and dine." — John xxi. 12.

N these words the believer is invited to a holy *nearness to Jesus.* " Come and dine," implies the same table, the same meat; ay, and sometimes it means to sit side by side, and lean our head upon the Saviour's bosom. It is being brought into the banqueting-house, where waves the banner of redeeming love. " Come and dine," gives us a vision of *union with Jesus,* because the only food that we can feast upon when we dine with Jesus is *Himself.* Oh, what union is this! It is a depth which reason cannot fathom, that we thus feed upon Jesus. " He that ꞓateth My flesh, and drinketh My blood, dwelleth in Me, and I in him." It is also an invitation to enjoy *fellowship with the saints.* Christians may differ on a variety of points, but they have all one spiritual appetite; and if we cannot all *feel* alike, we can all *feed* alike on the bread of life sent down from heaven. At the table of fellowship with Jesus we are one bread and one cup. As the loving cup goes round we pledge one another heartily therein. Get nearer to Jesus, and you will find yourself linked more and more in spirit to all who are like yourself, supported by the same heavenly manna. If we were more near to Jesus we should be more near to one another. We likewise see in these words the *source of strength* for every Christian. To look at Christ is to live, but for strength to serve Him you must " come and dine." We labour under much unnecessary weakness on account of neglecting this precept of the Master. We none of us need to put ourselves on low diet; on the contrary, we should fatten on the marrow and fatness of the gospel that we may accumulate strength therein, and urge every power to its full tension in the Master's service. Thus, then, if you would realize *nearness* to Jesus, *union* with Jesus, *love* to His people and *strength* from Jesus, " come and dine " with Him by faith.

" With Thee is the fountain of life."—Psalm xxxvi. 9.

THERE are times in our spiritual experience when human counsel or sympathy, or religious ordinances, fail to comfort or help us. Why does our gracious God permit this? Perhaps it is because we have been living too much without Him, and He therefore takes away everything upon which we have been in the habit of depending, that He may drive us to Himself. It is a blessed thing to live at the fountain head. While our skin-bottles are full, we are content, like Hagar and Ishmael, to go into the wilderness; but when those are dry, nothing will serve us but " Thou God seest me." We are like the prodigal, we love the swine-troughs and forget our Father's house. Remember, we can make swine-troughs and husks even out of the forms of religion; they are blessed things, but we may put them in God's place, and then they are of no value. Anything becomes an idol when it keeps us away from God: even the brazen serpent is to be despised as " Nehushtan," if we worship it instead of God. The prodigal was never safer than when he was driven to his father's bosom, because he could find sustenance nowhere else. Our Lord favours us with a famine in the land that it may make us seek after Himself the more. The best position for a Christian is living wholly and directly on God's grace—still abiding where he stood at first —" Having nothing, and yet possessing all things." Let us never for a moment think that our standing is in our sanctification, our mortification, our graces, or our feelings, but know that because Christ offered a full atonement, therefore we are saved; for we are complete in Him. Having nothing of our own to trust to, but resting upon the merits of Jesus—His passion and holy life furnish us with the only sure ground of confidence. Beloved, when we are brought to a thirsting condition, we are sure to turn to the fountain of life with eagerness.

" And David said in his heart, I shall now perish one day by the hand of Saul."—1 Samuel xxvii. 1.

THE thought of David's heart at this time was a *false* thought, because he certainly had no ground for thinking that God's anointing him by Samuel was intended to be left as an empty unmeaning act. On no one occasion had the Lord deserted His servant ; he had been placed in perilous positions very often, but not one instance had occurred in which divine interposition had not delivered him. The trials to which he had been exposed had been varied ; they had not assumed one form only, but many—yet in every case He who sent the trial had also graciously ordained a way of escape. David could not put his finger upon any entry in his diary, and say of it, " Here is evidence that the Lord will forsake me," for the entire tenor of his past life proved the very reverse. He should have argued from what God *had* done for him, that God would be his defender still. But is it not just in the same way that *we* doubt God's help ? Is it not *mistrust without a cause?* Have we ever had the shadow of a reason to doubt our Father's goodness ? Have not His lovingkindnesses been marvellous ? Has He *once* failed to justify our trust ? Ah, no ! our God has not left us at any time. We have had dark nights, but the star of love has shone forth amid the blackness ; we have been in stern conflicts, but over our head He has held aloft the shield of our defence. We have gone through many trials, but never to our detriment, always to our advantage ; and the conclusion from our past experience is, that He who has been with us in six troubles, will not forsake us in the seventh. What we have known of our faithful God, proves that He will keep us to the end. Let us not, then, reason contrary to evidence. How can we ever be so ungenerous as to *doubt* our God ? Lord, throw down the Jezebel of our unbelief, and let the dogs devour it.

" He shall gather the lambs with His arm."—Isaiah xl. 11.

OUR good Shepherd has in His flock a variety of experiences, some are strong in the Lord, and others are weak in faith, but He is impartial in His care for all His sheep, and the weakest lamb is as dear to Him as the most advanced of the flock. Lambs are wont to lag behind, prone to wander, and apt to grow weary, but from all the danger of these infirmities the Shepherd protects them with His arm of power. He finds new-born souls, like young lambs, ready to perish—He nourishes them till life becomes vigorous ; He finds weak minds ready to faint and die—He consoles them and renews their strength. All the little ones He gathers, for it is not the will of our heavenly Father that one of them should perish. What a quick eye He must have to see them all ! What a tender heart to care for them all ! What a far-reaching and potent arm, to gather them all ! In His lifetime on earth He was a great gatherer of the weaker sort, and now that He dwells in heaven, His loving heart yearns towards the meek and contrite, the timid and feeble, the fearful and fainting here below. How gently did He gather me to Himself, to His truth, to His blood, to His love, to His church ! With what effectual grace did He compel me to come to Himself ! Since my first conversion, how frequently has He restored me from my wanderings, and once again folded me within the circle of His everlasting arm ! The best of all is, that He does it all Himself personally, not delegating the task of love, but condescending Himself to rescue and preserve His most unworthy servant. How shall I love Him enough or serve Him worthily ? I would fain make His name great unto the ends of the earth, but what can my feebleness do for Him ? Great Shepherd, add to Thy mercies this one other, a heart to love Thee more truly as I ought.

" Thy paths drop fatness."—Psalm lxv. 11.

MANY are " the paths of the Lord " which " drop fatness," but an especial one is the *path of prayer*. No believer, who is much in the closet, will have need to cry, " My leanness, my leanness ; woe unto me." Starving souls live at a distance from the mercy-seat, and become like the parched fields in times of drought. Prevalence with God in wrestling prayer is sure to make the believer strong—if not happy. The nearest place to the gate of heaven is the throne of the heavenly grace. Much alone, and you will have much assurance ; little alone with Jesus, your religion will be shallow, polluted with many doubts and fears, and not sparkling with the joy of the Lord. Since the soul-enriching path of prayer is open to the very weakest saint ; since no high attainments are required; since you are not bidden to come because you are an advanced saint, but freely invited if you be a saint at all ; see to it, dear reader, that you are often in the way of private devotion. Be much on your knees, for so Elijah drew the rain upon famished Israel's fields.

There is another especial path dropping with fatness to those who walk therein, it is the secret walk of *communion*. Oh! the delights of fellowship with Jesus! Earth hath no words which can set forth the holy calm of a soul leaning on Jesus' bosom. Few Christians understand it, they live in the lowlands and seldom climb to the top of Nebo : they live in the outer court, they enter not the holy place, they take not up the privilege of priesthood. At a distance they see the sacrifice, but they sit not down with the priest to eat thereof, and to enjoy the fat of the burnt offering. But, reader, sit thou ever under the shadow of Jesus ; come up to that palm tree, and take hold of the branches thereof; let thy beloved be unto thee as the apple-tree among the trees of the wood, and thou shalt be satisfied as with marrow and fatness. O Jesus, visit us with Thy salvation!

" Behold, to obey is better than sacrifice."—1 Samuel xv. 22.

SAUL had been commanded to slay utterly all the Amalekites and their cattle. Instead of doing so, he preserved the king, and suffered his people to take the best of the oxen and of the sheep. When called to account for this, he declared that he did it with a view of offering sacrifice to God; but Samuel met him at once with the assurance that sacrifices were no excuse for an act of direct rebellion. The sentence before us is worthy to be printed in letters of gold, and to be hung up before the eyes of the present idolatrous generation, who are very fond of the fineries of will-worship, but utterly neglect the laws of God. Be it ever in your remembrance, that to keep strictly in the path of your Saviour's command is better than any outward form of religion; and to hearken to His precept with an attentive ear is better than to bring the fat of rams, or any other precious thing to lay upon His altar. If you are failing to keep the least of Christ's commands to His disciples, I pray you be disobedient no longer. All the pretensions you make of attachment to your Master, and all the devout actions which you may perform, are no recompense for disobedience. " To obey," even in the slightest and smallest thing, " is better than sacrifice," however pompous. Talk not of Gregorian chants, sumptuous robes, incense, and banners; the first thing which God requires of His child is obedience; and though you should give your body to be burned, and all your goods to feed the poor, yet if you do not hearken to the Lord's precepts, all your formalities shall profit you nothing. It is a blessed thing to be teachable as a little child, but it is a much more blessed thing when one has been taught the lesson, to carry it out to the letter. How many adorn their temples and decorate their priests, but refuse to obey the word of the Lord! My soul, come not thou into their secret.

"Babes in Christ."—1 Cor. iii. 1.

ARE you mourning, believer, because you are so weak in the divine life : because your faith is so little, your love so feeble? Cheer up, for you have cause for gratitude. Remember *that in some things you are equal to the greatest and most full-grown Christian.* You are as much bought with blood as he is. You are as much an adopted child of God as any other believer. An infant is as truly a child of its parents as is the full-grown man. You are as completely justified, for your justification is not a thing of degrees: your little faith has made you clean every whit. You have as much right to the precious things of the covenant as the most advanced believers, for your right to covenant mercies lies not in your growth, but in the covenant itself ; and your faith in Jesus is not the measure, but the token of your inheritance in Him. You are as rich as the richest, if not in enjoyment, yet in real possession. The smallest star that gleams is set in heaven; the faintest ray of light has affinity with the great orb of day. In the family register of glory the small and the great are written with the same pen. You are as dear to your Father's heart as the greatest in the family. Jesus is very tender over you. You are like the smoking flax ; a rougher spirit would say, "put out that smoking flax, it fills the room with an offensive odour !" but the smoking flax *He* will not quench. You are like a bruised reed ; and any less tender hand than that of the Chief Musician would tread upon you or throw you away, but He will never break the bruised reed. Instead of being downcast by reason of what you are, you should triumph in Christ. Am I but little in Israel ? Yet in Christ I am made to sit in heavenly places. Am I poor in faith ? Still in Jesus I am heir of all things. Though "less than nothing I can boast, and vanity confess," yet, if the root of the matter be in me I will rejoice in the Lord, and glory in the God of my salvation.

" God, my Maker, who giveth songs in the night."
Job xxxv. 10.

NY man can sing in the day. When the cup is full, man draws inspiration from it. When wealth rolls in abundance around him, any man can praise the God who gives a plenteous harvest or sends home a loaded argosy. It is easy enough for an Æolian harp to whisper music when the winds blow—the difficulty is for music to swell forth when no wind is stirring. It is easy to sing when we can read the notes by daylight; but he is skilful who sings when there is not a ray of light to read by—who sings from his heart. No man can make a song in the night of himself; he may attempt it, but he will find that a song in the night must be divinely inspired. Let all things go well, I can weave songs, fashioning them wherever I go out of the flowers that grow upon my path; but put me in a desert, where no green thing grows, and wherewith shall I frame a hymn of praise to God? How shall a mortal man make a crown for the Lord where no jewels are? Let but this voice be clear, and this body full of health, and I can sing God's praise: silence my tongue, lay me upon the bed of languishing, and how shall I then chant God's high praises, unless He Himself give me the song? No, it is not in man's power to sing when all is adverse, unless an altar-coal shall touch his lip. It was a divine song, which Habakkuk sang, when in the night he said, "Although the fig-tree shall not blossom, neither shall fruit be in the vines; the labour of the olive shall fail, and the fields shall yield no meat; the flock shall be cut off from the fold, and there shall be no herd in the stalls: yet I will rejoice in the Lord, I will joy in the God of my salvation." Then, since our Maker gives *songs in the night*, let us wait upon Him for the music. O Thou chief musician, let us not remain songless because affliction is upon us, but tune Thou our lips to the melody of thanksgiving.

" *Grow up into Him in all things.*"—Ephesians iv. 15.

MANY Christians remain stunted and dwarfed in spiritual things, so as to present the same appearance year after year. No up-springing of advanced and refined feeling is manifest in them. They *exist* but do not "*grow up into Him in all things.*" But should we rest content with being in the "green blade," when we might advance to "the ear," and eventually ripen into the "full corn in the ear ?" Should we be satisfied to believe in Christ, and to say, "I am safe," without wishing to know in our own experience more of the fulness which is to be found in Him. It should not be so ; we should, as good traders in heaven's market, covet to be enriched in the knowledge of Jesus. It is all very well to keep other men's vineyards, but we must not neglect our own spiritual growth and ripening. Why should it always be winter time in our hearts ? We must have our seed time, it is true, but O for a spring time—yea, a summer season, which shall give promise of an early harvest. If we would ripen in grace, we must live near to Jesus— in His presence—ripened by the sunshine of His smiles. We must hold sweet communion with Him. We must leave the distant view of His face and come near, as John did, and pillow our head on His breast; then shall we find ourselves advancing in holiness, in love, in faith, in hope—yea, in every precious gift. As the sun rises first on mountain-tops and gilds them with his light, and presents one of the most charming sights to the eye of the traveller ; so is it one of the most delightful contemplations in the world to mark the glow of the Spirit's light on the head of some saint, who has risen up in spiritual stature, like Saul, above his fellows, till, like a mighty Alp, snow-capped, he reflects first among the chosen, the beams of the Sun of Righteousness, and bears the sheen of His effulgence high aloft for all to see, and seeing it, to glorify His Father which is in heaven.

" Keep not back."—Isaiah xliii. 6.

ALTHOUGH this message was sent to the south, and referred to the seed of Israel, it may profitably be a summons to ourselves. Backward we are naturally to all good things, and it is a lesson of grace to learn to go forward in the ways of God. Reader, are you unconverted, but do you desire to trust in the Lord Jesus? Then *keep not back*. Love invites you, the promises secure you success, the precious blood prepares the way. Let not sins or fears hinder you, but come to Jesus just as you are. Do you long to pray? Would you pour out your heart before the Lord? *Keep not back.* The mercy-seat is prepared for such as need mercy; a sinner's cries will prevail with God. You are invited, nay, you are commanded to pray, come therefore with boldness to the throne of grace.

Dear friend, are you already saved? Then *keep not back* from union with the Lord's people. Neglect not the ordinances of baptism and the Lord's Supper. You may be of a timid disposition, but you must strive against it, lest it lead you into disobedience. There is a sweet promise made to those who confess Christ—by no means miss it, lest you come under the condemnation of those who deny Him. If you have talents *keep not back* from using them. Hoard not your wealth, waste not your time; let not your abilities rust or your influence be unused. Jesus kept not back, imitate Him by being foremost in self-denials and self-sacrifices. *Keep not back* from close communion with God, from boldly appropriating covenant blessings, from advancing in the divine life, from prying into the precious mysteries of the love of Christ. Neither, beloved friend, be guilty of keeping others back by your coldness, harshness, or suspicions. For Jesus' sake go forward yourself, and encourage others to do the like. Hell and the leaguered bands of superstition and infidelity are forward to the fight. O soldiers of the cross, keep not back.

" The love of Christ constraineth us."—2 Cor. v. 14.

HOW much owest thou unto my Lord? Has He ever done anything for thee? Has He forgiven thy sins? Has He covered thee with a robe of righteousness? Has He set thy feet upon a rock? Has He established thy goings? Has he prepared heaven for thee? Has he prepared thee for heaven? Has He written thy name in His book of life? Has He given thee countless blessings? Has He laid up for thee a store of mercies, which eye hath not seen nor ear heard? Then do something for Jesus worthy of His love. Give not a mere wordy offering to a dying Redeemer. How will you feel when your Master comes, if you have to confess that you *did* nothing for Him, but kept your love shut up, like a stagnant pool, neither flowing forth to His poor or to His work. Out on such love as that! What do men think of a love which never shows itself in action? Why, they say, " Open rebuke is better than secret love." Who will accept a love so weak that it does not actuate you to a single deed of self-denial, of generosity, of heroism, or zeal! Think how *He* has loved you, and given Himself for you! Do you know the power of that love? Then let it be like a rushing mighty wind to your soul to sweep out the clouds of your worldliness, and clear away the mists of sin. " For Christ's sake " be this the tongue of fire that shall sit upon you : " for Christ's sake " be this the divine rapture, the heavenly afflatus to bear you aloft from earth, the divine spirit that shall make you bold as lions and swift as eagles in your Lord's service. Love should give wings to the feet of service, and strength to the arms of labour. Fixed on God with a constancy that is not to be shaken, resolute to honour Him with a determination that is not to be turned aside, and pressing on with an ardour never to be wearied, let us manifest the constraints of love to Jesus. May the divine loadstone draw us heavenward towards itself !

" Why are ye troubled? and why do thoughts arise in your hearts?"—Luke xxiv. 38.

"WHY sayest thou, O Jacob, and speakest O Israel, My way is hid from the Lord, and my judgment is passed over from my God?" The Lord cares for all things, and the meanest creatures share in His universal providence, but His particular providence is over His saints. "The angel of the Lord encampeth round about them that fear Him." "Precious shall their blood be in His sight." "Precious in the sight of the Lord is the death of His saints." "We know that all things work together for good to them that love God, to them that are the called according to His purpose." Let the fact that, while He is the Saviour of all men, He is specially the Saviour of them that believe, cheer and comfort you. You are His peculiar care; His regal treasure which He guards as the apple of His eye; His vineyard over which He watches day and night. "The very hairs of your head are all numbered." Let the thought of His special love *to you* be a spiritual pain-killer, a dear quietus to your woe: "I will never leave *thee*, nor forsake *thee*." God says that as much to you as to any saint of old. "Fear not, I am thy shield, and thy exceeding great reward." We lose much consolation by the habit of reading His promises for the whole church, instead of taking them directly home to ourselves. Believer, grasp the divine word with a personal, appropriating faith. Think that you hear Jesus say, "I have prayed for *thee* that thy faith fail not." Think you see Him walking on the waters of thy trouble, for He is there, and He is saying, "Fear not, it is I; be not afraid." Oh, those sweet words of Christ! May the Holy Ghost make you feel them as spoken to *you;* forget others for awhile—accept the voice of Jesus as addressed to you, and say, "Jesus whispers consolation; I cannot refuse it; I will sit under His shadow with great delight."

" I will love them freely."—Hosea xiv. 4.

HIS sentence is a body of divinity in miniature. He who understands its meaning is a
theologian, and he who can dive into its fulness is a true master in Israel. It is a condensa-
tion of the glorious message of salvation which was
delivered to us in Christ Jesus our Redeemer. The
sense hinges upon the word " freely." This is the
glorious, the suitable, the divine way by which love
streams from heaven to earth, a spontaneous love
flowing forth to those who neither deserved it, purchased it, nor sought after it. It is, indeed, the
only way in which God can love such as we are.
The text is a death-blow to all sorts of fitness :
" I will love them *freely.*" Now, if there were any
fitness necessary in us, then He would not love
us freely, at least, this would be a mitigation and a
drawback to the freeness of it. But it stands, " I will
love you *freely.*" We complain, "Lord, my heart
is so hard." " I will love you freely." " But I do
not feel my need of Christ as I could wish." " I
will not love you because you feel your need ; I will
love you freely." " But I do not feel that softening
of spirit which I could desire." Remember, the
softening of spirit is not a condition, for there are
no conditions ; the covenant of grace has no con-
ditionality whatever ; so that we without any fitness
may venture upon the promise of God which was
made to us in Christ Jesus, when He said, " He that
believeth on Him is not condemned." It is blessed to
know that the grace of God is free to us at all times,
without preparation, without fitness, without money, and
without price ! " I will love them freely." These words
invite backsliders to return: indeed, the text was specially
written for such—" I will heal their backsliding ; I will
love them freely." Backslider ! surely the generosity
of the promise will at once break your heart, and you
will return, and seek your injured Father's face.

" He shall take of Mine, and shall show it unto you."
John xvi. 15.

THERE are times when all the promises and doctrines of the Bible are of no avail, unless a gracious hand shall apply them to us. We are thirsty, but too faint to crawl to the water-brook. When a soldier is wounded in battle it is of little use for him to know that there are those at the hospital who can bind up his wounds, and medicines there to ease all the pains which he now suffers : what he needs is to be carried thither, and to have the remedies applied. It is thus with our souls, and to meet this need there is one, even the Spirit of truth, who takes of the things of Jesus, and applies them to us. Think not that Christ hath placed His joys on heavenly shelves that we may climb up to them for ourselves, but He draws near, and sheds His peace abroad in our hearts. O Christian, if thou art to-night labouring under deep distresses, thy Father does not give thee promises and then leave thee to draw them up from the word like buckets from a well, but the promises He has written in the word He will write anew on your heart. He will manifest His love to you, and by His blessed Spirit, dispel your cares and troubles. Be it known unto thee, O mourner, that it is God's prerogative to wipe every tear from the eye of His people. The good Samaritan did not say, "Here is the wine, and here is the oil for you;" he actually poured in the oil and the wine. So Jesus not only gives you the sweet wine of the promise, but holds the golden chalice to your lips, and pours the life-blood into your mouth. The poor, sick, way-worn pilgrim is not merely strengthened to walk, but he is borne on eagles' wings. Glorious gospel ! which provides everything for the helpless, which draws nigh to us when we cannot reach after it—brings us grace before we seek for grace ! Here is as much glory in the giving as in the gift. Happy people who have the Holy Ghost to bring Jesus to them.

" Will ye also go away ?"—John vi. 67.

MANY have forsaken Christ, and have walked no more with Him ; but *what reason have* YOU *to make a change?* Has there been any reason for it in the *past?* Has not Jesus proved Himself all-sufficient? He appeals to you this morning—" Have I been a wilderness unto you ?" When your soul has simply trusted Jesus, have you ever been confounded ? Have you not up till now found your Lord to be a compassionate and generous friend to you, and has not simple faith in Him given you all the peace your spirit could desire ? Can you so much as dream of a better friend than He has been to you ? Then change not the old and tried for new and false. As for *the present*, can that compel you to leave Christ ? When we are hard beset with this world, or with the severer trials within the Church, we find it a most blessed thing to pillow our head upon the bosom of our Saviour. This is the joy we have to-day that we are saved in Him ; and if this joy be satisfying, wherefore should we think of changing ? Who barters gold for dross ? We will not forswear the sun till we find a better light, nor leave our Lord until a brighter lover shall appear ; and, since this can never be, we will hold Him with a grasp immortal, and bind His name as a seal upon our arm. As for *the future*, can you suggest anything which can arise that shall render it necessary for you to mutiny, or desert the old flag to serve under another captain ? We think not. If life be long—He changes not. If we are poor, what better than to have Christ who can make us rich ? When we are sick, what more do we want than Jesus to make our bed in our sickness ? When we die, is it not written that " neither death, nor life, nor things present, nor things to come, shall be able to separate us from the love of God, which is in Christ Jesus our Lord !" We say with Peter, " Lord, to whom shall we go ?"

" Why sleep ye? rise and pray, lest ye enter into temptation."
Luke xxii. 46.

HEN is the Christian most liable to sleep? Is it not *when his temporal circumstances are prosperous?* Have you not found it so? When you had daily troubles to take to the throne of grace, were you not more wakeful than you are now? Easy roads make sleepy travellers. Another dangerous time is *when all goes pleasantly in spiritual matters.* Christian went not to sleep when lions were in the way, or when he was wading through the river, or when fighting with Apollyon, but when he had climbed half way up the Hill Difficulty, and came to a delightful arbour, he sat down, and forthwith fell asleep, to his great sorrow and loss. The enchanted ground is a place of balmy breezes, laden with fragrant odours and soft influences, all tending to lull pilgrims to sleep. Remember Bunyan's description: "Then they came to an arbour, warm, and promising much refreshing to the weary pilgrims; for it was finely wrought above head, beautified with greens, and furnished with benches and settles. It had also in it a soft couch, where the weary might lean." "The arbour was called the Slothful's Friend, and was made on purpose to allure, if it might be, some of the pilgrims to take up their rest there when weary." Depend upon it, it is in easy places that men shut their eyes and wander into the dreamy land of forgetfulness. Old Erskine wisely remarked, "I like a roaring devil better than a sleeping devil." There is no temptation half so dangerous as not being tempted. The distressed soul does not sleep; it is after we enter into peaceful confidence and full assurance that we are in danger of slumbering. The disciples fell asleep after they had seen Jesus transfigured on the mountain top. Take heed, joyous Christian, good frames are near neighbours to temptations: be as happy as you will, only be watchful.

" The trees of the Lord are full of sap."—Psalm civ. 16.

WITHOUT sap the tree cannot flourish or even exist. *Vitality* is essential to a Christian. There must be *life*—a vital principle infused into us by God the Holy Ghost, or we cannot be trees of the Lord. The mere name of being a Christian is but a dead thing, we must be filled with the spirit of divine life. This life is *mysterious.* We do not understand the circulation of the sap, by what force it rises, and by what power it descends again. So the life within us is a sacred mystery. Regeneration is wrought by the Holy Ghost entering into man and becoming man's life ; and this divine life in a believer afterwards feeds upon the flesh and blood of Christ and is thus sustained by divine food, but whence it cometh and whither it goeth who shall explain to us ? What a *secret* thing the sap is ! The roots go searching through the soil with their little spongioles, but we cannot see them suck out the various gases, or transmute the mineral into the vegetable ; this work is done down in the dark. Our root is Christ Jesus, and our life is hid in him ; this is the secret of the Lord. The radix of the Christian life is as secret as the life itself. How *permanently active* is the sap in the cedar ! In the Christian the divine life is always full of energy---not always in fruit-bearing, but in inward operations. The believer's *graces,* are not every one of them in constant motion? but his life never ceases to palpitate within. He is not always working for God, but his heart is always living upon Him. As the sap *manifests itself in producing the foliage and fruit of the tree,* so with a truly healthy Christian, his grace is externally manifested in his walk and conversation. If you talk with him, he cannot help speaking about Jesus. If you notice his actions you will see that he has been with Jesus. He has so much sap within, that it must fill his conduct and conversation with life.

" He began to wash the disciples' feet."—John xiii. 5.

THE Lord Jesus loves His people so much, that every day He is still doing for them much that is analogous to washing their soiled feet. Their poorest actions He accepts ; their deepest sorrow He feels ; their slenderest wish He hears, and their every transgression He forgives. He is still their servant as well as their Friend and Master. He not only performs majestic deeds for them, as wearing the mitre on His brow, and the precious jewels glittering on His breastplate, and standing up to plead for them, but humbly, patiently, He yet goes about among His people with the bason and the towel. He does this when He puts away from us day by day our constant infirmities and sins. Last night, when you bowed the knee, you mournfully confessed that much of your conduct was not worthy of your profession ; and even to-night, you must mourn afresh that you have fallen again into the selfsame folly and sin from which special grace delivered you long ago ; and yet Jesus will have great patience with you ; He will hear your confession of sin ; He will say, " I will, be thou clean ;" He will again apply the blood of sprinkling, and speak peace to your conscience, and remove every spot. It is a great act of eternal love when Christ once for all absolves the sinner, and puts him into the family of God ; but what condescending patience there is when the Saviour with much long-suffering bears the oft recurring follies of His wayward disciple ; day by day, and hour by hour, washing away the multiplied transgressions of His erring but yet beloved child ! To dry up a flood of rebellion is something marvellous, but to endure the constant dropping of repeated offences— to bear with a perpetual trying of patience, this is divine indeed ! While we find comfort and peace in our Lord's daily cleansing, its legitimate influence upon us will be to increase our watchfulness, and quicken our desire for holiness. *Is it so ?*

" For the truth's sake, which dwelleth in us, and shall be with us for ever."—II. John 2.

ONCE let the truth of God obtain an entrance into the human heart and subdue the whole man unto itself, no power human or infernal can dislodge it. We entertain it not as a guest but as the master of the house—this is a *Christian necessity,* he is no Christian who doth not thus believe. Those who feel the vital power of the gospel, and know the might of the Holy Ghost as He opens, applies, and seals the Lord's Word, would sooner be torn to pieces than be rent away from the gospel of their salvation. What a thousand mercies are wrapt up in the assurance that the truth will be with us for ever; will be our living support, our dying comfort, our rising song, our eternal glory; this is *Christian privilege,* without it our faith were little worth. Some truths we outgrow and leave behind, for they are but rudiments and lessons for beginners, but we cannot thus deal with Divine truth, for though it is sweet food for babes, it is in the highest sense strong meat for men. The truth that we are sinners is painfully with us to humble and make us watchful; the more blessed truth that whosoever believeth on the Lord Jesus shall be saved, abides with us as our hope and joy. Experience, so far from loosening our hold of the doctrines of grace, has knit us to them more and more firmly; our grounds and motives for believing are now more strong, more numerous than ever, and we have reason to expect that it will be so till in death we clasp the Saviour in our arms.

Wherever this abiding love of truth can be discovered, we are bound to exercise our love. No narrow circle can contain our gracious sympathies, wide as the election of grace must be our communion of heart. Much of error may be mingled with truth received, let us war with the error but still love the brother for the measure of truth which we see in Him; above all let us love and spread the truth ourselves.

*" She gleaned in the field after the reapers: and her hap was
to light on a part of the field belonging unto Boaz, who was
of the kindred of Elimelech."*—Ruth ii. 3.

HER *hap was.* Yes, it seemed nothing but an accident, but how divinely was it overruled! Ruth had gone forth with her mother's blessing, under the care of her mother's God, to humble but honourable toil, and the providence of God was guiding her every step. Little did she know that amid the sheaves she would find a husband, that he should make her the joint owner. of all those broad acres, and that she a poor foreigner should become one of the progenitors of the great Messiah. God is very good to those who trust in Him, and often surprises them with unlooked for blessings. Little do we know what may happen to us to-morrow, but this sweet fact may cheer us, that no good thing shall be withheld. Chance is banished from the faith of Christians, for they see the hand of God in everything. The trivial events of to-day or to-morrow may involve consequences of the highest importance. O Lord, deal as graciously with Thy servants as Thou didst with Ruth.

How blessed would it be, if, in wandering in the field of meditation to-night, our hap should be to light upon the place where our next Kinsman will reveal Himself to us! O Spirit of God, guide us to Him. We would sooner glean in His field than bear away the whole harvest from any other. O for the footsteps of His flock, which may conduct us to the green pastures where He dwells! This is a weary world when Jesus is away—we could better do without sun and moon than without Him—but how divinely fair all things become in the glory of His presence! Our souls know the virtue which dwells in Jesus, and can never be content without Him. We will wait in prayer this night until our hap shall be to light on a part of the field belonging to Jesus wherein He will manifest Himself to us.

" Ye looked for much, and, lo, it came to little; and when ye brought it home, I did blow upon it. Why? saith the Lord of hosts. Because of mine house that is waste, and ye run every man unto his own house."—Haggai i. 9.

CHURLISH souls stint their contributions to the ministry and missionary operations, and call such saving good economy; little do they dream that they are thus impoverishing themselves. Their excuse is that they *must* care for their own families, and they forget that to neglect the house of God is the sure way to bring ruin upon their own houses. Our God has a method in providence by which he can succeed our endeavours beyond our expectation, or can defeat our plans to our confusion and dismay; by a turn of His hand He can steer our vessel in a profitable channel, or run it aground in poverty and bankruptcy. It is the teaching of Scripture that the Lord enriches the liberal and leaves the miserly to find out that withholding tendeth to poverty. In a very wide sphere of observation, I have noticed that the most generous Christians of my acquaintance have been always the most happy, and almost invariably the most prosperous. I have seen the liberal giver rise to wealth of which he never dreamed; and I have as often seen the mean, ungenerous churl descend to poverty by the very parsimony by which he thought to rise. Men trust good stewards with larger and larger sums, and so it frequently is with the Lord; He gives by cartloads to those who give by bushels. Where wealth is not bestowed the Lord makes the little much by the contentment which the sanctified heart feels in a portion of which the tithe has been dedicated to the Lord. Selfishness looks first at home, but godliness seeks first the kingdom of God and His righteousness, yet in the long run selfishness is loss, and godliness is great gain. It needs faith to act towards our God with an open hand, but surely He deserves it of us; and all that we can do is a very poor acknowledgment of our amazing indebtedness to His goodness.

" All the rivers run into the sea ; yet the sea is not full ; unto the place from whence the rivers come, thither they return again."—Ecclesiastes i. 7

EVERYTHING sublunary is on the move, time knows nothing of rest. The solid earth is a rolling ball, and the great sun himself a star obediently fulfilling its course around some greater luminary. Tides move the sea, winds stir the airy ocean, friction wears the rock : change and death rule everywhere. The sea is not a miser's storehouse for a wealth of waters, for as by one force the waters flow into it, by another they are lifted from it. Men are born but to die : everything is hurry, worry, and vexation of spirit. Friend of the unchanging Jesus, what a joy it is to reflect upon thy changeless heritage ; thy sea of bliss which will be for ever full, since God Himself shall pour eternal rivers of pleasure into it. We seek an abiding city beyond the skies, and we shall not be disappointed.

The passage before us may well teach us gratitude. Father Ocean is a great receiver, but he is a generous distributor. What the rivers bring him he returns to the earth in the form of clouds and rain. That man is out of joint with the universe who takes all but makes no return. To give to others is but sowing seed for ourselves. He who is so good a steward as to be willing to use his substance for his Lord, shall be entrusted with more. Friend of Jesus, art thou rendering to Him according to the benefit received ? Much has been given thee, what is thy fruit ? Hast thou done all ? Canst thou not do more ? To be selfish is to be wicked. Suppose the ocean gave up none of its watery treasure, it would bring ruin upon our race. God forbid that any of us should follow the ungenerous and destructive policy of living unto ourselves. Jesus pleased not Himself. All fulness dwells in Him, but of His fulness have all we received. O for Jesu's spirit, that henceforth we may live not unto ourselves !

" It is a faithful saying."—2 Timothy ii. 11.

AUL has four of these *"faithful sayings."* The
first occurs in 1 Timothy i. 15, "This is a faithful saying, and worthy of all acceptation, that
Christ Jesus came into the world to save sinners."
The next is in 1 Timothy iv. 6, "Godliness is profitable unto all things, having the promise of the life
that now is, and of that which is to come. This is a
faithful saying, and worthy of all acceptation." The
third is in 2 Timothy ii. 12, "It is a faithful saying—
If we suffer with Him we shall also reign with Him;"
and the fourth is in Titus iii. 3, "This is a faithful
saying, that they which have believed in God might
be careful to maintain good works." We may trace
a connection between these faithful sayings. The first
one lays the foundation of our eternal salvation in
the free grace of God, as shown to us in the mission
of the great Redeemer. The next affirms the double
blessedness which we obtain through this salvation—
the blessings of the upper and nether springs—of time
and of eternity. The third shows one of the duties to
which the chosen people are called; we are ordained
to suffer for Christ with the promise that "if we suffer,
we shall also reign with Him." The last sets forth
the active form of Christian service, bidding us diligently to maintain good works. Thus we have the
root of salvation in free grace; next, the privileges of
that salvation in the life which now is, and in that
which is to come; and we have also the two great
branches of suffering with Christ and serving with
Christ, loaded with the fruits of the Spirit. Treasure
up these faithful sayings. Let them be the guides of
our life, our comfort, and our instruction. The apostle
of the Gentiles proved them to be faithful, they are
faithful still, not one word shall fall to the ground;
they are worthy of all acceptation, let us accept them
now, and prove their faithfulness. Let these four faithful sayings be written on the four corners of My house.

" We are all as an unclean thing."—Isaiah lxiv. 6.

THE believer is a new creature, he belongs to a holy generation and a peculiar people—the Spirit of God is in him, and in all respects he is far removed from the natural man ; but for all that the Christian is a sinner still. He is so from the imperfection of his nature, and will continue so to the end of his earthly life. The black fingers of sin leave smuts upon our fairest robes. Sin mars our repentance, ere the great Potter has finished it, upon the wheel. Selfishness defiles our tears, and unbelief tampers with our faith. The best thing we ever did apart from the merit of Jesus only swelled the number of our sins ; for when we have been most pure in our own sight, yet, like the heavens, we are not pure in God's sight ; and as He charged His angels with folly, much more must He charge us with it, even in our most angelic frames of mind. The song which thrills to heaven, and seeks to emulate seraphic strains, hath human discords in it. The prayer which moves the arm of God is still a bruised and battered prayer, and only moves that arm because the sinless One, the great Mediator, has stepped in to take away the sin of our supplication. The most golden faith or the purest degree of sanctification to which a Christian ever attained on earth, has still so much alloy in it as to be only worthy of the flames, in itself considered. Every night we look in the glass we see a sinner, and had need confess, "We are all as an unclean thing, and all our righteousnesses are as filthy rags." Oh, how precious the blood of Christ to such hearts as ours ! How priceless a gift is His perfect righteousness ! And how bright the hope of perfect holiness hereafter ! Even now, though sin dwells in us, *its power is broken.* It has no dominion ; it is a broken-backed snake ; we are in bitter conflict with it, but it is with a vanquished foe that we have to deal. Yet a little while and we shall enter victoriously into the city where nothing defileth.

"I have chosen you out of the world."—John xv. 19.

ERE is distinguishing grace and discriminating regard; for some are made the special objects of divine affection. Do not be afraid to dwell upon this high doctrine of election. When your mind is most heavy and depressed, you will find it to be a bottle of richest cordial. Those who doubt the doctrines of grace, or who cast them into the shade, miss the richest clusters of Eshcol; they lose the wines on the lees well refined, the fat things full of marrow. There is no balm in Gilead comparable to it. If the honey in Jonathan's wood when but touched enlightened *the eyes*, this is honey which will enlighten *your heart* to love and learn the mysteries of the kingdom of God. Eat, and fear not a surfeit; live upon this choice dainty, and fear not that it will be too delicate a diet. Meat from the King's table will hurt none of his courtiers. Desire to have your mind enlarged, that you may comprehend more and more the eternal, everlasting, discriminating love of God. When you have mounted as high as election, tarry on its sister mount, the covenant of grace. Covenant engagements are the munitions of stupendous rock behind which we lie entrenched; covenant engagements with the surety, Christ Jesus, are the quiet resting-places of trembling spirits.

> "His oath, His covenant, His blood,
> Support me in the raging flood;
> When every earthly prop gives way,
> This still is all my strength and stay."

If Jesus undertook to bring me to glory, and if the Father promised that He would give me to the Son to be a part of the infinite reward of the travail of His soul; then, my soul, till God himself shall be unfaithful, till Jesus shall cease to be the truth, thou art safe. When David danced before the ark, he told Michal that election made him do so. Come, my soul, exult before the God of grace and leap for joy of heart.

" His head is as the most fine gold, His locks are bushy, and black as a raven."—Solomon's Song v. 11.

COMPARISONS all fail to set forth the Lord Jesus, but the spouse uses the best within her reach. By *the head* of Jesus we may understand His deity, " for the head of Christ is God ;" and then the ingot of purest gold is the best conceivable metaphor, but all too poor to describe one so precious, so pure, so dear, so glorious. Jesus is not a grain of gold, but a vast globe of it, a priceless mass of treasure such as earth and heaven cannot excel. The creatures are mere iron and clay, they all shall perish like wood, hay, and stubble, but the everliving Head of the creation of God shall shine on for ever and ever. In Him is no mixture, nor smallest taint of alloy. He is for ever infinitely holy and altogether divine. *The bushy locks* depict His manly vigour. There is nothing effeminate in our Beloved. He is the manliest of men. Bold as a lion, laborious as an ox, swift as an eagle. Every conceivable and inconceivable beauty is to be found in Him, though once He was despised and rejected of men.

> "His head the finest gold;
> With secret sweet perfume,
> His curled locks hang all as black
> As any raven's plume."

The glory of His head is not shorn away, He is eternally crowned with peerless majesty. *The black hair* indicates youthful freshness, for Jesus has the dew of His youth upon Him. Others grow languid with age, but He is for ever a Priest as was Melchisedek ; others come and go, but He abides as God upon His throne, world without end. We will behold Him to-night and adore Him. Angels are gazing upon Him—His redeemed must not turn away their eyes from Him. Where else is there such a Beloved? O for an hour's fellowship with Him! Away, ye intruding cares! Jesus draws me, and I run after Him.

"*After this manner therefore pray ye: Our Father which art in heaven, etc.*"—Matthew vi. 9.

THIS prayer begins where all true prayer must commence, with the spirit of *adoption*, "Our Father." There is no acceptable prayer until we can say, "I will arise, and go unto my Father." This child-like spirit soon perceives the grandeur of the Father "in heaven," and ascends to *devout adoration*, "Hallowed be Thy name." The child lisping, "Abba, Father," grows into the cherub crying, "Holy, Holy, Holy." There is but a step from rapturous worship to the *glowing missionary spirit*, which is a sure outgrowth of filial love and reverent adoration—"Thy kingdom come, Thy will be done on earth as it is in heaven." Next follows the heartfelt *expression of dependence* upon God—"Give us this day our daily bread." Being further illuminated by the Spirit, he discovers that he is not only dependent, but sinful, hence he *entreats for mercy*, "Forgive us our debts as we forgive our debtors:" and being pardoned, having the righteousness of Christ imputed, and knowing his acceptance with God, he humbly *supplicates for holy perseverance*, "Lead us not into temptation." The man who is really forgiven, is anxious not to offend again ; the possession of justification leads to an anxious desire for sanctification. "Forgive us our debts," that is justification ; "Lead us not into temptation,.but deliver us from evil," that is sanctification in its negative and positive forms. As the result of all this, there follows a *triumphant ascription of praise*, "Thine is the kingdom, the power, and the glory, for ever and ever, Amen." We rejoice that *our* King reigns in providence and shall reign in grace, from the river even to the ends of the earth, and of His dominion there shall be no end. Thus from a sense of adoption, up to fellowship with our reigning Lord, this short model of prayer conducts the soul. Lord, teach us thus to pray.

"But their eyes were holden that they should not know Him."
Luke xxiv. 16.

THE disciples ought to have known Jesus, they had heard His voice so often, and gazed upon that marred face so frequently, that it is wonderful they did not discover Him. Yet is it not so with you also? You have not seen Jesus lately. You have been to His table, and you have not met Him there. You are in a dark trouble this evening, and though He plainly says, "It is I, be not afraid," yet you cannot discern Him. Alas! our eyes are holden. We know His voice; we have looked into His face; we have leaned our head upon His bosom, and yet, though Christ is very near us, we are saying " O that I knew where I might find Him!" We should know Jesus, for we have the Scriptures to reflect His image, and yet how possible it is for us to open that precious book and have no glimpse of the Wellbeloved! Dear child of God, are you in that state? Jesus feedeth among the lilies of the word, and you walk among those lilies, and yet you behold Him not. He is accustomed to walk through the glades of Scripture, and to commune with His people, as the Father did with Adam in the cool of the day, and yet you are in the garden of Scripture, but cannot see Him, though He is always there. And why do we not see Him? It must be ascribed in our case, as in the disciples', to unbelief. They evidently did not expect to see Jesus, and therefore they did not know Him. To a great extent in spiritual things we get what we expect of the Lord. Faith alone can bring us to see Jesus. Make it your prayer, " Lord, open Thou mine eyes, that I may see my Saviour present with me." It is a blessed thing to *want* to see Him; but oh! it is better far to gaze upon Him. To those who seek Him He is kind; but to those who find Him, beyond expression is He dear!

" I will praise Thee, O Lord."—Psalm ix. 1.

PRAISE should always follow answered prayer ;
as the mist of earth's gratitude rises when the
sun of heaven's love warms the ground. Hath
the Lord been gracious to thee, and inclined his ear
to the voice of thy supplication ? Then praise Him
as long as thou livest. Let the ripe fruit drop upon
the fertile soil from which it drew its life. Deny not a
song to Him who hath answered thy prayer and given
thee the desire of thy heart. To be silent over God's
mercies is to incur the guilt of ingratitude ; it is to act
as basely as the nine lepers, who after they had been
cured of their leprosy, returned not to give thanks unto
the healing Lord. To forget to praise God is to refuse
to benefit ourselves ; for praise, like prayer, is one great
means of promoting the growth of the spiritual life.
It helps to remove our burdens, to excite our hope, to
increase our faith. It is a healthful and invigorating
exercise which quickens the pulse of the believer, and
nerves him for fresh enterprises in his Master's service.
To bless God for mercies received is also the way to
benefit our fellow-men ; "the humble shall hear thereof
and be glad." Others who have been in like circumstances shall take comfort if we can say, "Oh ! magnify
the Lord with me, and let us exalt His name together ;
this poor man cried, and the Lord heard him." Weak
hearts will be strengthened, and drooping saints will
be revived as they listen to our "songs of deliverance."
Their doubts and fears will be rebuked, as we teach
and admonish one another in psalms and hymns and
spiritual songs. They too shall "sing in the ways
of the Lord," when they hear us magnify His holy
name. Praise is the most heavenly of Christian duties.
The angels pray not, but they cease not to praise
both day and night ; and the redeemed, clothed in
white robes, with palm-branches in their hands, are
never weary of singing the new song, "Worthy is
the Lamb."

" Thou that dwellest in the gardens, the companions hearken to Thy voice: cause me to hear it."—Solomon's Song viii. 13.

MY sweet Lord Jesus remembers well the garden of Gethsemane, and although He has left that garden, He now dwells in the garden of His church: there He unbosoms Himself to those who keep His blessed company. That voice of love with which He speaks to His beloved is more musical than the harps of heaven. There is a depth of melodious love within it which leaves all human music far behind. Ten of thousands on earth, and millions above, are indulged with its harmonious accents. Some whom I well know, and whom I greatly envy, are at this moment hearkening to the beloved voice. O that I were a partaker of their joys! It is true some of these are poor, others bedridden, and some near the gates of death, but O my Lord, I would cheerfully starve with them, pine with them, or die with them, if I might but hear Thy voice. Once I did hear it often, but I have grieved Thy Spirit. Return unto me in compassion, and once again say unto me, "I am thy salvation." No other voice can content me; I know Thy voice, and cannot be deceived by another, let me hear it, I pray thee. I know not what Thou wilt say, neither do I make any condition, O my Beloved, do but let me hear Thee speak, and if it be a rebuke I will bless Thee for it. Perhaps to cleanse my dull ear may need an operation very grievous to the flesh, but let it cost what it may I turn not from the one consuming desire, cause me to hear Thy voice. Bore my ear afresh; pierce my ear with Thy harshest notes, only do not permit me to continue deaf to Thy calls. To-night, Lord, grant Thine unworthy one his desire, for I am Thine, and Thou hast bought me with Thy blood. Thou hast opened mine eye to see Thee, and the sight has saved me. Lord, open Thou mine ear. I have read Thy heart, now let me hear Thy lips.

" Renew a right spirit within me."—Psalm li. 10.

BACKSLIDER, if there be a spark of life left in him will groan after restoration. In this renewal the same exercise of grace is required as at our conversion. We needed repentance then ; we certainly need it now. We wanted faith that we might come to Christ at first; only the like grace can bring us to Jesus now. We wanted a word from the Most High, a word from the lip of the loving One, to end our fears then; we shall soon discover, when under a sense of present sin, that we need it now. No man can be renewed without as real and true a manifestation of the Holy Spirit's energy as he felt at first. because the work is as great, and flesh and blood are as much in the way now as ever they were. Let thy personal weakness, O Christian, be an argument to make thee pray earnestly to thy God for help. Remember, David when he felt himself to be powerless, did not fold his arms or close his lips, but he hastened to the mercy-seat with "renew a right spirit within me." Let not the doctrine that you, unaided, can do nothing, make you sleep; but let it be a goad in your side to drive you with an awful earnestness to Israel's strong Helper. O that you may have grace to plead with God, as though you pleaded for your very life—"Lord, renew a right spirit within me." He who *sincerely* prays to God to do this, will prove his honesty by using the means through which God works. Be much in prayer; live much upon the Word of God ; kill the lusts which have driven your Lord from you ; be careful to watch over the future uprisings of sin. The Lord has His own appointed ways ; sit by the wayside and you will be ready when He passes by. Continue in all those blessed ordinances which will foster and nourish your dying graces ; and, knowing that all the power must proceed from Him, cease not to cry, "Renew a right spirit within me."

" I did know thee in the wilderness, in the land of great drought."—Hosea xiii. 5.

ES, Lord, Thou didst indeed know me in my *fallen state*, and Thou didst even then choose me for Thyself. When I was loathsome and self-abhorred, Thou didst receive me as Thy child, and Thou didst satisfy my craving wants. Blessed for ever be Thy name for this free, rich, abounding mercy. Since then, *my inward experience* has often been a wilderness; but Thou hast owned me still as Thy beloved, and poured streams of love and grace into me to gladden me, and make me fruitful. Yea, when my *outward circumstances* have been at the worst, and I have wandered in a land of drought, Thy sweet presence has solaced me. Men have not known me when scorn has awaited me, but Thou hast known my soul in adversities, for no affliction dims the lustre of Thy love. Most gracious Lord, I magnify Thee for all Thy faithfulness to me in trying circumstances, and I deplore that I should at any time have forgotten Thee and been exalted in heart, when I have owed all to Thy gentleness and love. Have mercy upon Thy servant in this thing!

My soul, if Jesus thus acknowledged thee in thy low estate, be sure that thou own both Himself and His cause now that thou art in thy prosperity. Be not lifted up by thy worldly successes so as to be ashamed of the truth or of the poor church with which thou hast been associated. Follow Jesus into the wilderness: bear the cross with Him when the heat of persecution grows hot. He owned thee, O my soul, in thy poverty and shame—never be so treacherous as to be ashamed of Him. O for more shame at the thought of being ashamed of my best Beloved! Jesus, my soul cleaveth to Thee.

> "I'll turn to Thee in days of light,
>   As well as nights of care,
> Thou brightest amid all that's bright!
>   Thou fairest of the fair!"

" The Church in thy house."—Philemon 2.

IS there a Church in this house? Are parents, children, friends, servants, all members of it? or are some still unconverted? Let us pause here and let the question go round—*Am I a member of the Church in this house?* How would father's heart leap for joy, and mother's eyes fill with holy tears if from the eldest to the youngest all were saved! Let us pray for this great mercy until the Lord shall grant it to us. Probably it had been the dearest object of Philemon's desires to have all his household saved; but it was not at first granted him in its fulness. He had a wicked servant, Onesimus, who, having wronged him, ran away from his service. His master's prayers followed him, and at last, as God would have it, Onesimus was led to hear Paul preach; his heart was touched, and he returned to Philemon, not only to be a faithful servant, but a brother beloved, adding another member to the Church in Philemon's house. Is there an unconverted servant or child absent this morning? Make special supplication that such may, on their return to their home, gladden all hearts with good news of what grace has done! Is there one present? Let him partake in the same earnest entreaty.

If there be such a Church in our house, let us order it well, and let all act as in the sight of God. Let us move in the common affairs of life with studied holiness, diligence, kindness, and integrity. More is expected of a Church than of an ordinary household; family worship must, in such a case, be more devout and hearty; internal love must be more warm and unbroken, and external conduct must be more sanctified and Christlike. We need not fear that the smallness of our number will put us out of the list of Churches, for the Holy Spirit has here enrolled a family-church in the inspired book of remembrance. As a Church let us now draw nigh to the great head of the one Church universal, and let us beseech Him to give us grace to shine before men to the glory of His name.

*" And knew not until the flood came, and took them all away:
so shall also the coming of the Son of man be."*—Matt. xxiv. 39.

UNIVERSAL was the doom, neither rich nor poor escaped: the learned and the illiterate, the admired and the abhorred, the religious and the profane, the old and the young, all sank in one common ruin. Some had doubtless ridiculed the patriarch—where now their merry jests? Others had threatened him for his zeal which they counted madness—where now their boastings and hard speeches? The critic who judged the old man's work is drowned in the same sea which covers his sneering companions. Those who spoke patronisingly of the good man's fidelity to his convictions, but shared not in them, have sunk to rise no more, and the workers who for pay helped to build the wondrous ark, are all lost also. The flood swept them *all* away, and made no single exception. Even so, out of Christ, final destruction is sure to every man of woman born; no rank, possession, or character, shall suffice to save a single soul who has not believed in the Lord Jesus. My soul, behold this wide-spread judgment and tremble at it.

How marvellous the general apathy! they were all eating and drinking, marrying and giving in marriage, till the awful morning dawned. There was not one wise man upon earth out of the ark. Folly duped the whole race, folly as to self-preservation—the most foolish of all follies. Folly in doubting the most true God—the most malignant of fooleries. 'Strange, my soul, is it not? All men are negligent of their souls till grace gives them reason, then they leave their madness and act like rational beings, but not till then.

All, blessed be God, were safe in the ark, no ruin entered there. From the huge elephant down to the tiny mouse all were safe. The timid hare was equally secure with the courageous lion, the helpless cony as safe as the laborious ox. All are safe in Jesus. My soul, art thou in Him?

" I am the Lord, I change not."—Malachi iii. 6.

IT is well for us that, amidst all the variableness of life, there is One whom change cannot affect; One whose heart can never alter, and on whose brow mutability can make no furrows. All things else have changed—all things are changing. The sun itself grows dim with age; the world is waxing old; the folding up of the worn-out vesture has commenced; the heavens and earth must soon pass away; they shall perish, they shall wax old as doth a garment; but there is One who only hath immortality, of whose years there is no end, and in whose person there is no change. The delight which the mariner feels, when, after having been tossed about for many a day, he steps again upon the solid shore, is the satisfaction of a Christian when, amidst all the changes of this troublous life, he rests the foot of his faith upon this truth—*" I am the Lord, I change not."*

The stability which the anchor gives the ship when it has at last obtained a hold-fast, is like that which the Christian's hope affords him when it fixes itself upon this glorious truth. With God " is no variableness, neither shadow of turning." Whatever His attributes were of old, they are now; His power, His wisdom, His justice, His truth, are alike unchanged. He has ever been the refuge of his people, their stronghold in the day of trouble, and He is their sure helper still. He is unchanged in His *love.* He has loved his people with " an everlasting love;" He loves them now as much as ever He did, and when all earthly things shall have melted in the last conflagration, His love will still wear the dew of its youth. Precious is the assurance that He changes not! The wheel of providence revolves, but its axle is eternal love.

> " Death and change are busy ever,
> Man decays, and ages move;
> But His mercy waneth never;
> God is wisdom, God is love."

" Horror hath taken hold upon me because of the wicked that forsake Thy law."—Psalm cxix. 53.

MY soul, feelest thou this holy shuddering at the sins of others? for otherwise thou lackest inward holiness. David's cheeks were wet with rivers of waters because of prevailing unholiness; Jeremiah desired eyes like fountains that he might lament the iniquities of Israel, and Lot was vexed with the conversation of the men of Sodom. Those upon whom the mark was set in Ezekiel's vision, were those who sighed and cried for the abominations of Jerusalem. It cannot but grieve gracious souls to see what pains men take to go to hell. They know the evil of sin experimentally, and they are alarmed to see others flying like moths into its blaze. Sin makes the righteous shudder, because it violates a holy law, which it is to every man's highest interest to keep; it pulls down the pillars of the commonwealth. Sin in others horrifies a believer, because it puts him in mind of the baseness of his own heart: when he sees a transgressor he cries with the saint mentioned by Bernard, "He fell to-day, and I may fall to-morrow." Sin to a believer is horrible, because it crucified the Saviour; he sees in every iniquity the nails and spear. How can a saved soul behold that cursed kill-Christ sin without abhorrence? Say, my heart, dost thou sensibly join in all this? It is an awful thing to insult God to his face. The good God deserves better treatment, the great God claims it, the just God will have it, or repay His adversary to his face. An awakened heart trembles at the audacity of sin, and stands alarmed at the contemplation of its punishment. How monstrous a thing is rebellion! How direful a doom is prepared for the ungodly! My soul, never laugh at sin's fooleries, lest thou come to smile at sin itself. It is thine enemy, and thy Lord's enemy—view it with detestation, for so only canst thou evidence the possession of holiness, without which no man can see the Lord

" Behold, he prayeth."—Acts ix. 11.

PRAYERS are instantly noticed in heaven. The moment Saul began to pray the Lord heard him. Here is comfort for the distressed but praying soul. Oftentimes a poor broken-hearted one bends his knee, but can only utter his wailing in the language of sighs and tears; yet that groan has made all the harps of heaven thrill with music; that tear has been caught by God and treasured in the lachrymatory of heaven. "Thou puttest my tears into thy bottle," implies that they are caught as they flow. The suppliant, whose fears prevent his words, will be well understood by the Most High. He may only look up with misty eye; but " prayer is the falling of a tear." Tears are the diamonds of heaven; sighs are a part of the music of Jehovah's court, and are numbered with " the sublimest strains that reach the majesty on high." Think not that your prayer, however weak or trembling, will be unregarded. Jacob's ladder is lofty, but our prayers shall lean upon the Angel of the covenant and so climb its starry rounds. Our God not only *hears* prayer but also *loves* to hear it. " He forgetteth not the cry of the humble." True, He regards not high looks and lofty words; he cares not for the pomp and pageantry of kings; He listens not to the swell of martial music; He regards not the triumph and pride of man; but wherever there is a heart big with sorrow, or a lip quivering with agony, or a deep groan, or a penitential sigh, the heart of Jehovah is open; He marks it down in the registry of His memory; He puts our prayers, like rose leaves, between the pages of His book of remembrance, and when the volume is opened at last, there shall be a precious fragrance springing up therefrom.

> " Faith asks no signal from the skies,
>   To show that prayers accepted rise,
>   Our Priest is in His holy place,
>   And answers from the throne of grace."

"Their prayer came up to His holy dwelling place, even unto heaven."—2 Chronicles xxx. 27.

PRAYER is the never-failing resort of the Christian in any case, in every plight. When you cannot use your sword you may take to the weapon of all-prayer. Your powder may be damp, your bow-string may be relaxed, but the weapon of all-prayer need never be out of order. Leviathan laughs at the javelin, but he trembles at prayer. Sword and spear need furbishing, but prayer never rusts, and when we think it most blunt it cuts the best. Prayer is an open door which none can shut. Devils may surround you on all sides, but the way upward is always open, and as long as that road is unobstructed, you will not fall into the enemy's hand. We can never be taken by blockade, escalade, mine, or storm, so long as heavenly succours can come down to us by Jacob's ladder to relieve us in the time of our necessities. Prayer is never out of season : in summer and in winter its merchandize is precious. Prayer gains audience with heaven in the dead of night, in the midst of business, in the heat of noonday, in the shades of evening. In every condition, whether of poverty, or sickness, or obscurity, or slander, or doubt, your covenant God will welcome your prayer and answer it from His holy place. Nor is prayer ever *futile*. True prayer is evermore true power. You may not always get what you ask, but you shall always have your real wants supplied. When God does not answer His children according to the letter, He does so according to the spirit. If thou askest for coarse meal, wilt thou be angered because He gives thee the finest flour? If thou seekest bodily health, shouldst thou complain if instead thereof He makes thy sickness turn to the healing of spiritual maladies? Is it not better to have the cross sanctified than removed? This evening, my soul, forget not to offer thy petition and request, for the Lord is ready to grant thee thy desires.

" For my strength is made perfect in weakness."
2 Cor. xii. 9.

PRIMARY qualification for serving God with any amount of success, and for doing God's work well and triumphantly, is a sense of our own weakness. When God's warrior marches forth to battle, strong in his own might, when he boasts, "I know that I shall conquer, my own right arm and my conquering sword shall get unto me the victory," defeat is not far distant. God will not go forth with that man who marches in his own strength. He who reckoneth on victory thus has reckoned wrongly, for "it is not by might, nor by power, but by my Spirit, saith the Lord of hosts." They who go forth to fight, boasting of their prowess, shall return with their gay banners trailed in the dust, and their armour stained with disgrace. Those who serve God must serve Him in His own way, and in His strength, or He will never accept their service. That which man doth, unaided by divine strength, God can never own. The mere fruits of the earth He casteth away ; He will only reap that corn, the seed of which was sown from heaven, watered by grace, and ripened by the sun of divine love. God will empty out all that thou hast before He will put His own into thee ; He will first clean out thy granaries before He will fill them with the finest of the wheat. The river of God is full of water ; but not one drop of it flows from earthly springs. God will have no strength used in His battles but the strength which He Himself imparts. Are you mourning over your own weakness ? Take courage, for there must be a consciousness of weakness before the Lord will give thee victory. Your emptiness is but the preparation for your being filled, and your casting down is but the making ready for your lifting up.

"When I am weak then am I strong,
　Grace is my shield and Christ my song."

NO lips can tell the love of Christ to the heart
till Jesus Himself shall speak within. De-
scriptions all fall flat and tame unless the
Holy Ghost fills them with life and power; till our
Immanuel reveals Himself within, the soul sees Him
not. If you would see the sun, would you gather
together the common means of illumination, and seek
in that way to behold the orb of day? No, the wise
man knoweth that the sun must reveal itself, and only
by its own blaze can that mighty lamp be seen. It is
so with Christ. "Blessed art thou, Simon Bar-jona:"
said He to Peter, "for flesh and blood hath not revealed this unto thee." Purify flesh and blood by any
educational process you may select, elevate mental
faculties to the highest degree of intellectual power,
yet none of these can reveal Christ. The Spirit of God
must come with power, and overshadow the man with
His wings, and then in that mystic holy of holies the
Lord Jesus must display Himself to the sanctified eye,
as He doth not unto the purblind sons of men. Christ
must be His own mirror. The great mass of this
blear-eyed world can see nothing of the ineffable glories
of Immanuel. He stands before them without form
or comeliness, a root out of a dry ground, rejected by
the vain and despised by the proud. Only where the
Spirit has touched the eye with eye-salve, quickened
the heart with divine life, and educated the soul to a
heavenly taste, only there is He understood. "To you
that believe He is precious;" to you He is the chief
corner-stone, the Rock of your salvation, your all in
all; but to others He is "a stone of stumbling and a
rock of offence." Happy are those to whom our Lord
manifests Himself, for His promise to such is that
He will *make His abode with them.* O Jesus, our
Lord, our heart is open, come in, and go out no more
for ever. Show Thyself to us now! Favour us with
a glimpse of Thine all-conquering charms.

" No weapon that is formed against thee shall prosper."
Isaiah liv. 17.

THIS day is notable in English history for two
great deliverances wrought by God for us.
On this day the plot of the Papists to destroy
our Houses of Parliament was discovered, 1605.

" While for our princes they prepare
In caverns deep a burning snare,
He shot from heaven a piercing ray,
And the dark treachery brought to day."

And secondly—to-day is the anniversary of the
landing of King William III., at Torbay, by which
the hope of Popish ascendancy was quashed, and
religious liberty was secured, 1688.

This day ought to be celebrated, not by the satur-
nalia of striplings, but by the songs of saints. Our
Puritan forefathers most devoutly made it a special
time of thanksgiving. There is extant a record of the
annual sermons preached by Matthew Henry on this
day. Our Protestant feeling, and our love of liberty,
should make us regard its anniversary with holy gratitude. Let our hearts and lips exclaim, " We have
heard with our ears, and our fathers have told us
the wondrous things which Thou didst in their day,
and in the old time before them." Thou hast made
this nation the home of the gospel ; and when the
foe has risen against her, Thou hast shielded her.
Help us to offer repeated songs for repeated deliverances. Grant us more and more a hatred of Antichrist,
and hasten on the day of her entire extinction. Till
then and ever, we believe the promise, " No weapon
that is formed against thee shall prosper." Should it
not be laid upon the heart of every lover of the gospel
of Jesus on this day to plead for the overturning of
false doctrines and the extension of divine truth ?
Would it not be well to search our own hearts, and
turn out any of the Popish lumber of self-righteousness which may lie concealed therein ?

"Be thankful unto Him, and bless His name."—Psalm c. 4.

OUR Lord would have all His people rich in high and happy thoughts concerning His blessed person. Jesus is not content that His brethren should think meanly of Him; it is His pleasure that His espoused ones should be delighted with His beauty. We are not to regard Him as a bare necessary, like to bread and water, but as a luxurious delicacy, as a rare and ravishing delight. To this end He has revealed Himself as the "pearl of great price" in its peerless beauty, as the "bundle of myrrh" in its refreshing fragrance, as the "rose of Sharon" in its lasting perfume, as the "lily" in its spotless purity.

As a help to high thoughts of Christ, remember the estimation that Christ is had in beyond the skies, where things are measured by the right standard. Think how God esteems the Only Begotten, His unspeakable gift to us. Consider what the angels think of Him, as they count it their highest honour to veil their faces at His feet. Consider what the blood-washed think of Him, as day without night they sing His well deserved praises. High thoughts of Christ will enable us to act consistently with our relations towards Him. The more loftily we see Christ enthroned, and the more lowly we are when bowing before the foot of the throne, the more truly shall we be prepared to act our part towards Him. Our Lord Jesus desires us to think well of Him, that we may submit cheerfully to His authority. High thoughts of Him increase our love. Love and esteem go together. Therefore, believer, think much of your Master's excellencies. Study Him in His primeval glory, before He took upon Himself your nature! Think of the mighty love which drew Him from His throne to die upon the cross! Admire Him as He conquers all the powers of hell! See Him risen, crowned, glorified! Bow before Him as the Wonderful, the Counsellor, the mighty God, for only thus will your love to Him be what it should.

" I will pour water upon him that is thirsty."—Isaiah xliv. 3.

WHEN a believer has fallen into a low, sad state of feeling, he often tries to lift himself out of it by chastening himself with dark and doleful fears. Such is not the way to rise from the dust, but to continue in it. As well chain the eagle's wing to make it mount, as doubt in order to increase our grace. It is not the law, but the gospel which saves the seeking soul at first; and it is not a legal bondage, but gospel liberty which can restore the fainting believer afterwards. Slavish fear brings not back the backslider to God, but the sweet wooings of love allure him to Jesus' bosom. Are you this morning thirsting for the living God, and unhappy because you cannot find him to the delight of your heart? Have you lost the joy of religion, and is this your prayer, " Restore unto me the joy of Thy salvation "? Are you conscious also that you are barren, like the dry ground ; that you are not bringing forth the fruit unto God which He has a right to expect of you ; that you are not so useful in the Church, or in the world, as your heart desires to be ? Then here is exactly the promise which you need, " I will pour water upon him that is thirsty." You shall receive the grace you so much require, and you shall have it to the utmost reach of your needs. Water refreshes the thirsty : you shall be refreshed ; your desires shall be gratified. Water quickens sleeping vegetable life : your life shall be quickened by fresh grace. Water swells the buds and makes the fruits ripen ; you shall have fructifying grace : you shall be made fruitful in the ways of God. Whatever good quality there is in divine grace, you shall enjoy it to the full. All the riches of divine grace you shall receive in plenty ; you shall be as it were drenched with it : and as sometimes the meadows become flooded by the bursting rivers, and the fields are turned into pools, so shall you be—the thirsty land shall be springs of water.

"Saying, This is the blood of the testament which God hath enjoined unto you."—Hebrews ix. 20.

THERE is a strange power about the very name of blood, and the sight of it is always affecting. A kind heart cannot bear to see a sparrow bleed, and unless familiarised by use, turns away with horror at the slaughter of a beast. As to the blood of men, it is a consecrated thing : it is murder to shed it in wrath, it is a dreadful crime to squander it in war. Is this solemnity occasioned by the fact that the blood is the life, and the pouring of it forth the token of death ? We think so. When we rise to contemplate the blood of the Son of God, our awe is yet more increased, and we shudder as we think of the guilt of sin, and the terrible penalty which the Sin-bearer endured. Blood, always precious, is priceless when it streams from Immanuel's side. The blood of Jesus seals the *covenant* of grace, and makes it for ever sure. Covenants of old were made by sacrifice, and the everlasting covenant was ratified in the same manner. Oh, the delight of being saved upon the sure foundation of divine engagements which cannot be dishonoured ! Salvation by the works of the law is a frail and broken vessel whose shipwreck is sure ; but the covenant vessel fears no storms, for the blood ensures the whole. The blood of Jesus made His *testament* valid. Wills are of no power unless the testators die. In this light the soldier's spear is a blessed aid to faith, since it proved our Lord to be really dead. Doubts upon that matter there can be none, and we may boldly appropriate the legacies which He has left for His people. Happy they who see their title to heavenly blessings assured to them by a dying Saviour. But has this blood no voice to us ? Does it not bid us sanctify ourselves unto Him by whom we have been redeemed ? Does it not call us to newness of life, and incite us to entire consecration to the Lord ? O that the power of the blood might be known, and felt in us this night !

"Behold, I have graven thee upon the palms of my hands."
Isaiah xlix. 16.

NO doubt a part of the wonder which is concentrated in the word "*Behold,*" is excited by
the unbelieving lamentation of the preceding
sentence. Zion said, "The Lord hath forsaken me,
and my God hath forgotten me." How amazed the
divine mind seems to be at this wicked unbelief!
What can be more astounding than the unfounded
doubts and fears of God's favoured people? The
Lord's loving word of rebuke should make us blush;
He cries, "How can I have forgotten thee, when I have
graven thee upon the palms of my hands? How darest
thou doubt my constant remembrance, when the memorial is set upon my very flesh?" O unbelief, how
strange a marvel thou art! We know not which most
to wonder at, the faithfulness of God or the unbelief of
His people. He keeps His promise a thousand times,
and yet the next trial makes us doubt Him. He never
faileth; He is never a dry well; He is never as a setting sun, a passing meteor, or a melting vapour; and
yet we are as continually vexed with anxieties, molested with suspicions, and disturbed with fears, as
if our God were the mirage of the desert. "Behold,"
is a word intended to excite admiration. Here, indeed,
we have a theme for marvelling. Heaven and earth
may well be astonished that rebels should obtain so
great a nearness to the heart of infinite love as to be
written upon the palms of His hands. "I have graven
thee." It does not say, "Thy name." The name is
there, but that is not all: "I have graven *thee.*" See
the fulness of this! I have graven thy person, thine
image, thy case, thy circumstances, thy sins, thy
temptations, thy weaknesses, thy wants, thy works;
I have graven *thee,* everything about thee, all that
concerns thee; I have put thee altogether there.
Wilt thou ever say again that thy God hath forsaken
thee when He has graven *thee* upon His own palms?

"And ye shall be witnesses unto Me."—Acts i. 8.

IN order to learn how to discharge your duty as a witness for Christ, look at His example. He is always witnessing: by the well of Samaria, or in the Temple of Jerusalem: by the lake of Gennesaret, or on the mountain's brow. He is witnessing night and day; His mighty prayers are as vocal to God as His daily services. He witnesses under all circumstances; Scribes and Pharisees cannot shut His mouth; even before Pilate He witnesses a good confession. He witnesses so clearly and distinctly that there is no mistake in Him. Christian, make your life a clear testimony. Be you as the brook wherein you may see every stone at the bottom—not as the muddy creek, of which you only see the surface—but clear and transparent, so that your heart's love to God and man may be visible to all. You need not *say*, "I am true:" *be* true. Boast not of integrity, but *be* upright. So shall your testimony be such that men cannot help seeing it. Never, for fear of feeble man, restrain your witness. Your lips have been warmed with a coal from off the altar; let them speak as like heaven-touched lips should do. "In the morning sow thy seed, and in the evening withhold not thine hand." Watch not the clouds, consult not the wind— in season and out of season witness for the Saviour, and if it shall come to pass that for Christ's sake and the gospel's you shall endure suffering in any shape, shrink not, but rejoice in the honour thus conferred upon you, that you are counted worthy to suffer with your Lord; and joy also in this—that your sufferings, your losses, and persecutions shall make you a platform, from which the more vigorously and with greater power you shall witness for Christ Jesus. Study your great Exemplar, and be filled with His Spirit. Remember that you need much teaching, much upholding, much grace, and much humility, if your witnessing is to be to your Master's glory.

" As ye have received Christ Jesus the Lord."—Col. ii. 6.

THE life of faith is represented as *receiving—an act which implies the very opposite of anything like merit.* It is simply the acceptance of a gift. As the earth drinks in the rain, as the sea receives the streams, as night accepts light from the stars, so we, giving nothing, partake freely of the grace of God. The saints are not, by nature, wells, or streams, they are but cisterns into which the living water flows ; they are empty vessels into which God pours His salvation. The idea of receiving implies *a sense of realization,* making the matter *a reality.* One cannot very well receive a shadow ; we receive that which is substantial : so is it in the life of faith, Christ becomes real to us. While we are without faith, Jesus is a mere name to us—a person who lived a long while ago, so long ago that His life is only a history to us now ! By an act of faith Jesus becomes a real person in the consciousness of our heart. But receiving also means *grasping* or *getting possession of.* The thing which I receive becomes my own : I appropriate to myself that which is given. When I receive Jesus, He becomes *my* Saviour, so mine that neither life nor death shall be able to rob me of Him. All this is to receive Christ—to take Him as God's free gift ; to realize Him in my heart, and to appropriate Him as mine.

Salvation may be described as the blind receiving sight, the deaf receiving hearing, the dead receiving life ; but we have not only received these blessings, we have received CHRIST JESUS Himself. It is true that He gave us life from the dead. He gave us pardon of sin ; He gave us imputed righteousness. These are all precious things, but we are not content with them ; we have received *Christ Himself.* The Son of God has been poured into us, and we have received Him, and appropriated Him. What a heartful Jesus must be, for heaven itself cannot contain Him !

"The Master saith, Where is the guestchamber, where I shall eat the passover with My disciples?"—Mark xiv. 14.

JERUSALEM at the time of the passover was one great inn; each householder had invited his own friends, but no one had invited the Saviour, and He had no dwelling of His own. It was by His own supernatural power that He found Himself an upper room in which to keep the feast. It is so even to this day—Jesus is not received among the sons of men save only where by His supernatural power and grace He makes the heart anew. All doors are open enough to the prince of darkness, but Jesus must clear a way for Himself or lodge in the streets. It was through the mysterious power exerted by our Lord that the householder raised no question, but at once cheerfully and joyfully opened his guestchamber. Who he was, and what he was, we do not know, but he readily accepted the honour which the Redeemer proposed to confer upon him. In like manner it is still discovered who are the Lord's chosen, and who are not; for when the gospel comes to some, they fight against it, and will not have it, but where men receive it, welcoming it, this is a sure indication that there is a secret work going on in the soul, and that God has chosen them unto eternal life. Are you willing, dear reader, to receive Christ? then there is no difficulty in the way; Christ will be your guest; His own power is working with you, making you willing. What an honour to entertain the Son of God! The heaven of heavens cannot contain Him, and yet He condescends to find a house within our hearts! We are not worthy that He should come under our roof, but what an unutterable privilege when He condescends to enter! for then He makes a feast, and causes us to feast with Him upon royal dainties, we sit at a banquet where the viands are immortal, and give immortality to those who feed thereon. Blessed among the sons of Adam is he who entertains the angels' Lord.

" So walk ye in Him."—Colossians ii. 6.

IF we have received Christ Himself in our inmost hearts, our new life will manifest its intimate acquaintance with Him by a *walk of faith in Him.* Walking implies *action.* Our religion is not to be confined to our closet ; we must carry out into practical effect that which we believe.   If a man walks in Christ, then he so acts as Christ would act ; for Christ being in him, his hope, his love, his joy, his life, he is the reflex of the image of Jesus ; and men say of that man, " He is like his Master ; he lives like Jesus Christ." Walking signifies *progress.* " So walk ye in Him ;" proceed from grace to grace, run forward until you reach the uttermost degree of knowledge that a man can attain concerning our Beloved. Walking implies *continuance.*   There must be a perpetual abiding in Christ.   How many Christians think that in the morning and evening they ought to come into the company of Jesus, and may then give their hearts to the world all the day : but this is poor living ; we should always be with Him, treading in His steps and doing His will.   Walking also implies *habit.*   When we speak of a man's walk and conversation, we mean his habits, the constant tenour of his life.   Now, if we sometimes enjoy Christ, and then forget Him ; sometimes call Him ours, and anon lose our hold, that is not a habit ; we do not *walk* in Him.   We must keep to Him, cling to Him, never let Him go, but live and have our being in Him.   " As ye have received Christ Jesus the Lord, so walk ye in Him ;" persevere in the same way in which ye have begun, and, as at the first Christ Jesus was the trust of your faith, the source of your life, the principle of your action, and the joy of your spirit, so let him be the same till life's end ; the same when you walk through the valley of the shadow of death, and enter into the joy and the rest which remain for the people of God.   O Holy Spirit, enable us to obey this heavenly precept.

" His place of defence shall be the munitions of rocks: bread shall be given him; his waters shall be sure."—Isa. xxxiii. 16.

DO you doubt, O Christian, do you doubt as to whether God will fulfil His promise? Shall the munitions of rock be carried by storm? Shall the storehouses of heaven fail? Do you think that your heavenly Father, though He knoweth that you have need of food and raiment, will yet forget you? When not a sparrow falls to the ground without your Father, and the very hairs of your head are all numbered, will you mistrust and doubt Him? Perhaps your affliction will continue upon you till you dare to trust your God, and then it shall end. Full many there be who have been tried and sore vexed till at last they have been driven in sheer desperation to exercise faith in God, and the moment of their faith has been the instant of their deliverance; they have seen whether God would keep His promise or not. Oh, I pray you, doubt Him no longer! Please not Satan, and vex not yourself by indulging any more those hard thoughts of God. Think it not a light matter to doubt Jehovah. Remember, it is *a sin;* and not a little sin either, but in the highest degree criminal. The angels never doubt Him, nor the devils either: we alone, out of all the beings that God has fashioned, dishonour Him by unbelief, and tarnish His honour by mistrust. Shame upon us for this! Our God does not deserve to be so basely suspected; in our past life we have proved Him to be true and faithful to His word, and with so many instances of His love and of His kindness as we have received, and are daily receiving, at His hands, it is base and inexcusable that we suffer a doubt to sojourn within our heart. May we henceforth wage constant war against doubts of our God—enemies to our peace and to His honour; and with an unstaggering faith believe that what He has promised He will also perform. "Lord, I believe, help Thou mine unbelief."

" The eternal God is thy refuge"—Deut. xxxiii. 27.

THE word refuge may be translated " mansion," or " abiding-place," which gives the thought that *God is our abode, our home.* There is a fulness and sweetness in the metaphor, for dear to our hearts is our home, although it be the humblest cottage, or the scantiest garret; and dearer far is our blessed God, in whom we live, and move, and have our being. It is at home that we *feel safe:* we shut the world out and dwell in quiet security. So when we are with our God we " fear no evil." He is our shelter and retreat, our abiding refuge. At home, *we take our rest ;* it is there we find repose after the fatigue and toil of the day. And so our hearts find rest in God, when, wearied with life's conflict, we turn to Him, and our soul dwells at ease. At home, also, we *let our hearts loose;* we are not afraid of being misunderstood, nor of our words being misconstrued. So when we are with God we can commune freely with Him, laying open all our hidden desires ; for if the " secret of the Lord is with them that fear Him," the secrets of them that fear Him ought to be, and must be, with their Lord. Home, too, is the place of our *truest and purest happiness :* and it is in God that our hearts find their deepest delight. We have joy in Him which far surpasses all other joy. *It is also for home that we work and labour.* The thought of it gives strength to bear the daily burden, and quickens the fingers to perform the task ; and in this sense we may also say that God is our home. Love to Him strengthens us. We think of Him in the person of His dear Son ; and a glimpse of the suffering face of the Redeemer constrains us to labour in His cause. We feel that we must work, for we have brethren yet to be saved, and we have our Father's heart to make glad by bringing home His wandering sons ; we would fill with holy mirth the sacred family among whom we dwell. Happy are those who have thus the God of Jacob for their refuge !

" It is enough for the disciple that he be as His Master."
Matthew x. 25.

O one will dispute this statement, for it would be unseemly for the servant to be exalted above his Master. When our Lord was on earth, what was the treatment He received? Were His claims acknowledged, His instructions followed, His perfections worshipped, by those whom He came to bless? No; "He was despised and rejected of men." Outside the camp was His place : cross-bearing was His occupation. Did the world yield Him solace and rest? "Foxes have holes, and the birds of the air have nests; but the Son of man hath not where to lay His head." This inhospitable country afforded Him no shelter : it cast Him out and crucified Him. Such —if you are a follower of Jesus, and maintain a consistent, Christ-like walk and conversation—you must expect to be the lot of that part of your spiritual life which, in its outward development, comes under the observation of men. They will treat it as they treated the Saviour—they will despise it. Dream not that worldlings will admire you, or that the more holy and the more Christ-like you are, the more peaceably people will act towards you. They prized not the polished gem, how should they value the jewel in the rough? "If they have called the Master of the house Beelzebub, how much more shall they call them of His household?" If we were more like Christ, we should be more hated by His enemies. It were a sad dishonour to a child of God to be the world's favourite. It is a very ill omen to hear a wicked world clap its hands and shout "Well done" to the Christian man. He may begin to look to his character, and wonder whether he has not been doing wrong, when the unrighteous give him their approbation. Let us be true to our Master, and have no friendship with a blind and base world which scorns and rejects Him. Far be it from us to seek a crown of honour where our Lord found a coronet of thorn.

" Underneath are the everlasting arms."—Deut. xxxiii. 27.

OD—the eternal God—is Himself *our support* at all times, and especially when we are sinking in deep trouble. There are seasons when the Christian *sinks very low in humiliation*. Under a deep sense of his great sinfulness, he is humbled before God till he scarcely knows how to pray, because he appears, in his own sight, so worthless. Well, child of God, remember that when thou art at thy worst and lowest, yet " underneath " thee " are the everlasting arms." Sin may drag thee ever so low, but Christ's great atonement is still under all. You may have descended into the deeps, but you cannot have fallen so low as " the uttermost;" and to the uttermost He saves. Again. the Christian sometimes sinks very deeply in *sore trial from without*. Every earthly prop is cut away. What then? Still underneath him are " the everlasting arms." He cannot fall so deep in distress and affliction but what the covenant grace of an ever-faithful God will still encircle him. The Christian may be sinking under *trouble from within* through fierce conflict, but even then he cannot be brought so low as to be beyond the reach of the " everlasting arms "— they are underneath him ; and, while thus sustained, all Satan's efforts to harm him avail nothing.

This assurance of support is a comfort to any *weary but earnest worker* in the service of God. It implies a promise of strength for each day, grace for each need, and power for each duty. And, further, *when death comes*, the promise shall still hold good. When we stand in the midst of Jordan, we shall be able to say with David, " I will fear no evil, for Thou art with me." We shall descend into the grave, but we shall go no lower, for the eternal arms prevent our further fall. All through life, and at its close, we shall be upheld by the " everlasting arms "—arms that neither flag nor lose their strength, for " the everlasting God fainteth not, neither is weary."

"He shall choose our inheritance for us."—Psalm xlvii. 4.

BELIEVER, if your inheritance be a lowly one you should be satisfied with your earthly portion; for you may rest assured that it is the fittest *for you.* Unerring wisdom ordained your lot, and selected for you the safest and best condition. A ship of large tonnage is to be brought up the river; now, in one part of the stream there is a sandbank; should some one ask, "Why does the captain steer through the deep part of the channel and deviate so much from a straight line?" His answer would be, "Because I should not get my vessel into harbour at all if I did not keep to the deep channel." So, it may be, you would run aground and suffer shipwreck, if your divine Captain did not steer you into the depths of affliction where waves of trouble follow each other in quick succession. Some plants die if they have too much sunshine. It may be that you are planted where you get but little, you are put there by the loving Husbandman, because only in that situation will you bring forth fruit unto perfection. Remember this, had any other condition been better for you than the one in which you are, divine love would have put you there. You are placed by God in the most suitable circumstances, and if you had the choosing of your lot, you would soon cry, "Lord, choose my inheritance for me, for by my self-will I am pierced through with many sorrows." Be content with such things as you have, since the Lord has ordered all things for your good. Take up your own daily cross; it is the burden best suited for your shoulder, and will prove most effective to make you perfect in every good word and work to the glory of God. Down busy self, and proud impatience, it is not for you to choose, but for the Lord of Love!

> "Trials must and will befall—
> But with humble faith to see
> Love inscribed upon them all;
> This is happiness to me."

" The trial of your faith."—1 Peter i. 7.

FAITH untried may be true faith, but it is sure
to be little faith, and it is likely to remain
dwarfish so long as it is without trials. Faith
never prospers so well as when all things are against
her : tempests are her trainers, and lightnings are her
illuminators. When a calm reigns on the sea, spread
the sails as you will, the ship moves not to its harbour ; for on a slumbering ocean the keel sleeps too.
Let the winds rush howling forth, and let the waters
lift up themselves, then, though the vessel may rock,
and her deck may be washed with waves, and her mast
may creak under the pressure of the full and swelling
sail, it is then that she makes headway towards her
desired haven. No flowers wear so lovely a blue as
those which grow at the foot of the frozen glacier ; no
stars gleam so brightly as those which glisten in the
polar sky ; no water tastes so sweet as that which
springs amid the desert sand ; and no faith is so precious as that which lives and triumphs in adversity.
Tried faith brings experience. You could not have
believed your own weakness had you not been compelled to pass through the rivers ; and you would never
have known God's strength had you not been supported amid the water-floods. Faith increases in
solidity, assurance, and intensity, the more it is exercised with tribulation. Faith is precious, and its trial
is precious too.

Let not this, however, discourage those who are
young in faith. You will have trials enough without
seeking them : the full portion will be measured out
to you in due season. Meanwhile, if you cannot yet
claim the result of long experience, thank God for
what grace you have ; praise Him for that degree of
holy confidence whereunto you have attained : walk
according to that rule, and you shall yet have more
and more of the blessing of God, till your faith shall
remove mountains and conquer impossibilities.

"And it came to pass in those days, that He went out into a mountain to pray, and continued all night in prayer to God."—Luke vi. 12.

IF ever one of woman born might have lived without prayer, it was our spotless, perfect Lord, and yet none was ever so much in supplication as He! Such was His love to His Father, that He loved much to be in communion with Him: such His love for His people, that He desired to be much in intercession for them. *The fact* of this eminent prayerfulness of Jesus is a lesson for us—He hath given us an example that we may follow in His steps. *The time* He chose was admirable, it was the hour of silence, when the crowd would not disturb Him; the time of inaction, when all but Himself had ceased to labour; and the season when slumber made men forget their woes, and cease their applications to Him for relief. While others found rest in sleep, He refreshed Himself with prayer. *The place* was also well selected. He was alone where none would intrude, where none could observe: thus was He free from Pharisaic ostentation and vulgar interruption. Those dark and silent hills were a fit oratory for the Son of God. Heaven and earth in midnight stillness heard the groans and sighs of the mysterious Being in whom both worlds were blended. *The continuance* of His pleadings is remarkable; the long watches were not too long; the cold wind did not chill His devotions; the grim darkness did not darken His faith, or loneliness check His importunity. We cannot watch with Him one hour, but He watched for us whole nights. *The occasion* for this prayer is notable; it was after His enemies had been enraged—prayer was His refuge and solace; it was before He sent forth the twelve apostles—prayer was the gate of His enterprise, the herald of His new work. Should we not learn from Jesus to resort to special prayer when we are under peculiar trial, or contemplate fresh endeavours for the Master's glory? Lord Jesus, teach us to pray.

" The branch cannot bear fruit of itself."—John xv. 4.

HOW did you begin to bear fruit? It was when you came to Jesus and cast yourselves on His great atonement, and rested on His finished righteousness. Ah! what fruit you had then! Do you remember those early days? Then indeed the vine flourished, the tender grape appeared, the pomegranates budded forth, and the beds of spices gave forth their smell. Have you declined since then? If you have, we charge you to remember that time of love, and repent, and do thy first works. *Be most in those engagements which you have experimentally proved to draw you nearest to Christ,* because it is from Him that all your fruits proceed. Any holy exercise which will bring you to Him will help you to bear fruit. The sun is, no doubt, a great worker in fruit-creating among the trees of the orchard: and Jesus is still more so among the trees of His garden of grace. When have you been the most fruitless? Has not it been when you have lived farthest from the Lord Jesus Christ, when you have slackened in prayer, when you have departed from the simplicity of your faith, when your graces have engrossed your attention instead of your Lord, when you have said, " My mountain standeth firm, I shall never be moved ;" and have forgotten where your strength dwells—has not it been *then* that your fruit has ceased? Some of us have been taught that we have nothing out of Christ, by terrible abasements of heart before the Lord ; and when we have seen the utter barrenness and death of all creature power, we have cried in anguish, " From Him all my fruit must be found, for no fruit can ever come from me." We are taught, by past experience, that the more simply we depend upon the grace of God in Christ, and wait upon the Holy Spirit, the more we shall bring forth fruit unto God. Oh! to trust Jesus for fruit as well as for life.

"Men ought always to pray."—Luke xviii. 1.

IF *men* ought always to pray and not to faint, much more *Christian men.* Jesus has sent His church into the world on the same errand upon which He Himself came, and this mission includes intercession. What if I say that the church is the world's priest? Creation is dumb, but the church is to find a mouth for it. It is the church's high privilege to pray with acceptance. The door of grace is always open for her petitions, and they never return empty-handed. The veil was rent *for her*, the blood was sprinkled upon the altar *for her*, God constantly invites *her* to ask what she wills. Will she refuse the privilege which angels might envy her? Is she not the bride of Christ? May she not go in unto her King at every hour? Shall she allow the precious privilege to be unused? The church always has need for prayer. There are always some in her midst who are declining, or falling into open sin. There are lambs to be prayed for, that they may be carried in Christ's bosom? the strong, lest they grow presumptuous; and the weak, lest they become despairing. If we kept up prayer-meetings four-and-twenty hours in the day, all the days in the year, we might never be without a special subject for supplication. Are we ever without the sick and the poor, the afflicted and the wavering? Are we ever without those who seek the conversion of relatives, the reclaiming of backsliders, or the salvation of the depraved? Nay, with congregations constantly gathering, with ministers always preaching, with millions of sinners lying dead in trespasses and sins; in a country over which the darkness of Romanism is certainly descending; in a world full of idols, cruelties, devilries, if the church doth not pray, how shall she excuse her base neglect of the commission of her loving Lord? Let the church be constant in supplication, let every private believer cast his mite of prayer into the treasury.

" I will cut off them that worship and that swear by the Lord, and that swear by Malcham."—Zephaniah i. 5.

SUCH persons thought themselves safe because they were with both parties : they went with the followers of Jehovah, and bowed at the same time to Malcham. But duplicity is abominable with God, and hypocrisy his soul hateth. The idolater who distinctly gives himself to his false god, has one sin less than he who brings his polluted and detestable sacrifice unto the temple of the Lord, while his heart is with the world and the sins thereof. To hold with the hare and run with the hounds, is a dastard's policy. In the common matters of daily life, a double-minded man is despised, but in religion he is loathsome to the last degree. The penalty pronounced in the verse before us is terrible, but it is well deserved; for how should divine justice spare the sinner, who knows the right, approves it, and professes to follow it, and all the while loves the evil, and gives it dominion in his heart ?

My soul, search thyself this morning, and see whether thou art guilty of double-dealing. Thou professest to be a follower of Jesus—dost thou truly love Him ? Is thy heart right with God ? Art thou of the family of old Father Honest, or art thou a relative of Mr. By-ends ? A name to live is of little value if I be indeed dead in trespasses and sins. To have one foot on the land of truth, and another on the sea of falsehood, will involve a terrible fall and a total ruin. Christ will be all or nothing. God fills the whole universe, and hence there is no room for another god ; if, then, He reigns in my heart, there will be no space for another reigning power. Do I rest alone on Jesus crucified, and live alone for Him ? Is it my desire to do so ? Is my heart set upon so doing ? If so, blessed be the mighty grace which has led me to salvation ; and if not so, O Lord, pardon my sad offence, and unite my heart to fear Thy name.

"And Laban said, It must not be so done in our country, to give the younger before the firstborn."—Genesis xxix. 26.

WE do not excuse Laban for his dishonesty, but we scruple not to learn from the custom which he quoted as his excuse. There are some things which must be taken in order, and if we would win the second we must secure the first. The second may be the more lovely in our eyes, but the rule of the heavenly country must stand, and the elder must be married first. For instance, many men desire the beautiful and well-favoured Rachel of joy and peace in believing, but they must first be wedded to the tender-eyed Leah of repentance. Every one falls in love with happiness, and many would cheerfully serve twice seven years to enjoy it, but according to the rule of the Lord's kingdom, the Leah of real holiness must be beloved of our soul before the Rachel of true happiness can be attained. Heaven stands not first but second, and only by persevering to the end can we win a portion in it. The cross must be carried before the crown can be worn. We must follow our Lord in His humiliation, or we shall never rest with Him in glory.

My soul, what sayest thou, art thou so vain as to hope to break through the heavenly rule? Dost thou hope for reward without labour, or honour without toil? Dismiss the idle expectation, and be content to take the ill-favoured things for the sake of the sweet love of Jesus, which will recompense thee for all. In such a spirit, labouring and suffering, thou wilt find bitters grow sweet, and hard things easy. Like Jacob, thy years of service will seem unto thee but a few days for the love thou hast to Jesus; and when the dear hour of the wedding feast shall come, all thy toils shall be as though they had never been—an hour with Jesus will make up for ages of pain and labour.

> Jesus, to win Thyself so fair,
> Thy cross I will with gladness bear:
> Since so the rules of heaven ordain,
> The first I'll wed the next to gain.

" The Lord's portion is His people."—Deuteronomy xxxii. 9.

HOW *are they His?* By His own sovereign *choice.* He chose them, and set His love upon them. This He did altogether apart from any goodness in them at the time, or any goodness which He foresaw in them. He had mercy on whom He would have mercy, and ordained a chosen company unto eternal life ; thus, therefore, are they His by His unconstrained election.

They are not only His by choice, but by *purchase.* He has bought and paid for them to the utmost farthing, hence about His title there can be no dispute. Not with corruptible things, as with silver and gold, but with the precious blood of the Lord Jesus Christ, the Lord's portion has been fully redeemed. There is no mortgage on His estate ; no suits can be raised by opposing claimants, the price was paid in open court, and the Church is the Lord's freehold for ever. See the blood-mark upon all the chosen, invisible to human eye, but known to Christ, for " the Lord knoweth them that are His ;" He forgetteth none of those whom He has redeemed from among men ; He counts the sheep for whom He laid down His life, and remembers well the Church for which He gave Himself.

They are also His by *conquest.* What a battle He had in us before we would be won ! How long He laid siege to our hearts ! how often He sent us terms of capitulation ! but we barred our gates, and fenced our walls against Him. Do we not remember that glorious hour when He carried our hearts by storm ? when He placed His cross against the wall, and scaled our ramparts, planting on our strongholds the blood-red flag of His omnipotent mercy ? Yes, we are, indeed, the conquered captives of His omnipotent love. Thus chosen, purchased, and subdued, the rights of our divine possessor are inalienable : we rejoice that we never can be our own ; and we desire, day by day, to do *His* will, and to show forth *His* glory.

"Strengthen, O God, that which thou hast wrought for us."
Psalm lxviii. 28.

IT is our wisdom. as well as our necessity, to beseech God continually to strengthen that which He has wrought in us. It is because of their neglect in this, that many Christians may blame themselves for those trials and afflictions of spirit which arise from unbelief. It is true that Satan seeks to flood the fair garden of the heart and make it a scene of desolation, but it is also true that many Christians leave open the sluice-gates themselves, and let in the dreadful deluge through carelessness and want of prayer to their strong Helper. We often forget that the Author of our faith must be the Preserver of it also. The lamp which was burning in the temple was never allowed to go out, but it had to be daily replenished with fresh oil; in like manner, our faith can only live by being sustained with the oil of grace, and we can only obtain this from God Himself. Foolish virgins we shall prove, if we do not secure the needed sustenance for our lamps. He who built the world upholds it, or it would fall in one tremendous crash; He who made us Christians must maintain us by His Spirit, or our ruin will be speedy and final. Let us, then, evening by evening, go to our Lord for the grace and strength we need. We have a strong argument to plead, for it is *His own work of grace* which we ask Him to strengthen—*"that which Thou hast wrought for us."* Think you He will fail to protect and sustain *that?* Only let your faith take hold of His strength, and all the powers of darkness, led on by the master fiend of hell, cannot cast a cloud or shadow over your joy and peace. Why faint when you may be strong? Why suffer defeat when you may conquer? Oh! take your wavering faith and drooping graces to Him who can revive and replenish them, and earnestly pray, "Strengthen, O God, that which thou hast wrought for us."

" The Lord is my portion, saith my soul."—Lam. iii. 24.

T is not " The Lord is *partly* my portion," nor
" The Lord is *in* my portion ;" but He Himself makes up the sum total of my soul's inheritance. Within the circumference of that circle lies
all that we possess or desire. The *Lord* is my portion.
Not His grace merely, nor His love, nor His covenant,
but Jehovah Himself. He has chosen us for His
portion, and we have chosen Him for ours. It is true
that the Lord must first choose our inheritance for
us, or else we shall never choose it for ourselves ;
but if we are really called according to the purpose
of electing love, we can sing—

> " Lov'd of my God for Him again
> With love intense I burn ;
> Chosen of Him ere time began,
> I choose Him in return."

The Lord is our *all-sufficient* portion. God fills Himself; and if God is all-sufficient in Himself, He must
be all-sufficient for us. It is not easy to satisfy man's
desires. When he dreams that he is satisfied, anon he
wakes to the perception that there is somewhat yet
beyond, and straightway the horse-leech in his heart
cries, " Give, give." But all that we can wish for is
to be found in our divine portion, so that we ask,
" Whom have I in heaven but Thee ? and there is
none upon earth that I desire beside Thee." Well
may we " delight ourselves in the Lord " who makes
us to drink of the river of His pleasures. Our faith
stretches her wings and mounts like an eagle into
the heaven of divine love as to her proper dwelling-
place. " The lines have fallen to us in pleasant
places ; yea, we have a goodly heritage." Let us
rejoice in the Lord always ; let us show to the world
that we are a happy and a blessed people, and thus
induce them to exclaim, " We will go with you, for
we have heard that God is with you."

" Thine eyes shall see the King in His beauty."—Is. xxxiii. 17.

THE more you know about Christ the less will you be satisfied with superficial views of Him; and the more deeply you study His transactions in the eternal covenant, His engagements on your behalf as the eternal Surety, and the fulness of His grace which shines in all His offices, the more truly will you see the King in His beauty. Be much in such outlooks. Long more and more to see Jesus. *Meditation and contemplation* are often like windows of agate, and gates of carbuncle, through which we behold the Redeemer. Meditation puts the telescope to the eye, and enables us to see Jesus after a better sort than we could have seen Him if we had lived in the days of His flesh. Would that our conversation were more in heaven, and that we were more taken up with the person, the work, the beauty of our incarnate Lord. More meditation, and the beauty of the King would flash upon us with more resplendence. Beloved, it is very probable that we shall have such a sight of our glorious King as we never had before, *when we come to die.* Many saints in dying have looked up from amidst the stormy waters, and have seen Jesus walking on the waves of the sea, and heard Him say, "It is I, be not afraid." Ah, yes! when the tenement begins to shake, and the clay falls away, we see Christ through the rifts, and between the rafters the sunlight of heaven comes streaming in. But if we want to see face to face the "King in His beauty," *we must go to heaven* for the sight, or the King must come here in person. O that he would come on the wings of the wind! He is our Husband, and we are widowed by His absence; He is our Brother dear and fair, and we are lonely without Him. Thick veils and clouds hang between our souls and their true life: when shall the day break and the shadows flee away? Oh, long-expected day, begin!

" To whom be glory for ever. Amen"—Romans xi. 36.

"TO whom be glory for ever." This should be *the single* desire of the Christian. All other wishes must be subservient and tributary to this one. The Christian may wish for prosperity in his business, but only so far as it may help him to promote this—" To Him be glory for ever." He may desire to attain more gifts and more graces, but it should only be that "To Him may be glory for ever." You are not acting as you ought to do when you are moved by any other motive than a single eye to your Lord's glory. As a Christian, you are "of God, and through God," then live "to God " Let nothing ever set your heart beating so mightily as iove to Him. Let this ambition fire your soul ; be this the foundation of every enterprise upon which you enter, and this your' sustaining motive whenever your zeal would grow chill ; make God your *only* object. Depend upon it, where self begins sorrow begins ; but if God be my supreme delight and only object,

> " To me 'tis equal whether love ordain
>   My life or death—appoint me ease or pain."

Let your desire for God's glory be a *growing* desire. You blessed him in your youth, do not be content with such praises as you gave Him then. Has God prospered you in business ? give Him more as He has given you more. Has God given you experience ? Praise Him by stronger faith than you exercised at first. Does your knowledge grow ? Then sing more sweetly. Do you enjoy happier times than you once had ? Have you been restored from sickness, and has your sorrow been turned into peace and joy ? Then give Him more music ; put more coals and more sweet frankincense into the censer of your praise. Practically in your life give Him honour, putting the "Amen" to this doxology to your great and gracious Lord, by your own individual service and increasing holiness.

"He that cleaveth wood shall be endangered thereby."
Ecclesiastes x. 9.

OPPRESSORS may get their will of poor and needy men as easily as they can split logs of wood, but they had better mind, for it is a dangerous business, and a splinter from a tree has often killed the woodman. Jesus is persecuted in every injured saint, and He is mighty to avenge His beloved ones. Success in treading down the poor and needy is a thing to be trembled at : if there be no danger to persecutors here there will be great danger hereafter.

To cleave wood is a common every-day business, and yet it has its dangers; so then, reader, there are dangers connected with your calling and daily life which it will be well for you to be aware of. We refer not to hazards by flood and field, or by disease and sudden death, but to perils of a spiritual sort. Your occupation may be as humble as log splitting, and yet the devil can tempt you in it. You may be a domestic servant, a farm labourer, or a mechanic, and you may be greatly screened from temptations to the grosser vices, and yet some secret sin may do you damage. Those who dwell at home, and mingle not with the rough world, may yet be endangered by their very seclusion. Nowhere is he safe who thinks himself so. Pride may enter a poor man's heart ; avarice may reign in a cottager's bosom ; uncleanness may venture into the quietest home ; and anger, and envy, and malice may insinuate themselves into the most rural abode. Even in speaking a few words to a servant we may sin; a little purchase at a shop may be the first link in a chain of temptations; the mere looking out of a window may be the beginning of evil. O Lord, how exposed we are ! How shall we be secured ! To keep ourselves is work too hard for us : only Thou Thyself art able to preserve us in such a world of evils. Spread Thy wings over us, and we, like little chickens, will cower down beneath Thee, and feel ourselves safe !

" A spring shut up, a fountain sealed."—Canticles iv. 12.

IN this metaphor, which has reference to the inner life of a believer, we have very plainly the idea of *secrecy.* It is a spring *shut up:* just as there were springs in the East, over which an edifice was built, so that none could reach them save those who knew the secret entrance ; so is the heart of a believer when it is renewed by grace : there is a mysterious life within which no human skill can touch. It is a secret which no other man knoweth ; nay, which the very man who is the possessor of it cannot tell to his neighbour. The text includes not only secrecy, but *separation.* It is not the common spring, of which every passer-by may drink, it is one kept and preserved from all others ; it is a fountain bearing a particular mark—a king's royal seal, so that all can perceive that it is not a common fountain, but a fountain owned by a proprietor, and placed specially by itself alone. So is it with the spiritual life. The chosen of God were separated in the eternal decree ; they were separated by God in the day of redemption ; and they are separated by the possession of a life which others have not ; and it is impossible for them to feel at home with the world, or to delight in its pleasures. There is also the idea of *sacredness.* The spring shut up is preserved for the use of some special person : and such is the Christian's heart. It is a spring kept for Jesus. Every Christian should feel that he has God's seal upon him—and he should be able to say with Paul, " From henceforth let no man trouble me, for I bear in my body the marks of the Lord Jesus." Another idea is prominent—it is that of *security.*· Oh ! how sure and safe is the inner life of the believer ! If all the powers of earth and hell could combine against it, that immortal principle must still exist, for He who gave it pledged His life for its preservation. And who " is He that shall harm you," when God is your protector ?

" Thou art from everlasting."—Psalm xciii. 2.

CHRIST is EVERLASTING. Of Him we may sing with David, "Thy throne, O God, is for ever and ever." Rejoice, believer, in Jesus Christ, the same yesterday, to-day, and for ever. Jesus always *was.* The Babe born in Bethlehem was united to the Word, which was in the beginning, by whom all things were made. The title by which Christ revealed Himself to John in Patmos was, "Him which is, and which was, and which is to come." If He were not God from everlasting, we could not so devoutly love Him; we could not feel that He had any share in the eternal love which is the fountain of all covenant blessings; but since He was from all eternity with the Father, we trace the stream of divine love to Himself equally with His Father and the blessed Spirit. As our Lord always *was,* so also he *is* for evermore. Jesus is not dead; "He ever liveth to make intercession for us." Resort to Him in all your times of need, for He is waiting to bless you still. Moreover, Jesus our Lord ever *shall be.* If God should spare your life to fulfil your full day of threescore years and ten, you will find that His cleansing fountain is still opened, and His precious blood has not lost its power; you shall find that the Priest who filled the healing fount with His own blood, lives to purge you from all iniquity. When only your last battle remains to be fought, you shall find that the hand of your conquering Captain has not grown feeble—the living Saviour shall cheer the dying saint. When you enter heaven you shall find Him there bearing the dew of His youth; and through eternity the Lord Jesus shall still remain the perennial spring of joy, and life, and glory to His people. Living waters may you draw from this sacred well! Jesus always was, He always is, He always shall be. He is eternal in all His attributes, in all His offices, in all His might, and willingness to bless, comfort, guard, and crown His chosen people.

"Avoid foolish questions."—Titus iii. 9.

OUR days are few, and are far better spent in doing good, than in disputing over matters which are, at best, of minor importance. The old schoolmen did a world of mischief by their incessant discussion of subjects of no practical importance; and our Churches suffer much from petty wars over abstruse points and unimportant questions. After everything has been said that can be said, neither party is any the wiser, and therefore the discussion no more promotes knowledge than love, and it is foolish to sow in so barren a field. Questions upon points wherein Scripture is silent; upon mysteries which belong to God alone; upon prophecies of doubtful interpretation; and upon mere modes of observing human ceremonials, are all foolish, and wise men avoid them. Our business is neither to ask nor answer foolish questions, but to avoid them altogether; and if we observe the apostle's precept (Titus iii. 8) to be careful to maintain good works, we shall find ourselves far too much occupied with profitable business to take much interest in unworthy, contentious, and needless strivings.

There are, however, some questions which are the reverse of foolish, which we must not avoid, but fairly and honestly meet, such as these : Do I believe in the Lord Jesus Christ? Am I renewed in the spirit of my mind? Am I walking not after the flesh, but after the Spirit? Am I growing in grace? Does my conversation adorn the doctrine of God my Saviour? Am I looking for the coming of the Lord, and watching as a servant should do who expects his master? What more can I do for Jesus? Such enquiries as these urgently demand our attention; and if we have been at all given to cavilling, let us now turn our critical abilities to a service so much more profitable. Let us be peacemakers, and endeavour to lead others both by our precept and example, to " avoid foolish questions."

"O that I knew where I might find Him!"—Job xxiii. 3.

IN Job's uttermost extremity he cried after the Lord. The longing desire of an afflicted child of God is once more to see his Father's face. His first prayer is not "O that I might be healed of the disease which now festers in every part of my body!" nor even "O that I might see my children restored from the jaws of the grave, and my property once more brought from the hand of the spoiler!" but the first and uppermost cry is, "O that I knew where I might find HIM, who is my God! that I might come even to His seat!" God's children run home when the storm comes on. It is the heaven-born instinct of a gracious soul to seek shelter from all ills beneath the wings of Jehovah. "He that hath made his refuge God," might serve as the title of a true believer. A hypocrite, when afflicted by God, resents the infliction, and, like a slave, would run from the Master who has scourged him; but not so the true heir of heaven, he kisses the hand which smote him, and seeks shelter from the rod in the bosom of the God who frowned upon him. Job's desire to commune with God was intensified by the failure of all other sources of consolation. The patriarch turned away from his sorry friends, and looked up to the celestial throne, just as a traveller turns from his empty skin bottle, and betakes himself with all speed to the well. He bids farewell to earthborn hopes, and cries, "O that I knew where I might find my God!" Nothing teaches us so much the preciousness of the Creator, as when we learn the emptiness of all besides. Turning away with bitter scorn from earth's hives, where we find no honey, but many sharp stings, we rejoice in Him whose faithful word is sweeter than honey or the honeycomb. In every trouble we should first seek to realise God's presence with us. Only let us enjoy His smile, and we can bear our daily cross with a willing heart for His dear sake.

" O Lord, Thou hast pleaded the causes of my soul."
Lamentations iii. 58.

OBSERVE how *positively* the prophet speaks. He doth not say, " I hope, I trust, I sometimes think, that God hath pleaded the causes of my soul ;" but he speaks of it as a matter of fact not to be disputed. " Thou *hast* pleaded the causes of my soul." Let us, by the aid of the gracious Comforter, shake off those doubts and fears which so much mar our peace and comfort. Be this our prayer, that we may have done with the harsh croaking voice of surmise and suspicion, and may be able to speak with the clear, melodious voice of full assurance. Notice how *gratefully* the prophet speaks, ascribing all the glory to God alone ! You perceive there is not a word concerning himself or his own pleadings. He doth not ascribe his deliverance in any measure to any man, much less to his own merit ; but it is " *thou* "—" O Lord, Thou hast pleaded the causes of my soul; *Thou* hast redeemed my life." A grateful spirit should ever be cultivated by the Christian ; and especially after deliverances we should prepare a song for our God. Earth should be a temple filled with the songs of grateful saints, and every day should be a censer smoking with the sweet incense of thanksgiving. How *joyful* Jeremiah seems to be while he records the Lord's mercy. How triumphantly he lifts up the strain ! He has been in the low dungeon, and is even now no other than the weeping prophet ; and yet in the very book which is called " Lamentations," clear as the song of Miriam when she dashed her fingers against the tabor, shrill as the note of Deborah when she met Barak with shouts of victory, we hear the voice of Jeremy going up to heaven—"Thou hast pleaded the causes of my soul ; thou hast redeemed my life." O children of God, seek after a vital experience of the Lord's lovingkindness, and when you have it, speak positively of it ; sing gratefully ; shout triumphantly.

"The conies are but a feeble folk, yet make they their houses in the rocks."—Proverbs xxx. 26.

CONSCIOUS of their own natural defenceless-ness, the conies resort to burrows in the rocks, and are secure from their enemies. My heart, be willing to gather a lesson from these feeble folk. Thou art as weak and as exposed to peril as the timid cony, be as wise to seek a shelter. My best security is within the munitions of an immutable Jehovah, where His unalterable promises stand like giant walls of rock. It will be well with thee, my heart, if thou canst always hide thyself in the bulwarks of His glorious attributes, all of which are guarantees of safety for those who put their trust in Him. Blessed be the name of the Lord, I have so done, and have found myself like David in Adullam, safe from the cruelty of my enemy; I have not now to find out the blessedness of the man who puts his trust in the Lord, for long ago, when Satan and my sins pursued me, I fled to the cleft of the rock Christ Jesus, and in His riven side I found a delightful resting-place. My heart, run to Him anew to-night, whatever thy present grief may be; Jesus feels for thee; Jesus consoles thee; Jesus will help thee. No monarch in his impregnable fortress is more secure than the cony in his rocky burrow. The master of ten thousand chariots is not one whit better protected than the little dweller in the mountain's cleft. In Jesus the weak are strong, and the defenceless safe; they could not be more strong if they were giants, or more safe if they were in heaven. Faith gives to men on earth the protection of the God of heaven. More they cannot need, and need not wish. The conies cannot build a castle, but they avail themselves of what is there already: I cannot make myself a refuge, but Jesus has provided it, His Father has given it, His Spirit has revealed it, and lo, again to-night I enter it, and am safe from every foe.

" Grieve not the Holy Spirit."—Eph. iv. 30.

ALL that the believer has must come from Christ,
but it comes solely through the channel of the
Spirit of all grace. Moreover, as all blessings
thus flow to you through the Holy Spirit, so also no
good thing can come out of you in holy thought, devout worship, or gracious act, apart from the sanctifying operation of the same Spirit. Even if the good
seed be sown in you, yet it lies dormant except He
worketh in you to will and to do of His own good
pleasure. Do you desire to speak for Jesus—how
can you unless the Holy Ghost touch your tongue?
Do you desire to pray? Alas! what dull work it is
unless the Spirit maketh intercession for you! Do
you desire to subdue sin? Would you be holy?
Would you imitate your Master? Do you desire
to rise to superlative heights of spirituality? Are
you wanting to be made like the angels of God, full
of zeal and ardour for the Master's cause? You
cannot without the Spirit—"Without me ye can
do nothing." O branch of the vine, thou canst have
no fruit without the sap! O child of God, thou hast
no life within thee apart from the life which God
gives thee through His Spirit! Then let us not
grieve Him or provoke Him to anger by our sin.
Let us not quench Him in one of His faintest motions in our soul; let us foster every suggestion,
and be ready to obey every prompting. If the Holy
Spirit be indeed so mighty, let us attempt nothing
without Him; let us begin no project, and carry on
no enterprise, and conclude no transaction, without
imploring His blessing. Let us do Him the due
homage of feeling our entire weakness apart from
Him, and then depending alone upon Him, having
this for our prayer, "Open Thou my heart and my
whole being to Thine incoming, and uphold me with
Thy free Spirit when I shall have received that Spirit
in my inward parts."

"Lazarus was one of them that sat at the table with Him."
John xii. 2.

HE *is to be envied.* It was well to be Martha and serve, but better to be Lazarus and commune. There are times for each purpose, and each is comely in its season, but none of the trees of the garden yield such clusters as the vine of fellowship. To sit with Jesus, to hear His words, to mark His acts, and receive His smiles, was such a favour as must have made Lazarus as happy as the angels. When it has been our happy lot to feast with our Beloved in His banqueting-hall, we would not have given half a sigh for all the kingdoms of the world, if so much breath could have bought them.

He is to be imitated. It would have been a strange thing if Lazarus had not been at the table where Jesus was, for he had been dead, and Jesus had raised him. For the risen one to be absent when the Lord who gave him life was at his house, would have been ungrateful indeed. We too were once dead, yea, and like Lazarus stinking in the grave of sin ; Jesus raised us, and by His life we live—can we be content to live at a distance from Him? Do we omit to remember Him at His table, where He deigns to feast with His brethren? Oh, this is cruel! It behoves us to repent, and do as *He* has bidden us, for His least wish should be law to us. To have lived without constant intercourse with one of whom the Jews said, "Behold how He loved him," would have been disgraceful to Lazarus, is it excusable in us whom Jesus has loved with an everlasting love? To have been cold to Him who wept over his lifeless corpse, would have argued great brutishness in Lazarus. What does it argue in us over whom the Saviour has not only wept, but bled? Come, brethren, who read this portion, let us return unto our heavenly Bridegroom, and ask for His Spirit that we may be on terms of closer intimacy with Him, and henceforth sit at the table with Him.

" Israel served for a wife, and for a wife he kept sheep."
Hosea xii. 12.

JACOB, while expostulating with Laban, thus describes his own toil, " This twenty years have I been with thee. That which was torn of beasts I brought not unto thee : I bare the loss of it ; of my hand didst thou require it, whether stolen by day, or stolen by night. Thus I was ; in the day the drought consumed me, and the frost by night ; and my sleep departed from mine eyes." Even more toilsome than this was the life of our Saviour here below. He watched over all His sheep till He gave in as His last account, " Of all those whom Thou hast given me I have lost none." His hair was wet with dew, and His locks with the drops of the night. Sleep departed from His eyes, for all night He was in prayer wrestling for His people. One night Peter must be pleaded for ; anon, another claims His tearful intercession. No shepherd sitting beneath the cold skies, looking up to the stars, could ever utter such complaints because of the hardness of his toil as Jesus Christ might have brought, if He had chosen to do so, because of the sternness of His service in order to procure His spouse—

> " Cold mountains and the midnight air,
>   Witnessed the fervour of His prayer ;
>   The desert His temptations knew,
>   His conflict and His victory too."

It is sweet to dwell upon the spiritual parallel of Laban having required all the sheep at Jacob's hand. If they were torn of beasts, Jacob must make it good ; if any of them died, he must stand as surety for the whole. Was not the toil of Jesus for His Church the toil of one who was under suretiship obligations to bring every believing one safe to the hand of Him who had committed them to His charge ? Look upon toiling Jacob, and you see a representation of Him of whom we read, " He shall feed His flock like a shepherd."

"The power of His resurrection."—Philippians iii. 10.

THE doctrine of a risen Saviour is exceedingly precious. The resurrection is the corner-stone of the entire building of Christianity. It is the key-stone of the arch of our salvation. It would take a volume to set forth all the streams of living water which flow from this one sacred source, the resurrection of our dear Lord and Saviour Jesus Christ; but to *know* that he has risen, and to have fellowship with Him as such—communing with the risen Saviour by possessing a risen life—seeing Him leave the tomb by leaving the tomb of worldliness ourselves, this is even still more precious. The doctrine is the basis of the experience, but as the flower is more lovely than the root, so is the experience of fellowship with the risen Saviour more lovely than the doctrine itself. I would have you *believe* that Christ rose from the dead so as to sing of it, and derive all the consolation which it is possible for you to extract from this well-ascertained and well-witnessed fact; but I beseech you, rest not contented even there. Though you cannot, like the disciples, see Him visibly, yet I bid you aspire to see Christ Jesus by the eye of faith; and though, like Mary Magdalene, you may not "touch" Him, yet may you be privileged to converse with Him, and to know that He is risen, you yourselves being risen in Him to newness of life. To know a crucified Saviour as having crucified all my sins, is a high degree of knowledge; but to know a risen Saviour as having justified me, and to realise that He has bestowed upon me new life, having given me to be a new creature through His own new-ness of life, this is a noble style of experience: short of it, none ought to rest satisfied. May you both "know Him, and the power of His resurrection." Why should souls who are quickened with Jesus, wear the grave-clothes of worldliness and unbelief? Rise, for the Lord is risen.

WHEN we were united by faith to Christ, we were brought into such complete fellowship with Him, that we were made one with Him, and His interests and ours became mutual and identical. We have fellowship with Christ in His *love*. What He loves we love. He loves the saints—so do we. He loves sinners—so do we. He loves the poor perishing race of man, and pants to see earth's deserts transformed into the garden of the Lord—so do we. We have fellowship with Him in His *desires*. He desires the glory of God—we also labour for the same. He desires that the saints may be with Him where He is—we desire to be with Him there too. He desires to drive out sin—behold we fight under His banner. He desires that His Father's name may be loved and adored by all His creatures—we pray daily, " Let Thy kingdom come and Thy will be done on earth, even as it is in heaven." We have fellowship with Christ in His *sufferings*. We are not nailed to the cross, nor do we die a cruel death, but when He is reproached, we are reproached ; and a very sweet thing it is to be blamed for His sake, to be despised for following the Master, to have the world against us. The disciple should not be above His Lord. In our measure we commune with Him in His *labours*, ministering to men by the word of truth and by deeds of love. Our meat and our drink, like His, is to do the will of Him who hath sent us and to finish His work. We have also fellowship with Christ in His *joys*. We are happy in His happiness, we rejoice in His exaltation. Have you ever tasted that joy, believer ? There is no purer or more thrilling delight to be known this side heaven than that of having Christ's joy fulfilled in us, that our joy may be full. His *glory* awaits us to complete our fellowship, for His Church shall sit with Him upon His throne, as His well-beloved bride and queen.

" Get thee up into the high mountain."—Isaiah xl. 9.

EACH believer should be thirsting for God, for the living God, and longing to climb the hill of the Lord, and see Him face to face. We ought not to rest content in the mists of the valley when the summit of Tabor awaits us. My soul thirsteth to drink deep of the cup which is reserved for those who reach the mountain's brow, and bathe their brows in heaven. How pure are the dews of the hills, how fresh is the mountain air, how rich the fare of the dwellers aloft, whose windows look into the New Jerusalem! Many saints are content to live like men in coal mines, who see not the sun; they eat dust like the serpent when they might taste the ambrosial meat of angels; they are content to wear the miner's garb when they might put on king's robes; tears mar their faces when they might anoint them with celestial oil. Satisfied I am that many a believer pines in a dungeon when he might walk on the palace roof, and view the goodly land and Lebanon. Rouse thee, O believer, from thy low condition! Cast away thy sloth, thy lethargy, thy coldness, or whatever interferes with thy chaste and pure love to Christ, thy soul's Husband. Make Him the source, the centre, and the circumference of all thy soul's range of delight. What enchants thee into such folly as to remain in a pit when thou mayst sit on a throne? Live not in the lowlands of bondage now that mountain liberty is conferred upon thee. Rest no longer satisfied with thy dwarfish attainments, but press forward to things more sublime and heavenly. Aspire to a higher, a nobler, a fuller life. Upward to heaven! Nearer to God!

> " When wilt Thou come unto me, Lord ?
>   Oh come, my Lord most dear!
> Come near, come nearer, nearer still,
>   I'm blest when Thou art near."

*" The glorious Lord will be unto us a place of broad rivers
and streams."*—Isaiah xxxiii. 21.

BROAD rivers and streams produce fertility,
and abundance in the land. Places near broad
rivers are remarkable for the variety of their
plants and their plentiful harvests. God is all this to
His Church. Having God she has *abundance*. What
can she ask for that He will not give her? What want
can she mention which He will not supply? " In this
mountain shall the Lord of Hosts make unto all
people a feast of fat things." Want ye the bread of
life? It drops like manna from the sky. Want ye
refreshing streams? The rock follows you, and that
Rock is Christ. If you suffer any want it is your own
fault; if you are straitened you are not straitened in
Him, but in your own bowels. Broad rivers and
streams also point to *commerce*. Our glorious Lord is
to us a place of heavenly merchandize. Through our
Redeemer we have commerce with the past; the wealth
of Calvary, the treasures of the covenant, the riches
of the ancient days of election, the stores of eternity,
all come to us down the broad stream of our gracious
Lord. We have commerce, too, with the future. What
galleys, laden to the water's edge, come to us from the
millennium! What visions we have of the days of
heaven upon earth! Through our glorious Lord we have
commerce with angels; communion with the bright
spirits washed in blood, who sing before the throne;
nay, better still, we have fellowship with the Infinite
One. Broad rivers and streams are specially intended
to set forth the idea of *security*. Rivers were of old
a defence. Oh! beloved, what a defence is God to
His Church! The devil cannot cross this broad
river of God. How he wishes he could turn the
current, but fear not, for God abideth immutably the
same. Satan may worry, but he cannot destroy us;
no galley with oars shall invade our river, neither
shall gallant ship pass thereby.

" Yet a little sleep, a little slumber, a little folding of the hands to sleep: so shall thy poverty come as one that travelleth; and thy want as an armed man."—Proverbs xxiv. 33, 34.

THE worst of sluggards only ask for a little slumber; they would be indignant if they were accused of thorough idleness. A little folding of the hands to sleep is all they crave, and they have a crowd of reasons to show that this indulgence is a very proper one. Yet by these littles the day ebbs out, and the time for labour is all gone, and the field is grown over with thorns. It is by little procrastinations that men ruin their souls. They have no intention to delay for years—a few months will bring the more convenient season—to-morrow if you will, they will attend to serious things ; but the present hour is so occupied and altogether so unsuitable, that they beg to be excused. Like sands from an hourglass, time passes, life is wasted by driblets, and seasons of grace lost by little slumbers. Oh, to be wise, to catch the flying hour, to use the moments on the wing ! May the Lord teach us this sacred wisdom, for otherwise a poverty of the worst sort awaits us, eternal poverty which shall want even a drop of water, and beg for it in vain. Like a traveller steadily pursuing his journey, poverty overtakes the slothful, and ruin overthrows the undecided : each hour brings the dreaded pursuer nearer ; he pauses not by the way, for he is on his master's business and must not tarry. As an armed man enters with authority and power, so shall want come to the idle, and death to the impenitent, and there will be no escape. O that men were wise betimes, and would seek diligently unto the Lord Jesus, or ere the solemn day shall dawn when it will be too late to plough and to sow, too late to repent and believe. In harvest, it is vain to lament that the seed time was neglected. As yet, faith and holy decision are timely. May we obtain them this night.

" To preach deliverance to the captives."—Luke iv. 18.

NONE but Jesus can give deliverance to captives Real liberty cometh from Him only. It is a liberty *righteously bestowed ;* for the Son, who is Heir of all things, has a right to make men free. The saints honour the justice of God, which now secures their salvation. It is a liberty which has been *dearly purchased.* Christ speaks it by His power, but He bought it by His blood. He makes thee free, but it is by His own bonds. Thou goest clear, because He bare thy burden for thee : thou art set at liberty, because He has suffered in thy stead. But, though dearly purchased, *He freely gives it.* Jesus asks nothing of us as a preparation for this liberty. He finds us sitting in sackcloth and ashes, and bids us put on the beautiful array of freedom ; He saves us just as we are, and all without our help or merit. When Jesus sets free, the liberty is *perpetually entailed ;* no chains can bind again. Let the Master say to me, " Captive, I have delivered thee," and it is done for ever. Satan may plot to enslave us, but if the Lord be on our side, whom shall we fear ? The world, with its temptations, may seek to ensnare us, but mightier is He who is for us than all they who be against us. The machinations of our own deceitful hearts may harass and annoy us, but He who hath begun the good work in us will carry it on and perfect it to the end. The foes of God and the enemies of man may gather their hosts together, and come with concentrated fury against us, but if God acquitteth, who is he that condemneth ? Not more free is the eagle which mounts to his rocky eyrie, and afterwards outsoars the clouds, than the soul which Christ hath delivered. If we are no more under the law, but free from its curse, let our liberty be *practically exhibited* in our serving God with gratitude and delight. " I am Thy servant, and the son of thine handmaid : Thou hast loosed my bonds." " Lord, what wilt Thou have me to do ?"

" For He saith to Moses, I will have mercy on whom I will have mercy, and I will have compassion on whom I will have compassion."—Romans ix. 15.

IN these words the Lord in the plainest manner claims the right to give or to withhold His mercy according to His own sovereign will. As the prerogative of life and death is vested in the monarch, so the Judge of all the earth has a right to spare or condemn the guilty, as may seem best in His sight. Men by their sins have forfeited all claim upon God ; they deserve to perish for their sins—and if they all do so, they have no ground for complaint. If the Lord steps in to save any, He may do so if the ends of justice are not thwarted ; but if He judges it best to leave the condemned to suffer the righteous sentence, none may arraign Him at their bar. Foolish and impudent are all those discourses about the rights of men to be all placed on the same footing ; ignorant, if not worse, are those contentions against discriminating grace, which are but the rebellions of proud human nature against the crown and sceptre of Jehovah. When we are brought to see our own utter ruin and ill desert, and the justice of the divine verdict against sin, we no longer cavil at the truth that the Lord is not bound to save us ; we do not murmur if He chooses to save others, as though He were doing us an injury, but feel that if He deigns to look upon us, it will be His own free act of undeserved goodness, for which we shall for ever bless his name.

How shall those who are the subjects of divine election sufficiently adore the grace of God? They have no room for boasting, for sovereignty most effectually excludes it. The Lord's will alone is glorified, and the very notion of human merit is cast out to everlasting contempt. There is no more humbling doctrine in Scripture than that of election, none more promotive of gratitude, and, consequently, none more sanctifying. Believers should not be afraid of it, but adoringly rejoice in it.

" Whatsoever thy hand findeth to do, do it with thy might."—
Ecclesiastes ix. 10.

"WHATSOEVER thy hand findeth to do."
refers to works that are *possible*.   There
are many things which our *heart* findeth
to do which we never shall do.   It is well it is in our
heart ; but if we would be eminently useful, we must
not be content with forming schemes in our heart,
and talking of them ; we must practically carry out
"whatsoever our hand findeth to do."   One good deed
is more worth than a thousand brilliant theories.   Let
us not wait for large opportunities, or for a different
kind of work, but do just the things we "find to do"
day by day.   We have no other time in which to live.
The past is gone ; the future has not arrived ; we never
shall have any time but time *present*.   Then do not
wait until your experience has ripened into maturity
before you attempt to serve God.   Endeavour now to
bring forth fruit.   Serve God now, but be careful as
to the way in which you perform what you find to
do—" *do it with thy might.*"   Do it *promptly;* do not
fritter away your life in thinking of what you intend
to do to-morrow as if that could recompense for the
idleness of to-day.   No man ever served God by
doing things to-morrow.   If we honour Christ and
are blessed, it is by the things which we do *to-day*.
Whatever you do for Christ throw your whole soul
into it.   Do not give Christ a little slurred labour,
done as a matter of course now and then ; but when
you do serve Him, do it with heart, and soul, and
strength.

But where is the might of a Christian?   It is not
in himself, for he is perfect weakness.   His might
lieth in the Lord of Hosts.   Then let us seek His
help ; let us proceed with prayer and faith, and when
we have done what our " hand findeth to do," let us
wait upon the Lord for his blessing.   What we do
thus will be well done, and will not fail in its effect.

" They shall rejoice, and shall see the plummet in the hand of Zerubbabel."—Zechariah iv. 10.

SMALL things marked the beginning of the work in the hand of Zerubbabel, but none might despise it, for the Lord had raised up one who would persevere until the headstone should be brought forth with shoutings. *The plummet was in good hands.* Here is the comfort of every believer in the Lord Jesus; let the work of grace be ever so small in its beginnings, the plummet is in good hands, a master builder greater than Solomon has undertaken the raising of the heavenly temple, and He will not fail nor be discouraged till the topmost pinnacle shall be raised. If the plummet were in the hand of any merely human being, we might fear for the building, but the pleasure of the Lord shall prosper in Jesus' hand. The works did not proceed irregularly, and without care, for *the master's hand carried a good instrument.* Had the walls been hurriedly run up without due superintendence, they might have been out of the perpendicular; but the plummet was used by the chosen overseer. Jesus is evermore watching the erection of His spiritual temple, that it may be built securely and well. We are for haste, but Jesus is for judgment. He will use the plummet, and that which is out of line must come down, every stone of it. Hence the failure of many a flattering work, the overthrow of many a glittering profession. It is not for us to judge the Lord's church, since Jesus has a steady hand, and a true eye, and can use the plummet well. Do we not rejoice to see judgment left to Him ?

The plummet was in active use—it was in the builder's hand ; a sure indication that he meant to push on the work to completion. O Lord Jesus, how would we indeed be glad if we could see Thee at Thy great work. O Ziona, the beautiful, thy walls are still in ruins ! Rise, Thou glorious Builder, and make her desolations to rejoice at Thy coming.

" Joshua the high priest standing before the angel of the Lord."—Zechariah iii. 1.

IN Joshua *the high priest* we see a picture of each and every child of God, who has been made nigh by the blood of Christ, and has been taught to minister in holy things, and enter into that which is within the veil. Jesus has made us priests and kings unto God, and even here upon earth we exercise the priesthood of consecrated living and hallowed service. But this high priest is said to be *" standing* before the angel of the Lord," that is, standing to minister. This should be the perpetual position of every true believer. Every place is now God's temple, and His people can as truly serve Him in their daily employments as in His house. They are to be always " ministering," offering the spiritual sacrifice of prayer and praise, and presenting themselves a "living sacrifice" But notice where it is that Joshua stands to minister, it is *before the angel* of Jehovah. It is only through a mediator that we poor defiled ones can ever become priests unto God. I present what I have before the messenger, the angel of the covenant, the Lord Jesus; and through Him my prayers find acceptance wrapped up in *His* prayers; my praises become sweet as they are bound up with bundles of myrrh, and aloes, and cassia from Christ's own garden. If I can bring Him nothing but my tears, He will put them with His own tears in His own bottle, for He once wept; if I can bring Him nothing but my groans and sighs, He will accept these as an acceptable sacrifice, for He once was broken in heart, and sighed heavily in spirit. I myself, standing in Him, am accepted in the Beloved; and all my polluted works, though in themselves only objects of divine abhorrence, are so received, that God smelleth a sweet savour. He is content and I am blessed. See, then, the position of the Christian—" a priest—standing—before the angel of the Lord."

"The forgiveness of sins, according to the riches of His grace."—Ephesians i. 7.

COULD there be a sweeter word in any language than that word "forgiveness," when it sounds in a guilty sinner's ear, like the silver notes of jubilee to the captive Israelite? Blessed, for ever blessed be that dear star of pardon which shines into the condemned cell, and gives the perishing a gleam of hope amid the midnight of despair! Can it be possible that sin, such sin as mine, can be forgiven, forgiven altogether, and for ever? Hell is my portion as a sinner—there is no possibility of my escaping from it while sin remains upon me—can the load of guilt be uplifted, the crimson stain removed? Can the adamantine stones of my prison-house ever be loosed from their mortices, or the doors be lifted from their hinges? Jesus tells me that I may yet be clear. For ever blessed be the revelation of atoning love which not only tells me that pardon is possible, but that it is secured to all who rest in Jesus. I have believed in the appointed propitiation, even Jesus crucified, and therefore my sins are at this moment, and for ever, forgiven by virtue of His substitutionary pains and death. What joy is this! What bliss to be a perfectly pardoned soul! My soul dedicates all her powers to Him who of His own unpurchased love became my surety, and wrought out for me redemption through His blood. What riches of grace does free forgiveness exhibit! To forgive at all, to forgive fully, to forgive freely, to forgive for ever! Here is a constellation of wonders; and when I think of how great my sins were, how dear were the precious drops which cleansed me from them, and how gracious was the method by which pardon was sealed home to me, I am in a maze of wondering worshipping affection. I bow before the throne which absolves me, I clasp the cross which delivers me, I serve henceforth all my days the Incarnate God, through whom I am this night a pardoned soul.

" For I rejoiced greatly, when the brethren came and testified of the truth that is in thee, even as thou walkest in the truth."
3 John 3.

THE truth was in Gaius, and Gaius walked in the truth. If the first had not been the case, the second could never have occurred; and if the second could not be said of him the first would have been a mere pretence. Truth must enter into the soul, penetrate and saturate it, or else it is of no value. Doctrines held as a matter of creed are like bread in the hand, which ministers no nourishment to the frame ; but doctrine accepted by the heart, is as food digested, which, by assimilation, sustains and builds up the body. In us truth must be a living force, an active energy, an indwelling reality, a part of the woof and warp of our being. If it be *in us*, we cannot henceforth part with it. A man may lose his garments or his limbs, but his inward parts are vital, and cannot be torn away without absolute loss of life. A Christian can die, but he cannot deny the truth. Now it is a rule of nature that the inward affects the outward, as light shines from the centre of the lantern through the glass : when, therefore, the truth is kindled within, its brightness soon beams forth in the outward life and conversation. It is said that the food of certain worms colours the cocoons of silk which they spin : and just so the nutriment upon which a man's inward nature lives gives a tinge to every word and deed proceeding from him. To walk in the truth, imports a life of integrity, holiness, faithfulness, and simplicity—the natural product of those principles of truth which the gospel teaches, and which the Spirit of God enables us to receive. We may judge of the secrets of the soul by their manifestation in the man's conversation. Be it ours to-day, O gracious Spirit, to be ruled and governed by Thy divine authority, so that nothing false or sinful may reign in our hearts, lest it extend its malignant influence to our daily walk among men.

"Seeking the wealth of his people."—Esther x. 3.

MORDECAI was a true patriot, and therefore, being exalted to the highest position under Ahasuerus, he used his eminence to promote the prosperity of Israel. In this he was a type of Jesus, who, upon His throne of glory, seeks not His own, but spends His power for His people. It were well if every Christian would be a Mordecai to the church, striving according to his ability for its prosperity. Some are placed in stations of affluence and influence, let them honour their Lord in the high places of the earth, and testify for Jesus before great men. Others have what is far better, namely, close fellowship with the King of kings, let them be sure to plead daily for the weak of the Lord's people, the doubting, the tempted, and the comfortless. It will redound to their honour if they make much intercession for those who are in darkness and dare not draw nigh unto the mercy seat. Instructed believers may serve their Master greatly if they lay out their talents for the general good, and impart their wealth of heavenly learning to others, by teaching them the things of God. The very least in our Israel may at least *seek* the welfare of his people; and his desire, if he can give no more, shall be acceptable. It is at once the most Christlike and the most happy course for a believer to cease from living to himself. He who blesses others cannot fail to be blessed himself. On the other hand, to seek our own personal greatness is a wicked and unhappy plan of life, its way will be grievous and its end will be fatal.

Here is the place to ask thee, my friend, whether thou art to the best of thy power seeking the wealth of the church in thy neighbourhood? I trust thou art not doing it mischief by bitterness and scandal, nor weakening it by thy neglect. Friend, unite with the Lord's poor, bear their cross, do them all the good thou canst, and thou shalt not miss thy reward.

*" Thou shalt not go up and down as a talebearer among thy
people. . . . Thou shalt in any wise rebuke thy neighbour
and not suffer sin upon him.*—Leviticus xix. 16, 17.

TALE-BEARING emits a threefold poison; for it injures the teller, the hearer, and the person concerning whom the tale is told. Whether the report be true or false, we are by this precept of God's Word forbidden to spread it. The reputations of the Lord's people should be very precious in our sight, and we should count it shame to help the devil to dishonour the Church and the name of the Lord. Some tongues need a bridle rather than a spur. Many glory in pulling down their brethren, as if thereby they raised themselves. Noah's wise sons cast a mantle over their father, and he who exposed him earned a fearful curse. We may ourselves one of these dark days need forbearance and silence from our brethren, let us render it cheerfully to those who require it now. Be this our family rule, and our personal bond—SPEAK EVIL OF NO MAN.

The Holy Spirit, however, permits us to censure sin, and prescribes the way in which we are to do it. It must be done by rebuking our brother to his face, not by railing behind his back. This course is manly, brotherly, Christlike, and under God's blessing will be useful. Does the flesh shrink from it? Then we must lay the greater stress upon our conscience, and keep ourselves to the work, lest by suffering sin upon our friend we become ourselves partakers of it. Hundreds have been saved from gross sins by the timely, wise, affectionate warnings of faithful ministers and brethren. Our Lord Jesus has set us a gracious example of how to deal with erring friends in His warning given to Peter, the prayer with which He preceded it, and the gentle way in which He bore with Peter's boastful denial that he needed such a caution.

"Spices for anointing oil."—Exodus xxxv. 8.

MUCH use was made of this anointing oil under the law, and that which it represents is of primary importance under the gospel. The Holy Spirit, who anoints us for all holy service, is indispensable to us if we would serve the Lord acceptably. Without His aid our religious services are but a vain oblation, and our inward experience is a dead thing. Whenever our ministry is without unction, what miserable stuff it becomes! nor are the prayers, praises, meditations, and efforts of private Christians one jot superior. A holy anointing is the soul and life of piety, its absence the most grievous of all calamities. To go before the Lord without anointing is as though some common Levite had thrust himself into the priest's office—his ministrations would rather have been sins than services. May we never venture upon hallowed exercises without sacred anointings. They drop upon us from our glorious Head; from His anointing we who are as the skirts of His garments partake of a plenteous unction.

Choice spices were compounded with rarest art of the apothecary to form the anointing oil, to show forth to us how rich are all the influences of the Holy Spirit. All good things are found in the divine Comforter. Matchless consolation, infallible instruction, immortal quickening, spiritual energy, and divine sanctification all lie compounded with other excellencies in that sacred eye-salve, the heavenly anointing oil of the Holy Spirit. It imparts a delightful fragrance to the character and person of the man upon whom it is poured. Nothing like it can be found in all the treasuries of the rich, or the secrets of the wise. It is not to be imitated. It comes alone from God, and it is freely given, through Jesus Christ, to every waiting soul. Let us seek it, for we may have it, may have it this very evening. O Lord, anoint Thy servants.

" And Amaziah said to the man of God, But what shall we do for the hundred talents which I have given to the army of Israel? And the man of God answered, The Lord is able to give thee much more than this."—2 Chronicles xxv. 9.

A VERY important question this seemed to be to the king of Judah, and possibly it is of even more weight with the tried and tempted Christian. To lose money is at no times pleasant, and when principle involves it, the flesh is not always ready to make the sacrifice. " Why lose that which may be so usefully employed? May not the truth itself be bought too dear? What shall we do without it? Remember the children, and our small income!" All these things and a thousand more would tempt the Christian to put forth his hand to unrighteous gain, or stay himself from carrying out his conscientious convictions, when they involve serious loss. All men cannot view these matters in the light of faith; and even with the followers of Jesus, the doctrine of " we must live " has quite sufficient weight.

The Lord is able to give thee much more than this is a very satisfactory answer to the anxious question. Our Father holds the purse-strings, and what we lose for His sake He can repay a thousand-fold. It is ours to obey His will, and we may rest assured that He will provide for us. The Lord will be no man's debtor at the last. Saints know that a grain of heart's-ease is of more value than a ton of gold. He who wraps a threadbare coat about a good conscience has gained a spiritual wealth far more desirable than any he has lost. God's smile and a dungeon are enough for a true heart; His frown and a palace would be hell to a gracious spirit. Let the worst come to the worst, let all the talents go, we have not lost our treasure, for that is above, where Christ sitteth at the right hand of God. Meanwhile, even now, the Lord maketh the meek to inherit the earth, and no good thing doth He withhold from them that walk uprightly.

"Michael and his angels fought against the dragon; and the dragon fought and his angels."—Revelation xii. 7.

WAR always will rage between the two great sovereignties until one or other be crushed. Peace between good and evil is an impossibility; the very pretence of it would, in fact, be the triumph of the powers of darkness. *Michael will always fight;* his holy soul is vexed with sin, and will not endure it. Jesus will always be the dragon's foe, and that not in a quiet sense, but actively, vigorously, with full determination to exterminate evil. All His servants, whether angels in heaven or messengers on earth, will and must fight; they are born to be warriors—at the cross they enter into covenant never to make truce with evil; they are a warlike company, firm in defence and fierce in attack. The duty of every soldier in the army of the Lord is daily, with all his heart, and soul, and strength, to fight against the dragon.

The dragon and his angels will not decline the affray; they are incessant in their onslaughts, sparing no weapon, fair or foul. We are foolish to expect to serve God without opposition: the more zealous we are, the more sure are we to be assailed by the myrmidons of hell. The church may become slothful, but not so her great antagonist; his restless spirit never suffers the war to pause; he hates the woman's seed, and would fain devour the church if he could. The servants of Satan partake much of the old dragon's energy, and are usually an active race. War rages all around, and to dream of peace is dangerous and futile.

Glory be to God, we know the end of the war. The great dragon shall be cast out and for ever destroyed, while Jesus and they who are with Him shall receive the crown. Let us sharpen our swords to-night, and pray the Holy Spirit to nerve our arms for the conflict. Never battle so important, never crown so glorious. Every man to his post, ye warriors of the cross, and may the Lord tread Satan under your feet shortly!

" Thou hast made summer and winter."—Psalm lxxiv. 17.

MY soul begin this wintry month with thy God. The cold snows and the piercing winds all remind thee that He keeps His covenant with day and night, and tend to assure thee that He will also keep that glorious covenant which He has made with thee in the person of Christ Jesus. He who is true to His Word in the revolutions of the seasons of this poor sin-polluted world, will not prove unfaithful in His dealings with His own well-beloved Son.

Winter in the soul is by no means a comfortable season, and if it be upon thee just now it will be very painful to thee : but there is this comfort, namely, that *the Lord* makes it. He sends the sharp blasts of adversity to nip the buds of expectation : He scattereth the hoarfrost like ashes over the once verdant meadows of our joy : He casteth forth his ice like morsels freezing the streams of our delight. He does it all, He is the great Winter King, and rules in the realms of frost, and therefore thou canst not murmur. Losses, crosses, heaviness, sickness, poverty, and a thousand other ills, are of the Lord's sending, and come to us with wise design. Frosts kill noxious insects, and put a bound to raging diseases ; they break up the clods, and sweeten the soil. O that such good results would always follow our winters of affliction !

How we prize the fire just now ! how pleasant is its cheerful glow ! Let us in the same manner prize our Lord, who is the constant source of warmth and comfort in every time of trouble. Let us draw nigh to Him, and in Him find joy and peace in believing. Let us wrap ourselves in the warm garments of His promises, and go forth to labours which befit the season, for it were ill to be as the sluggard who will not plough by reason of the cold ; for he shall beg in summer and have nothing.

" O that men would praise the Lord for His goodness, and for His wonderful works to the children of men."—Ps. cvii. 8.

IF we complained less, and praised more, we should be happier, and God would be more glorified. Let us daily praise God for *common mercies*—common as we frequently call them, and yet so priceless, that when deprived of them we are ready to perish. Let us bless God for the eyes with which we behold the sun, for the health and strength to walk abroad, for the bread we eat, for the raiment we wear. Let us praise Him that we are not cast out among the hopeless, or confined amongst the guilty; let us thank Him for liberty, for friends, for family associations and comforts; let us praise Him, in fact, for everything which we receive from His bounteous hand, for we deserve little, and yet are most plenteously endowed. But, beloved, the sweetest and the loudest note in our songs of praise should be of *redeeming love*. God's redeeming acts towards His chosen are for ever the favourite themes of their praise. If we know what redemption means, let us not withhold our sonnets of thanksgiving. We have been redeemed from the power of our corruptions, uplifted from the depth of sin in which we were naturally plunged. We have been led to the cross of Christ—our shackles of guilt have been broken off; we are no longer slaves, but children of the living God, and can antedate the period when we shall be presented before the throne without spot or wrinkle or any such thing. Even now by faith we wave the palm-branch and wrap ourselves about with the fair linen which is to be our everlasting array, and shall we not unceasingly give thanks to the Lord our Redeemer? Child of God, canst thou be silent? Awake, awake, ye heritors of glory, and lead your captivity captive, as ye cry with David, "Bless the Lord, O my soul : and all that is within me, bless His holy name." Let the new month begin with new songs.

" Thou art all fair, my love."—Sol. Song iv. 7.

THE Lord's admiration of His Church is very wonderful, and His description of her beauty is very glowing. She is not merely *fair*, but *" all* fair." He views her in Himself, washed in His sin-atoning blood and clothed in His meritorious righteousness, and He considers her to be full of comeliness and beauty. No wonder that such is the case, since it is but his own perfect excellency that He admires; for the holiness, glory, and perfection of His Church are His own glorious garments on the back of His own well-beloved spouse. She is not simply pure, or well-proportioned; she is positively lovely and fair! She has actual merit! Her deformities of sin are removed; but more, she has through her Lord obtained a meritorious righteousness by which an actual beauty is conferred upon her. Believers have a positive righteousness given to them when they become " accepted in the beloved." (Eph. i. 6.) Nor is the Church barely lovely, she is *superlatively so.* Her Lord styles her "Thou fairest among women." She has a real worth and excellence which cannot be rivalled by all the nobility and royalty of the world. If Jesus could exchange His elect bride for all the queens and empresses of earth, or even for the angels in heaven, He would not, for He puts her first and foremost— " fairest among women." Like the moon she far outshines the stars. Nor is this an opinion which he is ashamed of, for he invites all men to hear it. He sets a " behold " before it, a special note of exclamation, inviting and arresting attention. *" Behold*, thou art fair, my love; *behold*, thou art fair." (Sol. Song iv. 1.) His opinion He publishes abroad even now, and one day from the throne of His glory He will avow the truth of it before the assembled universe. " Come, ye blessed of my Father," (Matt. xxv. 34,) will be His solemn affirmation of the loveliness of His elect.

"Behold, all is vanity."—Ecclesiastes i. 14.

NOTHING can satisfy the entire man but the Lord's love and the Lord's own self. Saints have tried to anchor in other roadsteads, but they have been driven out of such fatal refuges. Solomon, the wisest of men, was permitted to make experiments for us all, and to do for us what we must not dare to do for ourselves. Here is his testimony in his own words: "So I was great, and increased more than all that were before me in Jerusalem: also my wisdom remained with me. And whatsoever mine eyes desired I kept not from them, I withheld not my heart from any joy; for my heart rejoiced in all my labour: and this was my portion of all my labour. Then I looked on all the works that my hands had wrought, and on the labour that I had laboured to do: and, behold, all was vanity and vexation of spirit, and there was no profit under the sun." "Vanity of vanities, all is vanity." What! the whole of it vanity? O favoured monarch, is there nothing in all thy wealth? Nothing in that wide dominion reaching from the river even to the sea? Nothing in Palmyra's glorious palaces? Nothing in the house of the forest of Lebanon? In all thy music and dancing, and wine and luxury, is there nothing? "Nothing," he says, "but weariness of spirit." This was his verdict when he had trodden the whole round of pleasure. To embrace our Lord Jesus, to dwell in His love, and be fully assured of union with Him—this is all in all. Dear reader, you need not try other forms of life in order to see whether they are better than the Christian's: if you roam the world around, you will see no sights like a sight of the Saviour's face; if you could have all the comforts of life, if you lost your Saviour, you would be wretched; but if you win Christ, then should you rot in a dungeon, you would find it a paradise; should you live in obscurity, or die with famine, you will yet be satisfied with favour and full of the goodness of the Lord.

" There is no spot in thee."—Sol. Song iv. 7.

HAVING pronounced His Church positively full of beauty, our Lord confirms His praise by a precious negative, " There is no spot in thee." As if the thought occurred to the Bridegroom that the carping world would insinuate that He had only mentioned her comely parts, and had purposely omitted those features which were deformed or defiled, He sums up all by declaring her universally and entirely fair, and utterly devoid of stain. A spot may soon be removed, and is the very least thing that can disfigure beauty, but even from this little blemish the believer is delivered in his Lord's sight. If He had said there is no hideous scar, no horrible deformity, no deadly ulcer, we might even then have marvelled ; but when He testifies that she is free from the slightest spot, all these other forms of defilement are included, and the depth of wonder is increased. If He had but promised to remove all spots by-and-by, we should have had eternal reason for joy ; but when he speaks of it as already done, who can restrain the most intense emotions of satisfaction and delight ? O my soul, here is marrow and fatness for thee ; eat thy full, and be satisfied with royal dainties.

Christ Jesus has no quarrel with His spouse. She often wanders from Him, and grieves His Holy Spirit, but He does not allow her faults to affect His love. He sometimes chides, but it is always in the tenderest manner, with the kindest intentions: it is " my love " even then. There is no remembrance of our follies, He does not cherish ill thoughts of us, but He pardons and loves as well after the offence as before it. It is well for us it is so, for if Jesus were as mindful of injuries as we are, how could He commune with us ? Many a time a believer will put himself out of humour with the Lord for some slight turn in providence, but our precious Husband knows our silly hearts too well to take any offence at our ill manners.

" The Lord mighty in battle."—Psalm xxiv. 8.

ELL may our God be glorious in the eyes of
His people, seeing that He has wrought such
wonders for them, in them, and by them.
For them, the Lord Jesus upon Calvary routed every
foe, breaking all the weapons of the enemy in pieces
by His finished work of satisfactory obedience; by
His triumphant resurrection and ascension He completely overturned the hopes of hell, leading captivity
captive, making a show of our enemies openly, tri-
umphing over them by His cross. Every arrow of
guilt which Satan might have shot at us is broken, for
who can lay anything to the charge of God's elect?
Vain are the sharp swords of infernal malice, and the
perpetual battles of the serpent's seed, for in the
midst of the church the lame take the prey, and the
feeblest warriors are crowned.

The saved may well adore their Lord for His conquests *in them,* since the arrows of their natural hatred
are snapped, and the weapons of their rebellion broken.
What victories has grace won in our evil hearts! How
glorious is Jesus when the will is subdued, and sin
dethroned! As for our remaining corruptions, they
shall sustain an equally sure defeat, and every temptation, and doubt, and fear, shall be utterly destroyed.
In the Salem of our peaceful hearts, the name of Jesus
is great beyond compare: He has won our love, and
He shall wear it. Even thus securely may we look
for victories *by us.* We are more than conquerors
through Him that loved us. We shall cast down
the powers of darkness which are in the world, by
our faith, and zeal, and holiness; we shall win sinners
to Jesus, we shall overturn false systems, we shall
convert nations, for God is with us, and none shall
stand before us. This evening let the Christian warrior chant the war song, and prepare for to-morrow's
fight. Greater is He that is in us than he that is in the
world.

HIS should be a great encouragement to try to do good, since God has among the vilest of the vile, the most reprobate, the most debauched and drunken, an elect people who *must* be saved. When you take the Word to them, you do so because God has ordained you to be the messenger of life to their souls, and *they must* receive it, for so the decree of predestination runs. They are as much redeemed by blood as the saints before the eternal throne. They are Christ's property, and yet perhaps they are lovers of the ale-house, and haters of holiness ; but if Jesus Christ purchased them He will have them. God is not unfaithful to forget the price which His Son has paid. He will not suffer His substitution to be in any case an ineffectual, dead thing. Tens of thousands of redeemed ones are not regenerated yet, but regenerated they must be ; and this is our comfort when we go forth to them with the quickening Word of God.

Nay, more, these ungodly ones are prayed for by Christ before the throne. "Neither pray I for these alone," saith the great Intercessor, " but for *them also which shall believe* on Me through their word." Poor, ignorant souls, they know nothing about prayer for themselves, but Jesus prays for them. Their names are on his breastplate, and ere long they must bow their stubborn knee, breathing the penitential sigh before the throne of grace. "The time of figs is not yet." The predestinated moment has not struck ; but, when it comes, *they shall obey*, for God will have His own ; *they must*, for the Spirit is not to be withstood when He cometh forth with fulness of power—*they must* become the willing servants of the living God. "My people shall be willing in the day of my power." "He shall justify many." "He shall see of the travail of His soul." "I will divide him a portion with the great, and He shall divide the spoil with the strong."

" Even we ourselves groan within ourselves, waiting for the adoption, to wit, the redemption of our body."—Rom. viii. 23.

THIS groaning is universal among the saints: to a greater or less extent we all feel it. It is not the groan of murmuring or complaint: it is rather the note of desire than of distress. Having received an earnest, we desire the whole of our portion; we are sighing that our entire manhood, in its trinity of spirit, soul, and body, may be set free from the last vestige of the fall; we long to put off corruption, weakness, and dishonour, and to wrap ourselves in incorruption, in immortality, in glory, in the spiritual body which the Lord Jesus will bestow upon His people. We long for the manifestation of our adoption as the children of God. "We groan," but it is *"within ourselves."* It is not the hypocrite's groan, by which he would make men believe that he is a saint because he is wretched. Our sighs are sacred things, too hallowed for us to tell abroad. We keep our longings to our Lord alone. Then the apostle says we are *"waiting,"* by which we learn that we are not to be petulant, like Jonah or Elijah, when they said, "Let me die;" nor are we to whimper and sigh for the end of life because we are tired of work, nor wish to escape from our present sufferings till the will of the Lord is done. We are to groan for glorification, but we are to wait patiently for it, knowing that what the Lord appoints is best. Waiting implies being ready. We are to stand at the door expecting the Beloved to open it and take us away to Himself. This "groaning" is a *test.* You may judge of a man by what he groans after. Some men groan after wealth—they worship Mammon; some groan continually under the troubles of life—they are merely impatient; but the man who sighs after God, who is uneasy till he is made like Christ, that is the blessed man. May God help us to groan for the coming of the Lord, and the resurrection which He will bring to us.

" Ask, and it shall be given you."—Matthew vii. 7.

WE know of a place in England still existing, where a dole of bread is served to every passer-by who chooses to ask for it. Whoever the traveller may be, he has but to knock at the door of St. Cross Hospital, and there is the dole of bread for him. Jesus Christ so loveth sinners that He has built a St. Cross Hospital, so that whenever a sinner is hungry, he has but to knock and have his wants supplied. Nay, He has done better; He has attached to this Hospital of the Cross a bath; and whenever a soul is black and filthy, it has but to go there and be washed. The fountain is always full, always efficacious. No sinner ever went into it and found that it could not wash away his stains. Sins which were scarlet and crimson have all disappeared, and the sinner has been whiter than snow. As if this were not enough, there is attached to this Hospital of the Cross a wardrobe, and a sinner making application simply as a sinner, may be clothed from head to foot; and if he wishes to be a soldier, he may not merely have a garment for ordinary wear, but armour which shall cover him from the sole of his foot to the crown of his head. If he asks for a sword, he shall have that given to him, and a shield too. Nothing that is good for him shall be denied him. He shall have spending-money so long as he lives, and he shall have an eternal heritage of glorious treasure when he enters into the joy of his Lord.

If all these things are to be had by merely knocking at mercy's door, O my soul, knock hard this morning, and ask large things of thy generous Lord. Leave not the throne of grace till all thy wants have been spread before the Lord, and until by faith thou hast a comfortable prospect that they shall be all supplied. No bashfulness need retard when Jesus invites. No unbelief should hinder when Jesus promises. No cold-heartedness should restrain when such blessings are to be obtained.

"And the Lord shewed me four carpenters."—Zech. i. 20.

IN the vision described in this chapter, the prophet saw four terrible horns. They were pushing this way and that way, dashing down the strongest and the mightiest; and the prophet asked, "What are these?" The answer was, "These are the horns which have scattered Israel." He saw before him a representation of those powers which had oppressed the church of God. There were four horns; for the church is attacked from all quarters. Well might the prophet have felt dismayed; but on a sudden there appeared before him *four carpenters.* He asked, "What shall these do?" These are the men whom God hath found to break those horns in pieces. *God will always find men for His work,* and He will find them *at the right time.* The prophet did not see the carpenters *first,* when there was nothing to do, but first the "horns," and then the "carpenters." Moreover, the Lord finds *enough men.* He did not find *three* carpenters, but *four;* there were four horns, and there must be four workmen. God finds *the right men;* not four men with pens to write; not four architects to draw plans; but four carpenters to do rough work. Rest assured, you who tremble for the ark of God, that when the "horns" grow troublesome, the "carpenters" will be found. You need not fret concerning the weakness of the church of God at any moment; there may be growing up in obscurity the valiant reformer who will shake the nations: Chrysostoms may come forth from our Ragged Schools, and Augustines from the thickest darkness of London's poverty. The Lord knows where to find His servants. He hath in ambush a multitude of mighty men, and at His word they shall start up to the battle; "for the battle is the Lord's," and He shall get to Himself the victory. Let us abide faithful to Christ, and He, in the right time, will raise up for us a defence, whether it be in the day of our personal need, or in the season of peril to His Church.

"As is the heavenly, such are they also that are heavenly."—
1 Cor. xv. 48.

THE head and members are of one nature, and
not like that monstrous image which Nebuchadnezzar saw in his dream. The head was
of fine gold, but the belly and thighs were of brass,
the legs of iron, and the feet, part of iron and part of
clay. Christ's mystical body is no absurd combination
of opposites; the members were mortal, and therefore
Jesus died; the glorified head is immortal, and therefore the body is immortal too, for thus the record
stands, "Because I live, ye shall live also." As is
our loving head, such is the body, and every member
in particular. A chosen Head and chosen members;
an accepted Head, and accepted members; a living
Head, and living members. If the head be pure
gold, all the parts of the body are of pure gold also.
Thus is there a double union of nature as a basis
for the closest communion. Pause here, devout
reader, and see if thou canst without ecstatic amaze-
ment, contemplate the infinite condescension of the
Son of God in thus exalting thy wretchedness into
blessed union with his glory. Thou art so mean
that in remembrance of thy mortality, thou mayest
say to corruption, "Thou art my father," and to
the worm, "Thou art my sister;" and yet in Christ
thou art so honoured that thou canst say to the
Almighty, "Abba, Father," and to the Incarnate God,
"Thou art my brother and my husband." Surely if
relationships to ancient and noble families make men
think highly of themselves, *we* have whereof to glory
over the heads of them all. Let the poorest and
most despised believer lay hold upon this privilege;
let not a senseless indolence make him negligent to
trace his pedigree, and let him suffer no foolish attachment to present vanities to occupy his thoughts
to the exclusion of this glorious, this heavenly honour
of union with Christ.

" Girt about the paps with a golden girdle."—Rev i. 13.

"ONE like unto the Son of Man" appeared to John in Patmos, and the beloved disciple marked that he wore a girdle of gold. *A girdle*, for Jesus never was ungirt while upon earth, but stood always ready for service, and now before the eternal throne He stays not His holy ministry, but as a priest is girt about with "the curious girdle of the ephod." Well is it for us that He has not ceased to fulfil His offices of love for us, since this is one of our choicest safeguards that He ever liveth to make inter‑cession for us. Jesus is never an idler ; His garments are never loose as though His offices were ended ; He diligently carries on the cause of His people. *A golden girdle*, to manifest the superiority of His service, the royalty of His person, the dignity of His state, the glory of His reward. No longer does He cry out of the dust, but He pleads with authority, a King as well as a Priest. Safe enough is our cause in the hands of our enthroned Melchisedek.

Our Lord presents all His people with an example. We must never unbind our girdles. This is not the time for lying down at ease, it is the season of service and warfare. We need to bind the girdle of truth more and more tightly around our loins. It is a golden girdle, and so will be our richest ornament, and we greatly need it, for a heart that is not well braced up with the truth as it is in Jesus, and with the fidelity which is wrought of the Spirit, will be easily entangled with the things of this life, and tripped up by the snares of temptation. It is in vain that we possess the Scriptures unless we bind them around us like a girdle, surrounding our entire nature, keeping each part of our character in order, and giving com‑pactness to our whole man. If in heaven Jesus un‑binds not the girdle, much less may we upon earth. Stand, therefore, having your loins girt about with truth.

" Base things of the world hath God chosen."—1 Cor. i. 28.

WALK the streets by moonlight, if you dare, and you will see sinners then. Watch when the night is dark, and the wind is howling, and the picklock is grating in the door, and you will see sinners then. Go to yon jail, and walk through the wards, and mark the men with heavy over-hanging brows, men whom you would not like to meet at night, and there are sinners there. Go to the Reformatories, and note those who have betrayed a rampant juvenile depravity, and you will see sinners there. Go across the seas to the place where a man will gnaw a bone upon which is reeking human flesh, and there is a sinner there. Go where you will, you need not ransack earth to find sinners, for they are common enough; you may find them in every lane and street of every city, and town, and village, and hamlet. It is for such that Jesus died. If you will select me the grossest specimen of humanity, if he be but born of woman, I will have hope of him yet, because Jesus Christ is come to seek and to save *sinners.* Electing love has selected some of the worst to be made the best. Pebbles of the brook grace turns into jewels for the crown-royal. Worthless dross he transforms into pure gold. Redeeming love has set apart many of the worst of mankind to be the reward of the Saviour's passion. Effectual grace calls forth many of the vilest of the vile to sit at the table of mercy, and therefore let none despair.

Reader, by that love looking out of Jesus' tearful eyes, by that love streaming from those bleeding wounds, by that faithful love, that strong love, that pure, disinterested, and abiding love ; by the heart and by the bowels of the Saviour's compassion, we conjure you turn not away as though it were nothing to you ; but believe on Him and you shall be saved. Trust your soul with Him and He will bring you to His Father's right hand in glory everlasting.

" I am made all things to all men, that I might by all means save some."—1 Corinthians ix. 22.

PAUL'S great object was not merely to instruct and to improve, but to save. Anything short of this would have disappointed him ; he would have men renewed in heart, forgiven, sanctified, in fact, *saved.* Have our Christian labours been aimed at anything below this great point ? then let us amend our ways, for of what avail will it be at the last great day to have taught and moralised men if they appear before God unsaved ? Blood-red will our skirts be if through life we have sought inferior objects, and forgotten that men needed to be saved. Paul knew the ruin of man's natural state, and did not try to educate him, but to save him ; he saw men sinking to hell, and did not talk of refining them, but of saving from the wrath to come. To compass their salvation, he gave himself up with untiring zeal to telling abroad the gospel, to warning and beseeching men to be reconciled to God. His prayers were importunate and his labours incessant. To save souls was his consuming passion, his ambition, his calling. He became a servant to all men, toiling for his race, feeling a woe within him if he preached not the gospel. He laid aside his preferences to prevent prejudice ; he submitted his will in things indifferent, and if men would but receive the gospel, he raised no questions about forms or ceremonies : the gospel was the one all-important business with him. If he might save some he would be content. This was the crown for which he strove, the sole and sufficient reward of all his labours and self-denials. Dear reader, have you and I lived to win souls at this noble rate ? Are we possessed with the same all-absorbing desire ? If not, why not ? Jesus died for sinners, cannot we live for them ? Where is our tenderness ? Where our love to Christ, if we seek not His honour in the salvation of men ? O that the Lord would saturate us through and through with an undying zeal for the souls of men.

" Thou hast a few names even in Sardis which have not defiled their garments ; and they shall walk with me in white: for they are worthy."—Revelation iii. 4.

WE may understand this to refer to *justification*. "They shall walk in white ;" that is, they shall enjoy a constant sense of their own justification by faith ; they shall understand that the righteousness of Christ is imputed to them, that they have all been washed and made whiter than the newly-fallen snow.

Again, it refers to *joy and gladness :* for white robes were holiday dresses among the Jews. They who have not defiled their garments shall have their faces always bright ; they shall understand what Solomon meant when he said, " Go thy way, eat thy bread with joy, and drink thy wine with a merry heart. Let thy garments be always white, for God hath accepted thy works." He who is accepted of God shall wear white garments of joy and gladness, while he walks in sweet communion with the Lord Jesus. Whence so many doubts, so much misery, and mourning ? It is because so many believers defile their garments with sin and error, and hence they lose the joy of their salvation, and the comfortable fellowship of the Lord Jesus, they do not here below walk in white.

The promise also refers to *walking in white before the throne of God.* Those who have not defiled their garments here shall most certainly walk in white up yonder, where the white-robed hosts sing perpetual hallelujahs to the Most High. They shall possess joys inconceivable, happiness beyond a dream, bliss which imagination knoweth not, blessedness which even the stretch of desire hath not reached. The " undefiled in the way " shall have all this—not of merit, nor of works, but of grace. They shall walk with Christ in white, for He has made them " worthy." In His sweet company they shall drink of the living fountains of waters.

"Thou, O God, hast prepared of Thy goodness for the poor."
Psalm lxviii. 10.

ALL God's gifts are prepared gifts laid up in store for wants foreseen. He anticipates our needs; and out of the fulness which He has treasured up in Christ Jesus, He provides of His goodness for the poor. You may trust Him for all the necessities that can occur, for He has infallibly foreknown every one of them. He can say of us in all conditions, "I knew that thou wouldst be this and that." A man goes a journey across the desert, and when he has made a day's advance, and pitched his tent, he discovers that he wants many comforts and necessaries which he has not brought in his baggage. "Ah!" says he, "I did not foresee this: if I had this journey to go again, I should bring these things with me, so necessary to my comfort." But God has marked with prescient eye all the requirements of His poor wandering children, and when those needs occur, supplies are ready. It is goodness which He has prepared for the poor in heart, goodness and goodness only. "My grace is sufficient for thee." "As thy days, so shall thy strength be."

Reader, is your heart heavy this evening? God knew it would be; the comfort which your heart wants is treasured in the sweet assurance of the text. You are poor and needy, but He has thought upon you, and has the exact blessing which you require in store for you. Plead the promise, believe it and obtain its fulfilment. Do you feel that you never were so consciously vile as you are now? Behold, the crimson fountain is open still, with all its former efficacy, to wash your sin away. Never shall you come into such a position that Christ cannot aid you. No pinch shall ever arrive in your spiritual affairs in which Jesus Christ shall not be equal to the emergency, for your history has all been foreknown and provided for in Jesus.

" Therefore will the Lord wait that He may be gracious unto you."—Isaiah **xxx.** 18.

GOD often DELAYS IN ANSWERING PRAYER. We have several instances of this in sacred Scripture. Jacob did not get the blessing from the angel until near the dawn of day—he had to wrestle all night for it. The poor woman of Syrophenicia was answered not a word for a long while. Paul besought the Lord *thrice* that " the thorn in the flesh " might be taken from him, and he received no assurance that it should be taken away, but instead thereof a promise that God's grace should be sufficient for him. If thou hast been knocking at the gate of mercy, and hast received no answer, shall I tell thee why the mighty Maker hath not opened the door and let thee in ?   Our Father has reasons peculiar to Himself for thus keeping us waiting.   Sometimes it is to show His power and His sovereignty, that men may know that Jehovah has a right to give or to withhold.   More frequently the delay is for our profit.   Thou art perhaps kept waiting in order that thy desires may be more fervent.   God knows that delay will quicken and increase desire, and that if He keeps thee waiting thou wilt see thy necessity more clearly, and wilt seek more earnestly ; and that thou wilt prize the mercy all the more for its long tarrying.   There may also be something wrong in thee which has need to be removed, before the joy of the Lord is given.   Perhaps thy views of the Gospel plan are confused, or thou mayest be placing some little reliance on thyself, instead of trusting simply and entirely to the Lord Jesus.   Or, God makes thee tarry awhile that He may the more fully display the riches of His grace to thee at last. Thy prayers are all filed in heaven, and if not immediately answered they are certainly not forgotten, but in a little while shall be fulfilled to thy delight and satisfaction.   Let not despair make thee silent, but continue instant in earnest supplication.

" My people shall dwell in quiet resting places."
Isaiah xxxii. 18.

PEACE and rest belong not to the unregenerate, they are the peculiar possession of the Lord's people, and of them only. The God of Peace gives perfect peace to those whose hearts are stayed upon Him. When man was unfallen, his God gave him the flowery bowers of Eden as his quiet resting places; alas! how soon sin blighted the fair abode of innocence. In the day of universal wrath when the flood swept away a guilty race, the chosen family were quietly secured in the resting-place of the ark, which floated them from the old condemned world into the new earth of the rainbow and the covenant, herein typifying Jesus, the ark of our salvation. Israel rested safely beneath the blood-besprinkled habitations of Egypt when the destroying angel smote the first-born; and in the wilderness the shadow of the pillar of cloud, and the flowing rock, gave the weary pilgrims sweet repose. At this hour we rest in the promises of our faithful God, knowing that His words are full of truth and power; we rest in the doctrines of His word, which are consolation itself; we rest in the covenant of His grace, which is a haven of delight. More highly favoured are we than David in Adullam, or Jonah beneath his gourd, for none can invade or destroy our shelter. The person of Jesus is the quiet resting-place of His people, and when we draw near to Him in the breaking of bread, in the hearing of the word, the searching of the Scriptures, prayer, or praise, we find any form of approach to Him to be the return of peace to our spirits.

" I hear the words of love, I gaze upon the blood,
  I see the mighty sacrifice, and I have peace with God.
'Tis everlasting peace, sure as Jehovah's name,
'Tis stable as His steadfast throne, for evermore the same :
The clouds may go and come, and storms may sweep my sky,
This blood-sealed friendship changes not, the cross is
    ever nigh."

" So shall we ever be with the Lord."—1 Thess. iv. 17.

VEN the sweetest visits from Christ, how short they are—and how transitory! One moment our eyes see Him, and we rejoice with joy unspeakable and full of glory, but again a little time and we do not see Him, for our beloved withdraws Himself from us; like a roe or a young hart he leaps over the mountains of division; He is gone to the land of spices, and feeds no more among the lilies.

> " If to-day he deigns to bless us
> With a sense of pardoned sin,
> He to-morrow may distress us,
> Make us feel the plague within."

Oh, how sweet the prospect of the time when we shall not behold Him at a distance, but see Him face to face : when He shall not be as a wayfaring man tarrying but for a night, but shall eternally enfold us in the bosom of His glory. We shall not see Him for a little season, but

> " Millions of years our wondering eyes,
> Shall o'er our Saviour's beauties rove ;
> And myriad ages we'll adore,
> The wonders of his love."

In heaven there shall be no interruptions from care or sin; no weeping shall dim our eyes; no earthly business shall distract our happy thoughts; we shall have nothing to hinder us from gazing for ever on the Sun of Righteousness with unwearied eyes. Oh, if it be so sweet to see Him now and then, how sweet to gaze on that blessed face for aye, and never have a cloud rolling between, and never have to turn one's eyes away to look on a world of weariness and woe! Blest day, when wilt thou dawn? Rise, O unsetting sun! The joys of sense may leave us as soon as they will, for this shall make glorious amends. If to die is but to enter into uninterrupted communion with Jesus, then death is indeed gain, and the black drop is swallowed up in a sea of victory.

" Whose heart the Lord opened."—Acts xvi. 14.

IN Lydia's conversion there are many points of interest. It was brought about by *providential circumstances.* She was a seller of purple, of the city of Thyatira, but just at the right time for hearing Paul we find her at Philippi ; providence, which is the handmaid of grace, led her to the right spot. Again, *grace was preparing her soul for the blessing*— grace preparing for grace. She did not know the Saviour, but as a Jewess, she knew many truths which were excellent stepping-stones to a knowledge of Jesus. Her conversion took place in the use of the means. On the Sabbath she went when prayer was wont to be made, and there prayer was heard. Never neglect the means of grace ; God *may* bless us when we are not in His house, but we have the greater reason to hope that He *will* when we are in communion with His saints. Observe the words, "Whose heart *the Lord* opened." She did not open her own heart. Her prayers did not do it ; Paul did not do it. The Lord Himself must open the heart, to receive the things which make for our peace. He alone can put the key into the hole of the door and open it, and get admittance for Himself. He is the heart's master as He is the heart's maker. The first outward evidence of the opened heart was *obedience.* As soon as Lydia had believed in Jesus, she was baptized. It is a sweet sign of a humble and broken heart, when the child of God is willing to obey a command which is not essential to his salvation, which is not forced upon him by a selfish fear of condemnation, but is a simple act of obedience and of communion with his Master. The next evidence was *love,* manifesting itself in acts of grateful kindness to the apostles. Love to the saints has ever been a mark of the true convert. Those who do nothing for Christ or His church, give but sorry evidence of an "opened" heart. Lord, evermore give me an opened heart.

" Faithful is He that calleth you, who also will do it."
1 Thessalonians v. 24.

HEAVEN is a place where we shall never sin; where we shall cease our constant watch against an indefatigable enemy, because there will be no tempter to ensnare our feet. There the wicked cease from troubling, and the weary are at rest. Heaven is the "undefiled inheritance;" it is the land of perfect holiness, and therefore of complete security. But do not the saints even on earth sometimes taste the joys of blissful security? The doctrine of God's word is, that all who are in union with the Lamb are safe; that all the righteous shall hold on their way; that those who have committed their souls to the keeping of Christ shall find him a faithful and immutable preserver. Sustained by such a doctrine we can enjoy security even on earth; not that high and glorious security which renders us free from every slip, but that holy security which arises from the sure promise of Jesus that none who believe in Him shall ever perish, but shall be with Him where He is. Believer, let us often reflect with joy on the doctrine of the perseverance of the saints, and honour the faithfulness of our God by a holy confidence in Him.

May our God bring home to you a sense of your safety in Christ Jesus! May He assure you that your name is graven on His hand; and whisper in your ear the promise, " Fear not, I am with thee." Look upon Him, the great Surety of the covenant, as faithful and true, and, therefore, bound and engaged to present you, the weakest of the family, with all the chosen race, before the throne of God; and in such a sweet contemplation you will drink the juice of the spiced wine of the Lord's pomegranate, and taste the dainty fruits of Paradise. You will have an antepast of the enjoyments which ravish the souls of the perfect saints above, if you can believe with unstaggering faith that " faithful is He that calleth you, who also will do it."

"Ye serve the Lord Christ."—Colossians iii. 24.

O what choice order of officials was this word spoken? To kings who proudly boast a right divine? Ah, no! too often do they serve themselves or Satan, and forget the God whose sufferance permits them to wear their mimic majesty for their little hour. Speaks then the apostle to those so-called "right reverend fathers in God," the bishops, or "the venerable the archdeacons"? No, indeed, Paul knew nothing of these mere inventions of man. Not even to pastors and teachers, or to the wealthy and esteemed among believers, was this word spoken, but to servants, ay, and to slaves. Among the toiling multitudes, the journeymen, the day labourers, the domestic servants, the drudges of the kitchen, the apostle found, as we find still, some of the Lord's chosen, and to them he says, "Whatsoever ye do, do it heartily, as to the Lord, and not unto men; knowing that of the Lord ye shall receive the reward of the inheritance: for ye serve the Lord Christ." This saying ennobles the weary routine of earthly employments, and sheds a halo around the most humble occupations. To wash feet may be servile, but to wash *His* feet is royal work. To unloose the shoe-latchet is poor employ, but to unloose the great Master's shoe is a princely privilege. The shop, the barn, the scullery, and the smithy become temples when men and women do all to the glory of God! Then "divine service" is not a thing of a few hours and a few places, but all life becomes holiness unto the Lord, and every place and thing, as consecrated as the tabernacle and its golden candlestick.

"Teach me, my God and King, in all things Thee to see;
And what I do in anything to do it as to Thee.
All may of Thee partake, nothing can be so mean,
Which with this tincture, *for Thy sake*, will not grow bright and clean.
A servant with this clause makes drudgery divine;
Who sweeps a room, as for Thy laws, makes that and the action fine."

" *His ways are everlasting.*"—Habakkuk iii. 6.

HAT He hath done at one time, He will do yet again. Man's ways are variable, but God's ways are everlasting. There are many reasons for this most comforting truth: among them are the following—the Lord's ways are *the result of wise deliberation;* He ordereth all things according to the counsel of His own will. Human action is frequently the hasty result of passion, or fear, and is followed by regret and alteration; but nothing can take the Almighty by surprise, or happen otherwise than He has foreseen. His ways are *the outgrowth of an immutable character,* and in them the fixed and settled attributes of God are clearly to be seen. Unless the Eternal One Himself can undergo change, His ways, which are Himself in action, must remain for ever the same. Is He eternally just, gracious, faithful, wise, tender?—then His ways must ever be distinguished for the same excellences. Beings act according to their nature : when those natures change, their conduct varies also; but since God cannot know the shadow of a turning, His ways will abide everlastingly the same. Moreover there is no reason from without which could reverse the divine ways, since they are *the embodiment of irresistible might.* The earth is said, by the prophet, to be cleft with rivers, mountains tremble, the deep lifts up its hands, and sun and moon stand still, when Jehovah marches forth for the salvation of His people. Who can stay His hand, or say unto him, What doest Thou ? But it is not might alone which gives stability ; God's ways are *the manifestation of the eternal principles of right,* and therefore can never pass away. Wrong breeds decay and involves ruin, but the true and the good have about them a vitality which ages cannot diminish.

This morning let us go to our heavenly Father with confidence, remembering that Jesus Christ is the same yesterday, to-day, and for ever, and in Him the Lord is ever gracious to His people.

"They have dealt treacherously against the Lord."—Hosea v. 7.

BELIEVER, here is a sorrowful truth! Thou art the beloved of the Lord, redeemed by blood, called by grace, preserved in Christ Jesus, accepted in the Beloved, on thy way to heaven, and yet, "thou hast dealt treacherously" with God, thy best friend; treacherously with Jesus, whose thou art; treacherously with the Holy Spirit, by whom thou hast been quickened unto life eternal! How treacherous you have been in the matter of vows and promises. Do you remember the love of your espousals, that happy time—the springtide of your spiritual life? Oh, how closely did you cling to your Master then! saying, "He shall never charge me with indifference; my feet shall never grow slow in the way of His service; I will not suffer my heart to wander after other loves; in Him is every store of sweetness ineffable. I give all up for my Lord Jesus' sake." Has it been so? Alas! if conscience speak, it will say, "He who promised so well has performed most ill. Prayer has oftentimes been slurred—it has been short, but not sweet; brief, but not fervent. Communion with Christ has been forgotten. Instead of a heavenly mind, there have been carnal cares, worldly vanities and thoughts of evil. Instead of service, there has been disobedience; instead of fervency, lukewarmness; instead of patience, petulance; instead of faith, confidence in an arm of flesh; and as a soldier of the cross there has been cowardice, disobedience, and desertion, to a very shameful degree." "Thou hast dealt treacherously." Treachery to Jesus! what words shall be used in denouncing it? Words little avail: let our penitent thoughts execrate the sin which is so surely in us. Treacherous to Thy wounds, O Jesus! Forgive us, and let us not sin again! How shameful to be treacherous to Him who never forgets us, but who this day stands with our names engraven on His breastplate before the eternal throne.

" Salt without prescribing how much."—Ezra vii. 22.

SALT was used in every offering made by fire unto the Lord, and from its preserving and purifying properties it was the grateful emblem of divine grace in the soul. It is worthy of our attentive regard that, when Artaxerxes gave salt to Ezra the priest, he set no limit to the quantity, and we may be quite certain that when the King of kings distributes grace among His royal priesthood, the supply is not cut short by *Him*. Often are we straitened in ourselves, but never in the Lord. He who chooses to gather much manna will find that he may have as much as he desires. There is no such famine in Jerusalem that the citizens should eat their bread by weight and drink their water by measure. Some things in the economy of grace are measured; for instance our vinegar and gall are given us with such exactness that we never have a single drop too much, but of the salt of grace no stint is made, "Ask what thou wilt and it shall be given unto thee." Parents need to lock up the fruit cupboard, and the sweet jars, but there is no need to keep the salt-box under lock and key, for few children will eat too greedily from that. A man may have too much money, or too much honour, but he cannot have too much grace. When Jeshurun waxed fat in the flesh, he kicked against God, but there is no fear of a man's becoming too full of grace: a *plethora* of grace is impossible. More wealth brings more care, but more grace brings more joy. Increased wisdom is increased sorrow, but abundance of the Spirit is fulness of joy. Believer, go to the throne for a large supply of heavenly salt. It will season thine afflictions, which are unsavoury without salt; it will preserve thy heart which corrupts if salt be absent, and it will kill thy sins even as salt kills reptiles. Thou needest much; seek much, and have much.

"I will make thy windows of agates."—Isaiah liv. 12.

THE church is most instructively symbolised by a building erected by heavenly power, and designed by divine skill. Such a spiritual house must not be dark, for the Israelites had light in their dwellings; there must therefore be windows to let the light in and to allow the inhabitants to gaze abroad. These windows are *precious* as agates: the ways in which the church beholds her Lord and heaven, and spiritual truth in general, are to be had in the highest esteem. Agates are *not the most transparent* of gems, they are but semi-pellucid at the best:

> "Our knowledge of that life is small,
> Our eye of faith is dim."

Faith is one of these precious agate windows, but alas! it is often so misty and beclouded, that we see but darkly, and mistake much that we do see. Yet if we cannot gaze through windows of diamonds and know even as we are known, it is a glorious thing to behold the altogether lovely One, even though the glass be hazy as the agate. *Experience* is another of these dim but precious windows, yielding to us a subdued religious light, in which we see the sufferings of the Man of Sorrows, through our own afflictions. Our weak eyes could not endure windows of transparent glass to let in the Master's glory, but when they are dimmed with weeping, the beams of the Sun of Righteousness are tempered, and shine through the windows of agate with a soft radiance inexpressibly soothing to tempted souls. *Sanctification,* as it conforms us to our Lord, is another agate window. Only as we become heavenly can we comprehend heavenly things. The pure in heart see a pure God. Those who are like Jesus see Him as He is. Because we are so little like Him, the window is but agate; because we are somewhat like Him, it is agate. We thank God for what we have, and long for more. When shall we see God and Jesus, and heaven and truth, face to face?

" They go from strength to strength."—Psalm lxxxiv. 7.

THEY go *from strength to strength*. There are various renderings of these words, but all of them contain the idea of progress.

Our own good translation of the authorized version is enough for us this morning. "They go from strength to strength." That is, they grow stronger and stronger. Usually, if we are walking, we go from strength to weakness ; we start fresh and in good order for our journey, but by-and-by the road is rough, and the sun is hot, we sit down by the wayside, and then again painfully pursue our weary way. But the Christian pilgrim having obtained fresh supplies of grace, is as vigorous after years of toilsome travel and struggle as when he first set out. He may not be quite so elate and buoyant, nor perhaps quite so hot and hasty in his zeal as he once was, but he is much stronger in all that constitutes real power, and travels, if more slowly, far more surely. Some gray-haired veterans have been as firm in their grasp of truth, and as zealous in diffusing it, as they were in their younger days ; but, alas, it must be confessed it is often otherwise, for the love of many waxes cold and iniquity abounds, but this is their own sin and not the fault of the promise which still holds good : "The youths shall faint and be weary, and the young men shall utterly fall, but they that wait upon the Lord shall renew their strength ; they shall mount up with wings as eagles, they shall run and not be weary, and they shall walk and not faint." Fretful spirits sit down and trouble themselves about the future. "Alas !" say they, "we go from affliction to affliction." Very true, O thou of little faith, but then thou goest from strength to strength also. Thou shalt never find a bundle of affliction which has not bound up in the midst of it sufficient grace. God will give the strength of ripe manhood with the burden allotted to full-grown shoulders.

" I am crucified with Christ."—Galatians ii. 20.

THE Lord Jesus Christ acted in what He did as a great public representative person, and His dying upon the cross was the virtual dying of all His people. Then all His saints rendered unto justice what was due, and made an expiation to divine vengeance for all their sins. The apostle of the Gentiles delighted to think that as one of Christ's chosen people, he died upon the cross in Christ. He did more than believe this doctrinally, he accepted it confidently, resting his hope upon it. He believed that by virtue of Christ's death, he had satisfied divine justice, and found reconciliation with God. Beloved, what a blessed thing it is when the soul can, as it were, stretch itself upon the cross of Christ, and feel, "I am dead; the law has slain me, and I am therefore free from its power, because in my Surety I have borne the curse, and in the person of my Substitute the whole that the law could do, by way of condemnation, has been executed upon me, for I am crucified with Christ."

But Paul meant even more than this. He not only believed in Christ's death, and trusted in it, but he actually felt its power in himself in causing the crucifixion of his old corrupt nature. When he saw the pleasures of sin, he said, "I cannot enjoy these: I am dead to them." Such is the experience of every true Christian. Having received Christ, he is to this world as one who is utterly dead. Yet, while conscious of death to the world, he can, at the same time, exclaim with the apostle, "Nevertheless I live." He is fully alive unto God. The Christian's life is a matchless riddle. No worldling can comprehend it; even the believer himself cannot understand it. Dead, yet alive! crucified with Christ, and yet at the same time risen with Christ in newness of life! Union with the suffering, bleeding Saviour, and death to the world and sin, are soul-cheering things. O for more enjoyment of them!

" Orpah kissed her mother-in-law; but Ruth clave unto her."
Ruth i. 14.

BOTH of them had an affection for Naomi, and
therefore set out with her upon her return to
the land of Judah. But the hour of test came ;
Naomi most unselfishly set before each of them the trials
which awaited them, and bade them if they cared for
ease and comfort to return to their Moabitish friends.
At first both of them declared that they would cast in
their lot with the Lord's people ; but upon still further
consideration Orpah with much grief and a respectful
kiss left her mother in law, and her people, and her
God, and went back to her idolatrous friends, while
Ruth with all her heart gave herself up to the God of her
mother in law. It is one thing to love the ways of the
Lord when all is fair, and quite another to cleave to
them under all discouragements and difficulties. The
kiss of outward profession is very cheap and easy, but
the practical cleaving to the Lord, which must show
itself in holy decision for truth and holiness, is not so
small a matter. How stands the case with us, is our
heart fixed upon Jesus, is the sacrifice bound with cords
to the horns of the altar ? Have we counted the cost,
and are we solemnly ready to suffer all worldly loss for
the Master's sake ? The after gain will be an abundant
recompense, for Egypt's treasures are not to be compared with the glory to be revealed. Orpah is heard
of no more ; in glorious ease and idolatrous pleasure
her life melts into the gloom of death ; but Ruth lives
in history and in heaven, for grace has placed her in
the noble line whence sprung the King of kings.
Blessed among women shall those be who for Christ's
sake can renounce all ; but forgotten and worse than
forgotten shall those be who in the hour of temptation
do violence to conscience and turn back unto the world.
O that this morning we may not be content with the
form of devotion, which may be no better than Orpah's
kiss, but may the Holy Spirit work in us a cleaving of
our whole heart to our Lord Jesus.

"And lay thy foundations with sapphires."—Isaiah liv. 11.

NOT only that which is seen of the church of God, but that which is unseen, is fair and precious. Foundations are out of sight, and so long as they are firm it is not expected that they should be valuable; but in Jehovah's work everything is of a piece, nothing slurred, nothing mean. The deep foundations of the work of grace are as sapphires for preciousness, no human mind is able to measure their glory. We build upon *the covenant of grace,* which is firmer than adamant, and as enduring as jewels upon which age spends itself in vain. Sapphire foundations are eternal, and the covenant abides throughout the lifetime of the Almighty. Another foundation is *the person of the Lord Jesus,* which is clear and spotless, everlasting and beautiful as the sapphire; blending in one the deep blue of earth's ever rolling ocean and the azure of its all embracing sky. Once might our Lord have been likened to the ruby as He stood covered with his own blood, but now we see Him radiant with the soft blue of love, love abounding, deep, eternal. Our eternal hopes are built upon *the justice and the faithfulness of God,* which are clear and cloudless as the sapphire. We are not saved by a compromise, by mercy defeating justice, or law suspending its operations; no, we defy the eagle's eye to detect a flaw in the groundwork of our confidence— our foundation is of sapphire, and will endure the fire.

The Lord Himself has laid the foundation of His people's hopes. It is matter for grave enquiry whether *our* hopes are built upon such a basis. Good works and ceremonies are not a foundation of sapphires, but of wood, hay, and stubble; neither are they laid by God, but by our own conceit. Foundations will all be tried ere long: woe unto him whose lofty tower shall come down with a crash, because based on a quicksand. He who is built on sapphires may await storm or fire with equanimity, for he shall abide the test.

" Come unto me."—Matt. xi. 28.

THE cry of the Christian religion is the gentle word, "Come." The Jewish law harshly said, "Go, take heed unto thy steps as to the path in which thou shalt walk. Break the commandments, and thou shalt perish ; keep them, and thou shalt live." The law was a dispensation of terror, which drove men before it as with a scourge ; the gospel draws with bands of love. Jesus is the good Shepherd going before His sheep, bidding them follow Him, and ever leading them onwards with the sweet word, " Come." The law repels, the gospel attracts. The law shows the distance which there is between God and man ; the gospel bridges that awful chasm, and brings the sinner across it.

From the first moment of your spiritual life until you are ushered into glory, the language of Christ to you will be, " *Come, come* unto me." As a mother puts out her finger to her little child and woos it to walk by saying, "Come," even so does Jesus. He will always be ahead of you, bidding you follow Him as the soldier follows his captain. He will always go before you to pave your way, and clear your path, and you shall hear His animating voice calling you after Him all through life ; while in the solemn hour of death, His sweet words with which He shall usher you into the heavenly world shall be—" Come, ye blessed of my Father."

Nay, further, this is not only Christ's cry to you, but, if you be a believer, this is your cry to Christ— "Come ! come !" You will be longing for his second advent ; you will be saying, "Come quickly, even so come Lord Jesus." You will be panting for nearer and closer communion with Him. As His voice to you is "Come," your response to Him will be, " Come, Lord, and abide with me. Come, and occupy alone the throne of my heart ; reign there without a rival, and consecrate me entirely to Thy service."

"*Yea, thou heardest not; yea, thou knewest not; yea, from that time that thine ear was not opened.*"—Isaiah xlviii. 8.

IT is painful to remember that, in a certain degree, this accusation may be laid at the door of *believers*, who too often are in a measure *spiritually insensible.* We may well bewail ourselves that *we* do not hear the voice of God as we ought, "Yea, thou heardest not." There are gentle motions of the Holy Spirit in the soul which are unheeded by us : there are whisperings of divine command and of heavenly love which are alike unobserved by our leaden intellects. Alas ! we have been *carelessly ignorant—* "Yea, thou knewest not." There are matters within which we ought to have seen, corruptions which have made headway unnoticed ; sweet affections which are being blighted like flowers in the frost, untended by us ; glimpses of the divine face which might be perceived if we did not wall up the windows of our soul. But we "have not known." As we think of it we are humbled in the deepest self-abasement. How must we adore the grace of God as we learn from the context that all this folly and ignorance, on our part, was *foreknown by God*, and, notwithstanding that foreknowledge, He yet has been pleased to deal with us in a way of mercy ! Admire the marvellous sovereign grace which could have chosen us in the sight of all this ! Wonder at the price that was paid for us when .Christ knew what we should be ! He who hung upon the cross foresaw us as unbelieving, backsliding, cold of heart, indifferent, careless, lax in prayer, and yet He said, "I am the Lord thy God, the Holy One of Israel, thy Saviour. . . . Since thou wast precious in My sight, thou hast been honourable, and I have loved thee : therefore will I give men for thee, and people for thy life" ! O redemption, how wondrously resplendent dost thou shine when we think how black we are ! O Holy Spirit, give us henceforth the hearing ear, the understanding heart !

" I remember thee."—Jer. ii. 2.

ET us note that Christ delights to think upon
His Church, and to look upon her beauty.
As the bird returneth often to its nest, and as
the wayfarer hastens to his home, so doth the mind
continually pursue the object of its choice.   We cannot look too often upon that face which we love ; we
desire always to have our precious things in our sight.
It is even so with our Lord Jesus.   From all eternity
"His delights were with the sons of men;"   His
thoughts rolled onward to the time when His elect
should be born into the world ; He viewed them in
the mirror of His foreknowledge.   "In Thy book,"
He says, "all my members were written, which in
continuance were fashioned, when as yet there was
none of them." (Ps. cxxxix. 16.)   When the world
was set upon its pillars, He was there, and He set the
bounds of the people according to the number of the
children of Israel.   Many a time before his incarnation, He descended to this lower earth in the similitude of a man ; on the plains of Mamre, (Gen. xviii.)
by the brook of Jabbok, (Gen. xxxii. 24—30,) beneath
the walls of Jericho, (Josh. v. 13,) and in the fiery
furnace of Babylon, (Dan. iii. 19, 25,) the Son of Man
visited His people.   Because His soul delighted in
them, He could not rest away from them, for His
heart longed after them. Never were they absent from
His heart, for He had written their names upon His
hands, and graven them upon His side.   As the breastplate containing the names of the tribes of Israel was
the most brilliant ornament worn by the high priest,
so the names of Christ's elect were His most precious
jewels, and glittered on His heart.   We may often
forget to meditate upon the perfections of our Lord,
but He never ceases to remember us.   Let us chide
ourselves for past forgetfulness, and pray for grace ever
to bear Him in fondest remembrance.   Lord, paint
upon the eyeballs of my soul the image of thy Son.

"I am the door: by Me if any man enter in, he shall be saved, and shall go in and out, and find pasture."—John x. 9.

JESUS, the great I AM, is the entrance into the true church, and the way of access to God Himself. He gives to the man who comes to God by Him four choice privileges.

1. *He shall be saved.* The fugitive manslayer passed the gate of the city of refuge, and was safe. Noah entered the door of the ark, and was secure. None can be lost who take Jesus as the door of faith to their souls. Entrance through Jesus into peace is the guarantee of entrance by the same door into heaven. Jesus it the only door, an open door, a wide door, a safe door; and blessed is he who rests all his hope of admission to glory upon the crucified Redeemer.

2. *He shall go in.* He shall be privileged to go in among the divine family, sharing the children's bread, and participating in all their honours and enjoyments. He shall go in to the chambers of communion, to the banquets of love, to the treasures of the covenant, to the storehouses of the promises. He shall go in unto the King of kings in the power of the Holy Spirit, and the secret of the Lord shall be with him.

3. *He shall go out.* This blessing is much forgotten. We go out into the world to labour and suffer, but what a mercy to go in the name and power of Jesus! We are called to bear witness to the truth, to cheer the disconsolate, to warn the careless, to win souls, and to glorify God; and as the angel said to Gideon, "Go in this thy might," even thus the Lord would have us proceed as His messengers in His name and strength.

4. *He shall find pasture.* He who knows Jesus shall never want. Going in and out shall be alike helpful to him: in fellowship with God he shall grow, and in watering others he shall be watered. Having made Jesus his all, he shall find all in Jesus. His soul shall be as a watered garden, and as a well of water whose waters fail not.

"Rend your heart, and not your garments."—Joel ii. 13.

GARMENT-RENDING and other outward signs of religious emotion, are *easily manifested* and are *frequently hypocritical:* but to feel true repentance is far more difficult, and consequently far less common. Men will attend to the most multiplied and minute ceremonial regulations—for such things are *pleasing to the flesh*—but true religion is too humbling, too heart-searching, too thorough for the tastes of carnal men ; they prefer something more ostentatious, flimsy, and worldly. Outward observances are *temporarily comfortable;* eye and ear are pleased ; self-conceit is fed, and self-righteousness is puffed up : but they are *ultimately delusive,* for in the article of death, and at the day of judgment, the soul needs something more substantial than ceremonies and rituals to lean upon. Apart from vital godliness all religion is *utterly vain;* offered without a sincere heart, every form of worship is a solemn sham and an impudent mockery of the majesty of heaven.

HEART-RENDING is *divinely wrought* and *solemnly felt.* It is a secret grief which is *personally experienced,* not in mere form, but as a deep, soul-moving work of the Holy Spirit upon the inmost heart of each believer. It is not a matter to be merely talked of and believed in, but keenly and sensitively felt in every living child of the living God. It is *powerfully humiliating,* and *completely sin-purging;* but then it is *sweetly preparative* for those gracious consolations which proud unhumbled spirits are unable to receive ; and it is *distinctly discriminating,* for it belongs to the elect of God, and to them alone.

The text commands us to rend our hearts, but they are naturally hard as marble : how, then, can this be done ? We must take them to Calvary : a dying Saviour's voice rent the rocks once, and it is as powerful now. O blessed Spirit, let us hear the death-cries of Jesus, and our hearts shall be rent even as men rend their vestures in the day of lamentation.

---

*" Be thou diligent to know the state of thy flocks, and look
well to thy herds."*—Proverbs xxvii. 23.

EVERY wise merchant will occasionally hold a
stock-taking, when he will cast up his accounts, examine what he has on hand, and
ascertain decisively whether his trade is prosperous
or declining. Every man who is wise in the kingdom
of heaven, will cry, " Search me, O God, and try me ;"
and he will frequently set apart special seasons for
self-examination, to discover whether things are right
between God and his soul. The God whom we worship is a great heart-searcher ; and of old His servants knew Him as "the Lord which searcheth the
heart and trieth the reins of the children of men."
Let me stir you up in His name to make diligent
search and solemn trial of your state, lest you come
short of the promised rest. That which every wise
man does, that which God Himself does with us all, I
exhort you to do with yourself this evening. Let
the oldest saint look well to the fundamentals of his
piety, for grey heads may cover black hearts : and let
not the young professor despise the word of warning,
for the greenness of youth may be joined to the
rottenness of hypocrisy. Every now and then a
cedar falls into our midst. The enemy still continues
to sow tares among the wheat. It is not my aim
to introduce doubts and fears into your mind ; nay,
verily, but I shall hope the rather that the rough
wind of self-examination may help to drive them away.
It is not security, but carnal security, which we would
kill ; not confidence, but fleshly confidence, which we
would overthrow ; not peace, but false peace, which we
would destroy. By the precious blood of Christ, which
was not shed to make you a hypocrite, but that sincere
souls might show forth His praise, I beseech you,
search and look, lest at the last it be said of you,
" Mene, Mene, Tekel : thou art weighed in the balances,
and art found wanting."

" The lot is cast into the lap, but the whole disposing thereof is of the Lord."—Prov. xvi. 33.

IF the disposal of the lot is the Lord's, whose is the arrangement of our whole life? If the simple casting of a lot is guided by Him, how much more the events of our entire life—especially when we are told by our blessed Saviour: " The very hairs of your head are all numbered: not a sparrow falleth to the ground without your Father." It would bring a holy calm over your mind, dear friend, if you were always to remember this. It would so relieve your mind from anxiety, that you would be the better able to walk in patience, quiet, and cheerfulness as a Christian should. When a man is anxious he cannot pray with faith; when he is troubled about the world, he cannot serve his Master, his thoughts are serving himself. If you would " seek first the kingdom of God and His righteousness," all things would then be added unto you. You are meddling with Christ's business, and neglecting your own when you fret about your lot and circumstances. You have been trying "providing" work and forgetting that it is yours to obey. Be wise and attend to the obeying, and let Christ manage the providing. Come and survey your Father's storehouse, and ask whether He will let you starve while He has laid up so great an abundance in His garner? Look at His heart of mercy; see if that can ever prove unkind! Look at His inscrutable wisdom; see if that will ever be at fault. Above all, look up to Jesus Christ your Intercessor, and ask yourself, while He pleads, can your Father deal ungraciously with you? If He remembers even sparrows, will He forget one of the least of His poor children? " Cast thy burden upon the Lord, and He will sustain thee. He will never suffer the righteous to be moved."

> My soul, rest happy in thy low estate,
> Nor hope nor wish to be esteem'd or great;
> To take the impress of the Will Divine,
> Be that thy glory, and those riches thine.

" And there was no more sea."—Revelation xxi. 1.

SCARCELY could we rejoice at the thought of losing the glorious old ocean: the new heavens and the new earth are none the fairer to our imagination, if, indeed, literally there is to be no great and wide sea, with its gleaming waves and shelly shores. Is not the text to be read as a metaphor, tinged with the prejudice with which the Oriental mind universally regarded the sea in the olden times? A real physical world without a sea it is mournful to imagine, it would be an iron ring without the sapphire which made it precious. There must be a spiritual meaning here. In the new dispensation there will be no *division*—the sea separates nations and sunders peoples from each other. To John in Patmos the deep waters were like prison walls, shutting him out from his brethren and his work: there shall be no such barriers in the world to come. Leagues of rolling billows lie between us and many a kinsman whom to-night we prayerfully remember, but in the bright world to which we go there shall be unbroken fellowship for all the redeemed family. In this sense there shall be no more sea. The sea is the emblem of *change;* with its ebbs and flows, its glassy smoothness and its mountainous billows, its gentle murmurs and its tumultuous roarings, it is never long the same. Slave of the fickle winds and the changeful moon, its instability is proverbial. In this mortal state we have too much of this; earth is constant only in her inconstancy, but in the heavenly state all mournful change shall be unknown, and with it all fear of *storm* to wreck our hopes and drown our joys. The sea of glass glows with a glory unbroken by a wave. No tempest howls along the peaceful shores of paradise. Soon shall we reach that happy land where partings, and changes, and storms shall be ended! Jesus will waft us there. Are we in Him or not? This is the grand question.

" Yea, I have loved thee with an everlasting love."
Jer. xxxi. 3.

SOMETIMES the Lord Jesus tells His Church His love thoughts. "He does not think it enough behind her back to tell it, but in her very presence He says, 'Thou art all fair, my love.' It is true, this is not His ordinary method; He is a wise lover, and knows when to keep back the intimation of love and when to let it out; but there are times when He will make no secret of it; times when He will put it beyond all dispute in the souls of His people."* The Holy Spirit is often pleased, in a most gracious manner, to witness with our spirits of the love of Jesus. He takes of the things of Christ and reveals them unto us. No voice is heard from the clouds, and no vision is seen in the night, but we have a testimony more sure than either of these. If an angel should fly from heaven and inform the saint personally of the Saviour's love to him, the evidence would not be one whit more satisfactory than that which is borne in the heart by the Holy Ghost. Ask those of the Lord's people who have lived the nearest to the gates of heaven, and they will tell you that they have had seasons when the love of Christ towards them has been a fact so clear and sure, that they could no more doubt it than they could question their own existence. Yes, beloved believer, you and I have had times of refreshing from the presence of the Lord, and then our faith has mounted to the topmost heights of assurance. We have had confidence to lean our heads upon the bosom of our Lord, and we have no more questioned our Master's affection to us than John did when in that blessed posture; nay, nor so much: for the dark question, "Lord, is it I that shall betray thee?" has been put far from us. He has kissed us with the kisses of His mouth, and killed our doubts by the closeness of His embrace. His love has been sweeter than wine to our souls.

* R. Erskine's Sermons.

" Call thy labourers, and give them their hire."
Matt. xx. 8.

GOD is a good paymaster; He pays His servants
while at work as well as when they have done
it; and one of His payments is this, *an easy
conscience.* If you have spoken faithfully of Jesus to
one person, when you go to bed at night you feel happy
in thinking, " I have this day discharged my conscience
of that man's blood." There is a great *comfort in
doing something for Jesus.* Oh, what a happiness to
place jewels in His crown, and give Him to see of the
travail of His soul! There is also very great reward
in *watching the first buddings of conviction in a soul!*
To say of that girl in the class, " She is tender of
heart, I do hope that there is the Lord's work within."
To go home and pray over that boy, who said something in the afternoon which made you think he
must know more of divine truth than you had feared!
Oh, the joy of hope! But as for *the joy of success!*
it is unspeakable. This joy, overwhelming as it is,
is a hungry thing—you pine for more of it. To be
a soul-winner is the happiest thing in the world.
With every soul you bring to Christ, you get a new
heaven upon earth. But who can conceive the bliss
which awaits us above! Oh, how sweet is that
sentence, " Enter thou into *the joy of thy Lord!*" Do
you know what the joy of Christ is over a saved sinner? This is the very joy which we are to possess in
heaven. Yes, when He mounts the throne, you shall
mount with Him. When the heavens ring with " Well
done, well done," you shall partake in the reward;
you have toiled with Him, you have suffered with
Him, you shall now reign with Him; you have sown
with Him, you shall reap with Him; your face was
covered with sweat like His, and your soul was
grieved for the sins of men as His soul was, now shall
your face be bright with heaven's splendour as is His
countenance, and now shall your soul be filled with
beatific joys even as His soul is.

" Yet He hath made with me an everlasting covenant."
2 Samuel xxiii. 5.

THIS covenant is *divine in its origin.* "HE hath
made with me an everlasting covenant." Oh
that great word HE! Stop, my soul. God,
the everlasting Father, has positively made a covenant
with thee ; yes, that God who spake the world into existence by a word ; He, stooping from His majesty, takes
hold of thy hand and makes a covenant with thee. Is
it not a deed, the stupendous condescension of which
might ravish our hearts for ever if we could really
understand it ? " HE hath made with me a covenant."
A king has not made a covenant with me—that were
somewhat ; but the Prince of the kings of the earth,
Shaddai, the Lord All-sufficient, the Jehovah of
ages, the everlasting Elohim, "He hath made with
me an everlasting covenant." But notice, *it is particular in its application.* "Yet hath he made with
ME an everlasting covenant." Here lies the sweetness of it to each believer. It is nought for me that
He made peace for the world ; I want to know whether
He made peace for *me!* It is little that He hath
made a covenant, I want to know whether He has
made a covenant *with me.* Blessed is the assurance
that He hath made a covenant with me! If God the
Holy Ghost gives me assurance of this, then His salvation is mine, His heart is mine, He himself is mine—
He is my God.

This covenant is *everlasting in its duration.* An
everlasting covenant means a covenant which had no
beginning, and which shall never, never end. How
sweet amidst all the uncertainties of life, to know
that " the foundation of the Lord standeth sure," and
o have God's own promise, "My covenant will I
not break, nor alter the thing that is gone out of my
lips." Like dying David, I will sing of this, even
though my house be not so with God as my heart
desireth.

"I clothed thee also with broidered work, and shod thee with badgers' skin, and I girded thee about with fine linen, and I covered thee with silk."—Ezekiel xvi. 10.

SEE with what matchless generosity the Lord provides for His people's apparel. They are so arrayed that the divine skill is seen producing an unrivalled *broidered work*, in which every attribute takes its part and every divine beauty is revealed. No art like the art displayed in our salvation, no cunning workmanship like that beheld in the righteousness of the saints. Justification has engrossed learned pens in all ages of the church, and will be the theme of admiration in eternity. God has indeed "curiously wrought it." With all this elaboration there is mingled utility and durability, comparable to our being *shod with badgers' skins.* The animal here meant is unknown, but its skin covered the tabernacle, and formed one of the finest and strongest leathers known. The righteousness which is of God by faith endureth for ever, and he who is shod with this divine preparation will tread the desert safely, and may even set his foot upon the lion and the adder. Purity and dignity of our holy vesture are brought out in *the fine linen.* When the Lord sanctifies His people, they are clad as priests in pure white ; not the snow itself excels them ; they are in the eyes of men and angels fair to look upon, and even in the Lord's eyes they are without spot. Meanwhile the royal apparel is delicate and rich as *silk.* No expense is spared, no beauty withheld, no daintiness denied.

What, then ? Is there no inference from this ? Surely there is gratitude to be felt and joy to be expressed. Come, my heart, refuse not thy evening hallelujah ! Tune thy pipes ! Touch thy chords !

> " Strangely, my soul, art thou arrayed
>   By the Great Sacred Three !
> In sweetest harmony of praise
>   Let all thy powers agree."

" I will strengthen thee."—Isaiah xli. 10.

GOD has a strong reserve with which to discharge this engagement ; for he is able to do all things. Believer, till thou canst drain dry the ocean of omnipotence, till thou canst break into pieces the towering mountains of almighty strength, thou never needest to fear. Think not that the strength of man shall ever be able to overcome the power of God. Whilst the earth's huge pillars stand, thou hast enough reason to abide firm in thy faith. The same God who directs the earth in its orbit, who feeds the burning furnace of the sun, and trims the lamps of heaven, has promised to supply thee with daily strength. While He is able to uphold the universe, dream not that He will prove unable to fulfil His own promises. Remember what He did in the days of old, in the former generations. Remember how He spake and it was done ; how He commanded, and it stood fast. Shall He that created the world grow weary ? He hangeth the world upon nothing ; shall He who doth this be unable to support His children ? Shall He be unfaithful to His word for want of power ? Who is it that restrains the tempest ? Doth not He ride upon the wings of the wind, and make the clouds His chariots, and hold the ocean in the hollow of His hand ? How can He fail thee ? When He has put such a faithful promise as this on record, wilt thou for a moment indulge the thought that He has outpromised Himself, and gone beyond His power to fulfil ? Ah, no ! Thou canst doubt no longer.

O thou who art my God and my strength, I can believe that this promise shall be fulfilled, for the boundless reservoir of Thy grace can never be exhausted, and the overflowing storehouse of Thy strength can never be emptied by Thy friends or rifled by Thine enemies.

> " Now let the feeble all be strong,
> And make Jehovah's arm their song."

" The spot of His children."—Deuteronomy xxxii. 5.

WHAT is the secret spot which infallibly betokens the child of God? It were vain presumption to decide this upon our own judgment; but God's word reveals it to us, and we may tread surely where we have revelation to be our guide. Now, we are told concerning our Lord, "to as many as *received Him,* to them gave He power to become the sons of God, even to as many as believed on His name." Then, if I have received Christ Jesus into my heart, I am a child of God. That reception is described in the same verse as *believing on the name of Jesus Christ.* If, then, I believe on Jesus Christ's name—that is, simply from my heart trust myself with the crucified, but now exalted, Redeemer, I am a member of the family of the Most High. Whatever else I may not have, if I have this, I have the privilege to become a child of God. Our Lord Jesus puts it in another shape. "My sheep hear My voice, and I know them, and they follow Me." Here is the matter in a nutshell. Christ appears as a shepherd to His own sheep, not to others. As soon as He appears, His own sheep perceive Him—they trust Him, they are prepared to follow Him; He knows them, and they know Him—there is a mutual knowledge—there is a constant connection between them. Thus the one mark, the sure mark, the infallible mark of regeneration and adoption is a hearty faith in the appointed Redeemer. Reader, are you in doubt, are you uncertain whether you bear the secret mark of God's children? Then let not an hour pass over your head till you have said, "Search me, O God, and know my heart." Trifle not here, I adjure you! If you must trifle anywhere, let it be about some secondary matter: your health, if you will, or the title deeds of your estate; but about your soul, your never-dying soul and its eternal destinies, I beseech you to be in earnest. Make sure work for eternity.

" Friend, go up higher."—Luke xiv. 10.

WHEN first the life of grace begins in the soul, we do indeed draw near to God, but it is with great fear and trembling. The soul conscious of guilt, and humbled thereby, is overawed with the solemnity of its position ; it is cast to the earth by a sense of the grandeur of Jehovah, in whose presence it stands. With unfeigned bashfulness it takes the lowest room.

But, in after life, as the Christian grows in grace, although he will never forget the solemnity of his position, and will never lose that holy awe which must encompass a gracious man when he is in the presence of the God who can create or can destroy ; yet his fear has all its terror taken out of it ; it becomes a holy reverence, and no more an overshadowing dread. He is called up higher, to greater access to God in Christ Jesus. Then the man of God, walking amid the splendours of Deity, and veiling his face like the glorious cherubim, with those twin wings, the blood and righteousness of Jesus Christ, will, reverent and bowed in spirit, approach the throne ; and seeing there a God of love, of goodness, and of mercy, he will realize rather the covenant character of God than his absolute Deity. He will see in God rather His goodness than His greatness, and more of His love than of His majesty. Then will the soul, bowing still as humbly as aforetime, enjoy a more sacred liberty of intercession ; for while prostrate before the glory of the Infinite God, it will be sustained by the refreshing consciousness of being in the presence of boundless mercy and infinite love, and by the realisation of acceptance "in the beloved." Thus the believer is bidden to come up higher, and is enabled to exercise the privilege of rejoicing in God, and drawing near to Him in holy confidence, saying, "Abba, Father."

> " So may we go from strength to strength,
> And daily grow in grace,
> Till in Thine image raised at length,
> We see Thee face to face."

"The night also is Thine."—Psalm lxxiv. 16.

YES, Lord, Thou dost not abdicate Thy throne when the sun goeth down, nor dost Thou leave the world all through these long wintry nights to be the prey of evil; Thine eyes watch us as the stars, and Thine arms surround us as the zodiac belts the sky. The dews of kindly sleep and all the influences of the moon are in Thy hand, and the alarms and solemnities of night are equally with Thee. This is very sweet to me when watching through the midnight hours, or tossing to and fro in anguish. There are precious fruits put forth by the moon as well as by the sun : may my Lord make me to be a favoured partaker in them.

The night of affliction is as much under the arrangement and control of the Lord of Love as the bright summer days when all is bliss. Jesus is in the tempest. His love wraps the night about itself as a mantle, but to the eye of faith the sable robe is scarce a disguise. From the first watch of the night even unto the break of day the eternal Watcher observes His saints, and overrules the shades and dews of midnight for His people's highest good. We believe in no rival deities of good and evil contending for the mastery, but we hear the voice of Jehovah saying, "I create light and I create darkness; I, the Lord, do all these things."

Gloomy seasons of religious indifference and social sin are not exempted from the divine purpose. When the altars of truth are defiled, and the ways of God forsaken, the Lord's servants weep with bitter sorrow, but they may not despair, for the darkest eras are governed by the Lord, and shall come to their end at His bidding. What may seem defeat to us may be victory to Him.

> "Though enwrapt in gloomy night,
> We perceive no ray of light;
> Since the Lord Himself is here,
> 'Tis not meet that we should fear."

" For your sakes he became poor."—2 Cor. viii. 9.

THE Lord Jesus Christ was eternally *rich*, glorious, and exalted; but "though *He was rich*, yet for your sakes He became poor." As the rich saint cannot be true in his communion with his poor brethren unless of his substance he ministers to their necessities, so (the same rule holding with the head as between the members), it is impossible that our Divine Lord could have had fellowship with us unless He had imparted to us of His own abounding wealth, and had become poor to make us rich. Had He remained upon His throne of glory, and had we continued in the ruins of the fall without receiving His salvation, communion would have been impossible on both sides. Our position by the fall, apart from the covenant of grace, made it as impossible for fallen man to communicate with God as it is for Belial to be in concord with Christ. In order, therefore, that communion might be compassed, it was necessary that the rich kinsman should bestow his estate upon his poor relatives, that the righteous Saviour should give to His sinning brethren of His own perfection, and that we, the poor and guilty, should receive of his fulness grace for grace; that thus in giving and receiving, the one might descend from the heights, and the other ascend from the depths, and so be able to embrace each other in true and hearty fellowship. Poverty must be enriched by Him in whom are infinite treasures before it can venture to commune; and guilt must lose itself in imputed and imparted righteousness ere the soul can walk in fellowship with purity. Jesus must clothe His people in His own garments, or He cannot admit them into His palace of glory; and He must wash them in His own blood, or else they will be too defiled for the embrace of His fellowship.

O believer, herein is love! For *your sake* the Lord Jesus "became poor" that He might lift you up into communion with Himself.

" The glory of the Lord shall be revealed, and all flesh shall see it together."—Isaiah xl. 5.

WE anticipate the happy day when the whole world shall be converted to Christ; when the gods of the heathen shall be cast to the moles and the bats; when Romanism shall be exploded, and the crescent of Mohammed shall wane, never again to cast its baleful rays upon the nations; when kings shall bow down before the Prince of Peace, and all nations shall call their Redeemer blessed. Some despair of this. They look upon the world as a vessel breaking up and going to pieces, never to float again. We know that the world and all that is therein is one day to be burnt up, and afterwards we look for new heavens and for a new earth; but we cannot read our Bibles without the conviction that—

> " Jesus shall reign where'er the sun
> Does his successive journeys run."

We are not discouraged by the length of His delays; we are not disheartened by the long period which He allots to the church in which to struggle with little success and much defeat. We believe that God will never suffer this world, which has once seen Christ's blood shed upon it, to be always the devil's stronghold. Christ came hither to deliver this world from the detested sway of the powers of darkness. What a shout shall that be when men and angels shall unite to cry, " Hallelujah, hallelujah, for the Lord God Omnipotent reigneth!" What a satisfaction will it be in that day to have had a share in the fight, to have helped to break the arrows of the bow, and to have aided in winning the victory for our Lord! Happy are they who trust themselves with this conquering Lord, and who fight side by side with Him, doing their little in His name and by His strength! How unhappy are those on the side of evil! It is a losing side, and it is a matter wherein to lose is to lose and to be lost for ever. On whose side are you?

" Behold, a virgin shall conceive, and bear a son, and shall call his name Immanuel."—Isaiah vii. 14.

ET us to-day go down to Bethlehem, and in company with wondering shepherds and adoring Magi, let us see Him who was born King of the Jews, for we by faith can claim an interest in Him, and can sing, *"Unto us* a child is born, *unto us* a son is given."* Jesus is Jehovah incarnate, our Lord and our God, and yet our brother and friend; let us adore and admire. Let us notice at the very first glance *His miraculous conception.* It was a thing unheard of before, and unparalleled since, that a virgin should conceive and bear a Son. The first promise ran thus, *"The seed of the woman,"* not the offspring of the man. Since venturous woman led the way in the sin which brought forth Paradise lost, she, and she alone, ushers in the Regainer of Paradise. Our Saviour, although truly man, was as to His human nature the Holy One of God. Let us reverently bow before the holy Child whose innocence restores to manhood its ancient glory; and let us pray that He may be formed in us, the hope of glory. Fail not to note *His humble parentage.* His mother has been described simply as " a virgin," not a princess, or prophetess, nor a matron of large estate. True the blood of kings ran in her veins; nor was her mind a weak and untaught one, for she could sing most sweetly a song of praise; but yet how humble her position, how poor the man to whom she stood affianced, and how miserable the accommodation afforded to the new-born King!

Immanuel, God with us in our nature, in our sorrow, in our lifework, in our punishment, in our grave, and now with us, or rather we with Him, in resurrection, ascension, triumph, and Second Advent splendour.

"And it was so, when the days of their feasting were gone about, that Job sent and sanctified them, and rose up early in the morning, and offered burnt offerings according to the number of them all: for Job said, It may be that my sons have sinned, and cursed God in their hearts. Thus did Job continually."—Job i. 5.

WHAT the patriarch did early in the morning, after the family festivities, it will be well for the believer to do for himself ere he rests to-night.   Amid the cheerfulness of household gatherings it is easy to slide into sinful levities, and to forget our avowed character as Christians.   It ought not to be so, but so it is, that our days of feasting are very seldom days of sanctified enjoyment, but too frequently degenerate into unhallowed mirth.   There is a way of joy as pure and sanctifying as though one bathed in the rivers of Eden : holy gratitude should be quite as purifying an element as grief.   Alas! for our poor hearts, that facts prove that the house of mourning is better than the house of feasting.   Come, believer, in what have you sinned to-day ?   Have you been forgetful of your high calling ?   Have you been even as others in idle words and loose speeches ?   Then confess the sin, and fly to the sacrifice.   The sacrifice sanctifies.   The precious blood of the Lamb slain removes the guilt, and purges away the defilement of our sins of ignorance and carelessness.   This is the best ending of a Christmas-day—to wash anew in the cleansing fountain.   Believer, come to this sacrifice continually ; if it be so good to-night, it is good every night.   To live at the altar is the privilege of the royal priesthood ; to them sin, great as it is, is nevertheless no cause for despair, since they draw near yet again to the sin-atoning victim, and their conscience is purged from dead works.

Gladly I close this festive day,
  Grasping the altar's hallow'd horn ;
My slips and faults are washed away,
  The Lamb has all my trespass borne.

" The last Adam."—1 Cor. xv. 45.

JESUS is the federal head of his elect. As in Adam, every heir of flesh and blood has a personal interest, because he is the covenant head and representative of the race as considered under the law of works ; so under the law of grace, every redeemed soul is one with the Lord from heaven, since he is the Second Adam, the Sponsor and Substitute of the elect in the new covenant of love. The apostle Paul declares that Levi was in the loins of Abraham when Melchizedek met him : it is a certain truth that the believer was in the loins of Jesus Christ, the Mediator, when in old eternity the covenant settlements of grace were decreed, ratified, and made sure for ever. Thus, whatever Christ hath done, he hath wrought for the whole body of His Church. We were crucified in Him and buried with Him, (Read Col. ii. 10—13,) and to make it still more wonderful, we are risen with Him and even ascended with Him to the seats on high. (Eph. ii. 6.) It is thus that the Church has fulfilled the law, and is " accepted in *the beloved*." It is thus that she is regarded with complacency by the just Jehovah, for he views her in Jesus, and does not look upon her as separate from her covenant head. As the Anointed Redeemer of Israel, Christ Jesus has nothing distinct from His Church, but all that He has He holds for her. Adam's righteousness was ours so long as he maintained it, and his sin was ours the moment that he committed it ; and in the same manner, all that the Second Adam is or does, is ours as well as His, seeing that He is our representative. Here is the foundation of the covenant of grace. This gracious system of representation and substitution, which moved Justin Martyr to cry out, " O blessed change, O sweet permutation !" this is the very groundwork of the gospel of our salvation, and is to be received with strong faith and rapturous joy.

" Lo, I am with you alway."—Matthew xxviii. 20.

THE Lord Jesus is in the midst of His church; He walketh among the golden candlesticks; His promise is, " Lo, I am with you alway." He is as surely with us now as He was was with the disciples at the lake, when they saw coals of fire, and fish laid thereon and bread. Not carnally, but still in real truth, Jesus is with us. And a blessed truth it is, for where Jesus is, *love becomes inflamed.* Of all the things in the world that can set the heart burning, there is nothing like the presence of Jesus! A glimpse of Him so overcomes us, that we are ready to say, " Turn away Thine eyes from me, for they have overcome me." Even the smell of the aloes, and the myrrh, and the cassia, which drop from His perfumed garments, causes the sick and the faint to grow strong. Let there be but a moment's leaning of the head upon that gracious bosom, and a reception of His divine love into our poor cold hearts, and we are cold no longer, but glow like seraphs, equal to every labour, and capable of every suffering. If we know that Jesus is with us, *every power will be developed,* and every grace will be strengthened, and we shall cast ourselves into the Lord's service with heart, and soul, and strength; therefore is the presence of Christ to be desired above all things. *His presence will be most realised by those who are most like Him.* If you desire to see Christ, you must grow in conformity to Him. Bring yourself, by the power of the Spirit, into union with Christ's desires, and motives, and plans of action, and you are likely to be favoured with His company. Remember *His presence may be had.* His promise is as true as ever. He delights to be with us. If He doth not come, it is because we hinder Him by our indifference. He will reveal Himself to our earnest prayers, and graciously suffer Himself to be detained by our entreaties, and by our tears, for these are the golden chains which bind Jesus to His people.

" Can the rush grow up without mire ?"—Job viii. 11.

THE rush is spongy and hollow, and even so is a hypocrite ; there is no substance or stability in him. It is shaken to and fro in every wind just as formalists yield to every influence ; for this reason the rush is not broken by the tempest, neither are hypocrites troubled with persecution. I would not willingly be a deceiver or be deceived ; perhaps the text for this day may help me to try myself whether I be a hypocrite or no. The rush by nature lives in water, and owes its very existence to the mire and moisture wherein it has taken root ; let the mire become dry, and the rush withers very quickly. Its greenness is absolutely dependent upon circumstances, a present abundance of water makes it flourish, and a drought destroys it at once. Is this my case ? Do I only serve God when I am in good company, or when religion is profitable and respectable ? Do I love the Lord only when temporal comforts are received from His hands ? If so I am a base hypocrite, and like the withering rush, I shall perish when death deprives me of outward joys. But can I honestly assert that when bodily comforts have been few, and my surroundings have been rather adverse to grace than at all helpful to it, I have still held fast my integrity ? then have I hope that there is genuine vital godliness in me. The rush cannot grow without mire, but plants of the Lord's right hand planting can and do flourish even in the year of drought. A godly man often grows best when his worldly circumstances decay. He who follows Christ for his bag is a Judas ; they who follow for loaves and fishes are children of the devil ; but they who attend him out of love to Himself are His own beloved ones. Lord, let me find my life in *Thee*, and not in the mire of this world's favour or gain.

"And the LORD shall guide thee continually."—Isa. lviii. 11.

"THE *Lord* shall guide thee." Not an angel, but JEHOVAH shall guide thee. He said He would not go through the wilderness before His people, an angel should go before them to lead them in the way; but Moses said, "If *Thy* presence go not with me, carry us not up hence." Christian, God has not left you in your earthly pilgrimage to an angel's guidance: He Himself leads the van. You may not see the cloudy, fiery pillar, but Jehovah will never forsake you. Notice the word *shall*—"The Lord shall guide thee." How certain this makes it! How sure it is that God will not forsake us! His precious "shalls" and "wills" are better than men's oaths. "I will never leave thee, nor forsake thee." Then observe the adverb *continually*. We are not merely to be guided sometimes, but we are to have a perpetual monitor; not occasionally to be left to our own understanding, and so to wander, but we are continually to hear the guiding voice of the Great Shepherd; and if we follow close at His heels, we shall not err, but be led by a right way to a city to dwell in. If you have to change your position in life; if you have to emigrate to distant shores; if it should happen that you are cast into poverty, or uplifted suddenly into a more responsible position than the one you now occupy; if you are thrown among strangers, or cast among foes, yet tremble not, for "the Lord shall guide thee continually." There are no dilemmas out of which you shall not be delivered if you live near to God, and your heart be kept warm with holy love. He goes not amiss who goes in the company of God. Like Enoch, walk with God, and you cannot mistake your road. You have infallible wisdom to direct you, immutable love to comfort you, and eternal power to defend you. "Jehovah"—mark the word—"Jehovah shall guide thee continually."

" The life which I now live in the flesh, I live by the faith of the Son of God."—Gal. ii. 20.

HEN the Lord in mercy passed by and saw us in our blood, He first of all said, " Live ;" and this he did *first,* because life is one of the absolutely essential things in spiritual matters, and until it be bestowed we are incapable of partaking in the things of the kingdom. Now the life which grace confers upon the saints at the moment of their quickening is none other than the life of Christ, which, like the sap from the stem, runs into us, the branches, and establishes a living connection between our souls and Jesus. Faith is the grace which perceives this union, having proceeded from it as its first-fruit. It is the neck which joins the body of the Church to its all-glorious Head.

" *O Faith!* thou bond of union with the Lord,
Is not this office thine ? and thy fit name,
In the economy of gospel types,
And symbols apposite—the Church's *neck;*
Identifying her in will and work
With Him ascended ?"

Faith lays hold upon the Lord Jesus with a firm and determined grasp. She knows his excellence and worth, and no temptation can induce her to repose her trust elsewhere ; and Christ Jesus is so delighted with this heavenly grace, that He never ceases to strengthen and sustain her by the loving embrace and all-sufficient support of His eternal arms. Here, then, is established a living, sensible, and delightful union which casts forth streams of love, confidence, sympathy, complacency, and joy, whereof both the bride and bridegroom love to drink. When the soul can evidently perceive this oneness between itself and Christ, the pulse may be felt as beating for both, and the one blood as flowing through the veins of each. Then is the heart as near heaven as it can be on earth, and is prepared for the enjoyment of the most sublime and spiritual kind of fellowship.

"I came not to send peace on earth, but a sword."—Matt. x. 34.

THE Christian will be sure to make enemies. It will be one of his objects to make none; but if to do the right, and to believe the true, should cause him to lose every earthly friend, he will count it but a small loss, since his great Friend in heaven will be yet more friendly, and reveal Himself to him more graciously than ever. O ye who have taken up His cross, know ye not what your Master said? "I am come to set a man at variance against his father, and the daughter against her mother; and a man's foes shall be they of his own household." Christ is the great Peacemaker; but before peace, He brings war. Where the light cometh, the darkness must retire. Where truth is, the lie must flee; or, if it abideth, there must be a stern conflict, for the truth cannot and will not lower its standard, and the lie must be trodden under foot. If you follow Christ, you shall have all the dogs of the world yelping at your heels. If you would live so as to stand the test of the last tribunal, depend upon it the world will not speak well of you. He who has the friendship of the world is an enemy to God; but if you are true and faithful to the Most High, men will resent your unflinching fidelity, since it is a testimony against their iniquities. Fearless of all consequences, you must do the right. You will need the courage of a lion unhesitatingly to pursue a course which shall turn your best friend into your fiercest foe; but for the love of Jesus you must thus be courageous. For the truth's sake to hazard reputation and affection, is such a deed that to do it constantly you will need a degree of moral principle which only the Spirit of God can work in you; yet turn not your back like a coward, but play the man. Follow right manfully in your Master's steps, for He has traversed this rough way before you. Better a brief warfare and eternal rest, than false peace and everlasting torment.

" Hitherto hath the Lord helped us."—1 Samuel vii. 12.

THE word "hitherto" seems like a hand pointing in the direction of the *past*. Twenty years or seventy, and yet, "hitherto the Lord hath helped!" Through poverty, through wealth, through sickness, through health, at home, abroad, on the land, on the sea, in honour, in dishonour, in perplexity, in joy, in trial, in triumph, in prayer, in temptation, "hitherto hath the Lord helped us!" We delight to look down a long avenue of trees. It is delightful to gaze from end to end of the long vista, a sort of verdant temple, with its branching pillars and its arches of leaves; even so look down the long aisles of your years, at the green boughs of mercy overhead, and the strong pillars of lovingkindness and faithfulness which bear up your joys. Are there no birds in yonder branches singing? Surely there must be many, and they all sing of mercy received "hitherto."

But the word also points *forward*. For when a man gets up to a certain mark and writes "hitherto," he is not yet at the end, there is still a distance to be traversed. More trials, more joys; more temptations, more triumphs; more prayers, more answers; more toils, more strength; more fights, more victories; and then come sickness, old age, disease, death. Is it over now? No! there is more yet—awakening in Jesu's likeness, thrones, harps, songs, psalms, white raiment, the face of Jesus, the society of saints, the glory of God, the fulness of eternity, the infinity of bliss. O be of good courage, believer, and with grateful confidence raise thy "Ebenezer," for—

He who hath helped thee hitherto
Will help thee all thy journey through.

When read in heaven's light how glorious and marvellous a prospect will thy "hitherto" unfold to thy grateful eye!

" What think ye of Christ?"—Matthew xxii. 42.

THE great test of your soul's health is, *What think you of Christ?* Is He to you "fairer than the children of men"—"the chief among ten thousand"—the "altogether lovely"? Wherever Christ is thus esteemed, all the faculties of the spiritual man exercise themselves with energy. I will judge of your piety by this barometer: does Christ stand high or low with you? If you have thought little of Christ, if you have been content to live without His presence, if you have cared little for His honour, if you have been neglectful of His laws, then I know that your soul is sick—God grant that it may not be sick unto death! But if the first thought of your spirit has been, How can I honour Jesus? if the daily desire of your soul has been, " O that I knew where I might find Him!" I tell you that you may have a thousand infirmities, and even scarcely know whether you are a child of God at all, and yet I am persuaded, beyond a doubt, that you are safe, since Jesus is great in your esteem. I care not for thy rags, what thinkest thou of *His* royal apparel? I care not for thy wounds, though they bleed in torrents, what thinkest thou of *His* wounds? are they like glittering rubies in thine esteem? I think none the less of thee, though thou liest like Lazarus on the dunghill, and the dogs do lick thee—I judge thee not by thy poverty: what thinkest thou of the King in His beauty? Has He a glorious high throne in thy heart? Wouldst thou set Him higher if thou couldst? Wouldst thou be willing to die if thou couldst but add another trumpet to the strain which proclaims His praise? Ah! then it is well with thee. Whatever thou mayst think of thyself, if Christ be great to thee, thou shalt be with Him ere long.

> " Though all the world my choice deride,
> Yet Jesus shall my portion be;
> For I am pleased with none beside;
> The fairest of the fair is He."

" *Better is the end of a thing than the beginning thereof.*"
Ecclesiastes vii. 8.

LOOK at David's Lord and Master; see His beginning. He was despised and rejected of men; a man of sorrows and acquainted with grief. Would you see the end? He sits at His Father's right hand, expecting until His enemies be made His footstool. " As H⁊ is, so are we also in this world." You must bear the cross, or you shall never wear the crown; you must wade through the mire, or you shall never walk the golden pavement. Cheer up, then, poor Christian. " Better is the end of a thing than the beginning thereof." See that creeping worm, how contemptible its appearance! It is the beginning of a thing. Mark that insect with gorgeous wings, playing in the sunbeams, sipping at the flower bells, full of happiness and life ; that is the end thereof. That caterpillar is yourself, until you are wrapped up in the chrysalis of death ; but when Christ shall appear you shall be like Him, for you shall see Him as He is. Be content to be like Him, a worm and no man, that like Him you may be satisfied when you wake up in His likeness. That rough-looking diamond is put upon the wheel of the lapidary. He cuts it on all sides. It loses much—much that seemed costly to itself. The king is crowned ; the diadem is put upon the monarch's head with trumpet's joyful sound. A glittering ray flashes from that coronet, and it beams from that very diamond which was just now so sorely vexed by the lapidary. You may venture to compare yourself to such a diamond, for you are one of God's people ; and this is the time of the cutting process. Let faith and patience have their perfect work, for in the day when the crown shall be set upon the head of the King, Eternal, Immortal, Invisible, one ray of glory shall stream from you. " They shall be Mine," saith the Lord, " in the day when I make up My jewels." " Better is the end of a thing than the beginning thereof."

"Knowest thou not that it will be bitterness in the latter end?"
2 Samuel ii. 26.

IF, O my reader! thou art merely a professor, and not a possessor of the faith that is in Christ Jesus, the following lines are a true sketch of thine end.

You are a respectable attendant at a place of worship; you go because others go, not because your heart is right with God. This is your beginning. I will suppose that for the next twenty or thirty years you will be spared to go on as you do now, professing religion by an outward attendance upon the means of grace, but having no heart in the matter. Tread softly, for I must show you the deathbed of such a one as yourself. Let us gaze upon him gently. A clammy sweat is on his brow, and he wakes up crying, "O God, it is hard to die. Did you send for my minister?" "Yes, he is coming." The minister comes. "Sir, I fear that I am dying!" "Have you any hope?" "I cannot say that I have. I fear to stand before my God; oh! pray for me." The prayer is offered for him with sincere earnestness, and the way of salvation is for the ten-thousandth time put before him; but before he has grasped the rope, I see him sink. I may put my finger upon those cold eyelids, for they will never see anything here again. But where is the man, and where are the man's true eyes? It is written, "In hell he lifted up his eyes, being in torment." Ah! why did he not lift up his eyes before? Because he was so accustomed to hear the gospel that his soul slept under it. Alas! if you should lift up your eyes there, how bitter will be your wailings. Let the Saviour's own words reveal the woe: "Father Abraham, send Lazarus, that he may dip the tip of his finger in water, and cool my tongue, for I am tormented in this flame." There is a frightful meaning in those words. May you never have to spell it out by the red light of Jehovah's wrath!

" In the last day, that great day of the feast, Jesus stood and cried, saying, If any man thirst, let him come unto Me and drink."—John vii. 37.

*P*ATIENCE had her perfect work in the Lord Jesus, and until the last day of the feast He pleaded with the Jews, even as on this last day of the year He pleads with us, and waits to be gracious to us. Admirable indeed is the longsuffering of the Saviour in bearing with some of us year after year, notwithstanding our provocations, rebellions, and resistance of His Holy Spirit. Wonder of wonders that we are still in the land of mercy!

Pity expressed herself most plainly, for Jesus *cried*, which implies not only the loudness of His voice, but the tenderness of His tones. He entreats us to be reconciled. "We *pray* you," says the Apostle, "as though God did *beseech* you by us." What earnest, pathetic terms are these! How deep must be the love which makes the Lord weep over sinners, and like a mother woo His children to His bosom! Surely at the call of such a cry our willing hearts will come.

Provision is made most plenteously; all is provided that man can need to quench his soul's thirst. To his conscience the atonement brings peace; to his understanding the gospel brings the richest instruction; to his heart the person of Jesus is the noblest object of affection; to the whole man the truth as it is in Jesus supplies the purest nutriment. Thirst is terrible, but Jesus can remove it. Though the soul were utterly famished, Jesus could restore it.

Proclamation is made most freely, that every thirsty one is welcome. No other distinction is made but that of thirst. Whether it be the thirst of avarice, ambition, pleasure, knowledge, or rest, he who suffers from it is invited. The thirst may be bad in itself, and be no sign of grace, but rather a mark of inordinate sin longing to be gratified with deeper draughts of lust; but it is not goodness in the creature which brings him the invitation, the Lord Jesus sends it freely, and without respect of persons.

Personality is declared most fully. The sinner must come to *Jesus*, not to works, ordinances, or doctrines, but to a personal Redeemer, who His own self bare our sins in His own body on the tree. The bleeding, dying, rising Saviour, is the only star of hope to a sinner. Oh for grace to come now and drink, ere the sun sets upon the year's last day!

No waiting or preparation is so much as hinted at. Drinking represents a reception for which no fitness is required. A fool, a thief, a harlot can drink; and so sinfulness of character is no bar to the invitation to believe in Jesus. We want no golden cup, no be-jewelled chalice, in which to convey the water to the thirsty; the mouth of poverty is welcome to stoop down and quaff the flowing flood. Blistered, leprous, filthy lips may touch the stream of divine love; they cannot pollute it, but shall themselves be purified. Jesus is the fount of hope. Dear reader, hear the dear Redeemer's loving voice as He cries to each of us,

"IF ANY MAN THIRST,

LET HIM

COME UNTO ME

AND DRINK."

" The harvest is past, the summer is ended, and we are not saved."—Jeremiah viii. 20.

NOT *saved!* Dear reader, is this your mournful plight? Warned of the judgment to come, bidden to escape for your life, and yet at this moment *not saved!* You know the way of salvation, you read it in the Bible, you hear in from the pulpit, it is explained to you by friends, and yet you neglect it, and therefore are *not saved.* You will be without excuse when the Lord shall judge the quick and dead. The Holy Spirit has given more or less of blessing upon the word which has been preached in your hearing, and times of refreshing have come from the divine presence, and yet you are without Christ. All these hopeful seasons have come and gone—your summer and your harvest have past—and yet you are *not saved.* Years have followed one another into eternity, and your last year will soon be here: youth has gone, manhood is going, and yet you are *not saved.* Let me ask you—*will you ever be saved?* Is there any likelihood of it? Already the most propitious seasons have left you unsaved; will other occasions alter your condition? Means have failed with you—the best of means, used perseveringly and with the utmost affection—what more can be done for you? Affliction and prosperity have alike failed to impress you; tears and prayers and sermons have been wasted on your barren heart. Are not the probabilities dead against your ever being saved? Is it not more than likely that you will abide as you are till death for ever bars the door of hope? Do you recoil from the supposition? Yet it is a most reasonable one: he who is not washed in so many waters will in all probability go filthy to his end. The convenient time never has come, why should it ever come? It is logical to fear that it never will arrive, and that Felix like, you will find no convenient season till you are in hell. O bethink you of what that hell is, and of the dread probability that you will soon be cast into it!

Reader, suppose you should die unsaved, your doom no words can picture. Write out your dread estate in tears and blood, talk of it with groans and gnashing of teeth: you will be punished with everlasting destruction from the glory of the Lord, and from the glory of His power. A brother's voice would fain startle you into earnestness. O be wise, be wise in time, and ere another year begins, believe in Jesus, who is able to save to the uttermost. Consecrate these last hours to lonely thought, and if deep repentance be bred in you, it will be well; and if it lead to a humble faith in Jesus, it will be best of all. O see to it that this year pass not away, and you an unforgiven spirit. Let not the new year's midnight peals sound upon a joyless spirit! *Now*, Now, NOW believe, and live.

" Escape for thy life;

Look not behind thee,

Neither stay thou in all the plain;

Escape to the mountain,

Lest thou be consumed."

INDEX